CAMBRIDGE STUDIES IN EARLY MODERN HISTORY

Editors
J. H. ELLIOTT   H. G. KOENIGSBERGER

REFORM AND REVOLUTION
IN MAINZ
1743–1803

CAMBRIDGE STUDIES IN EARLY
MODERN HISTORY

Edited by J. H. Elliott and H. G. Koenigsberger

The idea of an 'early modern' period of European history from the fifteenth to the late eighteenth century is now widely accepted among historians. The purpose of the Cambridge Studies in Early Modern History is to publish monographs and studies which will illuminate the character of the period as a whole, and in particular focus attention on a dominant theme within it, the interplay of continuity and change as they are represented by the continuity of medieval ideas, political and social organisation, and by the impact of new ideas, new methods and new demands on the traditional structures.

REFORM AND REVOLUTION IN MAINZ
1743-1803

T. C. W. BLANNING
Fellow of Sidney Sussex College, Cambridge

CAMBRIDGE UNIVERSITY PRESS

Published by the Syndics of the Cambridge University Press
Bentley House, 200 Euston Road, London NW1 2DB
American Branch: 32 East 57th Street, New York, N.Y. 10022

© Cambridge University Press 1974

Library of Congress Catalogue Card Number: 73-93390

ISBN: 0 521 20418 6

First published 1974

Printed in Great Britain
at the University Printing House, Cambridge
(Brooke Crutchley, University Printer)

TO MY MOTHER AND FATHER

CONTENTS

Preface	*page* ix
Map	x

PART ONE   PROLOGUE
The 'German Problem' in the Eighteenth Century	1

PART TWO
The Electorate of Mainz in the Eighteenth Century (1743–1803)	39
Introduction	39
1. The Electorate of Mainz, the Empire and the Imperial Knights	46
2. Town and Country	70
3. Enlightened absolutism: Johann Friedrich Count von Ostein (1743–63) and Emmerich Joseph Freiherr von Breidbach zu Bürresheim (1763–74)	96
4. 1774: The aristocratic reaction	141
5. Enlightened absolutism: Friedrich Karl Freiherr von Erthal (1774–1802)	
Enlightenment from above	163
Enlightenment and reaction from below	193
6. Imperial adventures	210
7. 'Revolution': Aschaffenburg and Mainz 1790	241
8. Revolution: Mainz 1792–3	267

Contents

PART THREE   CONCLUSION

Germany and the French Revolution	*page* 303
Appendix. The Electors and Archbishops of Mainz 1695–1802	335
Bibliography	336
Index	347

PREFACE

The research conducted in German and Austrian archives, on which this book is based, was made possible in the first instance by the generous support of the *Institut für Europäische Geschichte* at Mainz, for which I am deeply grateful. Further work in England, France, Germany and Austria was financed by the Master and Fellows of Sidney Sussex College, to whom I am similarly indebted. I must also record my gratitude to the Freiherr von Franckenstein, the Count zu Eltz and the Count von Schönborn for allowing me to work in their family archives, and also to Karl Otmar Freiherr von Aretin for negotiating access to the archives of the Fürsten von der Leyen. Dr Ludwig Falck and Dr Elisabeth Darapsky of the *Stadtarchiv* in Mainz, Dr Wolfgang Wann of the *Bayerischen Staatsarchiv* in Würzburg, Gräfin Dr Anna Coreth of the *Haus-, Hof- und Staatsarchiv* in Vienna, Dr Leonhard Lenk of the *Freiherrlich zu Franckenstein'sches Archiv* and Dr Fritz Zobeley of the *Gräflich von Schönborn'sches Archiv* all gave me invaluable assistance. Although the responsibility for the various defects of this work is entirely my own, it has benefited greatly from the criticisms and suggestions of Dr Helmut Lippelt, Dr Klaus Scharf, Dr Helmut Mathy, Prof W. H. Bruford, Dr Derek Beales and the editors of the series.

Sidney Sussex College, T.C.W.B.
Cambridge

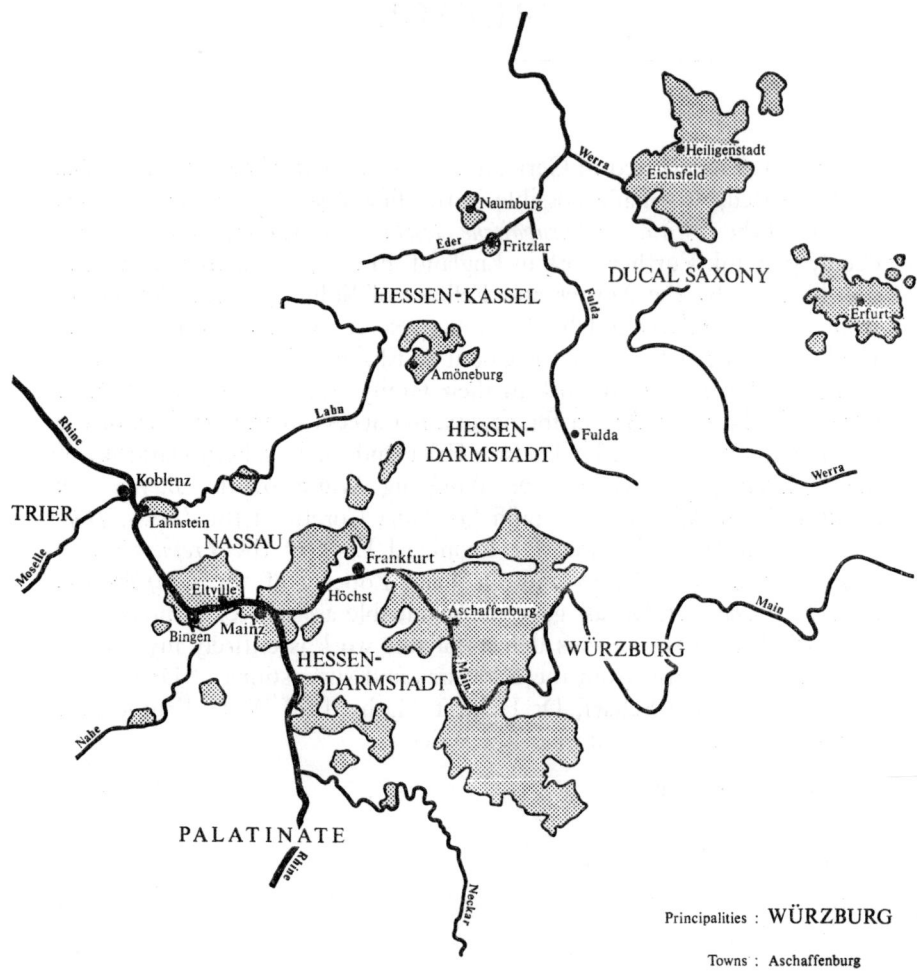

The Electorate of Mainz in the eighteenth century

Prologue

The 'German Problem' in the Eighteenth Century

I

The contrast between Germany and Western Europe in modern history has long been a subject of historical interpretation and research. The split in Europe, which has existed since the French Revolution and shook the continent to its foundations in the Industrial Revolution, had profound consequences. In two world wars it led not only to the political collapse of Germany as a great power but also to the end of Europe's hegemony in the world. Thus the split between Germany and the West will of necessity always be an important theme for historians. (Hajo Holborn, 'German Idealism in the light of Social History')[1]

Whether a source of pride, concern or neutral interest, the contrast which Holborn identified has never failed to engage the attention of the most powerful of German scholars in this century. Friedrich Meinecke, Ernst Troeltsch and Gerhard Ritter, to name only the most celebrated, all addressed themselves to the problem.[2] Nor, for obvious reasons, has interest subsided since the last war. Even those controversies which superficially are concerned only with national unification, the origins of the First World War or the rise of National Socialism are essentially concerned with the divergence between German-speaking areas and the West. Yet although the reality and unfading contemporaneity of 'The German Problem' are not in doubt, its location in time is a matter of considerable dispute. Earlier generations of historians concentrated their attention on the early nineteenth century and the development of Idealism; more recently, Ralf Dahrendorf has taken as his starting-point the Empire of 1871, while Leonard Krieger has gone back to the Reformation.[3]

Although on one level simply a history of the Electorate of Mainz during the last six decades of its existence, this book is intended to be a

[1] Reprinted in *Germany and Europe* (New York, 1971).
[2] Friedrich Meinecke, *Weltbürgertum und Nationalstaat*; *Werke*, ed. Hans Herzfeld, Carl Hinrichs and Walther Hofer, vol. 5 (Munich, 1962). Ernst Troeltsch, 'The Ideas of Natural Law and Humanity in World Politics', *Natural Law and the Theory of Society 1500–1800*, ed. Sir Ernest Barker (Cambridge, 1934). Gerhard Ritter, *Das deutsche Problem: Grundfragen deutschen Staatslebens gestern und heute* (Munich, 1962).
[3] Ralf Dahrendorf, *Society and Democracy in Germany* (London, 1968). Leonard Krieger, *The German Idea of Freedom, History of a Political Tradition* (Boston, 1957).

Prologue

contribution to this debate. It seeks to show how, behind the cosmopolitan façade of the eighteenth century, this part of Germany developed in a manner increasingly different from that of Western Europe. This is not an approach which will commend itself to everyone. French historians in particular have stressed the unity of a period which in their eyes was marked throughout Europe by the acceptance of French civilisation. Louis Réau began his book with the exclamation 'L'Europe française!', while part of the table of contents of another distinguished general history reads:

L'unité de l'Europe : L'Europe française – le français, langue européenne – l'art français, art européen – architecture française – musique française – sculpture française – costume française – cuisine française – L'invasion de l'Europe par la France – Cause de l'expansion française – la puissance française – la Cour de La France – Les salons – L'accueil français – L'émigration française – L'esprit féodal – Le cosmopolitisme – Le despotisme éclairé.[1]

The similarity of the metaphors *lumières*, *Aufklärung*, *Enlightenment* and *Illuminismo* has encouraged an over-emphasis on the characteristics enlightened thinkers held in common. Francocentric historians assume too readily that enlightened ideas current in Berlin or Vienna were but a reflection of those circulating in Paris. It is significant that in the work by Mousnier and Labrousse mentioned above, there are 28 references to Voltaire, 21 to Montesquieu, 14 to Diderot and 12 to D'Alembert, but only 8 to Kant, 6 to Herder, 2 to Wolff and none at all to Thomasius, Sonnenfels, Martini, Justi, Wieland or any other of the prominent figures of the Central European Aufklärung.[2] Even those historians who are aware of the variety of the Enlightenment feel obliged to pay periodic homage to its cosmopolitanism.

Few would disagree with Ernst Cassirer's view that:

the basic idea underlying all the tendencies of enlightenment was the conviction that human understanding is capable, by its own power and without recourse to supernatural assistance, of comprehending the system of the world and that this new way of understanding the world will lead it to a new way of mastering it.[3]

Yet even if the conceptual and methodological foundations and framework were similar, there was plenty of scope for individuals and groups to build fabrics which reflected regional, personal and chronological variations in style. Grouping Voltaire and Wolff under the enlightened um-

[1] Louis Réau, *L'Europe française au Siècle des lumières* (Paris, 1951), p. 1. Roland Mousnier and Ernest Labrousse, *Le XVIII Siècle: L'Époque des 'Lumières' (1715–1815)* (Paris, 1959), p. 569.
[2] Ibid., pp. 545–59.
[3] Quoted by Herbert Dieckmann, 'Themes and Structures of the Enlightenment', *Essays in Comparative Literature* (St Louis, 1961), p. 58.

brella is equivalent to classifying Borromini and Balthasar Neumann as 'baroque' architects: uncontroversial but unhelpful. In what follows the focus of attention will be the peculiar rather than the universal characteristics of Germany in general and Mainz in particular. Unlike many other investigations of the German Problem it will not be concerned exclusively with the movement of ideas. As Holborn pointed out in his brief but important article, German Idealism was not born in an act of spontaneous intellectual combustion, but was firmly rooted in Germany's social and political development.[1]

By contemporary standards, the Electorate of Mainz was only a middling state of the *Reich*, but its history in the eighteenth century illuminates a much wider area. In particular it illustrates what is intended to be the central theme of this book: the astonishing ability of the political and social establishment in Germany to absorb, adapt and even utilise progressive and potentially disruptive forces. If true, this generalisation is a paradox, for to both contemporaries and historians since the most obvious feature of the *Reich* was its decadence. Pufendorf's description – '*irregulare aliquod corpus et monstro simile*' – and Goethe's query – '*Das liebe heil'ge röm'sche Reich, Wie hält's nur noch zusammen?*' – are only two of a host of similar derogatory comments.[2] The fragility of the imperial institutions and the strength of the centrifugal forces are also too well known to require any detailed examination. The *Reichstag* was described by Sir George Etherege as 'only fit to entertain those insects in politics which crawl under the trees in St. James's Park'; the *Reichskammergericht* and *Reichshofrat*, hampered by lack of funds, accumulated an enormous backlog of untried cases and were accused of Protestant and Catholic bias respectively; the *Reichskreise* organisations were not even instituted in a large part of the *Reich*; the *Reichsarmee*, never more than a fraction of its nominal strength, mobilised late and demobilised early.[3]

These weaknesses, however obvious, should not lead one to overestimate the *Reich's* senility. Like any other political institution with roots several centuries deep, it possessed surprising reserves of stamina.[4] As several aspiring tyrants, notably the Dukes of Mecklenburg and Württem-

---

[1] Holborn, 'German Idealism', p. 3.
[2] Pufendorf's occurs in *De Statu Imperii Germanici* and Goethe's in *Faust*, Part One.
[3] F. L. Carsten, 'The Empire after the Thirty Years War', *The New Cambridge Modern History*, vol. 5, ed. F. L. Carsten (Cambridge, 1961), pp. 446–7. Fritz Hartung, *Deutsche Verfassungsgeschichte vom 15. Jahrhundert bis zur Gegenwart*, 8th ed. (Stuttgart, 1964), pp. 147–62. The most recent general summary of constitutional developments in the *Reich* between 1648 and 1806 is in *Handbuch der deutschen Geschichte*, ed. Herbert Grundmann, 9th ed. (Stuttgart, 1970), vol. 2, pp. 376–94.
[4] Despite periodic predictions of their imminent downfall, the Ottoman, Habsburg and Romanoff empires survived into the twentieth century and, in the last two cases, fell only after a particularly destructive foreign war.

Prologue

berg, discovered to their cost, the imperial institutions had not lost all their teeth.[1] Nor should it be forgotten that many subjects of the *Reich* were prepared to speak up loudly in its defence.[2] Even some of its severest critics found it preferable to the alternatives. Wieland commented that 'despite its undeniable faults and defects, the present constitution of the German *Reich* is incomparably more conducive to the domestic peace and prosperity of the nation as a whole and better suited to its character and the level of culture it has reached than the French democracy'.[3]

Until the French revolutionary armies threw every European frontier and institution into the melting pot, it was not at all clear that the *Reich* faced any fundamental changes. After 1648 the threat from outside naturally diminished. Although keen to tidy up his Eastern frontiers, Louis XIV was not likely to overturn a settlement which, in the words of a French diplomat, was 'one of the finest jewels in the French crown'.[4] His supine successors were enfeebled by growing financial difficulties and diverted by colonial ambitions. In the East, Poland, Sweden and the Ottoman Empire changed from predators into prey. The growing power of Russia never posed a real threat to the *Reich's* integrity. Like her French colleagues, Catherine the Great appreciated that its continued existence was the best possible check on undue Habsburg or Hohenzollern expansion. The best illustration of this way of thinking was the Franco-Russian guarantee of the Peace of Teschen in 1779 and with it the German *status quo*.

A much more potent danger to the *Reich* was the spectre of partition from within. Edmund Burke observed in December 1791:

As long as those princes (of Austria and Prussia) are at variance, so long the liberties of Germany are safe. But, if ever they should so far understand one another, as to be persuaded that they have a more direct and more certainly defined interest in a proportional, mutual aggrandisement, than in a reciprocal reduction, that is, if they come to think that they are more likely to be enriched by a division of spoil, than to be rendered secure by keeping to the old policy of preventing others from being spoiled by either of them, from that moment the liberties of Germany are no more.[5]

---

[1] F. L. Carsten, 'The German Estates in the Eighteenth Century', *Recueils de la Société Jean Bodin pour l'Histoire Comparative des Institutions*, volume XXV, pp. 227–38. See also the same author's *Princes and Parliaments in Germany from the Fifteenth to the Eighteenth Century* (Oxford, 1959). For a discussion of the achievements of the *Reichskreise* in Swabia and Franconia see Karl Otmar Freiherr von Aretin, *Heiliges Römisches Reich*, Vol. I, *Veröffentlichungen des Instituts für Europäische Geschichte Mainz*, Vol. 38 (Wiesbaden, 1967), pp. 70–6.
[2] A particularly good example was the speech made by Franz Wilhelm Freiherr von Spiegel, curator of the University of Bonn, shortly after the outbreak of the French Revolution. It is reprinted by Joseph Hansen, *Quellen zur Geschichte des Rheinlandes im Zeitalter der französischen Revolution*, vol. I (Bonn, 1931), pp. 478–83.
[3] Aretin, *Heiliges Römisches Reich*, I, p. 96.
[4] Quoted in G. Barraclough, *The Origins of Modern Germany* (Oxford, 1957), p. 385.
[5] 'Thoughts on French Affairs etc. etc. Written in December 1791', in *The Works and Correspondence of the Right Honourable Edmund Burke*, Vol. IV (London 1852), p. 563.

Particularly vulnerable were the weaker members of the *Reich*: the smaller princes, Imperial Counts, Imperial Knights and the Prince-Bishops. Plans for the secularisation of the ecclesiastical states were drawn up during the brief reign of the Wittelsbach Emperor Charles VII and again during the Seven Years War.[1] On both occasions they were foiled by the opposition of Austria.

The situation changed radically therefore when the Habsburgs themselves adopted policies hostile to the *Reich*. Joseph II came to the conclusion that the imperial title was a liability not an asset and in particular obstructed his attempt to turn his various dominions into a unitary state. From the late 1770s he was thinking in terms of abdicating as Emperor and severing all Austrian ties with the *Reich*.[2] Yet this removal of the *Reich*'s main protector did not lead to its slaughter, for when the Austrian shepherd became a wolf, the Prussian wolf became a shepherd. In view of the deep antagonism between the two states, this was inevitable; as Kaunitz observed drily on another occasion, if the Catholics were to become Protestants overnight, the Protestants would equally quickly become Catholics.[3] When Joseph abandoned the traditional Habsburg rôle, he both enabled and forced Frederick the Great to become an anti-emperor (*Gegenkaiser*). The two rulers could agree on the partition of Poland, but not on the partition of Germany. Indeed, the last decade of Frederick's life was dominated by his determination to prevent his rival exchanging the Netherlands for Bavaria. The Convention of Reichenbach of 1790 was a desperate attempt by Leopold II to save his inheritance, not a preparation for mutual aggrandisement.[4] Only a shotgun as menacing as the French Revolution could have forced this ill-matched couple into a *mariage de convenance*. It showed immediate signs of dissolution and ended in acrimonious divorce in 1795.[5] This is not to deny the existence or even growing strength of centrifugal forces: not only Austria and Prussia but also lesser states such as Saxony and Hanover began to believe that they had more to gain from the *Reich*'s destruction than from its preservation. But only in fortuitous alliance with French victories, French ideology and French designs on the left bank of the Rhine could these forces bring the *Reich* to its knees.

---

[1] Heribert Raab, *Clemens Wenzeslaus von Sachsen und seine Zeit (1739–1812)*, Vol. I, *Dynastie, Kirche und Reich im 18. Jahrhundert* (Freiburg, Basle, Vienna, 1962), pp. 121–8.
[2] Aretin, *Heiliges Römisches Reich*, I, p. 13.
[3] Aretin, 'Die Konfessionen als politische Kräfte rm Ausgang des alten Reichs', in *Festgabe Joseph Lortz*, ed. E. Iserloh and P. Manns, Vol. 2 (Baden-Baden, 1958), p. 182.
[4] Adam Wandruszka, *Leopold II*, Vol. II (Vienna, Munich, 1965), pp. 262–72.
[5] Hansen, *Quellen*, II, p. 880, III, pp. 31–4, 83–4, 491–5.

Prologue

II

The third potential threat to the *Reich* – internal subversion – proved to be the weakest of the three. Inevitably more complex than foreign aggression or princely ambition, it requires a more detailed examination. A more leisurely approach can also be justified on the grounds that an explanation of the feebleness of the subversive forces does much to illuminate the 'German Problem' identified at the beginning of this chapter.

Any explanation must start with Germany's economic and social development after 1648. In recent years the dispute as to whether the Thirty Years War was a catastrophe or an aggravated phase of a linear development has subsided, as economic historians have denied the existence of a 'German Economy' and have emphasised instead regional variations. The weight of evidence still suggests however that the military campaigns by themselves did not produce a sharp break.[1]

The war's most serious effect was on population. Günther Franz's summary-map shows losses of over 50% in the Palatinate, Württemberg, Thuringia, Pomerania and Mecklenburg, over 40% in Swabia, Franconia, Hessen and Brandenburg and over 30% in Bavaria. Only the Austrian Hereditary Lands, Lower Saxony, Holstein, Friesland and parts of Westphalia escaped lightly or with no losses.[2] If the *Reich* had also shared in the general European decline in the birth-rate, economic recovery would have been delayed indefinitely. In the event, the area proved to be a demographic exception. Although the losses had been so severe that a complete return to pre-war levels took more than a century, recovery did begin as soon as the war was over. Symbolic of German virility and fecundity was the achievement of Hans Bosshardt, who married his fourth wife at the age of eighty and had three children by her, the youngest being born the same year its 66-year-old stepbrother died.[3]

Trade and industry could not boast such formidable powers of regeneration. Although it is now accepted that earlier estimates were exaggerated and that something approaching normal activity returned to most areas within a few decades of the end of the war, the halcyon days of the sixteenth century had gone never to return. Trade between North Italy and South Germany, which had made the latter region one of the most prosperous in Europe, declined to a negligible point. Exports of grain and textiles from the Baltic ports never regained previous levels. Rhineland commerce, already decaying in 1618, did not show an upward trend until

---

[1] For a recent survey of the problem, see Henry Kamen, 'The Economic and Social Consequences of the Thirty Years War', *Past and Present*, 39 (1968), p. 61.
[2] Günther Franz, *Der dreißigjährige Krieg und das deutsche Volk*, Quellen und Forschungen zur Agrargeschichte, Vol. 7, 3rd ed. (1961), p. 8.
[3] Ibid., p. 49. After Hans' death at the age of 100 his widow quickly remarried.

the second quarter of the eighteenth century.[1] The effect on manufacturing, throughout the *Reich*, was even more serious: reduction of investment capital, disruption of supplies of raw material, destruction of equipment and contraction of markets.[2] This was not of course due entirely to disruption caused by the war. The long-term shift of the axis of the European economy away from Central Europe to the Atlantic Seaboard, the growing influence of colonial possessions, the decline of the Mediterranean, even the climatic changes which obstructed the Alpine passes, would have made and were making trading conditions progressively less favourable for German merchants and manufacturers, even had there been no war.

However the responsibility is apportioned, one conclusion is inescapable – the *Reich* of 1650 was a great deal poorer than it had been a hundred years earlier. To describe the next 150 years as a period of recovery is misleading, for it implies a return to the conditions which had existed previously. In fact what emerged was very different, the most striking novelty being a decline in the importance of the individual financier, merchant or manufacturer. The great entrepreneurs of the fifteenth and sixteenth centries, who had made the *Reichsstädte* the most flourishing cities of Europe, were not reincarnated. The most successful families, like the Fuggers, acquired noble status, bought landed estates and settled down to a *rentier* existence; others went bankrupt, died out or simply disappeared. Their place was taken by the princes, who appreciated that *rétablissement* of the economy was a necessary precondition for the *rétablissement* of revenue.

The attempt to play a more positive rôle in the economy was not only a response to changed circumstances; it also reflected the development of political absolutism. The complexities of that much-debated topic 'mercantilism' are beyond the scope of this study, but it does not seem in dispute that this period saw a significant general increase in state intervention in the economy; although to a lesser extent in England and the United Provinces than in France and to a lesser extent in France than in Germany. This greater degree of control was due partly to the more depressed state of the German economy but mainly to the ubiquity of secular authority. If there had been a sovereign prince in every English, Dutch or French provincial town, their economies would have enjoyed (or suffered) a great deal more interference. Quite apart from the various forms of direct assistance – credits, subsidies, exemptions from taxation or customs dues, cheap or even free raw materials and fuel, and so on – the princes exercised considerable indirect influence on the form of the economic re-

---

[1] See below, p. 72.
[2] Friedrich Lütge, *Deutsche Sozial- und Wirtschaftsgeschichte*, 2nd ed. (Berlin, Göttingen, Heidelberg, 1960), pp. 289-95.

Prologue

vival by their increased expenditure on courts, administrations and armies.[1] Louis XIV's Versailles created a fashion for display which brought many princes to the point of bankruptcy but which also injected large sums into circulation. The most distinctive characteristic of the German economy after 1648 was the growth in importance of the residential city, the prince's *Residenzstadt*. With one or two exceptions, such as Hamburg and Bremen, the Imperial Cities (*Reichsstädte*) never regained their predominant position. Now it was not Nuremberg, Augsburg, Ulm, Aachen, Cologne or Frankfurt am Main that were the centres of growth and vitality, but Munich, Vienna, Mannheim, Stuttgart, Berlin and Hanover.[2]

The growth of courts and administrations was accompanied by a growth in the number of people directly dependent on the prince for their livelihood. In both Weimar and Munich, for example, they formed more than a third of the city's total population.[3] Of the remainder a large number were indirectly dependent, on account of the colossal sums spent by the government and the other privileged orders. There grew up a host of manufacturing and service industries moulded in the image of their paymasters. The princes allowed their subjects no political independence, but they did provide them with employment. In his comparative study of a number of German cities Hans Mauersberg wrote: 'For the residential cities the second half of the eighteenth century was an epoch of not inconsiderable expansion for their industrial sector, an expansion which was increased still further by the directive measures of the eighteenth century absolute state.'[4]

More than at any time in the past, the *Reich*'s economy was moulded from above. This has been recognised even by Marxist historians; in the course of his study of industrial development in Bohemia after 1648, Klima observed that

> the Austrian absolute monarchy of the eighteenth century played an important rôle in the development of the manufacturing industry and at the same time supported the rise of new industrial relationships within the feudal order. The absolute monarchical state helped to bring about economic advance and the victory of new social relations over old ones.[5]

As a result, there was a wide difference between the independent entrepreneur of the sixteenth (or nineteenth) century and the *Partikulier* of the

---

[1] Ibid., p. 309.
[2] Heinrich Bechtel, *Wirtschaftsgeschichte Deutschlands*, Vol. II, *Vom Beginn des 16. bis zum Ende des 18. Jahrhunderts* (Munich, 1952), p. 80.
[3] W. H. Bruford, *Culture and Society in Classical Weimar 1775–1806* (Cambridge, 1962), p. 67; Hans Mauersberg, *Wirtschafts- und Sozialgeschichte zentraleuropäischer Städte in neuerer Zeit* (Göttingen, 1960), p. 207.   [4] Ibid., p. 217.
[5] A. Klima, 'Industrial development in Bohemia 1648–1781', *Past and Present*, 11 (1957), p. 94.

eighteenth, heavily dependent on the initiative and continuing support of his ruler.¹ Nor was this new relationship confined to the manufacturing sector; merchants also found that in the bleak conditions prevailing after 1648 only government contracts could keep large-scale trade in motion.² The mining industry, in the past a bastion of private enterprise, was taken over by the state.³ To a large extent the princes were filling a vacuum rather than invading territory already held; referring generally to the period 1648–1800 Wolfgang Zorn wrote: 'Far from being the repression of private initiative, state mercantilism was in reality a substitute for initiative which either was lacking entirely or was too weak.'⁴

To portray this period as one of unrelieved domination by the state would of course be exaggerated. As the economic war-wounds healed, so did private enterprise revive. In the course of the eighteenth century many large units, especially for the production of textiles, were founded and developed. It has been estimated that by the 1790s there were over 1,000 concerns employing 10 or more people, and of these only 60 were run directly by the state.⁵ Entrepreneurs such as Bolongaro, the Frankfurt tobacco merchant, and Schüle, the Augsburg 'Cotton King', amassed very respectable fortunes.⁶ The most celebrated were the von der Leyens of Krefeld, who imported skilled workers from Holland and even introduced machines for mechanical weaving.⁷ In some areas, notably Bohemia, Silesia and the Lower Rhine, significant industrial concentrations evolved. Although most of them were part-time spinners, almost 10% of Bohemia's population were engaged in some form of industrial activity by the middle of the century.⁸

These developments were reflected in structural changes. Although still numerous and powerful, the guilds suffered a relative decline. Increasingly, wealth and technological progress lay with other forms of organisation: putting-out (*Verlag*) and manufacturing (*Manufaktur*).⁹ As the guilds

---

¹ Bechtel, *Wirtschaftsgeschichte*, pp. 261–2; Lütge, *Sozial- und Wirtschaftsgeschichte*, p. 323.
² For a good example of this new type of entrepreneur, see W. O. Henderson's account of the Berlin firm of Splittberger and Daum. *Studies in the Economic Policy of Frederick the Great* (London, 1963), pp. 1–16.
³ Lütge, *Sozial- und Wirtschaftsgeschichte*, p. 317.
⁴ *Handbuch der deutschen Wirtschafts- und Sozialgeschichte*; Vol. I, *Von der Frühzeit bis zum Ende des 18. Jahrhunderts*, ed. Hermann Aubin & Wolfgang Zorn (Stuttgart, 1971), p. 573.
⁵ Ibid., pp. 549–50.   ⁶ Ibid.
⁷ Bechtel, *Wirtschaftsgeschichte*, p. 266.
⁸ Hermann Freudenberger, 'Industrialisation in Bohemia and Moravia in the Eighteenth Century', *Journal of Central European Affairs*, 19 (1960), p. 350. Between 1775 and 1788 the number of workers employed in weaving in Bohemia and Moravia increased from 39,000 to 66,000. Ibid., p. 354.
⁹ For the distinction between *Handwerk*, *Manufaktur* and *Fabrik*, see J. Kuczynski, *Die Bewegung der deutschen Wirtschaft von 1800 bis 1946*, 2nd ed. (Meisenheim, 1948), p. 22. There is a good deal of unjustified use of the term *Fabrik*, when *Manufaktur* would be more

became more restrictive, more introverted and more conservative, they attracted the hostile attention of the state. Part symptom and part cause was the *Reich* law relating to guilds of 1731. Although its efficacy depended entirely on the attitude of the individual princes, it doubtless hastened the growth in the number of manufacturing enterprises outside the guild framework.[1]

Yet when every qualification has been made and every exemption noted, the fact remains that German entrepreneurs were markedly weaker in numbers, wealth and independence than their counterparts in Western Europe. One interesting indication of this peculiarity was the prominent entrepreneurial rôle played by the nobility. In some areas they established a virtual monopoly. Of the 243 mines in Upper Silesia in 1785, 191 belonged to nobles, 20 to the King of Prussia, 14 to various other princes, and only 2 to private citizens of Breslau.[2] As Frederick the Great commented, 'the greatest entrepreneur of his age' was the Emperor Francis I, acting as a private individual.[3]

Accurate or not, that such a comment was possible stresses the peculiar character of German economic development. One hesitates to use the adjective 'backward', for this would imply a teleological and fundamentally unsound notion of economic 'progress'. Heinrich Bechtel has rightly pointed out the inapplicability of the term 'pre-capitalism' to describe this period: to see any period simply as the forerunner of another is analogous to denying a child its individuality by viewing it simply as a 'pre-adult'.[4] Global, European and German conditions gave the economy of the *Reich* a characteristic form between around the middle of the seventeenth century and around the end of the next. It was a form which helped to produce equally characteristic social, cultural and political results.

III

Although economic conditions and developments after 1648 made for a weak commercial and industrial middle class, they did not leave a total vacuum between privileged orders and lower classes. The gap was filled

---

accurate. In the opinion of Wolfgang Zorn the first real *Fabrik* was not founded in Germany until 1784. *Handbuch der Wirtschafts- und Sozialgeschichte*, p. 553.

[1] Lütge, *Sozial- und Wirtschaftsgeschichte*, p. 312; Bechtel, *Wirtschaftsgeschichte*, pp. 271–6.

[2] Lütge, *Sozial- und Wirtschaftsgeschichte*, p. 329. This is not to deny that in other European countries, in particular France, noble entrepreneurs were also common – G. V. Taylor, 'Types of Capitalism in 18th Century France', *English Historical Review*, 79 (1964), pp. 489–90, 495–6. There is insufficient evidence for any precise comparison, but general accounts give a very firm impression that the German nobility's entrepreneurial rôle was relatively more important.

[3] Lütge, *Die wirtschaftliche Situation in Deutschland und Oesterreich um die Wende vom 18. zum 19. Jahrhundert*, Forschungen zur Sozial- und Wirtschaftsgeschichte (Stuttgart, 1964), Vol. 6.

[4] Bechtel, *Wirtschaftsgeschichte*, p. 19.

by the hundreds of thousands of state employees. *Beamtentum* cannot be translated satisfactorily into any other language, for the simple reason that only in the *Reich* did this class reach such a highly developed stage. In large measure this was due to the *Reich*'s territorial complexity: not only the 300-odd *Reichsstände*, but also most of the Imperial Counts and Knights, needed officials of one kind or another. The German equivalent of the English noble's 'man of business' enjoyed public authority, public responsibilities and public status. Writing during the Second Empire, not a notably unbureaucratic era, Karl Biedermann estimated that one hundred years earlier there had been *twice* as many officials.[1] By the eighteenth century moreover they had formed themselves into a separate and relatively homogeneous *Beamtenstand*.[2]

The class of officials (*Amts-Bürgertum*) had attained a position in society which in terms of status was greatly superior to that of the commercial and manufacturing classes.[3] A report from the Hanover Commerce Commission of 1786 lamented that:

The people who organise and run manufacturing establishments do not enjoy enough social advantages to encourage our own men of means, who are in a position to do so, to give their children the right kind of education to equip them for a career in business: the social gap between those who serve their country and those who earn for it is still too great.[4]

The special character of the German officials however derived not so much from their numbers or elevated social status as from their close relationship with the intellectual establishment. This in turn stemmed from the extraordinary dominance exercised by the universities in German cultural life. In 1800 there were nearly fifty institutions of higher education in the *Reich*, as compared with 22 in France and 2 in England.[5] More important than their number was their vitality. While Oxford, Cambridge and the Sorbonne stagnated and even declined during the eighteenth century, many German universities adapted both structure and curricula to meet changing social needs.[6] Particularly striking was the rash of new founda-

---

[1] Karl Biedermann, *Deutschland im 18. Jahrhundert*, 2nd ed., Vol. 1 (Leipzig, 1880), p. 102. He cites as an example the principality of Leiningen, which employed a central authority of 50 councillors, 18 secretaries and 54 subordinate personnel to rule its 70,000 subjects.
[2] See Gustav Schmoller's summary of the reasons for this development, quoted in Grundmann, *Handbuch der deutschen Geschichte*, pp. 538–9.
[3] Grete Klingenstein, *Staatsverwaltung und kirchliche Autorität im 18. Jahrhundert: Das Problem der Zensur in der theresianischen Reform* (Vienna, 1970), p. 84.
[4] Mauersberg, *Wirtschafts- und Sozialgeschichte*, p. 339. For a literary example of the respect paid to officials, see Goethe's *Wilhelm Meisters Lehrjahre*, Book I, Chapter 14.
[5] *Großer Historischer Weltatlas*, Vol. 3, *Neuzeit*, ed. Josef Engel (Munich, 1957), p. 120.
[6] For a detailed description of this development, see two old but still very valuable books by Frederick Paulsen, *The German Universities and University Study* (London, 1906) and *German Education Past and Present* (London, 1908). For a description of the reforms under-

tions – 24 between 1600 and 1800, compared with 3 in France and none in England.[1] They included Giessen (1607), Kassel (1632), Halle (1694), Göttingen (1737), Erlangen (1743), Münster (1780) and Bonn (1786).

The vigour of the universities was both reflected in and responsible for the fact that most innovation in the German intellectual world proceeded within the universities, while in France and England the salons, academies and informal groups of the capital dominated. Although there were academies in the *Reich*, notably at Berlin, Göttingen, Erfurt and Munich, they never threatened the universities' hegemony. Halle and Königsberg, not Berlin, were the intellectual centres of Prussia, as was illustrated when Christian Wolff, recalled from exile by Frederick the Great, declined a post at the Berlin Academy in favour of a return to his chair at Halle.[2] A recital of the careers of some of the leading figures of the *Aufklärung* reinforces this observation: Thomasius was a professor at Halle, Wieland at Erfurt, Kant at Königsberg, Schlözer, Lichtenberg and Michaelis at Göttingen, Martini, Riegger and Sonnenfels at Vienna, Wolff at Halle and Marburg. Of course many German universities remained backward, many reforms were not implemented fully and there was much enterprising intellectual activity outside the academic world. Nevertheless, one is justified in describing German culture in the eighteenth century as university-dominated and -oriented, at least in relative terms.

The very large number of universities in the *Reich* reflected the princes' need for trained officials, rather than any simple enthusiasm for the promotion of scholarship. It is characteristic that only two universities were located in *Reichsstädte*: all the others were founded, maintained and directed by the princes. For this reason it is virtually impossible to make any clear distinction between academic and administrative officials.[3] The professors were appointed, paid, promoted and dismissed by the state. All of them, even those of foreign extraction, took an oath of loyalty to the sovereign. There was no academic freedom in the sense of self-government: the most powerful figure in a German University was not a vice-chancellor elected by his colleagues, or the heads of the various faculties, but the curator, a non-academic bureaucrat who made sure that the interests of the state always took precedence.[4]

---

taken in the Catholic Universities, see Robert Haass, *Die geistige Haltung der katholischen Universitäten Deutschlands im 18. Jahrhundert* (Freiburg, 1952).

[1] The figure for France includes Strasbourg, taken from the *Reich* by Louis XIV.

[2] Paulsen, *German Universities*, p. 46.

[3] 'The civil-servant caste included in the broadest sense, professors, secondary-school teachers, and pastors, for schools were state institutions and the churches – including the Catholic – were closely bound up with the courts and the aristocracy.' Holborn, 'German Idealism', p. 8.

[4] S. d'Irsay, *Histoire des Universités françaises et étrangères*, Vol. 2, *Du XVIe Siècle à 1860* (Paris, 1935), pp. 91–5.

The 'German Problem' in the Eighteenth Century

This increasing intimacy between politics and learning was also reflected in the new chairs created during the seventeenth and eighteenth centuries, for most of them – notably those for law and the various branches of 'cameralism' – had an obvious practical application.[1] Nor did the theological or philosophical faculties suffer a decline, for the training of both Catholic and Protestant priests, who exercised many more public responsibilities than their counterparts in other European countries, was conducted in the universities, not in separate seminaries.[2] Thus the German University became the most important formative influence on the German state of the eighteenth century. As Sir Ernest Barker observed, the German professors

> not only contributed to the general development of German political thought: they also played an active part in the development of law, and we may almost say, of the State, in Germany itself. There were no Inns of Court in Germany to control the teaching of law and the development of the legal system...they (the professors) could furnish from their own ranks, or train among the ranks of their pupils, the judges, statesmen, the officials and the ambassadors who were urgently needed by the German states. The legal faculties of the Universities were the reservoirs of the German *Beamtentum* (one of the greatest creations of the German genius), in its highest and widest sense.[3]

As Barker suggested, the professors' influence on public affairs extended from instruction to participation. Many of them moved frequently from university to government and back again, or were active in both simultaneously. Thomasius, Wolff, Goethe, Wieland, Martini, Sonnenfels, Riegger, Jacobi and many others held an administrative post at some time during their careers. Probably the best example of this mobility was the career of Joseph von Sonnenfels. After a false start as a soldier he entered public service as assistant to a member of the Austrian Supreme Court. Appointed to the chair of Political Science at the University of Vienna, he continued to sit on various government commissions. Even when the volume of his work as censor and councillor obliged him to resign his university post, he continued to publish his scholarly works and eventually set the seal on this fusion of theory and practice by becoming Rector of

---

[1] Grundmann, *Handbuch der deutschen Geschichte*, p. 307.
[2] Paulsen, *German Universities*, p. 48. Paulsen argues that the foundation of the episcopal seminaries in France after the Council of Trent was largely responsible for the decline of French universities.
[3] In his introduction to Gierke's *Natural Law and the Theory of Society*, pp. xiii–xiv. 'All the important Prussian civil servants of the eighteenth century were trained at Halle, and that characteristic tendency towards the rational, useful and practical, which everywhere is revealed in Prussian legislation and administration, is only the application of doctrines imbibed at Halle.' – An anonymous historian quoted in W. H. Bruford, *Germany in the Eighteenth Century* (Cambridge, 1965), p. 243.

Prologue

Vienna University.[1] Conversely, the officials themselves made an important contribution to the literary life of the *Reich*.[2]

More than anything else, it was this academic–bureaucratic predominance which distinguished German culture in the eighteenth century. Nowhere else in Europe did the literate classes have so many thousands of opportunities for state employment. This profusion of offices also played an important assimilatory rôle, for it brought the officials and intellectuals into close everyday contact not only with the princes but also with the nobles. More than in any other European country, the German nobility was a service nobility, both west and east of the Elbe. It was rare to find a family with either the means or the desire to enjoy an entirely *rentier* existence. In part this was due to the distribution of power within the *Reich*; the German equivalent of a French or English peer was a territorial prince, whose estates were a state and whose public authority could be abused but not discarded. Their younger sons, together with the lesser princes, Imperial Counts and Imperial Knights, sought employment as court officials, diplomats, army officers and administrators in the prince-bishoprics and larger secular states. The indigenous (*landständische*) nobles also had ample opportunity to find a niche in the civil services of their various states.

Simple contact between noble and commoner bureaucrats did not of course mean that they became identical. The former never relinquished their monopoly of the more prestigious and better-paid posts. Nor was there any real mobility between the groups. The German nobility's hypersensitivity on questions of rank invariably attracted comment from foreign visitors. *Mésalliances*, common in England and not rare in France, were greeted with horror.[3] Yet there is clear evidence that the gulf in outlook and attitudes was diminishing, as increasingly nobles sought an education which would qualify them for state employment.[4]

---

[1] Frederick Hertz, *The Development of the German Public Mind*, Vol. 2, *The Age of Enlightenment* (London, 1962), pp. 375–8.

[2] This is revealed by even the most cursory examination of J. G. Meusel's *Das gelehrte Teutschland oder Lexikon der jetzt lebenden teutschen Schriftsteller*, 5th ed. (Lemgo, 1796), a directory of contemporary German authors published in the 1780s and 1790s. In most cases the occupation of the author was listed.

[3] See below, p. 200. For a good literary example see Schiller's *Kabale und Liebe*.

[4] Leonard Krieger, for example, has written of 'the marriage of aristocracy and bureaucracy': *German Idea of Freedom*, p. 22. See below, pp. 201–3. Barnard has argued that during this period the German social and political élites were *consciously* 'reconstructed', as intellectual attainments rather than birth became accepted as the crucial criterion of individual worth, 'Thomasius' "Practical Philosophy"', *Journal of the History of Ideas*, 32 (1971), p. 246. Wieland commented that 'there are no class distinctions in polite society; a gentleman can go everywhere *tête levée*...and one does not become a gentleman by birth but through one's personal qualities'. Quoted in Hans-Jürgen Haferkorn, 'Der freie Schriftsteller: Eine literatursoziologische Studie über seine Entstehung und Lage in Deutschland zwischen 1750 und 1800', *Archiv für Geschichte des Buchwesens*, 5 (1964), p. 585.

The 'German Problem' in the Eighteenth Century

Even though this union was rarely if ever consummated sexually, commoners gained much reflected glory through their official – and often social – intercourse with the leaders of the social hierarchy. The most successful of them could even gain hereditary noble status. This did not make them any more acceptable as marriage partners, but the use of the prefix 'von' did lend a certain distinction. Indeed the very existence of a *Dienstadel* symbolised the social fusion.

For these reasons the attitude of most commoners towards the nobility was emulation rather than resentment. As Holborn wrote:

All groups accepted the nobleman as the type possessing the highest social graces and modelled their own style of life as much as possible according to the manners of the nobility...the German burgher had to crawl from under the shadow of the German nobleman, and he never fully succeeded in doing so, not even in the nineteenth century.[1]

IV

It is not surprising that these distinctive economic, social and political conditions engendered distinctively German attitudes towards the state. Some historians, notably Barker and Troeltsch, believe that the real watershed came in the late eighteenth and early nineteenth centuries, with the emergence of Idealism and the transition from Natural Law to Historical Law.[2] Although the cultural divergence between Germany and the West became particularly acute during these decades, it is also clear that in political philosophy at least the breach had occurred a great deal earlier. It was not the Idealists' deification of the state that gave German political thought its peculiarly authoritarian character, for this had been discernible for centuries. As with every intangible object, the pursuit of an intellectual trend is easier to sense than to describe. It is possible that individual thinkers illustrate more than influence the flow of opinion, but only by using them as landmarks can its passage be identified. The illustrations which follow are necessarily selective but not untypical or unrepresentative. Thinkers advocating authoritarian political systems could of course be identified in every country in Europe, but their assembled ranks would

[1] Hajo Holborn, *A History of Modern Germany 1648–1840* (London, 1965), p. 307.
[2] Barker, introduction to Gierke's *Natural Law and the Theory of Society*, p. l–liii. 'German thought...whether in politics or in history or in ethics, is based on the ideas of the Romantic Counter-Revolution. This was a movement which began by seeking to clear away the postulates of west-European thought, along with the scientific basis of mathematico-physical principles on which they rested. It proceeded to erect, both in the sphere of the State and in that of Society at large, the "organic" ideal of a group-mind (*Gemeingeist*) – an ideal half-aesthetic and half religious, but instinct throughout with a spirit of antibourgeois liberalism. Finally, on the basis of this ideal, and in order to give it form and substance, Romanticism sought to remedy the political disunity of Germany by the erection of a powerful unitary state.' Troeltsch, *The Ideas of Natural Law*, pp. 203–4.

Prologue

be neither as numerous nor as formidable nor as coherent as their counterparts in the *Reich*.

Invariably Martin Luther is singled out for special responsibility. His close alliance with the territorial princes and the decisive influence he and his followers exercised on the Protestant universities ensured that his political conservatism survived him. Elsewhere in Europe the need for dissenting minorities to defend themselves against persecution also obliged them to develop theoretical justifications of resistance. In Germany the application of *cuius regio ejus religio* and the opportunities for emigration to Catholic, Lutheran or even Calvinist principalities created a relatively monolithic situation. It is characteristic that the Pietist movement, which began in the late seventeenth century and became enormously influential in the next, was radical only in religious matters; politically, it was as conservative as the old Lutheran orthodoxy it sought to replace.[1]

Not even Luther's sturdy shoulders however can bear such a weight of personal responsibility. Although undeniably powerful, his contribution does not help to explain, for example, why theories of monarchical absolutism were also developed in the Catholic states. In his ingenious and persuasive study *The German Idea of Freedom*, Leonard Krieger argued that Luther's rôle has been exaggerated because it has been discussed in isolation from his background.[2] The central argument of his long and closely-argued book is that the Empire's peculiar structure and development, and in particular its territorial disintegration, led to the paradoxical notion of *Libertät*, the association by Germans of political liberty with the very authority of the state. Because the princes had a dual function – as executives within their own state, but as *representatives* within the *Reich* – and because the theorists enjoyed such a close relationship with the establishment, political debate did not proceed on the assumption that there was a natural antagonism between subjects and central authorities. As a result, there was no development in Germany of ideas of constitutional liberty, while spiritual liberties (freedom of belief and expression) and material liberties (economic, social and juridical) were never organised in a single system of rights.

This can clearly be seen in the political views of Leibniz, whose enormous influence inoculated his German successors against British or French empiricism. Although in theory he believed that only the wisest men in a state should rule, when it came to considering implementation Leibniz was prepared to accept significant qualifications. In view of the difficulty of defining 'wisdom' and the danger of choosing wrongly, he expressed a strong preference for hereditary monarchy. However un-

---

[1] Ritter, *Das deutsche Problem*, pp. 13–20.
[2] Krieger, *German Idea of Freedom*, p. 6.

reliable as a selector of ability, it did provide the best guarantee of internal and external security. Leibniz was aware of the temptations to which absolute rulers were susceptible, but was reluctant to agree to any limitations on their authority, because restrictions created a danger of anarchy without providing any compensating checks on abuses. The subjects of a state enjoyed no right of resistance: 'because usually the evil caused by the insurrection is incomparably greater than that which caused it'; 'because usually rebellions are more dangerous than bad government'; 'because such a remedy is worse than the complaint'. Only if expressly ordered to act contrary to the divine laws could they resist. If they were simply the passive objects of princely injustice they had to suffer in silence.[1]

Leibniz was not of course concerned primarily with directly political problems. Until late in the eighteenth century political thought in the *Reich* was dominated by three great exponents of Natural Law, with neatly overlapping careers – Samuel Pufendorf (1632–94); Christian Thomasius (1655–1728) and Christian Wolff (1679–1754). The Natural Law they expounded however did not have the liberal and constitutional overtones it acquired in Western Europe.[2] All of them postulated a contractual basis for the state, all of them believed in civil rights and all of them called for reforms of the existing structure; but none of them insisted on constitutional safeguards. Pufendorf held that only the ruler was competent to judge what did or did not contravene the natural laws and that 'therefore the supreme sovereign can rightfully force citizens to all things which he judges to be of any advantage to the public good'. However monstrous his behaviour, no sovereign could be deposed, 'because such obscurity usually surrounds civil acts that the common sort cannot recognise their equity or necessity' and 'there is always a presumption of justice on the part of the prince'.[3]

This authoritarian note was echoed with undimmed resonance in the works of his successors. Christian Thomasius railed against all manner of social evils – the persecution of 'witches', Jews, religious dissenters and unmarried mothers, the barbaric penal codes, legal discrimination against the poor, and so on. Yet although opposed to any patrimonial attitude on the part of the princes and prepared to advocate a new 'style' of politics, he

---

[1] Karl Herrmann, *Das Staatsdenken bei Leibniz*, Schriften zur Rechtslehre und Politik, Vol. 10 (Bonn, 1958), especially pp. 56–62.

[2] Troeltsch held that the authoritarianism and conservatism of Luther were responsible for the fact that 'the natural law ideas of western Europe only affected Germany in the sadly attenuated form of enlightened despotism; and even the theoretical protagonists of that law such as Wolff and Kant, proclaimed its principles with considerable reservations – reservations in favour of the actual historical environment which, as it impinges upon those principles, gradually subjects them to a rational process of modification'. *The Ideas of Natural Law*, p. 210.

[3] Krieger, *German Idea of Freedom*, p. 58.

did not progress to constitutionalism, indeed explicitly disdained it. There were to be no institutional safeguards for the subjects' individual liberties; they were to be enjoyed only at the prince's discretion.[1] The passage of time brought no dilution. Christian Wolff's absolutism was 'even more of a leviathan than the intellectual creations of Pufendorf and Thomasius'.[2] Repeating the former almost word for word, Wolff stated that 'he who exercises the civil power has the right to establish everything that appears to him to serve the public good'. Any division of powers was anathema to him: his prince was legislature, executive and judicature combined.[3]

The views of this great triumvirate, and of the thousands of lesser disciples drawn along in their wake, were not mere academic exercises. The peculiarities of the *Reich*'s political, educational and social structure, described in the previous section, ensured that their influence reached out through the medium of the universities to the individual states. Significantly, all three were professors: Pufendorf at Heidelberg and Lund, Thomasius at Leipzig and Halle, Wolff at Halle and Marburg. Official support for the school was expressed in the rash of new chairs for Natural Law and cameralism created during the first half of the eighteenth century.[4] Wolff's syntheses in particular achieved an astonishing ascendancy. Even Frederick the Great admired him, recalled him from exile and accepted with gratitude the dedication of his *Ius Naturae Methodo Scientifica Pertractatum*.[5]

The cameralist–Natural Law school did not however regard the state simply as an instrument of repression, whose sole object was the maintenance of order at home and abroad. They deduced from the social contract a host of positive functions for the state to perform. Christian Wolff again supplied the most complete statement. In his *Rational Thoughts on the Social Life of Mankind* (*Vernünftige Gedanken von dem gesellschaftlichen Leben der Menschen*), usually known as 'The Politics', he advocated a legislative programme of quite extraordinary detail. He expected the authorities to organise and direct every sector of the economy, to establish a national system of schools, universities and academies of arts and sciences, to set up pre-natal clinics, hospitals, institutions for unmarried mothers, poorhouses, orphanages, old people's homes, and so on, and so

---

[1] Barnard, 'Thomasius' "Practical Philosophy"'. Barnard argues that although he did nothing to alter the *structure* of absolutism, Thomasius did 'transmute profoundly its operative ethos, its *source* of authority'.
[2] Krieger, *German Idea of Freedom*, p. 67.   [3] Ibid.
[4] Hans von Voltelini, 'Die naturrechtlichen Lehren und die Reformen des 18. Jahrhunderts', *Historische Zeitschrift*, 105 (1910), pp. 69–70.
[5] Voltelini, 'Die naturrechtlichen Reformen'. For a recent account of Frederick's views on Wolff, see Carl Hinrichs, *Preußentum und Pietismus: Der Pietismus in Brandenburg-Preussen als religiös-soziale Reformbewegung* (Göttingen, 1971), pp. 435–41.

on.[1] As this selection suggests, Wolff's state existed to serve and influence not only the subjects' material appetites but also their intellects; it was a *Kulturstaat* as well as a *Wohlfahrtsstaat*. Wolff was only the most celebrated of a host of writers of similar bent. Nor was the belief in massive and detailed state intervention restricted denominationally; in the Catholic states also the same ideas were preached, and implemented. This was due partly to better contacts, as increasing numbers of Catholics were attracted to the more progressive Protestant universities, and partly to the continuing growth of indigenous strains. In the Habsburg territories, for example, the enduring influence of seventeenth century theorists such as P. W. Hörnigk and J. J. Becher suffices to show that development here was more than pale and belated imitation.

Eventually the degree of regimentation demanded became excessive. J. H. G. von Justi, for example, maintained that:

A properly constituted state must be exactly analogous to a machine, in which all the wheels and gears are precisely adjusted to one another; and the ruler must be the foreman, the mainspring or the soul – if one may use the expression – which sets everything in motion.[2]

It is not surprising that during the second half of the eighteenth century an increasing number of intellectuals found this sterile social engineering unacceptable. They turned from the rationality, practicality and immutable framework of the exponents of cameralism and Natural Law to emotion, spontaneity, individuality and deliberate naïvety. Although this reaction found expression in, perhaps even gave rise to, an extraordinary number of works of genius, and had a profound effect on German culture, it did not introduce any radical change in the way in which Germans regarded political authority. This is a paradox, for the *Weltanschauung* of the literary revival seemed favourable to political liberalism. The *Sturm und Drang* movement, for example, produced plays such as Schiller's *Die Räuber*, *Fiesko* and *Don Carlos*, Goethe's *Egmont* and *Götz von Berlichingen* and Lenz's *Der Hofmeister*, all of which had apparently obvious political implications. Yet in relation to their own immediate environment, the *Stürmer und Dränger* were almost entirely apolitical; their few explicit political pronouncements were invariably reactionary.[3]

The *Sturm und Drang* was inevitably short-lived. Most of its adherents turned out to be staunch conservatives when the outbreak of the French Revolution obliged them to articulate their political instincts. The same

---

[1] Christian Wolff, *Vernünftige Gedanken von dem gesellschaftlichen Leben der Menschen* (Halle, 1756), pp. 212–17, 257, 345, 348, 350, 353, 357, 371.
[2] Quoted in Geraint Parry, 'Enlightened Government and its Critics in Eighteenth Century Germany', *Historical Journal*, 6 (1963), p. 182.
[3] Roy Pascal, *The German Sturm und Drang* (Manchester, 1963), pp. 42–55.

could not be said of the two men who provided the most powerful alternatives to the prevailing systems – Herder and Kant. Herder's organic views on the state and political development were clearly incompatible with the existing regime in the *Reich*. However enlightened, absolute power was repugnant to him, for he believed that for one man to exercise authority over another was an affront to human dignity. Herder's ideal state would have had a written republican form of constitution, no single focus of power and no permanent administrative body:

> The *Volk*-State is conceived as a territorial community with its own language, laws and customs. It is the 'natural' social framework within which various sectional bodies and associations cooperate, and not an administrative machine. Indeed government is virtually reduced (or elevated) to 'co-operation'. There are no 'rulers'. Their existence is regarded as a denial of the rule of law.[1]

These views were certainly radical, but Herder was no threat to the established order, as the authorities recognised by leaving him in peace. Like other supporters of an organic view of the state, Herder had some difficulty in distinguishing between what had happened, what was happening, what would happen and what he wanted to happen; he was clear however that revolution was unacceptable: 'My motto remains gradual, natural, reasonable evolution of things; not revolution.'[2] Quite apart from his abhorrence of violence, it is impossible to imagine Herder leading a radical movement. He was no activist; any thought of disturbing the Olympian calm of Weimar, where he was employed as *Generalsuperintendent* of the clergy, never appears to have crossed his mind. His taste for controversy was reserved for the correspondence columns and the book-review sections of the learned journals. Nor were his published works likely to unleash agitation in spite of their author, for they were always long, always dense, always difficult and often confused. It was not until the armies of the French Revolution destroyed the old *Reich* that a nationalist movement reflecting some of Herder's ideas began to emerge. Even then Fichte, Schlegel, Gentz and Görres mined only the conservative vein in his works, leaving the liberalism untouched.

At first sight Kant seemed much more likely to give intellectual stimulus to a radical political movement. In the introduction to a recent compilation of his political essays Hans Reiss wrote that:

> Kant has rightly been called the philosopher of the French Revolution. There is, indeed, an analogy between the spirit of Kant's philosophy and the ideas of the French and American revolutions: for Kant asserted the independence of the individual in

---

[1] F. M. Barnard, *Herder's Social and Political Thought: From Enlightenment to Nationalism* (Oxford, 1965), pp. 65–7.
[2] Ibid., p. 83. See also *Herder on Social and Political Culture*, edited by F. M. Barnard (Cambridge, 1969), pp. 52–3.

face of authority, and the problem of human freedom was at the very core of his thought.¹

Kant did not of course approve of the way in which Herder developed, and wrote an intensely hostile review of the *Ideen zur Philosophie der Geschichte der Menschheit*, but his views on the state were as incompatible with the *status quo* as were those of his former pupil: he was opposed to cameralism in theory and enlightened absolutism in practice. Particularly radical was his advocacy of the division of powers, an elected representative assembly and participation in politics by a substantial part of the population.² Yet no more than Herder did Kant become the direct or indirect inspiration of a subversive movement. Nothing could have been less inflammatory than his philosophical treatises, from which explicit political pronouncements could be extracted only with difficulty and only by the keenest minds. It is significant that Kant's shortest, simplest, most celebrated and most influential tract – *Was ist Aufklärung?* – can be seen as an *apologia* for Frederick the Great's brand of enlightened absolutism. The distinction he drew in it between the public and private use of one's reason implied political quietism. He argued that the current age was distinguished by a marked erosion of the obstacles which prevented man's emergence from self-incurred immaturity and paid explicit tribute to his king and employer. He also advanced the paradox that the state of a strong ruler with 'a well-disciplined and numerous army' could provide more liberty than a republic:

A high degree of civil freedom seems advantageous to a people's *intellectual* freedom, yet it also sets up insuperable barriers to it. Conversely, a lesser degree of civil freedom gives intellectual freedom enough room to expand to its fullest extent.³

Nor did Kant ever allow the right of revolution. He managed to reconcile this with his approval of the French Revolution by arguing ingeniously if unconvincingly that the latter had not been a revolution at all.⁴ His cautious attitude towards existing political authority was reflected in his own actions. When he became involved in a dispute over censorship he submitted the moment he was ordered directly to do so, with the words: 'to recant and deny one's inner convictions is base; but to remain silent in a case like the present is the duty of a subject, and if everything one says must be the truth, one does not have the same duty to say all the truth in public'. He communicated this decision to Frederick William II as his 'most loyal subject'.⁵

¹ Hans Reiss, *Kant's Political Writings* (Cambridge, 1970), p. 3.
² Ibid., pp. 3–33.   ³ Ibid., p. 59.
⁴ For a recent discussion of Kant's attitude towards revolution, see the symposium in *Journal of the History of Ideas*, 32 (1971).
⁵ Wilhelm Dilthey, 'Der Streit Kants mit der Zensur über das Recht freier Religionsforschung', in *Gesammelte Schriften*, vol. IV (Leipzig and Berlin, 1921), p. 307.

Prologue

One also searches in vain at a lower level for radical impulses. In the second half of the eighteenth century an increasing number of journals devoted to public affairs were founded. Although many of them criticised individual abuses and individual princes, they did not progress to an attack on the system *per se* or to demands for constitutional reforms. The most important was A. L. Schlözer's *Staatsanzeigen*, which achieved a circulation of 4,000, the highest of any German journal in this period. Its editor's nose for political scandal and mordant pen made it the scourge of the more reactionary German princes. Yet typically Schlözer was monarchical to the core, and wanted reform only from above. He also displayed a number of distinctly illiberal traits, defending *lettres de cachet*, attacking both the idea of popular sovereignty and actual revolts, dismissing republics as 'aristocratic' and expressing the fear that meritocracy would degenerate into plutocracy.[1] Schlözer moreover took the English side in the American War of Independence; which was not surprising in view of the fact that he was a Professor at Göttingen and thus a subject and employee of George III. As Lessing said: 'the tame horse is fed in his stable but must serve; the wild horse is free in his wilderness but perishes of hunger and misery'.[2] Lessing was one of the few German intellectuals to make a conscious decision to live by his pen alone, but even a man of his eminence could not survive without a salaried post.[3] The choice was not in fact as simple as he suggested. It was not the case that German intellectuals deliberately smothered their radicalism for the sake of their jobs; rather that they were brought up within the academic–bureaucratic ethos and inevitably reflected the fact in their writings.

Government patronage was important in countries other than Germany but to such a lesser extent as to create a difference in kind. In both England and France the existence of one great capital, a higher degree of literacy and the concentration of political power meant that private patronage was immensely more important. The German equivalent of the Earl of Chesterfield or the Prince de Conti was a sovereign ruler of a state. Moreover, government patronage in England and France was dispensed mainly

---

[1] Fritz Valjavec, *Die Entstehung der politischen Strömungen in Deutschland, 1770–1815* (Munich, 1951), p. 101. Although prepared to label Schlözer and others like him, such as Schubart, Grossing, Winkopp and Wekhrlin as 'pre-' or 'early liberals', Valjavec was impressed neither by their radicalism nor their influence. He began his book with the words 'The liberal and democratic impulses in Germany before 1815 are in many ways self-contradictory, vague and without any real significance for their time. For the history of state activity during the period they are therefore meaningless.' Ibid., p. 4. Schultze has shown that the attacks by commoners on nobles in the journals shared the same specific and basically unpolitical character – *Die Auseinandersetzung zwischen Adel und Bürgertum in den deutschen Zeitschriften der letzten drei Jahrzehnte des 18. Jahrhunderts*, Historische Studien, vol. 163 (Berlin, 1925).
[2] Quoted in Haferkorn, *Der freie Schriftsteller*, p. 667.
[3] Holborn, *History of Modern Germany*, III, p. 320.

in the form of pensions, not as responsible posts in the administrations or universities.

In Germany on the other hand opportunities for active employment were so numerous that no division developed comparable to that between 'High Enlightenment' and 'Grub Street' in France. In Paris there developed during the course of the century a literary proletariat, living on the breadline and consumed by a fierce hatred of the world they had failed to penetrate – the court, the nobility, the Church, the academies, the salons, and of course those figures of the High Enlightenment who had found their niches in the establishment. They expressed their rage, bred by economic misery out of social frustration, in the *libelle*: a combination of crude pornography and political radicalism.[1] In Germany also there were doubtless many aspirant writers who failed to find the employment they thought they deserved but nowhere does one find groups of destitute radicals and pornographers comparable with the French *libellistes*.

V

One further distinctive characteristic of the *Aufklärung* needs to be discussed: its concern, one might also say obsession, with metaphysics, religion and ethics. In the seventeenth and eighteenth centuries German intellectuals were influenced much less by empiricism than their colleagues in Western Europe. There was no German Voltaire to popularise Bacon, Locke and Newton. There was no German Bayle or Simon to sow the seeds of scepticism. There was no German Shaftesbury to dismiss intellectual systems as the most ingenious way known to man of becoming foolish, or Voltaire to deride metaphysics as a minuet in which the dancer displays much skill and grace but ends up exactly where he started.

German thinkers did not of course live in a totally isolated world of their own; the reception of foreign influences, especially French, English and Italian, can be charted through internal evidence, translations and reviews in the learned journals.[2] Yet although such various figures as Rousseau, Locke and Muratori could arouse fervent admiration in Germany, they could not alter the prevailing attitude to politics. The reception of Montesquieu, an especially popular figure, provided an excellent

---

[1] See three recent articles by Robert Darnton, 'In Search of Enlightenment: Recent Attempts to Create a Social History of Ideas', *Journal of Modern History*, 43 (1971), 'The High Enlightenment and the Low-Life of Literature in Pre-Revolutionary France', *Past and Present*, 51 (1971), 'Reading, Writing and Publishing in Eighteenth Century France: A Case Study in the Sociology of Literature', *Daedalus*, December 1970.

[2] See, for example, L. Reynaud, *Histoire générale de l'influence française en Allemagne* (Paris, 1914), Raymond Trousson, 'J.-J. Rousseau et son œuvre dans la presse périodique allemande de 1750 à 1800', *Dix-huitième Siècle*, 1 (1969); G. Zart, *Einfluß der englischen Philosophie seit Bacon auf die deutsche Philosophen des 18. Jahrhunderts* (Berlin, 1881).

example of the ability of German thinkers to adapt liberal impulses to fit their immutable structure of monarchical absolutism.[1] On the question of the division of powers, for example, many were prepared to argue that this existed already. J. S. Pütter held that the relationship between Emperor and Empire or Prince and Estates was fundamentally similar to that between King and Parliament in England. Others managed to combine admiration for Montesquieu's views in general with the belief that his advocacy of limitations on royal power was unimportant. Justi held that representative government had a natural tendency to degenerate into oligarchy and/or chaos: 'I doubt whether a single people can show convincingly that it has gained anything by restricting the royal power'. He doubted whether even Great Britain had derived much benefit from her much-vaunted constitution. The best solution was to give the rulers unlimited power, but also 'to place them in such circumstances and to give them such motivation (*Triebfeder*) that of their own volition they exert all their effort to make their people happy and to rule with goodness and wisdom'. Rudolf Vierhaus concluded that Montesquieu's influence 'contributed to the fact that Wieland, Schiller, Kant, that Schlözer, Spittler and many others welcomed the initial stages of the French Revolution, which appeared to put an end to "despotism". But when the French proceeded to construct a new constitution according to abstract principles of reason and to realise the principles of popular sovereignty, Montesquieu then offered arguments for the rejection of such an enterprise.'[2]

Quite apart from the particular field of politics, indigenous German philosophical strains proved robust enough to retain their separate identity. Largely this was due to the enormous and continuing influence of Leibniz:

> The turn towards empiricism and materialism which Western Enlightenment took in the course of the century, except for Frederick of Prussia, found only a weak echo in Germany. What made the philosophy of Leibniz well-liked in Germany was its combination of a reformatory spirit with an attitude which kept intact existing institutions, such as state and Church, and also intellectual patterns, such as the belief in a personal God and transcendental ethics.[3]

Separate intellectual development was reinforced by social and political considerations. Isolated by background, education and function from the rest of the Third Estate, the academic–bureaucratic elite reserved its creative energies for the inner realm of the spirit.[4] The division of the

---

[1] Rudolf Vierhaus, 'Montesquieu in Deutschland: Zur Geschichte seiner Wirkung als politischer Schriftsteller im 18. Jahrhundert', *Collegium Philosophicum: Studien Joachim Ritter zum 60. Geburtstag* (Basle and Stuttgart, 1965), *passim*.   [2] Ibid., p. 437.
[3] Holborn, *History of Modern Germany*, II, p. 161; cf. Barnard, *Herder's Social and Political Thought*, p. 7.
[4] Krieger, *German Idea of Freedom*, p. 41.

The 'German Problem' in the Eighteenth Century

Reich into a 'Protestant' and 'Catholic' party and the tendency for political controversy to proceed along denominational lines, often using religious terminology, also helped to keep religion a live issue.

For these reasons, German intellectual appetites could never be satisfied by a diet of empiricism, sensationalist psychology and utilitarianism. They needed more ambitious fare, as even the most superficial review shows. Most of them agreed with Goethe's sneering comment on empiricism:

> *Daß ihr den sichersten Pfad gewählt, wer möchte das läugnen?*
> *Aber ihr tappet nur blind auf dem gebahntesten Pfad.*[1]

Even Thomasius, the most 'empirical' of the *Aufklärer*, wrote two substantial works on metaphysics. Christian Wolff was *critical* of what he considered to be the unsystematic and empiricist aspects of Thomasius. His own system was intended to contain nothing which did not proceed from self-evident axioms or preceding truths. Kant took a professional interest in the natural sciences and had the greatest respect for empirical fact, but believed that empiricism as a method was inadequate. Both in science and morality, *a priori* principles and judgments were necessary for explanation and understanding.[2] Even Herder, who denied reality to Kant's 'practical synthetic *a priori* judgments' and who claimed to be a complete empiricist, allotted a central role to the metaphysical forces he called '*Kräfte*'. As Barnard has observed 'Herder...was not a thoroughgoing empiricist at all. At heart, whether he knew it or not, he was not only a metaphysician, but a religious metaphysician at that.'[3] The desire to penetrate beyond the shadows in the cave was reflected in their view of the state. However different their approaches or destinations, they were all agreed that the state was more than an association for the promotion of security and material welfare. The attention they paid to the state's religious, moral and cultural rôle–identity distinguished them sharply from Western European political theorists.[4]

This metaphysical bent revealed itself most clearly in the unfading vitality of religion. In an article entitled 'What is Enlightenment?', published in the *Berlin Journal for Enlightenment*, G. N. Fischer wrote:

Many people think *only* of religion when they hear of *Aufklärung*. No reasonable man will deny...that *Aufklärung* is of course of the greatest importance in the field of religion...But it must not be confined to this field; indeed one cannot conceive a thorough religious *Aufklärung* without the prior triumph of *Aufklärung* in many other

---
[1] Werke, vol. v, pt. 1, *Aus den Tabulae Votivae* (Weimar, 1893), p. 306.
[2] Reiss, *Kant's Political Writings*, pp. 17–18.
[3] Barnard, *Herder's Social and Political Thought*, p. 53.
[4] Krieger, *German Idea of Freedom*, pp. 46–80.

Prologue

fields of human life. The term [*Aufklärung*] extends far beyond the comparatively narrow field of religion.[1]

It is difficult to imagine Voltaire or Diderot feeling obliged to remind their audience that the Enlightenment was not concerned exclusively with religion.

The most violent intellectual controversies of the eighteenth century in Germany – between Wolff and the Pietists or between Lessing and Goeze – were about religion. Nor did these struggles represent a confrontation between belief and unbelief. It is significant that Wolff, the dominant figure of the *Aufklärung*, believed that revelation and reason could be reconciled. Although his attitude was a good deal more ambiguous than most of his contemporaries, even Lessing cannot be compared with the French anti-clericals: 'Lessing spent his life hoping that Christianity was true and arguing that it was not.'[2] There is a disagreement among historians on the degree of peculiarity Germany displayed in this respect. The contrast usually drawn is that between the virulent anti-clericalism of France and the more even-tempered relationship between Enlightenment and religion of other countries.[3] To allow the obvious uniqueness of France does not however prohibit further differentiation. The German attitude towards religion was a great deal more serious and committed than it was in England, for example. It is impossible to imagine Pope's *Essay on Man* or Hume's *Natural History of Religion* written by a German.[4]

This concern with religion did not wane as the century progressed. Chateaubriand commented in 1797: 'When all other nations have given up their respect for religion, it will find a haven among the Germans.'[5] Apart from the sympathetic social background and intellectual tradition, this was due to the remarkable vitality of religious institutions. Protestantism was saved from ossification by the Pietist movement which emerged in the second half of the seventeenth century. Its origins lay in the radical reaction to the Thirty Years War. The appalling devastation and

---

[1] Quoted in Klaus Epstein, *The Genesis of German Conservatism* (Princeton, 1966), p. 35.
[2] Henry Chadwick, 'Lessing', *Encyclopedia of Philosophy*, vol. IV (London and New York, 1967), p. 445.
[3] Dieckmann, *Themes and Structures of the Enlightenment*, p. 70.
[4] 'The belief in a personal God of supreme wisdom and benevolence, the creator of a perfect world, who had planted in the immortal human soul the power to rise – through moral virtue – to the highest objectives of the universe, was not questioned by any serious German thinker. Philosophical materialism, which became one of the important schools of thought in France, found no place in Germany. There was also much reluctance to follow the development towards an epistemological scepticism and empiricism that took place in England from Locke to Hume.' – Holborn, *History of Modern Germany*, II, p. 311; cf. the same author's 'German Idealism', pp. 13–14.
[5] Quoted in G. P. Gooch, *Germany and the French Revolution* (London, 1920, reprinted 1965), p. 71.

suffering caused by the campaigns and God's failure to give the 'right' side any decisive assistance were seen as a divine judgment on the Protestant establishment. This immediate discontent was coupled to long-term dissatisfaction with orthodox Lutheranism. Men such as Philip Spener (1635–1705), August Hermann Francke (1663–1727) and Count Nicolaus Ludwig von Zinzendorf (1700–60) believed that the abuses Luther had ejected had been allowed gradually to creep back in again. Contrary to the wishes of its founder, they held, Lutheranism had become doctrinally dogmatic and institutionally rigid. Pietism came to assume many forms, but every variation was characterised by a desire to return to a simpler and more personal faith. Just as Luther had by-passed the Catholic Church in his attempt to establish direct communication with God, so did Pietists spurn orthodoxy. Like him, they followed the road of asceticism, mortification and introspection, via a profound sense of human depravity and personal sin to the destination of repentance, conversion and regeneration. Pietism's very strong subjective accent often took its members into mysticism but did not remove them from the world altogether. From the start the movement was imbued with a strong social reformatory spirit. Wherever groups of Pietists gathered, orphanages, workhouses and schools quickly followed. Of Francke's great complex of institutions at Halle the first two were an orphanage and a school for paupers.[1]

This combination of practical charity and personal religion proved so potent that within the space of a few decades Pietism came to dominate Protestant intellectual circles. Although founded only in 1694 the University of Halle quickly acquired the reputation of being the most progressive in the *Reich*, and expanded accordingly. Through the appointment of his pupils to chairs at other universities, Francke in particular wielded an extraordinary degree of influence. This phase of complete ascendancy was of relatively short duration. Some Pietists were unable to resist the temptation to allow their subjective approach to degenerate into emotional excess. After they had acquired wealth, power and prestige, the leaders began to slip into the same faults for which they had rebuked Lutheran orthodoxy so sternly. The ascetic and theocentric character of the movement as a whole was increasingly at odds with the secular Enlightenment.

Yet although Pietism as a direct force was clearly in decline by 1740, its indirect influence permeated German culture throughout the eighteenth century and into the next. The *Aufklärer* and the Pietists engaged each other in a number of bitter controversies, notably that which led to the expulsion of Christian Wolff from Halle in 1723, but their relationship had not always been acrimonious. Before the Pietists became conservative in every respect, their individualism, dislike of dogma and professed sup-

[1] Hinrichs, *Preußentum und Pietismus*, p. 18.

port for religious toleration were all attractive to their later opponents. Thomasius and even Wolff were never entirely free of the effects of their early encounter with the movement. Its enormous influence on education in the Protestant territories of the *Reich* meant that an unconscious Pietist residue remained in the minds of many who at first sight seem diametrically opposed. Indeed it is difficult to find a single Protestant intellectual of whom it is *not* said that Pietism played a formative rôle in his youth.[1] Carl Hinrichs closed his classic study of Pietism in Prussia with the words:

> One result of [Pietism's] struggles with Wolff was that the German Enlightenment did not bear any irreligious or non-Christian characteristics, and that in Halle a new scientific theology grew out of the fusion of Pietism and Wolffism, the theology of Baumgarten, Semler and Nösselt. The victory of the Enlightenment in Prussia was sealed, but the inheritance of Pietism continued to be effective.[2]

The controversies with the *Aufklärung* also pushed the Pietists increasingly towards doctrinal conservatism and an alliance with their former enemy, Lutheran orthodoxy. Politically any such change was unnecessary, for the movement had always been explicitly conservative. They inherited from Luther a belief in the total depravity of the world and the impossibility of mixing religion with politics. Unlike the English Puritans, with whom they had certain characteristics in common, the Pietists refused even to contemplate the use of secular means to establish God's kingdom on earth. Far from posing a threat to the existing order, Pietism proved to be a powerful extra prop. Duty, obedience and self-discipline were the *leitmotive* of the movement's secular message, expressed most clearly in the simple command: 'Pray and work!'[3]

The authorities soon came to appreciate the Pietist potential. In Prussia in particular a close alliance was formed, as both Frederick I and Frederick William I lent the movement official support in return for help in dealing with problems of education and social welfare. Initially Francke and his group at Halle were fired with the ambition of converting the world, but this dream faded rapidly as they were absorbed into the Prussian state. This relationship was by no means one-sided, for the Pietists did not hesitate to call on the state for assistance in their various disputes, with orthodox Lutherans, provincial nobles or enlightened thinkers such as Wolff, ex-

---

[1] 'Whereas Pietism as a distinct movement ran its course before the middle of the eighteenth century, its indirect influence through men like Kant continued long after it had ceased to be an important element in the religious life of Germany.' T. M. Greene, in his introduction to Kant's *Religion Within the Limits of Reason Alone* (New York, 1960), p. xiv.
[2] Hinrichs, *Preußentum und Pietismus*, p. 441. For a discussion of the relationship between Pietism and the *Aufklärung* with special reference to Lessing, see W. H. Bruford, *Theatre, Drama and Audience in Goethe's Germany* (London, 1950), pp. 117–22.
[3] Ritter, *Das deutsche Problem*, pp. 19–20.

pelled from Halle at their instigation in 1723. With the help of Berlin, for example, they infiltrated, influenced and then took control of the ecclesiastical and educational system of East Prussia.[1] The accession of Frederick the Great checked any further expansion of Pietism but did not signal its demise. Although he found the movement's doctrines distasteful in the extreme, the new king was as aware as his predecessors of the services it performed for his state. Even had he attempted to uproot Pietism, it would have lived on in the generations of nobles, officials, academics and burghers educated in its schools and universities.

Although it has attracted far less attention, there was a similar movement of renewal within the Catholic Church. It had two sides, which were held to be interdependent by its supporters: an 'external' movement for greater episcopal independence from Rome and an 'internal' movement for improving the quality of religious life. Although the German bishops had been in the van of the Conciliar Movement against the papacy, there had been a lull in hostilities between the middle of the fifteenth century and the end of the seventeenth. By the early eighteenth century however, the decline in interdenominational strife in the *Reich*, the example set by French Gallicanism, the growing influence of 'Jansenism' and the development of political absolutism all combined to redirect the episcopacy's attention to relations with Rome. As disputes with the papacy grew in frequency and intensity, so did the need for a theoretical justification of the prince-bishops' demands. This was provided by a group of anti-papal canonists, who with the help of their episcopal employers attained a dominant position in both the universities and vicariates of the ecclesiastical states by the middle of the century.[2] They were united in the belief that a combination of papal usurpation, episcopal weakness and the sheer passage of time had distorted the constitution of the Church. In particular they held that a programme of historical research was required to establish a distinction between the *essentialia* of papal power, which rested on divine institution, and the *accessoria*, which rested on mere prescription. Once the latter excrescences had been pruned, a return to the essence of the Church – the *ecclesia primitiva* – would be possible. This structural reorganisation would be accompanied by internal renewal, by means of a Jansenist reform of priesthood and liturgy.

This movement cannot however be understood purely in ecclesiastical terms. The prince-bishops never forgot that they were rulers as well as successors of the Apostles and responded to the same influences as their secular

---

[1] Hinrichs, *Preußentum und Pietismus*, ch. 3.
[2] On the development of the episcopalist programme, see Heribert Raab, *Die Concordata Nationis Germanicae in der kanonistischen Diskussion des 17. bis 19. Jahrhunderts: Ein Beitrag zur Geschichte der episkopalistischen Theorie in Deutschland* (Wiesbaden, 1956).

colleagues. The development of absolutism in a number of European countries in the seventeenth century did not pass unnoticed in the ecclesiastical states, although their response was usually hesitant and delayed. Due partly to the elective, non-dynastic nature of their states and partly to the fact that many of them were Imperial Knights, the prince-bishops tended to be more committed to the *Reich* constitution than the Protestant princes who sought to turn their territories into sovereign states. The development of the secularised and rationalistic Natural Law, which replaced the medieval web of interlocking authorities with the omnicompetent state, took place at Protestant universities, not at Mainz, Trier or Würzburg. Nevertheless, the differences between Protestant, Catholic and ecclesiastical states were of emphasis, not of kind, and it is not surprising that by the 1750s there was a general response. This was reflected in the changing view of Church–State relations. While the Jesuits dominated higher education, canon law was closely tied to theology, but as the eighteenth century progressed it fell under the sway of the Natural Law and political thought of the Enlightenment.[1]

There was also a growing feeling among Catholics that they had been overtaken by the Protestants. This was not simply a reaction to Frederick the Great's military success, but a more general sense of cultural inferiority. The achievements of scholars at universities in Hanover, Saxony and Prussia made their Catholic colleagues seem parochial and old-fashioned. D'Alembert wrote that when one travelled from a Catholic to a Protestant university in Germany one felt that one had travelled four hundred miles in the hour or had lived through four hundred years.[2] The growing gulf was indeed especially marked in the field of education. In higher education it was the Protestant universities which adapted their curricula to changing social needs, while their Catholic counterparts remained dominated by the Jesuits and their scholastic theology and philosophy. It was Protestant Göttingen, founded in 1737, that led the way in the humanities, mathematics, natural sciences and medicine.[3] The Italian Carlantonio Pilati observed that: 'the Protestant Germans are infinitely more enlightened than the Catholics' and explained the difference by reference to their respective educational systems.[4]

The problem was recognised in Catholic Germany long before any solution was attempted. Increasingly, young German scholars protested with

[1] Ibid., p. 80.
[2] Quoted in Helmut Mathy, 'Ein Schriftstück zur Mainzer Universitätsreform aus dem Jahre 1779', *Jahrbuch der Vereinigung 'Freunde der Universität Mainz'*, 9 (1960), p. 67.
[3] Bruford, *Germany in the 18th Century*, p. 245.
[4] Franco Venturi, 'History and Reform in the Middle of the Eighteenth Century', in *The Diversity of History: Essays in honour of Sir Herbert Butterfield*, ed. J. H. Elliott and H. G. Koenigsberger (London, 1970), p. 238.

their feet and drifted away to the Protestant universities of the North.[1] The same pattern was repeated in primary education. Johann Bernard Basedow (1723-90), the founder of the 'philanthropist' schools and the most influential pedagogue of the eighteenth century, was born at Hamburg and worked for most of his life at Dessau.[2] Most of the Catholic schools remained in the hands of ill-paid and semi-literate teachers, who were often the village bell-ringer and sexton as well. As the gap between Protestants and Catholics widened it was perhaps inevitable that eventually the latter would start to put their own house in order.

The most important characteristic of Catholic reform was that it proceeded inside the Church. The movement was not only approved, it was led by the hierarchy. The climax was the Congress of Ems of 1786, organised by the Archbishops of Mainz, Trier, Cologne and Salzburg and conducted by their delegates. This meeting was more than just another salvo in the centuries-old campaign against the Curia. Two documents were produced: not only the celebrated *Punctatio*, which was the episcopalist manifesto, but also the *Reformdekret*, a long and detailed programme for the reform of the Church.[3] This alliance between reform and the leadership of the Church was facilitated by the familiar fusion of academic theory and administrative practice. Invariably those who wrote about reform were also active members of their several vicariates. Johann Nicolaus von Hontheim *alias* Febronius, for example, was simultaneously a Professor at Trier University and a suffragan bishop.

In the event, the 'external' side of the movement could find no way of surmounting papal intransigence, but reform from within did make progress. In almost every diocese serious attempts were made by the prince-bishops to improve the training and status of parish priests, to make services more intelligible to the common man, to purge the 'excesses' of baroque piety and to curb the power and wealth of the monastic orders. Profligate rakes such as Johann Theodor of Liège were far outnumbered by conscientious reformers such as Max Franz of Cologne, Clemens Wenzeslaus of Trier, Frederick Karl of Mainz, Heinrich of Fulda, Franz Ludwig of Würzburg and Bamberg, August of Speyer and Hieronymus of Salzburg. Although in the ecclesiastical states the dual secular and ecclesiastical status of the prince-bishops ensured a firm link between theory and practice, the relationship was also close in most of the secular states. This was even the case in the Habsburg Monarchy, commonly regarded as a permanent battle-ground for Church and State. Recent research has established that Archbishop Trautson of Vienna and his successor Migazzi were keen to cooperate with the Austrian state in the

---

[1] See below, p. 103. [2] Hertz, *German Public Mind*, pp. 384-6.
[3] For further discussion of the Congress of Ems, see below, ch. 6.

work of reform. It was not until the 1770s and especially the 1780s that the growing radicalism of Kaunitz and Joseph created serious tension.[1]

This vitality of the established Churches in the *Reich* contrasted sharply with the decadence of the Catholic Church in France and rather less sharply with the complacency of the Anglican Church in England. The upper echelons of the French hierarchy were characterised by opposition to reform of any kind, non-residence and in some cases even scepticism.[2] The wide and bitter gulf which opened between the upper and lower clergy made a vital contribution to the collapse of the old order. The Anglican Church was not as somnolent as is sometimes assumed but neither was it marked by any progressive energy. The most potent religious force in England was Methodism, which began within the established Church but eventually was forced outside it. In both countries, but especially in France, the intellectuals found the traditional forms of belief increasingly unsatisfactory.

In Germany, on the other hand, very few felt obliged to desert the Church into which they were born. Even those who could not accept the literal truth of the Christian Gospel did not turn on the faith, but journeyed on into further metaphysical realms. Indeed the most striking single difference between the French and German Enlightenments was the respective incidence of anti-clericalism. The attacks on the Catholic Church published in Germany were written not but anti-Christians but by Protestants and were a continuation of the polemical – and predominantly political – battle waged by the two sides since the Reformation.

VI

As this account of the Catholic reform movement has sought to show, there was a close relationship between theorists and administrators. As was implied by the preceding sections dealing with the formation of the academic–bureaucratic class and the development of its attitudes towards the state, the same alliance operated in politics. Like any other statement on the relationship between thought and action in the period, this revives once again the aged problem of 'Enlightened Absolutism'. A full discussion of the issues or even the literature involved would devour a substantial volume without difficulty, but in the context of the present discussion one or two rudimentary observations need to be made.

Few would disagree that in the course of the eighteenth century a new *style* of politics developed in the *Reich*. The princes abandoned their

[1] Klingenstein, *Staatsverwaltung und kirchliche Autorität*, pp. 85, 92–5, 106–18, 156, 167.
[2] A. Soboul, *La France à la Veille de la Révolution* (Paris, 1966), p. 112; R. R. Palmer, *Catholics and Unbelievers in Eighteenth Century France* (Princeton, 1939), p. 26.

patrimonial view of the state in favour of one based on a social contract. In the words of Frederick the Great, they became the 'first servants' of the state rather than its owners. The individual principalities were held to be associations for the promotion of the security and welfare of those living within their boundaries. At the same time princes great and small began to introduce reforms of striking homogeneity: administrative, judicial, social, economic, educational, religious. The reality of these development is not in doubt; it is only when an attempt is made to trace a causal connection between them, or between either of them and the wider Enlightenment, that controversy arises.

Quite apart from its inherent improbability, any idea of a reign of philosopher-kings has been subjected to a number of potent criticisms. Many historians have argued that only the absolutism of 'Enlightened Absolutism' was real. Although decked out with all the trimmings of Enlightenment terminology, the 'enlightened' policies stemmed from practical considerations. They have been seen variously as an attempt to modernise the state and more specifically to increase revenue, as the 'westernisation' of Central and Eastern Europe, or as a simple continuation of old policies under new names.[1]

All these qualifications can be supported by an impressive weight of evidence and command respect. Certainly they carry more conviction than the chronological and geographical excesses of the International Commission of Historical Sciences of 1937, which pushed Enlightened Absolutism back to Pericles, forwards to Napoleon III and sideways to Turkey, India and China.[2] Yet now the pendulum has swung too far in the opposite direction. So anxious are some historians to avoid a charge of naïvety, that they have thrown out the enlightened baby with the *raison d'état* bathwater.[3] In the sense defined by Fritz Hartung – 'a form of government strongly influenced by the philosophy, and particularly by the political philosophy of the Enlightenment'.[4] Enlightened Absolutism can be identified in the *Reich*, although probably nowhere else.[5]

---

[1] Charles Morazé, 'Finance et despotisme: Essai sur les Despotes Éclairés', *Annales, Économies, Sociétés, Civilisations*, 13 (1948); Darnton, 'In Search of Enlightenment', p. 122; M. S. Anderson, *Europe in the Eighteenth Century 1713–1783* (London, 1961), pp. 121–3.

[2] *Bulletin of the International Committee of Historical Sciences* IX (1937).

[3] The comment of Sir Herbert Butterfield on the Namier School's interpretation of English history in the late eighteenth century is also appropriate here: 'Here is an interpretation of history which, through an anxiety to avoid being hoaxed, is in danger of refusing to realise the operative force of ideas'–'George III and the Namier School', *Encounter*, 8, 4 (1957), p. 74.

[4] Fritz Hartung, *Enlightened Despotism* (London, 1957), p. 8.

[5] 'A tendency that in other countries proved to be inconsistent, unstable, or derivative from other considerations, enlightened absolutism was in Germany from Pufendorf to the pre-revolutionary Kant, anchored securely in the tradition of the state.' – Krieger, *German Idea of Freedom*, p. 50.

Prologue

Three sources of confusion have obscured this identification. Firstly, it has been assumed too readily that there was a natural antagonism between the Enlightenment and the demands of the state. If any measure can be shown to have enhanced the power of the state, it is concluded that it can have had nothing to do with the Enlightenment.[1] Such an axiom would only be possible if the Enlightenment had been characterised by a mistrust of the state and an attachment to liberalism. This was signally not the case. The central rôle the philosophes allotted the legislator, their adoption of the *thèse royale* in France and their ambivalent relationship with authoritarian régimes elsewhere in Europe do not allow such a conclusion. Although none of them, with the dubious exception of the physiocrats, advanced a coherent theory of enlightened absolutism, their attitude to the central authorities was not hostile in principle.

This was even more clearly the case in the German-speaking territories. Not only did the *Aufklärer* deny subjects any right of resistance, they advocated a state with a monopoly of public authority and vastly increased responsibilities.[2] The German prince who increased his own power by reducing that of the Church, provincial estates or municipal councils, was fulfilling, not denying, the political aspirations of the *Aufklärung*. This is to argue only that there was no necessary antagonism, not that clashes could never occur. Frequently they did, and in any struggle for precedence between *Staatsräson* and *Aufklärung* it was invariably the latter that went to the wall. Even so, this friction was possible only in the few states large enough to nurture ambitions for expansion. In most of the states which made up the *Reich* there was no temptation to subordinate plans for reform to the needs of the military.[3]

This source of confusion has a social corollary: the belief that the Enlightenment was a 'bourgeois' movement, in contradistinction to the 'feudal' or 'aristocratic' established order. Certainly many of the attitudes enlightened thinkers held in common were hostile to privilege, but even the most perfunctory review of the philosophes' backgrounds, patrons and social habits reveals that such a simple social categorisation is erroneous: 'By 1778, when all of Paris was salaaming before Voltaire, the last generation of philosophes had become pensioned, petted and completely integrated in high society...It has been argued recently that, far from rising with the middle class, liberalism descended from a long line of aristocrats,

---

[1] 'Ils [the philosophes], ne virent pas que les souverains n'avaient pris dans le programme de l'Encyclopédie que les points qui leur étaient utiles; ou plus exactement, que dans ce que les "despotes éclairés" avaient fait et que n'avait rien de bien nouveau, il y avait des mesures qui coincidaient avec des points du programme encyclopédiste; ils ne virent pas que le but des souverains était seulement la puissance de leurs États pour dominer, envahir et démembrer.' – Mousnier and Labrousse, *Le XVIIIe Siècle*, p. 173.
[2] See above, pp. 17–19.
[3] Hartung, *Deutsche Verfassungsgeschichte*, p. 140.

and so did the Enlightenment.'¹ This fusion was given pictorial expression in Lemonnier's painting of Madame Geoffrin's salon, in which D'Alembert, Helvétius, Diderot, Quesnay, Rousseau and Raynal, among others, rub shoulders with the Duc de Nivernais, the Duchess d'Anville, the Prince de Conti, the Comtesse d'Houdetot, Maréchal de Richelieu and the Duc de Choiseul. Also present are the Baron de L'Aulne (Turgot) and the Baron de Montesquieu.²

In the *Reich* the cement which bound *Aufklärung* and Establishment was even stronger. Whereas most French nobles could play little part in the government of their country and became correspondingly more restive, their German counterparts were either sovereigns in their own right or high-ranking civil servants.³ Similarly the links between the German intellectuals and their states were much closer. The *Aufklärung* sought change, but was not a subversive movement; it developed within and in support of the established order, not outside and against it.⁴

The second main source of confusion which has obscured enlightened absolutism in the *Reich* has been a failure to distinguish between French Enlightenment and German *Aufklärung*, or rather an assumption that they were the same.⁵ To search for direct evidence of French ideas flourishing in German administrations is to invite inevitable disappointment. Many historians have suffered in particular from an obsession with the ideas of the physiocrats, a group with limited influence in their own country and virtually none outside it. The similarity between their '*despotisme légal*' and '*despotisme éclairé*', which was more terminological than substantive, has allowed the great physiocratic red herring to be dragged across the tracks whenever the problem is discussed.⁶ As I argued above, in the *Reich* enlightened ideas, and particularly political ideas, acquired their own distinctive character, as a result of the special background and status of their creators. The connection between theory and practice was so close that a separate classification of 'intellectuals' and 'administrators' is

---

¹ Darnton, 'In Search of Enlightenment', p. 119.
² The best easily accessible reproduction can be found in *The Eighteenth Century: Europe in the Age of Enlightenment*, ed. Alfred Cobban (London, 1969), pp. 262–3. A key to all those present is provided on p. 277. For further criticism of the notion of a 'bourgeois' Enlightenment see Miss Behrens' penetrating review article '"Straight History" and "History in Depth": the experience of writers on eighteenth century France', *Historical Journal*, VIII, 1 (1965), especially p. 123. See also below, p. 196.   ³ See above, p. 14.
⁴ See below, Chs 3 and 5.   ⁵ See above, pp. 2–3.
⁶ Even Fritz Hartung maintained that 'there is no ground for contesting the view that the characteristic doctrines of *Despotisme éclairé* developed in France in the sixties of the eighteenth century, as a political off-shoot of the economic doctrines of the Physiocrats', although he also allows that 'side by side with this French doctrine, the followers of which were avowed adherents of Enlightened Despotism, the ideas advanced by the eighteenth century writers on administration in Germany deserve attention in the history of Enlightened Absolutism'. *Enlightened Despotism*, pp. 9–10.

Prologue

always difficult and often impossible.[1] Those who deny the reality of 'enlightened absolutism' neatly evade this difficulty by denying that the thinkers in question were 'enlightened': 'What is true of France applies even more to the rest of Europe, where "enlightened absolutism"...had little relation to the Enlightenment. Most sovereigns reformed in order to maximise power. They reformed with cameralists, not philosophes, drawing on a tradition of bureaucratic rationalising that went back to the seventeenth, and sometimes the sixteenth century.'[2] Any definition of the Enlightenment which excluded from its ranks Thomasius, Wolff, Sonnenfels, Justi or Martini, must surely be unjustifiably narrow. Their links with the cameralists of an earlier period would disqualify them only if their views were identical with their predecessors', and that was patently not so.[3] Certainly the *Aufklärer* did not spring out Athene-like, ready-armed with the weapons of the Enlightenment, but neither for that matter did the philosophes.

More than half a century ago Hans von Voltelini pointed out that the reforms of the German enlightened rulers had only a tenuous connection with the ideas of the French Enlightenment, but were rooted firmly in the indigenous school of Natural Law, exemplified in the eighteenth century by Christian Wolff.[4] Unfortunately, his article has been sadly neglected, even in his own country. Only when the *Aufklärung* is allowed its own proper individuality, and is not viewed as a pale reflection of the philosophes, can enlightened absolutism be seen in its proper perspective.

A final fundamental error which usually creeps in when enlightened absolutism is discussed is the assumption that the policies enacted in a given state were the personal responsibility of the ruler. Enlightened Absolutism in Prussia, for example, is discussed usually in terms only of Frederick the Great, his relationship with his father, his *Anti-Machiavel* and the Political Testaments, his treatment of Voltaire, his perpetuation of the social hierarchy, his attitude towards popular education, his belief in the primacy of *Staatsräson*, his antipathy towards German culture, and so on. To a certain extent such an approach can be justified. In theory at least the absolute princes had the absolute power to impose their will on their territories. In theory at least their officials were the instruments of

---

[1] See above, pp. 11–15.   [2] Darnton, 'In Search of Enlightenment', p. 122.
[3] This is shown in great detail by Karl-Heinz Osterloh, *Joseph von Sonnenfels und die österreichische Reformbewegung im Zeitalter des aufgeklärten Absolutismus: Eine Studie zum Zusammenhang von Kameralwissenschaft und Verwaltungspraxis*, Historische Studien, vol. 409 (Hamburg, Lübeck, 1970).
[4] Voltelini, *Die naturrechtlichen Reformen*; the same point has been made recently by Ernst Walder, 'Zwei Studien über den aufgeklärten Absolutismus', *Schweizer Beiträge zur allgemeinen Geschichte*, 15 (1957).

The 'German Problem' in the Eighteenth Century

their will and their subjects passive recipients. Yet even in such individual creations as Frederick's Prussia or Joseph's Austria there was plenty of scope for individual officials to influence the formation and conduct of policy. Only if one pays due attention to the achievements and intellectual background of this group can one appreciate the practical strength of the *Aufklärung*.

In Prussia the attention paid to Frederick's conservatism, militarism and cynicism needs to be counterbalanced by a consideration of the work of Cocceji, Carmer and Suarez.[1] In the Habsburg Monarchy the influence exerted by the enlightened *Beamtentum* was far greater. In the past two or three decades it has come to be realised just how little 'Josephism' had to do with Joseph II.[2] Both the ideological basis and the legislative programme had been worked out long before Joseph became co-regent with his mother.[3] The introduction of enlightened reforms during the reign of the bigoted Maria Theresa is a paradox only if one ignores the work of Kaunitz, Sonnenfels, van Swieten, Riegger, and the others.[4] In the smaller German states, where few of the princes possessed Frederick's or Joseph's energy and personality, the bureaucrat–academics enjoyed correspondingly more scope.

This sketch of the *Reich* in the eighteenth century has sought to show that in several important respects it differed from Western Europe and particularly from France. The political, social, economic and cultural developments which elsewhere brought innovation, gradual or violent, from below, either passed the *Reich* by or were adapted by the established order for its own purposes. For all their apparently irrational, archaic and oppressive characteristics, both the *Reich* as a whole and its component principalities were going concerns when the French Revolution struck. Now the masses received the opportunity to overturn the old order, but they failed to take it. The isolated outbreaks of violence cracked only the paint of the *Reich*, they made no impression on the structure.[5] Although the resolution could destroy the *Reich* in its physical manifestations, it

---

[1] Otto Hintze, 'Preußens Entwicklung zum Rechtsstaat', *Forschungen zur brandenburgisch-preußischen Geschichte*, 32 (1920).

[2] See especially, Fritz Valjavec, *Der Josefinismus: Zur geistigen Entwicklung Oesterreichs im achtzehnten und neunzehnten Jahrhundert*, 2nd ed. (Munich, 1945); Winter, *Josefinismus*; Ferdinand Maass, *Der Josephinismus: Quellen zu seiner Geschichte in Oesterreich 1760–1790*, vol. I, *Ursprung und Wesen des Josephinismus 1760–1769* (Vienna, 1951). For a particularly intelligent recent discussion, see Klingenstein, *Staatsverwaltung und kirchliche Autorität*.

[3] Osterloh, *Sonnenfels*, p. 79.

[4] In his first work on Josephism, Ferdinand Maass identified Kaunitz as the chief 'culprit' responsible for its development. In a more recent work he has sought to show that Maria Theresa must also carry a large share of the blame – *Der Frühjosephinismus* (Vienna and Munich, 1969); see also Klingenstein, *Staatsverwaltung und kirchliche Autorität*, pp. 77–9.

[5] See below, Part 3.

could not destroy overnight attitudes and habits which had grown up over centuries. Neither the *Reichsdeputationshauptschluß* of 1803 nor the formal abolition of the *Reich* in 1806 nor the foundation of the German *Bund* in 1815 marked a decisive break in German history. The traditional ideals of religion, duty and obedience continued to dominate public life. What follows is an attempt to show how in one part of Germany these ideals adjusted to changing circumstances, without their essence being diluted.

The Electorate of Mainz in the Eighteenth Century (1743-1803)

Introduction

MENTZ, an archbishopric and electorate in Germany. It lies on the banks of the river Mayne, between the electorate of Trier on the west, the Palatinate on the south, Franconia on the east, and the Wetteraw on the north. It is about 60 miles in length from north east to south west and about 50 in breadth.[1]

As the Electorate of Mainz was the largest, wealthiest and most important ecclesiastical state in the *Reich*, it is surprising that no unified account of its history in the eighteenth century has been written. Partly this has been due to the obsession of many historians of Germany with the struggle for supremacy between Austria and Prussia and their failure to recognise the existence of a 'Third Germany'.[2] Because so many of the principalities which made up the latter were of limited size, resources and influence, their collective importance has been overlooked. It is forgotten that although literally hundreds of states disappeared from the map during the various territorial reorganisations of 1803-15, the people who lived in them did not. Although they now became Prussians, Bavarians, Nassauers, Hessians, or whatever, their attitudes did not change overnight, or indeed from one generation to another. Even a state with such a clearly defined ethos as Prussia could not absorb such formidable amounts of territory without both physical and psychological change. This alone is justification enough for paying attention to the political units which perished with the *Reich* in 1803-6.

The particular neglect of Mainz has been due to the city's vulnerability in war-time and the resulting dispersal of its archives. Until very recently histories of Mainz were based almost entirely on the collections in the *Stadtarchiv* and *Stadtbibliothek* there, which although substantial represent only a small proportion of the total available.[3] The most im-

---

[1] *Encyclopaedia Britannica*, 2nd ed. (Edinburgh, 1781), pp. 48,96.
[2] For a discussion of the historiography of this point, see Helmut Mathy, 'Über das Mainzer Erzkanzleramt in der Neuzeit: Stand und Aufgaben der Forschung', *Geschichtliche Landeskunde*, 2 (1965).
[3] See, for example, the works by Bockenheimer, Cremer, Dael, Goldschmidt, Schrohe and

The Electorate of Mainz in the Eighteenth Century

portant source for the history of the Electorate, in the eighteenth century at least, is the *Mainzer Erzkanzler Archiv*, now in the *Haus-, Hof- und Staatsarchiv* at Vienna, and it is largely on this that this present work relies.[1]

For most historians, and particularly for most non-German historians, Mainz acquires meaning only in the context of the French occupation of the city in 1792–3, the foundation of a revolutionary club, the convocation of a Rhenish-German National Convention and the request for annexation to France. Almost every general history of revolutionary Europe contains an obligatory reference to the 'Mainz Jacobins'. It is one of the aims of this book to show that the Electorate's experience during this crucial period is incomprehensible without a thorough investigation of what went before and that in the light of this knowledge the manifold misconceptions and apparent paradoxes in which the episode of the French occupation abounds dissolve without resistance. At the same time, it is also the aim of this book to show that the decades before 1792 did not constitute simply an incubatory phase but had an identity and a validity of their own.

To many Germans living in the late eighteenth century however, and in particular to those who subscribed to the political philosophy of the Enlightenment, the Electorate of Mainz seemed an anomaly.[2] They viewed it, together with all the other ecclesiastical states, as an unhappy reminder of those dark centuries of clerical domination when the *sacerdotium* had dominated by usurping the rightful powers of the *imperium*. The combination in one man of both prelate and prince seemed the very apotheosis of *l'infâme*. Subsequent historians have re-echoed this verdict with varying degrees of vehemence, depending on their political or religious affiliation, but the dual status of the Electorate's ruler has also been a source of confusion and some explanatory remarks are necessary.

Although ruled by the same Archbishop-Elector, the boundaries of the Archbishopric and those of the Electorate did not coincide. As Archbishop and Metropolitan, his authority was restricted to ecclesiastical

---

Scholl listed in the bibliography. Even the recent work on the demography and social structure of the city by M. Dreyfus (*Sociétés et mentalités à Mayence dans la seconde moitié du 18e siècle* [Paris, 1968]) relies very heavily on the *Stadtarchiv*.

[1] It appears from his bibliography that M. Dreyfus did not use the *Mainzer Erzkanzler Archiv* at all. Helmut Mathy has made extensive use of the Vienna archives and what remains of the University archives, now at Darmstadt, in writing many interesting and scholarly articles on the history of the University and the revolutionary period. See particularly *Die Geschichte des Mainzer Erzkanzlerarchivs 1782–1815*, Recht und Geschichte, vol. 5 (Wiesbaden, 1969).

[2] Peter Wende, *Die geistlichen Staaten und ihre Auflösung im Urteil der zeitgenössischen Publizistik*, Historische Studien, vol. 396 (Lübeck and Hamburg, 1966). For a discussion of the historiography of the ecclesiastical states, see Heribert Raab, *Clemens Wenzeslaus von Sachsen und seine Zeit 1739–1812* (Freiburg, Basle and Vienna, 1962), pp. 9–21.

Introduction

jurisdiction over the dioceses of Worms, Speyer, Constance, Strasbourg, Augsburg, Chur, Würzburg, Eichstätt, Paderborn and Hildesheim.[1] As Elector, however, he was secular ruler of the Electorate of Mainz and although its area was much smaller than the arch-diocese, his rights were the same as those enjoyed by all the other princes of the *Reich* in their own states.

The geography of this Electorate was a good deal more complicated than the brief description from the *Encyclopaedia Britannica* would suggest. Roughly it can be divided into three areas: firstly, the Lower Electorate (*Unterstift*), centred on Mainz and comprising a number of villages south of the city, the Rheingau, the area surrounding Bingen and a long strip of territory extending north-east of Mainz into the Taunus, as far as the fortress of Königstein; secondly, the Upper Electorate (*Oberstift*), a large and unbroken rectangle, stretching from Seligenstadt in the north to Walldürn in the south, bisected by the river Main and with its administrative capital at Aschaffenburg; and finally the Thuringian possessions, which consisted of two separate blocks of territory around Heiligenstadt and Erfurt respectively, the former region bearing the collective name 'The Eichsfeld'. There were in addition a number of other smaller parcels of territory dotted about Hessen and the Rhineland, such as the area around Amöneburg, sandwiched between Hessen-Kassel and Hessen-Darmstadt; the area on the *Bergstraße* (the road between Darmstadt and Heidelberg), which had been mortgaged to the Palatinate in 1463 but redeemed in 1624, and Oberlahnstein, at the mouth of the river Lahn.[2]

Although the Elector usually spent the summer at his Aschaffenburg residence and although there was a special Statthalter in Erfurt for the Thuringian provinces, the 350,000 subjects[3] living in this scattered collection of territories were ruled from the city of Mainz. As a site of continuous habitation since the first century A.D. and as the seat of the first Archbishop of the Empire, Mainz offered the eighteenth century tourist a great deal. As J. G. Keysler noted in his guide book of 1751 'a curious traveller will meet there several things worthy of his notice'.[4] The Austrian and Prussian bombardment during the siege of 1793 and the bombing of the Second World War have left only a few isolated reminders of the city's former

---

[1] *Recht und Verfassung des Reiches in der Zeit Maria Theresias*, ed. Hermann Conrad, Wissenschaftliche Abhandlungen der Arbeitsgemeinschaft für Forschung des Landes Nordrhein-Westfalen, vol. 28 (Cologne and Opladen, 1964), p. 491. Other suffragans formerly subject to Mainz were Prague, raised to metropolitan status by Clement XI, and Halberstadt and Verden, whose secularisation was recognised by the Peace of Westphalia.

[2] For a complete description, see A. F. Büsching, *A New System of Geography*, vol. 4 (London, 1762), pp. 523–42.

[3] Dreyfus, *Mayence*, p. 14.

[4] J. G. Keysler, *Travels through Germany, Bohemia, Hungary, Switzerland, Italy and Lorrain*, 2nd ed. (London, 1757) p. 269.

glory and an effort of imagination is required to visualise it as it was at the end of the eighteenth century.[1]

Most visitors approached the city from the east, either across the pontoon bridge from the fortified village of Kastel on the right bank of the Rhine, or by means of the 'market-ship', which plied regularly between Mainz and Frankfurt am Main. Their first impression would have been of a heavily fortified walled town, dominated by its massive red sandstone cathedral. Less than one hundred miles from the French frontier and designated an 'imperial fortress' (*Reichsfestung*), Mainz received periodic grants from imperial funds for the maintenance and development of the fortifications. The massive walls, which surrounded the city on four sides, were interrupted only by a separate fortress (the *Zitadelle*) in the southwestern sector and the gate-towers. Until the campaigns of 1792–3 however, the military value of the city was not put to the test in the eighteenth century and as the Elector's army never numbered more than 3,000, and was usually considerably less, Mainz did not give the impression of being a garrison town.

Far more striking was its ecclesiastical character. The great crossing-tower of the Cathedral Church of St. Martin was only one of a thicket of the towers and spires of parish churches, monasteries, convents, collegiate foundations, seminaries and chapels which formed the city's sky-line. The ubiquity of the clerical institutions was rivalled only by the large number of town houses belonging to the nobility. Many wealthy Imperial Knights (*Reichsritter*), although they were not subjects of the Electorate, maintained permanent establishments in the city, leaving only to spend the summer on their estates in the country. Their palatial residences, most of which dated from the late seventeenth or eighteenth century, gave the city a decidedly aristocratic tone. This was further enhanced by the houses of the canons of the cathedral chapter, all of whom were Imperial Knights. Although less grandiose than the residences of their secular relations, the cluster of baroque buildings around the Cathedral typified that combination of the ecclesiastical and the aristocratic in Mainz which struck visitors so forcibly.

Not even the largest residence, however, could compete in size with the electoral palace, although many were its superiors aesthetically. A curious combination of medieval fortress and baroque residence, it was located in the north-east corner of the city, looking out over the Rhine. Together with the other government buildings, it served as a reminder that the clergy and the nobility were there because Mainz was the seat of the Archbishop-Elector. The latter also had at his disposal the '*Favorite*', an

[1] Karl Heinz Esser's *Mainz* (Munich and Berlin, 1961) contains some excellent photographs by Helga Schmidt-Glassner of the old buildings which remain.

Introduction

exquisite complex of formal gardens and pavilions, which was situated outside the city walls on the south, opposite the point where the Main flows into the Rhine. Built by the Elector Lothar Franz von Schönborn (1695–1729), whose celebrated 'building-worm' was also responsible for Pommersfelden and the episcopal residence at Bamberg, it was much admired by contemporaries. Keysler wrote: 'The palace where the Elector resides has nothing remarkable. But the *Favorite* is a modern edifice; and for its situation and prospect over the Rhine and Maine, the architecture, and the disposition of the garden, which is adorned by pyramids, statues, cascades, and other water works, is a most elegant and delightful place.'[1] It was destroyed by the French during the siege of 1793.

The residence of the privileged classes may have dictated the general character of the city but they only constituted a small part of the whole. With the exception of the wealthier merchants and officials, who had built themselves new houses, the rest of the population lived in dwellings which took little account of changing architectural styles. At the beginning of the eighteenth century, three long straight streets had been laid out in the north of the city, with a grid of other streets intersecting at right angles, but this piece of town planning was unique. Every other quarter was a confusing tangle of narrow streets, small squares, alleys and cul-de-sacs. Perhaps this contrast between baroque elegance and medieval squalor accounted for the varying impressions of Mainz recorded by visitors, 'some describing it as a sink, and others as one of the best towns in Germany'.[2] An anonymous representative of the former school wrote in 1779: 'Taken as a whole, the city is badly built, and most of the streets are twisting, indeed some of them are so narrow that the houses, whose gables are built in the old tasteless style, almost touch across the street'.[3]

Many other aspects of life in Mainz must also have struck the eighteenth century observer as medieval. There were no factories, only the small workshops of the guildmasters, their journeymen and their apprentices. Even the largest warehouse on the banks of the Rhine owed its existence to the medieval right of staple, which required all goods passing through Mainz to be off-loaded and offered for sale before continuing their journey. The rich robes of the prelates and the habits of the monks were not the only evidence of the city's Roman Catholicism; the many colourful religious processions, organised by the lay brotherhoods and in which large sections of the population took part, indicated that the Enlightenment had yet to progress beyond the lecture-halls of the University or the salons of the nobility. No city enjoying such geographical advantages as Mainz

---

[1] Keysler, *Travels*, p. 270.
[2] J. K. Risbeck, *Travels through Germany*, vol. 3 (London, 1787), p. 203.
[3] Paul Lemcke, 'Ein Besuch in Mainz vor 104 Jahren', *Mainzer Anzeiger*, nos. 100 and 101 (1883).

could be totally without the bustle of commerce, but visitors were always more impressed by its administrative, residential or ecclesiastical character.

Mainz was worth a visit, but although the city expanded in wealth and population during the eighteenth century, relatively it had declined from the eminence it had attained in the High Middle Ages. Its humble origins lay in the military camp established in c. 12 B.C. by the Roman general Drusus, the step-son of Augustus. Due to its strategic position, the initial cluster of tents expanded rapidly to become, in A.D. 90, *Mogontiacum*, the seat of the Roman governor of Upper Germany. Although there were Christian bishops in the city from the early fourth century, the waves of invaders from the east – Vandals, Alemans and Huns – interrupted the sequence and it was not until the middle of the sixth century that the see was refounded by Bishop Sidonius.

Its elevation to metropolitan status in 746, with St Boniface as its first archbishop, not only made Mainz an important ecclesiastical centre but also provided a basis from which future archbishops could expand their political influence. With the development of the institutions of the Holy Roman Empire, their dual role as spiritual leader and secular prince became increasingly apparent. In the High Middle Ages, Mainz was the scene both of councils of the Church and diets of the Empire. The archbishop was made archchancellor of the Empire at the end of the thirteenth century and received official recognition as one of the seven electors of the emperor in the Golden Bull of 1356.

Imperial influence was accompanied by growing prosperity. Situated at the junction of the Rhine and the Main, and on the land-route which linked Asia with France, via Russia, Kiev, Cracow, Prague and Regensburg, Mainz was in an admirable position to benefit from the general increase in European trade. By the time Mainz assumed leadership of the *Rheinischer Staedtebund* (League of Rhenish Cities) in 1254, the city was one of the richest in Germany. From the middle of the twelfth century it boasted the proud title of '*aurea Maguntia*' (Golden Mainz). Civic wealth bred civic ambition and in the course of the twelfth, thirteenth and fourteenth centuries the citizens wrested from their archbishop-electors a series of economic and political privileges. Although these made the citizens quasi-autonomous, the city was never established finally as a Free Imperial City (*Reichsstadt*), that is directly and solely subject to the emperor. This inability, or lack of ambition, to follow the example of other formerly episcopal cities, such as Cologne, Speyer, Worms or Augsburg, was later to prove disastrous.

The most important single achievement of medieval Mainz occurred around the middle of the fifteenth century, when Johannes Gutenberg produced the first book printed with movable metal type. Paradoxically,

Introduction

this came at a time when the city was in full decline, economically and politically. At the end of the fourteenth and at the beginning of the fifteenth century, violent disputes between the patrician merchants and the guilds had led to the victory of the latter, the departure of the former and the impoverishment of the city. Public bankruptcies followed in 1429 and 1456 and the *coup de grâce* was delivered by the contested archiepiscopal election of 1461. Unwisely, the citizens opted for Diether von Isenburg and suffered accordingly when Adolf von Nassau asserted the primacy of his claims by force of arms. Having captured the city in 1462, Adolf proceeded to abolish all its privileges, to subject all municipal administration to his viceroy and to expel many of the citizens.

The interaction of economic decline and political defeat changed the city completely; from this time on, the administrative and residential, rather than the commercial, character of Mainz was assured. During the next three centuries the implications were worked out, with the extension of the fortifications and the erection of churches, monasteries, a new electoral palace and the town-houses of the nobility. Occasionally, the construction of a new warehouse or crane served as a reminder that commerce was still carried on in Mainz but the days when the great patrician merchants ruled the city had gone for ever.

Even had Mainz been established as a Free Imperial City, trading conditions would have become increasingly difficult. The decline of Cologne in the sixteenth and seventeenth centuries is an illustration of the general depression of Rhenish trade. The misfortunes of war after 1618 accelerated the downward trend. Long periods of foreign occupation and exploitation – by the Swedes (1631–6) and by the French (1644–8 and 1688–9) – brought further impoverishment and further depopulation. Although recovery was slow and often interrupted by fresh attacks of war, plague and famine, by the middle of the eighteenth century the losses of the seventeenth had been made good,[1] and until the French occupation of 1792 the city continued to expand in numbers and in wealth. Even so, there was never even a remote possibility that Mainz would regain the pre-eminence it had enjoyed in the High Middle Ages. The gold of '*aurea Maguntia*' had long been outshone by Vienna and Berlin, or even by Hanover, Munich or Dresden. Yet Mainz did not decline to the museum-like status of some other important medieval cities, such as Bruges; unlike Bruges, its river did not silt up, it remained a town of vital strategic importance and above all it was capital of the archbishop and elector of Mainz, the archchancellor of the Holy Roman Empire.

[1] Dreyfus, *Mayence*, pp. 85–6, 236–8.

I

The Electorate of Mainz, The Empire and the Imperial Knights

The direction of the affairs of the *Reichstag*, the Electoral College and the Electoral Rhenish Circle belongs to the Electorate of Mainz. As Chancellor of the Empire in Germany, the Elector of Mainz has the right to conduct a direct inspection of the administration of justice in the Empire, whether it concerns the *Reichskammergericht* or the *Reichshofrat*, and the authority of his position also makes itself felt when there is an election of an Emperor or King of the Romans. For it is the task of the Elector of Mainz on this occasion to convene the electors and to direct their deliberations, both concerning the election itself and the capitulation which the new Emperor has to sign and swear to, on his accession to the Empire. Other prerogatives, both important and extensive, ensure that this Elector is justly regarded as the first defender of the laws and constitutions which guarantee the liberty of the German Body politic. *Mémoire pour servir d'instruction au Sr. Michel Villebois allant de la part du Roy auprès de l'électeur de Mayence* (1729).[1]

I

Long after power has shrivelled, the ceremonial husk remains, and in an age especially fond of pomp and circumstance, the Elector of Mainz had ample opportunity to conceal his impotence behind a façade of etiquette and honorific powers. Nowhere was this more apparent than at an imperial election. It was the Elector of Mainz, as Archchancellor and Director of the Electoral College, who summoned the other Electors to Frankfurt for the election, who verified the credentials of the ambassadors, who chaired the discussions about the new capitulation of election, who collected the electors' votes and who consecrated and anointed the new emperor.[2] A good example of the charisma which still attached to him was Goethe's description of the arrival in Frankfurt of the Elector Emmerich Joseph von Breidbach zu Bürresheim for the election of the Archduke Joseph as

---

[1] *Recueil des Instructions données aux Ambassadeurs et Ministres de France depuis les Traités de Westphalie jusqu'à la Révolution française*, 28: États Allemands, vol. 1: L'Électorat de Mayence, ed. Georges Livet (Paris, 1962), p. 140.
[2] *Recht und Verfassung des Reiches in der Zeit Maria Theresias*, ed. Hermann Conrad, Wissenschaftliche Abhandlungen der Arbeitsgemeinschaft für Forschung des Landes Nordrhein-Westfalen, vol. 28 (Cologne and Opladen, 1964), pp. 436–46.

The Electorate, the Empire and the Imperial Knights

King of the Romans: 'The entry of the Elector of Mainz followed on 21 March. Now there began the firing of salutes, which later were to deafen us on many occasions. In the series of ceremonies this was an important occasion: because all the men we had seen appear so far, however senior they may have been, had been after all only subordinates; but here there appeared a sovereign, an independent prince, the first after the Emperor, ushered in and accompanied by a large retinue, as befitted his status.'[1] Goethe was only fifteen years old in 1764 and never became a conspicuously political animal, but even so it is unlikely that when he described Emmerich Joseph as 'first after the emperor' he really meant that he was more important than Frederick the Great. In terms of the Empire, the Elector of Mainz was first because he had always been first, and the fact that the Prussian army was fifty times larger was irrelevant.

The key to the Elector's prestigious position was the archchancellorship. As the constitutional lawyer Christian August von Beck taught the future Joseph II: 'The Elector of Mainz is archchancellor throughout Germany and therefore participates in all important affairs of the Empire.'[2] In this capacity he was also the titular head of the Imperial Chancellery, although day-to-day business was in the hands of the Vice-Chancellor (*Reichsvizekanzler*). In theory he appointed the latter, as well as the subordinate personnel, but in practice his choice was limited. The Chancellery was situated in Vienna, not in Mainz, and clearly the appointment of a Vice-Chancellor who was fundamentally opposed to the Habsburgs was out of the question; indeed the successful candidate swore an oath of fealty to both the Emperor and the Elector of Mainz. The Vice-Chancellor formed the official link between Emperor and Empire; through him were channelled the complaints and demands of the individual princes, he played a leading part at all imperial investitures and he prepared digests for the Emperor of all the most important business transacted at the *Reichstag* or in the imperial courts. All this made the Vice-Chancellorship a very desirable office and one which was hotly competed for, but it did not bring the Elector of Mainz any closer to real influence in the Empire. Once the Vice-Chancellor had been appointed, he was there for life and in any conflict between the interests of the courts of Mainz and Vienna it was always the former which were sacrificed. In any case, the most important creator and instrument of Habsburg policy in the Empire was the Chancellery of State, a purely Austrian institution and in no way subordinated to the Archchancellor.

In a formal sense the Elector of Mainz was also the most important man

---

[1] J. W. von Goethe, *Dichtung und Wahrheit*, pt. 1, bk. 5.
[2] Conrad, *Recht und Verfassung*, p. 461.

at the *Reichstag*.¹ As director, he received all incoming official business, sifted it and then referred it to the appropriate college for discussion. He also controlled the *Reichstag*'s archive. In the two central imperial courts – the *Reichshofrat* and the *Reichskammergericht* – he enjoyed a similarly elevated position; in the former he had the right to make a triennial inspection and was represented permanently by the Vice-Chancellor, while in the latter he appointed all the subordinate personnel.²

A final means of making his influence felt in the *Reich* was his leadership of the Electoral-Rhenish Circle. The Imperial circles were geographical groupings of principalities and Imperial Cities, formed in the fifteenth century to provide more effective collective security against internal and external aggresion and to facilitate the implementation of imperial laws. There were ten of these circles, each of them led by a convening prince (*kreisausschreibender Fürst*) and a director. The latter took the chair at Circle meetings and administered the secretariat and the archive; the former called the meetings, prepared the agenda, supervised the implementation of common policies, organised assistance for members threatened from within or without, and attempted to ensure that decisions of the *Reichstag* or the imperial courts were observed. The Elector of Mainz was both convening prince and director of the Electoral-Rhenish Circle which, apart from himself, included the electors of Cologne, Trier and the Palatinate. Usually the Elector of Mainz was also Prince-Bishop of Worms and in this capacity he was director and joint convening prince of the Upper-Rhenish Circle.³

The elaborate titles – Archbishop and Elector, Archchancellor of the Holy Roman Empire throughout Germany, Director and Convening Prince of the Electoral-Rhenish Circle – roll grandiosely off the tongue but reveal little of his real relationship with the emperor or his fellow princes. Clearly it would be foolish to divorce Goethe's judgement from its context and claim him literally as 'the first after the emperor'; on the other hand it would also be wrong to ignore entirely his imperial functions. Imperial politics did still matter in the eighteenth century and consequently the Elector of Mainz was still an important figure. The energy with which Prussia tried to entice him into the League of Princes and the energy with which Austria tried to stop him⁴ are sufficient evidence of this.

---

¹ There seems little point in using cumbersome English translations such as imperial diet, imperial aulic council or imperial cameral tribunal, when the German equivalents – *Reichstag, Reichshofrat*, and *Reichskammergericht* are comprehensible and more concise.
² Conrad, *Recht und Verfassung*, pp. 461–3.
³ Ibid., pp. 419–24.
⁴ See below, Ch. 6.

The Electorate, the Empire and the Imperial Knights

II

In the period after the Reformation there was a striking continuity in the way in which successive Archbishop-Electors exercised their imperial functions. This was due largely to the fact that most of them were Imperial Knights, a section of the German nobility with clearly defined traditions, aims and enemies. The exact origins of this uniquely German group are lost in the mists surrounding the dissolution of the Carolingian Empire, although it seems likely that as a group they owed their existence to the desire by successive emperors to check over-mighty dukes and counts by employing subordinate nobles. In particular, the use by the Salian emperors of *ministeriales* and the subsequent progress of the latter from the status of vassal to that of noble[1] assisted the formation of an independent class.

What distinguished the Imperial Knights from all other German nobles was their claim to be 'immediate' (*reichsunmittelbar*), that is directly and solely subject to the Emperor. Technically they had not gained full princely status, because they were not represented in the *Reichstag* and exercised only limited criminal jurisdiction, but their essential parity with the princes was recognised by both constitutional lawyers and imperial courts alike.[2] Whatever their origins or precise legal status, the Imperial Knights exercised a decisive influence not only on the Electorate's imperial policies but also on its domestic policies and its social and economic structure. To a large extent the history of Mainz in the eighteenth century is the history of the Imperial Knights, and an examination of their relationship with the Electorate is indispensable.

Although Imperial Knights had sat in the cathedral chapters of the ecclesiastical states for many centuries, it was not until the Reformation that they gained a predominant position. Of the great dynasties, only the Wittelsbachs and Habsburgs remained Catholics[3] and so princely domination of the ecclesiastical states failed for want of candidates. The way was left open for those lesser nobles who remained Catholic and they seized the opportunity gratefully.[4] In Mainz the last archbishop who was also a scion of a great princely house was Albrecht II of Brandenburg, who ruled from 1514 until 1545.

The Imperial Knights did not succeed in monopolising all the prince-

---

[1] P. Schnepp, 'Die Reichsritterschaft', *Deutsche Geschichtsblätter*, 14 (1913), pp. 157–94, 215–25.
[2] H. H. Hofmann, *Adelige Herrschaft und souveräner Staat*, Studien zur bayerischen Verfassungs- und Sozialgeschichte, vol. 2 (Munich, 1962), p. 96.
[3] The Wettiner of Saxony were re-converted to Catholicism in 1697.
[4] Karl Otmar Freiherr von Aretin, *Heiliges Römisches Reich 1776–1806*, vol. 1 (Wiesbaden, 1967), p. 8.

bishoprics; for example, those surrounded by Bavarian territory, such as Regensburg and Freising, were dominated by Bavarian nobles, and those surrounded by Austrian territory, such as Salzburg and Brixen, were dominated by Austrian nobles. Membership of the Cathedral Chapter of Cologne was restricted to Imperial Counts, while in Liège more than half the canons were commoners. Nevertheless, the Imperial Knights took the lion's share and, once they controlled a cathedral chapter and through it the election of the prince-bishop, they took great care to keep interlopers at bay by means of stringent membership qualifications. By the beginning of the eighteenth century the Imperial Knights dominated the prince-bishoprics of the Rhineland (except Cologne), Franconia and Swabia. Understandably, the canons usually elected one of their own number and consequently a series of Imperial Knights ascended the episcopal thrones in Constance, Speyer, Worms, Trier, Würzburg, Bamberg, Eichstätt and Mainz.[1]

The special interest taken by the Imperial Knights in the ecclesiastical states was due to a combination of economic, political and social considerations. In economic terms, their interest represented a need to find sources of revenue in addition to the income they derived from their estates. Like all other Germans who derived their income from the land, the Imperial Knights had been affected severely by the devastation of the Thirty Years War and by the agrarian depression which lasted throughout Europe until well into the eighteenth century.[2] Because all the sons of an Imperial Knight took their father's title and status, because primogeniture was by no means the rule and because families were often very large, many estates suffered from excessive fragmentation and division.[3] Although the eighteenth century saw a marked increase in both the price of agricultural produce and land values, it seems likely that the Imperial Knights' expenditure at least kept pace with any extra income. Before the Thirty Years War they had lived mainly on their estates and a modest income sufficed to maintain them in a manner befitting a nobleman, but as the refined tastes of Versailles percolated into Germany they felt obliged to respond. They tore down what were now seen to be 'barbaric monuments to gothic ignorance' and erected in their place rococo palaces set in formal gardens or later 'English' parks. Increasingly they spent the winters in the towns, which necessitated the building of additional town houses. The

---

[1] Karl Heinrich Freiherr Roth von Schreckenstein, *Geschichte der ehemaligen Reichsritterschaft in Schwaben, Franken und am Rheinstrome*, vol. 2 (Tübingen, 1871), p. 419.

[2] W. Abel, *Geschichte der deutschen Landwirtschaft vom frühen Mittelalter bis zum 19. Jahrhundert* (Stuttgart, 1962), p. 244.

[3] For a good example, see the description of the estates of the Freiherren von Erthal in Kittel, 'Geschichte der freiherrlichen Familie von und zu Erthal', *Archiv des historischen Vereins von Unterfranken und Aschaffenburg*, 17 (1865), p. 137.

The Electorate, the Empire and the Imperial Knights

Rhineland and Franconia still abound in splendid urban and rural residences dating from the eighteenth century, monuments to their builders' extravagance and good taste.

Nevertheless, some families enjoyed very large fortunes. The Schönborn family, for example, which supplied Mainz with two Electors and innumerable canons, courtiers and officials, assembled an enormous income by means of a combination of sensible marriages, fortunate inheritances and much imperial patronage. Their estates in the Rhineland and Franconia were extensive enough to be subdivided into eleven separate administrative districts. That centred on Mainz alone included property, tithes and dues in 44 villages varying in value from tithes at Dietenbergen worth a couple of thousand gulden to vineyards at Hattenheim worth over 30,000 gulden. Their average annual gross income from their German estates between 1745 and 1753 was 112,720 gulden.[1] There is some evidence that the wealth of the Schönborns was not unique. In the middle of the eighteenth century a Freiherr von Groschlag drew 45,000 gulden each year from his estates, while his close relations the Counts von Stadion owned property in Swabia alone valued at one-and-a-half million gulden.[2] When the left bank of the Rhine was ceded to France by the Treaty of Lunéville in 1801, the Counts von der Leyen lamented that they lost thereby 'eight square miles of land, sixty three villages, 20,000 inhabitants, 24 castles and administrative buildings, 145 farms and mills, together with many thousands of acres of forest; iron, coal, glass and several other industrial establishments'.[3] Some families also owned large estates in Austria, Bohemia and Hungary, usually acquired as gifts from the Habsburgs for diplomatic, political or military services. The Counts von Stadion owned three estates in Bohemia valued at 300,000 gulden in 1700, the Counts von Ostein drew 30–40,000 gulden per annum from their land there, while in 1918 the Czechoslovak government confiscated 500,000 acres from the Schönborns.[4]

These very large incomes were of course matched by very large expenditure, and not infrequently by too large expenditure. An imperial commission of inquiry, chaired by the Elector of Mainz, discovered in 1750 that Rudolf Franz Erwein Count von Schönborn owed various creditors 570,254 gulden, plus unpaid interest of 258,269

---

[1] Wiesentheid, *Abteilung XVa*, 13.
[2] Helmut Rössler, *Graf Johann Philipp Stadion: Napoleons deutscher Gegenspieler*, vol. 1 (Vienna, 1966), pp. 29–31, 115.
[3] A. G. Scharwarth, 'Die Fürsten von der Leyen und der Wiener Kongreß', *Rheinische Vierteljahrsblätter*, 33 (1969), p. 140. Eight German square miles equal 170 English square miles – see the conversion table in W. H. Bruford, *Germany in the Eighteenth Century* (Cambridge, 1965), p. 332.
[4] Rössler, *Stadion*, p. 29. PRO, SP.88.61. 21 April 1743, Thomas Villiers to Lord Carteret. E. J. Hobsbawm, *The Age of Revolution* (London, 1962), p. 15.

gulden.¹ Another notorious spendthrift was Franz Georg Count von Metternich, the father of the later Austrian Chancellor Clement. His family was obliged to sell their territory of Ochsenhausen to the Duke of Württemberg for 1,300,000 gulden to settle his debts.² Even the wealthiest Imperial Knight therefore was interested to acquire any additional form of revenue that might be available.

A particular problem was posed by daughters and younger sons, for like all other social classes the Imperial Knights were often blessed with large families. Although a number of children succumbed to the rigours of eighteenth century midwifery, enough survived to pose a serious problem of employment. In particular there was an acute shortage of eligible bachelors with the dual qualifications of Catholic faith and noble birth, for many of them obtained benefices which required a vow of celibacy. Girls without dowries or compensating physical charms were obliged therefore to seek their livelihood in the many convents and collegiate foundations reserved for noble ladies.³ Their brothers of course had a much wider range of options, for every prince in the *Reich* needed courtiers, diplomats, administrators and army officers. In most states however the Imperial Knights faced fierce competition for places from the indigenous nobility, who were naturally given preference by their rulers. Occasionally the Knights obtained important posts in the secular states – the families of both Stein and Metternich were Imperial Knights by origin – but it was only in the ecclesiastical states that they could establish a virtual monopoly.

In Mainz it was of crucial importance for the Imperial Knights that they had no competitors. As Johann Jakob Moser recorded in 1755: 'There is no nobility subject to the sovereignty and jurisdiction of the Electorate of Mainz, the nobles there belong to the body of immediate Imperial Knights'.⁴ The only other nobles were the officials of the *Dienstadel*, socially indistinguishable from commoners, and treated as such.⁵ As a result, the Knights had a free run of the many splendid employment opportunities the Electorate offered.

The richest prize an Imperial Knight in Mainz could win was of course

---

¹ Wiesentheid, *Bestand Joseph Franz Bonaventura*, pp. 46, 57.
² G. A. C. Sandeman, *Metternich* (London, 1911), p. 10.
³ For description of two typical *Damenstifter*, see Adelheid Simon, *Philippine von Guttenberg – die letzte Äbtissin von Eibingen vor der Säkularisation (1734–1804)*, Veröffentlichungen der Gesellschaft für fränkische Geschichte, 9th series, vol. 13, and Max Domarus, *Äbtissin Eva Theresia von Schönborn und das adelige Damenstift zur heiligen Anna in Würzburg*, Quellen und Forschungen zur Geschichte des Bistums und Hochstifts Würzburg, vol. 16 (Würzburg, 1964).
⁴ J. J. von Moser, *Einleitung in das Churfürstlich-Maynzische Staatsrecht* (Frankfurt am Main, 1755), p. 274.
⁵ The *Hofrat* of the Electorate, for example, was divided into noble and commoner 'benches'. The *Dienstadel* belonged to the latter.

The Electorate, the Empire and the Imperial Knights

the electorate itself. Not only did this bring power and prestige in the *Reich*,[1] it could also lead to the permanent enrichment of his family. Virtually all patronage in the Electorate was in the gift of its ruler and no Elector resisted the temptation to lavish sinecures on his relations. The most valuable gifts at his disposal however were not offices but the fiefs which reverted to the Electorate when the families which had held them died out. This was an infrequent but highly desirable occurrence, for nothing could prevent the Elector from bestowing the fiefs on his own family. A comparison of the fief registers before and after the reign of Johann Friedrich von Ostein (1743–63), for example, reveals a dramatic improvement in his family's fortunes. From holding no fiefs of Mainz it ended by holding land and buildings in fifteen villages, three villages complete, a castle, jurisdictional rights in another village, grazing rights in another and tithes in another.[2] The French minister in Mainz wrote in 1742: 'The ecclesiastical electorates are regarded by their possessors as little more than temporary benefices, from which they draw for themselves and their families all the benefits they can – honours, dignities, benefices, concessions and privileges from the Emperor.'[3]

But although most Electors were middle-aged when elected, vacancies occurred infrequently and the actuarial chances of any particular Imperial Knight becoming Elector were remote. His most promising source of revenue was the Cathedral Chapter and its twenty-four canonries. The Chapter indeed owned what amounted to a separate state, directly subject to the Emperor and for which it was in no way accountable to the Elector. The territory included large landed estates, the town of Bingen and seven other substantial villages.[4] Like the Imperial Knights, the Chapter was not *reichsständisch*, i.e. it did not have a seat in the *Reichstag*, but it ruled its territories as a sovereign nevertheless. It also owned extensive estates within the Electorate and in other principalities and to administer both types of property had developed its own civil service.

These possessions were not only extensive, they were located in the most fertile part of a fertile region. The town of Bingen, lying at the junction of the Nahe and the Rhine, had 4,500 inhabitants and was described in 1786 as 'a pleasant and prosperous little town', drawing its income from shipping and the wine trade.[5] The Chapter also owned the customs there,

---

[1] See above, pp. 46–8.
[2] Würzburg, *MRA*, Lehensakten, 139–40. Vienna, *MEA*, GK, Fasc. 85a, 550–4.
[3] Livet, *Recueil*, p. lxiv.
[4] A. F. Büsching, *A New System of Geography*, vol. 4 (London, 1762), pp. 531–2.
[5] P. W. Gercken, *Reisen durch Schwaben, Baiern, die angränzende Schweiz, Franken, die Rheinische Provinzen und an der Mosel in den Jahren 1779–1785* vol. 3 (Stendal, 1786), p. 93. His opinion was confirmed by [A. W. Schreiber], 'Streiferei von Mainz nach Münster im Junius 1792', *Streifereien durch einige Gegenden Deutschlands vom Verfasser der 'Szenen aus Fausts Leben'* (Leipzig, 1795), pp. 195–6.

which yielded 30,000 gulden *per annum*.¹ The village of Hochheim, on the East bank of the Rhine, produced some of the most celebrated wine in Germany; in a good year the value of the harvest reached 12,000 gulden.² It is not possible to calculate the Chapter's annual income with any precision; the most reliable proportional estimate is that it was one fifth of the Electorate's income. This would mean that in 1785, for example, the Chapter's income was approximately 375,000 gulden.³

For a corporate body with only twenty-four full members, this was a very respectable sum, and indeed the wealth of the individual canons was legendary. Risbeck described them in 1780 as 'the richest in Germany' and another traveller, K. L. von Knebel, also referred to their 'excessive incomes'.⁴ Moreover the canonries were not the only benefices available. Technically a canon was allowed to hold only one benefice unless it was too meagre to maintain him, but – as one might expect and as Moser records – this regulation was not enforced.⁵ In 1789 only four of the twenty-four canons did not have some sort of extra income. Fifteen of them sat in other cathedral chapters, four of them in more than one.⁶ The benefices at Trier were worth 3,000 gulden per annum, at Würzburg 1,500–2,000 gulden and at Bamberg 2,500 gulden.⁷ Further supplements were provided by the large number of less important collegiate foundations in Franconia and the Rhineland. Yet another source of income were the secular offices in the Electorate reserved for canons. The salaries were not large but they were useful little sinecures nevertheless.

The best example of what an enterprising canon could achieve was provided by the Provost Hugo Franz Karl Count von Eltz, who assembled a total income in excess of 75,000 gulden.⁸ As the chief minister of his uncle, the Elector Philipp Karl (1732–43) he had been the fortunate

---

[1] *Compendiöse Statistik von Maynz, Trier und Cöln, samt ihren Nebenländern* (Leipzig, 1798), p. 49.
[2] Eduard Vehse, *Geschichte der deutschen Höfe seit der Reformation*, vol. 45 (Hamburg, 1859), pp. 192–3.
[3] Wilhelm Herse, *Kurmainz am Vorabend der Revolution* (Berlin dissertation, 1907), pp. 15–17. Cf. Mainz, *Abteilung 6*, Fasc. 904.
[4] J. K. Risbeck, *Travels through Germany*, vol. 3 (London, 1787), p. 211. K. G. Bockenheimer, *Das öffentliche Leben in Mainz am Ende des 18. Jahrhunderts* (Mainz, 1902), p. 12.
[5] J. J. von Moser, *Einleitung in das Churfürstlich-Maynzische Staatsrecht* (Frankfurt am Main, 1755), p. 200.
[6] *Hof- und Staatskalender 1789*.
[7] Sophie-Matilde, Gräfin zu Dohna, *Die ständischen Verhältnisse am Domkapitel von Trier vom 16. bis zum 18. Jahrhundert*, Schriftenreihe zur trierischen Landesgeschichte und Volkskunde, vol. 6 (Trier, 1960), p. 27. There were residential qualifications and those permanently domiciled in Mainz could draw only part of their second benefices. Thus the provost of Mainz Hugo Karl von Eltz could receive only 1,250 gulden from his Trier benefice, where the residential requirement was 6 months – Hermann Nottarp, 'Ein Mindener Dompropst des 18. Jahrhunderts (Hugo Franz Karl von Eltz)', *Westfälische Zeitschrift*, 103–4 (1954), 124.
[8] Nottarp, *Eltz*, p. 123.

recipient of much imperial patronage. Among other lucrative benefices, Charles VI gave him the provostship of Pecsvarad in Hungary, which yielded over 40,000 gulden per annum.[1] He collected over 2,000 paintings, including works by Jordaens, Rembrandt, Rubens, Veronese, Holbein, Poussin, Tintoretto, Tiepolo, Dürer, Cranach and Canaletto, and made lavish gifts both to his family and to various spiritual foundations.[2] When he died his estate was valued at almost quarter of a million gulden.[3]

Eltz was almost certainly an exception. The little evidence I have been able to find suggests that the average canon was well-off but not extravagantly so. Franz Philipp von Franckenstein's benefice at Mainz, for example, brought him only 2,172 gulden in 1751. It rose to 2,502 gulden in 1756, fell to 2,325 in 1761, rose again to 2,452 in 1764 and finally reached 3,271 gulden in 1771. As arch-priest of the Chapter he received in addition 220 gulden per annum. Franz Philipp was also however Provost of St Victor in Mainz, canon of St Alban in Mainz and St Ferruti in Bleidenstadt and President of the Electorate's Exchequer. These additional offices brought his total income up to about 6,000 gulden, a very respectable figure at a time when 400 gulden was thought to be the *ideal* annual salary for a parish priest and a senior commoner official earned 600 gulden.[4]

Further evidence of the canons' wealth is supplied by the inventories of their estates, compiled after their death. The Kustos of the Chapter, Melchior Friedrich Count von Schönborn, owned jewels worth 11,144 gulden, silver worth 11,273 gulden, eight horses, seven coaches and wine worth 12,629 gulden. His total estate (net) amounted to 52,441 gulden.[5] His colleague Joseph Franz Count von Kesselstadt lived in similar comfort. His estate included sixty-two different items of silver, paintings by Caravaggio, Rembrandt, Holbein and Rubens, 117 shirts, six horses, five carriages, thirty-one guns and pistols for the chase, and some clothes which sound hardly suitable for a cleric – for example, 'a summer suit decorated with gold and silver *point d'Espagne*' and 'a blue coat, with silk waistcoat and breeches, embroidered with gold'.[6]

Although not as lucrative as has sometimes been supposed, the canonries represented highly desirable 'careers' for the younger and even eldest sons

---

[1] Ibid., p. 124.
[2] A. L. Veit, *Mainzer Domherren vom Ende des 16. bis zum Ausgang des 18. Jahrhunderts* (Mainz, 1924), p. 140. F. W. E. Roth, *Geschichte der Herren und Grafen zu Eltz*, vol. 2 (Mainz 1890), pp. 109–118.
[3] Nottarp, *Eltz*, p. 149.
[4] Vienna, *MEA*, GK, Fasc. 32, 546. Hans Goldschmidt, *Zentralbehörden und Beamtentum im Kurfürstentum Mainz vom 16. bis zum 18. Jahrhundert*, Abhandlungen zur mittleren und neueren Geschichte, vol. 7 (Berlin and Leipzig, 1908), Table 3. Ullstadt, 003948.
[5] Wiesentheid, *Bestand Melchoir Friedrich der jüngere (Domkustos)*, 34.
[6] Trier, 3708.

of Imperial Knights, and there was intense competition for any benefice which fell vacant. The Imperial Knights did not however all start the race equally handicapped, for the vacancies were filled by co-option – the Elector and the canons took it in turns to appoint the 'domicellars', the junior members of the Chapter who succeeded to full canonries in order of seniority. Understandably, the Elector or canon whose turn it was, nominated a nephew or some other close relation, with the result that the Chapter was dominated by a small group of families: during the period 1740–92 three Bettendorfs, three Dalbergs, three Franckensteins, three Kesselstadts and three Metternichs sat in the Chapter and frequently overlapped.[1] If one includes the twenty-four canons already in residence in 1740, there were seventy-two vacancies during the same period; over half of them (37) were filled by members of only sixteen families.

The twenty-four canonries were not the only rewards at stake. Influence in the Chapter meant patronage in the state. Apart from the rewards handed out to his supporters and their families by a new Elector, it was natural that he should favour his former colleagues and their relations. The Court Almanach reveals that a family's success in gaining secular posts in the Electorate was in direct proportion to its success in bringing its members into the Chapter. The families with members in the Chapter, or 29·6% of all noble families active in Mainz possessed 59·7% of all the offices held by nobles. Sixteen families or 9·2% had more than one member in the Chapter and they held 31·5% of all noble offices.[2]

But although an élite within the Imperial Knights took a disproportionate share of the pickings, there were plenty of secular offices left. There were approximately 130 offices in the Electorate's administration reserved exclusively for the Imperial Knights, ranging in importance from Chief Justice down to Hunting Boy. Some, such as Adviser to the Commission on Fire Insurance, were probably unpaid, but the majority carried real salaries. The amounts involved were useful but not princely: at the end of the eighteenth century the President of the Treasury received 1,200 gulden per annum and a Councillor 900 gulden.[3]

Even so, the duties were not commensurate with the returns. In every office of state there was a noble figurehead who drew the salary and a commoner assistant who did the work. The Chief Justice and President of the High Court, for example, held other posts in the administration and treated their judicial offices as sinecures.[4] In 1753 the Elector Johann Friedrich recognised the situation and made the senior commoner Director of the Court, because 'We find that contrary to our wishes the Chief Justice and President do not attend sessions of the Court, for the reason

[1] *Hof- und Staatskalender*, 1740–1792.
[2] *Hof- und Staatskalender*, 1740–1792.
[3] Goldschmidt, *Zentralbehörden*, p. 196.
[4] Ibid., pp. 154–5.

that they are engaged on other official business and for other reasons, such as their own personal unsuitability and the like.'[1] A similar situation existed at a local level. Most of the highly paid noble magistrates (*Amtsmänner*) never visited their districts and left the conduct of business to their assistants. Their official instructions recognised and sactioned this: 'The electoral magistrate is never obliged to be present in the electoral magistracy or to perform any official functions, unless he is specifically ordered to do so by the electoral government...and if he is not present he is not to meddle in the affairs of the magistracy, whatever they may be, nor is he to require written information or answers to his queries from the electoral officials.'[2]

Another useful source of employment was the court, where about sixty-five positions were reserved for the Imperial Knights. There were six main offices, carrying really substantial salaries by the end of the eighteenth century: Grand Master (6,000 gulden per annum), Grand Chamberlain (5,000), Grand Marshal (4,500), Grand Master of the Stables (4,500), Court Marshal (3,000) and Grand Chamberlain of the Silver (2,500).[3] Much less well-paid were the gentlemen-of-the-bedchamber (*Kammerherren*), stewards (*Truchsessen*), pages (*Edelknaben*), and cavaliers (*Hofkavalieren*). The total salary of a gentleman-of-the-bedchamber amounted to only 1,000 gulden and there was an average delay of seven years before it was paid in full. Yet the posts conferred a certain status and there is some evidence that an interim payment of some kind was made until a full salary became available. Additional perquisites such as free quarters at court were available and there was always the chance of promotion to the more remunerative positions.[4]

Every other German state had its court and its sinecures of course, but the court at Mainz seems to have been more flamboyant and relatively larger than most. In 1790 its total complement was 466, including the servants; as Risbeck had observed ten years earlier 'the expense of this establishment is very disproportionate to the revenue of the state'.[5] Dr John Moore, who was accompanying the Duke of Hamilton on his Grand Tour, expressed a wish to visit the Mainz court, but the Duke vetoed the idea, saying 'a court of clergymen must be more dismal and tedious than any other'.[6] Other English tourists received exactly the opposite impression. Thomas Pennant recorded the following impression of

---

[1] F. J. Hartleben, *Iurisdictio Moguntina* (Moguntiae [Mainz], 1782), p. 30.
[2] Ibid., p. 20.
[3] Würzburg, *MGKA*, 222: 38–9, 43, 53, 269, 306, 310, 343, 364.
[4] Ibid., 59, 66–7, 69–70, 79, 96, 178, 187, 203, 211, 249, 260, 268, 279.
[5] Risbeck, *Travels*, p. 240.
[6] John Moore, *A View of the Society and Manners in France, Switzerland and Germany*, vol. I (London, 1779), p. 410.

his visit to the Elector Emmerich Joseph in 1765: 'He was at dinner in public and had about thirty at table with him; in the antichamber was a band of Musick. He had a vast attendance, was served by a sort of footmen called Heydukes [haiduks] dressed in laced jackets, a great sash around their waists and cloth boots; great deal of meat, vast noise and no appearance of anything ecclesiastick, the elector and his clerical gentry being in embroidered coats.'[1] Extravagance is not of course a synonym of pleasure, though it was probably fashionable *ennui* which prompted the Countess von Pergen to report from Mainz to her husband 'at court one derives one's entire pleasure from spending five hours at table, three hours gambling and two hours doing nothing...you can have no idea of the boredom one is subjected to here; the company is always the same, one day is just like another, and generally I defy even a royal court to display more boredom'.[2] This comment notwithstanding, the Mainz court was renowned for being, as Metternich wrote, 'the best-appointed court in Germany'.[3] This had a considerable impact on the social and economic structure of the city, for it attracted to Mainz the great magnates among the Imperial Knights. Like most of their less fortunate colleagues, they did not – could not – rely entirely on the various sinecures available, but they did need a centre for urbane social intercourse and of all the ecclesiastical courts Mainz had the most to offer.

Imperial Knights who failed to find their niche in the administration or at court were given a third chance by the army. In 1792 it consisted only of 2,800 infantry, 50 hussars, 50 fusiliers, 120 artillerymen, six miners and six sappers, but was grotesquely over-officered, with a commander-in-chief, five full generals and seven major-generals.[4] As Risbeck observed, the army was designed to provide sinecures for the nobility rather than to serve any military purpose.[5] Between 1729 and 1796 no commoner became commander-in-chief, and only 15% of the generals, 22% of the major-generals, 25% of the colonels, $32\frac{1}{2}$% of the lieutenant-colonels and 44.4% of the majors were commoners.[6] In addition, the lifeguard, which saw action only at court ceremonies, was the exclusive preserve of the Imperial Knights. It was thought necessary to have five of them to com-

[1] Thomas Pennant, *A Tour on the Continent 1765*, ed. Sir G. R. de Beer (London, 1948), p. 141. For other descriptions of the luxury of the Mainz court, see: F. Schneider, 'Ein päpstlicher Gesandte über Mainz, 1762 und 1764', *Mainzer Journal*, 21 (1898). Correspondence on the French Revolution, ed. Charles Popham Miles, vol. 1 (London, 1890), p. 130. *Mémoires du Comte de Bray*, ed. F. de Bray (Paris, 1911), p. 122.
[2] Vienna, *Reika*, Fasc. 21, 224.
[3] *Aus Metternichs nachgelassenen Papieren*, ed. Fürst Richard Metternich-Winneburg, pt. 1, vol. 1 (Vienna, 1880), p. 16.
[4] Arthur Chuquet, *Les Guerres de la Révolution*, vol. 6 (Paris, n.d.), p. 28. Herse, *Kurmainz*, p. 18.
[5] Risbeck, *Travels*, p. 241.   [6] Würzburg, *MGKA*, 226.

mand its seven N.C.O.s, three musicians and thirty-five privates.[1] The salaries were moderate but useful; in 1779 a major received 951 gulden, a lieutenant-colonel 1,071 gulden, a colonel 1,702 gulden and a major-general 2,299 gulden.[2] As the army's chief function was ceremonial, it enjoyed close connections with the court, and noble officers had a good chance of obtaining further positions at court. Between 1729 and 1796 35% of them succeeded in doing so.[3]

III

The Imperial Knights' interest in Mainz was political as well as social and economic. Together with all the other ecclesiastical states they controlled, the Electorate helped them to survive as an independent order, subject only to the Emperor.[4] In the eighteenth century, as in the past, the Imperial Knights faced the hostility of the princes, who resented their autonomous position and sought to subject them to their rule. The Imperial Knights' territories formed irritating enclaves in the great and not-so-great states of Southern and Western Germany, and were seen by the princes as affronts to their sovereignty.[5] The Imperial Knights' titles to their property were often confused and there was plenty of opportunity for any prince wishing to pursue a 'policy of reunions'. Between 1521 and 1712, for example, the Dukes of Württemberg repossessed or secured in one way or another 106 estates which previously had belonged to Imperial Knights.[6]

In view of the greater resources of the princes, the Imperial Knights would have been subjected long before, had not successive emperors come to their assistance. In the face of princely particularism the emperors were glad to find allies anywhere, and a close alliance between the two harassed parties grew up. The emperors had authorised the Imperial Knights to form themselves into cantons and circles, promised in every imperial capitulation of election to defend their position and gave the imperial courts standing orders to protect them against encroachments by the

---

[1] Vienna, *MEA*, Militaria, Fasc. 96, 6.
[2] Richard Harms, *Landmiliz und stehendes Heer in Kurmainz, namentlich im 18. Jahrhundert* (Göttingen Dissertation, 1909), Anhang.
[3] Würzburg, *MGKA*, 223, *passim*. *Hof- und Staatskalender des Kurfürstentums Mainz 1740–1792*.
[4] See above, p. 49.
[5] Karl Heinrich Freiherr Roth von Schreckenstein, *Geschichte der ehemaligen Reichsritterschaft in Schwaben, Franken und am Rheinstrom*, vol. 2 (Tübingen, 1871), p. 498. For details of the constitutional issues at stake in the dispute between princes and Imperial Knights, see Gerhard Pfeiffer, 'Studien zur Geschichte der fränkischen Reichsritterschaft', *Jahrbuch für fränkische Landesforschung*, 22 (1962), *passim*.
J. F. Brandis, *Über das reichsritterschaftliche Staatsrecht und dessen Quellen* (Göttingen, 1788), p. 21.

princes.¹ For their part, the Imperial Knights supported the emperor with grants of money, served in his army, administration and diplomatic corps, and took an oath 'in all submission and obedience' recognising the emperor as their 'sole direct temporal superior, protector and patron'.² The Imperial Knights appreciated that their independence would perish with the *Reich* and closed their ranks in support of the Habsburgs. In 1787 the Freiherr von Soden posed the question: 'Why must Germany have an emperor?' and in reply argued that he was essential for the continued existence of the smaller states.³

Neither individually nor collectively did the Imperial Knights amount to very much; indeed they were not represented in the *Reichstag*. It was only through their control of many of the ecclesiastical states – and particularly of Mainz – that they were able to exert any influence on imperial affairs and to gain the support of the emperor; and it was to a large extent this political need which dictated the Imperial Knights' constant vigilance against any attempts by outsiders to disturb their control.

The key to their control of Mainz was of course their control of the Cathedral Chapter. The Chapter's regulations governing the admission of new members stated that a candidate had to be a member of one of the three circles of Imperial Knights – the Rhenish, Franconian or Swabian – and also had to be indisputably 'immediate' (*reichsunmittelbar*), that is directly and solely subject to the emperor. In addition he had to prove that his sixteen great-great-grandparents were all 'of ancient German knightly origin'. The family tree submitted to support this claim was to be examined by eight Imperial Knights listed as members of the three circles mentioned above.⁴ This exclusiveness was quite undiscriminating: they were as opposed to the admission of nobles who were not Imperial Knights as they were to the admission of commoners.

Not surprisingly, other German nobles attempted to break the Imperial Knights' monopoly, but without success.⁵ A particularly dangerous threat was posed by the younger sons of princely houses in pursuit of lucrative benefices. In the past this had come mainly from members of the Wittelsbach family, which had dominated the Electorate of Cologne, for example, from 1583 until 1761. But by the middle of the eighteenth century the Wittelsbachs were experiencing difficulty in keeping their own line going and had no younger sons to spare. After 1760 however a new

---

¹ C. C. F. von Strantz, *Geschichte des deutschen Adels*, vol. 3 (Breslau, 1845), p. 36.
² Hofmann, *Adelige Herrschaft*, p. 99.
³ Aretin, *Heiliges Römisches Reich*, vol. 1, p. 68.
⁴ A. L. Veit, 'Geschichte und Recht der Stiftmäßigkeit auf die ehemals adeligen Domstifte von Mainz, Würzburg und Bamberg', *Historisches Jahrbuch*, 33 (1912), p. 355.
⁵ For a recent discussion of their campaign, see Friedrich Keinemann, 'Das Domstift Mainz und der mediate Adel', *Historisches Jahrbuch*, 89 (1969).

danger loomed in the shape of Clemens Wenzeslaus, the youngest son of Augustus III of Saxony. He was exceptionally well-connected: his mother, Maria Josepha, was a daughter of the late Emperor Joseph I, and of his numerous sisters Maria Amalia was married to Charles III of Spain, Maria Josepha was married to the Dauphin and Maria Anna was married to the Elector Max III of Bavaria.[1] This formidable combination of Bourbon–Habsburg–Wittelsbach–Wettiner influence was difficult to resist and despite rebuffs from the chapters of Cologne, Münster, Paderborn, Liège, Hildesheim and Passau, Clemens Wenzeslaus collected Freising, Regensburg, Augsburg and Trier. When it became clear, in 1767, that he was bound to succeed at Trier, the Imperial Knights in the Chapter of adjacent Mainz stirred uneasily. When rumours then began to spread that Mainz was next on Clemens Wenzeslaus' shopping-list, they formed what became known as the '*Mainzer Ligue*' to deal with any actual attempt. With the help of the diplomats sent by Great Britain and the United Provinces, the Chapter succeeded. Saxon influence was confined to Trier and the Imperial Knights retained their grasp on Mainz until secularisation in 1803.[2]

The Imperial Knights thus dominated the Chapter, and through the Chapter they dominated the Electorate, not only because the Chapter elected the Archbishop-Elector but also because of the Chapter's special constitutional position. Indeed, during the period between the death of one elector and the election of another, the Chapter ruled the state directly. Although the interregnum could not last longer than three months and was usually much shorter, the canons ensured their continued political influence by compelling the new elector to sign a document listing and confirming their ancient – and in some cases recently acquired – privileges. It was this document, known as the capitulation of election (*Wahlkapitulation*) which was the Electorate's constitution, inasmuch as it had one.

The capitulation of election attained its most complete form with the 'perpetual' capitulation of 1787, drawn up by the Chapter for the election of a coadjutor in the same year.[3] It had two parts; in the first the Elector confirmed the Chapter's special privileges, which – as the canons admitted – had nothing to do with the Electorate as a whole. The second part, on

---

[1] Heribert Raab, *Clemens Wenzeslaus von Sachsen und seine Zeit 1739–1812*, vol. 1 (Freiburg, Basle and Vienna, 1962), pp. 41–51.

[2] For a detailed account of this episode, see the reports of George Cressener, London: *P.R.O.*, SP.81.147, and Albert Schulte, *Ein englischer Gesandte am Rhein: George Cressener als bevollmächtigter Gesandter an den Höfen der geistlichen Kurfürsten und beim Niederrheinisch-Westfälischen Kreis 1763–1781* (Bonn Dissertation 1954), p. 111.

[3] See below, pp. 228–31 and Manfred Stimming, *Die Wahlkapitulationen der Erzbischöfe und Kurfürsten von Mainz 1233–1788* (Göttingen, 1909), p. 86. Although conducted during the lifetime of the current incumbent, the coadjutor election was in effect an archiepiscopal election, since the coadjutor was elected *cum spe successionis*.

the other hand, was intended to become the permanent fundamental law of the land.[1]

The canons were well-aware of their special constitutional position and stated explicitly their claim to be the estates of the realm.[2] They argued that if they had the right to give the people a prince then they were certainly entitled to represent them over and against the prince. Without their consent the Elector could not alienate or mortgage any part of his state, could not reallocate any escheated fiefs and could not incur any debts.[3] Restrictions on his domestic policies were few: he was obliged to 'maintain' the Catholic religion, to give preference to native-born Catholics when making official appointments, not to tolerate heretics, to maintain the city's medieval right of staple, and not to impose excessive customs dues or crane fees. In foreign policy he was obliged to maintain good relations with the Pope and the 'eternal alliance' with the Habsburgs.[4]

The Chapter did not however possess any legislative veto; its only sanction was financial. No taxes could be increased and no new ones created without the canons' permission. The annual accounts of the exchequer, the war department and all other public bodies had to be presented to them for their inspection and approval.[5] Yet although these restrictions made an ambitious foreign policy impossible, the regular income from taxes and the extensive electoral domains were sufficient to allow any but the most extravagant Elector to pursue an independent policy. Equally ineffectual was the Chapter's control of certain high offices of state. The capitulation of election dictated that only canons could become Vicar General, President of the Council, Exchequer or Municipal Court, and Statthalter of the Erfurt or Eichsfeld territories, or of Mainz if the Elector were absent.[6] These positions however only involved administrative functions: decisions on policy belonged to the Elector and his inner circle of advisers, and nothing could force him to admit canons to this informal group if he did not want them. It is indicative of the failure of the Chapter to gain any real influence on the Electorate's government that in 1787 those with most influence on the Elector were just those people the perpetual capitulation sought to exclude from the state – Protestant foreigners.[7]

Of the sixty articles of the perpetual capitulation of election, the majority

[1] As Stimming writes (Ibid.), the ultimate fate of the perpetual capitulation of election is unknown. He is wrong, however, when he suggests that its terms have been lost. The text, together with the attendant correspondence between the Elector and the Chapter, can be found in Vienna, *MEA*, GK, Fasc. 85a, 454–570.
[2] Ibid., 532–3.   [3] Ibid., 510–12, 516.
[4] Ibid., 502, 506, 507, 514.
[5] Ibid., 516, Stimming, *Wahlkapitulationen*, pp. 122–8.
[6] Vienna, *MEA*, GK, Fasc. 85a, 518.
[7] E.g. Johann Friedrich Freiherr von Stein, Johannes Müller, Frau von Coudenhove, Frau von Ferrette. See below, Chs. 6–8.

protected the privileges and immunities of the Chapter and few concerned the subjects it claimed to represent. Of those that did, the most important were article twenty-seven, which forbade the admission of foreign troops to any part of the Electorate without the Chapter's permission, article thirty-one which forbade the hiring-out of the Electorate's troops to other states as mercenaries and article thirty-three which ordered that care should be taken to ensure uniformity of tax-assessment methods. The chief protection accorded to the subject was paragraph twenty and its requirement that due processes of law be observed and justice denied to no-one. As the judicial system was controlled entirely by the Elector and the judges were appointed and dismissed at his discretion, this was not a very impressive safeguard.[1]

Like their equivalents in other European countries, the *lois fondamentales* of Mainz were difficult to define and even more difficult to enforce, but they were not completely meaningless. Although the situation never arose, it seems reasonable to suggest that the existence of a capitulation of election would have made it easier for canons and subjects to resist a tyrannical Elector. There was however nothing new in the perpetual capitulation of election and it can hardly be seen as part of any 'aristocratic resurgence', especially since it was drawn up at the request of the Elector.

The accompanying treaty suggested that far from representing the people against the Elector, the Chapter formed a state within a state. It enjoyed civil and criminal jurisdiction over its members and servants – except in the case of major crimes, when the offender was judged by the Elector and a representative of the Chapter. Over the centuries the canons had also wrested a whole series of important exemptions – from fees in both the Mainz and *Reich* chancelleries, from customs dues for goods brought from its estates for consumption in the city, from the cattle toll, from the bridge toll, from the wine toll and – above all – from taxation, in that all direct and indirect taxes collected in its territories were paid to the Chapter and not to the state. In addition there were some rather more quaint examples of the canons' exploitation of the Electorate; where the Elector did not possess the right of enclosure they enjoyed all hunting rights and every year the electoral huntsmen were to deliver a specified amount of game to each of them. In the unlikely event of their having forgotten any, a final blanket clause confirmed all their traditional privileges.[2]

Like the perpetual capitulation of election, the treaty was accompanied by a lengthy supplement which supplied arguments and documentation in support of the individual clauses. Unlike the capitulation's appeal to canon

[1] Vienna, *MEA*, GK, Fasc. 85a, 509, 512–14.
[2] Ibid., 484, 486–8, 494–6, 500.

and imperial law however, the treaty was based solely on past practice and was supported only by a list of precedents. This was probably the reason for dividing the capitulation into two parts in the first place, for the legal status of the capitulation was highly doubtful. After a test-case in the Prince-Bishopric of Würzburg in 1695, Pope Innocent XII had forbidden all capitulations of election. The Emperor Leopold I had added his confirmation three years later.[1]

Capitulations continued to be presented and continued to be signed, but they had lost their effectiveness. In any future dispute between chapter and prince-bishop, the latter could probably count on papal and imperial support; in 1772 the French minister at Mainz wrote: 'the capitulation is no longer rigorously obligatory for the ecclesiastical electors, because the Chapter's capitulation does not have the force of law, as it is authorised neither by the imperial courts nor by the *Reichstag*'.[2] The bishops appended their signatures and ignored its provisions; at the height of the dispute between the Elector Emmerich Joseph and the Chapter,[3] the canons were very reluctant to expose their case to the unsympathetic imperial courts. It is difficult to see what other sanctions they possessed. The natural wealth of the country and the abundance of traditional sources of revenue made its financial control largely illusory. A direct appeal to the people was out of the question and never considered.

IV

The Electorate of Mainz therefore can hardly be described as a constitutional state; it bore a much closer resemblance to an absolute monarchy. Yet although the Imperial Knights could not dictate an Elector's policies, their dominance was clearly reflected, particularly in the policies adopted by successive Electors towards the Empire, the Emperor and the individual princes. It was appreciated clearly by all concerned with imperial politics that the survival of both the Imperial Knights and the ecclesiastical states depended on the survival of the Empire. If the great secular princes were ever allowed to break away from the Empire and establish complete sovereignty, then mediatisation,[4] secularisation and partition could not be far behind. Consequently the electors of Mainz were loyal supporters of the Habsburg emperors throughout this period, although occasionally a clash of interests could bring a temporary estrangement.

---

[1] Hans Erich Feine, *Die Besetzung der Reichsbistümer vom Westfälischen Frieden bis zur Säkularisation 1648–1803*, Kirchenrechtliche Abhandlungen, vols. 97 and 98 (Stuttgart, 1921), pp. 343–4. Fritz Hartung, *Deutsche Verfassungsgeschichte*, 7th ed. (Stuttgart, 1959), p. 144–5.
[2] Livet: *Recueil*, p. 193.   [3] See below, pp. 126–38.
[4] This refers to the Imperial Knights – they feared that they would be 'mediatised', i.e. subjected to a prince other than the Emperor; this is of course what happened in 1806.

Earlier attempts by Austria to establish a hegemonial position in Germany had driven Mainz into the arms of France, but once the Habsburgs had accepted the Westphalian settlement there were no further grounds for conflict. The validity of this general observation is not negated by the defection of 1785, when Mainz joined Frederick the Great's League of Princes.[1] The Elector was moved to break with tradition only by monumental tactlessness on Joseph II's part and by the belief that Austria no longer took any interest in the preservation of the *Reich*. Even so, a majority of the Chapter refused to ratify the step. The basic antagonism between Prussia and Mainz soon became apparent, and, after the death of his brother, Leopold II found it comparatively simple to woo Mainz back into the Habsburg fold.

This essential bias towards the Habsburg Emperor meant that when a vacancy occurred in the Electorate, and the diplomats gathered to attempt to secure the election of a candidate favourably disposed to their courts, it was the Austrian ambassador who enjoyed a head-start and who usually won. The fact that many of the canons' relations sought or had found positions in imperial service lent him considerable persuasiveness. Those numerous canons who owned estates within the Habsburg Monarchy also welcomed the opportunity to display their loyalty. In 1743 the English diplomat Thomas Villiers surmised correctly that the newly elected Johann Friedrich von Ostein would be very much attached to Austria because his estates there yielded 30–40,000 gulden per annum.[2]

The victory of a Habsburg-sponsored candidate was not however inevitable. It would have been most remarkable if the twenty-four canons had all waived their own chances of election in favour of some shining paragon. It would have been equally remarkable if diplomats opposed to Austria had refrained from exploiting the natural factiousness and jealousies of so numerous a body. As they did not possess the same initial advantages possessed by their Austrian colleague, they usually turned to simple bribery. When the French minister Blondel arrived in Mainz in 1732 he found that the Chapter entertained 'extreme hostility' towards Versailles; he described as follows how he employed his 'usual methods': 'The Elector was pleased to accept some tobacco and others accepted Italian liqueurs, chocolate, burgundy and champagne.' He concluded plaintively that 'it is the only way I know to make friends'.[3]

It was the reports of French diplomats like Blondel which have been largely responsible for the conventional – and exaggerated – picture of the ecclesiastical states as sinks of iniquity in which venal canons happily

---

[1] See below, pp. 210–220.
[2] London, *P.R.O.*, SP. 88.61, 21 April 1743, Thomas Villiers to Lord Carteret.
[3] Livet, *Recueil*, p. 159.

wallowed. It was they who coined the phrase '*point d'argent, point d'Allemagne*', and made remarks such as 'You will be aware that the Germans are extremely venal, and especially the majority of those who make up the cathedral chapters of Germany; they place alongside their principal emoluments the money they receive on the occasion of the various elections.'[1] Canons who delayed their decision as to which candidate to support until the last possible moment, holding out for the maximum price for their vote, were said to be 'waiting for the inspiration of the Holy Ghost'. In other words, the Austrian candidate was never assured of an easy victory; during the election at Mainz in 1743, the exasperated Austrian ambassador Count Cobenzl commented 'I think that the heretics who abolished the bishops must have been ambassadors at an episcopal election.'[2]

Apart from anything else, the enormous sum of money which could change hands during an episcopal election indicated that the great powers still attached considerable importance to the ecclesiastical states. In 1780 the Habsburgs paid out almost one million gulden to secure the election of the Archduke Max Franz at Cologne.[3] Despite the strictures of the French however, the canons could not always be bought and sold like cattle. If they believed that the election of a certain candidate constituted a threat to the Imperial Knights or the ecclesiastical states, then not all the gold of France, Prussia or the Maritime Powers could make them think otherwise. In 1787 the Prussians failed to secure the election of the Freiherr von Dienheim as coadjutor to the Elector Friedrich Karl, despite the expenditure of 180,000 gulden.[4] The successful candidate, Dalberg, was elected on his own very obvious merits; indeed he had asked all foreign courts not to intervene on his behalf. Personal rivalry and sheer greed could induce temporary confusion, but the cord of interest which linked Imperial Knights and Habsburg Emperor was never finally severed.

V

For the Imperial Knights therefore, the Electorate of Mainz was simultaneously a weapon for the defence of their order, a social centre and a source of outdoor relief. It would be tempting, but only partly correct, to

---

[1] Ibid., p. xi.
[2] Adolf Carl Michels, 'Die Wahl des Grafen Johann Friedrich Karl von Ostein zum Kurfürsten und Erzbischof von Mainz (1743)', *Archiv für hessische Geschichte und Altertumskunde*, new series, vol. 16, pt. 1 (1930), p. 551.
[3] Max Braubach, *Maria Theresias jüngster Sohn Max Franz, letzter Kurfürst von Köln und Fürstbischof von Münster* (Vienna and Munich, 1961), p. 64.
[4] Karl Otmar Freiherr von Aretin, 'Dalberg zwischen Kaiser und Fürstenbund: Actenstücke zur Koadjutorwahl in Mainz 1787', *Archiv für mittelrheinische Kirchengeschichte* (1964), p. 332.

The Electorate, the Empire and the Imperial Knights

assume that such an aristocratic vessel was bound to founder in the egalitarian currents which ran with increasing strength after the 1780s. It was certainly the case that criticism became more frequent and more bitter. Not surprisingly it was the canons of the Chapter who bore the brunt, for their combination of both noble and clerical status was uniquely suited to excite the wrath of the revolutionaries. The German Jacobin Karl Clauer, for example, wrote in 1791:

> The French have stopped believing that to be a teacher or priest of a religion whose founder had nothing, it is necessary to be rich enough to maintain a court, lackeys, mistresses and a stable full of thoroughbreds. They say that the founder of the Christian religion was not called Baron von Christ; they have stopped believing that to be a bishop it is necessary to have a stud-book like an Arab stallion.[1]

It is also clear that Germans whose views were less extreme than those of Clauer saw in the canons clerical parasitism personified. The expression 'with the belly of a canon' was a popular substitute for 'as fat as a pig'. Typical of the many anecdotes which circulated about them was the following recounted by Pilati di Tassulo after a visit to Mainz: two canons were promenading in front of the Dalberg palace '*en tenant des propos galants*', when they were approached by a beggar who addressed them as 'excellencies', which was the correct way of addressing a canon. Impressed but surprised, the canons asked how he knew that they were 'excellencies'; the beggar replied that he could tell by their topic of conversation.[2]

When the Cathedral Chapter disappeared into oblivion along with the Electorate in 1803, few lamented its passing. Its obsession with aristocratic exclusiveness, its manifold privileges justified only by prescription and its position as a state within a state contradicted its claim to be the estates and representatives of the people. To men like Clauer the canons were caricatures of the *ancien régime*. Yet apart from the occasional reprobate, they do not appear to have been more or less virtuous than other members of their order, and there were few complaints about individuals in the Mainz revolutionary Club in 1792–3. Enlightened intellectuals like Dalberg rubbed shoulders with conservatives like Eltz; most of them drifted through life, shooting their game and collecting their paintings, doing little good but also little harm.

It is important to remember when assessing contemporary attitudes towards the Chapter, and especially the attitudes of people actually living in Mainz, that the canons dispensed very large sums among the merchants, tradesmen and craftsmen of the city, and moreover that those very large

---

[1] Claus Träger, *Mainz zwischen Schwarz und Rot: Die Mainzer Revolution in Schriften, Reden und Briefen* (Berlin, 1963), p. 56.
[2] Pilati di Tassulo, *Voyages en differens Pays de l'Europe en 1774, 1775 et 1776*, vol. 1 (La Haye, 1777), p. 42.

sums derived from estates which were often far away. It is doubtful whether those who benefited from such expenditure spared many thoughts for the peasants who had made it possible. This should be sufficient warning against assuming automatically that high tension crackled between an overprivileged clergy and an underprivileged laity. Perhaps the canons' most appropriate epitaph was provided by the English tourist Dr Moore when he wrote:

> The streets swarm with ecclesiastics, some of them in fine coaches, and attended by a great number of servants. I remarked also many genteel airy abbés; who, one could easily see, were the most fashionable people and give the tone at this place...though it is most evident that in this electorate the clergy have taken exceeding good care of themselves; yet, in justice to them, it must also be acknowledged that the people also seem to be in an easy situation.[1]

The canons' secular relations attracted similarly hostile attention. In 1792, after the city had been captured and occupied by the French, a young supporter of the Revolution, Nicolaus Müller, published a play called *Der Aristokrat in der Klemme* (The Aristocrat in a Jam). The central character is a suitably repulsive baron, in debt to the tune of 22,000 gulden. When his creditor demands immediate repayment, the baron attempts to pacify him as follows:

> I thought we were agreed that I was to use the influence of my three relations in the treasury to get your eldest son a position as financial councillor at 5,000 gulden *per annum*. My sister, the Lady von Hoven,[2] who can make a certain member of the Cathedral Chapter do anything she wants, was to secure a benefice of at least 2,000 gulden for the youngest son. Your daughter was to receive a financial secretary's position worth 3,000 gulden a year and then seek her own husband to fill it. Your nephew can have a post in the administration of the lottery and you yourself, whether you need it or not, can have a pension of 100 Carolins.[3]

But the baron has failed to appreciate that such abuses were possible only under the old régime; the revolution has swept away the old corruption and a meritocracy has taken its place.

Yet at the same time as Müller was writing his play, Daniel Dumont, the leader of the merchants of the city, was composing a letter to the French general in charge of the occupying forces. Dumont protested *against* the planned abolition of the nobility, because:

> You know as well as I do that although the nobles who live in Mainz have some estates in the Electorate, most of their possessions lie elsewhere. An inevitable result will be that they will leave a city where the large sums they spend are regarded with envy and

---

[1] John Moore, *A View of the Society and Manners in France, Switzerland and Germany*, vol. 1 (London, 1779), p. 409.
[2] This refers to the Baroness von Coudenhove, the niece of the Elector Friedrich Karl. There were rumours that she was also his mistress. See below, p. 244 n 2.
[3] [N. Müller], *Der Aristokrat in der Klemme* (Mainz, 1792), p. 24.

contempt. In this way money will be removed from the state which previously circulated to the benefit of all citizens.[1]

As events were to show, the majority of the citizens preferred Dumont's economic realism to Müller's radical idealism.

[1] *Schreiben an Custine, General der französischen Armeen, veranlaßt durch seine entehrende Aufrufungen an die Bürger und Soldaten deutscher Nation, verfaßt von einem Manne, der ein Feind von allem Despotismus ist, der aber für das Beste seines Vaterlandes, für das Wohl seiner Mitbürger, für die Ehre Deutschlands Fürsten, sein Leben aufzuopfern bereit ist* (1792), p. 19.

2

Town and Country

The town and country of Mentz ought to be a spot most favourable to the powers and purposes of man – if with all the prime ingredients in hand for external ease and consolation, he could be left at liberty to mix and compound them as he would wish – if the waste of folly did not bring to nought the wantonness of fortune – if the froward impositions of human violence did not thwart and frustrate the blessings of nature! Those blessings of nature are here no less affluent than they are kind. In the best glories of all land, in corn and wine, in milk and honey – with concurring rivers, the Maine and the Rhine, streaming magnificently at the bottom – with the fruitful mountains, of the Rhinegau, are glittering to the top![1]

On any eighteenth century map of the Empire the various pieces of territory which made up the Electorate of Mainz are scattered across the Rhineland, Franconia and Thuringia to make a pattern as confused as an archipelago.[2] There was, however, a pivot around which all economic and social activity revolved and that pivot was the city of Mainz. Before the revolutionary wars disrupted its economy and decimated its population, Mainz was a prosperous and expanding community with approximately 30,000 inhabitants.[3] This figure was the result of a demographic recovery which had progressed slowly and spasmodically since the disasters of the Thirty Years War, when the city had lost between a third and a half of its population.[4] In the late seventeenth and early eighteenth century, plague, war and dearth brought frequent interruptions to the upward trend, but after about 1730 the rate of increase became both faster and more consistent. Rather surprisingly, this increase was not due to a corresponding increase in the birth-rate and/or decrease in the death rate. In only twenty-five years between 1729 and 1792 were there more births than deaths.[5] The

[1] Charles Este, *A Journey in the Year 1793 through Flanders, Brabant and Germany to Switzerland* (London, 1795), p. 291.   [2] See above, p. 41.
[3] The demography and social structure of the city have been the subject of an exhaustive study by François Dreyfus, *Société et Mentalités à Mayence dans la seconde moitié du 18. siècle* (Paris, 1968). See also his article 'Prix et Population à Trèves et à Mayence au XVIIIe siècle', *Revue d'histoire économique et sociale*, 34 (1956).
[4] Georg Mentz, *Johann Philipp von Schönborn, Kurfürst von Mainz, Bischof von Würzburg und Worms, 1605–1673*, vol. 2 (Jena, 1899), pp. 147–8.
[5] Dreyfus, *Mayence*, p. 265. Connoisseurs of the *Annales* school will not be surprised to learn that M. Dreyfus has established that *coitus interruptus* was the method of birth control favoured by most citizens of Mainz.

missing thousands were immigrants, peasants from Franconia, the Hunsrück and the Eifel, who had been forced off the land by the pressure of over-population and had been attracted to Mainz by the city's growing prosperity. After the middle of the century, the increasingly tolerant religious policies of the electors led to the immigration of surprisingly large numbers of Protestants. Most of them came from the neighbouring Palatinate, Nassau or Hessen, although in the 1770s the catchment-area expanded to include Württemberg, Thuringia and Saxony. Finally, there was a small but constant influx of foreigners, predominantly French and Italian.[1] With its 30,000 inhabitants Mainz was quite a large city by contemporary German standards. It was much smaller than Vienna, Hamburg or Berlin and somewhat smaller than Munich, Dresden or Frankfurt am Main, but was larger than Aachen, Hanover, Stuttgart, Düsseldorf, Mannheim or Kassel.[2] In terms of relative population, Mainz was far more important in the eighteenth century than it is today.

The people who lived in Mainz and the immigrants who flocked in to join them found all sorts of ways of making a living. The city's most obvious economic asset was its geographical position. Control of the confluence of the Main and the Rhine ensured an important share of the trade of both rivers. River-borne traffic between Holland and Switzerland or between Franconia and Alsace had to go through Mainz. The value of this outstanding natural advantage was much reduced, however, by human avarice. From Neuenburg, just north of Basle, to Rotterdam, there were thirty-eight customs posts, administered by nineteen different authorities.[3] In the absence of metalled roads and mechanised transport, the river should have been the quickest and cheapest means of transport, but on the Rhenish princes' list of priorities fiscal considerations came before commerce. During the Thirty Years War their need for ready cash had forced up customs dues, and rates were not reduced substantially after 1648. In 1700 two hundred sacks of salt cost 400 *Reichsthalers* in Cologne; by the time they reached Frankfurt their price had increased to 712 *Reichsthalers*.[4] Merchants turned to land-routes or to less obstructed rivers. Goods destined for Central Germany were frequently shipped from the United Provinces to Bremen or Hamburg and from there down the Weser or Elbe. In 1700 the transport of twenty-four tons of herrings from Cologne to Frankfurt cost 133 *Reichsthalers*, but only 96 *Reichsthalers* if taken from Bremen to Frankfurt.[5]

[1] Ibid., pp. 271–4.
[2] W. H. Bruford, *Germany in the Eighteenth Century: The Social Background to the Literary Revival* (Cambridge, 1965), pp. 333–6.   [3] Dreyfus, *Mayence*, p. 174.
[4] K. Schwarz, *Der wirtschaftliche Konkurrenzkampf zwischen der Reichsstadt Frankfurt und der kurfürstlichen Stadt Mainz* (Mainz, 1932), p. 23. Customs dues accounted for 225 *Reichsthalers* of the increase, transportation costs for the rest.   [5] Ibid., p. 23.

The volume of trade passing up and down the Rhine in the second half of the seventeenth century fell absolutely as well as relatively. Although economic historians continue to debate the relationship between the Thirty Years War and the general European depression, there is no doubt that Rhenish trade was affected severely by both.[1] Günther Franz has shown that no part of Germany suffered more than the territory between the Moselle and the Rhine, with population losses of over 50%.[2] The Upper Rhine escaped more lightly but even here the decline in population in Alsace and the Breisgau is estimated at between 40 and 50%.[3] War, general depression and the customs posts conspired to paralyse Europe's most important waterway; in 1648 there were only four shippers operating out of Mainz.[4]

The owners of the customs appreciated that a joint agreement on the reduction of tariffs was the only way to resurrect the golden goose, but unanimity proved to be elusive. This was not surprising, in view of the heterogeneity of their membership; the King of France, the Cathedral Chapter of Cologne, the Emperor, the King of Prussia, the Elector of Mainz, the United Provinces or the Imperial City of Cologne had little in common. Nor did they all take an equal interest in the promotion of Rhenish trade. The Landgraf of Hessen-Kassel, for example, who owned only one post on the Rhine (as opposed to the Palatinate's seven or the Elector of Cologne's five), was more concerned to divert traffic eastwards to the Weser. In the autumn of 1777 a dispute between him and the city of Cologne brought shipping on the Rhine to a standstill for almost three months.[5]

Although interruptions of this kind were frequent, in the course of the eighteenth century conditions in general improved. The War of the Austrian Succession and the Seven Years War were unwelcome, but were incomparably less damaging than the Thirty Years War or Louis XIV's campaigns in the Palatinate. Rhenish trade also benefited from the general growth of the European economy after the second quarter of the eighteenth century. Agreements between states bordering on the Rhine to improve navigation or to reduce customs dues were infrequently made and less frequently observed but even in this sector some progress was made.[6] Consequently, as M. Dreyfus has shown,[7] the 'decadence' of the Rhenish

---

[1] Henry Kamen, 'The Economic and Social Consequences of the Thirty Years War', *Past and Present*, 39 (1968).
[2] G. Franz, *Der dreißigjährige Krieg und das deutsche Volk*, Quellen und Forschungen znr Agrargeschichte, vol. 7 (1961), p. 8.   [3] Ibid.
[4] H. Scholl, *Kurmainzische Wirtschaftspolitik (1648–1802)* (Frankfurt am Main Dissertation, 1924), p. 76.
[5] Vienna, *Staka*, Fasc. 186, 195–6, 200–1, 203.
[6] Scholl, *Wirtschaftspolitik*, p. 78.   [7] Dreyfus, *Mayence*, pp. 177–9.

economy in the eighteenth century is a myth. Although erratic, there was a perceptible trend upwards after 1740 and this increase became more marked after 1770.

One of the most serious of the man-made obstacles to trade on the Rhine was the right of staple (*Stapelrecht*) enjoyed by Mainz and Cologne. For Mainz this meant that all goods passing through the city had to be unloaded, offered for sale and then reloaded in Mainz ships to be transported to their final destinations.[1] This apparently outrageous monopoly had some sort of practical justification. Its defenders argued that as different parts of the Rhine required different kinds of boats and different kinds of skills, Cologne and Mainz were obvious points of transfer.[2] However anachronistic this sort of argument may have been at the end of the eighteenth century, it does at least explain how Mainz came to own the right of staple; practice became tradition, tradition was elevated into a right, the right was supported by compulsion and was consummated finally by an imperial privilege of 1495.[3] Not surprisingly, the staple was opposed vigorously and continuously by the other interested parties. The merchants of Frankfurt, in particular, complained about the expense, delay and damage to goods involved.[4] Control of the mouth of the Main gave Mainz an unbeatable hand and successive electors had little difficulty in maintaining the principle of the staple intact until the very end. When they agreed to specific exemptions they were careful to ensure that the electoral treasury did not suffer. In the course of the eighteenth century, France and the Palatinate obtained agreements whereby their ships were allowed to travel directly to Frankfurt, without offloading in Mainz, but they continued to pay the old dues in full.[5] The revival of trade led to a relaxation of the requirement that goods be offered for sale for three days. An increasing number of commodities were allowed to be loaded straight on to the Mainz ships for further transport, the right of staple (*Stapelrecht*) thus becoming simply a right of transfer (*Umschlagsrecht*).[6]

The Mainz right of staple clearly had a stultifying effect on Rhenish commerce in general but it also produced certain obvious benefits for the Electorate's treasury, in the shape of the various fees foreign merchants and shippers were compelled to pay. The other main beneficiary was the guild of shippers, which was presented with a guaranteed market, and

---

[1] K. Bockenheimer, 'Mainzer Handel und Schiffahrt in der Zeit von 1648 bis 1831', *Festschrift zur Erinnerung an die Eröffnung des neuen Zoll- und Binnenhafens in Mainz* (1887), p. 17.
[2] H. Daniels, *Über das Stapelrecht zu Köln und Mainz* (Cologne, 1804), *passim*.
[3] Schwarz, *Konkurrenzkampf*, p. 8.
[4] A. Dietz, *Frankfurter Handelsgeschichte*, vol. 4 (Frankfurt am Main, 1925), p. 25.
[5] Schwarz, *Konkurrenzkampf*, pp. 26–7.
[6] In 1700 almost all goods were required to be unloaded but by 1792 this regulation applied only to timber floated down the Main from Franconia – Scholl, *Wirtschaftspolitik*, p. 84.

The Electorate of Mainz in the Eighteenth Century

Mainz was indeed a centre of the transport industry. Some contemporaries did not feel, however, that this was an unqualified blessing. They argued that the easy pickings afforded to haulage contractors by the staple dissuaded citizens from engaging in commerce on their own account: 'there is no really genuine favourable balance of trade here; what there is here consists for the most part in transport'.[1] This verdict was somewhat exaggerated when it was written but it would certainly have been accurate in 1750.

The absence of wholesale commercial establishments was not entirely due to the rival attractions of the transport industry, for its roots went back several centuries. In 1332, 1411 and 1423 there were mass emigrations of the patrician merchants, after violent and unsuccessful struggles with the craft guilds for control of the city. The contemporaneous expansion of Frankfurt turned Mainz into an economic backwater, a development which was confirmed by the abolition of municipal liberties after 1462.[2] The economy continued in a depressed state until well into the eighteenth century. Around 1750, however, the vigorous mercantilist policies of the Elector Johann Friedrich (1743-63) and his ministry initiated a revival of trade. Although trading conditions in general were becoming increasingly favourable, there can be little doubt that the new fairs, warehouses, cranes and various fiscal incentives played an important part.[3] When the Elector Lothar Franz von Schönborn (1695-1729) combined all the Mainz tradesmen in one guild at the beginning of the century he called it the retailers' guild (*Krämerzunft*); Ostein, on the other hand, was able to found a separate guild of wholesalers (*Handelsstand*), which continued to increase in size, wealth and importance up to the revolutionary wars.[4]

Mainz never became a manufacturing city, but it did emerge from the shadow cast by Frankfurt and became an important centre for local distribution and collection. Then as now, the slopes of the Rheingau produced the best wines in Germany and the Mainz wine market, established on a permanent footing in 1750, did brisk business. In 1789 wine to the value of 300,000 gulden was sent down the Rhine to Holland.[5] The remarkable fertility of the area surrounding the city provided a wide variety of agricultural produce for export. Tobacco, madder, hemp, millet, fruit, dried

---

[1] P. W. Gercken, *Reisen durch Schwaben, Baiern, die angränzende Schweiz, Franken, die Rheinische Provinzen und an der Mosel in den Jahren 1779-1785*, vol. 3 (Stendal, 1786), p. 71. See also Paul Lemcke, 'Ein Besuch in Mainz vor 104 Jahren', *Mainzer Anzeigen*, 100 and 101 (1883).
[2] See above, pp. 44-5.
[3] For a full account of Ostein's economic policies, see below, pp. 98-101.
[4] P. Gottschämmer, *Geschichte der Organisation der wirtschaftlichen Interessenvertretungen in Hessen* (Giessen Dissertation, 1912), p. 8.
[5] P. A. Winkopp & J. D. A. Höck, *Magazin für Geschichte, Statistik, Literatur und Topographie der sämmtlichen deutschen geistlichen Staaten*, vol. 1 (Zürich, 1790), p. 11.

fruit, fruit wine, fruit vinegar, woad, potash and various kinds of nuts were sold at the Mainz market for export.[1] Perhaps most important of all, the region produced a surplus of grain. In years of crisis, French merchants travelled from Besançon, Nancy or Strasbourg to Mainz to buy emergency supplies.[2] Another important natural product was timber from the forests of the Taunus and the Spessart. The trunks were bound together to form an enormous raft or *Flooz* and were then floated down the Main, through Mainz and on down the Rhine to their final destination in Holland.[3] Finally, the city also re-exported goods brought from Strasbourg: pork, tobacco, paper, cheese and Alsatian wine.[4]

Although usually they commented that trade on the Rhine was not as flourishing as it should have been, several contemporary travellers were impressed by the amount of agricultural produce being carried down the Rhine in Mainz ships. J. C. Risbeck wrote:

> The earth yields uncommon returns, and the corn of this country is imported [*sic*] far and wide on the Rhine. There are also large quantities of fruits and greens of all kinds; excellent asparagus and cabbage are the food of the most common people: nor is there a place in Germany where the people are so fond of them, or have a greater supply of provisions of this kind. Great shiploads of their cabbages, as well raw as pickled are carried down the Lower Rhine as far as Holland. The little city of Croneberg, situated on an eminence six miles off the main road, drives a trade with Holland to the amount of eight thousand guilders a-year for apples, cyder, and chestnuts, of which last it has large groves. All the villages of the country lie in orchards of trees and command large fields of corn below.[5]

Dreyfus has demonstrated convincingly that between the 1730s and the revolutionary wars Mainz participated in the general economic expansion of western Germany. The average annual traffic between Mainz and Strasbourg grew by 70% between 1740–9 and 1780–9, the rise becoming especially marked after 1770.[6] That this increase was not confined to one sector of the Rhine is shown by the receipts from the crane fees, which increased from 47,035 francs in 1770 to 61,790 francs in 1780 to 82,000 francs in 1789, although they fell back to 64,000 francs in 1790 and 1791.[7] It is also clear that, relatively, trade in Mainz expanded faster than elsewhere. Between 1730 and 1790 its population grew twice as fast as that of Frankfurt or Cologne.[8] Ever since the early fourteenth century Frankfurt

---

[1] Ibid., p. 11. A. L. Schlözer, *Staatsanzeigen*, vol. 1 (Göttingen, 1781), p. 16.
[2] Dreyfus, *Mayence*, p. 163.
[3] Ibid., pp. 164–5. Schlözer, *Staatsanzeigen*, vol. 1, p. 16.
[4] Dreyfus, *Mayence*, p. 188.
[5] J. K. Risbeck, *Travels through Germany*, vol. 3 (London, 1787), p. 188.
[6] Dreyfus, *Mayence*, p. 179.
[7] Ibid., p. 179. The corresponding figures quoted by Lehne in the *Historisch-Statistisches Jahrbuch des Departments von Donnersberg für das Jahr 9 der fränkischen Republik* (Mainz, n.d.) are 1770: 21,827, 1780: 28,674, 1789: 30,878, 1790: 29,737, 1791: 30,098.
[8] Dreyfus, *Mayence*, p. 191.

had been economically superior to Mainz in all departments, but towards the end of the eighteenth century the tide began to turn.[1] It is significant that it was Mainz, not Frankfurt, that benefited most from the considerable growth in the prosperity of the Main region. Treaties with Würzburg and Ansbach established a direct link with Franconia and by the end of this period Mainz had captured two thirds of the Main trade.[2] Almost continuous warfare between 1792 and 1814, accompanied by the long French occupation of the city, brought this encouraging development to an abrupt halt. After the restoration Mainz passed back into the shadow of Frankfurt and has never re-emerged.

The city's commercial expansion was based on the natural produce of its hinterland, not on the manufactured products of its workshops or factories. A major reason for the disappointing rate of industrial growth was the survival of archaic forms of organisation. Although certain qualifications have to be made, generally it can be stated that at the end of the eighteenth century the urban economy was still dominated by the craft guilds. Technically, the *Handelsstand* and the *Krämerzunft* mentioned above[3] were guilds, but in reality they were merely associations of wholesalers and retailers respectively. They were much larger, easier to join, and exercised much less control over their members than did the craft guilds. Merchants, shopkeepers and master craftsmen did, however, have one thing in common: they were all full citizens (*Bürger*). Indeed, although in theory it was possible to acquire rights of citizenship separately, in practice only members of a guild could become *Bürger*. As such they enjoyed certain rights and privileges: if accused of a criminal offence they had to be tried according to traditional procedure; they could deal in wine, whatever their nominal profession, if they paid the excise; they could purchase houses and land in the city; they were personally free and, together with their families, were exempt from military service, and the state labour dues (*Fronen*); they could graze their cattle and horses on the common pastures; if they paid the various taxes, which for a *Bürger* were immutable, for forty years they gained total exemption; they were eligible for appointment to the various honorific municipal bodies; they paid no excise on beer brewed for consumption at home; they had a right to a free bed at the St Rochus hospital in case of destitution, illness or old age; and so on.[4]

In the later Middle Ages the craft guilds had ruled the city of Maizn but

---

[1] H. Aubin, 'Frankfurt und Mainz', *Historische Vierteljahresschrift*, 25/4 (1931).
[2] Dreyfus, *Mayence*, p. 184. For a discussion of the vigorous commercial policies of the Mainz electors, which helped to make this possible, see below, pp. 99–100, 111.
[3] See above, p. 74.
[4] Heinrich Schrohe, *Die Stadt Mainz unter kurfürstlicher Verwaltung, 1462–1792*, Beiträge zur Geschichte der Stadt Mainz, vol. 5 (Mainz, 1920), pp. 184–5.

since 1462 they had succumbed to princely absolutism. The election by each guild of its own representatives (*Brüdermeister*) had become a purely formal gesture. A member of the municipal council, appointed by the elector, had to be present at all guild meetings and no decision could be taken without his consent. In 1782 this control was strengthened when two police commissars were authorised to attend all guild meetings and to inspect all records and accounts.[1] By the end of the eighteenth century, the guilds were simply organs of the state.

The most important privilege enjoyed by the masters, their journeymen and their apprentices was of course a monopoly of production. Once absolute, this monopoly had been eroded by the growth of two other groups of producers: the *Beisassen* and the *Tolerierten*. The former were foreigners who were allowed into Mainz to work at a trade for a limited period only. As their name suggests, the *Tolerierten* were Protestants and thus ineligible for admission to the craft guilds or the rights of citizenship.[2] Both groups paid fewer taxes than the *Bürger* but, on the other hand, their only right was to earn their living in the city. In practice this was no great hardship. Electors frequently waived the regulations to allow them to buy property, for example, and they were not conscripted into the army or forced to perform state labour dues. As the electoral economic and religious policies became increasingly liberal, membership of a guild became decreasingly attractive. The increase of their rivals reflected the failure of the guilds to maintain a closed shop; by 1792 there were 290 *Beisassen* and 89 *Tolerierten* in Mainz.[3]

Like so many other organisations founded for pecuniary gain, the craft guilds had a built-in tendency towards ossification. By the eighteenth century they were not merely irrelevant, they were positively obstructive. They showed all the negative conservatism of a vested interest overtaken by events: dogged devotion to old techniques, suspicion of innovation, resentment of competition and xenophobia. The masters concentrated on keeping their own numbers as small as possible. In this task they were assisted greatly by the complicated regulations governing admission to the guilds. The aspiring craftsman first had to serve an apprenticeship in Mainz of three years. As a journeyman, he then left the city to travel from one German town to another, collecting *en route* testimonials from his various employers. These *Wanderjahre* usually lasted two years. On his return to Mainz he was not allowed to apply immediately for admission to the ranks of the masters. First he had to work for another two years or so as a simple journeyman. He was then permitted to submit his masterpiece

---

[1] Friedrich Schmitt, *Das Mainzer Zunftwesen und die französische Herrschaft* (Frankfurt am Main and Darmstadt, 1929), p. 41.
[2] Schrohe, *Mainz*, pp. 145–69, 185.
[3] Ibid., p. 173.

to the guild and, if it were approved, to pay the substantial fees and become a master. This is a very generalised account; the process was often very much longer or, especially if the candidate concerned were a close relation of an existing master, shorter.[1] This long and complicated procedure gave the guilds ample opportunity to keep their numbers down, the regulations governing the presentation of masterpieces being an especially potent weapon.[2]

It is an indication of the region's economic backwardness that throughout Central Europe the guilds were still alive and kicking at the end of the eighteenth century, while in England, France and the United Provinces they were at most moribund. Partly this was due to the political disunity of the Empire. In 1731 the *Reichstag* had issued general imperial regulations for the reform, reorganisation and conduct of the guilds.[3] Theoretically applicable to the whole Empire, their actual implementation depended on the will of the individual princes. In Mainz there were two bursts of reforming legislation. Around the middle of the century, the Elector Johann Friedrich and his minister Count Stadion accompanied their ambitious commercial policies with an attack on the worst guild abuses. In 1747, 1748 and 1751, for example, edicts were issued against the practice of requiring very expensive, difficult and useless masterpieces. At the same time the lavish entertaining demanded from new masters was prohibited.[4] The second wave came in the 1780s, when the Elector Friedrich Karl removed the last vestiges of the guilds' control of their own affairs. Plans were also drafted for their total abolition.[5]

In fact the guilds survived until the French occupation of the city, but in a much truncated form. The electors did not deliver the *coup de grâce*, they simply ignored and marched past the opposition. This outflanking-manœuvre consisted simply in allowing citizens of Mainz or foreigners to set up manufacturing establishments in the city without having to join a guild. Indeed, positive incentives were offered to encourage them to do so. These included a reduction of customs, crane and warehouse fees, free entry for raw materials, free export for manufactured articles, interest-free loans, *ad hoc* payments for individual years, premiums for long periods of uninterrupted activity, tax concessions, a monopoly of trade in the city or certain areas elsewhere and occasionally the *privilegium exclusivum* for the whole Electorate.[6] Many of the entrepreneurs who sought to benefit

---

[1] F. G. Dreyfus, 'Les corporations à Mayence au XVIIIe siècle', *Cahier d'Études Comtoises*, 3 (1961), 156.
[2] Bockenheimer, *Zünfte*, p. 46.
[3] Friedrich Lütge, *Deutsche Sozial- und Wirtschaftsgesichte*, 2nd ed. (Berlin, Göttingen and Heidelberg, 1960), p. 310.
[4] Schmitt, *Zunftwesen*, pp. 38–9.   [5] See below, pp. 181–2.
[6] Schrobe, *Mainz*, p. 140. Scholl, *Wirtschaftspolitik*, pp. 153–60.

from these concessions were citizens of Mainz seeking to evade guild restrictions, but they were also joined by Frenchmen, Austrians, Italians and Belgians. Their establishments produced a great variety of commodities: ribbon and braid, cotton, pencils, chocolate, gold and silver chain, hats, silk, surgical instruments, playing cards, sewing needles, Spanish noodles, soap, parchment, cosmetics, taffeta, chintz, etc.[1] There is not enough reliable evidence to allow the prosperity or even longevity of these enterprises to be quantified but it does appear that after about 1770 the survival rate improved and that during the 1770s and 1780s production in Mainz increased substantially.[2]

It is doubtful whether the electoral treasury benefited greatly from these non-guild concerns. Indeed, the history of the most important of them – the porcelain factory at Höchst and the glass works at Lohr and Emmerichsthal – suggests the reverse. The pattern of events was similar in all three cases – persistent unprofitability punctuated by crises surmounted only by subsidies from the central government. Although today Höchst porcelain, even if not mentioned in the same breath as Meissen or Nymphenburg, commands much respect and high prices, at the time it could not be produced at a profit. The first entrepreneur secured all kinds of concessions from the Elector, including the *privilegium exclusivum*, but in 1756, ten years after beginning production, he was bankrupt. By 1777 the factory owed almost 20,000 gulden to the electoral treasury and 40,000 gulden to the Elector personally and was still on the brink of insolvency.[3] It lurched on to the end of the Electorate but continued to require periodic transfusions from the treasury. Although producing for the popular market, Emmerichsthal was equally unremunerative. The first entrepreneur suffered the same fate as his fellow trader at Höchst and was declared bankrupt in 1776, with total liabilities to the state of 16,902 gulden.[4] It is difficult to see who gained what from these enterprises. The treasury lost money, most of the entrepreneurs lost money, the glass dealers complained about the quality of the glass they were forced to buy and the prices charged to the public were higher than those of comparable foreign products.

Waste, inefficiency and unprofitability were doubtless features of many of these concerns but they did capture a growing share of the market. The increase in the city's population and prosperity meant that the market itself was expanding but there is some evidence that the old craft guilds suffered absolutely as well as relatively. An official survey of 1785 pre-

---

[1] Schrohe, *Mainz*, pp. 140–1.   [2] Dreyfus, *Mayence*, pp. 168–9.
[3] Scholl, *Wirtschaftspolitik*, pp. 139–44.
[4] August Amrhein, 'Die kurmainzische Glashütte Emmerichsthal bei Burjossa', *Archiv des historischen Vereins von Unterfranken und Aschaffenburg* (1900), pp. 191–2.

sented a most depressing picture. Only two of the ten master-masons were employed regularly, the rest having 'almost no livelihood'; only six of the twenty house-painters were fully occupied, the others working as day-labourers; all eight armourers were under-employed; and so on. There were complaints about foreign competition, about the Jews and pedlars who bought their goods elsewhere, and, of course, about the entrepreneurs who were not members of a guild.[1] The guilds had also declined in a more general sense. At the beginning of the eighteenth century it was vital for anyone wishing to carry on a trade to be a full citizen and thus a member of a guild. The life of the city was dominated by a hierarchy, which began with the Elector and proceeded down through clergy, nobility, citizens, journeymen and apprentices to the day-labourers. By the end of this period this traditional structure was riddled with exceptions; businessmen and merchants who were not members of the craft-guilds were often much wealthier than the master-craftsmen and in practice enjoyed the same privileges.[2]

But the guilds were not as 'decadent' as Dreyfus maintains. There can be no doubt that the guilds faced increasingly severe competition from outside, that in some trades there were simply too many masters and that in the 1770s and 1780s a number of them went to the wall. This did not mean that the guild system was on the point of collapse. In some trades, especially those concerned with the production of luxury goods, guild membership expanded rapidly in the course of the century.[3] The complaints made by the masters to the government inquiry in 1785 should be regarded with some suspicion. It would have been most remarkable if they had not taken advantage of the opportunity to portray their position in the darkest hues available. Perhaps most impressive of all, it is clear that the overwhelming majority of the masters were firmly attached to the guild organisation. The electors' reluctance to abolish the guilds altogether was due largely to their fear of the citizens' probable reaction.[4]

The economic and political conservatism of the guilds was due partly at least to the nature of their clientele. For Mainz was above all a *Residenzstadt*, a city whose economy depended on the presence within its walls of

---

[1] Scholl, *Wirtschaftspolitik*, pp. 110–15.   [2] Dreyfus, *Mayence*, p. 301.
[3] Josef Cremer, *Die Finanzen in der Stadt Mainz im 18. Jahrhundert: Ein Beitrag zur Finanzgeschichte der Stadt Mainz* (Giessen Dissertation, 1932), p. 24.
[4] When given a chance during the first French occupation of the city in 1792–3, the guilds remained obstinately attached to the old order. See below, pp. 289–93. In this respect Mainz was not exceptional. As T. S. Hamerow has written: 'Whereas by 1789 the guilds of England and France had lost much of their economic importance, in the Holy Roman Empire they still enjoyed full possession of their ancient rights. It was the French Revolution which opened a new era in the development of Germany by violently thrusting upon it the tenets of liberalism, nationalism and industrial freedom.' – *Restoration, Revolution, Reaction: Economics and Politics in Germany, 1815–1871* (Princeton, 1958), p. 22.

the elector, his court, his administration, the nobility and the clergy. The privileged orders were exempt from most forms of taxation and made little positive contribution to the Electorate's economy, but they were large employers and voracious consumers. Their parasitism was so striking that it is often forgotten that they constituted the main and often the only source of livelihood for a very considerable number of people. The biggest employer in Mainz was not a corn merchant, glass manufacturer or master-butcher, but the elector. On the eve of the Revolution about a quarter of the city's population were nobles, clergymen, officials and government employees of one kind or another, and their dependents.[1]

The elector also exercised considerable indirect influence on the economy through his expenditure. The court needed food, drink and entertainment; the electoral palaces and government buildings had to be maintained; the various offices of state needed a thousand different commodities. The following extract from the electorate's accounts for 1785 illustrates the wide range of beneficiaries:

	gulden
For music and the musicians:	4,465
For jewels, silver, porcelain and furniture:	19,144
For linen and for the washing and sewing of the same:	3,125
For the court kitchens:	75,944
For the court confectionery:	7,130
For the electoral gardens and avenues:	15,990
For building materials, tools and other necessary equipment:	35,593
For the upkeep of the electoral horses and carriages:	39,290
For the craftsmen and for goods bought from the retailers:	32,204
For the clothing of the liveried officials and servants:	32,204
For wine:	8,737[2]

Although the elector was the biggest single consumer in the city, in terms of total value he was eclipsed by the nobility as a class. The electorate had no ancient nobility of its own, but for political, economic and social reasons,[3] many Imperial Knights made Mainz their home. At the end of the eighteenth century at least twenty-seven families maintained permanent establishments in the city; in addition some courtiers were given rooms in the electoral palace and many others rented houses or lodgings for the season.[4] Their numbers were augmented further by the

---

[1] Dreyfus, *Mayence*, p. 329. An anonymous traveller reported from Mainz in December, 1773: 'There is really an abundance of everything here...the city is very populous, because the Elector's residence is here and apart from that because so many canons of the Cathedral Chapter and other gentlemen of the first rank live here.' – *Bemerkungen eines Reisenden durch Deutschland, Frankreich, England und Holland in Briefen an seine Freunde*, vol. 1 (Altenburg, 1775), p. 67. [2] Mainz, *Abteilung* 6, Fasc. 904. [3] See above, pp. 50–9.
[4] Clemens Kissel, 'Alte historische Adelshöfe in Mainz', *Mainzer Journal*, 260 and 263 (1898). A. L. Veit, *Mainzer Domherren vom Ende des 16. bis zum Ausgang des 18. Jahrhunderts* (Mainz, 1924), p. 84.

canons and domicellars of the exclusively noble Cathedral Chapter. No other city in the Empire, apart from Vienna, could boast such a distinguished concentration of impeccable breeding. Eduard Vehse, the historian of the German courts, called it: 'The Eldorado of the German nobility, the German Venice'.[1] Contemporary travellers rarely failed to comment on both the number and the wealth of the Mainz nobles. Lang, for example, observed: 'The nobility here is the most numerous and wealthy on the Rhine and is considered to be the oldest and purest in Germany. One can easily imagine their number when I say that one evening, on the occasion of a court ball, I counted over eighty carriages.'[2]

The presence in the city of this free-spending group of consumers had obvious economic repercussions: the Mainz which developed after the Thirty Years War clearly bore an aristocratic imprint. When spent in the city, the nobles' revenues from their landed estates created an economy in the image of their needs and desires. There were, for example, forty-six *marchandes de mode et de galanteries* in the city.[3] The local newspapers were filled with advertisements for luxury goods: 'fine hair powder... English night-lights...all kinds of paintings by famous masters...East Indian porcelain...large fine mirrors with beautifully gilded frames... silk stockings...fine liqueurs...chocolate...pomade from Provence... clothes made of the finest French cloth'.[4] One contemporary estimated that the nobility put 2½ million gulden into circulation each year, although this must have been a very rough guess.[5]

A more precise illustration of the effects of the presence of the nobles is provided by their domestic accounts. The Counts von Eltz, for example, had always had close connections with the Electorate and divided their time between their country residence in Eltville and their town house in Mainz. Their expenditure fluctuated considerably, possibly according to the degree of extravagance of the head of the family and the length of his actual sojourn in the city. It was nevertheless enormous: 13,684 gulden in 1752; 11,912 in 1761; 38,361 in 1771 and 29,537 in 1781.[6] The highly detailed accounts indicate that the money was scattered across a wide cross-section of the working population. There are lists of payments to all kinds of tradesmen, from goldsmiths to chemists, to the theatre for the rent of a box, to the Italian language teacher of the children, to carpenters

---

[1] Eduard Vehse, *Geschichte der deutschen Höfe seit der Reformation*, vol. 45 (Hamburg, 1859), p. 195.
[2] J. G. Lang, *Reise auf dem Rhein*, vol. 1, p. 21.
[3] Dreyfus, *Mayence*, p. 284, n. 26.
[4] *Kurfürstliche Mainzische gnädigst privileg. Anzeigen von verschiedenen Sachen*, den 11ten März 1780.
[5] [P. A. Winkopp], *Über die Verfassung von Mainz, oder Vergleich des alten und neuen Mainz* ('Deutschland', 1792), p. 15.
[6] Eltville, *Hausrechnungen*, 1752, 1761, 1771, 1781.

and glaziers for repairs to the residence, and so on. The kitchen accounts alone ran at about 350 gulden per month in 1781. Twenty-five servants were in attendance, including a huntsman, a hairdresser and a tutor. In 1781, 7,787 gulden were paid to various tradesmen, 4,163 to craftsmen, 2,494 to servants and 600 gulden in pensions to superannuated retainers. Included in the rubric headed 'miscellaneous' were payments to the poor, washerwomen, a seamstress, haulage contractors, carpenters and a hatter. Moreover, the dowager Countess von Eltz maintained a separate establishment; in 1781 her expenditure totalled 3,753 gulden. The desirability of the continued presence of the family in the city must have been apparent to everyone engaged in trade.

As the household accounts of other families have not survived, it is not possible to establish just how exceptional or typical the Eltzs were. The family was however only one of several listed by Risbeck as having incomes of between 30,000 and 100,000 gulden per annum.[1] The problem also arises as to how much of their income they derived from their estates and how much from their sinecures in the Electorate and consequently to what extent the tradesmen were merely repossessing, in the form of payment for goods bought, the taxes they had already paid. Anselm Casimir von Eltz, head of the Eltz family from 1736 until 1778, was Grand Chamberlain from 1746 until 1776, with a salary of 3,610 gulden, President of the Supreme Court from 1746 until 1776, with a salary of 1,500 gulden and Grand Master of the Court from 1776 until 1778, with a salary of 6,000 gulden.[2] His income from the state therefore never exceeded 8,000 gulden and in 1771 was only just over 5,000 gulden, while his expenditure in the same year was over seven times that sum. His son, Hugo Philipp, was Grand Master of the Stables and in 1771 drew 1,672 gulden from this post. Yet he spent 7,673 gulden on his separate establishment, the difference being met by an allowance from his father of 5,500 gulden and loans.[3] It is clear that for Imperial Knights whose estates had not been divided or alienated, salaries in the Electorate represented a supplementary rather than an essential part of their income. In 1785 Friedrich Joseph von Franckenstein was paid 3,000 gulden as Court Marshal but collected 10,472 gulden from his estates.[4] In terms of hard cash, the city gained far more than it lost by the presence of the nobility.

Despite their clerical status, the canons of the Cathedral Chapter had the same expensive tastes as their secular brothers and cousins. The

---

[1] Risbeck, *Travels*, p. 209.
[2] *Hof- und Staatskalender*, 1740–1778. Hans Goldschmidt, *Zentralbehörden und Beamtentum im Kurfürstentum Mainz vom 16. bis zum 18. Jahrhundert*, Abhandlungen zur mittleren und neueren Geschichte, vol. 7 (Berlin and Leipzig, 1908), pp. 211–12.
[3] Eltville, *Rechenbuch des Grafen Hugo Philipp Karl pro 1770–1773*.
[4] Ullstadt, 002371.

private accounts of the canon Franz Philipp von Franckenstein, for example, reveal that as his income from his various benefices mounted[1] so did his expenditure – from 2,380 gulden in 1752, to 3,138 gulden in 1761, to 4,653 gulden in 1771. His piety was not of the self-denying kind and there are numerous entries referring to visits to the theatre, concerts, the Italian opera and *bals masqués* and also to heavy losses at cards. The following extracts from his accounts illustrate the way in which a large number of Mainz tradesmen benefited from his extravagance:

	gulden	kreuzers
6 pairs of shoes	10	–
Entrance fees to 13 balls held during Carnival-time	31	19
To the tailor Jean Schnetterheim	19	20
To the Countess von Bassenheim, on account of a lost wager, a piece of Höchst porcelain	11	6
12 pairs of under-stockings	11	–
3 pairs of black silk stockings	16	25
Batiste for a dozen pairs of sleeves	14	7
14 *Ehlen* of cloth for the servants	17	22
50 bottles of 1750 Asmannshausen Red	20	–
To the apothecary Wacker	37	28
To surgeon Wehers for letting a vein	2	6
To painter Dischbein for a portrait	27	–
For cloth	98	–
To the button-maker	10	24
7 pairs of shoes	11	20

The economic importance of the court, administration, nobility and clergy was demonstrated clearly when they departed. There were two periods of French occupation: from October 1792 until July 1793 and from December 1797 until January 1814. The overthrow of the *ancien régime* may have brought significant social, political or cultural benefits but it did not lead to economic expansion. The population of the city in 1792 was approximately 30,000; by 1801 it had fallen to 21,615.[2] Although disruption caused by war doubtless made a major contribution to this decline, in 1815 the population was still only 23,000.[3] This is all the more striking in that throughout the period Mainz was not only an important French garrison town but was also the administrative capital of the *département* of Mont Tonnerre. The missing thousands had followed their sources of livelihood into exile at the courts of Franconia and Bavaria.

Before 1792, abundant natural resources, expanding commerce and the presence of many conspicuous consumers had made Mainz a wealthy city.

[1] See above, p. 55. [2] Lehne, *Jahrbuch*, p. 116.
[3] A. W. Schreiber, *Manuel pour les Voyageurs sur le Rhin* (Heidelberg, 1816), p. 93.

The prosperity of the individual citizens was enhanced further by the relatively mild system of taxation. There were three forms of direct taxation. The first was the *Schatzung*, a proportional tax levied on the assessed value of real estate and on income. The rates were low: 0·4% for houses and 1% for vineyards, pasture and arable fields. The tax on income (*Nahrungsschatzung*) varied between 1 gulden and 1 gulden 30 kreuzers for labourers and widows, between two and three gulden for craftsmen and between four and five gulden for wealthy merchants and brewers.[1] The second direct tax was a simple hearth-tax (*Herdschilling*) which was imposed on every citizen's household at a flat rate of fifty-four kreuzers per annum. More substantial was the *Servicegeld*, paid *in lieu* of billeting. Merchants paid between 20 kreuzers and three gulden per month, guild masters between 10 kreuzers and 1 gulden, *Beisassen* between 10 and 15 kreuzers, and *Tolerierte*[2] between 10 kreuzers and 3 gulden. In each case the exact amount paid depended on the financial circumstances of the man concerned.[3] In addition, certain specific dues were raised from various groups in the city. The Jews were taxed separately, new citizens had to contribute to funds set up to finance the fire-service and a new town-hall and had to purchase exemption from military service, all emigrants paid the *Nachsteuer* or 10% of the property they were taking with them and all citizens unable or unwilling to perform watch duty paid a special tax.[4]

This system had several inequitable features, of which the most striking was the number of exemptions. All nobles, clergy and electoral officials were exempt from the *Schatzung, Nahrungsschatzung, Herdschilling* and *Servicegeld*. These three privileged groups also received preferential treatment over the excise. Nobles, for example, could import free of charge sufficient grain for their domestic consumption, while the clergy could do the same for all the produce of their rural estates.[5] There was also a serious discrepancy between the amounts raised by direct and indirect taxation. In the 1780s the *Schatzung* and *Nahrungsschatzung* yielded about 8,000 gulden, the *Herdschilling* just over 2,000 and the *Servicegeld* just over 8,000; in 1785 the excise yielded over 42,000 gulden.[6] As the excise charges could only be recouped by additions to retail prices, it is clear that proportionally they bore most heavily on the poorer classes. Relatively, the wealthier a citizen became, the lighter his burden. It has been estimated that the most prosperous merchant paid no more than thirty gulden per annum in direct taxation.[7]

[1] Cremer, *Finanzen*, pp. 22–3.
[2] See above, p. 77.
[3] Cremer, *Finanzen*, p. 30.
[4] Ibid., pp. 31–5.
[5] Ibid., pp. 36–40.
[6] Ibid., pp. 24, 29, 30, 40.
[7] Scholl, *Kurmainzische Wirtschaftspolitik*, p. 169.

Despite these inequalities, taxation does not appear to have been oppressive. There were exemptions which spared the wealthy, but there were also exemptions which spared the poor. The *Schatzung, Herdschilling* and *Servicegeld* were paid only by full citizens (*Bürger*), only the *Nahrungsschatzung* was paid by all commoners. Whatever their legal status, paupers paid no direct taxes at all.[1] Partly for this reason, the problem of poverty did not assume the same appalling dimensions as in France, although there were paupers in the city. Indeed, during the 1770s and 1780s the government was sufficiently concerned to reorganise the welfare services.[2] Even so, the basic prosperity of the city, which appears to have increased at least as fast as the population, did not allow pauperism to reach an intolerable level. Dreyfus has estimated that in 1792 between 14% and 16% of the population needed relief of some kind.[3] When one takes into account the aged, the sick, the widows and orphans, this was not a particularly depressing percentage. It was certainly considerably lower than Strasbourg's (23%) or even Frankfurt's (21·5%).[4]

The evidence for the increasing wealth of the city is not confined to trade statistics, the accounts of noble households or inferences drawn from the fiscal structure. The many fine houses built in the second half of the century provide one kind of confirmation, the recorded impressions of contemporaries another. In 1785, for example, it was reported that: 'In a haberdashery here in October enough silk for 300 women's coats was bought, almost entirely by people who up till then had worn cotton.'[5] The estates of the deceased officials and merchants, as advertised for sale in the local papers, suggest that both their tastes and their means were similar to those of the nobles.[6] Eventually the Elector became alarmed by this conspicuous consumption on the part of mere commoners. In 1783 the Elector Friedrich Karl issued an ordinance against the 'exaggerated luxury' displayed by certain officials.[7] He recalled his earlier measures against excessive expenditure on jewels and gambling but noted with dismay that now 'clothes, the interior decoration of houses, household equipment, food, carriages, livery, the visiting of entertainments, in short almost everything seems to be affected by this dominant evil'. Luxury had

---

[1] Cremer, *Finanzen*, p. 22.   [2] See below, pp. 188–90.
[3] Dreyfus, *Mayence*, p. 353.
[4] Ibid. See also Olwen Hufton, 'Life and Death among the Very Poor', *The Eighteenth Century*, ed. Alfred Cobban (London, 1969), and also her book *Bayeux in the late Eighteenth Century* (Oxford, 1967). The difference between levels of poverty in Mainz and Bayeux – a town of similar size – is especially striking. I am grateful to Prof. J. H. Plumb for drawing my attention to the significance of this comparison.
[5] *Magazin der Philosophie und schönen Literatur*, 1 (1785), p. 84.
[6] Compare, for example, the estates of the merchant Steckmann and of the Cantor of the Cathedral Chapter Franz Philipp Freiherr von Franckenstein, advertised in the *Chur Mayntzische Wochentliche Frag- und Anzeigungs-Nachrichten*, 84 (1774).
[7] Mainz, *Abteilung* 26/1.

spread 'like a plague' from one class to another, ruining families and corrupting morals. Friedrich Karl announced that he did not intend to take coercive action but hoped that the warning that he would promote only those officials displaying healthy moderation would suffice. Predictably, his admonition had no effect and six years later von Lang commented on the liveliness of the citizens, 'the source of which may be ever-increasing luxury, which especially manifests itself in fastidious eating habits, expensive clothes and furniture in the Parisian style'.[1]

The leniency of the fiscal system in the city was made possible partly by the geographical location of the Electorate, partly by its natural resources and partly by the compulsory sacrifices of the rural population. The customs posts on the Rhine and Main and the various land routes yielded almost 200,000 gulden in 1785 or more than 10% of the Electorate's total revenue.[2] Dues imposed by virtue of the right of staple totalled approximately 75,000 gulden, while the bridge toll added more than 20,000 gulden.[3] Although some of these dues affected the citizens of Mainz directly or indirectly, the majority fell upon foreign merchants and travellers. The fertile and extensive state domains were another important source of income. In 1785 the rent of electoral houses, cellars, barns, gardens, arable land and pastures raised over 45,000 gulden. The sale of timber brought over 150,000 gulden, of salt 35,000 gulden and of venison and other forms of game 7,000 gulden.[4] The accounts for 1785 also include large sums realised by the sale of grain, wine, hay, straw and other agricultural produce, but although it is likely that some of this derived from the domains, it is also possible that some of it at least represented tithes or taxes paid in kind. Even disregarding this contribution, it is clear that the electors could afford a moderate burden of taxation.

The urban taxpayer was, however, much better placed than his rural counterpart. The crucial difference was that the former was confronted by only one lord (*Herr*): the elector as ruler of the state (*Landesherr*); but most peasants were subject to four – the lord who exercised political authority over him (*Landesherr*), the lord who exercised personal authority over him (*Gerichtsherr* and *Leibherr*), the lord who collected tithes from him (*Zehentherr*) and finally the lord who owned his land (*Grundherr*). Theoretically separate, two or more of these functions were often combined in the same man. Throughout the Electorate, the elector was always *Landesherr*, *Gerichtsherr* and *Leibherr*, often the *Grundherr* and in some places the *Zehentherr* as well. To draw a distinction between the four types of lords might seem, therefore, rather academic but the multiplicity had meaning for the peasant, because he paid dues to each of them. Most im-

[1] Lang, *Reise*, p. 15.   [2] Mainz, *Abteilung 6*, Fasc. 904.
[3] Ibid.   [4] Ibid.

portant was the direct tax or *Schatzung* paid to the *Landesherr*. As in the city of Mainz, this was divided into a tax on real estate and a tax on income. Rates for the latter or *Nahrungsschatzung*, however, appear to have been considerably higher in the country. Cremer[1] established that in the city even the wealthiest burgher paid no more than five gulden per annum, but in the Rheingau – the strip of territory on the right bank of the Rhine between Mainz and Rüdesheim – the basic rate was 4 gulden 5 kreuzers.[2] Rural craftsmen paid an additional $3\frac{1}{2}$ gulden and retailers paid between $3\frac{1}{2}$ and $10\frac{1}{2}$ gulden extra, the exact sum depending on their means. Day labourers and *Beisassen* paid a flat rate of seven gulden until they acquired property whose assessed rate was greater than that figure.[3] As in the city, temporary or permanent destitution brought exemption.

The *Schatzung* was the only tax common to both town and country, because the *Landesherr* was the only lord the town and country had in common. The most important dues demanded by the Elector as *Gerichtsherr* and *Leibherr* were the labour services or *Fronen* and the dues owed by virtue of the peasant's personal subordination (*Leibeigenschaft*). The former were of two kinds: those performed for the benefit of the community and those performed for the benefit of the electoral government. Of the latter category the most important and onerous concerned the upkeep of the roads. In certain areas local requirements brought additional services. The inhabitants of Nackenheim, for example, were obliged to maintain the banks of the Rhine, while in the forests of the Spessart the peasants were required to beat game for the hunts.[4] In the German territories west of the Elbe labour services were performed for the community or for the state, not for private individuals, as they were in the East. In Mainz, however, the electoral hunting rights were sometimes rented to nobles and so in this sense the peasants did perform labour services for individual nobles. It cannot now be established just how burdensome the labour services were. Doubtless there was a good deal of regional variation, but in some areas they appear to have been severe. Although the roads to and from the glass factory at Emmerichsthal[5] were in a very poor state, the electoral government expressed reluctance to contribute to their repair because the inhabitants of the region were already overburdened with labour services.[6] It was possible however to commute them for

[1] Cremer, *Finanzen*, p. 23.
[2] Winkopp & Höck, *Magazin*, vol. 2, p. 36. There were 60 kreuzers to a gulden.
[3] Ibid.
[4] Helmut Mathy, *Die Nackenheimer Revolution von 1792/1793*, Nackenheimer Heimatkundliche Schriftenreihe, vol. 14 (Nackenheim, 1967), p. 25. Wilhelm Herse, *Kurmainz am Vorabend der Revolution* (Berlin Dissertation, 1907), p. 19.
[5] See above, p. 79.
[6] Amrhein, *Emmerichsthal*, p. 151.

cash and under the last Elector a number of communities purchased total abolition.[1]

As the *Gerichtsherr* and the *Leibherr* were almost invariably the same person, the labour services were in practice only one of the obligations owed by the peasant by virtue of his *Leibeigenschaft*. This is usually translated as 'serfdom' but the 'serf' of western Germany had very little in common with his unfortunate counterpart in the eastern provinces of Prussia and the Habsburg Monarchy. In the fifteenth and sixteenth centuries more powerful protection from the princes of the western territories, together with their nobility's preference for service at court rather than commercial farming, prevented the development of great estates dependent on the labour services of the peasants.[2] In the Electorate of Mainz *Leibeigenschaft* took three main forms. If a peasant who was *leibeigen* wished to move to a town or village in the Electorate where *Leibeigenschaft* did not exist then he was obliged to pay a special tax (*Abkaufsgeld*), amounting to 5% of his total possessions. If he wished to leave the Electorate altogether, then the rate was raised to 15% and in addition he had to pay the regular emigration-tax (*Nachsteuer*) of 10%.[3] Secondly there was the *Besthaupt*, which had become a simple death duty of 5%, and finally there were regular annual dues which went under a variety of names (*Leib-Beet, Leib-Huhn, Fastnachthühner, Osterbraten* etc.).[4]

This form of *Leibeigenschaft* was widespread in western and central Germany and existed in most of the rural areas of the Electorate of Mainz, the chief exceptions being the Rheingau and the left bank of the Rhine. It is very difficult to estimate just how onerous these dues were. When the Elector Friedrich Karl announced the abolition of *Leibeigenschaft* in 1787 he also stated that it would be redeemable because the treasury could not be expected to suffer.[5] Although he did not specify the potential intensity of the suffering, the Electorate's accounts showed that in 1785 the *Abkaufsgeld* yielded a paltry 5,425 gulden and the *Besthaupt* 7,212 gulden.[6] The importance of *Leibeigenschaft* was more symbolic than substantive; it was a constant reminder of the dependent status of the peasantry and of the gulf between town and country.

In financial terms, much more important to the peasants were the tithes they were obliged to pay to the *Zehentherr*. There were three kinds of

[1] Mainz, *Kurmainzische Verordnungen*, 1te Sammlung, vol. 6, 1378.
[2] Friedrich Lütge, *Geschichte der deutschen Agrarverfassung vom frühen Mittelalter bis zum 19. Jahrhundert* (Stuttgart, 1963), p. 140.
[3] Winkopp & Höck, *Magazin*, vol. 2, p. 11. In 1785 it was ordered that, contrary to former practice, the *Nachsteuer* should be paid not on the gross estate but on the estate *after* the deduction of the *Abkaufsgeld*.
[4] Mainz, *Kurmainzische Verordnungen*, 3te Sammlung, vol. 3, 348. Herse, *Kurmainz*, p. 19.
[5] Würzburg, MRA, Leibeigenschaft, 27 K 168.
[6] Mainz, *Abteilung 6*, Fasc. 904.

tithes: the great tithes taken from the grain harvest, the lesser tithe taken from certain other specified crops, usually those grown on the fallow and wine, and a tithe taken from livestock. The Elector was the *Zehentherr* of comparatively few of his subjects, most of the tithe rights being owned by the clergy and the nobility.[1] The variety of tithe ownership is well illustrated by the registers of a group of seven small communities in Franconia. The owners listed were the electoral treasury, the Cathedral Chapter of Mainz and its Provost, the local electoral official, the collegiate foundation at Aschaffenburg, the Count von Schönborn, the Count von Ingelheim, Herr von Reuss, the heirs to the Hepp estate, the village of Grossostheim and the priests of the two parishes there.[2] The lion's share went to the Cathedral Chapter rather than the parish priests, but at least it remained in clerical hands of some kind. Only a very small proportion had been alienated to the secular nobility.[3]

It is clear that the tithe was still literally a tenth of the harvest and that a determined effort was made to collect it. In 1751 a general electoral ordinance decreed that the peasant should arrange his crop in groups of ten sheaves of equal size and that the *Zehentherr* should be allowed to select the tithe himself.[4] Throughout the eighteenth century the tithes remained a very lucrative source of income for their owners. The provost of the Mainz Cathedral Chapter owned two thirds of the grain tithe and two thirds of the wine tithe at Grossostheim in Franconia; in 1789 his agent there sent him 1,459 gulden as the net sum raised from the tithe that year.[5]

Finally, the peasants also paid dues to the *Grundherr* for the land they cultivated; only very few of them owned their land outright. Almost all the agricultural land in the Electorate belonged to the privileged orders: the Elector, the Cathedral Chapter, the monasteries or the Imperial Knights. As elsewhere in the Rhineland, the share of urban commoners was negligible.[6] There were two forms of tenure: the *Erbpacht* (or *Erbbestand*) and the *Zeitpacht* (or *Temporalbestand*). The former, which was in effect hereditary tenure, was particularly favourable to the peasant. He was obliged to pay all state taxes which attached to the land but, as the dues to the *Grundherr* were fixed, he benefited increasingly from the rising prices paid for agricultural produce. As its name suggests, the *Zeitpacht* was a limited form of tenure, the terms being reviewed at intervals of between six and twelve years.[7] The dues paid for land held in *Zeitpacht* could take

[1] In 1785 the electoral treasury collected only about 12,500 gulden in tithes – Ibid.
[2] Würzburg, *Rechnungen*, 27573, 27659, 27660, 27681.
[3] Ibid. This appears to have been the case throughout the Electorate – L. A. Veit, *Der Zusammenbruch des Mainzer Erzstuhles infolge der französischen Revolution* (Mainz, 1927), pp. 120–36.
[4] Mainz, *Kurmainzische Verordnungen*, bte Sammlung, vol. 6, 44.
[5] Würzburg, *Rechnungen*, 27573.   [6] Lütge, *Agrarverfassung*, p. 161.
[7] Veit, *Zusammenbruch*, p. 61.

a number of different forms but nowhere do they appear to have been particularly severe. In most areas twice the value of the seed employed was taken, which in the fertile lands of Franconia and the Rhine valley did not represent an intolerable burden.[1] Elsewhere rent was collected in the form of cash or a share of the harvest. The latter was invariably a third,[2] a smaller proportion than that paid by most French *métayers*.[3]

It is impossible to estimate precisely how much land was held in *Zeitpacht*, as opposed to the older hereditary form. Steinbach's figure for the Rhineland in general is a third,[4] but in the Electorate of Mainz at least the proportion appears to have been smaller. In the Rheingau most of the land was held on a hereditary basis and in the administrative district (*Oberamt*) of Starkenburg on the *Bergstraße* less than a fifth was held in *Zeitpacht*.[5] The peasants also, of course, had a share in the common meadows and forests. It is interesting that some communities, with the approval and assistance of the Elector, had partitioned much of their common land and re-allocated it to individual peasants.[6] Cleared forest land owned by the communities was distributed in a similar fashion. Winkopp commented in 1790: 'Its success and the apparently increasing wealth of previously landless citizens are eloquent praise for this measure.'[7]

Both fiscally and legally the peasants were the victims of discrimination on the part of the electoral government; compared with the towndwellers, the rural population was an underprivileged majority. There is a considerable amount of evidence, however, which suggests that at least in those parts of the Electorate which lay in Franconia and on the *Bergstraße*, the peasants enjoyed a certain and growing prosperity. This is partly explained by the ubiquity of hereditary tenure and fixed dues in an age of rising prices. The average price of grain in the decade 1780–9 was 80% higher than the average for 1730–40.[8] Another explanation lies in the increased productivity achieved by the widespread introduction of new crops, techniques and fertilisers. Particularly important was the increased use of forage crops such as red ('Brabant') clover, lucerne and esparsette, which in turn allowed more and better cattle to be kept, which produced more manure, which improved yields per acre.[9]

By the middle of the eighteenth century the planting of these artificial grasses and root crops on the fallow was widespread throughout the Rhine-

---

[1] Ibid.
[2] Winkopp & Höck, *Magazin*, vol. 2, p. 39.
[3] Albert Soboul, *La France à la Veille de la Révolution française*, vol. 1 (Paris, 1966), pp. 164–5.
[4] Franz Steinbach, 'Die rheinischen Agrarverhältnisse', *Tausend Jahre deutscher Geschichte und deutscher Kultur am Rhein*, ed. A. Schulte (Düsseldorf, 1925), p. 168.
[5] Winkopp & Höck, *Magazin*, vol. 2, pp. 11, 14, 39.
[6] Ibid., p. 13.   [7] Ibid.
[8] Dreyfus, *Mayence*, p. 108.
[9] H. Aubin, *Geschichte des Rheinlandes von der ältesten Zeit bis zur Gegenwart*, vol. 2 (Essen, 1922), pp. 134–5.

land, and Mainz was no exception. As early as 1765 Thomas Pennant, travelling through the Electorate from Aschaffenburg to Hanau, noted: 'In my road to Hanau passed thro' a flat rich country abounding with Indian Corn, Beets, Kidney Beans, Cabbages and Potatoes'.[1] The tithe registers still extant suggest that the new crops were produced in considerable quantities. At Grossostheim in 1789, for example, the Cathedral Chapter and Provost leased the potato tithes to Konrad Damrich and his wife for 280 Malters (approximately 1,100 bushels) of potatoes.[2] These agricultural improvements owed much to the initiative of the state. The last Elector, Friedrich Karl (1774–1802), was especially active in encouraging the introduction of new crops and the improvement of livestock.[3] His task was made easier not only by the favourable price structure but also by the high natural fertility of his dominions. In the 1740s Gundling had written: 'The Mainz territories are the most pleasant in the world. They produce everything that belongs to and could be desired for the needs and nourishment of mankind. There is no lack of grain, or of wine, or of cattle, or timber or game.'[4]

It seems to have been particularly important that the electorate did not suffer from '*la grande tare agricole française*': lack of manure.[5] The 3,000 inhabitants of the bailiwick (*Vogtei*) of Heppenheim in the *Oberamt* of Starkenburg shared, albeit unequally, 300 horses, 400 oxen and bulls, 1,000 cows and beef cattle and 1,400 pigs.[6] The neighbouring *Vogtei* of Furth, whose population was 2,800, was even better stocked: 740 horses, about the same number of oxen and bulls, 920 cows, 740 beef cattle, 502 calves, 2,230 sheep, 290 lambs and 180 goats.[7] P. A. Winkopp and J. D. A. Höck, who carried out a survey of the area at the end of the 1780s, reported: 'Since 1780 cattle-breeding has been improved extraordinarily, by encouragement to plant clover, by example and by concessions. It has increased to such an extent that the inhabitant who previously could not feed even two cows, can now not only support comfortably ten of the finest and best variety but can also harvest twenty cart-loads and more of clover-hay for winter fodder; and this is quite apart from his other hay...

---

[1] Thomas Pennant, *Tour on the Continent in 1765*, ed. Sir G. R. de Beer (London, 1948), p. 137. Conditions were similar in neighbouring territories. Cf. F. K. von Moser, 'Regierungsgeschichte des jezigen Herrn Fürsten-Bischofs Heinrichs des VIII zu Fulda', *Patriotisches Archiv für Deutschland*, 2 (1785). O. Berge, *Die Innenpolitik des Landgrafen Friedrich II von Hessen-Kassel* (Mainz Dissertation, 1952), p. 118.

[2] Wurzburg, *Rechnungen*, 27573. Dreyfus, *Mayence*, p. 600.

[3] See below, p. 186.

[4] Nicolaus Hieronymus von Gundling, *Discours über den vormaligen und itzigen Stand der deutschen Kurfürstenstaaten*, vol. 1, p. 429. See also above, pp. 70, 74–5.

[5] The phrase is Pierre Goubert's and appears in his chapter 'Les cadres de la vie rurale' in *Histoire économique et sociale de la France*, vol. 2, ed. Fernand Braudel and Ernest Labrousse (Paris, 1970), p. 97.

[6] Winkopp & Höck, *Magazin*, vol. 2, pp. 11, 16.   [7] Ibid., p. 23.

Town and Country

The district of Mörlebach deserves to be placed at the top of the list. To their own advantage, the inhabitants there have been captured by a certain ambition to have the finest cattle in their stall and they are encouraging the inhabitants of the other districts to follow their example.'¹ Throughout the *Oberamt* of Starkenburg this increase in the number of cattle, in turn made possible 'by a host of tasty turnips, beets and others of a similar kind', created a surplus of grain to be despatched to Mainz and other urban markets. Wine, dairy produce, nuts, apples, pears, dried figs, honey and timber were also exported.²

It would be misleading, however, to depict every area of the Electorate as a terrestrial paradise. There were also pockets of poverty, most notably and paradoxically in the Rheingau; paradoxically because the wines of the district were and are both the best and the most expensive in Germany. Relatively it must be one of the wealthiest strips of land in Europe, but it was the nobility and monasteries who in the late eighteenth century took the richest pickings. Their capital resources enabled them not only to survive the periodic poor vintages but also to take advantage of them by buying up cheaply the holdings of small peasant-producers reduced to destitution. Risbeck observed: 'It is a great misfortune for this country that, though restrained by law, the nobility are, through connivance of the elector, allowed to purchase as much land as they please.' He agreed that there were commoners there with annual incomes of 30, 40 or even 100,000 gulden per annum but argued that the exceptional few could not compensate 'for the sight of so many poor people with which the villages swarm'.³ Overpopulation⁴ had led to a progressive diminution in the size of holdings and almost total reliance on the vine, to a neglect of arable and pastoral. Consequently 'everyone, landowners as well as craftsmen (with the exception of the wealthy few) live for the most part from daylabouring'.⁵ Unfortunately, the demand for labour was very seasonal: the wine harvest was short, the winter was long. It was particularly ironic that this, the most depressed part of the Electorate, should have been technically the most free: there was no *Leibeigenschaft* and no state labour dues in the Rheingau.⁶

There were paupers both in the city of Mainz and in the rural areas of the Electorate but nowhere does one find evidence of poverty comparable

---

¹ Ibid., pp. 23–4.
² Ibid., pp. 14, 17, 25–6. Winkopp & Höck painted a similarly favourable picture of the *Oberamt* Steinheim am Main, in vol. 1, pp. 151–8.
³ Risbeck, *Travels*, p. 236. His dismal picture was repeated by other observers – Lang, *Reise*, p. 73. *Compendiöse Statistik von Maynz, Trier und Cöln samt ihren Nebenländern* (Leipzig, 1798), p. 37.
⁴ The *Encyclopaedia Britannica* of 1781 observed that the Rheingau 'is so populous that it looks like one entire town, intermixed with gardens and vineyards'.
⁵ Winkopp & Höck, *Magazin*, p. 41.
⁶ Ibid., p. 37.

to that which fuelled the *jacqueries* and *journées* in France. Travellers often only see what they want to see, but when several of them, from different backgrounds and even from different countries, agree substantially, then the historian is obliged to take their reports seriously. J. C. Risbeck, who was quick to comment on misery in the Rheingau when he found it and who was certainly no apologist for the ecclesiastical states, echoed the views of many of his contemporaries when he commented on Mainz: 'A peasant is in general extremely happy throughout the whole country. He is almost everywhere a freeman and oppressed with no hard taxes.'[1] Most important of all, at least in its political implications, the Electorate did not suffer from the '*crise quasi continue*' which afflicted various parts of France between 1770 and 1789.[2] In 1792 Johann Philipp Count von Stadion, a noble and canon of the Cathedral Chapter, but one who was in favour of the abolition of fiscal exemptions, who at least professed a belief in a 'free constitution' and who was critical of the electoral government, wrote that between 1770 and 1789 the peasants had prospered and that about 700,000 gulden worth of communal debts had been paid off.[3] Bad harvests could bring high prices, as in 1770–1 and 1788–9, for example, but the effects were cushioned by remedial action taken by the electoral government.[4] Ultimately of course, the proof of revolution is in the revolting. The most serious outbreak of rural discontent which occurred in this period in the Electorate came in 1787, when the peasants of the Rheingau protested against the introduction of a new German hymn book.[5]

For both the rural and the urban inhabitant of the Electorate of Mainz, the old maxim: '*Unter dem Krummstab ist gut zu wohnen*' (it is good to live under the episcopal crozier) was still valid in the late eighteenth century. It was not a dynamic or an expanding state, but if its citizens could not bask in the reflected glory of a warrior-king, at least they did not suffer the sacrifices which made his conquests possible. An anonymous English traveller concluded:

[1] Risbeck, *Travels*, p. 187. See also: [Francis Russell, 5th Duke of Bedford], *A Descriptive Journey through the Interior Parts of Germany and France, including Paris: with interesting and amusing Anecdotes. By a young English Peer of the Highest Rank, just returned from his Travels* (London, 1786), p. 22. Nicolai Karamsin, *Travels from Moscow through Prussia, Germany, Switzerland, France and England* (London, 1803), pp. 215–17. *The Letters of David Hume*, ed. J. Y. T. Greig, vol. 1 (Oxford, 1932), p. 121–2. P. W. Gercken, *Reisen durch Schwaben, Baiern, die angränzende Schweiz, Franken, die Rheinische Provinzen und an der Mosel in den Jahren 1779–1782*, vol. 4 (Worms, 1788), p. 354. *Kurze Beschreibung des gelobten Landes und der Mainzischen Kurlande*, p. 26. John Moore, *A View of Society and Manners in France, Switzerland and Germany*, vol. 1 (London, 1779), pp. 410. *Journal von und für Deutschland* (1784), Reisebeschreibungen. See also above, pp. 70, 74–5, and below, p. 95.
[2] Braudel and Labrousse, *Histoire*, p. 77.
[3] A. Jäger, *Daniel Dumont: Ein Beitrag zur Geschichte des mittelrheinischen Liberalismus* (Frankfurt am Main Dissertation, 1920), p. 224.
[4] See below, pp. 261–2.   [5] See below, pp. 207–9.

In the three ecclesiastical electorates, they know nothing of the heavy taxes under which the subjects of the temporal princes so heavily groan. They have raised the customs very little. No species of slavery is known here. There is no need of heavy taxes to portion out princesses. They have no overgrown armies, nor do they sell the sons of their farmers to foreign powers, nor have they taken any part in the civil or foreign disturbances of Germany. From all this it follows, that though they do not encourage arts and manufactures as much as they might do, agriculture has been carried to a height amongst them, which it has not reached in any other part of Germany.[1]

[1] *A Tour through Germany, containing full directions for travelling in that interesting Country: with Observations on the State of Agriculture and Policy of the different States: very particular Descriptions of the Courts of Vienna and Berlin, and Coblentz and Mentz* (London, n.d.), p. 41

3

Enlightened Absolutism:
Johann Friedrich Count von Ostein (1743–63) and Emmerich Joseph Freiherr von Breidbach zu Bürresheim (1763–74)

I

In 1738 the peripatetic Baron Pöllnitz passed through Mainz and observed that everything was rather quiet, as was usual in states ruled by ecclesiastical sovereigns.[1] The sovereign in question was Philipp Karl Count von Eltz, a prince more noted for personal piety than for intellect or energy. Already 67 years old when elected as a compromise candidate in 1732, his reign lasted only eleven years. Although the Wars of the Polish and Austrian Succession ensured that it was marked by a great deal of diplomatic activity, on the domestic front little was attempted and less was achieved.[2] The reign drew to a close in an atmosphere heavily pregnant with disaster. The last two wars had devastated the Electorate and decimated its finances; Philipp Karl had been forced to abandon the traditional alliance with the Habsburgs; more generally the Prussian seizure of Silesia had dramatised the weakness of the Catholic party in the Empire. Even more ominous were the plans for the secularisation of the ecclesiastical states mooted by the new Wittelsbach Emperor Charles VII.

1743 marked the bottom of the trough for the Electorate and the beginning of a sustained political, economic and cultural revival. After Philipp Karl's death on 21 March, the election campaign became a keenly fought contest between the diplomats Count Bünau and Blondel for the Franco-Bavarian party and Count Cobenzl for the Austrians. As their fortunes rose and fell rapidly in the maelstrom of the canons' conflicting interests, prejudices and convictions, the outcome remained uncertain until the eve of the election, when Johann Friedrich Karl Count

---

[1] Hans Hainebach, *Studien zum literarischen Leben der Aufklärungszeit in Mainz* (Giessen Dissertation, 1936), p. 1.
[2] F. W. E. Roth, *Geschichte der Herren und Grafen zu Eltz*, vol. 2 (Mainz, 1890), pp. 304–29.

von Ostein emerged as the strongest candidate.[1] His unanimous election on 2 April owed a good deal to both the moral and the military support of Austria and her allies. When Philipp Karl died, Mainz politics were dominated by Charles VII – who was still resident at Frankfurt am Main – and his French masters. The slow but steady approach of the 'Pragmatic Army' of British, Austrian and Hanoverian troops enabled the natural pro-Habsburg bias of the Cathedral Chapter to assert itself. The British diplomat Thomas Villiers, making the usual mistake of confusing a favourable choice with a free choice, commented: 'They are all here convinced that the Nearness of His Majesty's and the Queen of Hungary's troops secure to them a free election, and preserves them from Blows and Menaces.'[2] The Pragmatic Army crossed the Rhine at Neuwied on 12 April, Charles VII fled from Frankfurt on 17 April, Johann Friedrich von Ostein was elected on 22 April, and on 27 June the Pragmatic Army, commanded by George II, defeated the French at Dettingen, a small village on the Main belonging to Mainz.

The new Elector Johann Friedrich Karl Count von Ostein[3] owed his success more to his negative than to his positive qualities; he had made fewer personal enemies among the canons than his rivals. Although his election was welcomed in Vienna, he had not been the first choice. Thomas Villiers noted with approval that his family's large Austrian estates would keep Johann Friedrich in the allied camp but did not expect much from him as a ruler: 'It is to be apprehended that Ostein will let himself be governed by his mistress, the Bishop of Wurtzbourg, or some ill-chosen minister.'[4] Johann Friedrich was depicted by the various ambassadors as a gentle, cultured, pious man, with little knowledge and less experience of political matters.[5] A nephew of the Elector Lothar Franz von Schönborn (1695–1729), one of the greatest patrons of the Baroque, he devoted much time to the arts. He built a magnificent new palace for his family, a sumptuous town-house for his sister, the widowed Countess von Bassenheim, and was also the moving force behind the renovation and 'beautification' of numerous churches. An academy for painters, engravers, sculptors and stuccateurs was founded in 1747.[6]

If Johann Friedrich had decided to become ruler in practice as well as in name, then it is doubtful whether the Electorate's traditional torpor would have been disturbed. But in fact the virtual ruler of the state was his chief minister, Anton Heinrich Friedrich Count von Stadion. A member of one

---

[1] Adolf Carl Michels, 'Die Wahl des Grafen Johann Friedrich Karl von Ostein zum Kurfürsten und Erzbischof von Mainz (1743)', *Archiv für hessische Geschichte und Altertumskunde*, new series, 16 (1930), p. 566.   [2] P.R.O., SP.88.61, 16 April 1743.
[3] For the sake of brevity he will be referred to simply as Johann Friedrich in future.
[4] P.R.O., SP.88.61, 16 April 1743.   [5] Michels, 'Wahl', p. 531.
[6] Ibid., p. 571.

of the oldest and wealthiest Imperial Knight families, Stadion was 52 years old in 1743 and had already served the Electorate in a number of diplomatic and administrative capacities. Although his rise to power doubtless owed a great deal to the fact that he was the new Elector's cousin, in this case nepotism did not elevate incompetence. Stadion's rule not only proved to be a watershed in the history of Mainz, it also exerted influence on the development of Catholic Germany as a whole. Although violently opposed to both his principles and policies, the papal nuncio Oddi described him as 'without exception the first talent and minister in Germany'.[1] It was nothing new for an Elector of Mainz to be dominated by a more powerful relation; it was Stadion's attachment to the Enlightenment that brought a change.

Stadion's chief concern was the revival of the Electorate's economy, which had suffered severely as a result of almost continuous French military operations in the Rhineland between 1740 and 1748. Yet recovery from war-damage was inevitable in the long run; a more serious problem for Stadion was the limited number and limited horizons of the Mainz merchants. Gundling wrote in 1747:

> Trade consists largely in dealings in Franconian and Rhenish wines. Yet there is no doubt that many other branches of commerce could be raised to the same degree of activity; especially because neither the excise nor other obstacles stand in their way. Nothing is lacking apart from a good Prussian Commercial Director who would sort out and direct affairs. But it would be very difficult to persuade the people, who are too used to the good life under the episcopal crozier to think about the improvement of trade. They prefer to stay in the old rut and are satisfied if they can earn the same as their fathers and grandfathers.[2]

Consequently it was the depressed wholesale trade and the related dependence of Mainz on Frankfurt which became Stadion's main targets.

After a good deal of preliminary discussion, a Commerce Commission was established in 1746. One of its first actions was to set up a guild consisting exclusively of wholesalers (*Handelsstand*), 'for the greatest possible increase and encouragement of trade'.[3] A candidate for membership had to be a burgher of the city, a Roman Catholic and at least twenty years old; had to have the approval of the authorities, a certificate of baptism, a testimonial from a master-merchant and certificate of good conduct; and finally had to own a capital sum of not less than 5,000 gulden.[4] Initially

[1] H.-W. Jung, *Anselm Franz von Bentzel im Dienste der Kurfürsten von Mainz*, Beiträge zur Geschichte der Universität Mainz, vol. 7 (Wiesbaden, 1966), p. 5.
[2] Nicolaus Hieronymus von Gundling, *Discours über den vormaligen und itzigen Stand der deutschen Kurfürstenstaaten*, vol. 1 (Leipzig, 1747), p. 435.
[3] Mainz, *Kurmainzische Verordnungen*, 6te Sammlung, vol. 5, 85.
[4] P. Gottschämmer, *Geschichte der Organisation der wirtschaftlichen Interessenvertretungen in Hessen* (Giessen Dissertation, 1912), p. 16.

fifty-one merchants fulfilled these conditions and received the right to elect three directors, subject to the Elector's confirmation.[1]

Although the new organisation was structurally similar to a craft-guild, the electoral government went out of its way to stress that the merchants formed the élite of the Mainz economy. The *Handelsstand* took formal precedence over all other guilds, was supervised by the vicedom himself – the most senior official in the city – rather than a mere municipal councillor, and particularly successful merchants were distinguished with the honorary title of 'Commercial Councillor'. A more tangible privilege was a monopoly of wholesale trading in the city. The sense of exclusiveness was strengthened by the rejection of most candidates on the grounds of inexperience or lack of capital. The establishment of a primitive bourse was designed both to facilitate the conduct of business and to create a certain *esprit de corps*. As the award of the electoral titles suggested, Stadion envisaged close cooperation between merchants and government. The three directors of the *Handelsstand* were invited to the weekly sessions of the Commerce Commission, to represent the mercantile interest and to advise on the promotion of trade and industry.[2]

Until the fledgling Mainz merchants were able to emerge as independent importers and exporters, Stadion sought to reduce the city's dependence on Frankfurt for supplies of wholesale goods by the creation of three annual fairs. The detailed regulations published in February 1748 offered all sorts of inducements to attract foreign merchants: exhibition rooms were made available, religious toleration granted, Jews exempted from the special dues, loans at 5% offered, elaborate security precautions taken to safeguard property, market research conducted to discover the needs of the local retailers, imported goods exempted from customs dues, various entertainments organised, and so on.[3] Draconic ordinances were issued to ensure a sufficient supply of customers at the fairs. Mainz retailers were compelled to buy there and nowhere else, while foreign pedlars caught trying to operate independently of the fairs were fined 150 gulden and relieved of their goods.

The third fair was abandoned after 1748 but the other two, which took place before and thus posed a direct challenge to the Frankfurt fair, were surprisingly successful. Even the early fairs attracted between four and five hundred firms, from all over Germany and also from the United

---

[1] Richard Dertsch, 'Die Gründung des Mainzer Handelstandes im 18. Jahrhundert', *50 Jahre A. & E. Fischer, Mainz am Rhein* (Mainz, 1930), p. 26.
[2] E. Goldschmidt, 'Die Neubelebung der Mainzer Messen durch den Kurfürsten Johann Friedrich Karl', *Frankfurter Zeitung*, 15 February (1906).
[3] Mainz, *Kurmainzische Verordnungen*, 6te Sammlung, vol. 5, 86, 90-1, vol. 6, 7. Albert Kirnberger, *Die Handelsmesse in Mainz in der Zeit der merkantilistischen Politik unter der Regierung der drei letzten Kurfürsten von Mainz, 1743–1793* (Mainz, 1951), pp. 20-3.

The Electorate of Mainz in the Eighteenth Century

Provinces, Belgium, Alsace, Austria, Italy and Switzerland. At first they served only the Electorate's retailers but later expanded their clientele to include a much wider area.[1] The most reliable indication of the fairs' success was the reaction of the Frankfurt merchants. In 1757 they applied to the *Reichskammergericht* for an injunction restraining the Mainz government from damaging further the Frankfurt fairs, from placing a ban on visits by Mainz merchants to Frankfurt and from extending the Mainz fairs' catchment area beyond the Electorate. The imperial court agreed only to the second, but even this was rejected by Mainz, with the argument that it was a political matter and therefore did not fall within the *Reichskammergericht*'s competence.[2] As the Mainz wholesalers expanded their capital and confidence, the fairs became relatively less important but there can be little doubt that they had contributed to the revival of the economy.

The formation of the *Handelsstand* and the creation of the fairs were the main but not the only achievement of Stadion's Commerce Commission. The systematic rebuilding of the Electorate's arterial roads was begun in 1749, a permanent wine market was established in Mainz and a cattle market on the other side of the river at Kastel, new warehouses were erected on the banks of the Rhine, a loan bank was founded and a court to deal with commercial disputes was established. The agreement of 1748 that Bamberg would send its goods direct to Mainz, in return for guaranteed return freight, began the process which drew the Main trade away from Frankfurt to Mainz. A special attempt was made to develop the small town of Höchst. Agents were sent up and down the Rhine to encourage merchants and manufacturers to move to Höchst or to set up branches there, and they were assisted by advertisements in German, French and Belgian newspapers.[3]

Many historians are justly suspicious of the rôle played by 'policy' in creating economic expansion, but although general trading conditions throughout the Rhineland were improving in the 1740s and 1750s it seems reasonable to conclude that the government's encouragement had some effect. Certainly contemporaries were impressed by the Mainz example. The Prince-Bishop of Würzburg, Adam Friedrich von Seinsheim, sent a commission over to investigate, because 'The Elector Friedrich Karl of

---

[1] Ibid., p. 46.
[2] K. Schwarz, *Der wirtschaftliche Konkurrenzkampf zwischen der Reichsstadt Frankfurt und der kurfürstlichen Stadt Mainz* (Mainz, 1932), p. 56.
[3] Ibid., p. 59. See also, Gottfried Zoepfl, *Fränkische Handelspolitik im Zeitalter der Aufklärung*, Bayerische Wirtschafts- und Verwaltungsstudien, vol. 3 (Erlangen and Leipzig, 1894), pp. 152, 160–2; Niklas Vogt, *Geschichte des Verfalls und Untergangs der rheinischen Staaten des alten deutschen Reiches* (1833), p. 205; H. Scholl, *Kurmainzische Wirtschaftspolitik (1648–1802)* (Frankfurt am Main Dissertation, 1924), pp. 131–2; Mainz, *Kurmainzische Verordnungen*, 6te Sammlung, vol. 5, 97.

Enlightened absolutism, 1743–74

Mainz has revived the depressed Mainz trade. Wholesale trade flourishes there, many inhabitants derive direct and indirect benefit from it and the exchequer earns 40,000 gulden a year from it.'[1]

II

Measures of the kind described above have a very familiar ring; they would not have been out of place a century earlier. The creation of a guild of merchants or trade fairs seems almost anachronistic and serves only to illustrate the backward state of the Mainz economy. Taken in isolation, they do not permit the inference of any reception of the Enlightenment. Yet it was the 'enlightened' character of the reform programme in general which made Stadion's régime a watershed in Mainz history. His personal rôle must not be overestimated, for his period in office coincided with the growth of a reforming movement throughout Catholic Germany.[2] There was also a long reforming tradition within the Electorate, although it had been dormant for some decades. The formidable Elector Johann Philipp von Schönborn (1647–73), for example, was very much opposed to the Jesuits, introduced all manner of religious reforms, put a stop to the persecution of 'witches', paid particular attention to raising the level of parish priests and primary education and was involved in constant disputes with the Curia and the Papal Nuncio at Cologne.[3] It was certainly not the case that:

> Nature and Nature's laws lay hid in night:
> God said, *Let Stadion be!* and all was light!

The Electorate could not have remained insulated indefinitely from developments elsewhere in Catholic Germany, but Stadion did give the Enlightenment in Mainz a radical twist which throughout the century continued to distinguish it from that of the other ecclesiastical states. Stadion not only united in his person all the various streams discussed earlier, he also injected a flavour of the French secular Enlightenment. He had made frequent private and official visits to France and brought back with him a firm attachment to the philosophes. He met Voltaire on a number of occasions and, according to Wieland, admired him 'to the point of madness'.[4] Although he never attempted any constitutional reforms in the Electorate, he envied the British their constitution and was well-ac-

---

[1] Kirnberger, *Handelsmesse*, pp. 57–8.
[2] See above, pp. 29–32.
[3] Georg Mentz, *Johann Philipp von Schönborn, Kurfurst von Mainz, Bischof von Würzburg und Worms, 1605–1673*, vol. 2 (Jena, 1899), ch. 3, A. L. Veit, *Kirchliche Reformbestrebungen im ehemaligen Erzstift Mainz unter Erzbischof Johann Philipp von Schönborn, 1647–1673* (Freiburg, 1910), *passim*.
[4] Rudolf Asmus, *G. M. La Roche: Ein Beitrag zur Geschichte der Aufklärung* (Karlsruhe, 1899), p. 4.

quainted with the works of Locke and Shaftesbury.¹ Contemporaries agreed that Stadion himself was a formidable personality, whose intellectual power was allied to exceptional personal charm. Wieland offered the following description in a letter of 1762: 'Imagine an elderly man whose appearance and bearing are the same as he of whom Shakespeare says "that Nature might stand up and say: this is a man", who at seventy-two years old has all the fire of a Frenchman of fifty, joined to the simplicity, the way of thinking and the manners of an English nobleman; who is a statesman, amateur artist and a man of letters, as agreeable in conversation as it is possible to be.'² In his personal capacity he ruled the family territories in Swabia as a very model enlightened prince. One of his first actions on succeeding his father in 1742 was to release a 'witch' from the family dungeons and to compel the local priest to preach a sermon denouncing the injustice done to her.³ Wieland, himself a Protestant, commented: 'The Count hates nothing more than intolerance and superstition; in Württemberg he has a large territory with a small town, whose entirely Protestant population is well-pleased to have him for a master.'⁴

The group of intellectuals which gathered at Stadion's ancestral seat at Warthausen to engage in intellectual conversation, to browse in his enormous library and to read the latest enlightened works to each other, was especially important because it formed a meeting-place for the Protestant and Catholic Enlightenment. In 1753 Stadion's illegitimate son Georg Michael La Roche, whose very name indicates that his father's francophilic inclinations extended beyond the purely cultural sphere, married Sophie Gutermann, who until very recently had been engaged to Christoph Martin Wieland.⁵ After a temporary and understandable estrangement, Sophie and Wieland re-established friendly relations. In 1760 Wieland returned from Zürich to take up an official position in his home-town, the Imperial City of Biberach, which adjoined the Stadion territories. He became a frequent and welcome visitor at Warthausen and it was through him that the Stadion circle was drawn into closer contact with the Protestant world. In 1766, for example, he accompanied Sophie to Bad Lauchstädt, where she made the acquaintance of Gleim and J. C. Jacobi.⁶ Stadion's chief interest was the works of the French philosophes – his

---

[1] Helmut Rössler, *Graf Johann Philipp Stadion: Napoleons deutscher Gegenspieler*, vol. 1 (Vienna, 1966), p. 39.
[2] Asmus, *La Roche*, p. 31.   [3] Rössler, *Stadion*, p. 41.
[4] Adolf Bach, 'Graf Friedrich von Stadion, ein Aufklärer als Minister im katholischen Kurmainz', *Aus Goethes rheinischem Lebensraum* (Neuss, 1968), p. 35.
[5] There is some dispute as to whether La Roche was Stadion's bastard or simply his adopted son, but the former is most likely – Asmus, *La Roche*, pp. 5–9. On Sophie Gutermann's relationship with Wieland, see Gabriele Freiin von Koenig-Warthausen, 'Sophie La Roche', *Lebensbilder aus Schwaben und Franken*, vol. 10 (Stuttgart, 1966).
[6] Asmus, *La Roche*, p. 47.

evenings were often spent listening to extracts from the *Encyclopédie* read by his son or daughter-in-law – but even he responded to Wieland's influence. Wieland reported gleefully in 1764: 'Aurora has even converted my old, honourable patron, Count Stadion, away from his traditional prejudices against German poetry; he is greatly surprised that everything can be said in the German language; for up to now he knew the German language only from documents, charters and public papers.'[1] It was probably no Pauline flash of inspiration that directed Stadion's interest to the North; he had, for example, already sent his two sons to university at Göttingen.[2]

Stadion's personal attitude to the Roman Catholic religion remains something of a mystery. One of his most recent biographers has written that he was a Jansenist but never non-Christian, although it is not clear on what evidence this verdict is based.[3] It may be doubted whether a passionate admirer of Voltaire could also be a practising Christian, although the fact that he called his domestic chaplain 'Master Pangloss' is hardly conclusive. His pious wife eventually left him, but this could have been due as much to his philandering as to his scepticism, for Stadion acquired the reputation of being something of a sexual athlete. In *Dichtung und Wahrheit* Goethe wrote that Stadion used La Roche to write his love-letters.[4] Wieland reported that the day before he died Stadion expressed the desire to discuss the immortality of his soul, which does not imply any great confidence in the hereafter.[5]

It is certain, however, that he was opposed to the Jesuits and that he supported the nascent episcopalist movement. Of the former he wrote: 'As long as the Jesuits keep control of the lists of sins of great men and by means of the schools can beat or coax infantile prejudices and dogma into the heads of young people, they will always enjoy the support of the majority.'[6] Due probably to the timidity and piety of the Elector, Stadion did not become embroiled in a major dispute with Rome, but he did lend his support to individual episcopalists. The most important of these was Johann Baptist Horix, who was a native of Mainz but had studied at Göttingen. Through Stadion's patronage he was appointed to the chair of constitutional law at Mainz in 1758. In the same year he published the *Tractatiuncula de fontibus juris canonici Germanici* and announced his intention of using it as the basis of his lecture course for the following academic year.

[1] Ibid., p. 45.
[2] Rössler, *Stadion*, p. 54.
[3] Gabriele Freiin von Koenig-Warthausen, 'Friedrich Graf von Stadion', *Lebensbilder aus Schwaben und Franken*, vol. 8 (Stuttgart, 1962), p. 121.
[4] J. W. von Goethe, *Dichtung und Wahrheit*, pt. 3, bk. 13.
[5] Asmus, *La Roche*, pp. 48–9.   [6] Koenig-Warthausen, *Stadion*, p. 120.

Horix saw in the Pope only a centre of unity for the Church and was prepared to allow him only the minimum powers necessary for the performance of this function. Each national Church should enjoy complete jurisdictional autonomy. This would mean only a return to the purity of the *ecclesia primitiva*, before the constitution of the Church had been perverted by the Isidorean forgeries; indeed the whole elaborate superstructure of papal power was based on deceit and ignorance.[1] More than anything, it was the radical *tone* of Horix's strictures that distinguished his work from those of other contemporary episcopalists and which was to distinguish the movement in Mainz from that in other ecclesiastical states. It was not surprising that the Jesuit theological faculty of the University of Mainz was outraged by the *Tractatiuncula* and condemned its propositions as '*calumniosae, temerariae, male sonantes, scandalosae, haeresi proximae etc.*'.[2]

The Elector appears to have been shaken by the attack and Stadion was unable to save his protégé from temporary embarrassment. A commission of enquiry was ordered, Horix interrogated and the *Tractatiuncula* condemned. Although he was made to deny publicly that he had anything to do with it, it seems likely that Stadion not only had advance knowledge of the work but had also encouraged Horix to write it.[3] The professor's disgrace did not last long; by the beginning of the academic year 1759–60 he was back lecturing again. In view of the emphasis of the episcopalists on historical research as a weapon, it was very important that Stadion secured for Horix access to the imperial archives, which were controlled by the Elector of Mainz in his capacity as archchancellor of the Empire. His discovery there of the Mainz *Acceptatio* and his publication of it in 1763 – the year of Febronius – gave a powerful boost to the episcopalist movement. Indeed Raab has written that 'without the publication of the Mainz *Acceptatio* the Koblenz *Gravamina* of 1769, the *Punctatio* of Ems and the literary controversy over the Munich nuncio would have been unthinkable'.[4]

That Stadion was concerned with the internal state of the Church as well as its external relations was shown by the amortisation law of 1746.[5] Numerous amortisation laws – designed to prevent property passing into

---

[1] Heribert Raab, *Die Concordata Nationis Germanicae in der kanonistischen Diskussion des 17. bis 19. Jahrhunderts* (Wiesbaden, 1956), pp. 126–30.
[2] Anton Ph. Brück, *Die Mainzer theologische Fakultät im 18. Jahrhundert*, Beiträge zur Geschichte der Universität Mainz, vol. 2 (Wiesbaden, 1955), p. 26, n. 6.
[3] Raab, *Condordata*, p. 127.
[4] Ibid., p. 132.
[5] Mainz, *Kurmainzische Verordnungen*, 6e Sammlung, vol. 5, 52. Cf. Hans Illich, 'Maßnahmen der Mainzer Erzbischöfe gegen kirchlichen Gütererwerb (1462–1792)', *Mainzer Zeitschrift* 34 (1939), 56–7.

'the dead hands' of the monasteries – had been passed before, but this new version was a good deal sharper. The transfer to religious institutions of secular estates of any description was prohibited; if any such institution did receive land by means of a gift or a legacy, it was to be sold to a secular purchaser within a year. Failure to comply with this clause would lead to immediate confiscation of the offending property by the electoral treasury. Stiff penalties were threatened for monasteries which bid for land at public auctions or which lent money on the security of a piece of property and then allowed the debt to exceed its value, thus allowing foreclosure. Implementation proved difficult. In 1753 all officials in the Electorate were ordered to publicise the 1746 law, because of the recent increase in the amount of property passing into the dead hands.[1] This was not, however, Stadion's only attempt to redirect the wealth of the Church into secular channels. The considerable expenditure caused by the War of Austrian Succession was met partly by clerical taxation. During the interregnum of 1763 the Cathedral Chapter complained that the late elector had imposed repeated levies on the clergy, without regard for their privileged position, and a new clause was written in to the capitulation of election which called on his successor to spare them whenever possible.[2]

In matters affecting the Church Stadion was faced by the joint opposition of clergy and people. He also discovered that he could not rely on the Elector's unqualified support. Stadion had wished to clear a small square in front of the Cathedral (the *Höfchen*) to make room for more booths for the Mainz fairs. The operation immediately assumed religious overtones, for it involved the removal of the Mission Cross, originally erected by the Jesuits. It was also rumoured that a statue of St John Nepomuc, a saint especially favoured by the Jesuits and the patron saint of the Cathedral Chapter, would suffer the same fate. Opposition from both people and clergy found public expression when Father Winter S.J. delivered an inflammatory sermon in the Cathedral. At the end of a panegyric of the saint he cried: 'The Mission Cross has been taken away; St John beware that you too don't have to make way for the usurers and desecrators of the temple!'[3] Although Winter was disciplined for his plain-speaking, his immediate object had been attained. Accompanied by a great procession of schoolchildren, the guilds and clergy, singing hymns and chanting prayers, the Mission Cross, placed on a cart covered with red silk and drawn by six of the Elector's horses, was taken back to the *Höfchen* and solemnly re-erected.

[1] Ibid., p. 57.
[2] Manfred Stimming, *Die Wahlkapitulationen der Erzbischöfe und Kurfürsten von Mainz, 1213–1788* (Göttingen, 1909), p. 81.
[3] Vogt, *Verfall*, p. 205.

Lack of determined support from the Elector helps to explain the incomplete, even half-hearted nature of the reforms. This was especially the case in the field of education. Founded in 1477, the University of Mainz had reached a low ebb by the time Johann Friedrich was elected. Sporadic attempts at reform by previous electors had failed to halt a decline which was absolute as well as relative.[1] Although the Jesuits had performed sterling services in the past, they now acted as a powerful brake on any adaptation of curricula or teaching methods.[2] A group of Mainz Lullists attempted to break the Jesuits' monopoly of teaching posts, but without success.[3] Although the library was improved and the administrative structure was clarified by a new charter in 1746, no fundamental change was undertaken.[4] The appointment of Horix pointed the way to the future but the Jesuits were still in overall control at the end of Johann Friedrich's reign.

A more determined attempt was made to improve primary education. A general survey of the Electorate's schools in 1747 revealed all kinds of defects, especially mass truancy. During the summer the children were kept at home to help in the fields, while even during the winter they attended only fitfully. An ordinance of 1754 instructed all parish priests to preach sermons reminding parents of their duties, threatened the parents of truants with fines and ordered that people wishing to get married would have to make good any gaps in their religious education before the ceremony could be performed. Another similar ordinance of four years later specified that school attendance was compulsory for all children between the ages of seven and thirteen and repeated the threat of fines for failure to comply. At the same time questionnaires were sent out to establish just how many teachers there were, how and how much they were paid, whether they had other occupations, what they could teach and so on.

Although there was nothing new about trying to make children go to school the language used in the ordinances was distinctly more modern. The religious object of education still came first – indeed it was stressed that lack of it led to 'all forms of vice and sin, especially stealing and fornication, as well as cursing and swearing' – but secular considerations were also mentioned for the first time. The current system was criticised for producing not only a 'semi-Christian' for God and the Church but also a 'bad subject' for the sovereign and the community. True education should cultivate both a good Christian and a useful citizen-of-the-world (*Welt-*

---

[1] Leo Just & Helmut Mathy, *Die Universität Mainz, Grundzüge ihrer Geschichte* (Trautheim and Mainz, 1965), p. 25.
[2] Brück, *Theologische Fakultät*, p. 22.
[3] Anton Ph. Brück, 'Der Mainzer "Lullismus" im 18. Jahrhundert', *Jahrbuch für das Bistum Mainz* (1949).
[4] Just & Mathy, *Universität*, pp. 25–7.

bürger). It was particularly significant that also for the first time the clerical monopoly of education was broken by the creation of a joint commission of priests and secular officials.[1]

It is difficult to point to any individual measure taken during this period and identify any radically new or enlightened characteristic, but one does receive a very firm, if general, impression of accelerated change. Stadion and his officials formed a *parti de mouvement*, determined to drag the Electorate back to at least a position of parity with the secular states of the *Reich*. They were still working within a highly traditional and conservative framework and this fact should be remembered when considering the apparently archaic flavour of some of their reforms. Against the foundation of trade fairs and a guild of merchants should be set the encouragement of firms working outside the guild structure and the new amortisation law. That a new spirit had entered the Mainz political establishment is illustrated further by the wide scope of their reforms. Attempts were made to improve the *mont-de-piété*, the prisons, the coinage, the fire-services, public hygiene, the education of midwives and the care of the old, the sick and orphans.[2] Johann Jakob Moser, a Protestant and not a great admirer of the ecclesiastical states, wrote that a collection of ordinances, published in 1752, demonstrated the 'most laudable concern' of the Elector for the well-being of his subjects.[3] Although the repetition of these projects during the next two reigns suggest that they made little actual impact, the guide-lines had been laid down.

III

One year after his set-back over the Horix affair Stadion was rash enough to quarrel with the Elector's favourite nephew and heir to his personal fortune. The cause of the incident is not known but the upshot was that the Elector ordered Stadion to return to his estates in Swabia and not to return until he was called for.[4] Although he did not die until 1768, at the age of 76, he never went back to direct events in Mainz. His defeat and departure might well have signalled the Electorate's return to its traditional state of somnolence, but the break in continuity did not last long, for three years later, in 1763, the Elector Johann Friedrich died. As usual there was no shortage of candidates wishing to replace him: the provost Hugo Karl

---

[1] Anton Ph. Brück, *Kurmainzer Schulgeschichte*, Mainzer Beiträge zur Pädagogik, Historische Abteilung, vol. 1 (Wiesbaden, 1960), pp. 9–10. The ordinances of 1754 and 1758 are reprinted on pp. 22–5.
[2] Koenig-Warthausen, *Stadion*, p. 121.
[3] J. J. von Moser, *Einleitung in das Churfürstlich-Maynzische Staatsrecht* (Frankfurt am Main, 1755), p. 264.
[4] Hainebach, *Studien*, p. 4.

Count von Eltz, the dean Emmerich Joseph Freiherr von Breidbach zu Bürresheim, the cantor Lothar Franz Ignaz Freiherr von Specht zu Bubenheim and the canon Franz Philipp Freiherr von Franckenstein.[1] Eltz, who was popular with the clergy and was closely related to numerous members of the Cathedral Chapter, was a warm ante-post favourite.[2] There was considerable consternation in diplomatic quarters therefore when Breidbach, who at the outset had been sure of only one vote apart from his own, was elected unanimously on 5 July.[3]

Breidbach had been in the fortunate position of knowing that Specht and Franckenstein wanted Eltz even less than they wanted him and by threatening to give his own votes to Eltz he was able to win them over, together with their supporters and a few other waverers. Although a later historian of Mainz recorded that Specht had been inspired by the Holy Ghost to switch his votes to Breidbach, the English diplomat Cressener raised the possibility of a more secular kind of influence: 'Monsr. Schmiedberg confided to me that the French minister had received orders from his court the 22nd in Cypher, which he had imparted to him the 23rd, as he was then a Candidate, by which he was empowered by his Court to offer in his own name by way of loan to be repaid at his leisure (or never if it did not suit the person elected) one hundred thousand livres to Baron Breidbach, eighty thousand to Baron Schmiedberg and even greater sums if it was requisite.'[4] 'Schmiedberg' (Karl Joseph Adolf Schenk von Schmidburg), who was never a serious candidate, virtuously declined the bribe; it is not known how Breidbach responded. The Austrian ambassador Count Pergen had been very confident that Eltz would win and was not at all pleased by Breidbach's success. Before the election campaign had begun in earnest he had reported that the latter was 'lively' but did not possess that degree of devotion to the House of Austria that one looked for in a future elector of Mainz.[5] His worst fears were confirmed when an intercepted letter revealed that the French minister Kempfer had been instructed by Versailles to work for Breidbach's success.[6] Pergen's own hands were tied by instructions from Vienna that he should adopt a position of neutrality.

In terms of birth the new Elector Emmerich Joseph was exceptionally well-qualified. The Freiherren von Breidbach zu Bürresheim first emerged as *ministeriales* at the beginning of the thirteenth century and by the fifteenth members of the family appeared in Mainz both as secular officials and members of the Cathedral Chapter.[7] In any attempt to discuss Emmerich Joseph's personal qualifications to rule the Electorate it is necessary

[1] See above, p. 54-5, 84.
[2] Vienna, *Staka*, Fasc. 136, 76.
[3] P.R.O., SP.81.142, 6 July 1763.
[4] Ibid.
[5] Vienna, *Staka*, Fasc. 136, 76.
[6] Ibid., 84, 86.
[7] Weidenbach, 'Die Freiherren von Breidbach zu Bürresheim', *Annalen des historischen Vereins für den Niederrhein*, 24 (1872), p. 88.

Enlightened absolutism, 1743-74

but difficult to distinguish between legend and reality. Subsequent popular histories of Mainz are stuffed with anecdotes illustrating his popularity, simplicity, humility, charity, wisdom, justice, devotion to his subjects' welfare and ability to mix with people from every class.[1] Even his considerate attitude towards his servants was felt to be remarkable enough to merit a mention. The danger of making him appear a conventional cardboard saint was avoided by frequent reference to his twin passions of alcohol and hunting, although his chroniclers hastened to add that the peasants were not inconvenienced by the latter.

Obviously none of this folklore is properly documented and few of the anecdotes can be literally true, although at least some of the virtues ascribed to him are confirmed by contemporary admirers. The best summary was contained in the instructions given to the French diplomat Marquis de Clausonnette in 1775, the year after Emmerich Joseph's death, which described him as 'very enlightened, very knowledgeable of the laws, rights and duties of his position [as Archchancellor of the Empire] and to many other qualities he added a resolute will. Even the Protestants revered him on account of his enlightenment, his principles, his moderation, his impartiality. In domestic affairs the views of this prince were noble and just, and he struck at the roots of the abuses and the bad institutions which generally infect the educational system and the constitution of the ecclesiastical principalities.'[2] His reputation survived even the revolutionary epoch. The Mainz Jacobins of 1792 cited Emmerich Joseph as the exception which proved the rule that all electors were despotic parasites: 'Only you, honest Joseph von Breitenbach, the Mainz Ganganelli [i.e. Clement XIV], cannot be placed in this class. You loved your fatherland more than your principality and sought to destroy prejudices by bold policies and to improve the lot of your people by philanthropic education.'[3]

It was particularly important that Emmerich Joseph's unexpected election revived the influence of Stadion, after a gap of only three years. It was through the latter's patronage that the new Elector had received his first taste of public office twenty years earlier, when he had been appointed to the presidency of the Commerce Commission.[4] Later he also became a member of the Poor Law Commission and the War Council, and president

---

[1] See, for example, Franz Werner, *Der Dom von Mainz, nebst Darstellung der Schicksale der Stadt und der Geschichte ihrer Erzbischöfe*, vol. 3 (Mainz, 1836), pp. 174-230, and Vogt, *Verfall*, p. 208.

[2] Georges Livet, *Recueil des Instructions données aux Ambassadeurs et Ministres de France, depuis les traités de Westphalie jusqu'à la révolution française*, 28, États Allemands, vol. 1, L'Électorat de Mayence (Paris, 1962), p. 258.

[3] Friedrich Lehne, 'Mainz im Zeitalter der Aufklärung und der Revolution', *Mainz zwischen Schwarz und Rot: Die Mainzer Revolution in Schriften, Reden und Briefen*, ed. Claus Träger (Berlin, 1963), p. 51.

[4] Kirnberger, *Handelsmesse*, p. 25.

of the Council (*Hofrat*), the most important administrative body in the Electorate.¹ By the time of his election he had already won a reputation for being a just and able administrator.² His new status, however, gave him unlimited scope to indulge his hobbies and he had little time for day-to-day business. The papal nuncio wrote: 'He is a man of talent, of spirit, he speaks very well, but drinks even better, so that between this diversion and hunting he occupies much of the day, and thus has to allow his ministers to do everything. The country seems to be content with his government and in the ecclesiastical field also affairs go on in good order and the clergy are better looked after than in the other ecclesiastical states.'³

That these interests did not lead to the neglect of the Electorate was due largely to his choice of two other protégés of Stadion as his chief ministers: Karl Friedrich Willibald Freiherr von Groschlag and Anselm Franz Freiherr von Bentzel. Groschlag, who was only 34 in 1763, had studied law at two Protestant universities, Marburg and Göttingen, and his frequent visits to France, including a spell as Mainz ambassador at Versailles from 1758 to 1761, served as a link between the Stadion circle and the French Enlightenment. He made the acquaintance of Montesquieu, stayed with the Prince de Conti, reported on the current intellectual scene and sent back to Mainz copies of the latest works of the philosophes.⁴ Groschlag was not liked by everyone who met him, but in German intellectual and political circles he acquired a reputation as formidable as that of Stadion. The liberal publicist Christian Schubart, editor of the influential Württemberg journal *Deutsche Chronik*, wrote after a visit to Aschaffenburg in 1773: 'I had the good fortune to spend a whole day in the company of this excellent minister. Statesmanship, philosophy, history, literature and the arts, educational theory, languages, the study of human nature, religion – all lie within the circle which the magic staff of his genius has drawn about him.'⁵

Quite apart from any question of personality, both age and birth dictated that Groschlag would be the dominant partner. Anselm Franz von Bentzel was ten years younger, and compared with the Groschlags, whose line could be traced definitely to 1254, his family was *parvenue*. The first Bentzel had come to Mainz as a Swedish officer in the army of Gustavus Adolphus and it was not until 1732 that the family acquired a patent of imperial nobility. The title of Freiherr followed in 1746.⁶ After studying at the universities of Mainz, Erfurt and Vienna, Bentzel entered Mainz

---

¹ *Hof- und Staatskalender*. ² Vienna, *Staka*, Fasc. 136, 84, 86.
³ Heribert Raab, 'Die Breidbach Bürresheim in der Germania Sacra: Eine Skizze der Reichskirchenpolitik des Mainzer Kurfürsten Emmerich Joseph und seines Bruders Karl Ernst', *Mainzer Almanach* (1962), p. 93.
⁴ Karl Diel, *Ein Parkvorbild der Goethezeit: Der Lustgarten der Freiherren von Goschlag zu Dieburg* (Darmstadt, 1941), pp. 19, 107–9.   ⁵ Ibid., p. 126.
⁶ Jung, *Bentzel*, p. 8.

Enlightened absolutism, 1743–74

service in 1759 and was only twenty-four when Emmerich Joseph was elected. With one or two very rare exceptions, new electors did not immediately dismiss the ministry they inherited, but rather allowed it to fade away. As official positions in Mainz were usually vacated only by death or promotion the official structure of power as recorded in the state almanac often bore scant relation to reality. Thus Groschlag did not become Grand Master of the Court until Stadion's death in 1768, while Bentzel's titular progress was blocked by the longevity of Chancellor Vorster. Although the latter enjoyed both the status and the salary conferred by his position it was Bentzel who exercised the power. Count Neipperg, the Austrian ambassador, commented in 1768: 'Because of his skill, industry and experience, von Bentzel enjoys the complete confidence of the Elector.'[1] When Vorster finally died in 1770, Neipperg commented that his departure would have little effect on the conduct of business because as far as the ministry was concerned the Chancellor had been dead for a number of years.[2]

There is no evidence to explain why the election of his protégé did not herald the return of Stadion to head the ministry in Mainz. He was seventy-two in 1763 and may have felt that the leisurely pursuits of his Swabian estates were preferable to the bustle of Mainz politics. It is also possible that Emmerich Joseph wanted to go his own way, although clearly there had been no rupture between the two. Groschlag, Bentzel and a number of other Mainz officials were frequent guests at Warthausen and the continuity was maintained.[3] Links with Protestant intellectuals were, if anything, strengthened. In 1769 Wieland was appointed to a chair at Erfurt, the Electorate's second university, and he continued in his mediating rôle even after his move to Weimar three years later. Stadion's circle had been the crucible of the Mainz Enlightenment and his influence was clearly reflected in the reforms of the new reign.

As he had been the first president of his predecessor's Commerce Commission, it was to be expected that the new elector would take an interest in the economy. No fundamental reforms were attempted; existing lines of development were encouraged and a few obstacles to further progress were removed. In 1770, for example, a Highways Commission was established to supervise improvements throughout the Electorate. A coinage convention was arranged with Frankfurt, Trier, the Palatinate and Hessen-Darmstadt in 1765, which established a common currency level and removed debased coins from circulation. Agreements with Würzburg and Ansbach reduced tariffs by a third and established a direct link between Mainz and Eastern Franconia, bypassing Frankfurt.[4]

---

[1] Vienna, *Staka*, Fasc. 156, 187.
[2] Ibid. Fasc. 161, 365.
[3] Rössler, *Stadion*, p. 46.
[4] Scholl, *Kurmainzische Wirtschaftspolitik*, pp. 92–5; Schwarz, *Der wirtschaftliche Konkurrenzkampf*, pp. 60–1.

The most ambitious project was the attempt to stimulate the development of Höchst. In 1768 it was announced that Protestant immigrants would be welcomed there and would be permitted to practise their religion in private. When their numbers reached suitable proportions a church and school would be built at government expense and public worship allowed. The administration of the town was to be in the hands of the local official acting in cooperation with a council composed of equal numbers of Roman Catholics and Protestants. The mayor was to be chosen in turn by the Catholics, Lutherans and Calvinists. Although the concession applied only to Höchst and even there does not appear to have attracted a substantial number of immigrants, even this limited relaxation of orthodoxy by a prince-bishop – thirteen years before Joseph II's toleration edict – was striking enough. Mallet du Pan wrote to Voltaire four years later 'The Elector of Mainz has had a small town built on the Main; the only condition that he imposes on immigrants is that of Confucius: be just and believe what you like.'[1]

The end of the Seven Years War and the long-term improvement in the economic situation brought much-needed relief to the Electorate's finances. In a report prepared for the Austrian ambassador in 1764, Groschlag described them as having 'collapsed completely'.[2] At the time he was presenting a claim for food and cash supplied to the imperial troops during both the War of the Austrian Succession and the Seven Years War and so this verdict may have been somewhat exaggerated. Needless to say, the appeal evoked as little response in Vienna as did another similar claim in France.[3] Peace, careful accounting and relative economy managed to restore the situation without aid from outside. This is revealed in a document entitled 'Summary of all money and *naturalia*, converted to cash values, present on the death of His Electoral Grace Emmerich Joseph, of most blessed memory; also of those items of extraordinary expenditure which he met during his most glorious reign'. It was sent by the Austrian ambassador Count Neipperg to Kaunitz shortly after Emmerich Joseph's death.[4] Neipperg vouched for its authenticity and claimed that it had been presented to the Cathedral Chapter by the President of the Exchequer Franz Philipp von Franckenstein.[5] It revealed that debts totalling 153,000 gulden had been paid off and that there was a credit balance of 238,000 gulden in cash and 267,000 gulden worth of grain, wine and wood. It also listed those items of extraordinary expenditure which could be regarded

---

[1] *Voltaire's Correspondence*, ed. Theodore Besterman, vol. 81 (Geneva, 1963), p. 132.
[2] Vienna, *Staka*, Fasc. 142, 50.
[3] Ibid. Fasc. 147, 32, Fasc. 152, 7, Fasc. 154, 102, Fasc. 155, 161.
[4] Ibid. Fasc. 175, 600.
[5] The minutes of the Chapter for 2 June 1774 record the presentation of this document but do not list any figures.

as permanent assets. These included 87,000 gulden for the visitation of the *Reichskammergericht*, 66,000 gulden for new roads and 200,000 gulden for buildings.

A more precise illustration of the responsible nature of Emmerich Joseph's government was provided by his efforts to deal with the famine of 1771–2. A series of bad harvests after 1766 affected prices all over Germany and in Mainz the price of grain rose from an average of 4 gulden per *Malter* to 7.2 gulden in 1770 and 8.14 gulden in 1771.[1] Unusually wet weather in 1770 ruined the harvest and provoked a serious crisis. An official investigation in the spring of 1771 came to the conclusion that the shortage had been created artificially by 'the most disgraceful and deplorable avarice' of the grain-hoarders. The ordinance which followed fixed the price of grain and bread and threatened confiscation of the supplies of racketeers. As this proved insufficient, in December of the same year a commission was set up 'to alleviate the emergency and for the best of the country'. Large consignments of grain were purchased in Poland, shipped via Danzig and Amsterdam to Mainz and sold there at moderate prices.

These measures appeared to have had the desired effect, for the price of grain in Mainz, even in the worst months, was considerably less than in some other German cities. The Elector himself reported to the Cathedral Chapter at the end of 1772 that 'We have been comforted by observing that at a time when grain prices had reached a quite extraordinary level in almost every part of Germany, prices in our capital city, as well as throughout our electoral lands, have been held at a level which in present circumstances is moderate.' The commission financed its activities by loans from Frankfurt merchants, the difference between the cost of purchasing and transporting the grain and the price it was sold at in Mainz being met by the exchequer.[2] The Elector's efforts to avert disaster prompted an appreciative demonstration when he returned to the city after the crisis. His carriage was halted, the horses removed from their shafts and their places taken by a number of citizens. Moved to tears, so the report goes, the Elector was drawn through cheering crowds to his palace.[3]

---

[1] F. G. Dreyfus, 'Prix et Population à Trèves et à Mayence au XVIIIe siècle', *Revue d'histoire économique et sociale*, 34 (1956), 251.

[2] Mainz, *Kurmainzische Verordnungen*, 6te Sammlung, vol. 8, 21 May 1771; Vienna, *MEA*, Militaria, Fasc. 96.

[3] Werner, *Der Dom von Mainz*, p. 203. This is one of Werner's stories which seems to have a basis in fact, cf. *Dankrede an Ihro Kurfürstliche Gnaden zu Mainz bey Dero Höchsten Rückkehr von Höchst nach der Residenzstadt Mainz für Dero zur Steuer allgemeiner Fruchtteuerung mildestgetroffener Maasregeln und Fürsorg, abgestattet von unterthänigst-dankmüthigster Bürgerschaft zu Mainz* (Mainz, 1771).

IV

Beneficial though they were, the measures described so far reveal little more than careful husbandry and traditional paternalism. Although they give the lie to the cynical observations of French diplomats,[1] they do not suggest any great modernity of outlook. This was much more apparent in the Elector's efforts to reform the educational system. After much preparation a Schools Commission was set up at the end of 1770. Although the official chairman was Franz Xaver Maria von Hornstein, the real force behind it was Anselm Franz von Bentzel, who prepared the plans and supervised their execution.[2] They were aimed at two main targets: the teachers, and what they taught. The inadequate salary and low status attracted to the profession men who were often only semi-literate themselves. Their need to find supplementary income by digging graves or digging vegetables made them turn a blind eye to the mass-truancy which virtually closed rural schools for the summer.[3] When they did teach they confined the curriculum to a great deal of scriptural knowledge, some reading, writing and singing and very little else. An inquiry into the schools in the city of Mainz in 1771 revealed that only three out of seven taught arithmetic. Even the grammar school concentrated largely on religion and the classics, neglecting entirely German literature, foreign languages, mathematics or any of the natural sciences.[4]

The reformers believed that both syllabus and structure would have to be adapted to meet changing needs and that a major pre-requisite of this operation was the reduction of clerical influence. The Jesuits ruled the University and the grammar schools, while the archiepiscopal General Vicariate, through its powers of appointment and supervision, controlled rural and urban lower education. The new secular accent was made clear in the manifesto of the reformers: 'A Treatise Concerning the Improvement of the Education of Youth in the Electorate of Mainz', published in 1771. It was written by J. J. F. Steigentesch, who was Bentzel's most important collaborator and who translated the minister's general principles into legislative drafts and explanatory tracts.[5] The preface of the treatise began:

The administration of schools is the most important object of a sovereign's care and is the only means of binding the body politic into a *true whole*...public education is the *sole* means of uniting the *body politic* in a true whole; of diffusing one soul, a *common* spirit through members and veins; of making the tasks and the operation of

---

[1] See above, pp. 65–6.
[2] August Messer, *Die Reform des Schulwesens im Kurfürstentum Mainz unter Emmerich Joseph (1763–1774)* (Mainz, 1897), p. 13.
[3] See the various reports reprinted in Brück, *Kurmainzer Schulgeschichte*, pp. 31–77.
[4] Messer, *Reform*, pp. 75–89, 96, 113–14.   [5] Jung, *Bentzel*, p. 35.

a government infinitely more easy and of making the internal administration of a state, which as matters stand at the moment is the most onerous business in the world, a pleasant occupation. *Education of all members of the state according to fixed principles drawn from the nature of man and social life* creates for the highest ruler and his citizen a public treasure whose springs flow for ever and multiply indefinitely.[1]

By setting up a commission subject only to the secular government and with powers over all branches of education, Emmerich Joseph and his advisers went further than most Protestant princes in the exclusion of ecclesiastical influence from education. The first step in the addition of substance to this purely formal separation was the founding of a College of Education. It opened its doors to eleven selected candidates on 1 May 1771; two years later this number had grown to thirty-five.[2] Instruction was free and in cases of hardship a maintenance allowance was paid. The new director, Steigentesch, used the most modern enlightened text books, including works by Felbiger, Gellert, Muratori and Lessing. The aspiring teachers were taught that 'secular knowledge' must be made 'pleasant and attractive', that both reason and memory should be exercised and that the specific and practical value of general theories should always be illustrated. The old tyranny of 'memory the only object of school exercises and the Latin language the sole objective' was to be replaced by a much wider and more 'relevant' range of subjects. The usual trio of religion, reading and writing was to be joined by the four basic operations of arithmetic, and those various branches of natural science and natural history which would be useful to a countryman, such as soil-science and the use of artificial fertilizers or artificial meadows. The need to explain the duties of a subject – especially that of obedience – was also stressed.[3] After a course of two years successful graduates were despatched to spread enlightenment in the country schools of the Electorate. The Commission attempted to make these schools worthy of the training of the new incumbents by increasing the salary and thus preventing the need to pursue a second profession, and by improving the school buildings.[4]

In 1773 the Commission turned its attention to the municipal schools, which were divided into primary schools (*Trivialschulen*) for children between five and eight years old, and secondary schools (*Realschulen*) for children between nine and fifteen. As Bentzel reported to the Elector, great emphasis was laid on practical subjects with the object of making the children 'honest Christians and useful citizens'.[5] Although plans were also prepared for a similar reconstruction of the grammar schools, implementation was conditional on the removal of the Jesuits. At all stages of

---

[1] Brück, *Kurmainzer Schulgeschichte*, p. 78.   [2] Messer, *Reform*, pp. 15, 26.
[3] Brück, *Kurmainzer Schulgeschichte*, p. 11.   [4] Messer, *Reform*, p. 72.
[5] Ibid., pp. 95–6.

the reform the Commission was at pains to point out its orthodox religious character: the first essential characteristic of a teacher listed in the official instructions was 'true piety'.¹ Yet relatively religion retreated and the utilitarian ideal of 'the useful citizen' marched into the foreground. Although the spiritual and temporal welfare of the individual was always mentioned, for Bentzel at least the demands of the state were paramount. They determined not only the practical curricula of the primary and secondary schools but also the curious admissions system of the grammar school. The children of professional men – officials, academics, lawyers – were to be admitted freely, the children of burghers and craftsmen had to take an entrance examination and the luckless offspring of peasants were not to be admitted at all. Bentzel argued that although in principle it was wrong to bind a man to his estate, because this destroyed incentive, in practice a good peasant was more useful to the state in the country, spreading light in the stygian rural darkness, than learning to be an intellectual in the city.² The number of pupils was to be reduced from 500 to 300, for the state had no need of the 'swarms of half-educated young people' who streamed out of the schools annually and were only a burden to themselves and the community.³

In practice however this ambitious scheme ran into a number of serious difficulties. It had been intended that all future vacancies for teachers should be filled by graduates of the College of Education and that they should be paid a minimum annual salary of 300 gulden.⁴ Despite large contributions from the Elector's private purse the scheme suffered constantly from lack of funds. The annual salary aimed at was never achieved, the commission was forced to appoint unqualified teachers or to leave positions vacant and the College was obliged to accept unsuitable candidates. Although in 1773 he received an assistant in the shape of a pupil of Wieland from Erfurt, Steigentesch found that it took much longer than expected to train them as teachers. He complained that he had to waste a great deal of time teaching them how to speak properly, because of their 'corruption of native-taste and mother-tongue'.⁵

Although sensibly they had begun their reforms with the primary schools, Emmerich Joseph and Bentzel had for some time been eyeing the University, which had been in the hands of the Jesuits since their arrival in 1561. Again, the two main problems were seen as finance and curriculum. Not until the Jesuit monopoly of the theological and philosophical faculties had been broken and fresh sources of income found, could the University be adapted to meet the needs of the reformed Electorate. One

---

[1] Mainz, *Kurmainzische Verordnungen*, 6te Sammlung, vol. 8. 9 October 1773.
[2] Messer, *Reform*, p. 112.
[3] Jung, *Bentzel*, p. 41.
[4] Messer, *Reform*, p. 160.
[5] Hainebach, *Studien*, p. 33.

of Emmerich Joseph's first actions was to appoint a commission under the chairmanship of Bentzel to investigate ways of improving the University's finances.[1] In 1764 application was made to Rome for permission to increase the number of monasteries already obliged to contribute to the University. The Curia employed its usual delaying tactics and it was not until 1766 that a definite refusal was communicated. Although the Elector lacked the ruthless resolution of a Joseph II and declined to take unilateral action, projects of secularisation continued to be discussed throughout his reign. It seems very likely that by the time of his unexpected death in 1774, three monasteries had been earmarked for dissolution. The proceeds were intended to finance a major reconstruction of the University, which was to celebrate its 300th anniversary in 1777.[2]

The financial problem was thus never solved; but the power of the Jesuits was broken. Emmerich Joseph was not prepared to copy the Kings of France, Spain and Portugal and eject them altogether and contented himself with piecemeal tactics. He made his own position clear when he commented that some of the Jesuits' proposals for the reorganisation of the theological faculty 'sufficiently demonstrated...the thoroughly bad nature of their previous teaching methods'.[3] His views were probably strengthened by opposition to the Jesuits from within the University. In 1763 and again in 1764 the students complained bitterly about the teaching methods employed and demanded in particular that the simple dictation of theological propositions should be replaced by exposition. This incident, which ended with the Jesuits being instructed to abandon dictation, gave members of the other faculties the opportunity to air their general grievances against the Order.[4]

Although subjected to periodic harrassment[5] the Jesuits survived in Mainz until the total dissolution of the Order by Clement XIV in 1773. This at least gave Bentzel the chance to replace the teaching staff of the philosophical and theological faculties. In two drafts composed before the actual dissolution he had made his intentions clear: 'It is completely impossible to continue any longer the useless philosophical jumble [*Gewirr*], with which the Jesuits have concerned themselves up till now' and 'All the stuff the Jesuits teach is useless and incomprehensible to their pupils'.[6]

---

[1] Jung, *Bentzel*, p. 46.
[2] Ernst Jakobi, *Die Entstehung des Mainzer Universitätsfonds*, Beiträge zur Geschichte der Universität Mainz, vol. 5 (Wiesbaden, 1959), pp. 21–39.
[3] Brück, *Theologische Fakultät*, p. 38.
[4] Ibid., pp. 23–8.
[5] In 1768 the Jesuits of Aschaffenburg had declined to appear before an electoral commission, claiming they were exempt by reason of papal privilege. They were told that they would be fined heavily unless they appeared immediately. Two years later they were forbidden to conduct a mission among the soldiers of the Mainz garrison – Vienna, *MEA*, GK, Fasc. 63.
[6] Jung, *Bentzel*, p. 49.

The new appointments were to bring the University of Mainz into line with the most progressive Catholic universities and even to allow it to compete with the Protestants. The instructions given to the new Professor of Dogma, for example, constituted – in the opinion of one recent historian – 'a programme absolutely determined by rationalism, whose strict implementation would not have left much Catholic doctrine still standing'.[1] These changes were not simply the result of a predilection for enlightened thought on the part of Emmerich Joseph, Bentzel and the others, real though that was. They were expected to provide the state with tangible benefits. As in their plans for primary and secondary education, there was constant emphasis on the need for 'useful citizens'. Even the aim of theological study was stated to be 'practical Christianity'.

Emmerich Joseph also made an attempt to inject new life into the moribund university at Erfurt. Here too no fundamental improvement in the financial situation was achieved, but a number of new professors gave it a temporary lustre. The most important was Wieland, who was called to the chair of philosophy, apparently as a result of Groschlag's intercession.[2] The most interesting was Karl Friedrich Bahrdt, a Protestant and the *enfant terrible* of German enlightened theology, who rejected revelation, preached a purely 'natural' religion and amongst other things was a highly effective satirist. Others included Friedrich Justus Riedel, Heinrich Schmid, Friedrich Herel and Georg Meusel.[3] In his autobiography Bahrdt described how a battle royal raged between the intruders and the old guard.[4] Although the former enjoyed the support of the Elector, the latter proved to have greater staying-power. Tired of the endless bickering, Wieland departed for Weimar in 1772 to become tutor to the young Duke Carl August. He was preceded or soon followed by most of the others. Riedel moved to Vienna, Bahrdt and Schmid to Giessen and Herel returned to Nuremberg. Meusel lingered on until 1779 but his influence on university affairs was negligible.

Although their implementation was incomplete, Emmerich Joseph's educational reforms went a good deal further than those of his predecessors. The same pattern was repeated in the ecclesiastical sphere, for in 1769 there occurred the first major clash between the German archbishops and the Pope. Although the affair of the 'Koblenz *Gravamina*' was subsequently overshadowed by the Congress of Ems, all the principles and issues at stake in the latter had been well ventilated in the course of the

[1] Brück, *Theologische Fakultät*, p. 45.
[2] Rössler, *Stadion*, p. 58.
[3] V. Michel, *C. M. Wieland: la formation et l'évolution de son esprit jusqu'en 1772* (Paris, 1938), p. 404.
[4] K. F. Bahrdt, *Geschichte seines Lebens, seiner Meinungen und Schicksale*, vol. 2 (Berlin, 1791), pp. 5–20.

earlier conflict. The episcopalist movement had reached ideological maturity in the 1760s with the publication by Horix of the Mainz *Acceptatio* and by Hontheim *alias* Febronius of *De Statu Ecclesiae*.[1] It was something of a coincidence, however, that in 1768–9 all three Rhenish archbishops found good reason to translate their theoretical antipathy towards Rome into action. Max Friedrich of Cologne was upset by the interference of the nuncio in his attempts to reform the Weidenbach fraternity house. Clement Wenzeslaus of Trier was upset by Clement XIII's insistence that he resign his bishoprics of Regensburg and Freising when he acquired Augsburg. Emmerich Joseph of Mainz was upset by what seemed to him the exorbitant fees he was required to pay to Rome when he was elected bishop of Worms.[2]

As usual, the formulation of protests on these and other related specific issues gave rise to a more general exposition of the episcopalist programme. The time seemed ripe for the formation of a common front. Early in 1768 Max Friedrich approached a number of ecclesiastical states with a view to taking joint action for the 'recovery' of episcopal rights. There was an especially warm response from Mainz. But by the time Emmerich Joseph sent a detailed programme to Cologne the situation had changed. Max Friedrich was now engaged in delicate negotiations with Rome on another matter and the Mainz proposals were too strong for his taste. At the beginning of 1769, therefore, Emmerich Joseph took the initiative himself. In the course of the year his emissaries succeeded in overcoming the reservations of Trier and Cologne and in December a joint meeting was held at Koblenz.[3]

Usually known as the 'Koblenz *Gravamina*', the convention of 31 articles which finally emerged was the political expression of the researches of canonists like Neller and Horix. Indeed the presence of Hontheim, as the representative of Trier, underlined the close association between theory and practice. The five principles on which the Mainz position was based were expressed most clearly in the instructions given to the canon Damian von der Leyen when in the summer of 1770 he was sent to Bonn

---

[1] See above, p. 104.
[2] H. Schotte, 'Zur Geschichte des Emser Kongresses', *Historisches Jahrbuch*, 35 (1914), p. 87. Heribert Raab, *Clemens Wenzeslaus und seine Zeit, 1739–1812*, vol. 1 (Freiburg, Basle and Vienna, 1962), pp. 296–301. There is some dispute as to which of these grievances played the most important part. Heribert Raab, who has greater knowledge of the sources than any other living historian, is insistent that it was Emmerich Joseph's disgruntlement over the Worms fees that proved decisive. – Heribert Raab, 'Zur Geschichte der Aufklärung im Rhein-Main-Gebiet', *Historisches Jahrbuch*, 88 (1968), 434.
[3] For a detailed account of the events leading up to the meeting, see *Des kurtrierischen Rats H. A. Arnoldi Tagebuch über die zu Ems gehaltene Zusammenkunft der vier erzbischöflichen Herren Deputierten*, ed. M. Höhler (1915), pp. 26–30, 328–35. Indicative of the mood in Mainz was the banning in the same year of the ultramontane treatise of Cardinal Robert Bellarmine S.J., *De potestate summi pontificis in rebus temporalibus* – Raab, *Concordata*, p. 139, n. 59.

and Koblenz to reinforce the solidarity of the other two archbishops. It was claimed: firstly that the Pope, as supreme shepherd of the Church, possessed by virtue of divine institution all rights necessary for the unity of the Church; in all Church affairs he was the first and supreme chairman (*Vorsteher*). Secondly, the power to bind and loose had been bestowed by Christ on the Church as a whole, represented by a General Council. This Council alone possessed fundamental legislative power and was the supreme judicial instance, above the Pope and subject to no other human agency. Thirdly, as the successors of the Apostles, the bishops had been granted by God all powers necessary for the government of their dioceses. Neither the Pope, nor any other bishop, might interfere in diocesan affairs without the permission of the bishop concerned. Fourthly, provincial councils or the meetings of metropolitans and their suffragans were empowered to decide collectively on the business of the province. Fifthly, secular power was directly instituted by God and was entirely independent of the spiritual power.[1] The thirty-one *Gravamina* reflected the episcopacy's sense of being the victim of papal usurpation, for they were mainly negative demands. The emphasis was on abolition: of annates, of the exemption of monasteries and other privileged bodies from episcopal jurisdiction, of papal control of German benefices, of papal interference in dispensations, of the jurisdiction of papal nuncios, of papal encroachments on regular episcopal jurisdiction, and so on.[2]

It had proved quite difficult to obtain agreement on this programme; it proved to be quite impossible to implement it. As the three archbishops were not prepared to take unilateral action, thus risking an open schism, their only hope lay in forcing the Pope to make concessions. Even in alliance their combined pressure did not amount to very much and so they turned to the Emperor for reinforcement. Joseph II's answer, communicated on 4 October 1770, was a grave disappointment, although not entirely unexpected. Almost all that Joseph could expect from helping the archbishops was a further deterioration in his own relations with the papacy. As he himself was engaged on the reform of the Austrian Church such a course did not recommend itself. In a long but prevaricating reply he declined to intervene in Rome and commented that some of the *Gravamina* required action by the *Reichstag*, some could be dealt with by the bishops unilaterally, some by the Emperor alone and some by both of them together.[3] Particularly disheartening was his insistence that the archbishops should consult and act in concert with their suffragans. As Joseph knew full well, the German bishops did not wish to escape from the papal frying-pan into the metropolitan fire. Certainly they wanted

[1] Vienna, *MEA*, GK, Fasc. 71. [2] Höhler, *Ems*, pp. 31–3.
[3] Ibid., pp. 38–9.

independence from Rome but remained deeply suspicious of the archbishops' motives.[1]

The whole incident had also made it clear that episcopalism and Josephism had one essential difference, although they sprang from the same roots and used the same vocabulary. Joseph's attempts to establish a state-church brought him into conflict not only with Rome but also with the prince-bishops of the Empire whose diocesan jurisdiction extended into his territories. Because the contest was three-sided – between Pope, Emperor and secular Catholic princes, and the German episcopacy – the chances of the last-named and weakest contestant were negligible. Nothing daunted, Emmerich Joseph tried a new initiative in 1772. He proposed to his two colleagues that Damian von der Leyen be sent to Vienna to reopen negotiations. Although Max Friedrich of Cologne was in favour, the weak and vacillating Clemens Wenzeslaus first hesitated and then vetoed the project.[2] There the matter was allowed to rest for more than a decade.

V

Emmerich Joseph and his ministers also encountered serious difficulties on the domestic front. Their reforms represented a conscious effort to import and impose alien ideas and institutions; the Enlightenment in Mainz was the artificial creation of the aristocratic and bureaucratic élite. It had links with the past through the episcopalist tradition, for example, but links which stretched back only to that same élite's historical counterparts. Until the latter part of the eighteenth century it is simply impossible to discover any spontaneous secular literature in Mainz, apart from a few wretched eulogistical poems – often in Latin – to mark special occasions.[3] The Enlightenment in Mainz owed nothing to the mass of the people and so it is not surprising that the only response it evoked in them was hostility. The vast majority of both peasants and townspeople still looked exclusively to the Catholic Church for guidance on every issue, directly religious or not. And at its lower levels this Church was still governed by the baroque piety of the Counter Reformation. It was characterised by loyalty to the Pope, reluctance to tolerate heterodoxy, suspicion of intellectual innovation and an attachment to naïve and sensuous forms of worship. This may have been repugnant to Stadion, Groschlag, Bentzel or Emmerich Joseph but they were in a very small minority.

It is particularly important to remember that the flamboyant ceremonial

---

[1] Karl Otmar Freiherr von Aretin, *Heiliges Römisches Reich 1776–1806*, vol. 1 (Wiesbaden, 1967), pp. 378–9. This particular conflict of interests was to become even more apparent after the Congress of Ems, fifteen years later. See below, pp. 224–5.
[2] Höhler, *Ems*, pp. 43–4.
[3] Hainebach, *Studien*, p. 9.

of baroque piety was not simply imposed from above by a self-indulgent clergy; it both formed and reflected the religious aspirations of their congregations. A description of a Corpus Christi procession in Mainz in 1769, for example, by a visitor from Brunswick made it clear that practically the whole population participated.[1] And not only the lower classes participated in public religious life. There was, for example, the 'Congregation of the Blessed Virgin', a group of influential clergy and laymen which met for joint devotions and marched together in processions. Members were required to swear allegiance to the Tridentine decrees, to make their confession at least once a fortnight, to genuflect and bare their heads at the name of Mary and to attend the Congregation's services on the Virgin's festival.[2] In the second half of the eighteenth century there were signs that interest in the secular thought of the Enlightenment had extended to some of the ordinary citizens but it remained predominantly the concern of the nobility, the academics and the bureaucrats.[3]

Emmerich Joseph and his ministers were aware that the success of their reforms depended to a large extent on at least the acquiescence of the subjects and made strenuous efforts to obtain it. Before the educational reforms of the late 1760s, the chief instrument was a government-sponsored journal called 'The Citizen' (*Der Bürger*), edited and for the most part written by J. F. Steigentesch. The first issue appeared in June 1765, with the avowed intention of promoting 'good habits [*Sitten*] and what is known as...civic virtue [*bürgerliche Tugend*]'. Steigentesch was very aware of the intellectual superiority of the Protestant North and sought to persuade his fellow-citizens to emulate its achievements. Although he stressed that Roman Catholicism was not responsible for the backwardness of the South, he praised and reprinted Protestant literature and once proudly announced that three poems mistakenly attributed to himself had in fact been written by the Brunswick Intendant, Gieseke. In the best tradition of the French Enlightenment 'The Citizen' advocated a stream of projects, ranging from a stud-farm for horses to a new A.B.C. book. In 1769 the journal devoted its space to extracts from the works of Basedow and a discussion of educational reform. In the following year Steigentesch closed the journal down to take up his new position as director of the newly established College of Education and the practical promotion of 'civic virtue'.[4]

Emmerich Joseph was not prepared however to advance beyond the modest aims of simplified religion, better education and practical secular improvements. His aversion to anything that smacked of radicalism or im-

---

[1] Heinrich Schrohe, 'Ein Reisebericht über Mainz im Jahre 1769', *Hessische Volksbücher*, 48 (1922).
[2] Anton Ph. Brück, 'Das Buchapostolat der Mainzer "Congregatio maior academica" im 18. Jahrhundert', *Mainzer Zeitschrift*, 60/61 (1965/1966), pp. 70-3.
[3] See below, pp. 193-209.   [4] Hainebach, *Studien*, p. 18.

piety was well-illustrated by the curious case of the Abbé Laurens. Laurens, a Frenchman by birth, had been arrested in Frankfurt at the beginning of 1766 on suspicion of having written *L'Imirce ou la fille de la nature* and *La Chandelle d'Arras*, two works which featured the familiar French combination of anti-clericalism and pornography. As he was a priest he was handed over to the Mainz authorities and brought to trial. He pleaded guilty and was condemned to life imprisonment, a sentence which was immediately confirmed by the Elector. This is the only recorded prosecution of this kind and it is doubtful whether the radical Enlightenment penetrated to Mainz, at least at this stage.[1]

Far more alarming for the reformers was the dogged conservatism of the people they sought to enlighten. The somewhat melodramatic precautions taken on the occasion of the dissolution of the Jesuits indicated that they were fully aware of this obstacle. On 6 September 1773, the entire Mainz garrison turned out, occupied key positions throughout the city and patrolled the streets. The inquisitive crowds that gathered were dispersed. The Elector's commissars proceeded to the Jesuit College, divided its members into various carriages and accompanied them to monasteries outside the city.[2] It appears that the government's anxiety was well-founded. Niklas Vogt, in 1773 a 17 year-old pupil at the grammar school, wrote much later that 'the people saw this [the expulsion] with a mixture of dismay and disgust' and an anonymous chronicler recorded that the troops were called out 'to prevent an uprising'.[3] Rudolf Eickemeyer, a teacher of mathematics at the College of Education, wrote that large crowds gathered and that everywhere one saw anger, grief and lamentations; nuns fainted and a woman gave birth prematurely.[4]

This outburst of fidelity to the Jesuits was the climax of popular opposition to the ministry's reforms. Yet on many occasions the Elector and his ministers had gone out of their way to stress the orthodox nature of the measures. For all his admiration of the Protestant intellectuals, Steigentesch wrote that it was blasphemy to assert that Catholicism was the cause of 'prevailing ignorance' in the South and, although he criticised individual priests, he emphasised that nothing was more important that 'veneration of the clergy' as such. Despite the introduction of the new subjects, the Catholic religion stood four-square in the centre of the curriculum of the new schools. All pupils were to attend Mass daily and take the sacraments

---

[1] K. Schnelle, *Aufklärung und klerikale Reaktion: Der Prozess gegen den Abbé Henri Joseph Laurens*, Neue Beiträge zur Literaturwissenschaft, vol. 18 (Berlin, 1963). Schnelle asserts that there can be no doubt that pornography and radical French publications found their way to Mainz, but offers no supporting evidence.
[2] Vogt, *Verfall*, p. 210.
[3] Ibid., p. 210. *Mainzer Chronik aus der Zeit von 1767 bis 1782*, ed. Franz Heerdt (Mainz, 1879).
[4] *Denkwürdigkeiten des Generals Eickemeyer*, ed. Heinrich Koenig (Frankfurt am Main, 1845), p. 50.

more frequently. Public examinations were held to convince the suspicious public of 'the value, purity and orthodoxy of the school-system'.[1] The Commission set up to deal with the ex-Jesuits' estates could devote the proceeds only to the maintenance of the former owners, the costs of the new schools and the improvement of the seminary. So great was Emmerich Joseph's desire to avoid the suspicion of having benefited from the dissolution, that he forbade the exchequer to buy any of the excellent wine of the former noviciate.[2]

These attempts to improve public relations were fruitless; Steigentesch was the first to be burned in effigy on the death of his master. The public examinations at the schools served only to confirm their belief in the heretical nature of the proceedings. Eickemeyer described how at one of them he set a pupil a mathematical problem which involved the use of addition symbols. This at least was one sign the illiterate audience understood and a peasant roared from the back of the room: 'Go on and make crosses, make lots of them, the devil will get you anyway!'[3] The anti-clerical opinions of Bentzel and Steigentesch, as well as those of the teachers in the new schools such as Isenbiehl, Schwarz and Metternich, were well-known and the people refused to believe their protestations of orthodoxy.

As might have been expected, the clergy played a prominent part in fomenting discontent. In January 1773, Steigentesch complained to the Elector that Father Peter Conrad had attacked the Schools Commission in the most objectionable fashion in a sermon delivered at the Church of St Christopher. The Elector called for a report from the Vicariate and a copy of Conrad's sermon was obtained. Its style was certainly inflammatory. After a long purple passage on the golden age of faith and the godlessness of the present, he turned his fire on the College of Education:

> Is it not the greatest absurdity, folly and stupidity to use books whose authors are either well-known heretics or who don't even dare to put their names on the title pages; is it not the greatest absurdity, folly and stupidity to appoint as a teacher and instructor in the Faith, a man of whom one only knows that he is a worshipper of nature and a depraved scoundrel – Christ took pity on the children who are entrusted to such teachers: 'But whoso shall offend one of these little ones which believe in me, it were better for him that a millstone were hanged about his neck, and that he were drowned in the depth of the sea' [Matthew 18, 6]; and finally is it not the greatest absurdity, folly and stupidity to cast doubts on what has been believed for 1700 years and to ignore Holy Scripture, the Holy Fathers and many councils of the Church?[4]

Conrad was briskly despatched to the clerical prison at Marienborn, although he was released shortly afterwards and sent to the rural parish at

---

[1] Hainebach, *Studien*, p. 19. Wilhelm Herse, *Kurmainz am Vorabend der Revolution* (Berlin Dissertation, 1907), p. 32.
[2] Livet, *Recueil*, p. 227.   [3] Eickemeyer, *Denkwürdigkeiten*, p. 50.
[4] Vienna *MEA*, GK, Fasc. 37.

Trechtlingshausen.[1] It is clear that he enjoyed the support of his flock, for after his arrest a petition was sent to the Elector from the churchwardens and 'all the parishioners' of St Christopher's, citing Conrad's excellence as a priest, his beautiful services, his restoration of the parochial finances and his devotion to duty, and pleading for his release from custody.[2]

Another influential priest in Mainz was Hermann Goldhagen, S.J., who was a prolific publisher of educational works, though not of a kind likely to win the approval of Bentzel. His devotional anthology, entitled 'A Little Primer against the Danger of the Age, for a Pious Life and a Blessed Death' and published in 1772, launched a bitter attack on the present age 'where a shameless dissolute way of life has become the fashion and many people rush with bound eyes towards certain death and the hell which will just as certainly follow after'.[3] There could be little doubt as to the target of his fire and brimstone.

The rural peasantry, when they did find a means of expression, showed the same stolid conservatism as their fellow-countrymen in Mainz. In 1769 the Elector published an ordinance which drastically reduced the number of holy festivals observed in the Electorate. Some were abolished, others moved to Sundays. The reduction was based on the decline of the religious element in the festivals to the point where they were merely extra holidays: 'laudable enthusiasm has become light-hearted indifference and rest from manual labour has become sinful idleness'. As an essential corollary, the festivals which remained were made purely religious occasions and a further ordinance forbade any public merry-making.[4] Despite the religious phraseology of the ordinances, the motive of the Elector appears to have been economic. Although eighteen festivals had been abolished or moved, the peasants declined to take the opportunity to increase their wealth by honest labour. Accordingly, six months later it was ordered that on the former festivals the peasants were to perform labour services for the community, building roads and the like.[5] Predictably they resisted and a chronicler recorded in 1770 'Many were driven with blows and fines to work, until they got used to it.'[6] The superstitious peasants also doubted the orthodoxy of the new measures and blamed them for the poor harvests of 1770 and 1771.[7]

The peasants received another opportunity to parade their dislike of

---

[1] Messer, *Reform*, pp. 166–7.   [2] Vienna, *MEA*, GK, Fasc. 37.
[3] Hermann Goldhagen, *Denkbüchlein gegen die Gefahren der Zeit, um fromm zu leben und selig zu sterben* (Mainz, 1772).
[4] A. L. Veit, 'Emmerich Joseph von Breidbach-Bürresheim, Erzbischof von Mainz (1763–1774), und die Verminderung der Feiertage', *Festschrift Sebastian Merkle* Düsseldorf (1922). Vienna, *MEA*, GK, Fasc. 69, 356, 376.
[5] Ibid. Fasc. 69 (ii), 63.   [6] Heerdt, *Mainzer Chronik*.
[7] Veit, *Verminderung der Feiertage*, p. 364.

innovation when the new school system was introduced to the country. When Mathias Metternich, a graduate of the new College of Education, was sent to teach at the village of Dromersheim, he reported that very few children went to school and on one occasion none at all had turned up. He also wrote of the 'raging hostility' towards the new teaching methods and of the 'scoffers, who ought to be punished, who spread it around that the method is heretical'. His colleague at Hechtsheim complained to the School Commission that the villagers threw stones at him in the streets and refused to send their children to 'the new learning' as they called it.[1]

VI

Popular opposition to Emmerich Joseph's reforms could find only primitive expression in hostile demonstrations and passive resistance and was unlikely to have any influence on the government. It became a much more serious threat when allied with the Cathedral Chapter, the self-styled estates of the Electorate. A major clash between the Elector and the Chapter was delayed until 1772, although a few incidents before then had indicated worsening relations. In 1765, for example, Emmerich Joseph abolished the canons' exemption from the bridge-toll and promised instead an unspecified cash payment from the exchequer. The cessation of this and other exemptions was necessary for 'the preservation of the well-being of the country'.[2] It appears that a series of small incidents such as this led to a permanent souring of relations, for in 1767 Emmerich Joseph told the Austrian ambassador, Count Neipperg, that for some time he had been on bad terms with the Chapter.[3] He mentioned specifically that the canons had attempted to interfere with his conduct of imperial affairs. They had claimed that the rights of the Archchancellor of the Empire formed an inalienable possession of the Electorate and that therefore any action which might lead to their diminution came within the scope of the Chapter.[4] The real struggle began on 30 July 1771, with the publication of the 'Ordinance of His Electoral Grace of Mainz, Concerning the Monasteries of the Electoral Lands'.

The monasteries in Mainz presented a large target to the reformers. In the Electorate as a whole there were 96 monasteries and convents; in the city of Mainz alone ten monasteries, eight convents and nine collegiate

[1] Messer, *Reform*, pp. 57–66, 69.
[2] Vienna, *MEA*, GK, Fasc. 43, 238. Cf. a dispute over a petition from the lower clergy: Ibid. Fasc. 32, 349.
[3] Vienna, *Staka*, Fasc. 155, 142.
[4] By the capitulation of election the Elector was required to seek the consent of the Chapter for the alienation of any part of the Electorate, although this clause was clearly intended to apply to real estate only.

foundations.¹ Most were exceedingly well-endowed and it would appear from contemporary exposés that Mammon had tempted many of their members away from the Rule. Eickemeyer depicted them as debauched, drunken, lecherous and superstitious.² He was admittedly a very biased observer, but his hostile observations were confirmed by other reports. In 1765 Thomas Pennant observed that at the Carthusian house in Mainz 'Wine is sold here as in a tavern; many rooms being filled with company, tho' Sunday; the dress of the monks was a good fine cloth; and their cells elegant so that they seem to deviate much from their old austerity.'³ Dr John Moore, accompanying the Duke of Hamilton on his Grand Tour, wrote of the monks and friars:

However good Christians they might be, many of them had much the appearance of paying occasional homage to the ancient heathen deity Bacchus, without being restrained in their worship like the soldiers on parade in Mannheim. – One of them in particular appeared to have just arisen from this devotion – he moved along in the most unconcerned manner imaginable, without observing any direct course, or regarding whether he went to the right hand or to the left. He muttered to himself as he went – Does he repeat his pater-noster? said I – I rather imagine he prays from Horace, replied the D[uke] –

Quo me, Bacche, rapis tui
Plenum? Quae nemora, aut quos agor in specus
*Velox mente nova?*⁴

Outside the city of Mainz the wealthiest and the most celebrated monastery was the ancient Benedictine foundation at Eberbach in the Rheingau, where in 1780 Risbeck found magnificently furnished rooms, billiard tables, an excellent hunt, 'half-a-dozen beautiful singing-women' and 'a stupendous wine-cellar, the well-ranged batteries of which made me shudder'.⁵ It was to this sort of situation that Emmerich Joseph turned his attention in 1771, 'convinced of the disorders which ruled in the monasteries'.⁶

It is clear that a good deal of preparatory work had been done and a few preliminary decrees should have warned the monks of what was coming. In 1769 all monastic houses were forbidden to admit any new novices without the express permission of the Elector; to ensure observance the Vicariate was to draw up a list of the complement of each house, with the name, age and date of first vows of each member. A later directive instructed the Vicariate to discover the original number of members when

---

[1] Herse, *Kurmainz*, p. 23. Karl Klein, 'Mainz unter dem Kurfürsten Emmerich Joseph', *Mainzer Wochenblatt*, January 15–17, 20 (1869).
[2] Eickemeyer, *Denkwürdigkeiten*, p. 42.
[3] Thomas Pennant, *Tour on the Continent in 1765*, ed. Sir G. R. de Beer (London, 1948), p. 141.
[4] John Moore, *A View of the Society and Manners in France, Switzerland and Germany*, vol. 1 (London, 1779), p. 407.
[5] J. K. Risbeck, *Travels through Germany*, vol. 3 (London, 1787), p. 238.
[6] Vienna, *MEA*, GK, Fasc. 43, 417.

each establishment was founded or admitted to the Electorate. In 1770 the visitation of the large and wealthy monastery of Amorbach was ordered.[1] It had forty-three members and an annual income of 20,000 gulden; indeed the investigating commission found the secular affairs of the monasteries to be in 'the most flourishing state'. The spiritual condition of Amorbach however left much to be desired. The Prior was found guilty of favouritism, neglect of duties in the choir, slackness in the maintenance of discipline and of entertaining relations of a suspicious nature with the younger brothers. The commission advised that he be deposed at once. The other brothers also had many faults; Pater Willibald, for example, was generally considered to be the father of the illegitimate child of a village girl. Armed with statistical information and evidence of monastic shortcomings, the Elector went to work.

The ordinance published on 30 July 1771 was divided into four sections, each of which posed a definite threat to the continued existence of the Electorate's monastic houses.[2] The first dealt with the strict observance of the Rule – 'the best guide to monastic perfection'. The Rule was to be enforced rigorously: within six months heads of orders were to send in their constitutions and rules, together with an account of abuses which had crept in and suggestions for improvement. The second forbad the frequent practice of monks assuming the functions of parish priests and living outside their monasteries. Those who had done so were to return immediately. No monk was to leave his house unless accompanied by a colleague and under no circumstances was he to stay away longer than three weeks. The third section was a more direct assault. Over-expansion of numbers had led to pressure on resources and thus to abuses. The spiritual blackmail of dying men, to secure their estates, was cited as one example. Too much wealth, moreover, destroyed the very fibre of religious life. In future therefore no superior could accept money or any other goods from a novice, only subjects of the Electorate could be admitted and the number fixed at the time of foundation could not be exceeded. The final section was a further restriction on numbers. As, according to the Rule, only those with a true vocation might take vows, novices were to be at least twenty-three years old and were to be examined more severely.

Although all provisions of the ordinance were supported by reference to the decrees of the Council of Trent, the monks and their supporters rightly viewed its severity as a frontal assault on their position. Their worst suspicions were confirmed when a new amortisation law was published the following year.[3] As its framers were at pains to point out in the preamble, similar measures had been regularly enacted and regularly ignored.[4] But the severity and scope of the new law placed it in a different class alto-

[1] Ibid. Fasc. 72b.   [2] Ibid. Fasc. 43, 503.   [3] Ibid.   [4] See above, pp. 104–5.

gether. Henceforth no subject of the Electorate might bequeath any goods, moveable or immoveable, to monastic establishments. They in turn were forbidden to acquire such goods, whether by purchase or by foreclosing on mortgages. All title-deeds to property acquired since the law of 1615 were to be examined by electoral officials. If they did not constitute a valid *titulum possessionis* – that is including the permission of the Elector of the day – the land concerned was to be confiscated. Collegiate foundations were exempted, for the money paid to their members re-entered the economy and did not lie fallow in 'dead hands'. Acquisitions made in contravention of this ordinance were to be confiscated and a fine of 500 gulden was to be imposed on the offending monastery. Anyone who informed on an illegal purchase was to receive a third of the value of the goods concerned, 'together with concealment of his name'. A final clause struck at the traditional self-sufficiency of the monastic community and also revealed a political outlook potentially dangerous for all the other corporate bodies of the Electorate:

As it is contrary to a well-organised constitution if in a state individual groups are formed, which cut themselves off from general trade and industry in the supply of necessities, and at the same time think of themselves as separate states, it must be regarded as an intolerable encroachment and burden on the citizen's livelihood if the alms-collecting of various monasteries falls on the country-dwellers; if others intrude on secular professions by producing their own wine and administering their own estates and if many abbeys, religious houses and monasteries pursue almost all trades within their walls.

If the two ordinances were rigorously enforced – and there was every indication that they would be – the future of the monasteries was bleak indeed. A commission consisting of councillor Graccher and Georg Adam Freiherr von Fechenbach was set up to supervise the enforcement of the law.[1] Graccher had played a prominent part in the preparation and promulgation of the amortisation law and was fond of such remarks as 'the preservation of the whole is always more important than the preservation of the parts'. The commission soon encountered non-cooperation from the Vicariate, inefficiency from local officials and evasion from the monasteries. The Carthusians of Grünau applied to the commission for permission to keep a legacy and sought to strengthen their case by presenting the commissioners with six ducats. Untempted, they reported the matter to the Elector, who passed the six ducats on to the poorhouse and fined the Carthusians 100 ducats more, payable within fourteen days. Other monasteries opposed the ordinances more subtly. A group of Benedictine houses complained to the Congregation of Regular Clergy in Rome,

---

[1] Illich, *Maßnahmen*, p. 60ff. Dr Illich's account is based on the documents in the *Bayerischen Staatsarchiv* at Würzburg.

which called on the Mainz General Vicariate to explain its actions. On the instructions of the Elector, the Vicariate replied that it did not recognise the Congregation's right to interfere in the state's internal affairs.[1] The Cathedral Vicar Feuerstein decided on a more flamboyant protest. He built a hermitage in his garden and placed inside it statues of St Ignatius and St Bruno, holding copies of the ordinance of 1771. The offending documents bore the legend 'The Lord God knows nothing of this'. Threatened with imprisonment, Feuerstein apologised.[2] The Elector could afford to disregard eccentric forms of discontent of this kind, but the Chapter's counter-attack could not be ignored.

The first wave was a long remonstrance despatched to the Elector on 1 July 1772.[3] The canons argued that to forbid the monasteries to acquire property was to condemn them to death; to require them to prove the validity of title-deeds to property acquired since 1615 was manifestly unjust, for many had been destroyed by wars and natural disasters. They also voiced the fear that other German rulers would quickly follow suit, which would have serious consequences for all Mainz religious institutions owning property in other principalities – and not least of all the Cathedral Chapter itself.

As the remonstrance was written in respectful and courteous language, Emmerich Joseph may have thought that their opposition would not be serious. But simultaneously the Chapter had made a bold raid behind the Elector's lines. On 1 July they had instructed two of their members – the canon Georg Karl Freiherr von Fechenbach and the domicellar Hugo Franz Freiherr von Kerpen – and two of their officials – Bernard Gottfried Reider and Philipp Adam von Schultheiss – not to take part in any further legislation relating to the monasteries.[4] All four held posts in the secular government and had been intimately connected with the promulgation of the two ordinances. It was customary for members and officials of the Chapter to serve the state and both von Reider and von Schultheiss had obtained its prior permission to do so. Intentionally or not, the Chapter's attempt to suspend their loyalty to the state was a direct challenge to the Elector's authority. In fact the canons had miscalculated, for all four immediately referred the Chapter's orders to the Elector and asked him for further instructions.

At the time Emmerich Joseph was suffering from a serious illness, caused no doubt by his intemperate habits, although Count Neipperg believed it to be psychosomatic, a result of the strain caused by his long altercation

---

[1] Livet, *Recueil*, p. 227.
[2] Vogt, *Verfall*, p. 213.
[3] Vienna, *MEA*, Fasc. 43, 446. Würzburg, *MDP*, vol. 63, 1541.
[4] Vienna, *MEA*, GK, Fasc. 43, 450ff. Würzburg, *MDP*, vol. 63, 1541.

with the Chapter.¹ He was still well enough to summon a deputation from the Chapter, to berate them for their conduct, to forbid them to do anything further until he was fully recovered and to threaten to counter disobedience with force.² He also referred the matter to his two chief ministers – Groschlag and Bentzel – for a report. It appears that it had been the former who had been mainly responsible for the measures against the monasteries. In 1772 Hardenberg recorded in his memoires: 'Groschlag carries great weight with the Elector and has made all the arrangements for the reduction of the festivals and the restriction of the clergy, but he is very much hated by the latter.'³

Groschlag was certainly anti-clerical but he protested that he was not anti-religious. At the height of the amortisation dispute he wrote to his brother-in-law, Count Pergen, that he had always observed the external forms of the Catholic religion and that no man was in a position to judge the state of his soul; he continued: 'Unfortunately we live in an age in which the principles of our holy religion are confused with the vile interests of the priests and monks...Attachment to monasticism is often taken for religion itself. One is held to be irreligious if one opposes various scandalous practices, which are infamously used by religious orders to get money and privileges, and by which they seek to oppress the people and keep them in a state of beggary.'⁴ Groschlag's letters to Pergen reveal the bitterness which had crept into the struggle. He wrote of a 'war' between Elector and Chapter, blaming the canons' 'infamous' conduct on the pernicious influence of the monks, the fanaticism of the 'mad' provost (von Eltz), bribery and imbecility.

It was in this sort of mood that Groschlag sat down to write his report. Both he and Bentzel informed their master that while the Chapter might present remonstrances, their attempts to subvert the loyalty of his officials was nothing less than an 'appeal to rebellion'.⁵ They advised that the Chapter be proceeded against with all severity –'if [the Canons] do not see the injustice of the measures they have taken and correct them, then these must be countered with the necessary archiepiscopal and sovereign power'.⁶

Accepting their advice, the Elector sent three communications to the Chapter on 30 August.⁷ In the first he dismissed the objections contained in their remonstrance by reference to 'the true best of the working population, as the main pillar of every state'. In the other two he turned his attention to the attempt to subvert his ministers. Although he omitted Bentzel's and Groschlag's discourse on the constitutional issues involved, his tone

---

¹ Vienna, *Staka*, Fasc. 167, 468.   ² Ibid., 480.
³ *Denkwürdigkeiten des Staatskanzlers Fürsten von Hardenberg bis zum Jahre 1806*, ed. Leopold von Ranke (Leipzig, 1877), vol. 1, p. 23.
⁴ Vienna, *Reika*, Fasc. 21, 235.   ⁵ Vienna, *MEA*, GK, Fasc. 43, 412, 420.
⁶ Ibid., 414.   ⁷ Ibid., 476, 478, 480.

matched theirs. At first, he wrote, he would demand only an explanation of their actions, but 'would clearly be entitled to take immediately the measures available to us by virtue of our power and dignity'.[1] It is difficult to see how the Chapter could have resisted this thinly-veiled threat of force. The canons and officials concerned had made it clear that their first loyalty was to the Elector and the state. The Chapter might have appealed to the imperial courts but, in view of the mood prevailing in Vienna in 1772, it was highly improbable that they would have secured a favourable judgment.

What in fact ensued is best described in Bentzel's own words:

Today, the second of September, 1772, towards five-o'clock in the afternoon, the Right Reverend Dean von Dalberg, together with the canons Franz von Dalberg, von Metternich and von Bibra, arrived at the electoral *Favorite*, the Elector's summer residence, for an audience, and after they had been admitted by His Electoral Grace, the Dean declared that the entire Cathedral Chapter laid itself at the Elector's feet and that, in the monthly assembly of the Chapter held today, it had been decided that the orders given to the electoral councillor von Kerpen, and the ecclesiastical councillor Schultheiss some time ago should be revoked; and that the Dean and the other deputed canons here present had been instructed to inform the Elector, to his due satisfaction, and to request him to forget all that was past and to grant the Chapter the former electoral grace and favour.[2]

The Elector replied that he was very pleased to hear this and that he would restore his favour to the Chapter, hoping that in future they would behave properly and show themselves worthy of his trust. The delegation then left. Bentzel's meticulous record of the afternoon's events is understandable; it was a famous victory.

When von Groschlag cast aspersions on the integrity and the sanity of the canons who opposed him, he also mentioned that the most sensible of them were scandalised by their colleagues' behaviour.[3] This suggests that the Chapter was not monolithic in its opposition to the Elector, but the exact number of dissenters cannot be established. The minutes of the Chapter record only 'concluded unanimously' or 'concluded by a majority'. Yet on 15 July Karl Theodor von Dalberg and Franz Philipp von Walderdorff made separate declarations in the Chapter, dissociating themselves from the majority's decisions to put pressure on the members and servants in the Electorate's service. Dalberg called it an 'encroachment' on the Archbishop's powers and Walderdorff argued that the Chapter had only the power to remonstrate.[4] These two, together with the General Vicar von der Leyen, had been named by the French ambassador as a group favoured by the Elector and on particularly friendly terms with Groschlag.[5] Sophie La Roche also referred to Dalberg as an 'intimate friend'

[1] Ibid., 478.
[2] Ibid., 488.
[3] Vienna, *Reika*, Fasc. 21, 270.
[4] Würzburg, *MDP*, vol. 63, 1564.
[5] Livet, *Recueil*, p. 195.

of Groschlag.[1] However, they were all young men, had been full canons for only a few years and were unlikely to carry much weight in the General Assembly of the Chapter.

Even after its submission, the Chapter continued to make hostile noises. The canons repeatedly asked for 'more information' about the amortisation ordinance until an exasperated Elector told them he would discuss the matter no further.[2] The monastic commission continued to harass the monks: in 1773 the houses of the Dominicans of Mainz and Frankfurt, and of the Carthusians and Capuchins of Mainz were inspected.[3] The Benedictines of Seligenstadt resisted the commission and sent two of their members to Vienna to enlist imperial support. The investigation of the monastery was carried on regardless.[4] Indeed there was every indication that the Elector was preparing to go further; the smell of secularisation was in the air. As early as 1771 the Schools Commission had suggested that if all else failed a monastery could and should be dissolved to provide the funds for the new schools.[5] In 1773 an anonymous *pro-memoria* proposed the secularisation of the Cistercian abbey of Schönthal an der Jagst and the devotion of the annual income of 40,000 gulden to public projects.[6]

The canons had retired to lick their wounds, but they were resting, not dying, and at the beginning of 1774 they re-emerged to offer combat again. This time the occasion was the disposal of the estates of the ex-Jesuits. Emmerich Joseph had intended that the very considerable amount of land and money involved should form a fund for the newly reformed grammar schools, and set up a commission to administer the fund, headed by the canon Damian von der Leyen.[7] The commissioner recommended that the small and scattered estates of the Jesuits, where the income did not justify the costs of administration, should be sold and the money realised invested.[8] At the beginning of 1774 the Chapter's own exchequer recommended that a number of these estates be bought. The canons' reaction was swift and positive; not only did they forbid their officials to buy any of the estates, they also called for a report on the legality of the sale and requested the Elector to stop the auctions.[9] The Elector explained that it was in the interest of the fund itself to sell some of the smaller estates and declined to halt the sale.[10]

From this point the conflict escalated rapidly and the original issue was soon forgotten. The Chapter claimed that the estates of the Jesuits formed

[1] *Lettres de Sophie de La Roche à C.-M. Wieland*, ed. V. Michel (Paris, 1938), p. 58.
[2] Vienna, *MEA*, GK, Fasc. 43, 494–500.
[3] Ibid. Fasc. 72b. See also, Johannes Simmert, *Die Geschichte der Kartause zu Mainz*, Beiträge zur Geschichte der Stadt Mainz, vol. 16 (Mainz, 1958).
[4] Paris, vol. 64, 38.
[5] Messer, *Reform*, pp. 91–2.
[6] Vienna, *MEA*, GK, Fasc. 72b.
[7] Ibid. Fasc. 75.
[8] Vienna, *Reika*, Fasc. 21, 375.
[9] Würzburg, *MDP*, vol. 64, 732.
[10] Vienna, *Reika*, Fasc. 21, 359–60.

an inalienable part of the Electorate and that therefore they could not be disposed of without their consent. The canons also claimed that their consent was necessary for all matters affecting the Church, the Elector's successor, the Chapter and education. This somewhat arbitrary choice of topics represented a revolutionary expansion of the Chapter's rights, for – as the Elector rightly pointed out – the capitulation of election required that their consent be obtained only in case of alienation of part of the Electorate and new taxation or borrowing. The original issue was obscured further when the Chapter took the opportunity to attack the new school system as well.[1]

As the battle was fought out on paper, it appeared unlikely that the Chapter would make any progress. The Elector agreed to send the canons any documents they might require about the Jesuit estates, but refused to stop the auctions or to admit the necessity of obtaining their consent.[2] Yet the canons displayed much more resolution than they had done during the dispute over the monastic legislation. They announced that they would hold all officials working on the Jesuit affairs responsible for their actions, thus indicating their intention of punishing them when Emmerich Joseph died.[3] Emmerich Joseph claimed later that this had led immediately to the spread of 'deplorable discontent' among his officials. The Chapter also threatened that if the estates were sold without its consent it would regard the sale as illegal, publish a declaration to this effect and take any necessary legal steps. This could be taken as a warning to potential purchasers of the estates that they would be dispossessed by the Chapter on the death of the Elector. In a later general remonstrance to the Emperor, Emmerich Joseph also raised the spectre of mob support for the Chapter's demands. Doubtless this was a calculated appeal to Joseph II's authoritarian instincts, although other sources confirm that there was truth in the claim. As early as July 1772 Count Neipperg had reported: 'These continuing disputes between the Elector and his Cathedral Chapter make a very bad impression on the people here, who are discontented about both the abolition of the festivals and the edict issued against the monasteries, but who are especially and greatly enraged by the ministry here. The latter is generally accused of possessing little inclination for religion and of taking instead every opportunity to incite their master in an exaggerated fashion against the clergy. These unfortunate rumours are whispered against the ministry in every part of the country.'[4] In February 1774 the French ambassador, the Marquis d'Entraigues, had reported that the Chapter had decided to take the matter to the *Reichshofrat* in Vienna.[5]

[1] Ibid., 361–74.
[2] Ibid., 375–6. Paris, vol. 64, 85.
[3] Vienna, *Reika*, Fasc. 21, 375.
[4] Vienna, *Staka*, Fasc. 167, 480.
[5] Paris, vol. 64, 33.

Enlightened absolutism, 1743–74

The evidence of their various remonstrances suggests that the Chapter's opposition to the Elector's policies was both political and ideological. It is clear that they were strongly motivated by a desire to restrict the power of the Elector and make good their claim to be the estates of the realm. It is equally clear that most of the canons felt strongly that both the clergy and the Roman Catholic religion were threatened by Emmerich Joseph's educational and monastic reforms. This was well illustrated by the bizarre incident of the Eltz dinner party in July 1772. The height of the amortisation dispute happened to coincide with the election of a new dean of the Chapter. At first it appeared that there would be only two candidates – the elder von Dalberg and Franz Philipp von Franckenstein – but then a third – Philipp Karl von Hoheneck – emerged in rather extraordinary circumstances. Count Neipperg reported that on 26 July Hoheneck rode out to Hettersheim to dine with Hugo Franz von Eltz, the leader of the conservative party in the Chapter, and two monks. 'The wine and their enthusiasm for preserving the privileges of the clergy' brought the company into a state of high excitement. The meal reached a dramatic climax when Eltz seized Hoheneck's hand, kissed it, and cried *'Ecce Salvator Ecclesiae Moguntinae!* This man is the only prop of our Holy Church! If we didn't have him it would certainly collapse – the Elector is a really good man; but Cardinal Groschlag and the *Auditor Rotae* Bentzel ruin him; these two alone are responsible for the campaign against the clergy – I am sorry for the Elector's poor soul whenever I think of how he has been led astray by the two of them! and if only that were all! but even our young and innocent canons and domicellars are being used for such godless business!' The provost then filled his glass and continued: 'Let every true Christian drink this toast with me: *Vivat Salvator Ecclesiae Moguntinae et pereant Cardinalis Groschlag et Auditor Rotae!*' Neipperg observed caustically that the guests lost no time in identifying themselves as true Christians.[1]

One reason for the increased determination of the Chapter may have been the powerful leadership provided by two of the canons – Friedrich Karl Freiherr von Erthal and Franz Philipp Freiherr von Franckenstein. D'Entraigues went as far as to say: 'This body [The Chapter] would never have thought of opposing [the Elector's measures] if it had not been set in motion by Baron Erthal, always fanatical and always opposed to everything done without him.'[2] As Emmerich Joseph bitterly complained to the Vice-Chancellor of the *Reich*, Prince Colloredo, he had favoured Erthal and Franckenstein in the past, making the former Treasurer of the Chapter and the latter President of the Exchequer.[3] Erthal had been the Mainz ambassador in Vienna and had returned in July 1773 to direct the Chap-

[1] Vienna, *Staka*, Fasc. 167, 484. [2] Paris, vol. 64, 85.
[3] Vienna, *Reika*, Fasc. 21, 393–6.

ter's campaign. Whatever his and Franckenstein's motives may have been, they were not entirely ideological. There was a strong odour of political intrigue.

In rejecting one of the Chapter's numerous remonstrances, the Elector had cast aspersions on the integrity of their protests and had suggested that they sprang from 'other sources'.[1] Although the situation is not altogether clear, it appears that Erthal and Franckenstein were working with the Imperial Vice-Chancellor Prince Colloredo and his son the Count, with the primary object of securing the dismissal of Bentzel and especially of Groschlag. The feud, which was of several years' standing, stemmed from Groschlag's supposed adherence to the court of Versailles and his ambition to succeed Prince Colloredo as Vice-Chancellor, a post coveted by Count Colloredo. Through his brother-in-law, Count Pergen, Groschlag made fervent protestations of his loyalty to the Austrian court and had also avowed that he would not accept the position of Vice-Chancellor, even if it were offered to him.[2] Even his friends did not believe him. A French report on the subject concluded: 'Groschlag has set his sights on Prince Colloredo's position, which is in the gift of the Elector; it is even said that he has received a sort of promise; he has deluded himself into thinking that he is entitled to the support of the Court of Vienna, on account of the services he has rendered, but he gave the game away; all the Austrian candidates for the post of Vice-Chancellor have worked unceasingly to discredit Baron Groschlag in the eyes of [Joseph II]; and Count Neipperg, Count Pergen's successor, provides them with both the opportunity and the means.'[3]

By exerting pressure on the Elector through the Chapter, the Colloredos hoped to discredit Groschlag's policies and secure his dismissal. It is not certain that Neipperg consciously assisted them. Relations between Mainz and Vienna were highly volatile throughout Emmerich Joseph's reign. Periods of relative calm would suddenly be disrupted by a violent dispute over the visitation of the *Reichskammergericht*, navigation of the Rhine or some other imperial matter. Neipperg came to the conclusion that the Elector was basically sound but that his natural inclination toward Austria was frequently disturbed by the machinations of Groschlag and Bentzel. In report after report he painted a picture of a decent but feeble ruler perverted by his evil ministry. Although this certainly gave the Colloredos ample opportunity to denigrate the Mainz ministers, it is unlikely that Neipperg was privy to the plan to use the dispute over the monastic legislation to get rid of them. He was in complete agreement with the monastic ordinance of 1771 and, while officially neutral in internal disputes, described the Chapter's actions in the amortisation controversy as 'im-

[1] Ibid., 365-8. [2] Ibid., 235. [3] Livet, *Recueil*, pp. 198-9.

proper'.¹ His hearty dislike of Groschlag and Bentzel did, however, play straight into the hands of the Elector's opposition. On their return from a conference with Count Colloredo at Frankfurt, Erthal and Franckenstein told Emmerich Joseph that they had nothing against him personally and were opposed only to his ministers.² Erthal and Franckenstein's help to the Colloredos was not disinterested; their rewards were to come later.

This combination of internal pressure from the Chapter and external pressure from Vienna was a potent weapon. The Elector's position was, however, stronger than it seemed. Firstly the Chapter was not united in its opposition. The Marquis d'Entraigues reported that six canons were either neutral or supporters of the Elector, identifying von der Leyen and von Hornstein, President of the School Commission, as members of the latter group.³ Von Dalberg also supported his patron and placed on record in the minutes his protest at the Chapter's course of action. He asserted that the Chapter had the right of advice but not of consent, expressed his support for the Elector's measures and ended with a panegyric of the new educational system.⁴ Secondly, Emmerich Joseph showed a great deal more resolution in defence of his ministry than had been expected. During the amortisation campaign Groschlag had written to von Pergen that he might have to save the Elector from himself, and d'Entraigues also doubted his determination.⁵ Yet he informed the Chapter and Vienna, directly and through the Austrian ambassador Count Metternich, that Groschlag and Bentzel enjoyed his complete confidence, that their policies were his policies and that he would not dismiss them.⁶

Faced with this situation and the danger of alienating an important prince of the Empire, Austrian policy, as opposed to the machinations of the Colloredo family, began to change. Early in 1774 Count Neipperg informed the Elector, Groschlag and Bentzel that, although it had been thought in Vienna that the Chapter had had a case at the outset, their subsequent conduct, in the face of the Elector's moderation, had incurred the disapproval of all courts and of all honest men.⁷ Encouraged by this realignment and perhaps exasperated by the increasingly aggressive tone of the Chapter's remonstrances, Emmerich Joseph launched his counter-attack. On 27 May 1774, he despatched a long and detailed account of the whole affair to Prince Colloredo, together with complete copies of the Chapter's remonstrances and replies.⁸ He asked the Vice-Chancellor to place the matter in the hands of the Emperor and demanded peace in the

---

¹ Vienna, *Staka*, Fasc. 166, 429, Fasc. 167, 480.   ² Vienna, *Reika*, Fasc. 21, 393–6.
³ Paris, vol. 64, 74, 105. Count Neipperg added the names of Damian von der Leyen and Franz Philipp von Walderdorff – Vienna *Staka*, Fasc. 167, 484.
⁴ Würzburg, *MDP*, vol. 64, 940.   ⁵ Vienna, *Reika*, Fasc. 21, 270. Paris, vol. 64, 80.
⁶ Ibid.   ⁷ Ibid., 85.
⁸ Vienna, *Reika*, Fasc. 21, 375ff.

Electorate, due respect, honour and security for his officials and satisfaction for the insults he had suffered. He hinted at a possible use of force when he mentioned his reluctance to resort to 'open steps'. In an accompanying personal letter he reminded Colloredo of the favours he had shown him and upbraided the ungrateful conduct of Erthal and Franckenstein. According to d'Entraigues a second and more direct assault was planned. Under another pretext, von der Leyen was to be sent to Vienna as a plenipotentiary minister to enlist the supoprt of Joseph II. If he succeeded in this he was to proceed to Rome to obtain a papal brief, which would forbid the Chapter to interfere in the Electorate's government, on pain of excommunication. Considering Joseph II's views on church reform and the desirability of retaining the support of the Elector of Mainz, the success of this project was certainly a possibility. It was never put to the test. Just before five o'clock on the afternoon of 11 June, Emmerich Joseph collapsed and died as he was about to enter his carriage for his daily drive.[1] Back in the saddle once more, the Chapter began at once to dismantle both his legislation and his ministry. The 'aristocratic reaction' had begun.

VII

In political terms the thirty years covered by the reigns of Johann Friedrich and Emmerich Joseph were a unity. This continuity was largely a result of the personal and ideological affinities of the men who ruled Mainz during the period. Although their links with the past were clear and acknowledged, their sense of innovation was also justified. Although many of their reforms were incomplete, even abortive, a fundamental change had occurred. Expressed most generally, this change was a secularisation of the political outlook of the Elector and his ministry and a divorce between the archiepiscopal and sovereign functions. In the electoral ordinances it found expression in the constant emphasis on the subjects' secular welfare (*Wohlfahrt*) as the proper end of political activity. In the eyes of the reformers this required the fullest possible exploitation of the Electorate's resources, both natural and human. Institutions and laws had to be judged by their contribution to public welfare, not by their antiquity or the prescriptive rights of the beneficiaries. Any groups, religious or secular, which hampered this galvanisation of the Electorate's energies by their selfish interests, had to be swept aside. The central objective was always utilitarian, always practical. In view of the prevailing ecclesiastical predominance, this was bound to be an anti-clerical operation. A great deal of ink has been expended on the problem of whether or not the 'Catholic Enlightenment' was also – consciously or unconsciously – anti-

---

[1] Vienna, *Staka*, Fasc. 175, 584.

Enlightened absolutism, 1743–74

Christian.[1] As the question has been very well-ventilated in the past and as the answer depends largely on the observer's religious stand-point, I do not propose to discuss it here.

It is necessary, however, to make one or two brief remarks in conclusion about the general motivation of the reforms, for the simple observation that they were 'practical' does not take one very far. It is customary to view most of the reforms of the 'enlightened despots' in terms of an attempt to increase their countries' military potential. This at least played no part in Mainz. The Electorate's size, resources and location meant that it could never be in a position to think of territorial expansion. The army of a couple of thousand played an important ceremonial role at court, was a useful source of employment for the Imperial Knights but was in military terms nothing more than a police force. Indeed there is no evidence that either of the two electors or their ministers entertained any military delusions of grandeur.

A related general interpretation of 'enlightened despotism' is that which singles out the fiscal motive for predominant status.[2] It is highly likely that this played a part in the electors' calculations: the attempt to expand the economy, to encroach on clerical exemption from taxation and to reduce monastic land-holdings all brought, or would have brought, the treasury substantial benefit. Revenue is not, however, an end in itself; the desire to accumulate money *per se* is a psychiatric disorder and one from which the two electors in question clearly did not suffer. Normally the act of collecting money is neutral, it is the object of expenditure which determines one's view of the agent. Doubtless there was a healthy streak of hedonism in the electors' fiscal concerns. They maintained luxurious courts and bestowed a large number of favours of various kinds on their relations, but no more so than their predecessors. Partly of course it was a question of having to pay off debts accumulated during the wars, although this was achieved with relative ease.

Even if there were more personal evidence available, in the form of diaries, correspondence or private memoranda, it would be impossible to 'prove' that this or that consideration was uppermost in the reformers' minds. From the content and the style of the various pieces of legislation, however, it seems reasonable to infer that they were influenced by contemporary enlightened thought. As the links between the Stadion circle and contemporary intellectuals can be established and as the latters' theories

---

[1] Compare, for example, the very different views of H. Brück, *Die rationalistischen Bestrebungen im katholischen Deutschland, besonders in den drei rheinischen Erzbistümern* (Mainz, 1865) and Sebastian Merkle, *Ausgewählte Aufsätze und Reden*, ed. Theobald Freudenberger (Würzburg, 1965).

[2] Charles Morazé, 'Finance et despotisme, essai sur les despotes éclairés', *Annales, Économies, Sociétés, Civilisations*, 3 (1948), 279–96.

are mirrored in the former's practice, it requires an unusual degree of scepticism to deny any connection. As in most German states it is very difficult to distinguish between 'intellectuals' and 'government' in Mainz, because outside the latter there was little, if any, intellectual activity. The university must be included as part of the government, since it enjoyed no independence and since the professors often doubled as officials. This close relationship between thought and action was at its most apparent in the episcopalist movement, but it is clearly discernible in other fields as well.

The Mainz reformers were not working in a vacuum. All over Germany greater and lesser princes were initiating the same kind of reforms. Particularly potent was the example set by Austria, not only because it was a great power with which the Electorate had always had close ties but also because the problems were similar in both countries. By the mid 1760s the development by Kaunitz and others of what later came to be known as 'Josephism' was well under way. An amortisation law for Lombardy was issued in 1766, the minimum age for the admission of monks was raised to twenty-four in 1770 and in the following year an amortisation law for the Austrian lands was put into force.[1] These parallel lines of development were to become even clearer in the course of the 1780s. It was not entirely one-way traffic: one of the earliest 'Josephist' measures in the Habsburg Monarchy was based on a Mainz model, and it also appears that Count Pergen's educational plans were much influenced by his experience in the Electorate.[2]

In the second half of the eighteenth century most of the ecclesiastical states made strenuous efforts to catch up with their secular counterparts. In many cases they were consciously following a pattern already laid down by Stadion and his successors. In 1774 it seemed that just as these other states were beginning to reform, Mainz was going into reverse, for the untimely death of Emmerich Joseph marked the end of an era. For the majority of the Electorate's subjects events had moved too far too fast and certainly, in relation to its background, the programme of episcopalist, educational, economic and ecclesiastical reform was decidedly radical. In the sense that its members reflected the aspirations of the people, the Cathedral Chapter now at last made good its claim to be the estates of the Electorate, although – as events were to show – the canons' motives were by no means purely ideological. The Interregnum was to show how powerful an alliance between popular and aristocratic conservatism could be.

[1] Ferdinand Maass, *Der Josephinismus*, vol. 1 (Vienna, 1951), p. 54, vol. 2 (Vienna, 1953), pp. 11, 18–24.
[2] Ferdinand Maass, *Der Frühjosephinismus* (Vienna, Munich, 1969), p. 14. Rössler, *Stadion*, p. 87.

4

1774: The aristocratic reaction

The immediate reaction to the death of the Elector was aristocratic neither in style nor in substance. The long-repressed opposition of the common people to the enlightened reforms welled up and overflowed. A crowd of citizens gathered outside the lodgings of the director of the College of Education, J. F. Steigentesch, and demanded that he be handed over to them. It appears that he had sensed the imminent demise of his master, for his landlord informed the mob that their prey had left the city two days previously, with all his belongings. The frustrated lynching party then proceeded to erect a gallows in the street and to hang and burn Steigentesch in effigy.[1] They also took revenge on the director's pupils, severely mishandling those unfortunate enough to be caught on the streets. On this and succeeding days the desire of the bulk of the population to return to the old orthodoxy was well demonstrated. Pamphlets attacking the previous régime appeared: 'For all too long the devil has sat at his spinning wheel and the rope, by which we would all have been choked, was almost ready.'[2]

The Chapter's response was delayed until the following morning (12 June) but it was no less violent. Appropriately, its first legislative action as supreme ruler of the Electorate was to abolish the Schools Commission as 'contrary to the capitulation [of election] and the constitution'.[3] A new commission under the chairmanship of Friedrich Karl von Erthal, the leader of the opposition to the late Elector's education reforms, was set up to examine the existing system and to recommend ways of avoiding 'the moral dangers', to which the school-children were presently exposed. Acting on the Commission's advice, the Chapter proceeded to restore the status quo as it had existed before Bentzel began his work. On 17 June the ex-Jesuit Hermann Goldhagen was made temporary prefect of the schools. Although the decision as to whether ecclesiastical control of education

---

[1] *Denkwürdigkeiten des Generals Eickemeyer*, ed. Heinrich Koenig (Frankfurt am Main, 1845), p. 53.
[2] Wilhelm Herse, *Kurmainz am Vorabend der Revolution* (Berlin Dissertation, 1907), p. 35.
[3] Vienna, *MEA*, GK, Fasc. 71. This fascicle contains the minutes of the Chapter during the Interregnum. There is no pagination. The minutes can also be found at Würzburg, *MDP*, vol. 64.

was to be restored permanently was left to the next Elector, the canons struck a final blow when they abolished the College of Education on 12 July.[1]

Simultaneously the canons conducted a purge of the teaching staff of the new schools. On the day after Emmerich Joseph's death four teachers at the Grammar School, a University professor and Steigentesch were suspended. During the next few days several more were suspended and/or interrogated.[2] This abrupt change in official policy dismayed many educated people in the city, according to the Marquis d'Yves; he reported to his uncle that they hastened to hide papers and books which the new régime might consider offensive.[3]

At the same time the Chapter turned its attention to the monastic and amortisation ordinances. On the day after Emmerich Joseph's death the Commission which had been set up to enforce them was abolished. Two days later the Vicariate was instructed to examine the two ordinances and to mark any clauses contrary to the Electorate's constitution or otherwise objectionable. A similar order was issued to the secular government. Predictably, the Vicariate found much that was objectionable and recommended that the amortisation law be suspended and the monastic law radically altered. The Chapter confirmed the first recommendation but called for a more detailed report on the second.[4]

As in their assault on the new schools, the canons accompanied their legislative demolition by disciplinary action against the officials responsible. On 12 June the ecclesiastical councillors Schultheiss and Schumann, who had played a prominent part in the promulgation of the two ordinances, were suspended and all documents concerning their activities were sent to the suffragan bishop for a report. Two weeks later, tired of their uncertain position, they asked that they be either reinstated or proceeded against legally. The Chapter promptly dismissed them and told them to seek reinstatement from the next Elector.[5]

The last major piece of the late Elector's legislation to which the canons turned their attention was the fund consisting of the sequestered estates of the ex-Jesuits. The Commission set up to administer the fund was instructed to send in all its documents for investigation. It is not clear what the Chapter's final intentions were, for the interregnum was over before it had a chance to act, but it did demonstrate its sympathy for the former Jesuits in other ways. On 13 June they were allowed to return to the city from which they had been so brusquely removed the previous autumn, and ten days later were readmitted to their old college. Hopes of a complete

---

[1] Vienna, *MEA*, GK, Fasc. 71.
[2] Vienna, *MEA*, GK, Fasc. 71; *Staka*, Fasc. 175, 586–9; B. Seuffert, 'Wielands Schüler vor der Inquisition', *Euphorion*, 3 (1896), pp. 377–87, 726–34.
Vienna, *Staka*, Fasc. 175, 586.   [4] Vienna, *MEA*, GK, Fasc. 71.   [5] Ibid.

1774: The aristocratic reaction

restoration of their former position were encouraged when the Chapter ordered the Vicariate to report on whether the most able of the former Jesuits could be used as schoolteachers and whether others might be entrusted with parochial duties. Again, the election intervened before the report could be presented, although the petition of an individual ex-Jesuit to preach again was granted.[1]

On a lower level the Chapter intervened in individual cases to censure some priests or to pardon others convicted by the previous régime. On 12 June the priest Heittersdorff was ordered to stop the over-frequent visits of females to his house and to keep his newly-erected back-doors locked until further notice, while on the same day the priest Gertler was released from custody in the Mainz seminary and sent back to his parish at Bingen, where he was 'so loved and needed'. The interregnum had not been underway long before the case of the turbulent priest Peter Conrad,[2] smouldering in exile at Trechtlingshausen, was brought to the Chapter's attention. In a strongly-worded petition Conrad asserted his innocence, called on the Vicariate for support, alleged that Bentzel had been both his accuser and his judge and demanded repayment of his costs and restitution as priest of St Christopher's in Mainz.[3] He received further support from his old parishioners when on the following day they petitioned for his return. Instructed to examine the matter, the Vicariate reported that Conrad had been imprisoned and banished on the special orders of the Elector and against the will of the Vicariate. They believed that Conrad could justly claim reinstatement but added that his replacement at St Christopher's had done nothing wrong. The Chapter decided to leave the problem to the next Elector.

While persecuting the minor officials of the previous régime, the Chapter had not forgotten their deceased enemy's chief ministers. The day before his master's death, Groschlag had confided to the Marquis d'Yves that the Elector's death would unleash a bitter struggle in the state and expressed fears about his own future.[4] In view of Groschlag and Bentzel's share in the anti-clerical legislation and their views on the Chapter's rôle in the Electorate[5] it is hardly surprising that the canons took advantage of their new-found power to humiliate them. On 12 June they ordered all officials wishing to remain in the service of the Electorate to reapply for their confirmation, and while they gave this confirmation to five dignitaries of the court immediately, they ignored Groschlag and Bentzel.[6] When on the same day Chancellor Bentzel went to the Chapter to ask for instructions, he was told that he would be sent for when his services were required.[7] In

[1] Ibid.
[2] See above, pp. 124–5.
[3] Vienna, *MEA*, GK, Fasc. 71.
[4] Vienna, *Staka*, Fasc. 175, 585.
[5] See above, p. 131.
[6] Vienna, *MEA*, GK, Fasc. 71.
[7] Paris, vol. 64, 127.

a state of uneasy suspension, the two ministers stumbled along for the next few days, accused of nothing but clearly facing dismissal.

Groschlag attempted to strengthen his position by enlisting the support of the various diplomatic representatives in Mainz, but his fortunes were crumbling so obviously that he received only polite but transparently evasive answers to his entreaties. Although the French ambassador, the Marquis d'Entraigues, admired Groschlag's qualities and thought that he was the best German minister of recent years, he recommended that no protection be given him by Versailles.[1] Groschlag also tried to gain the support of Count Neipperg, professing his allegiance to the Austrian court in the most extravagant terms and claiming that he sought his last refuge in the ambassador's friendship. Neipperg evaded the issue by declaring that he was unable to interfere in the domestic affairs of the state.[2] Groschlag had said that there were three courses of action open to him: to resign and withdraw into private life, to resign and enter the service of another foreign power or to stay and await events quietly. In the event he chose the last course, hoping perhaps for a change of heart on the part of a majority of canons.

D'Entraigues reported to his court that the canons charged Groschlag with sowing dissension between Elector and Chapter and of acting arbitrarily, but that he would not be impeached, only dismissed from office. The reason for this reluctance to prosecute was the fear of alienating his fellow-nobles.[3] Groschlag of course belonged to one of the oldest families of Imperial Knights and was related to many of the leading Mainz families. The Bentzels on the other hand were originally service nobility and only the Chancellor's father had been made a Freiherr and admitted to the Imperial Knights. This explains perhaps why Groschlag's alleged misdemeanours went unexamined while Bentzel soon found himself facing a possible criminal action for misappropriating public funds. It is clear that the canons did not stumble across incriminating evidence during their investigation of some other facet of Bentzel's activity, for already on 12 June four local officials had been ordered to Mainz to attend the Chapter's investigation.[4] Rumours of Bentzel's corruption must have been circulating for some time before Emmerich Joseph's death. The affair caused a great stir in Mainz and the ambassadors predicted the most unfortunate consequences for the Chancellor.[5] The actual investigation showed that the rumours were exaggerated. Of the four officials interrogated, one denied that he had supplied Bentzel with anything, another had supplied him only

---

[1] Paris, vol. 64, 128.   [2] Vienna, *Staka*, Fasc. 175, 592.
[3] Paris, vol. 64, 130.
[4] Vienna, *MEA*, GK, Fasc. 71. The documents relating to the investigation of this case are to be found in the same fascicle as the minutes of the Chapter, but again there is no pagination.
[5] Paris, vol. 64, 125. Vienna, *Staka*, Fasc. 175, 588.

with grain and the other two had lent him about 45,000 gulden in cash over a six-year period. One of these claimed that the Elector had known all about it but had looked the other way. The sums still outstanding had been paid back that morning.[1] Although Bentzel had certainly behaved dishonestly, the possible connivance of the Elector and the fact that the money had been repaid probably convinced the Chapter that a trial would serve no useful purpose, for the whole affair was shelved.[2]

There were a number of other reasons for the unrelenting hostility shown towards Bentzel and Groschlag by the majority of the canons. The conservatives amongst them disapproved of the ministers' radical reform programme. Those outside the charmed circle of power, by virtue of inadequate blood-relationship or opposed political views, resented the grip which the Stadion circle had held on the Electorate's patronage for the past thirty years. But it was opposition to them from Vienna which was decisive in prompting first the suspension and then the dismissal of Groschlag and Bentzel. Although relations between Vienna and Mainz had been subject to periodic strain ever since Emmerich Joseph's election, until 1766 the Austrian ambassador in Mainz was Count Joseph von Pergen, who was married to Groschlag's sister and was naturally restrained in his comments on his brother-in-law. His successor, Count Neipperg, suffered from no such inhibitions. In his reports Groschlag assumed the proportions of an ogre, not only unsound in his opinions but also deceitful in his tactics. Neipperg resented especially Groschlag's pose as the honest but powerless pro-Austrian, struggling in vain to turn an erring Elector back into the Habsburg paths of righteousness, when in fact the rôles were reversed. The following extract from a report of 1768 is typical:

Von Bentzel is totally dependent on von Groschlag and is completely in cahoots with him; von Groschlag on the other hand tries to keep his hands clean as far as the Imperial Court is concerned and tries to build up credit for himself there, while at the same time trying to discredit the Elector, so that he can give the false impression that it is he who can make the Elector do what is acceptable to the Imperial Court, although in fact it is he who is mainly responsible for striving to prevent the Elector following his natural inclination to fall in with the imperial wishes in all possible circumstances.[3]

Groschlag was a peculiarly able diplomat, if dissimulation of intent is a characteristic of good diplomacy, but he succeeded only in persuading everybody that he was against them. Thus Vienna was against him because of his close connection with the French minister, the British minister welcomed his dismissal 'having found him on all occasions attached to the

---

[1] Vienna, *MEA*, GK, Fasc. 71.
[2] Ibid. Erthal's report to the Chapter of 21 June was marked '*Concl. solle noch zur Zeit auf sich beruhen*'.
[3] Vienna, *Staka*, Fasc. 156, 193.

Court of Vienna, and by no means a friend to the Maritime Powers', the Dutch ambassador welcomed his departure because he was 'devoted solely' to Versailles and the French ambassador declined to help him because he was a broken reed.[1] In offending none, Groschlag alienated all and, by arousing the suspicions of the Colloredo family,[2] he finally ensured that he would fail to survive the interregnum as first minister of the Electorate of Mainz. Although Groschlag was doubtless a slippery customer, it must be remembered that it was not gratuitous knavery that prompted him to oppose Vienna. Rather it was Joseph II's determination to sever his ties with the Holy Roman Empire, thus disrupting the status quo. In the various disputes over the visitation of the *Reichskammergericht* or the conduct of business in the Imperial Chancellery, it is clear that it was Joseph who was the aggressor.[3] From Neipperg's reports it is also clear that it was Emmerich Joseph who wished to make concessions for the sake of a quiet life and Groschlag and Bentzel who were determined not to submit to Joseph's bullying.

The violence of the Chapter's campaign against the former régime did not pass unnoticed by the rest of Germany. Immediately after Emmerich Joseph's death the rumour began to circulate that he had been poisoned by the Jesuits,[4] and Prince Carl of Hessen always believed that he had been smothered to death by two of the canons.[5] Fifteen years later a story was still circulating that he had been poisoned with arsenic.[6] The news of the reversal of Emmerich Joseph's reforms brought yelps of pain from numerous enlightened writers. Lavater deplored the 'terrible relapse of the Mainzers into the old barbarism' and Heinse wrote to a friend 'the monks and clerics are again crawling out of their nests, like the bats and owls which emerge when the sun has gone down'.[7] The tutor of the Freiherr von Stein, the later Prussian reformer, wrote from Göttingen: 'The death of the Elector of Mainz hit us like a clap of thunder...This event will have a great effect on German affairs and on the happiness of the inhabitants on the banks of the Rhine.'[8]

Simultaneously the Chapter was attacked in articles whose violence was

[1] Ibid. Fasc. 175, 586. P.R.O., SP.81.153. Paris, vol. 64, 125.
[2] See above, pp. 135–7.
[3] Heinrich Kretschmayr, 'Das deutsche Reichsvizekanzleramt', *Archiv für österreichische Geschichte*, 84 (1898), 461. Lothar Gross, *Die Geschichte der deutschen Reichshofkanzlei* (Vienna, 1933), pp. 87–92.
[4] Herse, *Kurmainz*, p. 34.
[5] Philipp Losch, *Kurfürst Wilhelm I, Landgraf von Hessen* (Marburg, 1923), p. 104.
[6] Øjvind Andreasen & Helmut Mathy, 'Frederik Münters Reise nach Mainz (1791)', *Mainzer Zeitschrift*, 62 (1967), p. 68.
[7] Hans Hainebach, *Studien zum literarischen Leben der Aufklärungszeit in Mainz* (Giessen Dissertation, 1936), p. 59.
[8] Freiherr von Stein, *Briefe und Amtliche Schriften*, vol. 1, ed. Walther Hubatsch (Stuttgart, 1957), p. 83.

only equalled by their inaccuracy. The canons were eventually moved to take counter-measures by a particularly extreme example of gutter-journalism, published in the *Courier du Bas-Rhin* of 6 July. Amidst a panegyric of the late Elector's measures and an attack on the Chapter's change of direction could be found a number of false assertions. It was alleged, for example, that von Groschlag had been ordered back to his estates at Dieburg, that von Bentzel was under house arrest, that the Jesuits had reentered their old College in triumph, in the carriages of the court, that priests had been ordered to attack the school reforms and that all priests who had cooperated with the previous régime were to be deprived of their benefices. The author concluded by saying that only a little *auto-da-fé* was needed to allow them to compete with the fourteenth and fifteenth centuries 'in extremism and barbarism'.[1] The canons responded promptly. Expressing themselves with equal vigour, they asserted the falsehood of the charges in a public declaration.[2] Although both of them disapproved of the Chapter's measures, Neipperg and d'Entraigues agreed that the charges were without foundation.[3] Memories of the interregnum still rankled long afterwards. In 1783, for example, A. L. Schlözer's *Staatsanzeigen* published an article which reminisced about the excellence of Emmerich Joseph's reforms and the tyranny of the Chapter, and asserted that the Chapter had acted illegally in requiring all officials to reapply for their positions.[4]

Illegal or not, the swift decline and fall of Bentzel and Groschlag, once their patron had died, was powerful evidence not only of the conservatism of most of the canons but also of the power of the Austrian court in the Mainz election campaign. As the twenty-four canons began to be canvassed after Emmerich Joseph's death, this power made itself felt no less forcibly than previously. It had been thought by the diplomats that four or five candidates would emerge: the Dean Karl Joseph von Dalberg, the Treasurer Friedrich Karl von Erthal, the Cantor Franz Philipp von Franckenstein, the Canon Philipp Karl von Hoheneck and possibly the aged Provost Hugo Karl von Eltz.[5] There was also a rumour that Vienna might try to secure the election of Arch-Duke Maximilian.[6] These predictions of a multi-sided, closely fought battle were upset when it emerged the day after Emmerich Joseph's death that Friedrich Karl von Erthal had already collected a majority. He had assured himself of the support of Eltz and Franckenstein, together with their supporters, and had also attracted two or three uncommitted voters. By 16 June Erthal felt sufficiently sure

[1] Vienna, *Staka*, Fasc. 175, 600. [2] Vienna, *MEA*, GK, Fasc. 71.
[3] Vienna, *Staka*, Fasc. 175, 600.
[4] A. L. Schlözer, *Staatsanzeigen*, 29 (Göttingen, 1785), p. 48.
[5] Paris, vol. 64, 125. [6] P.R.O., SP.81, 153.

of the size and reliability of his party to send a courier to Vienna, announcing in advance his certain victory.[1]

Compared with previous campaigns, the election of 1774 was a dull affair. Erthal made all the running and – despite the wishful thinking of the Dutch and French ambassadors – was never seriously challenged. There were a number of reasons for his remarkably conclusive success. The foundation of his support lay in the alliance with Eltz and Franckenstein. The former was seventy-three years old in 1774 and already enjoyed an enormous income. Even had he desired to become Elector, it is doubtful whether he could have gathered more support than he had in 1743 or 1763. Franckenstein was only fifty-two years old, had more supporters and according to d'Entraigues had planned to become Elector for the last ten years.[2] He was persuaded to abandon his claims by bad health[3] and the fact that the Franckensteins were the heirs of Erthal, who together with his two unmarried brothers was the last of his line.[4]

In view of later events, it is highly probable that the ambitions of Eltz and Franckenstein were blunted further by promises of lucrative positions for members of their respective families. For the same reason, Erthal with his solid core of eleven supporters was in an admirable position to attract the floating votes of hitherto uncommitted canons. The Elector controlled all patronage, and canons anxious to secure continued possession of their own and their relations' sincecures had nothing to gain from acting coyly once a clear favourite had emerged. Once a successful bandwagon had been launched, it rolled forward by its own momentum at ever-increasing velocity and unanimous support could be gathered very quickly. To the conservative majority of the Chapter, Erthal had given apparently ample evidence of his determination to restore and maintain the old order.

A final and perhaps decisive reinforcement was the support of the Austrian court. Erthal had probably taken advantage of his sojourn in Vienna as the Electorate's ambassador to convince Maria Theresa and Joseph II of his devotion and to secure a promise of their support in the event of a vacancy at Mainz. He had also gained the assistance of the Vice-Chancellor of the Reich, Prince Colloredo,[5] who was described by the British diplomat George Cressener as 'entirely devoted to Baron d'Erthal'.[6] Austrian support enabled Erthal to restrain a number of supporters who showed signs of wavering on the eve of the election. D'Entraigues recorded that, to disarm the conspiracy, all the canons had been shown a letter to Erthal from Maria Theresa, in which she congratulated him on obtaining

[1] Paris, vol. 64, 133. [2] Ibid., 125.
[3] He died on 3 October 1774.
[4] Franckenstein and Erthal were first cousins. Their mothers – Maria Margaretha *née* Bettendorf and Maria Eva *née* Bettendorf – were sisters.
[5] See above, pp. 135–7. [6] P.R.O., SP.81.153.

a majority.¹ Neipperg was indeed given direct instructions to help him and the ambassador intervened to halt a last-minute plot which he believed to have been instigated by the Dutch and French ambassadors. He visited each canon suspected of being involved, emphasised that Erthal was the Austrian choice and stated that their Imperial Majesties expected that the canon would not renege on an earlier promise to vote for him.²

Although it is possible that Erthal would have been elected at Mainz without this diplomatic assistance, it is certain that without it he would not have obtained the other prince-bishopric vacated by Emmerich Joseph's death – Worms. Because the Prince-Bishopric of Worms was one of the smallest ecclesiastical states, it was usually held by one of the more powerful and wealthy neighbouring Prince-Bishops – Mainz, Trier or Speyer. As soon as Erthal had gathered a majority in Mainz, he and Neipperg turned their attention to the lesser prize. They discovered that as expected both Trier and Speyer were candidates and that the latter, supported by the Elector of the Palatinate, had gained the votes of five of the thirteen canons.³ Erthal could probably count on the further allegiance of the five Mainz canons who also had benefices in the Chapter at Worms, and would certainly be backed by the Austrian Court. Two other considerations, however, made the Worms campaign particularly difficult. As Erthal was not yet actually elected in Mainz he could not canvass openly in Worms, for fear of alienating his supporters by a display of over-confidence.⁴ As he was not himself a member of the Worms Chapter and was not equipped with a papal *brevis eligibilitatis*, he had to fall back on election by postulation, which required a two-thirds majority or 9 votes.⁵ Despite these impediments, Erthal's campaign progressed smoothly; by 17 June Neipperg could report that 8 votes had been secured.⁶ This estimate was over-optimistic, for two days later Karl Anton von Dalberg broke ranks and declared himself a candidate.⁷ Undeterred by the pleadings of Neipperg and the threat that he would be opposed by Vienna, Dalberg set off for Schwetzingen to enlist the support of the Elector of the Palatinate. Perhaps encouraged by this desertion, another candidate in the shape of the Prince-Abbot of Fulda entered the lists.⁸ Erthal's pluralistic hopes seemed to be vanishing.

---

¹ Paris, vol. 64, 179.
² Vienna, *Staka*, Fasc. 175, 601. Helmut Rössler – *Graf Johann Philipp Stadion, Napoleons deutscher Gegenspieler*, vol. 1 (Vienna, 1966), p. 68 – states that the canon Johann Philipp von Stadion was asked by Joseph II in a personal note to assist Erthal's election.
³ Vienna, *Staka*, Fasc. 175, 587, 591. ⁴ Paris, vol. 64, 135.
⁵ Ibid., 141. On the requirements for postulation, see Hans Erich Feine, *Die Besetzung der Reichsbistümer vom Westfälischen Frieden bis zur Säkularisation, 1648–1803*, Kirchenrechtliche Abhandlungen, 97 and 98 (Stuttgart, 1921), p. 237.
⁶ Vienna, *Staka*, Fasc. 175, 591. ⁷ Ibid., 593.
⁸ Ibid., 594.

The recovery of his fortunes was due partly to the deficiencies of his opponents and partly to a more effective mobilisation of his own assets. As d'Entraigues pointed out, Dalberg never really stood a chance: because the tiny resources of Worms necessitated union with a large ecclesiastical state, because the Chapter liked to be ruled by an absentee bishop, because the Elector of Mainz had a great deal of patronage with which to reward his supporters, because Dalberg was too young and because the Palatinate would not back him.[1] More important was the fact that, as the day of the Mainz election drew nearer and as Erthal's victory became more and more certain, open canvassing on his behalf was made possible. That it was carried out by Neipperg, acting on the instructions of Vienna, explains its eventual success. When Emmerich Joseph died, the Dean of the Worms Chapter, the Freiherr von Mohr, wrote to Neipperg inquiring about the wishes of their Imperial Majesties.[2] The ambassador replied that as yet he had no precise instructions; in the meantime he hoped that von Mohr would seek to arrest any developments contrary to the imperial interest. Until Maria Theresa and Joseph II informed him of their choice, Neipperg sought to form an alliance of canons opposed to the election of the Prince-Bishop of Speyer.[3] By 25 June Neipperg had received his instructions and he spread among the canons by word of mouth the news that Erthal was the man favoured by Vienna. On the same day Erthal was able to inform the ambassador that he had secured the votes necessary for postulation. The other three soon joined and on 26 July the new Archbishop of Mainz was unanimously elected Prince-Bishop of Worms. Imperial support had been of decisive importance, although it is possible that simple bribery persuaded some of the canons.[4]

One of the reasons for the sweeping success of the Erthal–Vienna combination was the absence of any competition from the other ambassadors. Until a very late stage Erthal succeeded in concealing from the latter his adherence to Austria and by then it was too late for them to do anything about it. His success in misleading them was achieved simply by being all things to all men. On 8 July d'Entraigues reported that 'this canon [Erthal] has assured me that he is very desirous of justifying the good opinion of the King and of meriting his protection, by the exactitude with which he carries out the agreements of his predecessors with the Crown of France and by his devotion to anything which could please his Majesty'.[5] Erthal expressed himself in the same vein to Count Wartensleben, the Dutch ambassador, who wrote to his British colleague George Cressener: '[Erthal] has made me the most sweeping and fine promises of friendship

---

[1] Paris, vol. 64, 141.
[2] Vienna, *Staka*, Fasc. 175, 589.
[3] Ibid., 593.
[4] Ibid., 589, 595, 604.
[5] Paris, vol. 64, 167.

for the Maritime Powers', and on another occasion: 'I believe that we shall have every reason to be satisfied with the new Elector, in all respects.'[1] Cressener also had a very high opinion of Erthal, both as a man and as a potential elector. He was taking the waters at Spa when Emmerich Joseph died and the information he received from various correspondents in Mainz did nothing to disturb his opinion that his personal presence there was unnecessary. His belief that Erthal was attached to the Maritime Powers was confirmed by a letter from him which proclaimed his devotion in extravagantly subservient language. Cressener also believed that the pact between Erthal and Franckenstein had been made to reduce their dependence on Vienna and to ensure that they would be under no obligation after the election. Encouraged by the ambassador's glowing reports, the British government bestowed its official blessing on Erthal's candidature. The Earl of Suffolk praised the conduct of the Chapter 'and the propriety of their choice; Baron d'Erthal being by every account very deserving of the situation to which he will now be raised'.[2]

Meanwhile Erthal was making equally fervent protestations of allegiance to Neipperg, the difference being that this time he meant them. He declined, for example, to become a candidate for the Bishopric of Worms until Vienna had made its intentions clear.[3] Any hopes that after his election he might throw off the Austrian shackles, now his primary object had been attained, were soon shattered. At the beginning of October the Mainz delegates at the *Reichskammergericht* were ordered to follow the instructions of the Imperial Commission in all matters. The chance of obtaining further imperial patronage was a powerful incentive for continued support of the Habsburgs. One of Erthal's brothers was made an Imperial Privy Councillor and the other was promised all possible assistance in obtaining the Prince-Bishoprics of Würzburg and Bamberg, when they fell vacant.[4]

Of the foreign ambassadors it was the Marquis d'Entraigues who first suspected Erthal's duplicity. As early as 18 June he was aware that Vienna was conspiring in favour of Erthal but he did not attempt to form a rival party.[5] Perhaps he believed that the task was hopeless, or was lulled by Erthal's declarations of friendship or saw opposition as unnecessary, in that France and Austria were at least nominal allies. Cressener and Wartensleben slumbered on in their rose-tinted dreams until after the election was over. The first indication that Cressener received that something was amiss came from a certain Count Hatzfeld who passed through Spa and told him that Erthal had been attached to the Austrian interest ever since

[1] P.R.O., SP.81.153.
[2] Ibid.
[3] Vienna, *Staka*, Fasc. 175, 593.
[4] P.R.O., SP.81.153.
[5] Paris, vol. 64, 135.

his sojourn in Vienna as Mainz ambassador.[1] From this point rumours multiplied and in October Cressener travelled down to Mainz to find out for himself. His worst fears were soon confirmed. In his first report to the Earl of Suffolk he lamented: 'If I may credit what Count Wartensleben and the French minister tell me, the Elector is entirely guided by the Court of Vienna, and is as false as he is polite.' A week later and after a number of interviews with the new Elector, Cressener himself came to the conclusion that Erthal is 'absolutely a creature of the Court of Vienna'. Understandably, Cressener's blunders did not go unnoticed and a sharp letter of censure was despatched from St James.[2] Yet even if Wartensleben and Cressener had been perceptive enough to resist Erthal's unctuous flattery, it is very unlikely that they would have been able to find an alternative candidate. As early as 1767 Cressener had marked Erthal down as an aspirant Elector,[3] and indeed it is very probable that he began planning his campaign at this early stage. In the manipulation of the material, ideological and diplomatic considerations, he had shown a high degree of skill; his reward was the first electorship of the Empire.

The new Elector was fifty-six years old and like most of his predecessors came of an old family of Imperial Knights, with long connections with the Electorate.[4] After a conventional aristocratic education, which included periods of study at the universities of Mainz and Reims, he entered the Chapter in 1753. Although he emerged later as the leader of the party of conservatism, he enjoyed the patronage of both Johann Friedrich and Emmerich Joseph, becoming Rector of the University in 1754, Privy Councillor and President of the Council in 1758 and Treasurer of the Chapter in 1768.[5]

One pressing matter for Erthal's attention was the disposal of Groschlag and Bentzel, who were still technically Grand Master and Chancellor respectively, but had been forbidden by the Chapter to carry out the duties of their offices. Any hopes the two ministers may have had of reinstatement under the new régime were soon dashed when, shortly after his election, Erthal ordered them to refrain from performing official functions and to await further orders. Before making a final decision he consulted Vienna and, claiming that his only interest was that of 'the most glorious, most just head of the Empire', told Neipperg that he would abide by the decision of the Austrian Court. Mistrustful of Groschlag but unwilling to

[1] P.R.O., SP. 81.153.
[2] Ibid. The rebuke is mentioned in Cressener's despatch dated Bonn 17 November 1774.
[3] Ibid.
[4] Kittel, 'Geschichte der freiherrlichen Familie von und zu Erthal', *Archiv des historischen Vereins von Unterfranken und Aschaffenburg*, 17 (1865), p. 195. His father had been magistrate of the Mainz town and *Amt* of Lohr am Main.
[5] See above, p. 135.

become involved in the domestic affairs of the Electorate, Maria Theresa and Joseph adopted a neutral stand on the matter, which allowed Erthal to give full rein to his personal feelings.[1] Groschlag at least said he thought that Erthal had nothing against him personally but the Elector had a very different view of their relationship. His brother had advised him to forgive and forget old quarrels; Erthal rejoined that Groschlag had persecuted him for a dozen years and that he could think of no more agreeable use of his authority than to dismiss the two men he regarded as his enemies.[2] His antipathy towards Bentzel was equally acute. According to one of Neipperg's anonymous informants it stemmed from the time when, at the height of the amortisation dispute, Bentzel had advised Emmerich Joseph to warn Erthal that in the history of the Electorate there were many examples of canons being thrown into prison.[3]

As soon as he heard that the decision had been left to him, the new Elector dismissed both Groschlag and Bentzel. The latter was to have a pension of 2,000 gulden per annum; the former a similar sum, in addition to the retention of his two magistracies of Aschaffenburg and Dieburg, which together yielded 6,000 gulden annually.[4] Bentzel accepted his pension and departed, but Groschlag's ideas of correct noble behaviour kept him in Mainz for one last round. In his reply to the offer he thanked the Elector for his generosity but added that as no title or rank equivalent to the office he had lost had been offered and as no reasons had been advanced for his dismissal, he felt sure that the Elector would understand that he felt unable to accept the terms and that 'when it is a question of choosing between interest and honour, a gentleman does not need to reflect. So you will permit, My Lord, that I lay my position at court and my two Magistracies at your feet, reserving for myself the pleasure of remembering that I have served two Electors and the Electorate for twenty-two years, as a man of honour and honesty.' On this dignified note, Groschlag departed for Höchst, where he married Sophie Helena Countess von Stadion and then retired into private life.[5]

Erthal was in dire need of the positions vacated by Groschlag and Bentzel, for once the election was over he was obliged to fulfil his obligations to his supporters. Some years later a bizarre story was in circulation, purporting to describe how Erthal acquired the support of the Eltz party. The aged Provost Hugo Karl von Eltz held Erthal to be 'an atheist' and refused even to see him. Erthal bribed a lackey, made his way into the Provost's apartments, threw himself at his feet and cried: 'Help! The Religion! The

---

[1] Vienna, *Staka*, Fasc. 175, 592, 599, 603. [2] Paris, vol. 64, 184.
[3] Vienna, *Staka*, Fasc. 175, 589. [4] Ibid., 605.
[5] P.R.O., SP.81.153. Karl Diel, *Ein Parkvorbild der Goethezeit: Der Lustgarten der Freiherren von Groschlag zu Dieburg* (Darmstadt, 1941), pp. 19–20.

Religion!' Apparently overwhelmed by this demonstration, Eltz embraced Erthal and promised him his party's votes.¹ It seems far more likely that patronage rather than religion provided the cement for the alliance. Although there is no direct evidence of a bargain with Eltz and Franckenstein other than the observations of the ambassadors, the subsequent promotions certainly lend weight to their suspicions. The former Grand Chamberlain, Anselm Casimir von Eltz, became Grand Master, and his son, Johann Philipp Jakob von Eltz, became Statthalter of the Eichsfeld territory.² Franz Philipp von Franckenstein was put in charge of domestic affairs and his nephew was made President of the Council. Referring to this last appointment, Count Neipperg wrote: 'the young canon von Franckenstein, who is very young and rather inexperienced, is to receive the position of President of the Council, which the Elector previously held; this appointment seems to be incomprehensible unless it is a necessary result of the agreement His Electoral Grace was obliged to enter into with the Franckenstein family, to make his election absolutely certain; for subsequent events hardly allow any other interpretation, as this family and the Eltz family seek to divide the most important positions of the Electorate amongst themselves and to establish a kind of nepotism'.³

Although the distribution of offices between the two families may have been fairly equal, it was the Eltz family which gained most influence over Erthal and a marriage was planned between the Elector's brother and a Countess von Eltz.⁴ During his visit to Mainz in October Cressener reported that 'The Grand Prevot, Baron Eltze, the Grand Master Count Eltze, and his daughter Charlotte Eltze – Chanoinesse, are those who have the greatest influence on his electoral Highness.' The Franckensteins suffered another blow to their influence when the Cantor Franz Philipp died suddenly on 3 October.⁵ Neipperg's deputy, Sengwein, wrote that Erthal was upset at the loss of his 'intimate friend' but according to d'Entraigues, Franckenstein had died of disappointment at having to play second fiddle to the Eltz family.⁶

If the perceptive support of Erthal by some of the canons brought advantage to their families, his election was a severe blow to his opponents' hope of advancement. Erthal had assembled unanimous support very quickly but nevertheless there was a small but vocal minority, which although accepting the inevitability of his eventual victory, was determined to oppose the reactionary measures of his more revanchist supporters in the Chapter. During the first violent sessions of the Chapter, on the day

---

¹ Andreasen & Mathy, *Münters Reise*, p. 68.   ² P.R.O., SP.81.153.
³ Vienna, *Staka*, Fasc. 175, 608.   ⁴ Ibid., 615.
⁵ P.R.O., SP.81.153.
⁶ Paris, vol. 64, 266. Vienna, *Staka*, Fasc. 175, 612.

after Emmerich Joseph's death, Karl Theodor von Dalberg had intervened to announce that he reserved the right to have his vote entered in the minutes in written form.[1] As during the battles over the amortisation and monastic ordinances, he was supported by the General Vicar, von der Leyen, the President of the Municipal Court, von Walderdorff, and the canon von Hornstein. According to d'Entraigues, these four 'constantly resisted the Chapter's actions'.[2] Once the election was over Erthal made no attempt to accommodate them and sent to the General Vicariate a memorandum which violently attacked the measures of his predecessor, especially those relating to public education.[3] Unable to act according to the principles of the new régime, von der Leyen tendered his resignation and it was rumoured that Walderdorff and Dalberg would follow suit.[4] Hornstein was in no position to demonstrate his solidarity with the other three, for his office had already been abolished by the Chapter, along with the Schools Commission over which he had presided. Although their opposition testified to their enthusiastic support of the late Elector's policies, it failed to have any kind of practical effect on the Chapter's voting behaviour, or on Erthal's policies.

They were more successful in their attempts to confound the Chapter's plan of extending its power by the insertion of new clauses in the capitulation of election.[5] The claims to participation in government, first heard during the dispute over the Jesuit fund, were resurrected.[6] Predictably, the minority of four opposed any extension of the Chapter's powers and, more surprisingly, attacked the very principle of the capitulation itself. According to Dalberg and his supporters, far from being the constitution of the state, the capitulation was simoniacal, useless in every respect and condemned by the Pope and the imperial courts alike.[7] They succeeded in preventing the imposition of further restrictions on the Elector, although the capitulation itself survived. What innovations there were derived from the clerical conservatism of the majority of canons. Clause One, for example, required the Elector to convert all inhabitants of the Electorate unfortunate enough not to be Roman Catholics, albeit 'in a fair and modest way', and to take the firmest measures against 'the irreligion, unchristian principles and blasphemy which unfortunately are creeping in everywhere'.[8] The seminary fund, which had been a point of contention during the dispute over the Jesuits' assets, was to be restored to its former state

---

[1] Vienna, *MEA*, GK, Fasc. 71.
[2] Paris, vol. 64, 171.
[3] Ibid., 226.
[4] Vienna, *Staka*, Fasc. 175, 608.
[5] Manfred Stimming, *Die Wahlkapitulationen der Erzbischöfe und Kurfürsten von Mainz, 1233–1788* (Göttingen, 1909), p. 81, wrote that five canons opposed the capitulation in principle; the fifth is unknown to me.
[6] Paris, vol. 64, 141.
[7] Ibid., 171.
[8] Vienna, *MEA*, GK, Fasc. 11a.

and not to be altered without the Chapter's approval. The same applied to the fund composed of the old Jesuit estates. The only new constitutional provision was a singularly nebulous clause which urged the Elector to take a number of canons as his advisers and to 'use' them in state business. In the absence of any effective sanctions it is difficult to see how the Chapter expected to enforce this.

Supported by a large majority of canons and unhampered by any new constitutional restrictions, Erthal enjoyed a further advantage in the shape of his immense popularity with the common people. Even a week before his formal election Neipperg could write: 'I cannot pass over in silence the fact that the justifiable joy of all the Mainz subjects at the unanimous election of the Cathedral Cantor as their future ruler is so exceptionally great that such general applause can hardly ever have been experienced at an archiepiscopal election... or that the clergy and people have ever been so entirely of one mind.'[1] His actual election was greeted by the illumination of the city and jubilant demonstrations from the people.[2] The young Friedrich Lothar von Stadion was an eye-witness of the emotional scenes which followed and reported home:

> He [Erthal] talked to everyone, now walking round the table, now going to the window [to show himself] to the people, who constantly shouted 'Long live our father, our Elector!' Moved by their love, he replied, 'Yes, I do want to be your father!'; he thanked them and then went away to dry his tears of joy. His brother, the chevalier, wept and there was not a member of the company who was not moved and did not shed tears of joy. Dearest parents, if you had been there, oh how your good sensitive hearts would have been moved![3]

Popular aversion to religious innovation in the previous reign has already been described; indeed the people hoped that Erthal would complete the return to baroque piety already begun by the Chapter. Shortly after the election, a large group of citizens petitioned Erthal to restore the education system to the care of the Jesuits and Neipperg reported that the Mainz clergy also hoped for great things from the new Elector.[4] At least as far as his public behaviour went, they were not disappointed: Erthal set a perfect example to his flock. After a spiritual retreat of eight days, he was consecrated priest on 11 September and said his first Mass on the following day.[5] Unlike many of his episcopal colleagues, his devotion to duty was irreproachable; he marched at the head of processions, said Mass regularly,

---

[1] Vienna, *Staka*, Fasc. 175, 600.
[2] Niklas Vogt, *Geschichte des Verfalls und Untergangs der rheinischen Staaten des alten deutschen Reiches* (1833), p. 215.
[3] Rössler, *Stadion*, p. 69.
[4] Paris, vol. 64, 239. Vienna, *Staka*, Fasc. 175, 608.
[5] Karl Klein, *Geschichte von Mainz unter dem letzten Kurfürsten, Karl Friedrich Joseph von Erthal* (Mainz, 1870), p. 3.

attended theological disputations, conducted confirmation and ordination services and imposed an austere régime on his court.¹ In his speech of acceptance to the Chapter, having first expressed verbosely his failure to find words to express his joy, Erthal called on God to help him 'to preserve our Catholic religion, which in our time has sunk so deep' and pledged himself to a conservative policy, proclaiming to the canons: 'You have seen how, here among you, I have condemned everything which in any way might have harmed our constitution, which is worthy of veneration at all times, and I noticed with the greatest pleasure your most steadfast, patriotic and powerful support in maintaining it.'² It must have seemed that the clock had been put back to 1743.

Erthal's rule began in a blaze of popularity, yet by the end of 1774 all goodwill had been dissipated and affairs of state had ground almost to a halt. In the upper ranks of society this remarkable transformation was caused by disputes over the distribution of patronage and the break-up of the coalition which had secured Erthal's election. The success of the Eltz and Franckenstein families in monopolising the great offices of state gave rise to 'dissatisfaction and extreme jealousy in the rest of the nobility'.³ Erthal had made the fatal mistake of promising more offices than were at his disposal. Friedrich Lothar von Stadion, at the reception mentioned above, took the opportunity to ask Erthal to confer a benefice on the Stadions' tutor, Kolborn. Erthal replied: 'It would cause me the greatest pleasure to be of service to the Stadion family, because I know how much I owe them and I know how much they love me.' The young Stadion commented: 'That moved me so much that I almost wept in his face.' It was just as well he restrained his tear-ducts, because the benefice in question went to a protégé of someone else. Friedrich Lothar's next letter home had a quite different tone: 'What, would the Elector refuse such a trifle to his best friend, who so unselfishly gave him his vote for this archbishopric and [is prepared] to give his brother his vote for two bishoprics? Would it have been such an enormous favour for the Elector to have given a benefice to the Stadion family, which has performed so many services for the Electorate? And leaving all this aside, doesn't an honest clergyman deserve more than a cringing ex-Jesuit?' This particular branch of the Stadion family had been at loggerheads with the branch into which Groschlag was about to marry, but the rift was now healed and the Stadions were united in opposition to the new elector.⁴

---

¹ Franz Werner, *Der Dom von Mainz, nebst Darstellung der Schicksale der Stadt und der Geschichte ihrer Erzbischöfe*, vol. 3 (Mainz, 1836), p. 246. Clemens Theodor Perthes, *Politische Zustände und Personen in Deutschland zur Zeit der französischen Herrschaft*, vol. 1 (Gotha, 1862), p. 23.
² Vienna, *Staka*, Fasc. 175, 606.   ³ Ibid., 608.
⁴ Rössler, *Stadion*, pp. 69–70.

The Elector's party was fragmented further when the Eltz and Franckenstein factions quarrelled and became 'as much enemies as they were before friends'.[1] With the exception of two or three families, the entire nobility was 'astounded and revolted' by Erthal's vindictive treatment of Groschlag.[2] These considerations brought about a remarkable shift of opinion in the Chapter and the minority of four opposed to Erthal became a majority. Neipperg, who had every reason to be a dedicated supporter of the Austrophile Elector, reported as early as the beginning of September that the Privy Councillor von Strauss had declined to accept the position of Chancellor vacated by Bentzel's dismissal, because fourteen of the twenty-four canons had promised Bentzel that they would do all they could to secure his reappointment.[3] Only a month later he could add that the Count von Sickingen would turn down an appointment as Mainz foreign minister because of the violent opposition of many canons.[4] The halcyon days of unanimous support had gone for ever.

Erthal might have pleaded in his own defence that the supply of patronage was necessarily limited, that he was not responsible for internecine warfare among his own supporters and that in view of their violently opposed principles, the retention of Groschlag was a plain impossibility. Yet Erthal had contributed to his own misfortunes by violent statements on the one hand and chronic indecision on the other. The previous ministry had been cleared away, but as weeks and then months went by no new one was appointed to take its place. Positions at court were filled but the composition of the ministry remained a mystery.[5] Business began to pile up, the administrative machine to creak to a halt. By late October Neipperg was writing of 'general discontent'.[6] His French colleague was more specific: 'In four months of government he has decided nothing; he has no ministers; all his tribunals are without presidents; his court is in the greatest confusion; he replies constantly to everyone:"I'll find out about it, I shall have to see"... the bourgeoisie begins to murmur; the majority of canons are discontented; several of the most important families are thinking of leaving the city. Although the late Elector left a considerable sum of money, the payment of current expenses is beginning to fall behind. This is a great deal of destruction in little time and is the result of a passionate self-conceit, which seeks to change everything, and of an irresolute character, which knows how to complete nothing.'[7] At the same time Erthal's personal behaviour gave rise to fears for his mental

---

[1] P.R.O., SP.81.153. [2] Paris, vol. 64, 179.
[3] Vienna, *Staka*, Fasc. 175, 608. [4] Ibid., 613.
[5] One exception was the appointment of a certain Herr Haupt as referendar for Worms affairs. He was described by d'Entraigues as a 'ridiculous person', whose only qualification lay in being von Sickingen's bailiff – Paris, vol. 64, 239.
[6] Vienna, *Staka*, Fasc. 175, 614. [7] Paris, vol. 64, 304.

1774: The aristocratic reaction

stability. He appears to have developed a persecution complex and lived in perpetual fear of being poisoned. According to both Cressener and Neipperg's deputy, Sengwein, he threw a cup of chocolate out of the window because the froth was white, and on another occasion made a servant taste a glass of water he had brought.[1] After all the popular jubilation, it was a melancholy opening to the new reign.

1774 drew to a close with the Elector still fumbling for a ministry and the Chapter as factious as it had been under his predecessor. To many contemporaries it seemed as if the events of the last six months had marked a watershed in the history of the Electorate, a return to traditional conservatism after thirty years of innovation. This view of the period has been challenged strongly by Heribert Raab in a recent article.[2] He contends that the actions of the Chapter should be seen not as a blind reaction on the part of the canons, but rather an attempt to counter the dangers of a 'false, godless Enlightenment'.[3] They did not attempt to destroy everything but sought to preserve what was tried and tested by time, while at the same time preparing for an 'organic development' by certain reforms.[4] The conflict was thus not between clerical reaction and the Enlightenment, but between enlightened conservatism and radical impiety. By way of support and amplification of these assertions, Raab also argues that the Enlightenment perpetrated by Emmerich Joseph and his officials was a false Enlightenment, that among the University professors, nobility and cultured bourgeoisie opposition was growing to the protagonists of the Enlightenment and their methods, that the Commission set up by the Chapter to deal with the schools was not destructive but wished only to maintain continuity and wipe out abuses, and that Erthal was elected on his merits.[5]

The evidence produced in support of these statements derives from self-professed supporters of the Chapter and opponents of the former régime. His description of the Enlightenment in Mainz as 'impious' rests on the condemnation of Schwarz and Isenbiel by the Chapter, but the doubtful orthodoxy of a couple of the Elector's officials does not justify the branding of the whole process as irreligious.[6] For his claim that the upper classes in Mainz opposed the reforms, Raab cites no evidence and the contention has slight relevance to the point at issue anyway. Nor can the activities of the Chapter's Schools Commission be in any way described as 'constructive'. The minutes of the Chapter show that the Commission was used primarily as a tribunal to interrogate the professors and school-

---

[1] P.R.O., SP.81.153.
[2] Heribert Raab, 'Das Mainzer Interregnum', *Archiv für mittelrheinische Kirchengeschichte*, 14 (1962).   [3] Ibid., p. 178.   [4] Ibid.
[5] Ibid., pp. 176–9.   [6] See above, pp. 138–9.

teachers and that its only important proposal was the abolition of the College of Education.¹ The concern of the canons to persecute the teachers outweighed their concern for the educational welfare of the children. Many teachers were dismissed but none appointed in their place. When the Director Härdt complained that under these conditions teaching was impossible and discipline was collapsing, he was told to do the best he could.² The election of Erthal made very little difference to the confused situation. As Sengwein reported: 'In school affairs everything has reverted to the model of the well-known old jesuitical teaching method',³ while d'Entraigues thought that the state of the schools was 'nothing but an example of confusion and indiscipline'.⁴

In general the events of the interregnum indicate that, far from being a body of wise and moderate legislators, the Chapter was largely composed of frustrated men who had spent all too long in the political wilderness and were determined to seize their opportunity to exact revenge.⁵ The precipitate violence of the first few days after Emmerich's death supports this view, as do the opinions of the ambassadors, whatever their diplomatic affiliations. Wartensleben described 'the passions and violence' of the canons, the Marquis d'Yves wrote of their 'terrible persecutions' and Cressener concluded that they 'proceeded with all the violence an inflamed and mistaken zeal could inspire'.⁶

Raab sees the conflict between the Chapter and Emmerich Joseph, the interregnum and the election in ideological terms. Although differing opinions about Church–State relations certainly played a part in the controversies, the situation was far too complex to allow the isolation of any one particular issue. The canons' opposition to the reform programme was dictated at least partly by fears about the future of all corporate groups within the Electorate, of which the Cathedral Chapter was only the most powerful and prominent. This anxiety was exacerbated by thunder-clouds of secularisation, which, as the Chapter rightly pointed out, threatened its

---

[1] Raab's only two original sources of information are the tutor of the young Counts von Stadion and the papal nuncio Caprara. The former certainly visited the great houses in Mainz, with his charges, although it may be doubted whether his relatively low social status gained him access to important or reliable information. Caprara did not even visit Mainz during the period and, as Raab admits, was out of touch with affairs there because of the Elector's anti-papal policies.

[2] Vienna, *MEA*, GK, Fasc. 71.

[3] Vienna, *Staka*, Fasc. 175, 619.   [4] Paris, vol. 64, 239.

[5] H.-W. Jung – *Anselm Franz von Bentzel im Dienste der Kurfürsten von Mainz*, Beiträge zur Geschichte der Universität Mainz, vol. 7 (Wiesbaden, 1966), p. 63 – argued that the Chapter's actions should not be seen as revenge because Emmerich Joseph had already made concessions in educational matters before his death. Although he has worked in the *Mainzer Erzkanzlerarchiv* in Vienna, Jung appears to be unaware of the dispute over the Jesuit estates and the bitterness it aroused.

[6] P.R.O., SP.81.153.

own material position, if not through the direct action of the Electorate of Mainz, then certainly by the tempting prospect offered to neighbouring secular princes. The original issue was obscured still further by the introduction of constitutional arguments which amounted to claims of co-regency in the government of the state. In addition, the leaders of the agitation were involved in imperial politics and had set their sights at a target far beyond the defeat of Emmerich Joseph's domestic policy.[1]

Similarly, the events of the interregnum and the election of Erthal cannot be explained simply in terms of the canons' admiration of his personal qualities and their aversion to the brand of enlightened absolutism practised by Emmerich Joseph, Groschlag and Bentzel. Certainly some observers believed that Erthal was all an electoral candidate should be, but others had an entirely different opinion.[2] The Chapter's enthusiasm for his conservatism was assisted, if not dictated, by the support of the Court of Vienna, and counter-measures by the other ambassadors were prevented by the subtle if mendacious assurances of devotion. His successful wooing of the Erthal and Franckenstein factions, which enabled him to gain the all-important early lead over his rivals, was made possible by his prospective control of the Electorate's patronage, by 'interest'. The fragmentation of his supporters after the election was caused not by any deviation from the straight and narrow path of piety but by his own personal failings and the simple fact that there were not enough jobs to go round. It is impossible to understand this tangled thicket without reference to the ideological conflict between supporters and opponents of the Catholic Enlightenment, but it was not the sole or, indeed, the most important consideration.

The complexity of the issues in Mainz should guard against any attempt to relate the episode too closely to any general European movement. Some historians have identified a pattern of 'aristocratic reaction' to enlightened reforms in the second half of the eighteenth century, which in turn ushered in the democratic revolution. The most succinct formulation is Godechot's:

If sovereigns sought the support of the people, the privileged orders did not hesitate to do so too. Outbidding the rulers, the aristocrats proclaimed themselves to be the only defenders of the people... In general the people were encouraged not only by the philosophes but also by the privileged orders to enter into struggle against the sovereign. In most countries of the West the 'aristocratic reaction' inevitably led to a revolt of the nobility and soon thereafter to a revolt of the people.[3]

---

[1] See above, pp. 148–9.
[2] Raab quotes Caprara's following assessment of him: '*Erthall* [sic] *passa per uomo abile, aperto, capace di grandi intraprese, forse non totalmente lontano da piani intrapresi dal defonto*' (p. 175). The French, on the other hand, thought him 'vain, opinionated and feeble' – Livet, *Recueil*, p. 195. I see no reason why this judgment should be any more biased than that of the papal nuncio. Indeed, the months succeeding the election showed that it was more accurate.
[3] Jacques Godechot, *France and the Atlantic Revolution of the Eighteenth Century 1770–1799* (New York, 1965), p. 26.

There was certainly a reaction in Mainz from the only existing corporate body but it was not a reaction fuelled exclusively by resentment of enlightened reforms and political ambition. It should also be remembered that disputes between Elector and Chapter were a constant feature of the Electorate's history.[1] Nor did this particular clash lead on to popular revolt. The people wished only a return to the old religious and educational order; there is no evidence that they entertained any more ambitious political or social aims. As the events of the next reign were to show, the 1774 interregnum marked only a brief interruption in the Mainz experience of enlightened absolutism.

[1] Stimming, *Wahlkapitulationen, passim.*

5

Enlightened absolutism: Friedrich Karl von Erthal

ENLIGHTENMENT FROM ABOVE

I

The new Elector was fifty-six years old on his election. No other Elector of Mainz has received so much attention from historians and no other Elector of Mainz has been condemned so unanimously. This has been partly due to the many unfavourable comments made about his person by contemporaries. They ranged in detail and severity from Swinburne's description of him as 'a cross, ill-looking priest' to Stein's branding of him as 'vain, ambitious, jealous of his prestige and just as susceptible to mistrust as he is to boundless confidence'.[1] Arrogant, vain, both suspicious and credulous, susceptible to flattery, capricious, extravagant and a hypochondriac, Friedrich Karl was not the stuff of which historiographical heroes are made.[2] There is always a danger of reading into a portrait characteristics already suggested by literary sources, but Heinrich Füger's portrait of Friedrich Karl does seem to confirm this distinctly unappealing description.[3] Superficially flattering, it shows him swathed in his magnificent scarlet and ermine electoral robes, around his neck a scarlet sash supporting a large jewel-studded cross and medallion, on his finger an enormous diamond ring. Encased in a crisp white wig, his profile is undeniably impressive: a broad forehead, prominent eye-brows, dark brown eyes and a great hooked nose. His red, rather thin, lips, however, give him an air of petulance and irascibility, as he looks *down* at the viewer, with an expression of *hauteur* and disdain. Perhaps subsequent events were responsible for this interpretation, certainly they served to confirm it. Friedrich Karl seemed possessed by a restless demon, for ever sending him off in new directions, chasing but never catching fame and fashion. Carl August of Weimar wrote of him: 'Peace is death to him, but if there is a real

[1] Henry Swinburne, *The Courts of Europe at the Close of the Last Century*, vol. 1 (London, 1895), p. 366. K. G. Bockenheimer, *Mainz im Fürstenbunde* (Mainz, 1905), p. 15.
[2] See for example, the long description of him by the Austrian diplomat Ferdinand Count Trauttmansdorff – Vienna, Staka, Fasc. 214, 7.
[3] The best coloured reproduction can be found in Leo Just and Helmut Mathy, *Die Universität Mainz, Grundzüge ihrer Geschichte* (Trautheim and Mainz, 1965), facing p. 64.

hubbub of action, then he feels at home.'[1] Although he was destined to be the last Elector of Mainz, he was also destined to preside over the most turbulent period in the Electorate's long history.

The new reign had opened ingloriously, in an atmosphere of reaction and irresolution, but at the beginning of 1775 Friedrich Karl appointed to the vacancies in his administration and business began to get back to normal.[2] As stability returned to the conduct of affairs it also became clear that Friedrich Karl did not intend to allow his policies to be dictated by the conservative views of the canons who had voted him into office. His own views on the Chapter's actions during the interregnum must remain a mystery, although in view of later events it seems reasonable to conclude that his professed conservatism was born of tactics rather than conviction. His appointment by the late Elector Emmerich Joseph as President of the *Hofrat* and Rector of the University suggested that their outlook was at least similar. Within the University he had indeed supported the *anti-Jesuit* party; in 1768, for example, he had presented a report which was highly critical of the Order's teaching methods.[3] There is no direct evidence that his conservative stance during the election campaign of 1774 was a sham, although it is suggestive that no one appears to have been surprised when Friedrich Karl reverted to the enlightened policies of his predecessor. The Marquis d'Entraigues, the most intelligent of the foreign diplomats in Mainz, was convinced that Friedrich Karl was opposed in principle to the reactionary views of his supporters, gave them free rein only to ensure his election and at the same time sought to mitigate the effects of their actions. D'Entraigues also forecast that Friedrich Karl would change course as soon as the situation allowed.[4] His prophecy was soon fulfilled; by the end of the second year of the new reign there were clear signs that the break in continuity, which the interregnum had caused, was about to be repaired.

In view of the Chapter's brisk demolition of Emmerich Joseph's educational system, it was appropriate that it was in education that signs of a restoration first became apparent. Friedrich Karl signalled his intentions early when he appointed Ernst Xaver Turin to be 'General Director of the entire school-system throughout the Electorate of Mainz'. Like the reformers of the previous reign, Turin was an admirer of the Silesian pedagogue Johann Ignaz Felbiger, whose essential message was that 'one must strive in the schools to educate young people in such a way that with time

---

[1] *Briefe des Herzogs Carl August an seine Mutter die Herzogin Anna Amalia*, ed. Alfred Bergmann, Jenaer germanistische Forschungen, vol. 30 (Jena, 1938), p. 66.
[2] P.R.O., SP.81.154, 1.
[3] Anton Ph. Brück, *Die Mainzer theologische Fakultät im 18. Jahrhundert*, Beiträge zur Geschichte der Universität Mainz, vol. 2 (Wiesbaden, 1955), p. 37.
[4] Paris, vol. 64, 130, 141.

Enlightened absolutism, 1774–1802

they become: a. honest Christians; b. good citizens, that is faithful and obedient subjects of the authorities and c. useful people for the community'.[1] Shortly after his appointment Turin set down his thoughts on education in general in a long memorandum entitled 'Concerning the improvement of the primary schools in the Catholic provinces of Germany'.[2] He saw education as one of the most important responsibilities of the ruler:

> It is the duty of every honest sovereign to protect his people against beggary and to bring wealth and prosperity to his country by good administration, encouragement of agriculture, trade, the mechanical arts, the building of factories etc. He is prince for this reason, to make his people happy. Yet to allow a people to grow up in stupidity and ignorance and to attend to only their bodies and material needs is to perform only half the duties of a sovereign.

This should not be seen as a simple act of altruism, for Turin added:

> When I talk about schools, I do not mean just those which prepare our intellectuals, but also those which educate for the state rational, god-fearing and capable citizens and subjects.

Before the Electorate's schools could be in a position to fulfil these functions, Turin believed that four obstacles would have to be overcome: the shortage of schools and teachers, the existing teachers' ignorance of what and how to teach, the shortage of books and the shortage of money.

A number of decisions at the beginning of his reign suggested that Friedrich Karl was prepared to give Turin the necessary assistance. The College of Education was restored in 1776, with the proviso that in future all teaching vacancies would be filled by its graduates. At the same time laymen were readmitted to the Schools Commission. The ex-Jesuits who had been reappointed to the teaching posts at the Grammar School after the death of Emmerich Joseph were ejected again.[3] Turin's utilitarian bias was reflected in the creation of a special secondary school for potential merchants and manufacturers, with a curriculum which included bookkeeping, banking and salesmanship.[4] Within a few years the Enlightenment had returned officially to Mainz, as was shown by the banal eulogies of the Elector written by Ladrone, the headmaster of the Grammar School:

> Oh how my bosom swells
> At the name of Friedrich!

---

[1] Johann Ignaz Felbiger, *Eigenschaften, Wissenschaften und Bezeigen rechtschaffner Schulleute* (Bamberg and Würzburg, 1772), p. 21.
[2] Most of it is reprinted in Anton Ph. Brück, *Kurmainzer Schulgeschichte*, Mainzer Beiträge zur Pädagogik, Historische Abteilung, vol. 1 (Wiesbaden, 1960), pp. 84–96.
[3] Ibid., p. 13. Karl Klein, *Geschichte von Mainz unter dem letzten Kurfürsten Karl Friedrich Joseph von Erthal* (Mainz, 1870), p. 9.
[4] Maria Inviolata Helfrich, *Das Mainzer Bildungswesen 1774–1792* (Frankfurt am Main Dissertation, 1922), pp. 39–40.

The Electorate of Mainz in the Eighteenth Century

> It was dark – Let there be light
> He said – Darkness! Cease!
> And Light was there
> And Darkness not there[1]

Friedrich Karl's main interest, however, lay in higher education, and very few of Turin's ambitious plans were realised. As an ordinance of 1780 lamented, a major obstacle was the lack of interest in, even hostility towards, education on the part of the ordinary people. The constant reiteration of threats to punish the parents of truants had no effect; in 1797 the teachers were still complaining that in summer only 10% of the children went to school. A detailed survey of 1781 revealed that more than a third of the Electorate's school-teachers were badly paid. A number of plans to break the vicious circle of low salaries attracting poor teachers were discussed but never implemented. Consequently it remained normal for teachers to pursue a second profession. A report of 1782 revealed that in many villages the schools were in the hands of tailors, tithe-collectors, foresters, weavers, customs-officials, cobblers and cattle breeders.[2] Although the Elector could hardly be blamed for the peasants' passive resistance, it was depressing that rural education remained the Cinderella. While funds were lavished on the University at Mainz, the schoolmaster at Nackenheim, only a few miles away, was expected to exist on twenty gulden in cash, eleven bushels of grain and the proceeds from $1\frac{3}{4}$ *Morgen* of vineyard and $6\frac{1}{2}$ *Morgen* of arable land. As in many other villages, the grain had to be collected from each individual peasant household, a requirement which did nothing to enhance the teacher's popularity or social status. It is not surprising that in 1791 it was reported that the school-buildings at Nackenheim were falling down and that no examinations had been held for five years.[3]

The University on the other hand could complain of no such neglect. Friedrich Karl on his accession had shown his continuing interest in University affairs by retaining the position of *Rector Magnificus*. The 300th anniversary of the University's foundation in 1477 passed without official celebrations, the reason for this unusual reticence being lack of finance rather than lack of pride in past achievements. In fact plans were already afoot to remedy the deficiencies, although they proceeded at a leisurely pace. Reports were ordered in 1776, the secularisation of monastic property to provide the necessary funds was proposed in 1777, the Elector's approval was given in 1778 and the support of Joseph II was won in 1779.

---

[1] Hans Hainebach, *Studien zum literarischen Leben der Aufklärungszeit in Mainz* (Giessen Dissertation, 1936), p. 64.
[2] Brück, *Kurmainzer Schulgeschichte*, pp. 15–16, 48–53, 57.
[3] Helmut Mathy, *Die Nackenheimer Revolution von 1792/1793*, Nackenheimer Heimatkundliche Schriftenreihe, vol. 14 (Nackenheim, 1967), p. 26. A *Morgen* is rather less than an acre.

Enlightened absolutism, 1774–1802

This annual sequence was then broken by resistance from Rome, although not for long. In 1781 a papal bull authorised the dissolution of the Carthusian, Altmünster and Rich Clares houses in Mainz.[1]

It seemed that Friedrich Karl had solved at one blow the problem which had plagued the Mainz University since its foundation. For all his indignation at the sterile wealth of the 'dead hands', Emmerich Joseph had never considered officially secularisation as a path to general welfare. Now Friedrich Karl, the former leader of the conservatives, had dared to lay hands on three of the wealthiest religious foundations in the Electorate. The reaction of the Chapter was not delayed long. The canons had heard rumours of the impending dissolutions, but they had not been consulted and they were not given formal notification until the day before the commissars actually took possession of the monastic establishments.[2] On the following day Count Metternich, the Austrian ambassador, summoned the Dean of the Chapter and told him that the projected reorganisation of the University enjoyed the full support of the Emperor. When the Dean began to complain 'in an excited and immoderate tone', Metternich informed him curtly that he could not accept a protest against a project already graced with imperial approval. He added that the Chapter seemed determined to oppose every beneficial mesaure attempted by the Elector and suggested that this extraordinary behaviour sprang from 'dishonourable motives'.[3]

Armed with a supporting opinion from a Giessen lawyer, the canons resurrected the phraseology of the amortisation dispute, asserting their right to participation and consent.[4] The Elector sent only a terse reply, emphasising that the dissolutions derived their validity both from his archiepiscopal and sovereign authority and from papal and imperial approval. Under his predecessor this sort of reply might have led to a protracted and bitter series of exchanges; now the Chapter seemed to have lost much of its martial spirit. Old conservatives like Hugo von Eltz and Franz Philipp von Franckenstein had died and been replaced by younger men, who had been brought up in an era of enlightened reform and were more progressive than their predecessors. It is also likely that Count Metternich's timely intervention cooled their pugnacity. The majority of canons replied meekly that they had not wished to insult the Elector but only to make their motives clear. They also instructed their agent in Vienna to dispel any bad impression which inadvertently they might have made there.[5] Armed with the consent of both his temporal and his spiritual

---

[1] Ernst Jakobi, *Die Entstehung des Mainzer Universitätsfonds*, Beiträge zur Geschichte der Universität Mainz, vol. 5 (Wiesbaden, 1959), pp. 66ff. Vienna, *Reika*, Fasc. 22, 3. K. G. Bockenheimer, *Die Restauration der Mainzer Hochschule im Jahre 1784* (Mainz, 1884), p. 12.
[2] Würzburg, *MDP*, vol. 67, 1650.   [3] Vienna, *Staka*, Fasc. 197, 386.
[4] Würzburg, *MDP*, vol. 67, 1655.   [5] Ibid., 1711.

superior and not seriously threatened by the token yelps of the canons, Friedrich Karl was in a strong position to reconstruct higher education in his state.

It was hoped that the substantial assets of the three dissolved houses would more than cover the cost of the University's expansion and modernisation. In an article laconically entitled 'Poverty of the Monasteries', A. L. Schlözer's *Staats Anzeigen* reported that 1700 butts of wine, worth about 500,000 gulden, had been found in their cellars and that the convent of the Rich Clares owned a capital sum of 160,000 gulden in cash.[1] The joint annual income of the three houses was about 38,000 gulden, so that there was a good deal left to be added to the University funds, even after the dispossessed monks and nuns had been catered for.[2] In 1784 Friedrich Karl made a final raid on Church property when he ordered each of the seventeen collegiate foundations in the Electorate to reserve a benefice for one of the University professors in holy orders. The beneficiary was not required to carry out any of the duties of the foundation or to reside there; it was simply an expedient to lighten the burden the expansion imposed on the University funds.[3]

With the material basis assured, the structure and content of the new University could be determined. Any hopes or fears that the transformation of the scale of the institution might not be accompanied by equivalent changes in substance were dispelled on 9 September 1782, when it was announced that Anselm Franz Freiherr von Bentzel had been appointed curator, with the title of 'Excellency'.[4] Friedrich Karl's reappointment of the man he had dismissed so abruptly on his accession was the final proof that he had returned to the policies of his predecessors. It soon became clear that Bentzel's eight-year exile, spent quietly on his estates at Emmerichshofen near Hanau, had not changed his views on education. These were expressed most fully in his 'New Constitution of the Improved University at Mainz', an official publication issued just before the inauguration of the reformed institution in 1784. Although both the new curator and his master were self-conscious innovators, they retained theology as the pivotal subject in the curriculum. In his first petition to Joseph II, Friedrich Karl had stressed that the primary aim of the reorganisation was

[1] A. L. Schlözer, *Staatsanzeigen*, vol. 1 (Göttingen, 1782), p. 25.
[2] Ernst Jungk, *Zur Geschichte und Rechtsnatur des Mainzer Universitätsfonds*, Beiträge zur Geschichte der Stadt Mainz, vol. 12 (Mainz, 1938), p. 2.
[3] *Journal von und für Deutschland* (1784), 7 March.
[4] H.-W. Jung, *Anselm Franz von Bentzel im Dienste der Kurfürsten von Mainz*, Beiträge zur Geschichte der Universität Mainz, vol. 7 (Wiesbaden, 1966), p. 75. The third part of Jung's book contains a detailed account of Bentzel's actions as curator. The right to adopt the prefix 'Excellency' was a particularly rare mark of distinction, usually conferred only on foreign ambassadors and the highest court dignitaries and ministers of state. Unsuitable or insufficient use of the title could lead to unedifying squabbles.

to ensure that theology would be taught 'with exemplary thoroughness', while in his speech at the official opening he instructed the assembled professors to subordinate all the other disciplines to the service of religion.[1] This concern was reflected in the establishment of a theological faculty with no fewer than eleven chairs.

Yet although the University remained an essentially religious institution, the introduction of new disciplines reduced the relative predominance of the 'Queen of Sciences', as did the new emphasis on inter-disciplinary studies. All students were obliged to attend a general preparatory course of a year's duration, designed to sharpen their powers of judgment, widen their understanding and encourage them to think for themselves.[2] Theology did not play a large part in this course. To the traditional four-fold division of philosophy, theology, medicine and law, two new faculties were added: history and statistics, and cameralism. Among the new chairs created were those for politics, diplomacy, applied mathematics, botany, chemistry, veterinary science, land economy, commerce and accounting.[3] As his reform of the schools during the previous reign had suggested, Bentzel's view of education was dictated by an obsession with 'relevance'. Like many other worshippers of that elusive deity, he paid scant attention to the intellectual development of the individual student. He was not concerned with scholarship *qua* scholarship but with the production of useful citizens and especially of efficient and diligent officials. For Bentzel the University had to be utterly subordinated to the state:

> The so-called academic freedom is a relic of earlier misconceptions and is moreover completely unsuited to the needs of the present times. The state wishes and the parents expect that young people will be directed towards the fear of God, virtue, wisdom and the arts and sciences, so that they in their turn will be in a position to enlighten the mass of the people and to instil in them a better way of thinking, better habits and a better character. Discipline, integrity, temperance, order and true religion are the means of attaining this.[4]

In view of this list of moral priorities, it is not surprising that Bentzel was especially fond of using military metaphors when discussing educational or political matters. Criticisms of the severity of the courses were rejected with the comment: 'It doesn't matter if there are few [students], if only they are useful for the state.'[5] The later coadjutor, Karl Theodor Freiherr von Dalberg, had complained to Friedrich Karl that Bentzel believed:

> the University must be a machine, whose soul is the curator, whose limbs are the teachers and whose aim is the cultivation of those pupils needed by the state for

---

[1] Vienna, *Reika*, Fasc. 22, 19. Just and Mathy, *Universität Mainz*, p. 33. Cf. Bentzel's remarks: Brück, *Theologische Fakultät*, p. 67.
[2] The regulations were reprinted in A. L. Schlözer's *Staatsanzeigen*, vol. 3 (1783), pp. 23ff.
[3] Just and Mathy, *Universität Mainz*, p. 31.   [4] Jung, *Bentzel*, p. 87.
[5] Hainebach, *Studien*, p. 82.

administrative purposes. He believes that all this can be forced through by precise and detailed regulations, by the exact and mechanical obedience of the teachers and severe supervision of the students. But...in this way the teachers' independence, ability to think for themselves and spirit are lost.[1]

This austere vision of Bentzel, distinctly reminiscent of Joseph II's contemporaneous blitz on intellectual 'self-indulgence', was no personal quirk of the curator. His plans were always perused, occasionally modified but usually approved by the Elector. The logical conclusion of the reforms was an ordinance of 1785 which decreed that in future all vacancies in the Electorate's administration would be filled by graduates of the University of Mainz, because now all useful subjects could be studied there and so there was no excuse for going elsewhere.

Despite this grimly practical language, the reformed University was surprisingly liberal in some respects. The Elector freed the teaching staff from censorship, with the observation that knowledge could grow only if there was freedom of expression and communication.[2] A more radical step was the appointment of a number of distinguished Protestants, wooed away from North German universities by generous salaries. They included Sömmering, the anatomist; Müller, the Swiss historian; Forster, who had sailed round the world with Captain Cook; and Pfeiffer, the cameralist. The University's sub-title of *Alma Mater Moguntina semper catholica* did not prevent extensions of toleration. It was announced in 1786 that Protestants would be allowed to take degrees, except in the theological faculty, on condition that their dissertations contained nothing hostile to Roman Catholicism. Even more remarkable was the extension of this privilege to individual Jews.[3]

It was also intended that this new ecumenical spirit should inspire the Catholic members of the University. Both Bentzel and the influential suffragan bishop Heimes intended that through the University 'young and old priests, preachers and theological teachers should be deeply imbued with toleration, which accords so closely with the views of His Electoral Grace'.[4] This concern found expression in the new appointments, for even the theological faculty was staffed largely with men of an episcopalist and Jansenist bent.[5] The radical views of some of the theologians and philosophers at the University and the highly equivocal role some of them played during the revolutionary period prompted some nineteenth century historians to brand the whole institution as impious.[6] This was an un-

---

[1] Brück, *Theologische Fakultät*, p. 85. [2] Hainebach, *Studien*, p. 80.
[3] Helmut Mathy, 'Um die Promotion der Protestanten und Juden an der alten Mainzer Universität', *Jahrbuch der Vereinigung 'Freunde der Universität Mainz'* (1962), pp. 66, 69.
[4] Brück, *Theologische Fakultät*, p. 68.
[5] Ibid., pp. 69–75. 'Jansenist' is used in its most general sense, see above, pp. 29–32.
[6] The best example of this school is H. Brück, *Die rationalistischen Bestrebungen im katholischen Deutschland, besonders in den drei Erzbistümern* (Mainz, 1865).

reasonable charge, based on a confusion of secular with irreligious. As the historian of the theological faculty has argued,[1] the form of Enlightenment propagated at the University was one which remained faithful to Roman Catholicism. Only very few of the professors, then or later, deserted the faith for deism.

By the autumn of 1784 preparations were complete and the 'restored' University was officially opened on 15 November, to the accompaniment of lengthy and elaborate celebrations. There was some justification for this orgy of self-congratulation, for the reforms won much praise from intellectuals throughout Germany. Later in life former students of such widely differing political views as Prince Clemens von Metternich and Johann Weitzel recorded in their memoirs their recollection of the University's excellence.[2] After a visit to Mainz in 1789, the Prussian educational reformer Friedrich Gedike, who usually saw a bigoted monk round every Catholic corner, recorded with surprise that:

> Although I concluded from my observations that the journals have been too noisily enthusiastic about the present organisation of the University, I must admit on the other hand that this University's constitution has much in it that is excellent and even worthy of imitation by Protestant universities; and that it is vastly more distinguished than any other Catholic university. The dark monkish spirit which rules in other Catholic universities manifests itself here much more seldom.[3]

Even more than his predecessor, Friedrich Karl began to assume the proportions of a hero of the Catholic Enlightenment.

The bold optimism of 1784 was soon dissipated. Even before the official inauguration, Count Metternich reported that the 'more rational' people in Mainz appreciated that the proposed scale of the University bore no relation to the funds available.[4] His comment was doubtless motivated partly by political malice, but it proved to be correct. Less than a year after the official opening, Sömmering wrote to Müller that 'Everything is going badly here. *Eminentiss* [Friedrich Karl] said to me himself: "The fund has been weakened so much that nothing more can be drawn from it without making it bankrupt".'[5] A major cause of these difficulties was the failure to collect all the wealth of the three dissolved houses. Much of their land lay outside the Electorate and after secularisation was seized by the princes

---

[1] Brück, *Theologische Fakultät*, p. 93.
[2] *Aus Metternichs nachgelassenen Papieren*, ed. Fürst Richard Metternich-Winneburg, vol. 1 (Vienna, 1880), p. 14. Johann Ignaz Weitzel, *Das Merkwürdigste aus meinem Leben und aus meiner Zeit*, vol. 1 (Leipzig, 1821), p. 106.
[3] Leo Just, *Die alte Universität Mainz von 1477 bis 1798*, Beiträge zur Geschichte der Universität Mainz, vol. 4 (Wiesbaden, 1957), p. 61. For other similar opinions, see J. K. Risbeck, *Travels through Germany*, vol. 3, (London, 1787), p. 206, and Wilhelm von Humboldt, *Gessammelte Schriften*, vol. 14, ed. Albert Leitzmann (Berlin, 1922), p. 40.
[4] Vienna, Staka, Fasc. 210, 754. Metternich was already thoroughly disenchanted with Friedrich Karl's policies towards Vienna. [5] Just, *Universität Mainz*, p. 28.

concerned.[1] This experience inhibited any further dissolutions, for every substantial religious institution in the Electorate owned property in other principalities.

As the financial problem became more acute in the late 1780s, the morale of the University sank. This is reflected most clearly in the correspondence of Georg Forster, who replaced Johannes Müller as librarian in 1788, when the latter was appointed to a post in the administration.[2] He lamented to his father-in-law that the University's finances were in a state of chaos and that no sense of priorities was evinced in spending what they did have. Of the 50,000 volumes supposedly in the Library, only four to five thousand had been published since 1700 and about 35,000 were duplicates. As the six faculties were allowed only 100 gulden a year each for new purchases, Forster found himself besieged by book-sellers clamouring for the settlement of unpaid bills. He reported that the Elector was disenchanted by this transformation of a prestigious asset into a tiresome liability and could not bear to have the subject mentioned in his presence. Forster's despairing comments on the state of the library were echoed by others; the verdicts of two foreign visitors were 'pitiful' and 'wretched' respectively.[3]

Attempts to keep the University on an even keel were hampered further by internecine disputes, notably that between the Curator Bentzel and the Suffragan Bishop, Heimes.[4] This reached such a pitch of intensity that when Bentzel died suddenly in 1786 it was rumoured that he had been poisoned.[5] Certainly the University as it emerged from the reforms bore only a limited resemblance to the optimistic blueprint of 1784, but its defects should not be exaggerated. When the French occupation of the city in 1792-3 and the revolutionary wars brought about its final collapse, the reformed University of Mainz was still the most progressive and celebrated in Catholic Germany.[6]

[1] Jungk, *Universitätsfond*, pp. 16-22. A detailed account of the financial problems of the University can be found in Jung, *Bentzel*, pp. 140-1.
[2] Georg Forster, *Sämtliche Schriften*, vol. 8 (Leipzig, 1843), pp. 4, 26, 34, 36, 51, 57-8, 83, 86, 153, 164, 178, 198, 219.
[3] Øjvind Andreasen and Helmut Mathy, 'Frederik Münters Reise nach Mainz, (1791)', *Mainzer Zeitschrift*, 62 (1967), p. 72. *Briefe eines reisenden Dänen, geschrieben im Jahr 1791 und 1792 während seiner Reise durch einen Teil Deutschlands, der Schweiz und Frankreichs* (Züllichau, 1793), p. 95.
[4] Jung, *Bentzel*, pp. 142-5.
[5] His doctors felt obliged to publish a statement that he had died from natural causes – *Journal von und für Deutschland* (1786), 10.
[6] Although they criticised individual aspects, this was recognised by contemporaries. See, for example, Johann Nikolaus Becker, 'Über Mainz, in Briefen an Freund R.', *Mainz zwischen Schwarz und Rot*, ed. Claus Träger (Berlin, 1963), pp. 76-9. P. W. Gercken, *Reisen durch Schwaben, Baiern, die angränzende Schweiz, Franken, die Rheinische Provinzen und an der Mosel in den Jahren 1779-1785* (Stendal, 1786), p. 30. J. G. Lang, *Reise auf dem Rhein (von Mainz*

II

The Elector and his ministry's overriding concern with the education of the subjects was also shown when they turned their attention to ecclesiastical affairs. The driving force in this sector was Valentin Heimes, of whom the papal nuncio Bellisomi wrote: 'The suffragan bishop Heimes is the one who has control over all matters; a clever man with a bluff manner, he has risen from a very low condition to be firstly suffragan of Worms and then of Mainz and to acquire much influence over the Elector.'[1] Heimes' uncouth appearance and rough manners betrayed his peasant background but masked a sharp intellect. Count Metternich, the Austrian ambassador, described him as 'an exceedingly able, active and very perceptive man, free from all prejudices and selfish ambitions'.[2] Although Heimes had played an important part in the events leading up to the dissolution of the three monasteries for the benefit of the University, it was not until his appointment as Suffragan Bishop of Mainz in 1783 that he won full scope for his reforming energies. His plans were made quite clear in a memorandum presented to Metternich in the same year. He argued that the German Church had been infested with the same abuses for centuries, but that now, 'in the present enlightened times', there was an opportunity to uproot them once and for all. If only the Archbishop of Mainz would follow the trail blazed by the Josephists in Austria, he would draw after him all the other prince-bishops. Internal renewal, combined with the abolition of papal usurpations, would also lay the basis for the return of the Protestant Churches to the Catholic fold.[3]

As Heimes had been a *protégé* of the late Elector, it is not surprising that there was a considerable degree of continuity. This was especially apparent in the continuing efforts to impose restrictions on the monasteries and convents of the Electorate. A steady stream of ordinances sought to stop them acquiring any more property and to subject their internal affairs to the direct control of the General Vicariate.[4] Institutions thought to be incorrigibly corrupt were put to other uses – in 1789, for example,

---

bis Düsseldorf), vol. 1 (Frankfurt am Main, 1790), p. 16. *Compendiöse Statistik von Maynz, Trier und Cöln samt ihren Nebenländern* (Leipzig, 1798), p. 31. The growing prestige of the University was reflected in its growing numbers: 440 in 1783; 501 in 1784; 755 in 1785; 727 in 1786 – Jung, *Bentzel*, p. 145, n. 33.

[1] Heribert Raab, 'Die Finalrelation des Kölner Nuntius Carlo Bellisomi (1785–1786)', *Römische Quartalschrift für christliche Altertumskunde und Kirchengeschichte*, 51 (1956), 116.
[2] Vienna, *Staka*, Fasc. 205, 595. See also the description by Arnoldi, the Trier representative at the Congress of Ems, *Des kurtrierischen Rats H. A. Arnoldi Tagebuch über die zu Ems gehaltene Zusammenkunft der vier erzbischöflichen Herren Deputierten*, ed. M. Höhler (Mainz, 1915), p. 64.
[3] Vienna, *Staka*, Fasc. 205, 595.
[4] Mainz, *Kurmainzische Verordnungen*, 6te Sammlung, vols. 8–10. Vienna, *MEA*, GK, Fascs. 85a, 85b, 86.

the Dominican house in Mainz was converted into a home for retired priests.[1]

Pace the ultramontane critics, the reformers' chief concern was with the substance of religious life. The boisterous exhibitionism of baroque piety was no longer in vogue and just as the new generation of architects turned from the writhing complexities of the baroque to the severe lines of classicism, so the enlightened church reformers viewed with distaste the naïve enthusiasm of an earlier age. In the churches of Mainz, for example, it was customary on Ascension Day for a wooden figure of Christ to be hauled up into the roof and on Whit Sunday for a model or even a live dove to be let down into the church. Both ceremonies were banned by the General Vicariate in 1788.[2] Models of biblical scenes, such as the crib at Christmas or the Holy Sepulchre at Easter, the ringing of church bells during thunder storms, the placing of lighted candles on saints' tombs during Easter week and the dressing-up of dolls to represent the Virgin were also forbidden.[3] The Vicariate's distaste for anything smacking of idolatry was extended to include the chief proponents of these flamboyant customs – the lay brotherhoods (*Brüderschaften*). It was planned, in imitation of Joseph II, to amalgamate all of them in one centrally controlled body, but the revolutionary wars intervened before the reform could be carried out.[4]

More significant was the assault on pilgrimages. In 1784 the *Journal von und für Deutschland*, edited in Fulda by the Mainz councillor Freiherr von Bibra, published a long and detailed *exposé* of the pilgrimage to Walldürn.[5] Situated in the Franconian territory of the Electorate of Mainz and not far from the river Main, Walldürn owed its position as one of Germany's most popular Catholic pilgrimage places to a remarkable miracle which had occurred there in 1120. When a careless priest knocked over the chalice while celebrating Mass, the blood of Christ which fell on his corporal-cloth was immediately transformed into a pictorial transformation of the crucifixion, surrounded by eleven imprints of Christ's head on the cloth of St Veronica. The priest concealed the corporal-cloth under the altar, only revealing its whereabouts on his death-bed. Duly discovered and exhibited, the corporal-cloth was responsible for numerous miracles, but it

---

[1] Ibid. Fasc. 85b.
[2] G. L. C. Kopp, *Die katholische Kirche im 19. Jahrhundert* (Mainz, 1830), p. 233. The title of Kopp's book is very misleading. It is concerned almost exclusively with the ecclesiastical reforms of the prince-bishops in the last half of the eighteenth century and in particular with those of Friedrich Karl of Mainz. Kopp had been a member of the Mainz General Vicariate and claimed that as he had been able to collect all the relevant documents he was completely impartial. In fact he was an unquestioning supporter of his former employer's programme. However, as he prints almost all the ordinances and reports in full, his work has great value as source material.
[3] Ibid., pp. 229–32.   [4] Ibid., pp. 239–44.   [5] *Journal von und für Deutschland* (1784), 3.

was not until seventy years later that it was sent to Rome, investigated and confirmed as a genuine miracle. On its return to Walldürn crowds of pilgrims came from all over Germany to benefit from the corporal-cloth's curative powers.

As one might expect, the author of the article in the *Journal von und für Deutschland* poured scorn on what he considered to be a superstitious fable and with great relish described the ruthless exploitation of the naïve pilgrims by the rapacious Carthusian monks who looked after the church. At the same time he portrayed the pilgrims as unruly, drunken and lecherous and alleged that 'most girls lose their virginity during the journey'. Branding the whole affair as 'hateful, indeed disgusting' and 'a disgrace to our country and our century', he called on the Elector of Mainz to put an end to it. The latter's response was prompt and as conditions at Walldürn must have been known to the Vicariate, it is likely that the article was intended to prime public opinion. A commission of investigation was despatched to Walldürn and the theological faculty of the University of Mainz was ordered to examine the religious substance of the miracle.

In view of its popularity total abolition of the pilgrimage was out of the question. Instead, it was decreed that all pilgrimages which lasted overnight had to have the express permission of the Vicariate.[1] In practice this was a severe restriction; as most places of pilgrimage were in remote rural areas, only the local inhabitants could reach and return from them in a day. In addition a plan was drawn up for the investigation of every pilgrimage in the Electorate but was never implemented fully. Heimes and the Vicariate also intervened on a number of other occasions to deal with what they held to be outbreaks of superstition. In 1788, for example, a proclamation signed by Heimes announced that on investigation a rash of 'miracles' at Algesheim proved to be due entirely to natural causes or self-delusion. Parish priests were ordered to instruct their flocks accordingly.[2]

The reform programme was not confined to the abolition of abuses; the Elector and his ministers also wished to promote what they considered to be true Catholicism, a Catholicism freed from all gothic uncouthness and above all a Catholicism determined and dictated by the central ecclesiastical authorities. This entailed a new ritual. In 1788 a *Congregatio Rituum* was set up, with the task of introducing uniform services in all parishes and monastic churches.[3] With this aim in view a new breviary was prepared, although it came too late to be introduced.[4] At the same time another commission began work on the revision of the *Agenda*, the collection of directives from the Archbishop concerning the cure of souls.[5] Among other

---

[1] Kopp, *Katholische Kirche*, pp. 236–7.
[2] Mainz, *Kurmainzische Verordnungen*, 1te Sammlung, vol. 6, 1420.
[3] Vienna, *MEA*, GK, Fasc. 85b.   [4] Kopp, *Katholische Kirche*, p. 183.
[5] Ibid., pp. 166–9.

innovations, the new draft required that all ceremonies in which the common people took an active part, such as weddings, christenings and burials [*sic*], were to be conducted in German, and where Latin was used a translation was to be provided in a neighbouring column. Apart from devotional tracts, the reading material of the majority of subjects was confined to the various calendars, which combined practical information with moral homilies and unsophisticated literature. To secure a monopoly of this important means of communication, the electoral government forbade entry of all foreign calendars and published its own 'to influence through it the way of thinking and the education of the common man'.[1]

The abolition of certain external forms of worship should not be interpreted as indifference on the part of the government; indeed it paid closer attention to the imagined religious needs of the people than any of its predecessors. In addition to their weekly sermons, parish priests were ordered to offer religious instruction every Sunday afternoon and twice during the week. They were also urged to devote their spare time to the education of paupers' children.[2] In 1785 the Vicariate ordered parish priests to hold no fewer than five services on Sundays and festivals: Mass at 6 a.m., using the vernacular hymn book and including a brief commentary on the day's text, High Mass at 9.30, with a sermon of 30 minutes, an hour of religious instruction for young people at 2 p.m., an hour of prayer for all parishioners at 3 and evensong at 7.[3] In 1788 the General Vicariate was instructed to plan a three-year course in morality and religion for each and every subject in the Electorate, to be dispensed in half-hourly doses on Sundays and festivals.[4] Although the revolutionary wars prevented the introduction of this scheme, it does provide further evidence of the religious motivation of the reform programme.

As the reformers appreciated that much depended on the quality and training of the individual parish priests, in 1778 a new scheme for the vetting of newly appointed priests was introduced. Ten years later the *Mainzer Monatschrift von geistlichen Sachen* claimed that the scheme had led to a significant improvement in the standard of priests.[5] There is very little evidence to substantiate this claim, just as there is very little evidence to deny it. At the end of the 1780s an English tourist wrote that 'there is not a more regular clergy in all Germany than that of this place. There is no diocese, in which the regulations made by the Council of Trent have been more strictly adhered to, than here; the archbishops having made a

---

[1] *Journal von und für Deutschland* (1784), 10.
[2] Kopp, *Katholische Kirche*, p. 222. *Mainzer Monatschrift von geistlichen Sachen*, 5 (1789), pp. 92–7.
[3] Ibid. 1 (1785), pp. 1163–4.
[4] Vienna, *MEA*, GK, Fasc. 85b.
[5] *Mainzer Monatschrift von geistlichen Sachen*, 4 (1788), pp. 2–4.

Enlightened absolutism, 1774–1802

particular point of it, both at the time of the reformation, and ever since.'[1] This verdict is emphatic enough, although it is doubtful whether the author had either the opportunity or the inclination to investigate conditions in the rural parishes. It is significant, however, that during the revolutionary period there were no outbreaks of anti-clericalism comparable to those in France. Nor was there any evidence of that tension between the upper and lower echelons of the Church which played such an important part in the French Revolution. With one or two exceptions, the Mainz clergy remained loyal to the old régime.

The importance attached to ecclesiastical reform was illustrated by the rôle it played at the Congress of Ems in 1786. The document which authorised the Mainz representative, Heimes, to sign the final *Punctatio* listed three reasons for holding the Congress: the redefinition of the original rights of the archbishops and bishops, the grievances against Rome and the reform of the Church.[2] Although more time was spent on the last of these, historians have invariably equated the 'Congress of Ems' with the first two.[3] Two documents were signed by the representatives of Mainz, Cologne, Trier and Salzburg at Ems: the *Punctatio* of twenty three articles, which defined the archiepiscopal position over and against Rome, and the 'Reform Decree'. The headings into which the 103 clauses of the latter were divided give a good impression of the scope of the reformers' interests: encroachments on episcopal power; the improvement of the cure of souls, parish priests and parish services; the abolition of abuses in processions, in churches and indulgences; mendicant orders; monasteries; convents; foundations for the daughters of the nobility and privileged classes; and collegiate foundations.[4]

It is certainly true that internal reform was not the main reason for the Ems meeting. Friedrich Karl sent a representative in the short term because of the dispute over the papal nuncios and in the long term because of his ambition to found a National German Church under his leadership.[5] In his reports Heimes made it quite clear that the initiative for the discussion of the reform proposals came from the other delegates. At the same time, however, he pointed out rather smugly that no objection could be raised because most of the reforms had been implemented in Mainz al-

---

[1] *A Tour through Germany, containing full Directions for Travelling in that interesting Country, with Observations on the State of Agriculture and Policy of the Different States: very particular Descriptions of the Courts of Vienna and Berlin, and Coblentz and Mentz* (London, n.d.), p. 48. See also, Andreasen and Mathy, *Münters Reise*, p. 66.
[2] Vienna, *MEA*, Religionssachen, Fasc. 38, 369.
[3] Heimes' daily reports to Mainz on the progress of the Congress reveal that three days were spent on the first two (26–8 July), but four on the third (29–30 July, 1–2 August). E. Préclin and E. Jarry, for example, in the *Histoire de l'Église*, vol. 19, p. 777, do not mention the latter.
[4] The full text of this document and of the *Punctatio* is reprinted in Höhler, *Ems*, pp. 92–106.
[5] See below, pp. 220–8.

ready.¹ Later Heimes was more positive in his enthusiasm for this aspect of the Congress' activities. He argued that a joint reform programme, ratified by all four archbishops, would give added force to the individual measures, would reduce opposition and would make cathedral chapters, monasteries and other religious institutions think twice before complaining to the *Reichstag*. He concluded: 'for me this is the chief benefit of the present Congress: that the archbishops will be enabled to undertake important reforms without having to fear that at the end it will all have been in vain'.²

The climax of the reforms was intended to be a diocesan synod. Such a meeting had last been convened in Mainz in 1548 and in any German territory in 1609,³ but as a means of discussing, publicising and imposing reform it had gained recent prominence through the synod held in the Tuscan diocese of Pistoia in 1786. As many of the principles enunciated in the reform programme drawn up by Leopold and his ministers – the *Punti Ecclesiastici* – reappeared in its counterpart in Mainz, it seems likely that there was a direct influence.⁴ In a circular of 1789 the Elector ordered the Cathedral Chapter, the Vicariate, the theological faculty, all collegiate foundations and monasteries and the regional assemblies of parish priests to compile lists of desirable reforms. The purpose of the synod was threefold – the buttressing of faith and morals, the restoration of discipline and, where necessary, the alteration or amplification of ecclesiastical laws.⁵ Although the Cathedral Chapter and most of the monasteries believed that the *status quo* left little to be desired, the report from the Vicariate expounded a radical programme of reform. Some of the suggestions were repetitions of points made at the Congress of Ems, and were aimed at the reduction of papal influence. Others reiterated measures which had been taken already and proposed only that they be sharpened and extended. The Vicariate proposed, for example, that for nuns the 'solemn vows' be replaced by 'simple vows for a limited period of time', and that no monks should take their final vows before the age of twenty-five. Religious practices smacking of superstition were to be abolished, services reformed to encourage lay participation and where necessary the number of parishes and the salaries of their incumbents increased.⁶ Some individual members wanted to go further; indeed a majority of them proposed that a discussion of the modification of clerical celibacy be placed on the synod's agenda.⁷

---

¹ Vienna, *MEA*, Religionssachen, Fasc. 38, 253.
² Ibid., 280.   ³ Kopp, *Katholische Kirche*, p. 58.
⁴ Adam Wandruszka, *Leopold II*, vol. 2 (Vienna, 1965), pp. 111–39.
⁵ Brück, *Die rationalistischen Bestrebungen*, p. 125. Kopp, *Katholische Kirche*, p. 59.
⁶ Ibid., pp. 60–3 prints the Vicariate's report in full.
⁷ An English traveller wrote in September 1789: 'The Elector means to assemble a synod next winter in which it will be proposed that the clergy be permitted to marry' – W. A. Miles, *Correspondence on the French Revolution*, ed. Chas. Popham Miles, vol. 1 (London, 1890), p. 130.

Enlightened absolutism, 1774–1802

Others suggested that monastic vows should not be eternally binding, that saints who had either never existed or had set a bad example be erased from the calendar and even that 'the use of the chalice be restored to the laity, for without this a union with the Protestant Church can never be thought of'.[1]

News of the arrangements for the synod spread rapidly and, according to the Papal Nuncio in Cologne Pacca: 'dismayed the well-intentioned German bishops and aroused in all true Catholics a feeling of pain and depression, for they knew very well the way of thinking of the Elector, the erroneous and heterodox principles of his councillors and the godless opinions which predominated at the University there'.[2] Fearing a repetition of the Pistoia incident, Rome reacted sharply. Pius VI warned Friedrich Karl that, if the synod attempted to make changes in church discipline, it would be subjected to a papal investigation and condemned. Undeterred, and perhaps encouraged by this, the Elector pressed on with the arrangements and convened the synod for 1792. The coronation of the Emperor Franz II and the attendant ceremonies in the summer of that year necessitated its postponement; in October the arrival of the French armies dealt the final blow.

The reformers' concern to heal the breach with the Protestants, reflected in their discussion of clerical celibacy and the chalice for the laity, also found expression in their advocacy of religious toleration. The Electorate had emerged from the Reformation containing more Protestants than any other ecclesiastical state.[3] In the Erfurt and Eichsfeld territories, where most of them were located and where they were in a majority, they succeeded in asserting their right to worship in public. In the city of Mainz, where they were only 600 strong,[4] their position was much less favourable. With the special permission of the electoral government, a Protestant might live and carry on trade in Mainz, but he was not regarded as a full citizen. Even this limited permission was usually granted only on condition that the applicant promised to join the Catholic Church at a later date. His children were baptised by a Catholic priest and he was buried in the corner of a Catholic cemetery, without the accompaniment of a religious service.[5] Outside Erfurt and the Eichsfeld, public exercise of the Protestant religion was permitted only in the eternally embryonic manufacturing town of Höchst.

In view of his other ecclesiastical reforms and his appointment of

---

[1] Kopp, *Katholische Kirche*, pp. 63–6.
[2] Bartolomeo Pacca, 'Die Denkwürdigkeiten des Kardinals Pacca', *Frankfurter zeitgemäße Broschüren*, new series, 28 (1909), 75.
[3] J. J. von Moser, *Einleitung in das Churfürstlich Maynzische Staatsrecht* (Frankfurt am Main, 1755), p. 229.
[4] F. G. Dreyfus, 'Prix et Population à Trèves et à Mayence au XVIIIe siècle', *Revue d'histoire économique et sociale* 34 (1956), p. 242.
[5] Heinrich Schrohe, *Die Stadt Mainz unter kurfürstlicher Verwaltung (1462–1792)*, Beiträge zur Geschichte der Stadt Mainz, vol. 5 (Mainz, 1920), pp. 167–8, 185–6.

Protestants to high positions in the University and the state, it is not surprising that Friedrich Karl considered following Joseph II's example in this sphere also. Early in the reign he had set a personal example of toleration when he visited Erfurt in 1777. He banned the polemical *Controvers-Predigten*, which had been given by Catholic preachers in the cathedral there, visited Protestant churches and invited Protestant ministers to dine with him.[1] In Mainz, although the legal position of the Protestants remained unchanged, the regulations were relaxed in practice to allow an increasing number to settle in the city. Acting on the orders of the central government, the *Vicedom*'s office intervened on numerous occasions in the 1780s to grant special permission to individual Protestants to settle and carry on their trade.[2] However they were only admitted *ad instar civis* and for their religious services they were compelled to travel to Biebrich, in the neighbouring Protestant principality of Nassau.[3]

Friedrich Karl's liberal attitude towards their admission may have encouraged the Protestants to hope for the final removal of their disabilities, for in 1787 the Director of the Electoral Poor House, Rulffs, delivered a petition to the Elector on behalf of his co-religionists, asking that they be allowed to hold services in the city at their own expense.[4] He argued that 'as soon as permission is granted and publicised, many Protestants languishing in intolerant states will quickly desert the scenes of their oppression, and manufacturers and merchants will gladly flock to the fortunate Mainz territories, to live under a wise and tolerant government'.[5]

The Elector referred the matter to his council, which met on 31 December 1787 to consider a report drawn up by councillor Hoffner.[6] Hoffner considered that his master's enlightened views made it unnecessary to repeat abstract arguments in favour of toleration and addressed himself instead to three practical questions: was it advisable to introduce toleration to a German archbishopric and to set up a different religion alongside Roman Catholicism? Would such toleration affect the livelihood of the Electorate's Roman Catholic subjects? Could any material benefits be expected from toleration? As regards the first problem, he emphasised that it was not a question of tolerating a sect which was already established but of setting up an entirely different religion. It could be argued, as even

---

[1] Karl Freiherr von Beaulieu-Marconnay, *Karl von Dalberg und seine Zeit*, vol. 1 (Weimar, 1879), p. 19.   [2] Schrohe, *Stadt Mainz*, pp. 158–66.
[3] Joseph Hansen, *Quellen zur Geschichte des Rheinlandes im Zeitalter der französischen Revolution*, vol. 1 (Bonn, 1931), p. 87, n. 2.
[4] Hermann Stevens, *Toleranzbestrebungen im Rheinland während der Zeit der Aufklärung* (Bonn Dissertation, 1939), p. 16. For details of the signatories, see F. G. Dreyfus, *Sociétés et Mentalités à Mayence dans la seconde moitié du 18. siècle* (Paris, 1968), p. 306.
[5] L. Fronhauser, *Die Geschichte der evangelischen Gemeinde in Mainz* (Mainz, 1902), p. 306.
[6] Vienna, *MEA*, GK, Fasc. 85a. The documents in this fascicle, on which the following paragraphs are based, are not paginated.

Montesquieu had done in *De l'Esprit des Lois*, that two religions in a state created two parties and, especially where one was favoured at the expense of the other, envy and discord were the inevitable result. Having noted the objection, Hoffner dismissed it, by asserting that the Enlightenment which had spread during the last few decades had dispelled those regrettable prejudices which had raised citizen against citizen and brother against brother. He concluded optimistically that it was appreciated 'generally' that no-one had the right to hate members of a different denomination because they disagreed about matters which had no bearing on civic life. Although it was inevitable that certain exclusively Catholic benefices would remain closed to them, it was desirable and indeed essential that Protestants be granted full civil and religious rights.

Although he had stated his belief that there was general agreement on the desirability of toleration, Hoffner anticipated considerable opposition from the guilds. His reply was to take the war into the opposition's camp by arguing that the guilds were useless anachronisms, whose only effect on the economy was to stunt its growth. Although conceding that their total and immediate abolition was impracticable, he demanded that at least the guilds' membership restrictions be lifted; and of course the Protestants be admitted. Hoffner then passed on to the question of positive material benefits. By reference to the catastrophic effects of the revocation of the Edict of Nantes and the strenuous efforts made by contemporary rulers to attract immigrants, he predicted that an announcement of religious toleration in Mainz would woo large numbers of wealthy and industrious Protestants from the North. The Electorate's outstanding geographical position and its wealth of natural assets could also attract some of the Dutch merchants who had been forced to leave their country following the political unrest there. Full toleration could only bring great wealth to the state and its citizens.

The council to which this remarkable report was presented consisted of eight Imperial Knights, seven members of the service nobility and six commoners, including Hoffner. With some qualifications they approved his recommendations, although his outspoken comments on the utility of the guilds were referred to the *Vicedom*'s office for further comment. It was agreed to recommend to the Elector that Protestants be granted full civil rights, private but not public religious worship and the right to elect and pay a pastor and a schoolmaster, subject to electoral confirmation. A minority of five councillors voted that when the Protestants were sufficiently numerous they be allowed to worship in public. Hoffner's report, with the Council's decisions inserted in the margin, was despatched to Friedrich Karl for a final decision.

Although in the preamble to his report Hoffner had mentioned Rulffs' petition, it is possible that the Council was in fact considering a much more ambitious project. In Holland during 1787 the tension between the patriots of the *Frei Korps* and William V had erupted into open violence. The insurrection had only been suppressed with the help of 20,000 Prussian troops. The persecution, which followed the restoration of the Orange régime, forced many of the Patriots to flee to England, France and Germany. At the beginning of December, 1787, one of Friedrich Karl's chief ministers, Maximilian von Strauss, presented a report to him headed 'The utilisation of the present Dutch disorders for the Electorate'.[1] Von Strauss argued that if commercial concessions and the right of private worship were granted, large numbers of wealthy Dutch patriots could be attracted to Mainz. The former Carthusian monastery on the southern perimeter of the city, which had been dissolved to provide funds for the restored University, could be turned into a commercial centre for them. He proposed further that two agents be despatched to Holland to recruit immigrants on the spot. His plan was supported by the Coadjutor von Dalberg. It appears that Friedrich Karl was equally enthusiastic, for three days later the two agents had been selected and their instructions drawn up. Following the advice of von Strauss, the Elector announced his intention of making the Carthusian buildings the centre of a new industrial suburb, promised private and later public worship and offered very generous economic concessions. The two agents, the treasury official Pitschaft and the merchant Pestel, set out for Holland on the pretext of commercial business and arrived in Amsterdam on 27 December. Subsequently they reported that the situation was very confused, that 10,000 families had already fled the country and that although they had succeeded in infiltrating Patriot circles, they were unable to report any positive success. They did however make contact with a Patriot called Peter Ebeling, who according to Pitschaft was a 'half-millionaire' and prepared to help them. By the middle of January the two agents had returned to Mainz. In his final report Pitschaft recommended that Ebeling be made 'Resident Minister' in Holland, his brother given the title of Privy Councillor and that a general edict of toleration be published in various North German newspapers and then reprinted in Dutch and French for clandestine re-distribution in the Netherlands.

The ordinance of 30 January 1788 incorporated both the Council's recommendations and Pitschaft's proposals. Although only private worship was allowed, the seventeen other concessions represented positive encouragement rather than mere toleration.[2] What then happened is

[1] Ibid. Fasc. 84a. The exact date of this and other documents in the fascicle, on which the following paragraphs are based, is impossible to determine.
[2] The eighteen points were: 1. free private exercise of religion in Weisenau or public exercise in Höchst, 2. freedom to build, 3. exemption from customs dues for building materials, 4. cheap building sites, 5. full civil rights, 6. free import of all property, 7. right to leave with all

shrouded in mystery. On 23 March 1788 a Dutch doctor by the name of Van den Heuvell wrote to von Strauss, reminding him that they had once met when Van den Heuvell was passing through Mainz. He informed the minister that like many of his fellow-countrymen he had been forced to leave Holland and was now living in exile in Brussels. A communication purporting to come from the Elector of Mainz had circulated among the Dutch *émigrés* there, promising land for building and many other generous concessions. As a number of his compatriots had decided to accept the offer, Van den Heuvell wanted to know whether the communication was authentic and whether the Dutch could hope to support themselves by trade, manufacturing or professional services. At this point the documents fall silent.

Although it is probable that the number of Protestants in Mainz increased in the 1780s,[1] there is no evidence of a large influx of Dutch *émigrés*. Nor can it be established definitely that the Protestants already in the city were allowed the private exercise of their religion.[2] Almost two years later, in December 1789, an anonymous official was still repeating the desirability of attracting wealthy families to Mainz and thus the necessity of religious toleration.[3] It would appear therefore that although the ordinance of 30 January was published and distributed in the Netherlands, it did not attract many Protestants to Mainz. Many of the *émigrés* had escaped to France and were waiting only for the chance to return to their country and resume the struggle. The outbreak of the French Revolution and disturbances elsewhere in Europe must also have prompted the Elector and his government to consider whether the economic advantages to be expected might not be more than offset by the political radicalism of the immigrants.

belongings without paying customary emigration tax, 8. customs dues to be same as those paid by Mainz merchants, 9. freedom from all regular municipal fees for those settling in Mainz for the first time, 10. freedom from ground rent for all new houses, 11. the same rate of excise as that paid by the other citizens, 12. each denomination (i.e. Lutheran and Calvinist) shall choose one or two representatives for the municipal council, 13. both Lutherans and Calvinists will have the right to present to the Elector the names of two or three candidates to be their pastor, the final selection to be made by the Elector, 14. there will be no closed guilds and everyone will be allowed to pursue his trade freely, 15. to make their social life more pleasurable, state help will be given for the purchase of landed estates, country houses and gardens, 16. hunting or fishing enthusiasts will be allowed to rent electoral hunting and fishing rights, 17. other help and privileges will be granted on the basis of individual merit or need, 18. by way of information it is recorded that Protestants have already been appointed as officials and teachers in Mainz, that they may graduate from the University and that there are many other Protestants in the city carrying on their trade.

[1] Dreyfus, 'Prix et Population', 242.
[2] Stevens, *Toleranzbestrebungen*, p. 17. Fronhauser, *Geschichte der evangelischen Gemeinde*, wrote that nothing was known after the presentation of Rulff's original petition, but he had seen only the documents in the *Pfarrarchiv*.
[3] Vienna, *MEA*, GK, Fasc. 85a.

Although it is clear that they believed in religious toleration for its own sake, Friedrich Karl and his ministry did not support it out of pure altruism; they expected that it would bring very real economic benefits for the state. The same mixture of motives dictated their policy towards the Jews. As in most European countries, the Jews of the Electorate had been frequently persecuted and expelled and just as frequently readmitted. After a terrible pogrom in 1348 they did not begin to drift back until the seventeenth century. In 1672 two streets were sealed off by gates to form a ghetto and a nightly curfew was imposed.[1] Jews were only allowed to settle in the state if they could prove possession of a capital sum of 5,000 gulden. In addition to all regular forms of taxation they had to pay a special tax, which varied between 30 and 60 gulden per annum, according to rates of assessment. The Jews who resided in the city in 1783 were excluded from the guilds and schools, were subjected to all kinds of legal disabilities and were unable to buy property.[2]

The three ordinances issued by Friedrich Karl in 1783 and 1784 did not establish parity with the Electorate's Christian subjects but did ameliorate the Jews' condition considerably. The first reorganised all Jews under one rabbi and admitted them to the regular courts in all civil and criminal cases. All forms of legal discrimination were abolished and the officials were ordered 'most expressly, to provide the Jews, just as the Christians, with quick justice, to punish them in no way more severely than the other Christian subjects and to impose the same court fees'.[3] A second ordinance made arrangements for the holding of a General Jewish Assembly in Aschaffenburg to make financial provision for their Chief Rabbi, while a number of other measures were taken to bring the community under closer state supervision. At the same time, 'so as not to omit anything which might promote the education and future happiness of the Jews', all Jewish children were to be admitted to Christian schools. Local officials were ordered to help dispel any prejudices which might obstruct the introduction of this innovation. Greater security for Jewish property-owners was arranged; in all areas where guild regulations were not in force Jews were to be allowed to found industrial enterprises.[4] A final ordinance

---

[1] F. Dael, 'Die Bevölkerungsverhältnisse der Stadt Mainz von den ältesten bis zu den neuesten Zeiten', *Hübners Jahrbuch für Volkswissenschaft und Statistik* (1853), 29. Heinrich Wothe, *Mainz* (Mainz, 1928), p. 200.
[2] Josef Cremer, *Die Finanzen in der Stadt Mainz im 18. Jahrhundert* (Giessen dissertation, 1932), p. 32. There is considerable uncertainty as to the size of the Jewish community. Dael's estimate for the early 1780s is 8–900 – 'Bevölkerungsverhältnisse', 29. Dreyfus' estimate for 1773 is c. 300, although he is of the opinion that it grew: 'Prix et Population', 242. Schrohe notes that in 1778 the central government informed the *Vicedom*'s office that there were 101 Jews in the city, although this figure probably does not include their families, *Stadt Mainz*, p. 171. On the economic activity of the Jewish community, see Dreyfus, *Mayence*, pp. 308–20.   [3] A. L. Schlözer, *Staatsanzeigen*, vol. 6 (1784), p. 502.
[4] Ibid., p. 504.

of September 1784 emphasised particularly that Christian teachers should not treat their Jewish pupils with contempt. It also allowed Jews to buy property in all parts of the Electorate, except Mainz itself, and to cultivate the soil themselves.[1] In all three ordinances there were constant references to the Elector's attachment to religious toleration and his 'aversion to any restraint on the freedom of conscience'. Although the desire to bring the Jews under closer state control may have played a part, it is clear that Friedrich Karl's motive was also humanitarian. As in his policy towards the Protestants, he was following very much in the footsteps of Joseph II, who in 1782 had abolished many of the disabilities from which the Jews in the Habsburg Monarchy suffered.[2] Although the Jews in Mainz were still excluded from the guilds in the city and were still obliged to pay the *Judenschutzgelder*, compared with their co-religionists in other German territories their situation was distinctly favourable.[3]

III

Friedrich Karl was more ambitious and, at least on paper, more thorough than either of his predecessors, but in the reforms described so far he was only following lines laid down decades before by Stadion, Groschlag, Bentzel and others. Education and religion were of course common preoccupations of both theorists and practitioners of the German Enlightenment in general. Consequently, it represented a significant expansion of the traditional legislative scope of his office, when Friedrich Karl turned his attention to agriculture. Although the great majority of the inhabitants of the Electorate lived on the land, previous electors had neglected agriculture almost entirely in favour of the more obviously remunerative sectors of trade and industry. As usual, there is no evidence of a direct causal link between theory and practice, although it seems reasonable to surmise that Friedrich Karl's legislation reflected the great upsurge of interest in agriculture in the second half of the century.[4] The Elector and his ministry would certainly not have been ignorant of the new developments. In his *Manual of Economic and Cameral Science*, Johann Friedrich Pfeiffer, Professor of Cameralism at Mainz, devoted a good deal of space to agricultural improvements.

[1] Ibid., p. 509.
[2] Extracts from Joseph's legislation are reprinted in T. C. W. Blanning, *Joseph II and Enlightened Despotism* (London, 1970), pp. 142–4.
[3] See, for example, Nicolai Karamsin's horrifying description of the situation of the Jews in the Imperial City of Frankfurt am Main, in *Letters of a Russian Traveller, 1789–90*, tr. F. Jonas (Columbia, 1957), pp. 100–1.
[4] Wilhelm Abel, *Geschichte der deutschen Landwirtschaft vom frühen Mittelalter bis zum 19. Jahrhundert* (Stuttgart, 1962), pp. 185, 260–3.

Friedrich Karl's policy took the form of encouragement, advice and even direct assistance to 'improving' peasants. An ordinance of 1784, for example, observed that several communities, by enclosing their waste land and planting clover on it, had incurred the hostility of certain minority interests, especially shepherds. The electoral officials were instructed to make sure that the enclosures were not obstructed, because 'the best possible cultivation of the soil forms both the most important concern and the wealth of the state; the best possible cultivation of the soil, however, requires the best livestock, and it is impossible to get the best livestock without sufficient fodder'.[1] As a corollary of this argument, the export of manure was prohibited. A determined attempt was made to acquaint every community in the Electorate with the advantages of artificial pasture. A short guide praising and explaining the cultivation of clover was distributed free. Officials were authorised to give the peasants financial assistance to obtain the right kind of clover and to reward the successful innovators amongst them.[2]

Ease of cultivation, high yield-density and nutritional value made the potato a very attractive crop to governments ever-anxious about social unrest arising from erratic grain harvests. Unlike their French colleagues, the Rhenish peasants took to potatoes with alacrity; Thomas Pennant noted their cultivation in the Electorate as early as 1765.[3] Although private initiative was doubtless responsible for the first introduction of the plant, the government certainly did all it could to encourage its spread. Officials were again instructed to encourage potato cultivation, to help peasants obtain seed and to advance money for the purpose from the communal funds, because 'potatoes are an important food for humans and animals'.[4]

Perhaps it was the relatively small scale of the Electorate which enabled and encouraged its ruler to pay special attention to individual cases of hardship. Schlözer's *Staats Anzeigen*, normally hypercritical of anything connected with an ecclesiastical state, recorded approvingly that an impoverished village in the Erfurt territory had been exempted from taxation for six years and given an interest-free loan of 900 gulden for the purchase of livestock.[5] Throughout the Electorate, peasants afflicted by flood or fire were paid compensation from communal and government funds and from voluntary donations collected by local officials.[6]

---

[1] Mainz, *Kurmainzische Verordnungen*, 1te Sammlung, vol. 4, 999.
[2] Ibid. 3te Sammlung, vol. 1, 58.
[3] See above, pp. 91–3. The potato in France, on the other hand, was 'si peu répandue qu'elle ne figure même pas parmi les produits agricoles portés aux états de prix du Contrôle général' – Albert Soboul, *La France à la Veille de la Révolution* (Paris, 1966), p. 16.
[4] Mainz, *Kurmainzische Verordnungen*, 1te Sammlung, vol. 6, 1441.
[5] Schlözer, *Staatsanzeigen* (1782), 3, p. 308.
[6] Mainz, *Kurmainzische Verordnungen*, 1te Sammlung, vol. 3, 657, 3te Sammlung, vol. 3, 350.

Enlightened absolutism, 1774–1802

In 1787 Friedrich Karl announced his intention of abolishing *Leibeigenschaft*, necessarily but unsatisfactorily translated as 'serfdom'. He admitted that it existed 'in a considerable part' of his dominions, that the dues involved when a serf died or moved from his village were onerous and that as a result agriculture, population growth and the welfare of individual peasants suffered. He added, however, that the dues would be redeemable, since the treasury could not be expected to abandon this source of income.[1] Local officials were instructed to confer with the communities in their districts and agree upon a method of raising the necessary money. It was not until December 1791 that these consultations were concluded and the arrangements for abolition announced.[2] The rate of redemption fixed was twenty times the average annual sum paid by any community in *Leibeigenschaft* dues. The communities were authorised to borrow the sum necessary, or to cede to the electoral treasury communal property or rights of equivalent value.

It is impossible to gain any exact impression of the effect of this and the other measures designed to promote agriculture. Certainly there is clear evidence that most Mainz peasants were much less wretched than their French or East European counterparts,[3] although this was due in part to a more favourable environment. Nevertheless, Friedrich Karl's policies do mark a decisive break from the exclusively urban orientation of previous electors. As the educational and religious reforms had already indicated, the peasant was now regarded as being more than a fiscal *Milchkuh*. In this sphere again, Friedrich Karl was no innovator; somewhat belatedly he was following paths mapped out already by the secular princes, especially by Joseph II. Simultaneously, other prince-bishops were introducing similar pieces of legislation.[4] Even if the measures had no real effect on agricultural development, it seems likely that their mere enactment helped to draw the sting of rural discontent. There was no serious peasant disturbance in the Electorate in the 1780s and 1790s; indeed, during the latter decade thousands of peasants serving in the local militia conducted highly effective guerila warfare against the French revolutionary armies.[5]

Although Friedrich Karl's attention to the needs of the rural population marked a break with the past, his policy towards trade and industry did not. As with most of the German princes, his economic practice was still dictated by the mercantilist ideal of a self-sufficient state. Particular attention

[1] Würzburg, *MRA*, Leibeigenschaft, 27, K 168.
[2] Mainz, *Kurmainzische Verordnungen*, 6te Sammlung, vol. 11, 119.
[3] See above, pp. 91–5.
[4] Hildegunde Flurschütz, *Die Verwaltung des Hochstifts Würzburg unter Franz Ludwig von Erthal*, Veröffentlichungen der Gesellschaft für fränkische Geschichte, 9th series, vol. 19 (Würzburg, 1965), pp. 113–25. Braubach, *Max Franz*, pp. 141–4.
[5] Karl Rothenbücher, *Der Kurmainzer Landsturm in den Jahren 1799 und 1800* (Augsburg, 1878).

was paid to the natural resources of the Electorate. In 1775, for example, the export of wool was prohibited, following complaints about shortages from the weavers' guild.¹ Under the influence of the new cameralist faculty at the University, attempts were made to develop the state's extensive but hitherto neglected mineral resources.² Although the population of the Electorate was increasing both naturally and by immigration, the Elector followed the mercantilists in believing that the export of humans was as detrimental to the economy as the export of raw materials. An ordinance of 1784 forbade emigration without the express permission of the government.³

Friedrich Karl showed far less interest than either of his two predecessors in commerce. Of the few measures taken in this field during his reign, the most important were the construction of new quays for shipping on the banks of the Rhine and the conclusion of a treaty with Würzburg to regulate shipping on the Main and to arrange a mutual reduction of freight and customs tariffs.⁴ This relative neglect was probably due less to any basic lack of interest or to a belief in *laissez-faire* than to the fact that government interference was no longer felt to be necessary. For it was after 1770 that there was a marked acceleration in economic growth throughout the Rhineland.⁵ There were, however, occasional signs that Friedrich Karl was prepared to consider at least a modification of the Electorate's traditional economic structure. The guilds were not abolished entirely, but their last rights of self-government were removed, police commissars were appointed to supervise their activities and they were compelled to admit previously unwanted applicants, such as orphans, bastards and the sons of paupers. Simultaneous attempts were made to foster industrial enterprises outside the guild system.⁶

The attempts to improve both the lot and productivity of the peasantry were paralleled by a programme of social legislation for the urban poor of Mainz. This involved 'the secularisation of charity', the acquisition by the state of a monopoly of social responsibilities which in the past had been shared with the Church. As there is no evidence of any dereliction of duty on the part of the latter, it can be assumed with some confidence that here again contemporary ideology and contemporary example were decisive. In the Habsburg Monarchy, the source of so much of Friedrich Karl's

¹ Mainz, *Kurmainzische Verordnungen*, 6te Sammlung, vol. 8, 12 June 1775.
² Johann Friedrich Pfeiffer, *Von der Nothwendigkeit der in den kurmainzischen Landen auflebenden Berwerks- und Schmelzwissenschaften* (Mainz, 1784).
³ Mainz, *Kurmainzische Verordnungen*, 6te Sammlung, vol. 9, 192.
⁴ Karl Bockenheimer, *Das öffentliche Leben in Mainz am Ende des 18. Jahrhunderts* (Mainz, 1902), p. 24. Flurschütz, *Würzburg*, p. 145.
⁵ See above, pp. 72–6.
⁶ Friedrich Schmitt, *Das Mainzer Zunftwesen und die französische Herrschaft* (Frankfurt am Main and Darmstadt, 1929), pp. 34, 41–2. See above, p. 78.

domestic legislation, the process of secularisation was largely completed during the middle decades of the eighteenth century. Joseph II continued the process, paying special attention to the needs of the mentally and physically handicapped.¹ Both here and later in Mainz, the detailed legislation reflected the influence of the Italian reformer Lodovico Muratori, whose most important work in this field – *Christian Charity* – had been translated into German in 1761. In many German states reforming princes introduced schemes based on his general principles.²

The core of the reorganisation in Mainz was a new Poor Law, devised and implemented by August Friedrich Rulffs. Formerly a Hanoverian minister, Rulffs had made his name with two books on work-houses and orphanages. After his arrival in Mainz in April 1786, reforms based on his proposals followed quickly; in August a General Poverty Commission for the whole Electorate was set up, followed in October by a Special Poverty Commission for the city.³ Their instructions in the form of a General Poor Law were published at the beginning of the next year.⁴ The new ordinance made a sharp distinction between those who were destitute on account of physical disability and those who were able to work but unable to find employment. The paupers of the former category were to be admitted to the hospitals and other charitable foundations, or paid outdoor relief if they preferred to remain in their own homes. Poor people suffering temporary illness were to be provided with free medical attention and medicine. On the other hand, anyone physically capable of working was to be put to work in a factory controlled by the Poverty Commission. Citizens who were too proud to reveal their poverty could have the tools and materials fetched from the factory by a third person and could do their work in the privacy of their own homes. The under-employed, the unmarried mothers, and the prostitutes were also expected to form part of the factory's labour force. As it was held that provision had now been made for every conceivable kind of destitution, all begging without a special permit was to stop at once. Anyone caught giving alms to a beggar would be fined 5 gulden for a first offence and at the discretion of the courts for successive offences. Observant citizens who reported such illegal acts of philanthropy were to be rewarded with half of the fine.

Although the factory appears to have enjoyed considerable initial success, with over 900 people employed, by the end of 1789 it was in difficulties. Rulffs' combination of arrogance and wilfulness made many

---

[1] Grete Klingenstein, *Staatsverwaltung und kirchliche Autorität im 18. Jahrhundert* (Vienna, 1970), pp. 69–73. Eduard Winter, *Der Josefinismus* (Berlin, 1962), pp. 177–90.
[2] Lotte Koch, *Wandlungen der Wohlfahrtspflege im Zeitalter der Aufklärung* (Erlangen, 1933).
[3] F. Rösch, *Die Mainzer Armenreform vom Jahre 1786*, Arbeiten aus dem Forschungsinstitut für Fürsorgewesen in Frankfurt am Main, vol. 3 (Berlin, 1929), p. 19.
[4] Mainz, *Kurmainzische Verordnungen*, 6te Sammlung, vol. 10, 184.

enemies among the electoral officials concerned with the project and finally destroyed the confidence of the Elector.[1] Although local officials were ordered to buy cloth for the uniforms of their servants and the clothing of the inmates of the electoral prisons from the factory, the high cost of the raw materials and the incompetence of the workers destroyed original hopes that the venture could be run at a profit. Consequently plans to found similar factories elsewhere in the Electorate had to be abandoned. At the same time an ambitious plan to reorganise the collection of alms for the unemployable poor came to nothing.[2]

Other attempts to improve the condition of the Electorate's less fortunate subjects were more successful. After 1784 unmarried pregnant women were admitted free to the new maternity hospital for their confinement.[3] In 1786 an institution for the education of deaf-mutes was established. Its director had been sent to Paris at government expense to study at the institute of Charles Abbé de l'Épée, probably the most important of all the eighteenth century pioneers in this field.[4] In the same year a new set of regulations was issued to make prison conditions more humane. No one could be held in custody for longer than eight days without a hearing; local officials were ordered to make sure that prisoners sent to Mainz were adequately clothed; the use of irons was forbidden, and the regular inspection of prisons was arranged.[5] Corporal punishment required express government permission and a prior medical examination of the victim. Only a leather-covered cane could be used.[6] These measures appear to have had the desired effect, for in 1793 the English traveller Charles Este was full of praise for the Electorate's penal arrangements. Although he may only have been repeating the claims of the electoral officials, he reported that since the reforms of 1786, trials were quicker, fees were lower, capital punishment was almost unknown, as was imprisonment for debt, the prisons were inspected regularly, their object was correction rather than punishment and their inmates were well-fed.[7]

---

[1] Rösch, *Armenreform*, p. 22.
[2] Ibid., pp. 59, 91, 133–4.
[3] *Journal von und für Deutschland* (1784), p. 137.
[4] Helmut Mathy, 'Medizinhistorische Miniaturen aus dem Bereich der Mainzer Universität vom Ende des 18. Jahrhunderts', *Jahrbuch der Vereinigung 'Freunde der Universität Mainz'*, 12 (1963), p. 109.
[5] *Journal von und für Deutschland* (1786), 47–9.
[6] Mainz, *Kurmainzische Verordnungen*, 1te Sammlung, vol. 5, 1250.
[7] C. L. A. Este, *A Journey in the Year 1793 through Flanders, Brabant and Germany to Switzerland* (London, 1795), pp. 304–6. Two years earlier another traveller, Frederik Münter, had written 'The administration of justice is said to be good here and to contrast greatly with the wretched situation in the Palatinate' – Andreasen and Mathy, 'Münters Reise', 67.

IV

It was relatively simple for the Elector and his ministers, sitting in their offices in Mainz, to review the state of the Electorate, to identify its defects and to draw up long, elaborate and tedious reforming ordinances. It was less easy to goad the administration into actually carrying them out. The delay of four years between the original ordinance and the actual presentation of the reports on the abolition of serfdom, for example, indicated a marked lack of urgency among the officials in the localities. The central government was well aware of the shortcomings of its agents and admonitory ordinances throbbed with indignation at their neglect of duty: 'We have noticed with displeasure how much electoral officials ignore Our orders and presume to regard their implementation as a matter of no consequence, so that on several occasions the electoral officials themselves have had to be proceeded against.'[1] Despite threats of dire punishment or summary dismissal, the local officials ambled on regardless. In 1776, for example, it was decreed that all schoolmasters should in future be selected from the graduates of the Mainz College of Education.[2] Thirteen years later a furious ordinance noted that this particular measure had been ignored and that despite repeated reminders electoral educational policy had been carried out badly or not at all. In 1785 an ordinance listed no fewer than sixteen faults prevalent in local administration.[3]

With a highly ambitious brain and a fitfully responsive body, the Mainz body politic was suffering from multiple sclerosis, and throughout his reign Friedrich Karl made numerous attempts at radical surgery. The Council's conduct of business was rearranged, new departments were created, the number of officials was increased and new independent bodies were set up.[4] The patient was incurable. When the arrival of the French armies removed both the opportunity and the need for further reform, the old abuses remained. The Council was still overloaded, administration and justice were still intertwined, financial affairs were still confused and offices continued to be bought and sold.[5] In his detailed study of the Electorate's administration, Hans Goldschmidt dismissed Friedrich Karl's reforms and at the same time explained their failure by seeing them as a vainglorious attempt to give Mainz the appearance of a great state. The creation of new government bodies with bombastic titles but negligible

---

[1] Mainz, *Kurmainzische Verordnungen*, 1te Sammlung, vol. 4, 993.
[2] Ibid. 6te Sammlung, vol. 8, 26 August 1776.
[3] Ibid., vol. 11, 7, 1te Sammlung, vol. 5, 1155.
[4] Hans Goldschmidt, *Zentralbehörden und Beamtentum im Kurfürstentum Mainz vom 16. bis zum 18. Jahrhundert*, Abhandlungen zur mittleren und neueren Geschichte, vol. 7 (Berlin and Leipzig, 1908), pp. 82–8, 90–1, 120, 134–5, 163, 181–2.
[5] Ibid., pp. 105, 124, 139, 146, 168, 192.

duties and the growing discrepancy between the salaries of court and state officials lend considerable weight to this view. It is also reinforced by a comparison of the elaborate Mainz structure with the more modest counterparts in the other ecclesiastical states.[1]

Yet is would be a mistake to condemn the entire administrative reform as a *folie de grandeur*. Friedrich Karl certainly loved to play the part of the Great Monarch but, as two ordinances of 1788 showed, he was also genuinely concerned that his subjects be governed justly. The first announced that the Elector would hold general audiences every Monday at four in the afternoon. All subjects were entitled to attend and expound their grievances to their master in person. The second ordinance was a more direct warning to oppressive or negligent officials. Friedrich Karl asserted that his entire policy had been based on the premise that 'princes only exist to promote the well-being of their subjects', adding that this could not be realised without the assistance of his officials. The latter must not think that they had fulfilled the obligations of their office if they merely avoided censure; they were also required to keep a constant watch on 'the character, the morals, the physical condition, the order and the economic condition of their subjects'. To ensure that the officials proved worthy of their vocation, the supervision of their activities was to become more rigorous. At the end of every quarter the district offices were to send in lists of cases still outstanding in their territories and the reasons for the delays. The central judicial authorities were to report to the Elector on all cases involving abuses or negligence on the part of the officials. Although he stressed that nothing would please him more than to find everything functioning perfectly, Friedrich Karl announced his intention of conducting personal inspections of local districts.[2] That these two ordinances were necessary at all in 1788 was a reflection on the failure of his previous attempts at reorganisation.

Bureaucratic failure was not of course a problem peculiar to Mainz. Even in Prussia and Austria many of the local officials blithely ignored the elaborate legislation formulated by the central government and remained impervious to threats of retribution.[3] This was due partly to ignorance, partly to laziness, and partly to hostility to the law in question and partly to deference to the local nobility. As the gap widened between centre and periphery, between plan and execution, legislation *per se* became discredited. Wilhelm von Humboldt's *Ideen zu einem Versuch, die Grenzen der Wirksamkeit des Staats zu bestimmen* of 1792 was only one reflection of this malaise. Even in Mainz there was an echo. In 1793 the liberal canon

---

[1] See, for example, the situation in the Electorate of Cologne – Braubach, *Max Franz*, pp. 97–9.
[2] *Journal von und für Deutschland* (1788), 2.
[3] Hans Rosenberg, *Bureaucracy, Aristocracy & Autocracy: The Prussian Experience, 1660–1815* (Boston, 1958). On Austria, see Blanning, *Joseph II*, pp. 77–9.

Enlightened absolutism, 1774-1802

Johann Philipp Count von Stadion wrote to his friend Daniel Dumont that the two main faults of the Electorate were the failure of the administration to implement laws and 'the passion for innovation'. Later he wrote that the first rule of good government was 'do not govern too much. I believe that the multiplicity of laws, whether prohibitive or prescriptive, is a malaise of the present century.'[1] Johann Philipp was the son of Friedrich Count von Stadion, who more than any individual was responsible for the introduction to Mainz of omnicompetent 'enlightened absolutism'. The wheel had turned full circle.

ENLIGHTENMENT AND REACTION FROM BELOW

I

Quite apart from the question as to how much of the government's programme was actually implemented, there is a certain unreality in discussing legislation in isolation from the Electorate's subjects. This approach can be justified, because when this period began there was little or no intellectual activity outside government circles. Indeed the supposed backwardness of the Electorate was at least partly responsible for the institution of the reforms in the first place. By the 1780s, however, the efforts of Stadion, Groschlag, Bentzel and the others had begun to bear fruit. Signs proliferated that enlightened ideas were no longer the monopoly of government officials and university professors. In view of the strenuous efforts by three successive electors to propagate these ideas, through a reformed educational system, explanatory and admonitory ordinances and official publications such as *Der Bürger*,[2] this was hardly surprising.

One indication of this diffusion of the Enlightenment was the publication of a number of journals not directly sponsored by the government. Although their quality was mediocre in the extreme, their very existence testified to a certain intellectual self-consciousness. The first issue of the *Mainzer Anzeigen von gelehrten Sachen* asserted defiantly that Mainz was just as entitled at Göttingen, Leipzig, Jena or Tübingen to present to foreigners the products of its own intellectuals. It also claimed proudly that Mainz was the only Catholic University to publish a learned journal (*gelehrte Zeitung*).[3] The *Magazin der Philosophie und schönen Literatur*,

---

[1] A. Jäger, *Daniel Dumont* (Frankfurt am Main dissertation, 1920), pp. 224, 235. He was echoing – probably unknowingly – the words of Justus Möser: 'It is the general malaise of the present century that so many general laws are made and so few observed' – quoted in F. M. Barnard, *Herder's Social and Political Thought* (Oxford, 1965), p. 26.
[2] See above, p. 122.
[3] The *Mainzer Anzeigen von gelehrten Sachen* was published in Mainz from 1785 to 1791. A complete set of this and other journals can be found in the Mainz *Stadtbibliothek*.

which also appeared first in 1785, published poems, reviews and reports on events in Mainz of interest to academics, such as the opening of the reformed University. Deservedly, it perished after only four issues.[1]

By far the most important was the *Mainzer Monatschrift von geistlichen Sachen*. Although edited and for the most part written by members of the archiepiscopal Vicariate, it was not formally an official publication. Nevertheless, its editorial policy was always faithful to the enlightened Catholicism preached and practised by the Elector and his Suffragan Bishop, Heimes. During the dispute over the papal nuncios and the Congress of Ems, for example, it entered the polemical lists repeatedly to propagate the Mainz position. Government ordinances on ecclesiastical matters were both publicised and recommended. The *Monatschrift* was insistent that the reform of baroque piety was the only alternative to the decay of Catholicism. The ordinance requiring priests to offer their parishioners religious instruction[2] was accompanied by the observation that this measure was particularly necessary in view of the simultaneous elimination of monkish superstition and return to Christian simplicity: 'however loudly the selfish or short-sighted crowd of bigots may shout, this is inevitable if we do not wish to look on with indifference as all straight-thinking people turn further and further from religion'.[3] Special pride was taken in the Elector's tolerant outlook. A report on how the authorities fetched a Lutheran pastor from Nassau to tend to one of his co-religionists, who was dying in prison at Mainz, was heralded with the words: 'In Mainz the divine daughter of Heaven, toleration, is being diffused more and more.'[4]

The individual literary works produced were as closely connected with the political and academic establishment as the journals. Of the twenty-one books published in Mainz in 1787, nine were theological, legal or medical treatises written in Latin.[5] The rest consisted almost entirely of academic works on mineralogy, philosophy, archaeology, law, medicine, economics, natural history and educational theory. All the three works on philosophy were written by Anton Dorsch, of whom more later. One's general impression of the list is that the Mainz intellectual community was oriented very much towards sober scholarship; the only piece of fiction was a Latin edition of Aesop's fables.

A better indication of the growth of a spontaneous interest in the Enlightenment was the emergence of masonic and literary societies. An abortive start had been made in the 1760s. The papal bulls condemning free-

---

[1] *Magazin der Philosophie und schönen Literatur* (Mainz and Leipzig, 1785-6).
[2] See above, p. 176.
[3] *Mainzer Monatschrift von geistlichen Sachen*, 5 (1789), p. 393.
[4] Ibid., 1 (1785), p. 1008.
[5] The list is taken from the *Mainzer Anzeigen von gelehrten Sachen* of 1787.

Enlightened absolutism, 1774–1802

masonry were never published in the Electorate and in 1765 the lodge 'At the Three Thistles' was founded. When the Elector ordered its closure two years later it had attracted a membership of 44.[1] Subsequently Freemasons in Mainz were compelled to join lodges in neighbouring principalities, until the foundation of a new lodge in the city in 1789. As suggested by its name – 'Friedrich Karl Joseph At The Golden Wheel' – the new foundation enjoyed the Elector's blessing. By the time it was closed down by the French occupation authorities three years later, its membership had grown to about seventy.[2] Mainz was also the home of a branch of the *Illuminati*, that mysterious order held responsible by the Abbé Barruel for the French Revolution. Founded in the early 1780s, its membership of fifty was the largest in the Rhineland.[3] Finally there was a group of Rosicrucians (*Rosenkreuzerorden*) in the city, but no evidence has survived about its activities.[4] Any precise definition of the aims of these groups is made impossible by the exceedingly vague nature of the little evidence that has survived. Adam Weishaupt's definition of the *Illuminati*'s programme was typical: 'My aim is to help reason gain supremacy. The ideal of the Order is to diffuse light. We are fighters against darkness.'[5] All that can be said with confidence of the Mainz members of the Masons, *Illuminati* and perhaps Rosicrucians is that they were for 'enlightenment' and against 'superstition', which is little enough.

More important than these phantom groups was the Reading Club (*Lesegesellschaft*), which opened in 1781. Modelled on the clubs frequently found in North Germany, its expressed aim was 'to provide a suitable opportunity to read at a low cost new publications of all kinds and to enjoy social relationships in which literary and political knowledge will be exchanged'.[6] The Club's premises on the *Höfchen* near the Cathedral consisted of two reading rooms and two clubrooms for discussion and refreshment.[7] For an annual subscription of twelve gulden, a member could take his pick of twenty-three literary and twenty-four political newspapers, forty-one periodicals and a large number of serially issued works of reference.[8] A visitor to Mainz in 1783 reported that the Reading Club 'has no equal in Germany', that its 193 members included 'almost all ministers, canons of the Cathedral Chapter, the most enlightened section of the

---

[1] Hansen, *Quellen*, vol. 1, p. 71. [2] Ibid., p. 72.
[3] Ibid., p. 46. [4] Ibid., p. 72.
[5] Quoted in G. P. Gooch, *Germany and the French Revolution* (New Impression, London, 1965), p. 30.
[6] Hansen, *Quellen*, vol. 1, p. 16.
[7] D. J. P. Schunk, *Beiträge zur Mainzer Geschichte mit Urkunden* vol. 1 (Frankfurt and Leipzig, 1788), p. 9. Helmut Mathy, 'Gelehrte, okkulte und studentische Vereinigungen und Gesellschaften in Mainz am Ende des 18. Jahrhunderts', *Jahrbuch der Vereinigung 'Freunde der Universität Mainz'* (1969), p. 73.
[8] A complete list of the publications taken can be found in Hansen, *Quellen*, vol. 1, p. 17.

nobility and other important people' and that 'in short everything is so decorous and well-organised that it does Mainz an honour and is very well-worthy of imitation'.[1] This verdict was echoed by a number of members. The historian Niklas Vogt wrote at about the same time: 'All good political and academic newspapers, all celebrated journals etc. are read here, and in both conversation and argument there rules a truly British freedom, which pays tribute to both the government and the people.'[2]

The extent and spontaneity of popular interest in the Enlightenment can be well established. Far more important is its social composition. The Enlightenment is usually seen as a bourgeois phenomenon, fundamentally opposed to the nobility;[3] and indeed its basic assumptions and positive recommendations do seem antipathetic to any kind of privilege. The observation of the traveller quoted above that all the 'best' people in Mainz were members of the Reading Club indicates that the situation there was more complicated. Superficially there was every reason for a deep ideological divide between nobles and commoners. The severity of the Imperial Knights' marital regulations, probably the strictest of any European nobility, has already been discussed. Their caste-consciousness was doubtless heightened by their equally exclusive education. Either the young baron or count was taught by a private tutor and a series of specialised dancing, fencing and riding masters, or he was sent to a boarding school reserved for the higher nobility. The five young Counts von Kesselstadt combined both; after a preliminary course of study at Mainz with their tutor, they were sent on to the *Ritterakademie* at Vienna, where they mixed only with boys of their own class.[4] Final intellectual polish was added by a period at a university. The visit of three of the young Kesselstadts to the University of Strasbourg coincided with that of Goethe, but it may be doubted whether they moved in the same circles. The accounts of their expenditure there consist predominantly of visits to concerts, balls and the theatre and of depressingly regular losses at cards.[5]

Probably the most important part of the nobleman's education was the Grand Tour, designed to add the final embellishment of social grace. Although the itinerary of the Tour, which usually lasted at least two years,

[1] 'Auszug eines Briefes vom Rhein', *Neue Reisebemerkungen in und über Deutschland von verschiedenen Verfassern*, vol. 4 (Halle, 1787).
[2] Quoted in M. Herrmann, *Niklas Vogt, ein Historiker der Mainzer Universität* (Munich dissertation, 1916), p. 84.
[3] See, for example, Klaus Epstein, *The Genesis of German Conservatism* (Princeton, 1966), p. 61. Recently however this view has been challenged by, among others, Betty Behrens, '"Straight History" and "History in Depth": The Experience of Writers on Eighteenth Century France', *Historical Journal*, VIII, 1 (1965); Denis Richet, 'Autour des origines idéologiques lointaines de la Révolution française: élites et despotisme', *Annales, Économies, Sociétés, Civilisations*, 24, 1 (1969); Robert Darnton, 'In Search of Enlightenment: Recent attempts to create a social history of ideas', *Journal of Modern History*, 43 (1971).
[4] Trier, 3791–99.   [5] Ibid., 3800.

Enlightened absolutism, 1774–1802

varied considerably, it always included Paris and Versailles. Anselm Casimir Count von Eltz began his tour with nine months of legal studies at Leyden. He then progressed in a leisurely fashion through the courts and provincial towns of Holland, Brabant and Flanders, before arriving in Paris in February 1733. He spent six months there, living a life of fashion and spending a great deal of money. Perhaps because his uncle had become Elector of Mainz the year before, he was received by Fleury and Louis XV at Versailles. He also crossed over to England, where he visited Windsor, Oxford and Blenheim, went hunting at Richmond with the Duke of Hamilton and was presented to George II.[1] As an educational exercise, the tour's success obviously depended on the individual noble's proclivities. The journals of the two Counts von Eltz suggest that they spent most of their time visiting their fellow-nobles and ladies of fashion, which was doubtless an education in itself.

On his return to Mainz, the young noble had every opportunity to lead a social life entirely among members of his own class; at court, in the palaces or in the noble club on the *Große Bleiche*, the centre of Mainz high society.[2] Restricted of course to the Imperial Knights, membership of the latter fluctuated between sixty and seventy. There were two ballrooms and several rooms open each day for gaming. The climax of the season were the masked balls held in December, January and February, when two eight-piece bands performed in the ball-room, refreshments were provided and the inevitable gaming tables were laid out. These occasions appear to have been highly popular; eight balls held in February 1765 yielded 1,864 gulden in entrance money. They also allowed the committee to run the Club at a profit; by 1786 they had paid off the 18,000 gulden borrowed to buy the premises in 1762 and had amassed a further surplus of 18,000 gulden.

It is certain that the combination of snobbery and predilection for French culture paraded by many nobles irritated intellectuals intensely. In 1780 Risbeck wrote of the Mainz nobility: 'They all speak a wretched French jargon and are really ashamed of their mother-tongue; also very few of them have any close acquaintance with the literature of their fatherland, because on the other hand they know even the most trivial of our [i.e. French] authors.'[3] He observed that most of them brought home from the Grand Tour only the patois of the Parisian fish-women and a taste for French clothes.[4] Johann Becker's summary of their souvenirs

---

[1] Eltville, unnumbered manuscript.
[2] On the Club, see the *Protocolla cum Adjunctis de anno 1762 usque 1792, das adeliche Gesellschaftshaus betreffend*, now at Eltville.
[3] Quoted in Hainebach, *Studien*, p. 1. Risbeck was of course German, but in the anonymous edition of his *Travels* he pretended to be a Frenchman.
[4] Risbeck, *Travels*, p. 210.

was even more abrasive: 'venereal disease, dulled senses and dissipated powers'.[1]

Although doubtless many of the nobles richly deserved this abuse, it is not difficult to show that there were so many exceptions as to make these generalisations worthless. First and foremost there is the simple fact that the Enlightenment in Mainz was largely the creation of Imperial Knights or Counts: the three electors and their ministers Stadion, Groschlag and Bentzel. Certainly the reforms demanded by Becker, or even Risbeck, were a good deal more radical than those introduced in Mainz, but this in no way authenticates their depiction of the nobles as mindless consumers with no interests outside *galanterie à la mode*. The evidence against these generalisations is fragmentary but suggestive. The bills for their book purchases indicate that some nobles at least were not only interested in works on horse ailments and erotica. Between 1782 and 1786 Friedrich Joseph von Franckenstein spent almost 3,000 gulden on books. His library included Diderot and D'Alembert's *Encyclopédie* and works by Ovid, Milton, Pascal and Rousseau.[2] Hugo Philipp Karl von Eltz bought scores of works on history, politics, and philosophy, including the collected works of Sonnenfels and Rousseau. He subscribed to eleven literary and political periodicals, including the journal of the Illuminati.[3] One of the most voracious collectors was the Elector's brother, Lothar Franz von Erthal, who amassed 3,600 books and 18,000 etchings.[4] There were also some signs of an interest in the natural sciences. At the request of a group of nobles, the celebrated anatomist Sömmering obtained a piece of scientific equipment known as a Hygrometer. He wrote to his friend Johannes von Müller that: 'The Statthalter of Erfurt, Dalberg, intends to devote himself principally to the study of fire, Count Kesselstadt to air and Count Walderdorff to electricity. They are three magnificent men.'[5] Part of the entertainment at the von Franckenstein wedding was a lecture by Baron Gleichen on the discoveries he had made by observations through his microscope.[6]

The aggregate of these examples of noble cultural interests do not perhaps amount to very much, but it is clear that the nobility were entirely responsible for the lively theatrical life in Mainz during this period.[7] For all its exclusiveness, the Imperial Knights' Club performed a service for the whole city when, between 1766 and 1768, it built a theatre next door to the

---

[1] Johann Nicolaus Becker, *Über Mainz, in Briefen an Freund R.*, reprinted in Claus Träger (ed.), *Mainz zwischen Schwarz und Rot* (Berlin, 1963), p. 81.
[2] Ullstadt, 002438. [3] Eltville, *Hausrechnung*, 1791.
[4] Bockenheimer, *Mainzer Hochschule*, p. 49.
[5] Just, *Universität Mainz*, p. 28. [6] Ullstadt, Fasc. 3c.
[7] K. Schweickert, *Die Musikpflege am Hofe der Kurfürsten von Mainz im 17. und 18. Jahrhundert*, Beiträge zur Geschichte der Stadt Mainz, vol. 11 (Mainz, 1937), p. 80.

Club at a cost of 10,000 gulden.[1] In addition subsidies were paid to the companies which rented the theatre. Although the admission of the general public was an economic necessity, they were kept at arm's length. The Imperial Knights appropriated the boxes, the service nobility and electoral officials were allocated the circle, while the common citizens could take their choice of the gods or the pit.[2] Initially the nobility's immersion in French culture was reflected in the repertoire of largely French plays.[3] In the 1780s, however, an increasing number of plays and operas by modern German playwrights and composers were performed. *Clavigo, Götz von Berlichingen, Iphigenie in Tauris, Don Carlos* and *Figaro* and – more surprisingly in view of its theme – *Kabale und Liebe* were all presented shortly after their publication.[4] The quality of the productions appears to have been high. In 1789 the great actor Iffland wrote from Mannheim to his friend Ochsenheimer, who was performing in Mainz, that although he disliked the director, 'I must be fair and admit that yours is the best theatre in Germany, apart from ours.'[5]

The finest example of a cultured noble was Karl Theodor Freiherr von Dalberg, described by Goethe as 'the star of hope at that time of the Catholic world'.[6] A member of one of the oldest families of Imperial Knights, he became a canon of the Mainz Cathedral Chapter in 1768, was appointed Statthalter of the Erfurt territory in 1771 and was elected Coadjutor of Mainz in 1787. By all accounts Dalberg was a man of quite exceptional personal charm. He was the friend and correspondent of Schiller, Goethe, Wieland, Herder, Humboldt and Jean Paul, to mention only the most celebrated. From the innumerable tributes they paid him, he emerges as a man of great generosity, impeccable morals and intense intellectual curiosity. Schiller dedicated his *Über Anmuth und Würde* to him with a line from Milton: 'What there thou seest, fair creature, is thyself'.[7] Dalberg's education had included spells at Heidelberg and Göttingen, and throughout his life he maintained close links with the Protestant intellectual world. This was helped by the fact that his sojourn at Erfurt as Statthalter coincided with the classical age of neighbouring Weimar.

---

[1] Eltville, *Protocolla cum Adjunctis, passim.* Jakob Peth, *Geschichte des Theaters und der Musik zu Mainz* (Mainz, 1879), p. 32, wrote that the theatre had cost 30,000 gulden, but the minutes of the Club record expenditure of only 9,800 gulden and the building was insured for only 10,000 gulden.

[2] Peth, *Theater*, p. 83.

[3] This preference for the French theatre was not peculiar to Mainz. In Goethe's *Wilhelm Meisters Lehrjahre*, bk. 3, ch. 1, a Countess asks her husband to engage a troupe of players 'even though unfortunately they are only Germans'.

[4] Peth, *Theater*, pp. 48, 59, 67, 81.   [5] Ibid., p. 90.

[6] Quoted in W. H. Bruford, *Culture and Society in Classical Weimar, 1775–1806* (Cambridge, 1962), p. 55. For Goethe's own (favourable) opinion of Dalberg, see Beaulieu-Marconnay, *Dalberg*, vol. 1, pp. 52–6.

[7] Ibid., p. 180.

Although Dalberg was not a stupid man the thirty-six publications definitely attributed to him are not very distinguished. The very wide range of topics these slender volumes covered suggests dilettantism. His interest in politics, philosophy, poetry, painting, the natural sciences or archaeology was genuine, his understanding superficial.[1] Yet although of little originality, his political treatises illustrate very well the assumptions which underlay enlightened absolutism in Mainz. His two chief premises were 'the purpose of the state is the promotion of the happiness of those persons who by the union of their wills make up the state',[2] and 'political philosophy not only agrees with the general principles of moral philosophy, but may also be made perfectly consistent with the particular precepts of the latter'.[3] He conceded that certain aspects of modern life were unpleasant, such as the slave trade, but expressed the optimistic view that 'never were so many effects of refined notions felt, as we perceive in our days: for now, in many respects a glorious dawn begins, which promises to bring on that broad day-light so long wished for'.[4] He observed that it was now generally understood that war was evil, that 'an unnecessary and wanton limitation of liberty can do no good', that a state does not flourish because of its size but because of the quality of its government and that 'trade and the arts will be better promoted by encouraging merit, than by constraint and compulsion'. His conclusion suggested that a reign of philosopher-kings had begun: 'no former period of time has produced more monarchs, sovereigns, and statesmen, so deserving of respect from posterity...Hail! to the Statesman, whose actions are guided by the principles of general moral philosophy.'[5]

It is impossible to make even an approximate estimate of the number of nobles in Mainz influenced by enlightened ideas. Nor does it follow necessarily that a sense of intellectual affinity would be sufficient to prompt noblemen to mix socially with commoners. One or two incidents in the 1780s suggested that the rays of Dalberg's 'glorious dawn' had not yet touched every pocket of caste-consciousness. The unfortunate Freiherr von Greiffenklau discovered this to his cost when he was ostracised after contracting a mésalliance. Greiffenklau, moreover, had only slipped down one rung of the social ladder; his bride's father was a nobleman, had the title of Freiherr, and was a senior official at the *Reichshofrat*. All he lacked

---

[1] Otto Vossler, 'Carl von Dalberg', *Mainzer Zeitschrift*, 58 (1963), p. 82.
[2] *Von den wahren Grenzen der Wirksamkeit des Staats in Beziehung auf seine Mitglieder*, reprinted in Robert Leroux, *La théorie du despotisme éclairé chez Karl Theodor Dalberg*, Publications de la faculté des lettres de l'Université de Strasbourg, vol. 60 (Paris, 1932), p. 45. This was the most celebrated of the replies evoked by Humboldt's *Ideen zu einem Versuch, die Grenzen der Wirksamkeit des Staats zu bestimmen*. See above, p. 192.
[3] *The Connection between Moral and Political Philosophy*, considered by Charles, Baron Dalberg. An essay, read before the Academy of Useful Sciences at Erfurt, July the 3rd, 1786, p. 26.
[4] Ibid., p. 36.   [5] Ibid., p. 37.

Enlightened absolutism, 1774–1802

was status as an Imperial Knight.¹ Another example of this sort of mentality was the proposal of General Gudenus that 'to increase military splendour' in future only nobles be commissioned as officers.² Georg Forster, the University Librarian, believed that all the nobility were tarred with the same brush. He reported to his wife in 1788 that, as one might expect, the nobility lived entirely among themselves. In support of his opinion he described what was known in Mainz as a *Piroutschade*, which appears to have consisted simply of a tour of the city by the noblemen and their ladies in their *barouches*, while the common people looked on.³

Quite apart from the fact that Forster had only been in Mainz a few days when he passed this verdict, there is good reason to doubt its accuracy. A number of other commoners living in Mainz at the time, who were in no sense apologists for the established order, left evidence that there was much social intercourse between intellectual noble and intellectual commoner. In October 1787, the Protestant Professor of Anatomy, Sömmering, wrote to none other than Georg Forster concerning a voyage of exploration they proposed to undertake together. Among other things, he mentioned that they would have no problem of finding enough huntsmen to take with them because the Master of the Elector's Hunt, Count Kesselstadt, and his assistants, Freiherr von Hausen, Freiherr von Klot and Freiherr von Guttenberg, were all his 'special friends' and would compete among themselves to do him a favour.⁴ The degree of intimacy suggested by this letter does not appear to have been exceptional. The historian Niklas Vogt, who certainly did not approve in principle of a privileged aristocracy, moved in similar circles.⁵ Every decently dressed Erfurt citizen could attend Dalberg's *Assembleen*, held every Tuesday from five till eight p.m. in the Statthalter's residence, and play cards, listen to music or engage in conversation. Herder, Goethe, Wilhelm von Humboldt and especially Schiller were frequent visitors.⁶ C. M. Plümicke, who visited Erfurt in 1791, was greatly impressed and commented 'Nowhere can such a cultured and courteous nobility be found as easily as here.'⁷ Actors found a season in Mainz both lucrative and congenial. Opitz wrote to his friend J. A. Christ, who was thinking of accepting an offer from Mainz, that 'the public in Mainz is cultured and grateful, it consists almost entirely of nobles, people of

---
¹ Andreasen and Mathy, 'Münters Reise', 67.
² Richard Harms, *Landmiliz und stehendes Heer in Kurmainz, namentlich im 18. Jahrhundert* (Göttingen dissertation, 1909), p. 42.
³ Forster, *Sämtliche Schriften*, vol. 8, p. 11.
⁴ *Georg Forsters Briefwechsel mit S. Th. Sömmering*, ed. H. Hettner (Brunswick, 1877), p. 446.
⁵ Herrmann, *Vogt*, p. 27.
⁶ Alfred Overmann, 'Karl Anton Theodor Maria Freiherr von Dalberg', *Mitteldeutsche Lebensbilder*, vol. 3 (Magdeburg, 1928), p. 183.
⁷ C. M. Plümicke, *Briefe auf einer Reise durch Deutschland im Jahre 1791*, vol. 2 (1793), p. 39.

politest society, who treat and reward an artist in a manner befitting their refined discernment'.[1] Christ duly moved to Mainz, and found that his reaction was the same as his friend's. He became especially friendly with Franz Karl Count von Ingelheim, the Grand Master of the Court, and his family. He wrote of Ingelheim: 'The old Count, first Marshal, is an extremely good-natured gentleman, and in the circle which he honours with his company, whether they are noble or commoner, he completely forgets his high dignity and is just a friend.'[2]

The evidence provided by these personal impressions is given further reinforcement by the distribution of membership of the Reading Club, the intellectual focus of the city:

Groups	Number	%
Titled nobility without office or foreign diplomats	12	7.5
Nobles in the service of the Elector	35	21.87
Noble Officers	12	7.5
Higher regular and secular clergy	19	11
Lower regular and secular clergy	12	7.5
University Professors	16	10
Doctors and surgeons	12	7.5
Lawyers	9	5.62
Officials	19	11.87
Scholars, writers, artists	8	5
Manufacturing bourgeoisie	0	0
Commercial bourgeoisie	7	4.38
Total	161[3]	

There is a striking similarity between these figures and those for the Mainz branch of the Illuminati (see opposite).

It has been emphasised already that in the Mainz context, or indeed any other, the Enlightenment was not a creed, which required from its adherents acceptance of all its articles. It can be objected quite properly, therefore, that the Enlightenment was big enough to attract both commoners and nobles, while still allowing plenty of room for fundamental disagreement between them on social and political issues. It is certainly the case that the establishment never intended that the bases of state and society should be questioned. Outside the University, censorship continued unabated. This was made clear by the *Mainzer Monatschrift von geistlichen Sachen*, which can be regarded as the government's mouthpiece.

[1] *Schauspielerleben im 18. Jahrhundert: Erinnerungen von J. A. Christ*, ed. R. Schirmer (Munich, 1912), p. 236.   [2] Ibid., p. 252.   [3] Dreyfus, *Mayence*, p. 500.

Enlightened absolutism, 1774–1802

In an editorial of 1785 it commented that although the General Vicariate's decision to ban a work by the Austrian radical Joseph Eybel would doubtless surprise many people, it had never been the Elector's intention to introduce unlimited freedom of publication. For all his enthusiasm for 'true Enlightenment', it continued, Friedrich Karl would never neglect his duty to suppress books dangerous to the state, morality or religion. The journal reminded its readers that the Christians at Ephesus, under the direction of St Paul, had burnt godless works in public.[1]

Groups	Number	%
Titled nobility without office or foreign diplomats	4	8
Nobles in the service of the Elector	8	16
Noble Officers	4	8
Higher regular and secular clergy	4	8
Lower regular and secular clergy	5	10
University Professors	2	4
Doctors and surgeons	2	4
Lawyers	7	14
Officials	9	18
Scholars, writers, artists	2	4
Manufacturing bourgeoisie	0	0
Commercial bourgeoisie	1	2
Students	2	4
Total	50[2]	

Practical evidence of this attitude was supplied by an incident which occurred very soon afterwards. At the end of 1785 *Der deutsche Zuschauer* published a violent attack on certain unnamed ministers in Mainz for their part in the suspension of one of their colleagues. Friedrich Karl not only took immediate steps to discover and punish the journal's source of information but also issued a warrant for the arrest of its editor, P. A. Winkopp. The latter's attempt to flee to Switzerland was in vain; he was apprehended *en route*, returned to Mainz, interrogated and imprisoned.[3]

Censorship could of course cut both ways. In 1788 the Elector followed the example of Joseph II in banning the *Journal historique et littéraire*, edited by the ultraconservative and ultramontane ex-Jesuit Abbé Feller.[4]

[1] *Mainzer Monatschrift von geistlichen Sachen*, 1 (1785), p. 451. [2] Dreyfus, *Mayence*, p. 502.
[3] There is a detailed account of the incident in Jung, *Bentzel*, pp. 151–2. Winkopp was soon released. Ironically, not only did he then enter Mainz service, but during the revolutionary period he also became one of the old régime's most effective propagandists. See below, pp. 284–95.
[4] *Mainzer Monatschrift von geistlichen Sachen*, 4 (1788), p. 797.

As this restraint on both left and right suggested, the electoral government did not propose that public opinion should stray across the narrow boundaries marked down for it. It was probably inevitable that a number of intellectuals in Mainz would not be prepared to accept restrictions, especially when Friedrich Karl joined the camp of counter-revolution after 1789. Nevertheless, as this account has sought to show, attitudes towards the Enlightenment were not dictated solely by economic or social considerations. There was no straightforward confrontation between 'enlightened bourgeoisie' and 'conservative aristocracy'.

II

As during the previous reign, the main opposition to the Elector's reforms stemmed not from a feeling that they did not go far enough but rather from a feeling that they went too far. This was common to almost every section of society. When Friedrich Karl began to employ Protestants, for example, the officials who had hoped themselves for promotion to these positions began to discover that religious toleration in practice had its drawbacks. The first Protestants to arrive in Mainz were specialised academics like Sömmering and Pfeiffer, and Friedrich Karl could reasonably claim that there were no qualified Catholics available in their fields. This argument lost much of its force when applied to the appointment of Protestants to posts in the administration.

The Swiss historian Johannes Müller was called to Mainz in 1786 to become University Librarian. After quickly winning the confidence and affection of the Elector, he was employed increasingly on state business. As this forced him to neglect the library, although it was in urgent need of attention, in 1788 Friedrich Karl decided to clarify the situation by giving Müller a formal post in his government and appointing a new librarian.[1] At Müller's prompting, his choice fell on another Protestant, Georg Forster, who had accompanied Cook on one of his voyages, had taught in a number of German and Polish universities and was presently at Göttingen. Even before his arrival in Mainz, rumours of the furore caused by his appointment had reached Forster's ears.[2] Anxiously he wrote to Sömmering to ask whether or not it was believed in Mainz that he had taken the post from Councillor Zapf, and was suitably concerned when Sömmering replied in the affirmative.[3]

This was nothing, however, compared with the storm unleashed by Müller's promotion. In April 1788 Müller asked his brother to keep quiet about his part in the appointment of Forster, because he did not want to

[1] Hansen, *Quellen*, vol. 1, p. 322.   [2] Forster, *Sämtliche Schriften*, vol. 8, p. 17.
[3] Hettner, *Forster und Sömmering*, pp. 533–4.

add to the number of enemies already confronting him.¹ Denied any means of constitutional protest, Müller's opponents reached for their pens. In the summer of 1788 an anonymous publication appeared in Mainz, ostensibly concerned with the perpetual capitulation of election but primarily directed against the employment of Protestants in the state.² In fact written by the Councillor and Professor of *Reich* history, Peter Anton Frank, it proposed that all Protestants in Mainz be dismissed until such a time as Protestant princes employed an equal number of Catholics.³ Müller was well aware that the attack was directed at him and wrote to his mother that he was surrounded by 'envious men and evil tongues'.⁴ Assured of the Elector's support, he decided to carry on regardless.

Hostility composed of economic interest and religious conviction was also displayed by the guilds. Despite their claims that they were more efficient than the Protestants, they showed a marked reluctance to enter into competition with them. In 1779 a Protestant by the name of Jacob Arbeiter asked for permission to set up a factory for the manufacture of 'English wax', taffeta and linen.⁵ In its report to the central government, the *Vicedom*'s office enumerated many reasons in favour of the project but proposed that permission be made conditional on the applicant and his wife becoming Catholics, because 'the public would find it very objectionable... if a Protestant were allowed such a large business'. Arbeiter and his family appear to have agreed to this condition, for they were still in Mainz in 1788. Later the *Vicedom* paid less attention to the prejudices of the citizens and Protestants were admitted without any restrictions.

Although the protests of the guilds over individual cases were ignored, when the question of general toleration arose, their prospective opposition proved a powerful inhibition. The councillors who opposed their colleague Hoffner's plan⁶ were not against toleration in principle, they feared the wrath of the people. Indeed it was probably this consideration which persuaded Friedrich Karl not to carry out his plan to give the Protestants equal rights. The common people also made their opposition to the University and the Protestant professors felt. Georg Forster had hoped that the Jesuit Church could be turned into a badly-needed University Library, but the scheme was resolutely opposed by the city. One group of citizens was so incensed that it took the unusual step of sending a petition to

---

¹ Johannes von Müller, *Sämtliche Werke*, ed. Johann Georg Müller, vol. 5 (Tübingen, 1810), p. 211.
² (P. A. Frank), *Etwas über die Wahlkapitulationen in den geistlichen Staaten* (Frankfurt, 1788).
³ Frank appears to have modified his position somewhat, for in the following year he proposed that Protestants be appointed if the Elector could find no qualified Catholics – *Beiträge zu der beständigen Wahlkapitulation für das Maynzische Erzstift* (Frankfurt, 1789).
⁴ Müller, *Sämtliche Werke*, vol. 5, pp. 236, 245.
⁵ Schrohe, *Stadt Mainz*, p. 158.
⁶ See above, p. 180.

the government.[1] Forster informed his father-in-law that a threatening letter had been sent to the University, attacking the Protestants for repaying hospitality with attempts to deprive the people of their places of worship.[2]

These and other incidents after 1789 demonstrated the extent to which the Mainz Enlightenment was a fragile growth, sustained artificially by the ordinances of the government. The authentic voice of the people of Mainz was not to be found in the *Mainzer Monatschrift von geistlichen Sachen* or the *Magazin der Philosophie und schönen Literatur* but in the ex-Jesuit Hermann Goldhagen's *Religionsjournal*, which appeared between 1776 and 1792. It was the first German journal whose sole aim was hostility to the Enlightenment.[3] As Goldhagen stated when founding the journal, there were scores of anti-religious publications but none to defend 'true religion'.[4] Through its pages Goldhagen propagated a form of Roman Catholicism which would not have been out of place in 1618. He stood four-square behind a Church with an ultramontane exterior and a baroque interior. His formidable polemical gifts were employed against a wide range of opponents – deists, Protestants, 'materialists', 'epicureans', 'fatalists', 'optimists', 'tolerantists' etc. – but his special *bêtes noires* were the Illuminati. In three articles in 1787, for example, he accused them of atheism and materialism and arraigned them as threats to religion and the state.[5] The flavour of Goldhagen's editorial policy can be caught from the headings of some of his articles: 'The dangers to religion in the present age', 'A defence of religion against the current unbelief', 'Summary of the most important religious truths against Voltaire's philosophical dictionary', and so on. In an article entitled 'Of general toleration in religious matters' he wrote: 'The freedom to believe and to act as one likes is the song of victory of the closing years of the eighteenth century: this general toleration was an invention of the godless Bayle: on the pretext of an unlimited love he opens up the gates to Heaven to everyone who believes he is right; according to his presumption, all heretics, Jews, Mohammedans, and heathens can be on the road to salvation...this system condones all vices, brings no advantages to the fatherland and even contravenes the rights of princes.'[6] Not surprisingly, Goldhagen had frequent brushes with the

---

[1] A. Ruppel, 'Die Berufung des schweizer Geschichtsschreibers und späteren Staatsmannes Johannes von Müller zum Bibliothekar der Mainzer Universitätsbibliothek', *Stadt und Stift, Beiträge zur Mainzer Geschichte*, Festschrift für Heinrich Schrohe (Mainz, 1934), p. 126.
[2] Forster, *Sämtliche Werke*, vol. 8, p. 173.
[3] Valjavec, *Josephinismus*, p. xli.
[4] Johannes Hompesch, *Hermann Goldhagens Religionsjournal* (Cologne dissertation, 1923), p. 69.
[5] *Religionsjournal* (1787), 2, 3, 5.
[6] Quoted in H. Matzke, *Die Aufklärung im Kurerzbistum Mainz und ihre besondere Wirkung auf die Einführung des deutschen Kirchengesangs* (Mainz, 1920), p. 35.

electoral censorship. In 1782 he was ordered to show every copy of the *Religionsjournal* to ecclesiastical councillor Scheidel before publication, while in the following year he was told that any more attacks on the Elector's ecclesiastical policies would lead to the forfeit of the pension he enjoyed as an ex-Jesuit.[1] Nevertheless, his journal was the longest-lived of all the Mainz publications and also the most popular.[2] The Elector of Mainz may have deprecated such views but they represented the opinion of the great majority of his subjects.

The attachment of the common people to their traditional forms of worship was well illustrated by the incidents surrounding the Elector's attempt to introduce the use of the vernacular to Church services. In the general plan of reform sent to the Vicariate in 1784, he had stressed the need for a uniform liturgy and to this end proposed the introduction of a new German Hymn Book.[3] The project was taken in hand the following year by a commission consisting of members of the Vicariate and of the University's theological faculty.[4] They in turn deputed the task of assembling the hymns to the ecclesiastical councillor and parish priest of St Ignatius, Ernst Turin. His collection was submitted for censorship and approved in the latter part of 1786.

It is clear that the authorities expected trouble from the start. A laudatory review of an advance copy in the *Mainzer Monatschrift von geistlichen Sachen* mentioned that the compiler had asked them to stress that not a single line, let alone a whole verse, had been taken from a Protestant book. The journal also noted that some 'stupid criticisms' were already in circulation, such as that the collection did not include an *Ave Maria*.[5] These premonitions notwithstanding, supplies of the new book were sent out to the Electorate's parishes in February 1787, with an instruction to the priests to ensure that their flocks used them.[6] In many parishes the transition from Latin to German progressed smoothly, but in others the order to sing in a language everybody understood caused grave offence. The rumour spread rapidly that the new collection was heretical, the fact that it was written in German and the hymns were given numbers – like the Lutheran books – being regarded as particularly suspicious.[7] An official of the Vicariate also cast doubts on its orthodoxy. His criticisms were referred to the theological faculty, which reported that they were totally unfounded and that the collection was exemplary in every way.[8]

[1] Hompesch, *Goldhagen*, p. 71.
[2] Ibid., pp. 74–9.
[3] Vienna, *MEA*, GK, Fasc. 76.
[4] Ibid. Fasc. 85a 134. The preamble to this communication contained a résumé of the events leading up to the imposition of the Hymn Book.
[5] *Mainzer Monatschrift von geistlichen Sachen*, 1 (1785), 1222–5.
[6] Matzke, *Aufklärung*, p. 109.
[7] Ibid., p. 133.
[8] Vienna, *MEA*, GK, Fasc. 85a, 134.

This verdict on the book's orthodoxy appears to have been the right one. Perhaps foreseeing trouble, the Elector had ordered quite explicitly from the start that no Protestant hymns should be included because of the offence they would give.[1] Although stating that it was quite admissible to take over good things from the Protestants, the *Mainzer Monatschrift von geistlichen Sachen* denied angrily that on this occasion either form or content had been borrowed. It was prepared to concede only that the book contained some hymns which had been in existence before the Reformation and which the Protestants had been sensible enough to adopt.[2] The authorities attempted to bring this message home to the people by means of some simple propaganda. In a short pamphlet entitled *Dialogues about the Mainz Hymn Book*, for example, an enlightened supporter of the book, Herr Wahrmund, exposes the stupidity of its opponents – the imbecilic Frau Hammebambel, the drunken Father Schlauch and the crooked Dr Kloss. Their attempts to foment sedition are stoutly resisted by the honest labourer Kunz, who berates people 'who join all the brotherhoods, rush to all the services, wear consecrated girdles, put on scapulars, and are even in lower orders but who are of no use at all...and deceive and pull the wool over the eyes of their fellow-men where and how they can'.[3]

The dissidents remained unconvinced. In most parishes they were content simply to ignore the new Hymn Book and continue singing in Latin, but where the local priest insisted on carrying out the Vicariate's orders, a serious conflict arose. Copies which did find their way into the hands of the peasants were promptly torn up and burnt.[4] They were encouraged both by their priests and by the regular clergy. Eventually the Vicariate felt obliged to inform the provincial head of the Capuchins that if individual members continued to preach against singing hymns in German, action would be taken againt the Order as a whole.[5] In a number of villages in the Rheingau there were outbreaks of violence and intimidation, and at Rüdesheim something approaching an insurrection broke out. Led by a cooper called Kron, variously described by observers as 'inflated' and 'somewhat unbalanced',[6] the pious citizens took the law into their own hands. On a Sunday in June 1787, Kron and his supporters brushed aside a detail of soldiers outside the church and proceeded to conduct a service themselves in what they believed to be Latin. On the same evening one of the electoral officials was unwise enough to remonstrate with a group of dissidents and in the ensuing *mêlée* inflicted and received considerable

---

[1] H. Brück, 'Geschichte eines Gesangbuchs', *Der Katholik*, 46 (1866) p. 204.
[2] *Mainzer Monatschrift von geistlichen Sachen*, 3 (1787), pp. 530–1.
[3] Matzke, *Aufklärung*, p. 114.
[4] Ibid., pp. 112, 126.   [5] Brück, 'Gesangbuch', p. 207.
[6] See the report of a Neuwied paper printed in Hansen, *Quellen*, vol. 1, p. 201 and a contemporary account quoted in Matzke, *Aufklärung*, p. 126.

Enlightened absolutism, 1774–1802

personal damage.[1] The conflict reached a climax a few days later when a group of citizens broke into the local jail and freed one of their imprisoned leaders. At this point the central government in Mainz intervened, and despatched three hundred troops to quell the rising. They met with no resistance and were withdrawn by the end of September. The insurgents were treated lightly. Although a number of them received varying doses of corporal punishment, only Kron was sentenced to a long term of imprisonment.[2]

This and other disturbances, however, forced the authorities to adopt a more cautious attitude. A new edition of the Hymn Book was published in March 1788, but it was stated that neither 'force nor punishments' were to be used to secure its implementation.[3] More trouble brought more concessions. The Vicariate next allowed local priests to accommodate the prejudices of their flocks to the extent of using a mixture of German and Latin or the German and Latin form alternately. Yet in 1791 the authorities were still complaining that in many places the new Hymn Book had not been introduced and recognised their inability to impose their will by formally allowing the reintroduction of a purely Latin liturgy.[4]

This was the most serious disturbance to occur in the Electorate before 1789. It might be argued of course that the peasantry's assault on the new Hymn Book was only a symptom of much more deep-seated discontent. The Rheingau, the scene of most of the trouble, was certainly the most over-populated and economically depressed region of the country.[5] In the absence of any evidence of social, economic or political aims, however, such a conclusion must remain pure surmise. Even if this were the case, the incident would still show the depth of the peasantry's attachment to traditional forms of worship and the attention they paid to the views of their priests. When viewed together with the complex reaction of other sections of society to the Enlightenment, the Battle of the Hymn Books suggested that the Electorate's reaction to revolution was not likely to be straightforward.

[1] Matzke, *Aufklärung*, p. 127.
[2] Ibid., pp. 127–31.
[3] Mainz, *Kurmainzische Verordnungen*, 6te Sammlung, vol. 10, 263.
[4] Matzke, *Aufklärung*, p. 141. The affair recalls the comment of Sir Hugo Mallinger in George Eliot's *Daniel Deronda*: 'If you are to rule men, you must rule them through their own ideas; and I agree with the Archbishop of Naples who had a St. Januarius procession against the plague. It's no use having an Order in Council against popular shallowness. There is no action possible without a little acting.'
[5] See above, p. 93.

6

Imperial adventures

I

As archchancellors, the Electors of Mainz had always played a certain rôle in the *Reich*, although their importance had declined sadly since their days as kingmakers in the High Middle Ages. In the course of the 1780s there was a brief but dramatic reversal; indeed between 1785 and 1787 'the focal point of *Reich* politics moved from Regensburg to Mainz'.[1] The period was marked by intense diplomatic activity. The pot was kept on the boil by a series of controversial episodes: the Austrian proposal to exchange the Netherlands for Bavaria, the War of the Bavarian Succession, the League of Princes, the dispute between the United Provinces and Austria, the dispute over the papal nuncios, the Prussian intervention in the United Provinces, the Liège revolution, the war between the Turks and Austria and finally of course the French Revolution.

Although the eventual collapse of the *Reich* was not inevitable, the 1780s were certainly years of growing instability. France, the European power with the greatest interest in preserving the traditional structure, had withdrawn almost entirely from imperial affairs. Although not growing senile, Frederick of Prussia was growing old; no one knew what his indolent and bovine heir-apparent would do. Most important of all was the attitude of the Habsburg Emperor, for centuries the most important centripetal counterbalance to the centrifugal tendencies of the great princes.[2] Finally severed from his mother's apron-strings by Maria Theresa's death in 1780, Joseph II threw Habsburg policy into reverse. Ignoring the advice of his Chancellor, Kaunitz, he was determined to realise his view that the *Reich* was a useless and moribund anachronism, from which the new Austrian state should be separated.[3] In view of its turbulent character it is not surprising that the decade has attracted a great deal of attention from historians.[4] Even a general account of the League of Princes, the episode with

---

[1] Karl Otmar Freiherr von Aretin, *Heiliges Römisches Reich*, Veröffentlichungen des Instituts für Europäische Geschichte Mainz, vol. 38 (Wiesbaden, 1967), pt. 1, p. 159.
[2] See above, pp. 3–5.
[3] Aretin, *Reich*, pt. 1, pp. 13–14.
[4] Aretin's definitive work has a bibliography containing 2,233 entries.

which Mainz was most concerned, would be as lengthy as it is unnecessary. This chapter, therefore, must be confined to the fortunes of the Electorate.

Friedrich Karl had owed his election in 1774 to Habsburg influence, and in the early years of his reign he was a paradigm of gratitude. When the new Austrian ambassador, Franz Sigmund Freiherr von Lehrbach, arrived to take up his duties in 1775, he was greatly impressed by the honeymoon atmosphere which prevailed.[1] Even in an age of hyperbolic diplomacy, Friedrich Karl distinguished himself by the extravagance of his protestations of devotion to the Austrian court. The full weight of what authority he possessed as Archchancellor was thrown behind Habsburg policy. A ministerial note of 1779, for example, greeted Joseph's declaration on the Bavarian exchange with 'the most fervent applause'; it promised that every attempt would be made to bring the other princes of the *Reich* into line.[2] Imperial approval of the plan to secularise three monasteries to provide funds for the new University was probably a reward for this loyalty. Attempts by the Elector of Trier to draw Mainz into a common front against Joseph's ecclesiastical policies were curtly rebuffed. Lehrbach's successor Franz Georg Count von Metternich, reported to Kaunitz in 1782 that 'I feel confident that I can give you an assurance that there has never been a time when this court has been better-intentioned.'[3] Yet within three years Friedrich Karl had joined Frederick the Great's League of Princes.

The points of conflict between Mainz and Vienna were legion, but the real catalyst proved to be their sharply opposed attitudes towards the Imperial Chancellery (*Reichskanzlei*).[4] As it was Joseph's primary aim to turn the Habsburg Monarchy into a unified state, it was inevitable that imperial institutions would suffer. The Imperial Chancellery, located in Vienna but headed by the Elector of Mainz as Archchancellor, was clearly an affront to Joseph's concept of sovereignty. The existence of a separate and entirely Habsburg-run Chancellery (*Staatskanzlei*) greatly increased the chances of demarcation disputes. Less than a year after his accession as sole ruler, Joseph provided a foretaste when he transferred from the Imperial Chancellery to the Chancellery of State responsibility for examining the credentials of ambassadors. This was a clear breach of earlier agreements with the Archchancellor.[5] The issue seems petty enough, but men whose powers are largely honorific necessarily pay close attention to such *minutiae*.

Over the next two years a number of similar incidents stoked up resent-

[1] Vienna, *Staka*, Fasc. 180, 4.
[2] Ibid. Fasc. 191, 246. [3] Ibid. Fasc. 201, 433.
[4] Helmut Mathy, 'Über das Mainzer Erzkanzleramt in der Neuzeit: Stand und Aufgaben der Forschung', *Geschichtliche Landeskunde*, 2 (1965), 128.
[5] Ibid.

ment on both sides. At the beginning of 1783 Metternich complained to Friedrich Karl that the Mainz representative at the *Reichstag* appeared to be favouring the 'Protestant' (i.e. anti-Habsburg) party. The Elector replied that he attached great importance to maintaining friendly relations with the Emperor but feared that they would be disrupted if disputes over the Imperial Chancellery continued. Metternich countered with the curious argument that the Elector of Mainz exercised two functions – as Archchancellor and as a prince of the *Reich*, and that disputes over the former office should not be allowed to disturb the total relationship.[1] As Friedrich Karl was not inclined to become a political schizoid, the disputes continued. By now the scene of operations had switched to the *Reichstag*, for it was here that the Elector of Mainz enjoyed greatest scope for retaliation. When the Mainz representative at the *Reichstag*, Franz Gregorius Freiherr von Hauser, died in 1783, it was expected that the Bohemian representative, Ferdinand Count Trauttmansdorff, would succeed him. Friedrich Karl appointed instead Maximilian Joseph Freiherr von Karg, who soon proved a thorn in the Austrian flesh.[2] Metternich was instructed by Vienna to inform the Elector that in his conduct of business von Karg showed an unmistakable bias in favour of the Protestants and that the Emperor could place no trust in him.[3] An open breach yawned between Mainz and Vienna.

Disputes between the Emperor and Archchancellor were nothing new. What gave them extra spice in the 1780s was not only Joseph II's newly won freedom of action but also Friedrich Karl's extreme sensitivity. The diplomats preferred to call it vanity. With rare unanimity, they agreed that large helpings of flattery were required to handle him. Ferdinand Count Trauttmansdorff, who succeeded the discredited Metternich as Austrian ambassador in Mainz in 1785, reported to Kaunitz that:

> The Elector's ruling passion is his ambition, which is excessively developed and all too easy to arouse; this is the origin of his desire to take every opportunity to emulate the greater monarchs of Europe, or at least to play a really important and independent rôle in the *Reich*, by expanding *ad infinitum* his position as the first prince of the *Reich* and, as the first ecclesiastical elector, by proclaiming himself the supreme head of the entire *Reich* hierarchy; in these two capacities he will arrogate to himself the task of defending the rights both of the ecclesiastical and the secular princes.[4]

When explaining to Count Mercy, the Austrian ambassador in Paris, why Mainz had joined the League of Princes, Trauttmansdorff placed the Elector's *gloriole* high on the list.[5] This verdict was not only dictated by

---

[1] Vienna, *Staka*, Fasc. 205, 503.
[2] Aretin, *Reich*, p. 158. The Elector of Mainz was of course Director of the *Reichstag* and his representative (*Direktorialgesandte*) was a figure of considerable importance.
[3] Vienna, *Staka*, Fasc. 211, 771, Fasc. 212, 812.
[4] Ibid. Fasc. 214, 7.   [5] Ibid. Fasc. 216, 1.

the customary belief that princes who opposed the Habsburgs were morally as well as politically unsound. The Prussian diplomat Karl Freiherr von Stein concluded his successful mission to lure Friedrich Karl into the League of Princes with the observation that:

We can rely on this prince's firmness and the excellence of his principles and expect from him effective and consistent conduct, if we treat him with confidence and with a certain deference – he is vain, ambitious and jealous of his prestige, as susceptible to mistrust as he is to boundless confidence.[1]

Joseph II was certainly not the man to capitalise on Friedrich Karl's failings. For him the Elector of Mainz was a powerless symbol of the despised *Reich*, to be ordered and, if necessary, elbowed out of the way. The uncompromising character of his curt replies to protests would have enraged more humble men than Friedrich Karl. In thinly veiled language, the Austrian diplomats in Mainz complained bitterly that their efforts were constantly frustrated by the Emperor's pigheadedness. Metternich reported to Kaunitz that the breach between Mainz and Vienna could be healed overnight, if only some concession could be made to the Elector's wounded pride.[2] After he had joined the League of Princes, his suffragan bishop Valentin Heimes assured Trauttmansdorff that his defection was due solely to a feeling that the Emperor despised the *Reich* and especially its Archchancellor. It would never have occurred if even the slightest attention had been paid to the various remonstrances. Instead, they had been dismissed with ever-increasing harshness. A perfectly legitimate complaint about the passage of Austrian troops across the Electorate, for example, was countered by a threat to help the Protestants restrict the Elector's powers as Director of the *Reichstag*. Consequently, Heimes stated, Friedrich Karl had been driven into the arms of the Prussians.[3]

The dispute was more than a shouting-match about honorific powers between two headstrong and disagreeable rulers. There were some really substantive issues at stake, and of these the most important was Joseph's diocesan reorganisation. Basically this was an attempt to make the ecclesiastical and the administrative boundaries of his dominions coincide. This involved abolishing unilaterally the jurisdiction of bishops who were not Habsburg subjects. After the death of the Prince-Bishop of Passau in February 1783, those parts of the Passau diocese which extended into Austrian territory were severed and incorporated in two new bishoprics established at Linz and St Pölten. Furthermore, the estates of the Prince-

[1] G. H. Pertz, *Das Leben des Ministers Freiherrn vom Stein*, vol. 1 (Berlin, 1850), pp. 67 ff. Freiherr von Stein, *Briefe und Amtliche Schriften*, vol. 1, ed. Walther Hubatsch (Stuttgart, 1957), p. 223. For a similar judgment from the French ambassador Count O'Kelly, see K. G. Bockenheimer, *Kurmainz im Fürstenbunde* (Mainz, 1905), p. 15.
[2] Vienna, *Staka*, Fasc. 212, 816, 832.   [3] Ibid. Fasc. 216, 20.

Bishopric located there, comprising some two thirds of Passau's landholding, were confiscated. Although Joseph's desire to establish direct control of the Church in his state is certainly understandable, his action was no less certainly a blatant contravention of the *Reich* constitution, the Peace of Westphalia, the Imperial Capitulation of Election and a solemn undertaking given to Passau by Charles VI in 1728. Ecclesiastical opinion throughout the *Reich* was horrified, for Passau was only one of many Prince-Bishoprics whose dioceses extended into Habsburg territory.

The first reaction in Mainz was curiously muted, but by the summer of 1783 Metternich was expressing great anxiety about the Elector's 'improper' views on the subject.[1] The situation did not change after Joseph had managed to bully the new Prince-Bishop of Passau into accepting the situation, because he then transferred his attention to Salzburg, Regensburg, Freising and others. Friedrich Karl now took more decisive action. In the autumn of 1784 a remonstrance claiming that the Emperor's actions were contrary to the laws and constitution of the *Reich* was circulated among other prince-bishops for signature.[2] This unusually aggressive step showed how tense the situation had become, although in the event Metternich had little difficulty in persuading Max Franz of Cologne, Joseph's brother, and Clemens Wenzeslaus of Trier, Joseph's cousin, not to sign.[3] The incident also showed that Friedrich Karl had assumed the leadership of the prince-bishops against the Emperor's diocesan policies. A distinguished Austrian historian, Helmut Rössler, has explained Friedrich Karl's subsequent defection to the Prussian camp solely in terms of his 'blind hatred' of Joseph II.[4] He probably did hate Joseph for the wrong reasons, but he also opposed him for the right ones. No Elector of Mainz, unless bribed or coaxed into submission, could stand by idly and watch the Emperor trample on the Imperial Constitution. With their limited resources and elective constitutions, the prince-bishoprics were highly vulnerable to the great German dynasties. When the Habsburg Emperor, traditionally their surest defence against secular predators, abandoned them, secularisation loomed large.

There can be no doubt that the diocesan dispute caused grave offence in Mainz, but it was not the only reason for the rift. Friedrich Karl was thoroughly disenchanted with Joseph II long before the Passau affair. In a review of his years in Mainz, written just before his final departure, Metternich made it quite clear that it was the trouble over the Imperial Chancellery which had destroyed Friedrich Karl's earlier attachment to to Vienna.[5] A number of other less important issues helped to poison rela-

[1] Ibid. Fasc. 205, 527, 545, 547, 550, 552.
[2] Ibid. Fasc. 210, 719, 721, 744, 792.   [3] Ibid. Fasc. 212, 810.
[4] Hellmuth Rössler, *Graf Johann Philipp Stadion, Napoleons deutscher Gegenspieler*, vol. 1 (Vienna, 1966), p. 119.   [5] Vienna, *Staka*, Fasc. 212, 832.

tions further. Given plenty of ill-will on both sides, the most trivial of incidents could spark off a full-scale row. The activities of the Austrian recruiting-officers and the need for Austrian contingents to pass through the Electorate *en route* for the Netherlands provided an excellent example.[1] Navigation on the Rhine, a perennial source of controversy, became an issue once again.[2] In a situation of this kind it is difficult to apportion responsibility with any degree of precision, but certainly the Austrians were not behaving with any great finesse. In 1784 Metternich took grave exception to a dissertation on the *Reich* postal services, published on the occasion of the reopening of Mainz University. It is surprising enough that he should bother with so petty an issue; more startling were the language and tone of his protest, which seemed expressly designed to alienate the Elector.[3]

These minor incidents are probably best seen as symptoms of the more fundamental conflict over the Imperial Chancellery. More problematic is the relationship between the change in personnel at the top and the change in policy. During the early years of his reign Friedrich Karl's chief minister was Wilhelm Count von Sickingen. His appointment in 1775 was rightly regarded as a sign that his employer would be a faithful supporter of the Habsburgs. Consequently there was a disappointed reaction in Vienna when von Sickingen was dismissed in 1782.[4] The reasons for his departure remain obscure. It was reported that he was incompetent, that he himself had said 'when it comes to affairs of state, I am a blockhead', but this is based only on rumour.[5] It is certain, however, that he had become embroiled in one of the most malodorous scandals of the century: for many years he and his brother had kept their father incarcerated in his own castle. Although the father was both mentally deranged and compulsively extravagant, this made little impression on public opinion. The episode provided the plot for Schiller's *Die Räuber*, first published in 1781 and first performed at Mannheim early the following year, a few weeks before von Sickingen's dismissal.[6] There is no proof of any causal link between the two events, although the coincidence of the timing is suggestive, to say the least.

The story did not end there. Von Sickingen then proceeded to Vienna and, so it was rumoured later, turned Joseph II and Kaunitz against the

---

[1] Ibid. Fasc. 205, 613. *Politischer Briefwechsel des Herzogs und Großherzogs Carl August von Weimar*, ed. Willy Andreas, vol. 1 (Stuttgart, 1954), p. 116.
[2] Vienna, *Staka*, Fasc. 205, 613.   [3] Ibid. Fasc. 211, 777.
[4] Ibid. Fasc. 201, 398, 401. For Count Metternich's views on Sickingen's dismissal, see H. Mathy, 'Die Entlassung des österreichischen Gesandten Franz Georg von Metternich aus Mainz im Jahre 1785', *Mainzer Zeitschrift*, 66 (1971).
[5] W. M. Becker, 'Das Urbild des alten Moor in Schillers Räubern', *Zeitschrift für die Geschichte des Oberrheins*, new series, 43 (1930), 321.
[6] Ibid., p. 322.

Mainz régime by spreading all sorts of unedifying stories about the Elector and his entourage. These stories then found their way back to Mainz and helped to intensify Friedrich Karl's dislike of the Viennese court.[1] It is no longer possible to separate fact from gossip but, whatever the truth of the matter, von Sickingen's departure only served to accelerate the Elector's desertion of the Habsburg camp.

At first Metternich was not unduly worried. The Elector continued to chair cabinet meetings, while his brother, Lothar Franz Freiherr von Erthal, took over von Sickingen's special responsibilities. Although sixty-five years of age, in poor health and with no experience of or interest in affairs of state, in Metternich's eyes Lothar Franz von Erthal had one cardinal virtue – he was pro-Habsburg.[2] This amiable connoisseur of the arts was not the man to fill the gap left by von Sickingen; when the Elector fell under the sway of a new group, he retired swiftly, and perhaps gratefully, to the wings again. He was replaced by the Hatzfeldt family, led by the widowed Charlotte Sophie Countess von Hatzfeldt, the Elector's cousin. By far the most important member of the family was her daughter Sophie, who was married to a spendthrift nobleman from Liège, Georg Ludwig Freiherr von Coudenhove.[3] From about 1783 until the end of the decade Sophie von Coudenhove was the undisputed *éminence grise* of Mainz, and naturally attracted a great deal of notoriety. She was intelligent, energetic, determined, skilful and physically attractive. It remains doubtful whether or not she was Friedrich Karl's mistress, but it is certain that she exercised a great deal of influence over him.[4]

Although Sophie moved to Mainz soon after her uncle's election, it was not until after von Sickingen's dismissal that she began to make her political mark. By the end of 1783 Metternich found it advisable to mention in his despatches to Kaunitz the receptions she held several times a week attended by her brother, Franz Count von Hatzfeldt; the French ambassador, Count O'Kelly; and the Elector, but not, alas, by Metternich himself.[5] In the course of the following year Sophie's influence was consolidated. Metternich lamented that the Elector's company at his Aschaffenburg residence consisted almost entirely of the Hatzfeldt ladies, and regretted especially the baleful influence of the 'very scheming Frau von Coudenhove'.[6] His alarm was fully justified, for the entire Hatzfeld family

---

[1] Pertz, *Steins Leben*, p. 42.
[2] Vienna, *Staka*, Fasc. 201, 424, Fasc. 212, 832.
[3] The name was spelt in all sorts of different ways – Guttenhoven, Goudenhoven, etc. Coudenhove is the spelling used today.
[4] In 1806, long after Friedrich Karl's death, she denied vehemently that she had been his mistress – K. Schib, *Johannes von Müller 1752–1809* (Schaffhausen, 1967), p. 151, n. 55. A portrait of her can be found among the illustrations.
[5] Vienna, *Staka*, Fasc. 205, 613.   [6] Ibid. Fasc. 210, 736.

was devoted to the interests of Prussia. The Prussian envoy von Stein reported to Berlin that 'every time I name Madame de Coudenhove I should like to venture to repeat that she is without doubt the most excellent minister Your Majesty could have at the court of Mainz'.[1] Early in 1785 she received political support but perhaps unwelcome competition for the Elector's affections in the shape of a certain Frau von Ferrette from Alsace, 'a young and pretty woman, for whom it appears the Elector has particularly warm feelings'.[2]

The rise of Sophie von Coudenhove was accompanied by a precipitate fall in the personal stock of Count Metternich. Just before he left Mainz for good he composed a detailed account of his chequered career in the city.[3] He recalled that during the early years of the reign his relations with the Elector had been marked by a close personal friendship. He could call on him unannounced at any hour of the day, he spent his evenings with him and even gave him advice on purely personal matters. Even when the disputes with Joseph II brought a change of policy, Friedrich Karl assured him that he would never allow political disagreement to sour their personal relations. Metternich then made a very stupid mistake; he assumed that Friedrich Karl's attachment to Sophie could be dissolved by a man-to-man talk. 'As a friend', he warned him against that lady's intrigues and even suggested that a campaign was afoot to obtain a pro-French successor, by means of a coadjutor election. Metternich paid for his feeble grasp of psychology by losing overnight not only any residual political influence he may have had, but also the Elector's affection. Friedrich Karl also came to believe that Metternich was being devious as well as impertinent, that the Austrians wished to secure the election of a Habsburg Archduke as coadjutor and to facilitate their own campaign were deliberately spreading the false rumour of French designs.[4] After this incident it was only a matter of time before Vienna replaced an ambassador who was no longer on speaking terms with the ruler to whom he was accredited.

Metternich's negotiation of the confused situation at the Mainz court had not been very adroit, but navigation from the start had been made difficult by his master's intransigence. Joseph managed to incense the Elector on a petty personal level as well as on that of high politics. A fine example was the Coudenhove court case. In 1779 the *Reichskammergericht* found for the Coudenhove family in a suit involving 70–80,000 *Reichstalers*. After the defendant had fled to Vienna with all his possessions, the plain-

---

[1] Joseph Hansen, *Quellen zur Geschichte des Rheinlandes im Zeitalter der französischen Revolution*, vol. 1 (Bonn, 1931), p. 174, n. 4.
[2] Ibid., p. 178, n. 3. For a detailed description and analysis of Metternich's departure, see Mathy, 'Metternich'.
[3] Vienna, *Staka*, Fasc. 212, 832.   [4] Ibid. Fasc. 217, 152.

tiffs asked the Austrian Court Chancellery to proceed against him. Taking its stand on a special privilege, the Chancellery refused to cooperate, although there was no question as to the justice of the *Reichskammergericht*'s decision.[1] Not surprisingly, Friedrich Karl then attempted to persuade the Austrian authorities to help his niece and was suitably annoyed when Joseph declined to intervene. The affair remained a sensitive issue for a number of years. In the summer of 1785, just before Mainz joined the League of Princes, Trauttmansdorff reported that the Elector had worked himself into a frenzy about it, saying that Joseph's reply to his observation that sovereigns should implement judicial decisions had been so insulting that he would not expose himself to ridicule again but would seek satisfaction elsewhere.[2] Trauttmansdorff's belief that cooperation over the case would do much to woo Sophie von Coudenhove and thus her uncle out of the arms of Prussia was simply ignored in Vienna.

As the tide in Mainz ebbed, turned and flowed increasingly in the direction of Berlin, the salaried officials hastened to trim their sails accordingly. Here again Joseph's misguided sense of propriety gave powerful assistance to his enemies. On his accession as sole ruler in 1780 Joseph decided that the distribution of pensions and favours to prominent statesmen in the *Reich* had to stop. In 1783, when Austro-Mainz relations were disturbed but still fluid, Valentin Heimes, the highly influential suffragan bishop, asked to be appointed Imperial Book-Censor in Frankfurt, a post in the gift of the Emperor. Metternich forwarded the request to Vienna, with a strong recommendation that it be granted, for he considered Heimes to be the only genuinely pro-Habsburg minister in Mainz.[3] His advice was rejected.

At the same time Philipp Karl von Deel, the minister in charge of foreign affairs, reminded Metternich that some time before he had been promised an annual pension of 2,000 gulden. This had been made in return for his giving up a claim to a post at the *Reichskammergericht* in favour of a candidate sponsored by Vienna. Deel regretted that his domestic circumstances now made it necessary for him to ask that this promise be honoured.[4] Again Metternich recommended that this request be granted and again his advice was rejected. Two years later, with Mainz on the verge of joining the League of Princes, he reminded Vienna reproachfully of the ill effects which had followed this refusal. He even thought that Heimes' loyalty could be regained if only he were given the post at Frankfurt.[5] By this time Deel had placed himself beyond salvation by accepting Prussian money and by playing a leading part in steering Friedrich Karl into the Prussian

[1] Ibid. Fasc. 197, 355.
[2] Ibid. Fasc. 214, 4.
[3] Ibid. Fasc. 205, 595.
[4] Ibid.
[5] Ibid. Fasc. 212, 832.

League.¹ Doubtless he exaggerated his own importance, but Deel told Trauttmansdorff in 1786 that Mainz would never have deserted the Habsburgs if he had been given his pension.² Joseph's contempt for the *Reich* was never better illustrated than in this readiness to sacrifice two potential allies for the sake of a paltry 2,000 gulden and a minor post in the imperial administration.

On the rare previous occasions they had fallen foul of Vienna, the Electors of Mainz had sought the protection of France. This was no longer possible, for France was Austria's ally. Although this did not mean that Versailles was prepared to give Joseph II any real assistance, it did mean a policy of non-intervention. France moreover was teetering on the brink of bankruptcy. It was inevitable therefore that the Electorate should be drawn into the Prussian orbit, all the more so because the Prussians themselves were looking for allies. Joseph's *entente* with Russia in 1781, together with the French alliance, revived the nightmare of the coalition assembled by Kaunitz at the beginning of the Seven Years War. Perilously isolated, Frederick the Great sought to use the fears aroused in the *Reich* by Joseph's aggression to found a League of German Princes opposed to Habsburg expansion.

Frederick never intended that this League should be anything more than a stop-gap, to be discarded when Prussia found more powerful allies elsewhere, notably in Great Britain. But other Germans were more ambitious. A number of lesser princes – Karl Friedrich of Baden, Leopold of Anhalt-Dessau, Carl August of Weimar, Ernst of Gotha and Karl Wilhelm of Braunschweig-Wolfenbüttel – wanted the League to be a third force, to protect the smaller states against both Prussia and Austria. They also hoped that under its aegis the institutions of the *Reich* would be reformed and revived. While they appreciated that at the present time Joseph posed the main threat, all of them could remember a time when Frederick had been the aggressor. It was hoped therefore that Prussia would be a protector but not a member of their League.³ Whatever his motives, any prince interested in founding a league within the *Reich* was certain to be interested in recruiting the Archchancellor. The powers he exercised at the *Reichstag*, in the Imperial Chancellery and in the imperial courts made him a valuable ally, whether in obstructing the Habsburgs or in reforming the *Reich*.

After much preparation and a number of false starts the League of Princes (*Fürstenbund*) was eventually founded in the summer of 1785. Needless to say, it was created in the image desired by Frederick the Great, although the princes interested primarily in reform did join as well. The

¹ Pertz, *Steins Leben*, pp. 45, 54–7.   ² Vienna, *Staka*, Fasc. 216, 10.
³ Andreas, *Briefwechsel*, p. 8.

wooing of the Elector of Mainz did not reach a successful conclusion until October, although it had begun months, even years before. A Prussian envoy, Johann Friedrich von Stein, had been sent out to test opinion in the *Reich* as early as 1781. Although his visit to Mainz sent a first tremor of unease down Metternich's spine, nothing came of it.[1] Two years later the situation began to change, as Joseph's abrasive 'diplomacy' made itself felt. In December 1783 Wilhelm von Edelsheim, the chief minister of Karl Friederich of Baden, detected throughout the *Reich* a mood favourable to the formation of a League. In Mainz, he thought, both Deel and the Elector would support such a scheme. Almost exactly a year later the Duke of Brunswick wrote to Carl August of Weimar that 'our ecclesiastical princes make me very hopeful; they see the dangers which menace them and feel that their interests are almost the same as our own'.[2]

Prussian envoys continued to glide in and out of Mainz, but it was not until early 1785 that a really serious attempt was made to elevate Friedrich Karl's disenchantment with Vienna into a formal attachment to Berlin. After unofficial probing by Edelsheim and Carl August of Weimar, a formal approach was made by Karl von Stein, who arrived in Mainz at the beginning of July. The negotiations dragged on through the summer, as Friedrich Karl's natural indecision was reinforced by a diplomatic counter-offensive from Trauttmansdorff and his Russian and French colleagues. Their efforts only served to delay matters; on 18 October the Electorate of Mainz joined the League of Princes.[3]

II

Friedrich Karl's position, as the only prince-bishop in a predominantly Protestant and entirely anti-Habsburg alliance, was difficult enough. It was complicated further by his simultaneous involvement in a major dispute with the papacy. Since the failure of the Koblenz initiative in 1769-70,[4] the German episcopalist movement had been in the doldrums, sputtering only occasionally over minor grievances. It roared back into life in February 1785 when it was announced in Rome that a papal nuncio was to be sent to Munich at the request of the Elector of Bavaria, Karl Theodor. As the negotiations had been conducted in secret, it was even more of a shock when the news of their successful completion reached the German episcopacy.[5] The bishops viewed the existing nuncios with extreme distaste; the announcement of a new creation enraged them.

[1] Vienna, *Staka*, Fasc. 197, 346.
[2] Andreas, *Briefwechsel*, pp. 81-2, 112.
[3] Vienna, *Staka*, Fasc. 214, 21, 27, 43-4, 56, 60, 64. Pertz, *Steins Leben*, pp. 47-66.
[4] See above, p. 118.
[5] H. Schotte, 'Zur Geschichte des Emser Kongresses', *Historisches Jahrbuch*, 35 (1914), 91.

No one was more appalled than the Archbishop of Mainz. In a letter to his colleague at Salzburg on 11 March, he expressed the fear that the new nuncio would be equipped with the same powers as the nuncio at Cologne. He did not dispute the Pope's right to send diplomatic representatives to foreign courts, but claimed that it was illegal to send out agents with powers which encroached on the jurisdiction of the local bishops and archbishops. As a first step, he proposed that the Pope be asked whether the new nuncio was to hold the same brief as the nuncio at Cologne. An affirmative reply was to be countered by a joint protest from the entire German episcopacy. If that failed to have the desired effect at Rome, the help of the Emperor was to be enlisted. As a last resort the whole affair was to be referred to the *Reichstag*.[1]

This plan was applauded warmly by the Archbishop of Salzburg but did not receive unanimous support elsewhere. The Archbishop of Trier supposed naïvely that the Pope had appointed a nuncio simply as a matter of 'diplomatic convenience'.[2] Even after confirmation arrived in May that the Munich nuncio would be fully equipped, the German episcopacy could not form a united front. Both Friedrich Karl's attempt to enlist the support of his suffragans and his attempt to launch a concerted campaign at the *Reichstag* evoked a very mixed reception.[3] His chief adviser on ecclesiastical matters, Valentin Heimes, wrote in July that an alliance consisting of Mainz, Salzburg, Eichstätt, Würzburg, Bamberg and Freising could be formed but that the Archbishops of Cologne and Trier were dragging their feet.[4] It was not until the autumn of 1785 that the episcopalist protest acquired fresh momentum. Max Franz of Cologne had been equivocal not because he felt any enthusiasm for the papal position but because he hoped to exploit the situation to gain concessions over the nuncio at Cologne.[5] When he realised that Pius VI was utterly intransigent, he became more receptive to overtures from Mainz. Friedrich Karl's proposal in September that a joint approach be made to the Emperor was now given a warm welcome.[6] On 22 September an appeal was despatched from Mainz calling on Joseph II to help defend the German Church against Roman encroachments.[7] Max Franz gave powerful support by making a personal visit to Vienna to urge his brother to help. Joseph's reply, despatched to Mainz on 12 October, was entirely satisfactory. He informed Friedrich Karl that he would help the German Church not only to defend its existing rights but also to regain those usurped by the papacy on earlier occasions. He pledged that he would regard the nuncios as simple ambassadors,

---

[1] Vienna, *MEA*, Religionssachen, Fasc. 38, 12–15. [2] Ibid., 30–1.
[3] Ibid., 18–21, 58–9. [4] Ibid., 67.
[5] Schotte, 'Zur Geschichte des Emser Kongresses', p. 92.
[6] Vienna, *MEA*, Religionssachen, Fasc. 38, 96.
[7] Ibid., 102.

competent only to deal with secular business and not authorised to exercise any kind of jurisdiction.[1]

Following Joseph's advice, Friedrich Karl then sought the cooperation of his numerous suffragans. The response was discouraging. Only the Prince-Bishop of Eichstätt promised full support; the replies of the others bristled with qualifications.[2] For this reason it was decided in Mainz that the archbishops should take the initiative, in the hope that the rest of the episcopacy would be drawn after them. In January 1786 Valentin Heimes wrote to Waldenfels, the chief minister of Cologne, proposing that representatives of the four archbishops should meet to compose a common programme and devise a common strategy.[3] Although this met with cautious approval, it was not until March that formal invitations to attend a congress were despatched.[4] Another and longer delay followed, as four months were spent in haggling over the venue and terms of reference. Eventually, on 24 July, the four delegates and their assistants assembled at Bad Ems, a small spa on the river Lahn, not far from Koblenz.[5] The careful preparation now paid dividends; the Congress proper lasted only ten days. Agreement on the wording of the *Punctatio*, which defined the episcopal position, was reached on 28 July and on the wording of the 'Reform Decree', which was a programme of internal church reform, on 2 August. After a feeling in Cologne and Trier that the delegates had exceeded their brief caused a short delay, the final *Punctatio* was signed by the delegates on 25 August. Ratification by the four archbishops followed soon afterwards.[6]

Described by Ranke as 'probably the most remarkable document to proceed from the womb of the German Catholic Church since the Reformation',[7] the *Punctatio* of Ems is seen rightly as the climax of the German episcopalist movement. It did not, however, contain anything new. Quite self-consciously, the delegates at Ems took as their model the programme drawn up at Koblenz sixteen years earlier.[8] When Heimes sent back to Mainz the first points of the *Punctatio* on 27 July, he observed that 'at present we are taking as a basis the *Gravamina* collected back in 1769, and we shall also retain them, in so far as it is considered feasible and advisable'.[9] Both in detail and in general principles, there is a striking similarity

---

[1] Ibid., 116.   [2] Ibid., 139–46.
[3] *Des kurtrierischen Rats H. A. Arnoldi Tagebuch über die zu Ems gehaltene Zusammenkunft der vier erzbischöflichen Herren Deputierten*, ed. M. Höhler (1915), p. 49.
[4] Vienna, *MEA*, Religionssachen, Fasc. 38, 164. The replies are also enclosed, 170–5.
[5] Ibid., 177. This fascicle contains the reports Heimes sent daily to Mainz. Another day-by-day account, written by a member of the Trier delegation, has been reprinted by Höhler, *Ems*.
[6] Vienna, *MEA*, Religionssachen, Fasc. 38, 438, 474.
[7] Leopold von Ranke, *Die deutschen Mächte und der Fürstenbund*, 2nd ed. (Leipzig, 1875), p. 253.   [8] See above, p. 119.
[9] Vienna, *MEA*, Religionssachen, Fasc. 38, 191.

between the thirty-one articles agreed at Koblenz and the *Punctatio* of Ems. The latter's fundamental premise was stated in the preamble:

> The Roman Pope is and will always remain the supreme overseer (*Aufseher*) and primate of the entire Church, and is equipped by God with the jurisdiction necessary for this purpose. All Catholics must render him canonical obedience with complete veneration. On the other hand, all privileges and reserved powers which were not a part of this primacy during the first centuries but stem from the later Isidorean decrees, to the obvious detriment of the bishops, cannot now be brought within the scope of this jurisdiction, for the forgery and falsehood of these decrees have been adequately proved and are generally recognised.[1]

There followed twenty-three articles, with many sub-divisions; a detailed exposition and analysis would require a book in itself. Essentially, they represented an attempt to give practical expression to the principle that Christ had given to all his apostles, and their successors the bishops, unlimited power to bind and loose. The abolition of the nuncios, the abolition of any exemption from episcopal jurisdiction enjoyed by groups or individuals and the transfer from Rome to the individual dioceses of the right to dispense from the laws of the Church were three of the most important demands. If the Ems programme had been carried out, the German Church would have wrested an even greater degree of independence from Rome than its Gallican counterpart in France.

The Congress of Ems was the climax of the episcopalist movement in more senses than one. From that point disappointment followed disappointment. The most acute and decisive was the changed attitude of Joseph II. His early support, as expressed in his letter of 12 October 1785, had been dictated by a desire to keep Mainz out of the League of Princes and to accelerate negotiations with Salzburg over a new diocesan arrangement.[2] By the autumn of the following year, not only did these considerations no longer apply, they had been replaced by others which required a changed policy. It was Karl Theodor of Bavaria and the Palatinate who now needed humouring. He was, after all, the only major prince who had not yet joined the League of Princes. His consent would also be required for the exchange of Bavaria for the Netherlands, a plan Joseph was reluctant to abandon.[3] Joseph was also reluctant to give any assistance to a movement led by the Elector of Mainz, who the previous year had shown his gratitude for imperial support by joining an alliance whose avowed aim was the frustration of Habsburg policies. As Kaunitz observed when news of the proposed Congress of the Archbishops first filtered through to

---

[1] Ibid., 442. The *Punctatio* is reprinted in full in Höhler, *Ems*, pp. 171–83.
[2] Aretin, *Reich*, vol. 1, p. 389.
[3] Karl Otmar Freiherr von Aretin, 'Die Konfessionen als politische Kräfte am Ausgang des alten Reiches', *Festgabe Joseph Lortz*, ed. E. Iserloh and P. Manns, vol. 2 (Baden-Baden, 1958).

Vienna, Mainz would only use the nuncio dispute to detach the prince-bishops from Austria and lure them into the Prussian camp.[1]

The essential difference between the 'Josephism' of the Austrian secular state and the 'Febronianism' of the prince-bishops of the *Reich* was again illustrated. When the Gallican Church loosed its ties with Rome, it did so on the orders and with the support of the King of France. Because they were independent members of the *Reich*, the prince-bishops in Germany could expect no such support. Rather it was in the interest of the secular princes to emulate Bavaria, to persuade the Pope to give them their own ecclesiastical organisation and thus exclude the jurisdiction of 'foreign' prince-bishops.[2] Aware of these considerations and naturally averse to any cooperation with Joseph II, Friedrich Karl wanted to take the matter direct to the *Reichstag*. He was overruled by the other Archbishops, who insisted that imperial support was indispensable. Consequently, the *Punctatio* was drafted in the form of a communication to the Emperor and sent to him on 10 September 1786. In a covering letter the Archbishops asked Joseph to intervene in Rome on their behalf. If the Pope remained obstinate, they asked for a National Council to be summoned. If this proved impossible, they expressed the hope that Emperor and *Reichstag* would take joint action at least against Rome's temporal exactions.[3]

Joseph's reply, when it arrived after a delay of more than four months, was a bitter disappointment. He assured the Archbishops of his general support for their campaign, but also added a fatal qualification:

As regards the various points [of the *Punctatio*] you have enclosed with your joint communication, all I can say at present is that their chances of enforcement and the value one can expect from them depend to a large extent on a prior and firm agreement made by the Archbishops with the bishops who are exempt [from metropolitan jurisdiction], as well as with their suffragan bishops, and with the princes of the *Reich* whose territories form part of the episcopal diocese.[4]

As Joseph well knew, this was asking the impossible. Any doubts the Archbishops might have had about Joseph's attitude were soon dispelled by some more bad news from Vienna. The Trier *chargé d'affaires* reported Joseph as saying that while he would not obstruct the German episcopacy's attempt to regain powers usurped by the Papacy, he would then set about regaining for himself imperial powers usurped by the German episcopacy.[5]

As in 1769, the bishops proved to be more suspicious of the archbishops than they were of the Pope.[6] As long as the Munich nuncio remained the sole target, most of the bishops were prepared to give their general sup-

---

[1] Ibid., p. 222. Aretin, *Reich*, vol. 1, pp. 402–3.
[2] See above, pp. 213–14.
[3] Vienna, *MEA*, Religionssachen, Fasc. 38, 494.
[4] Ibid., 539.
[5] Höhler, *Ems*, p. 191.   [6] See above, p. 120.

port; but when the field of fire was extended to include all papal jurisdiction, they had second thoughts. August of Speyer, who was frequently embroiled in disputes with the Mainz General Vicariate, caused trouble from the start. In a letter to Friedrich Karl of April 1785, he argued that the nuncio at Cologne should be left alone and that any campaign against the new arrival at Munich would have no chance of success if the bishops stood to lose more on the archiepiscopal roundabouts than they gained on the papal swings.[1] Franz Ludwig of Bamberg and Würzburg, Friedrich Karl's younger brother, expressed the same anxiety, albeit less bluntly.[2]

In view of this antagonism, it is not surprising that Joseph's call for cooperation went unanswered. When the news that the four Archbishops had held a secret Congress at Ems leaked out, the bishops' mistrust intensified. August of Speyer sent to a number of his colleagues a detailed and hostile analysis of the *Punctatio*, and urged them to resist the metropolitan offensive.[3] Although the other prince-bishops were not as forthright in their condemnation of the Ems proposals, they were not prepared to assist the Archbishops. Franz Ludwig of Bamberg and Würzburg was evasive, Liège, Fulda, Hildesheim and Regensburg openly hostile.[4] Only insignificant Eichstätt and Chur pledged full support.[5]

For the reasons mentioned above, it was even more unlikely that the Archbishops could form an alliance with the secular princes. The interests of the German Church, with its curious combination of *temporalia* and *spiritualia*, and its intimate relationship with the Imperial Knights, could not be reconciled with those of the great princes wishing to turn their territories into sovereign states.[6] As the Archbishop of Salzburg pointed out, Joseph II had been an unmitigated disaster for the German Church. His reversal of Habsburg policy had left it virtually defenceless, while his diocesan reorganisation had pointed the way for the other German princes.[7] The latter's alliance with the Roman Curia went back to the Reformation, when their loyalty to Catholicism was rewarded by greater independence from the ecclesiastical jurisdiction of the bishops.[8] Certainly they had nothing to gain from helping the German episcopacy.

Cooperation with other sections of the *Reich* was made much more difficult by disagreements among the Archbishops themselves. In an early memorandum Valentin Heimes, the suffragan bishop of Mainz, observed

---

[1] Vienna, *MEA*, Religionssachen, Fasc. 38, 28.
[2] Ibid., 47.
[3] Ibid., Fasc. 39, 4.
[4] Ibid., 3, 22, 42, 216, 223.
[5] Ibid., 34. Schotte, 'Zur Geschichte des Emser Kongresses', pp. 105–6, wrote that only Speyer and Liège actively opposed the *Punctatio* and described the position of Regensburg, Eichstätt, Würzburg–Bamberg and Paderborn–Hildersheim as neutral. The documents in the *Mainzer Erzkanzler Archiv* show that such a categorisation is wrong.
[6] Aretin, *Reich*, vol. 1, p. 38.
[7] Vienna, *MEA*, Religionssachen, Fasc. 39, 220.
[8] Aretin, *Reich*, p. 47.

that Trier and Cologne could not be relied upon.¹ From the Mainz point of view he was right. Max Franz of Cologne and Clemens Wenzeslaus of Trier heartily resented Friedrich Karl's aspirations to primacy in the German Church and viewed his manipulation of the nuncio dispute with deep mistrust. In particular they suspected that he would exploit it in the interest of the League of Princes, and to the detriment of their Habsburg relations. Max Franz told his colleague at Trier that he would never agree to the holding of a congress in Mainz, because it would give the impression that the Primate of Germany was gathering the subordinate Archbishops around him.² The Cologne delegate to the Congress of Ems, Tautphäus, was ordered not to allow the discussion of anything directed against the Emperor.³

Quite apart from their dislike of the Prussian bias of Mainz policy, the two Archbishops were also opposed to the radical reform proposals made by Heimes at the Congress. There were many heated exchanges, for example, on the question of the power of the bishops to dispense from the laws on fasting.⁴ The Mainz proposals carried the day on this issue, but met defeat on the question of clerical celibacy. It was believed in Mainz that a relaxation of the laws regarding the latter was essential for a reconciliation with the Protestants, but Trier and Cologne were adamant that the *status quo* must be preserved.⁵ Although much more cooperative, in Mainz eyes the attitude of the fourth Archbishop, Hieronymus of Salzburg, also left a good deal to be desired. A member of one of the most prominent Austrian noble families and the son of the Imperial Vice-Chancellor, Rudolph Joseph Prince von Colloredo, Hieronymus was basically pro-Habsburg. He was certainly eager to take a strong line against the Munich nuncio, but was suspicious of anything which smacked of Prussian influence. When his dispute with Joseph II over diocesan reorganisation was settled, largely to Salzburg's satisfaction, there was no real cause for straying from the Habsburg fold.⁶

The Congress of Ems, and with it the German episcopalist movement, was a failure. Many of the proposals for Church reform contained in the 'Reform Decree' were implemented in individual dioceses, but relations between the German Church and Rome continued unaltered. In Mainz the sense of failure was more intense because the ministry's ambitions had been pitched so much higher. Although Friedrich Karl's opposition to the Munich nuncio and support for the reform programme was as whole-

---

¹ Vienna, *MEA*, Religionssachen, Fasc. 38, 67. ² Höhler, *Ems*, p. 49.
³ Vienna, *MEA*, Religionssachen, Fasc. 38, 177.
⁴ Ibid., 345, 347, 363. The Mainz minister von Deel commented cynically that the attitude of Trier and Cologne was dictated by their reluctance to lose customs revenue, for a relaxation of fasting would lead inevitably to a decline in the Dutch fish trade on the Rhine.
⁵ Aretin, *Reich*, vol. 1, pp. 390–1. ⁶ Ibid., p. 397.

hearted as that of any of his colleagues, these were only short-term and secondary considerations. The key to his policy was still the League of Princes: he hoped to attract the Prince-Bishops into the League by playing on their resentment of Joseph's diocesan reforms and the Pope's appointment of a new nuncio. He appreciated that paradoxically the German episcopacy's only possible allies were the Protestants. The Protestant princes were naturally anti-Habsburg and, as they themselves enjoyed complete control of ecclesiastical affairs, were opposed to any attempt by their Catholic rivals to claim the same privileged position. The League also had much to expect from a mass entry of the prince-bishops, for they formed the chief support of Habsburg influence in the *Reich*. Their desertion would certainly allow the Protestants to dominate the *Reichstag* and would even make the election of a non-Habsburg emperor possible.

In acting as its self-appointed recruiting officer, the Elector of Mainz was not guided by any pure enthusiasm for the League and its aims. It was part of a grand design to establish for Mainz a pre-eminent position in the *Reich*. This was to be achieved by the creation of a German National Church, with the Archbishop of Mainz as its Primate and with only formal ties with the Papacy. This new alliance would find political expression by the admission of its members to the League of Princes. No longer would Mainz be isolated and powerless as the only ecclesiastical member of the League, but instead, as the leader of a large bloc of princes, would hold the balance of power in the *Reich*. This was not all: the political union of the German prince-bishops and the Protestants would prepare the way for a religious fusion, for the return of the heretics to the Catholic fold. It would be a Catholic fold, however, which had been cleansed of the internal corruption and papal usurpation which had led to the original breach. A *Leitmotiv* of Febronius, this last aim lay behind the Mainz delegation's eagerness to have the modification of clerical celibacy placed on the Agenda at Ems. If all this could be realised, Mainz would become as important a capital as Vienna, Berlin or Hanover.[1]

In retrospect, this plan seems so far-fetched that it is difficult to believe that anyone could have taken it seriously. Yet it was not simply born of Friedrich Karl's delusions of grandeur; its most consistent and forceful exponent was the 'logical, lucid and clear-sighted' Valentin Heimes.[2] The quality of its parentage could not save a child doomed from conception. With one or two insignificant exceptions the prince-bishops could not be persuaded to abandon their traditional loyalty to the Habsburgs. It proved relatively easy to persuade the other Archbishops to make threatening gestures at Rome but impossible to entice them into the League. The

---

[1] This summary of Friedrich Karl's aims is based largely on Aretin, *Reich*, pp. 392–6 and Aretin, 'Confessionen', pp. 219–24.   [2] Aretin, *Reich*, vol. 1, p. 396.

especially high hopes held of Salzburg were soon dashed. During his visit to Mainz in July 1786, it became quite clear that Archbishop Hieronymus would not consider any action directed against the Emperor.[1] Given the intransigence of Trier and Cologne, this meant that for Mainz the chief reason for holding the Ems Congress had been invalidated before the delegates had even assembled. The plan to heal the Protestant–Catholic division, based on a total misunderstanding of the Reformation, had no chance of success anyway; the failure of Heimes' radical proposals meant that it did not even get underway.

The upheaval in *Reich* politics during the 1780s not only gave Friedrich Karl an opportunity to cut a figure in international diplomacy, it also gave him greater scope for making mistakes. The coincidence of the League of Princes, Joseph II and the nuncio dispute would have taxed the resources of a ministry far more powerful, able and experienced than that to be found in Mainz. From the Congress of Ems onwards, Friedrich Karl's policies were bedevilled by his simultaneous membership of the League of Princes, which was pro-Prussian, and the archiepiscopal alliance, which was anti-Prussian. By trying for everything he gained nothing. This was made clear by the fortunes of the Electorate after joining the League of Princes.

III

Even after persuading Frederich Karl to enlist, the League could not rest on its laurels. In view of the new member's advanced age and poor health, it was likely that the Electorate's adhesion to the League would be of short duration. Most of the canons of the Cathedral Chapter were pro-Austrian, or at least anti-Prussian, and – taking their stand on ancient treaties concluded between the Habsburgs and the Electorate – they refused to ratify Friedrich Karl's entry.[2] This meant that the next Elector would be entirely at liberty to take Mainz out of the League and back into the arms of Austria. The only way to achieve continuity was to secure during Friedrich Karl's lifetime the election of a *coadjutor cum spe successionis* (the equivalent of a crown-prince), who was prepared to sign the League's articles.

In the event, it took the League's diplomats almost two years to achieve this aim.[3] Finding a candidate who was not only a supporter of the League,

---

[1] Aretin, 'Confessionen', p. 224.   [2] Vienna, *Staka*, Fasc. 215, 80, 88.
[3] Full accounts of the Coadjutor Election of 1787 can be found in Aretin, *Reich*, vol. 1, pp. 198–211 and in two articles by the same author: 'Höhepunkt und Krise des deutschen Fürstenbundes: Die Wahl Dalbergs zum Coadjutor von Mainz (1787)', *Historische Zeitschrift*, 196 (1963) and 'Dalberg zwischen Kaiser und Fürstenbund: Actenstücke zur Koadjutorwahl in Mainz 1787', *Archiv für mittelrheinische Kirchengeschichte* (1964). Cf. Willy Andreas, 'Dalbergs Wahl zum Coadjutor von Mainz', *Archiv für Kulturgeschichte*, 42 (1960). Trauttmansdorff's regular and very full reports can be found in Vienna, *Staka*, Fasc. 222–4.

Imperial adventures

but also acceptable to both the Elector and the Chapter proved immensely difficult. The most obvious candidate was the Canon Karl Theodor Freiherr von Dalberg,[1] who commanded most support in the Chapter. Unfortunately, he was detested by the Elector. Nor was he entirely to the League's taste, for although a close friend of Carl August of Weimar, he was not prepared to commit himself to an explicitly anti-Habsburg combination. Dalberg liked to think of himself as a 'patriot', whose chief concern was *Reich* reform and the conciliation of Prussia and Austria. Eventually his woolly idealism exasperated the League to such an extent that they rejected him as their candidate and took up instead the pliable nonentity Christoph Karl Freiherr von Dienheim, who also had the advantage of being the Elector's favourite. Dienheim's following in the Chapter however was slender, and not all the gold of Prussia could provide the missing muscle. The intensive canvassing undertaken on his behalf in Mainz during March 1787 only served to show that only Dalberg could be elected. Bowing to the inevitable, the League switched their support, dragging a reluctant Elector after them.

As von Aretin has shown on a number of occasions, Dalberg's election was in no sense a victory for Prussia and the League, despite all their attempts to make it appear so.[2] Indeed, Kaunitz and Trauttmansdorff viewed the outcome of the election campaign with satisfaction. From their point of view it was particularly important that the Elector had not been able to impose any conditions on Dalberg when giving him his votes. They knew that subsequently attempts would be made to entice the new coadjutor into the League, but felt confident that they would fail. On 31 March Dalberg had given Trauttmansdorff the following assurance:

> If the lot falls to me I shall sign nothing, I shall commit myself to nothing and shall act as a good patriot who knows both the duties an Elector of Mainz owes to all the members of the *Reich* and those imposed on him separately *vis-à-vis* the Emperor by his office of Archchancellor.

Later in the conversation he added:

> So far I have spoken to you as a minister, but I want to repeat again as a friend that you will have reason to be satisfied with me.[3]

The election of Dalberg had also been a tribute to the incorruptibility of most of the canons. The Prussians had authorised the expenditure of large sums of money, but their generosity evoked only a faint response. As early

---

[1] See above, pp. 199–200.
[2] See, for example, Aretin, *Reich*, vol. 1, pp. 198–211. This myth has proved surprisingly durable, its longevity being due to the Prussian orientation of most historians of the period. Willy Andreas, for example, has stated that Trauttmansdorff was greatly surprised by Dalberg's success, when in fact exactly the reverse was the case – Andreas, 'Dalbergs Wahl', p. 333.
[3] Vienna, *Staka*, Fasc. 222. This unnumbered report is located between reports 55 and 56.

as 1785 Trauttmansdorff had predicted that only the younger and impecunious canons would be tempted.[1] Events proved him right; only one or two were induced to desert their natural preference. Among these was the *roué* von Kerpen, whose extravagance had reduced his income from 8,000 gulden to 600 and had made him correspondingly vulnerable.[2] Against this example of venality must be set Trauttmansdorff's report that the canons Franckenstein, Boos, Redwitz and Harff had rejected indignantly attempts to bribe them.[3] A later and perhaps unreliable source recorded that Ritter had rejected an approach from the Elector with the words 'Your Electoral Grace knows that I need money, but I shall not become a rogue for the sake of it.' His colleague Bettendorff said that he would give his support to another candidate – Fechenbach – because 'the food is good at his place' and was not tempted by mere financial inducements. He told the Elector 'I am a gentleman, and a gentleman must keep his word.'[4] Although the League spent more than 180,000 gulden, they could not gather more than ten votes for Dienheim, including his own.[5]

The election of Dalberg rather than Dienheim meant that the League was still far removed from its object of achieving continuity in Mainz policy. As Dalberg had refused to join the League to assist his election, it was not likely that he would do so now that the prize was his. It was at this point – and not for the first time – that Joseph II came to the aid of his enemies. During the next few months Joseph succeeded in driving the new coadjutor into the Prussian camp, by renewing his programme of diocesan reorganisation and by treating Dalberg's admittedly naïve appeals for help in reforming the *Reich* with studied contempt. Trauttmansdorff lamented to Kaunitz on a number of occasions that the Emperor's refusal to be even polite to Dalberg had snatched defeat from the jaws of victory.[6] As Carl

[1] Ibid. Fasc. 215, 89.
[2] Ibid. Fasc. 222, 28.   [3] Ibid., 57.
[4] Øjvind Andreasen and Helmut Mathy, 'Frederik Münters Reise nach Mainz (1791)', *Mainzer Zeitschrift*, 62 (1967), p. 66. Trauttmansdorff described poor Bettendorff as 'completely cretinous', even though he voted the right way. Earlier in his career his colleagues had attempted to exclude him from the Chapter on the grounds of his mental deficiencies – Vienna, *MEA*, GK, Fasc. 43, 546ff.
[5] Aretin, 'Dalberg', p. 332. Not all of them of course were purchased. Some were pledged because of family ties; some canons may even have voted for Dienheim because they thought he was the best candidate. This display of political virtue was not as unique as the conventional accounts of the ecclesiastical states lead one to suppose. See, for example, Raab's account of the elections at Cologne, Münster, Paderborn and Hildesheim in 1761–3 – *Clemens Wenzeslaus von Sachsen und seine Zeit, 1739–1812*, vol. 1 (Freiburg, Basle and Vienna, 1962), pp. 129–77. The 180,000 gulden were dispersed in Mainz as follows: 70,000 for votes purchased in Mainz, 60,000 to Dienheim for agreeing to transfer 'his' votes to Dalberg, 20,000 for the election at Worms and 30,000 for bribing subordinate officials and servants – Karl Freiherr von Beaulieu-Marconnay, *Karl von Dalberg und seine Zeit*, vol. 1 (Weimar, 1879), p. 97.
[6] Vienna, *Staka*, Fasc. 223, 100, 106, 128. Aretin, 'Dalberg', p. 350.

Imperial adventures

August of Weimar observed gleefully to Frederick William II: '*Joseph II se fait la guerre à lui-même.*'[1]

In their attempt to woo Dalberg into their ranks the League's diplomats also received powerful assistance from the Pope. Superficially this was surprising. The Elector of Mainz and his ministers had played a leading part in the campaign against the papal nuncios, while the League consisted almost entirely of Protestants. As so often in the past, political considerations dictated cooperation with the heretics. Joseph II had become such a menace that Pius VI was prepared to look for allies anywhere. Consequently, when the League applied to Rome for a *breve eligibilitatis* for the Mainz coadjutor there was an encouraging response. The Prussian diplomat Girolamo Marchese Lucchesini brought the negotiations to a successful conclusion on 18 April. He had agreed to only two conditions: that the Elector of Mainz would call a halt to the campaign against the nuncios and observe the *status quo*, and that the new coadjutor would join the League of Princes.[2] This gave the League a powerful hold over Dalberg and they lost no time in imposing it. If Joseph had paid even token attention to Dalberg's attempts to remain a man of the centre, he might still have been restrained from the final step, but the renewal of the diocesan encroachments and his general indifference left the new coadjutor no choice. On 11 June, the day after his formal election, Dalberg joined the League of Princes.[3]

It is no exaggeration to say that Dalberg's election and his subsequent admission to the League marked a watershed in *Reich* politics. An immediate result was a reshuffle of his former supporters in Vienna. Kaunitz lost all influence on imperial affairs; Trauttmansdorff was recalled from Mainz and sent to Brussels as Minister.[4] Any fresh initiative from Vienna would have to await the death of Joseph II. Superficially the situation in the opposing camp was just the reverse. Everyone knew that Dalberg was a member of the party which saw the League primarily as an instrument for the reform of the *Reich* and moreover that he was a close personal friend of this group's leader, Carl August of Weimar. Yet, although the process was more protracted, the pattern of events was the same as in Vienna. During the three years following the coadjutor election the reform movement faded away and power politics triumphed.

No one doubted that the less important members of the League were sincere in their desire to reform the *Reich*, but contemporary opinion was

---

[1] Andreas, *Briefwechsel*, p. 354.
[2] Max Immich, 'Preußens Vermittelung im Nuntiaturstreit 1787 bis 1789', *Forschungen zur brandenburgischen und preußischen Geschichte*, 8 (1895), pp. 144–7. The Pope also promised not to make any further encroachments on the metropolitan jurisdiction of Mainz.
[3] Aretin, *Reich*, vol. 1, p. 203.
[4] Aretin, *Reich*, vol. 1, p. 204.

less generous to the Elector of Mainz. The Prussian minister Finckenstein explained Friedrich Karl's decision to join in the following terms:

The Elector has been decided by his desire to shine with Your Majesty [Frederick the Great] in a rôle which is at the same time patriotic and popular, by his personal hatred of the Emperor, by their disputes over his rights as Archchancellor of the *Reich*, by the influence of his relations, the Coudenhove family...and finally by the advice of his three ministers von Deel, von Heimes and von Strauss.[1]

A conspicuous absentee from this list was any plan for the reform of the *Reich*. Yet it cannot be denied that Friedrich Karl expended a good deal of time and many thousands of words on the subject. He summarised his own view of the situation in a letter to Carl August at the end of 1787: 'The League of Princes...has as its main objectives the maintenance of the lawful and traditional powers and rights of each member of the *Reich*, the prevention of any illegal violation of the same, the improvement of the legislative process and the [prevention of] the exchange of Bavaria'.[2]

To propagate his views he found a remarkably gifted publicist in the Swiss historian Johannes Müller, who had been appointed University Librarian in 1786. Müller's definitive statement of the Mainz position was the massive 'Portrayal of the League of Princes' (*Darstellung des Fürstenbundes*), published in 1786.[3] After a long preparatory section dealing with the nature of liberty, the balance of power and the history of the *Reich*, he turned his attention to the present situation. His starting point was the belief that the *Reich* was not an instrument for conquest but 'a great confederation of members of varying sizes who have agreed jointly on a common system of law and mutual assistance'.[4] The League of Princes had been founded to defend the *Reich*'s essence against the encroachments of Joseph II, in no sense was it an aggressive association. Müller was particularly anxious to show that it was not a creature of Prussia, but rather a union of many princes, of whom Prussia happened to be one.[5] Needless to say, he also took the opportunity to eulogise the unselfish patriotism of the Elector of Mainz.[6] Müller's ambition extended beyond resisting aggression or improving *Reich* institutions. He also had a vision of national renewal under the auspices of the League. In a later treatise he exhorted the other Prince-Bishops to join, claiming that then the League would 'reawaken the Germans. National feeling has shrunk in the face of wretched partiality. We shall only be patriotic when, as citizens of a vigorous federal republic, under princes as defenders of the laws, everyone feels himself to be part of a fatherland.'[7]

[1] Ranke, *Fürstenbund*, p. 168, n. 1.   [2] Andreas, *Briefwechsel*, p. 405.
[3] Johannes von Müller, *Sämtliche Werke*, ed. J. G. Müller, vol. 9 (Tübingen, 1811).
[4] Ibid., p. 123.   [5] Ibid., pp. 271–2.   [6] Ibid., pp. 292–7.
[7] Max Lehmann, 'Eine Denkschrift von Johannes von Müller aus dem Jahre 1787', *Historische Zeitschrift*, 71 (1893), p. 73.

Imperial adventures

The most important practical expression of these general principles was the call for a Congress of the League, to be held in Mainz. This proposal was first raised by Friedrich Karl during the winter of 1786-7, shelved during the coadjutor election campaign, raised again in the summer, shelved during Prussia's intervention in Holland, and raised again at the end of 1787. Friedrich Karl told Carl August of Weimar in October that at the present time the League was a skeleton; only a Congress of its members could give it flesh and blood. If another year were allowed to slip away, enthusiasm for reform would dim.[1] Carl August was in full agreement and spent several weeks in Mainz during the winter helping to prepare a circular to the other princes of the League. To avoid the impression that an anti-*Reichstag* was being set up, it was proposed that individual members should authorise the diplomats already in Mainz to negotiate on their behalf.

Although apparently innocuous, this plan exposed the deep division within the League. Its three major powers – Prussia, Hanover and Saxony – were not interested in the reform of the *Reich*. Indeed their long-term aim to establish complete sovereignty within their territories made them fundamentally hostile towards the *Reich*. They had founded the League to resist Joseph II, and that was all. As Frederick William II was informed by his ministry 'the principal aim and object of the League is to prevent the dismembering of Bavaria and every other despotic or illegal action on the part of the leading power'. Saxony's views were the same, while Hanover had not wanted the ecclesiastical states in the League in the first place.[2] The opposition of the three Electors was of course decisive. The Congress was shelved again, this time for good.

The same fate befell Friedrich Karl's other main objective in the League: military expansion. While in Mainz attending the celebrations surrounding Dalberg's formal election as coadjutor, Carl August reported to Berlin that the Elector intended to ask Prussia and Hanover for subsidies to double the size of his army to 8,000 and to repair the city's fortifications. Friedrich Karl argued that in the event of war between the Elector and Austria, a strengthened Mainz would enjoy decisive strategic importance.[3] Carl August was appalled by this martial display; the rôle he envisaged for the Archchancellor was that of pacific reformer. Commenting that 'this project flatters infinitely the Elector's ambition and imagination', he advanced eleven arguments against the project. There was never any danger that such an expensive scheme would find support in Berlin, Hanover or Dresden. The three electors, and especially their ministers,

---

[1] Andreas, *Briefwechsel*, p. 376.
[2] Ibid., p. 422, 479. Ernst A. Runge, 'Die Politik Hannovers im deutschen Fürstenbund (1785–1790)', *Niedersächsisches Jahrbuch für Landesgeschichte*, 8 (1931), p. 16.
[3] Andreas, *Briefwechsel*, p. 356.

were well aware that by any military standards Mainz was a negligible quantity.

The incident was yet another instance of the incompatibility between the hierarchical *Reich* and the sovereign state. In terms of imperial law and tradition the Elector of Mainz, as Archchancellor, was a more important figure than the Elector of Brandenburg, Hanover or Saxony. In terms of power politics, on the other hand, his status in the League was that of a junior partner dealing with public relations, while the three senior partners took all the important decisions by themselves. The clearest indication of the relationship was the fact that Friedrich Karl was allowed to sign only the main treaty of the League and the first secret article, which related to preventing the exchange of Bavaria. He was not told about the other secret articles or any of those classified as 'top secret', which dealt with military precautions, the election of a King of the Romans, the possibility of a ninth (Protestant) elector, and so on.[1]

Irritation was the only response, therefore, when Friedrich Karl began to give himself airs and graces on the question of a Congress in Mainz or the military subsidies. Frederick William II remarked sourly that 'I hope the Elector will always act as an Archchancellor, but not as head of the League.'[2] Prussia certainly had some reason to start having doubts about the value of Mainz membership of the League. Friedrich Karl had failed to persuade any of his episcopal colleagues to follow his example in joining. His powers at the *Reichstag* were still useful – but Prussia was not interested in an initiative there anyway. The election of Dalberg moreover had not dispelled fears for the continuity of policy in Mainz.[3] After a brief honeymoon following the election, relations between Elector and coadjutor had reverted to their earlier tense condition.[4] In view of these considerations, there was no reason for the League to pay much attention to the ambitions of the Elector of Mainz.

Prussia's attitude towards Mainz, or even imperial reform, had not always been one of indifference. During the first part of Frederick William's reign Carl August of Weimar had been the dominant influence at Berlin and virtually Prussian Minister for the *Reich*. By late 1787, however, the regular ministers Hertzberg and Finckenstein were beginning to reassert their influence. They took little or no interest in the *Reich* and wished to steer Prussia back into the mainstream of European diplomacy, and in particular towards an alliance with Great Britain. Aware of their hostility, Carl August made a number of attempts to establish friendly

---

[1] Runge, 'Hannover', p. 43.   [2] Andreas, *Briefwechsel*, p. 441.
[3] This was one of the reasons for not admitting Friedrich Karl to the secret articles of the League. It was feared that during the interregnum which would follow his death the pro-Austrian canons would take the opportunity to publish them.
[4] Beaulieu-Marconnay, *Dalberg*, vol. 1, pp. 157–63.

relations with the two men.¹ His approaches were in vain; by the spring of 1788 he had lost virtually all influence on Prussian policy. In a letter to Sophie von Coudenhove he exclaimed: 'May the League go to the devil...I would be the first to go to hell, provided that I didn't meet any of my fellow-princes there.'² In another more playful letter to the widowed baroness he resorted to analogy to describe the progress of the League: 'In marriage the making of a child is much more pleasant than its birth, and both father and mother are much more delighted by the beginning of the affair than they are by its consequences.'³ To a less committed observer it would have been clear that the League had had its day; its purpose had been served. Joseph II had been checked and was now safely embroiled, together with Russia, in an enervating war with the Turks. His other ally France was clearly on the brink of bankruptcy and civil disorder. The disturbances in Holland had not only diverted Prussian interest away from the *Reich* but had also paved the way for a more permanent form of cooperation between Prussia and Great Britain. The agreement between the two powers, signed at Loo on 13 June 1788, was the beginning of the end for the League of Princes.⁴

The Mainz ministry may not have appreciated all the complexities of the situation, but they could see quite plainly that the League was going sour on them. In March 1788 the Hanoverian ambassador in Mainz, Steinberg, reported that Friedrich Karl had been annoyed greatly by the refusal of the League to hold a Congress in his capital.⁵ This disillusionment was reflected most clearly in a pamphlet by Johannes Müller, published in July and entitled 'What Germany expects from the League of Princes' (*Deutschlands Erwartungen vom Fürstenbund*). He recalled the optimism which had attended its foundation in 1785 and expressed disappointment that nothing had happened since. Although he repeated the hope that Mainz would become both the political and the military centre of the League, privately he knew that there was no chance of its realisation: 'I am in favour of the German League, but in the hope that it will be effective; if it is not, it can hold no interest for me.'⁶

In 1789 this rather negative disenchantment became active irritation. When it became clear that Joseph II was dying, a dispute arose over the powers to be exercised after his death by the *Reichsvikare*, who directed the conduct of imperial business between the death of one emperor and the election of his successor. The League of Princes was drawn into the fray because one of the *Reichsvikare* was the Elector of Saxony. As Archchancellor, the Elector of Mainz was naturally keen to restrict the powers

---
¹ Andreas, *Briefwechsel*, pp. 28–31.
² Ibid., p. 473.
³ Ibid., p. 484.
⁴ Aretin, *Reich*, pp. 212–17.
⁵ Andreas, *Briefwechsel*, p. 461.
⁶ Hansen, *Quellen*, vol. 1, pp. 301–3.

of the *Reichsvikare* as much as possible. He proposed that even before a vacancy should occur their powers should be defined by the *Reichstag*. Together with the Elector of Bavaria, his future fellow-*Reichsvikar*, the Elector of Saxony took violent exception to this proposal, and individual members of the League hastened to take sides. Although Hanover remained neutral, Prussia's decision to support the *Reichsvikare* showed Friedrich Karl that he could hope for nothing more from his nominal allies.[1] The League of Princes was not interred formally until the Declaration of Pillnitz of 1791, but it had been moribund for a long time before that.

IV

Dalberg's election as coadjutor was also a milestone in Friedrich Karl's ecclesiastical campaign. This had been directed in the short-term against the Munich nuncio and in the long-term towards the foundation of a German National Church under his leadership. Such an ambitious plan was probably quite impracticable anyway, but the promise made to Rome to observe the *status quo*, made in exchange for Dalberg's *breve eligibilitatis*, proved the final blow. Although this last episode in the history of the episcopalist movement was highly complex, its essentials can be quickly told.[2] During the year following the Congress of Ems, very little had been achieved. Following the Emperor's instructions, the four archbishops had consulted their suffragans, with predictably meagre results. During the first six months of 1787 attention in Mainz was concentrated on the coadjutor election, leaving little or no time for the nuncio dispute. Interest revived in November of that year when Pius VI authorised the Elector of Bavaria to impose a special levy of 10% on all ecclesiastical benefices. Similar concessions had been made many times in the past, but collection had always been organised by the bishops. On this occasion the Munich nuncio was to take their place.[3] In both Berlin and Mainz this was regarded as a serious breach of the agreement made at the time of Dalberg's election. The other three Archbishops, although they lacked this special motive, were also incensed. During the next few months many angry protests were sent to Rome, without having the slightest effect. It became clear that the Archbishops alone could not bring sufficient pressure to bear on the Pope.

With the Archbishop of Mainz neutralised by a separate and secret agreement, it seemed likely that the campaign against the nuncio would not advance beyond the level of pointless invective. During the winter of 1787–8, however, the Elector Max Franz of Cologne assumed control and

---

[1] On the *Reichsvikare* affair, see Andreas, *Briefwechsel*, pp. 520–2, and Runge 'Hannover', p. 49.
[2] The most detailed account is to be found in Schotte, 'Zur Geschichte des Emser Kongresses'.
[3] Ibid., p. 338.

Imperial adventures

injected fresh determination. When he went to Vienna at Christmas to officiate at the wedding of his nephew, the Archduke Franz, he took the opportunity to berate his brother Joseph for lack of support. By holding out the threat of following Mainz into the League of Princes, he won an assurance of more active help in the future.[1] In the meantime attempts by Mainz to negotiate a settlement with the Pope made no progress. Friedrich Karl's growing irritation at Roman intransigence was accompanied by a growing willingness to cooperate with Cologne in a fresh initiative. Both he and Clemens Wenzeslaus of Trier, however, wished to concentrate their fire on the new intruder at Munich; they were prepared to give tacit recognition to the Cologne nuncio.[2] For obvious reasons, Max Franz was not prepared to make this concession. He stuck to the principle established at Ems: that all nuncios equipped with powers of jurisdiction were illegal. It was an indication of the ascendancy he had achieved in the archiepiscopal alliance that at a meeting at Bonn on 18–19 July 1788 he managed to persuade his two Rhenish colleagues to expand their target.[3] Agreement was also reached on the tactics to be employed. After prompting and promises of support from Vienna, it was decided to take the affair to the *Reichstag*. An imperial decree of 9 August set the machinery in motion.

The mills of the Archbishops ground very slow, but they did not grind very fine, by way of compensation. It was not long before they stopped altogether. Pius VI had not been impressed by the Congress of Ems, nor by remonstrances from Vienna, nor by Prussian attempts to arrange a compromise. Even if support were forthcoming, it was not likely that the *Reichstag* would prove any more successful. Quite simply, the Pope was not prepared to make any concessions over the nuncios whatsoever, and the Archbishops had no means of making him do so. The Secretary of State, Cardinal Buoncompagni, wrote to the nuncio at Cologne: 'However unpleasant the political situation of the Church might be, the papal representatives must never lower themselves to being the slaves of the secular authorities and must never abandon the defence of dogma and the principles of the Church.'[4] There was special opposition to making any sort of a deal with the Elector of Mainz, who had assumed the proportions of an anti-Christ. Pacca's verdict, recorded in his memoirs, was: 'This Elector led an entirely secular life...and only remembered to be a bishop when an opportunity arose to upset the Pope or to oppose the Holy See.'[5]

---

[1] Braubach, *Max Franz*, pp. 199–200.
[2] There had been a nuncio at Cologne since the sixteenth century.
[3] Braubach, *Max Franz*, p. 201.
[4] Schotte, 'Zur Geschichte des Emser Kongresses', p. 319.
[5] Bartolomeo Pacca, 'Die Denkwürdigkeiten des Kardinals Pacca', *Frankfurter zeitgemäße Broschüren*, new series, 27 (1908), p. 201.

Rome's uncompromising attitude was strengthened by intermittent support from Berlin. The vacillation of Frederick William II was another reflection of the struggles within his ministry. Those who attached most importance to the reforming activities of the League of Princes advocated support for the Archbishops. Those who saw in the League only an anti-Habsburg device advocated support for the Pope. By the spring of 1788 this latter group had established complete ascendancy in the councils of the King. Their hand was strengthened by the simultaneous Austrian intervention on behalf of the Archbishops. It was natural that the more the Austrians attempted to draw the *Reichstag* into the affair, the more the Prussians would attempt to keep it out. Consequently, after the imperial decree of 9 August 1788, attempts were made by the League to persuade Friedrich Karl to resume direct negotiations with Rome. Although greatly irritated by Prussia's half-hearted support, he succumbed in December.

The unity of the Archbishops had been broken again, this time for good.[1] As it was clear that nothing could be expected now from the *Reichstag*, Salzburg and Cologne also made direct approaches to Rome. The answer took almost a year to arrive and when it did it proved to be completely negative. There was one further flurry of activity after the death of Joseph II, when a number of restrictions on the nuncio were incorporated in the new Emperor's capitulation of election. It had no practical value. By this time the outbreak of the French Revolution and disturbances within the *Reich* had made disputes about nuncios seem distinctly parochial. In a circular to his three archiepiscopal colleagues of 12 March 1790 Clemens Wenzeslaus announced that the current situation demanded unity between the head and the members of the Church and an example of submission to authority.[2] Germany's episcopalist movement was over.

Friedrich Karl's imperial adventures had ended in disappointment. When the French Revolution began a new and final era of the *Reich*'s history, both the League of Princes and the alliance of Archbishops were on the point of collapse. The extent of Friedrich Karl's failure can be judged only in terms of his aims, both professed and concealed. For public consumption he announced that the League had been founded to afford protection against imperial encroachments, to improve Reich institutions and to prevent the exchange of Bavaria. Only the third of these aims had been realised, and it may be doubted whether Mainz membership of the League had made a decisive contribution. For the great Protestant states Bavaria was the *raison d'être* of the League; the other two issues were ornaments and were never taken out of the window. The possibility of other prince-

[1] Hansen, *Quellen*, vol. 1, p. 340, n. 2. Immich, 'Preussens Vermittlung', p. 163.
[2] Schotte, 'Zur Geschichte des Emser Kongresses', p. 803.

Imperial adventures

bishops following Mainz into the Prussian camp may have slowed but certainly did not stop Joseph's diocesan reorganisation. The reform of the *Reich*, in which the Elector of Mainz as Archchancellor would have played a starring rôle, was never allowed to progress beyond nebulous statements of principle.

Many contemporaries, on the other hand, insisted that Friedrich Karl's real motive was a simple desire for prestige. If this were the case, he must have derived considerable satisfaction from his membership of the League, at least during its early stages. In 1786 Count Trauttmansdorff commented admiringly that the League had sent an army of high-ranking diplomats and princes to Mainz to encourage Friedrich Karl's high opinion of himself: the Dukes of Weimar and Gotha, the two Princes of Hessen-Darmstadt, the Margrave of Baden, both Freiherren von Stein, Böhmer, Steinberg, the two Edelsheims, Görtz, Hofenfels, and so on.[1] This idyllic period was of only brief duration. By the end of 1787 it had become clear that the Elector of Mainz would never play more than a subordinate rôle in the League. The plans he proposed for a Congress in his capital and military subsidies were rejected with thinly disguised contempt.

In retrospect, it is easy to see that the important position enjoyed by Friedrich Karl in the years 1785–7 had to be temporary. It was an Indian Summer, brought on by the uncertainty surrounding Frederick the Great's old age and death, Prussia's isolation and Joseph's maverick behaviour. When Prussia overcame her diplomatic isolation, the League of Princes was doomed. Not even this exceptional episode could conceal the growing discrepancy between the hierarchical constitution of the *Reich* and the ambitions of the powerful secular states.[2] In seeking to translate the theoretical supremacy of the Archchancellor into practice, Friedrich Karl was attempting to turn the clock back several hundred years. It was not surprising that his failure was total.

His ecclesiastical policies met with the same fate. Just as Friedrich Karl and Johannes Müller took a genuine interest in the reform of the *Reich*, so did Friedrich Karl and Valentin Heimes take a genuine interest in the programme drawn up at Ems. They were not simply bidding for more power by the exclusion of papal influence. As the determined and unpopular attempts to introduce reforms within the Electorate showed,[3] they were also concerned with improving the quality of religious life. It cannot be denied however that Friedrich Karl's position in the German Church was compromised seriously by his political ambitions. In his schedule of priorities the political always preceded the ecclesiastical. Well

[1] Vienna, *Staka*, Fasc. 216, 33.
[2] Aretin, *Reich*, pp. 23–5.
[3] See above, pp. 173–80, 204–9.

aware of the fact, his fellow bishops and archbishops viewed the machinations of his court with the utmost distrust. Far from founding a National Church, with himself as primate, Friedrich Karl stumbled into isolation; not one of his colleagues followed him into the League. Although his ambition, vanity and volatile temperament made his failures seem all the greater, it should be remembered that none of his more modest or able colleagues enjoyed any greater success.

Perhaps time was running out for all the ecclesiastical states. The same secular princes who scotched the plans for *Reich* reform were equally opposed to the *Reich*'s ecclesiastical organisation. Catholic princes, and Protestant princes with Catholic subjects, resented the independent status of the episcopacy. Every secular prince, whatever his denomination, looked at the rolling acres of the prince-bishoprics with a secularising glint in his eye. Short-term political considerations prompted Prussia to lend occasional support to the Archbishops, but this could only be temporary. If the two great German powers ever reached an agreement, the days of the ecclesiastical states would be numbered. Nor could the beleaguered Church of the *Reich* expect much sympathy or assistance from Rome. The German prince-bishops had been a thorn in the papacy's flesh for several decades. Cooperation with secular princes such as Karl Theodor of Bavaria seemed a much more attractive alternative. For all these reasons, the failure of the episcopalist movement left the prince-bishoprics in a highly vulnerable position. As Schotte remarked:

The tragi-comedy of Ems, which seemed to some to be the dawn of a better future, had become the *lever du rideau* of secularisation.[1]

[1] Schotte, 'Zur Geschichte des Emser Kongresses', p. 805.

7

'Revolution': Aschaffenburg and Mainz 1790

'July 14th in Paris was the finest day since the fall of the Roman Empire', wrote Johannes Müller to his brother on 14 August 1789, 'the previous generation aped French frivolity, the next will copy French courage'.[1] His friend and colleague Georg Forster shared his enthusiasm, interpreting the Revolution as a victory for philosophy.[2] Like many of their contemporaries, Forster and Müller expected that the French experience would soon be repeated in Germany. The many superficial similarities between the two countries certainly lent support to their predictions. It could have been argued that the situation in Germany was potentially more combustible. The contrast between overprivileged noble and underprivileged commoner was even more striking east than west of the Rhine, for here many of the nobles enjoyed virtually sovereign powers. East of the Elbe the peasants' condition amounted to slavery. The man-made barriers to the country's development were both more formidable and more irrational in Germany. The hundreds of governments, customs posts, armies and courts bore constant witness to the waste, inefficiency and political impotence of the *Reich*. The Electorate of Mainz, with its great pretensions but puny resources, was a microcosm of this wider discrepancy between potential and reality. To many it seemed ripe for an early imitation of 'French courage'.

One striking parallel between events at Versailles and Mainz was the gilded frame within which they occurred. Friedrich Karl's grandiose diplomatic adventures were accompanied by an enormous expansion in the size and opulence of his court. He began his reign in a muted atmosphere of pious austerity, but this did not last long.[3] The arrival of the sophisticated Wilhelm Count von Sickingen[4] brought a complete reversal. Over the next decade and a half Friedrich Karl unfolded a more active – and more expensive – aesthetic programme than the Electorate had seen

[1] Johannes von Müller, *Sämtliche Werke*, ed. J. G. Müller, vol. 5 (Tübingen, 1814), p. 269.
[2] Georg Forster, *Sämtliche Schriften*, vol. 8 (Leipzig, 1843), p. 85.
[3] The Austrian diplomats were greatly impressed by the economies he made during the first two years of his reign. Vienna, *Staka*, Fasc. 175, 620, 627, Fasc. 180, 4.
[4] See above, p. 215.

since the days of Lothar Franz von Schönborn (1695-1729), the legendary patron of the baroque. Three years after his accession he began the complete reconstruction of the interior of his palace at Mainz; it was still in progress nine years later.[1] The *Favorite*, a complex of gardens, pavilions and orangeries on the outskirts of the city, was extended, and a new summer residence was added. Yet another summer retreat was erected on an island in the Rhine.[2]

It was at Aschaffenburg, however, that Friedrich Karl really gave full rein to his artistic ambitions. The interior of the massive seventeenth-century castle was gutted. What took its place was described by Philip Gercken in 1785:

> One finds the most beautiful rooms, whole series, so that more than ten rooms follow in a row, and appointments which are even better than those in the palace at Mainz. Everything is magnificently furnished, in the latest style.[3]

Just outside the town he built a tiny but exquisite château – *Schönbusch* – which still exists and is an enduring monument to his extravagance and good taste.[4] It was surrounded by a large and studiously wild park in the English style, in which could be found numerous fashionable accoutrements such as a temple of friendship, a temple of philosophy, a gothic tower, a hermitage decorated with busts of the ancient philosophers, a model dairy-farm and a small classical building in which the Elector took his breakfast.[5] The close environs of Aschaffenburg also boasted a second English park, complete with terraces, an orangery, lakes, grottoes, waterfalls, a botanical garden, a concert-hall and the artificial ruins of a convent.[6] This verdant paradise was completed by a game-park and pheasantry, over the entrance to which stood a quotation from Shaftesbury: 'Receive me in your quiet sanctuaries and favour my retreat and thoughtful solitude.'[7]

---

[1] For a detailed description, see: [Francis Russell, 5th Duke of Bedford], *A Descriptive Journey through the Interior Parts of Germany and France, including Paris, with interesting and amusing anecdotes*, by a young English Peer of the Highest Rank, just returned from his Travels (London, 1786), pp. 25–6. Eduard Graf von Coudenhove-Erthal reprints a photograph of the main state-room, the *Akademiesaal*, as it looked before destruction by bombing in the Second World War – 'Die Kunst am Hofe des letzten Kurfürsten von Mainz (Friedrich Carl Joseph von Erthal) 1774-1802', *Wiener Jahrbuch für Kunstgeschichte*, 10 (1935), plate 69.

[2] Karl Klein, *Geschichte von Mainz unter dem letzten Kurfürsten Karl Friedrich Joseph von Erthal* (Mainz, 1870), pp. 13–14.

[3] P. W. Gercken, *Reisen durch Schwaben, Baiern, die angränzende Schweiz, Franken, die Rheinische Provinzen und an der Mosel in den Jahren 1779-1785*, vol 4 (Worms, 1788), p. 355.

[4] Erich Bachmann, *Schönbusch bei Aschaffenburg* (Munich, 1963).

[5] J. C. Dahl, *Geschichte und Beschreibung der Stadt Aschaffenburg* (Darmstadt, 1818), pp. 78–9. S. Behlen and J. Merkel, *Geschichte und Beschreibung von Aschaffenburg und dem Spessart* (Aschaffenburg, 1843), pp. 92–9. [6] Ibid., pp. 86–7.

[7] Ibid., p. 88. For Johannes von Müller's description of *les charmes de la vie* at Aschaffenburg, see Edgar Bonjour, *Johannes Müller, Briefe in Auswahl*, 2nd ed. (Basle, 1954), p. 159.

'Revolution': Aschaffenburg and Mainz 1790

Within this golden frame the Elector showed a highly developed taste for pageantry and opulent display. On the occasion of the election of Dalberg as coadjutor, for example, the celebrations lasted four days and included processions, banquets, firework displays, concerts, balls, illuminations and – somewhat incongruously – military manœuvres.[1] Even when the opportunity for such grand setpieces was lacking, the court continued its pursuit of pleasure unabated, and Mainz acquired the reputation of being one of the most worldly and glamorous courts in Germany.[2]

By itself a monarch's love of display did not necessarily generate social unrest, unless increased taxation was required to finance it. Indeed royal extravagance could bring considerable benefit to the tradesmen and service industries of his capital. In Mainz in the 1780s, however, it seemed to many that the Elector's sensualism was a symptom of a more general decadence. Although nepotism had always been a feature of the Electorate's political life, Friedrich Karl's rapacity was without precedent. His only surviving male relations were his two brothers: Franz Ludwig, who was Prince-Bishop of Würzburg and Bamberg and thus suitably catered for, and Lothar Franz, who was already satiated with Mainz sinecures.[3] The Elector's residual family affection was lavished on the Hatzfeldts. Various members of the family enjoyed rapid preferment at court, in the government, in the army and in the ecclesiastical institutions controlled by the Elector.[4]

This nepotist raid on the Electorate's resources, together with the simultaneous influx of other 'foreign nobles', caused deep resentment among those Imperial Knights who had come to regard Mainz as 'their' Electorate.[5] It also gave an extra edge to the political opposition, which had been growing in strength since the beginning of Friedrich Karl's reign. The core of this opposition was formed by Canons of the Cathedral Chapter who had been supporters and beneficiaries of the late Elector Emmerich Joseph's régime: Damian Count von der Leyen, Franz Philipp Count von Walderdorff, Franz Xaver Freiherr von Hornstein and Karl Anton Freiherr von Dalberg.[6] They came to be known as the *Emme-*

---

[1] Franz Werner, *Der Dom von Mainz, nebst Darstellung der Schicksale der Stadt und der Geschichte ihrer Erzbischöfe*, vol. 3 (Mainz, 1836), p. 263.
[2] See above, p. 57. See also Count Schlik's report to Kaunitz on the 'extraordinary expenditure' of the Elector – Vienna, *Staka*, Fasc. 224, 9.
[3] Kittel, 'Geschichte der freiherrlichen Familie von und zu Erthal', *Archiv des historischen Vereins von Unterfranken und Aschaffenburg*, 17 (1865).
[4] Würzburg, *MGKA*, Fasc. 226 (1), 34, 44, 108, 179. *Hof- und Staatskalender des Kurfürstentums Mainz*, 1774–1793.
[5] The *Hof- und Staatskalender* show that between Friedrich Karl's election in 1774 and 1793 members of 43 noble families – or more than a quarter of all noble families active in Mainz in the eighteenth century – appeared in Mainz for the first time.
[6] See above, pp. 132–33, 137, 154–5.

richianer. During the turbulent interregnum of 1774 they had resisted stoutly but unavailingly the conservative reaction and the election of Friedrich Karl. Although in a small minority at this point, their ranks were soon increased when the new Elector's supporters fell out over the distribution of the post-election spoils. One by one, the great families which had supported Friedrich Karl – the Franckensteins, the Eltzs, the Stadions – went into opposition.[1]

The strength of the opposition was shown by the Chapter's refusal to endorse the Elector's membership of the League of Princes. The Canons certainly resented Joseph II's diocesan reorganisation, but could not bring themselves to accept a combination led by Frederick the Great. The very fact that it was the Elector who moved towards Berlin was enough to push them in the opposite direction. This instinctive hostility was intensified by the change in the Elector's ministry. The Hatzfeldts, The Baronesses von Coudenhove and Ferrette, von Stein, Müller and all the other special envoys of the League were bound to excite disapproval in Mainz. Some of them were women, most of them were Protestants and all of them were outsiders. Moreover, many of them suffered from unsavoury personal reputations.[2]

It seems clear that in opposing the League of Princes the Canons reflected the view of most nobles in Mainz. In a very long and detailed report of May 1786 Trauttmansdorff explained the close links between the political interests of the great Mainz magnates and voting patterns in the Chapter.[3] He attached special importance to the closely-related Stadion and Schönborn families, who worked together against the Elector's party inside and outside the Chapter. Their family and political links with such influential canons as von der Leyen, Walderdorff and Dalberg played an important part the following year in frustrating the attempt by Friedrich Karl and the League of Princes to secure the election of Dienheim as co-

---

[1] See above, pp. 157–8.
[2] Not unnaturally – although perhaps incorrectly – most contemporaries assumed that Mesdames Coudenhove and Ferrette ('*les femmes électorales de Mayence*') were the Elector's mistresses. Sophie von Coudenhove was also thought to be simultaneously the mistress of the Prussian diplomat Johann Friedrich von Stein. Her brother Franz Count von Hatzfeldt was having an affair with Countess von Schlick, the wife of the Austrian ambassador. Johannes von Müller maintained a homosexual relationship with his manservant. *Recueil des Instructions données aux Ambassadeurs et Ministres de France, depuis les Traités de Westphalie jusqu'à la Révolution française*, section 18, États Allemands, vol. 1, L'Électorat de Mayence, ed. Georges Livet (Paris, 1962), p. 255; Wilhelm Lüdtke, 'Der Kampf zwischen Oesterreich und Preußen um die Vorherrschaft im "Reiche" und die Auflösung des Fürstenbundes (1788–91)', *Mitteilungen des oesterreichischen Instituts für Geschichtsforschung*, 45 (1931), p. 133, 144; Louis Joseph Amour Marquis de Bouillé, *Souvenirs et fragments pour servir aux mémoires de ma vie et de mon temps*, vol. 1 (Paris, 1906), p. 40; Øjvind Andreasen and Helmut Mathy, 'Frederik Münters Reise nach Mainz (1791)', *Mainzer Zeitschrift*, 62 (1967), p. 73. K. Henking, *Johannes von Müller*, vol. 2 (1928), pp. 72–4.
[3] Vienna, *Staka*, Fasc. 216, 60.

adjutor.¹ Dalberg's success was a victory for the *Emmerichianer* and provided further evidence of the opposition of the bulk of the Mainz nobility to the Elector, his policies and his advisers.

Although the Chapter's opposition was doubtless irritating, it did not pose any serious political threat. The canons had no legislative veto and no means of influencing the Elector's choice of advisers.² During an interregnum they ruled supreme, but during an Elector's lifetime they entered the political arena only on the rare occasion of a coadjutor election or when asked to authorise an increase in taxation. Their victory in the former proved to be only temporary, while the Electorate did not begin to run into financial difficulties until 1791.³ By this time the French Revolution had provided ample proof of the need for solidarity between sovereign and nobility. Not one of the canons, or indeed any of the nobles in Mainz, showed any sign of seeking an alliance with the Third Estate against their rulers. Nor was there any indication of a more general 'aristocratic resurgence' in the 1780s. Both the Chapter's determination and political ambition were far stronger in the crisis of 1773–4 than subsequently.⁴

Any cooperation between nobles and commoners was made difficult by the absence of any joint representative body, since the final demise of the estates after the Peasants' War of 1524–5. No one proposed that they should be revived. It was doubtful moreover whether there was any significant popular discontent for ambitious nobles to exploit. Neither in the city of Mainz nor in the Electorate at large was there any early attempt to imitate events in France. This was not due to ignorance. The newspapers of the Rhineland, including the *Mainzer Zeitung*, had reported fully on the Assembly of Notables, the summoning of the Estates General, the agitation for the doubling of the Third Estate and the fall of the Bastille.⁵ It seems likely that some version of what was happening in France penetrated even to the more remote and illiterate villages. The Rhineland as a whole was not uniformly calm. There were many reports of urban riots and peasants refusing to pay tithes. In Boppard, a town in the Electorate of Trier less than fifty miles from Mainz, an old dispute over the ownership of a forest threatened to become an insurrection. A harassed official reported that the dissidents had talked of following the example set by Paris.⁶ In

---

¹ Hellmuth Rössler, *Graf Johann Philipp Stadion, Napoleons deutscher Gegenspieler*, vol I (Vienna, 1966), pp. 121–5. ² See above, p. 62. ³ See below, p. 271. ⁴ See above, pp. 130–40.
⁵ Joseph Hansen, *Quellen zur Geschichte des Rheinlandes im Zeitalter der französischen Revolution*, vol. I (Bonn, 1931), pp. 338, 376.
⁶ Ibid., pp. 367, 394, 430, 566, 575. Although trouble constantly recurred, there was no actual outbreak of violence at Boppard. Kyösti Julku [*Die revolutionäre Bewegung im Rheinland am Ende des 18. Jahrhunderts*, vol. I (Helsinki, 1965), p. 101], erroneously assigns Boppard to the Electorate of Mainz. For an account of the disturbances in the Rhineland in 1789 based on Prussian reports, see Lüdtke, *Oesterreich und Preußen*, pp. 77–82. Lüdtke erroneously assigns Alzey to the Electorate of Mainz. In fact it was part of the Palatinate.

the autumn there was rioting in Koblenz and Trier.[1] Although not threatened immediately, the Elector of Mainz also began to show signs of nervousness.

At the end of August the semi-official *Mainzer Zeitung* published an appeal for calm. It painted a golden picture of present conditions in Germany, depicted the terrible anarchy in France and concluded: 'To the honour of our region let it be said that religion has too great an influence over the Rhinelanders to allow them to break the oath they have made to their princes – princes who have their well-being so much at heart.'[2] Propaganda was reinforced by action. Two ordinances warned local officials against wandering bands of French brigands and doubled the guards on the frontiers.[3] The summer passed without incident, although there was flurry of excitement at the end of October when a Wetzlar newspaper reported that the citizens of Aschaffenburg had risen in revolt, had broken all the windows in the electoral residence and razed the château *Schönbusch* to the ground.[4] The report was totally false and an indignant Friedrich Karl demanded a rigorous investigation from the Wetzlar authorities.

There were no more alarms, false or real, but the atmosphere remained tense. Throughout the autumn Johannes Müller, whose initial enthusiasm for the Revolution was on the wane, reported to his various correspondents that the revolutionary contagion was creeping into the *Reich* and that trouble might even be expected in Mainz.[5] Yet at the end of November Müller reported that far from being rebellious, the citizens of Mainz had greeted their Elector, on his return from Aschaffenburg, with unprecedented demonstrations of affection, as if they expressly wished to distinguish themselves by their loyalty.[6] As the winter passed without disturbances it seemed that Mainz could drift on undisturbed by the violence in France.

This calm was rudely broken in February 1790 when rumours reached Mainz that the citizens of Aschaffenburg and the peasants of the surrounding district were preparing a revolt. On 8 February, Will, the director of the Aschaffenburg *Vicedom*'s office, sent a report denying the danger of open rebellion but admitting that discontent existed.[7] Together with a second report, which described the situation in greater detail, this

---

[1] Hansen, *Quellen*, vol. 1, pp. 461, 469.
[2] Ibid., pp. 422–3.
[3] Mainz, *Kurmainzische Verordnungen*, 6te Sammlung, vol. 11, 33, 38.
[4] Vienna, *MEA*, Militaria, Fasc. 102B. The documents in this fascicle are not paginated, and many of them are not dated. Where possible, the date, author and destination have been given.
[5] Müller, *Sämtliche Werke*, vol. 5, pp. 270, vol. 16, p. 399.
[6] Hansen, *Quellen*, vol. 1, p. 507, n. 2.
[7] Vienna, *MEA*, Militaria, Fasc. 102B. *Aschaffenburg den 8ten Feb. 1790*, Will to the Elector.

'Revolution': Aschaffenburg and Mainz 1790

communication was sent to the Elector's ministers for their perusal. Their advice was far from unanimous. While von Keller and Heimes suggested that two councillors be sent to investigate the disturbances, von Deel urged greater discretion and proposed only that an agent be sent on another pretext. True to his military calling, Field Marshal Franz Count von Hatzfeldt adopted a much more aggressive tone. He agreed that a commission should be sent to examine the citizens' grievances but insisted that they be accompanied by a military force of at least 200 men. He criticised Will and the other Aschaffenburg officials for allowing the situation to develop, poured scorn on the idea that there was no real danger of a serious revolt and demanded that the disaffected citizens be made an example of the Elector's determination to stamp out any discontent. Hatzfeldt was supported by the same Johannes Müller who had greeted the French Revolution with such rapture six months previously.[1] Friedrich Karl agreed with the advocates of immediate repression, ordered von Hatzfeldt to make the necessary military preparations and appointed councillors von Linden and Wallmenich to form the commission of inquiry.

After attending Mass in the garrison church, the expeditionary force of 225 soldiers and eight musicians set off for Aschaffenburg on 14 February, under the leadership of Lieutenant-Colonel Freiherr von Fechenbach.[2] After an uneventful journey, during which the only casualty was a soldier who got out of step and spiked his eye on the bayonet of the soldier in front, they marched into Aschaffenburg on 16 February.[3] The bulk of the contingent formed up in front of the town-hall, while other details occupied key positions throughout the city. Von Linden and von Wallmenich, who had arrived earlier that morning, then proceeded to read an electoral proclamation from the steps of the town-hall. They announced that while the Elector would do everything in his power to redress properly presented and well-founded grievances, he would not tolerate any kind of subversive activity. Any complaints the citizens might have were to be presented to the commission and any attempt to take the law into their own hands would be punished most severely.[4]

There was never in fact the slightest indication that Lieutenant Colonel von Fechenbach's troops would be needed to restore order. Director Will reported to Mainz that the citizens were entirely peaceful when the soldiers arrived and, far from offering any resistance, were surprised and

---

[1] Ibid., *Die Beschwerden der Bürgerschaft zu Aschaffenburg in Ansicht des Marcktrechtes betrf.*, n.d.
[2] Ibid., *Verzeichniß des zum Aufmarsche bestimmten Commando des G: v: Hatzfeldischen Infanterie Rgts*, n.d.
[3] Ibid., *Aschaffenburg den 16ten Feb. 1790*, Will to the Elector.
[4] Ibid., *Mainz, am 13ten February 1790*.

dismayed.¹ As they were to pay for the upkeep of the troops, their emotions were fully understandable. Two alleged ringleaders were arrested, the soldiers were billeted on the citizens in groups of four and the commission began its work. Throughout the military occupation there were only two minor incidents – when the son of a local official shouted an obscenity at von Fechenbach and when a citizen and a soldier became involved in a brawl, the responsibility for which was shared equally.²

As the commission's investigation progressed, it became clear that the measures of the central government had been out of all proportion to the actual trouble involved. The origin of the citizens' discontent lay in the allocation of the right to sell goods at the Aschaffenburg market. The concessions were administered by a municipal official, *Stadtschultheiß* Giesen, and the fees were paid into the municipal treasury to be used for the benefit of the community. For some time local tradesmen had complained that Giesen carried out the duties of his office capriciously and inefficiently and there were even rumours of corruption. Led by the chemist Prator, the clock-maker Nitschner and the butcher Morhard, a group of citizens met to discuss their grievances. In an excitable atmosphere induced by the consumption of large quantities of Franconian wine, direct action was threatened.³ News of these clandestine meetings soon reached the regional *Vicedom*'s office, which had its seat at Aschaffenburg. Aware that some at least of the citizens' grievances were justified, its director, Will, invited a delegation to come to his office to discuss the matter. Together they worked out a new and mutually acceptable scheme for the distribution of the right to sell at the market. Will forwarded it to Mainz, with the recommendation that it be approved. He also described the agitation which had taken place but expressed the hope that time and the new plan would act as a sufficient palliative.⁴ It was at this point however that von Hatzfeldt and Müller intervened to persuade the Elector to send a military force.

Having established the origins of the disturbance, the commission proceeded to collect the citizens' other specific complaints.⁵ The first and most important concerned the market; the others gave a clear indication of the social and political aspirations of the town's burghers. They complained that there were too many tradesmen and craftsmen in Aschaffenburg and proposed that the number should be reduced. They asserted that their livelihood was also threatened by country people manufacturing

---

¹ Ibid., *Aschaffenburg den 16ten Feb. 1790*, Will to the Elector.
² Ibid., *Aschaffenburg vom 16ten Hornung 1790*, von Fechenbach to the Elector, *Bericht der Aschaffenburger Commissarien in Sachen des arretirten Schreinermeister Seitz betreff*.
³ Ibid., *Kurzer Innbegriff des zu Aschaffenburg im Monath Februar besorgten Auflaufes und dessen Hergang*, n.d.
⁴ Ibid., *Aschaffenburg, den 9ten Feb. 1790*, Will to the Elector.
⁵ Ibid., *Die Aschaffenburger Beschwerden betreffend*, n.d.

articles themselves and demanded that they should be forced to purchase their requirements in the town. For the same reason they criticised foreign and indigenous pedlars for selling their wares from door to door before and after the official market days. To strengthen the guilds, they proposed that no master be allowed to pursue a profession other than that for which he originally had been registered. No one who resided in the country should be allowed to carry on a trade in the town. A foreigner who wished to settle in Aschaffenburg should possess a capital sum of 700 gulden or 500 gulden if he married the daughter of a local citizen. The number of Jews in the town should be reduced. Citizens of thirty or forty years standing should be exempted from certain taxes without having to make a formal application. Grazing rights in the game-park and the Schmerlenbach forest should be restored. To reduce the costs of educating their children, the system as it existed before the dissolution of the Jesuits should be reintroduced. Negotiations between the Elector and the town over forestry rights should be reopened: If the Elector and his ministers had ever been afraid that the Aschaffenburg disturbance was a prelude to a revolution of the French variety, this list of grievances must have set their minds at rest.

Von Linden and von Wallmenich sent the list to Mainz, together with the observation that many of the complaints were justified and should be met.[1] Despite his earlier indignation at the insubordination of his Aschaffenburg subjects, Friedrich Karl agreed. He accepted the advice of the commission that the administration of the market should be taken away from *Stadtschultheiß* Giesen. In future it was to be conducted by a municipal councillor and two citizens elected by the masters of the guilds. He also admitted that the grazing rights had been taken away unjustly and promised that they would be restored. As regards the other complaints, it was decided that some were inadmissible, others were met already by general ordinances and others needed further investigation.[2] Precisely because the issues were so petty and practical, the Elector found it easy to make concessions and come to an agreement. Throughout their remonstrances there was not the slightest whisper of a revolutionary mood or of opposition based on principle, which might have justified the sledgehammer tactics adopted to deal with the disturbance. The commission also discovered that the peasant unrest in the surrounding district was as nebulous as the 'Aschaffenburg Revolution' itself. The evidence for it was finally reduced to the story of a few drunken peasants in an Aschaffenburg inn declaring that if the citizens of the town started a revolution they would march as well. Von Linden and von Wallmenich were unable to

[1] Ibid.
[2] Ibid., *Beschwerden der Bürgerschaft zu Aschaffenburg betreff.* Marked: *Placuit FCJ Churfürst.*

discover who the peasants were or indeed whether the story was true or not.[1]

In Mainz the commission's report and recommendations led to the same sort of wrangling which had preceded the original despatch of the troops. Heimes pointed out that the whole affair had been a false alarm, and that the arrest of Prator, Nitschner and Morhard had been illegal, because nothing had been proved against them beyond a few indiscreet remarks. The ministers who had pressed for immediate represssion sought to justify their heavy-handed approach by reference to the potential danger. Müller in particular argued that he would never have voted to send troops 'if we did not live in times when a fanaticism which is spreading everywhere has shattered all principles of social order'.[2] After some considerable dispute it was agreed that the costs of the military expedition and the commission of inquiry should be shared by the 'ring leaders', the citizens as a whole and the electoral treasury. All the ministers agreed that the troops should be recalled.[3]

The panic was over. At the beginning of May Müller gave his own highly-coloured version of the episode in a letter to his brother.[4] He described how he and von Hatzfeldt had stood out against the pusillanimity of the other ministers and how the swift use of force had reduced the insurgents to trembling obedience. He concluded smugly that the Aschaffenburg citizens were now the best subjects of the Electorate. The facts of the case accorded more closely with Heimes' dismissal of the affair as a little local difficulty. The actual grievances would not have been out of place in the fourteenth century and were of such a limited kind that they were easy to settle. It is possible that the Aschaffenburg burghers were moved to agitate for their demands by the example of the French or Belgian revolutionaries, but there is no evidence of any international stimulation. There was certainly very little in the Aschaffenburg remonstrance to remind one of the Declaration of the Rights of Man and Citizen.

Considering the social and economic structure of the town, this was not surprising. Although it had only 4,000 inhabitants, Aschaffenburg closely resembled Mainz. It derived considerable material benefit from the annual sojourn of the court, from the nobles who gathered there for the excellent hunting in the Spessart forests and from the numerous religious establishments which included the wealthy collegiate foundation of St Peter and St Alexander.[5] The economic activity of the town was organised in guilds, which were as averse to competition as their counter-

---

[1] Ibid., *Die Aschaffenburger Untersuchungs Sache betreffend*.
[2] Ibid. [3] Ibid.
[4] Müller, *Sämtliche Werke*, vol. 5, p. 330.
[5] Gercken, *Reisen*, p. 354. *Compendiöse Statistik von Maynz Trier und Cöln samt ihren Nebenländern* (Leipzig, 1798), p. 42.

'Revolution': Aschaffenburg and Mainz 1790

parts in Mainz. As the commission's report had shown, far from struggling against the archaic restrictions of the *ancien régime*, the chief ambition of the burghers was to make the guilds more exclusive and more xenophobic than before. By declining to eject the Jews, to deter foreigners from settling in the town or to forbid craftsmen to move from one profession to another, the government showed once again that it was more progressive than its subjects. Secure behind their special privileges, the citizens of Aschaffenburg could hope to gain nothing from a rebellion. When trying to pacify the citizens' anger, caused by the maladministration of the market, the most powerful deterrent Director Will could think of was to warn them that the first effect of disorders would be the immediate cancellation by the Elector of his annual stay in the town. Much more probable was an insurrection from the peasants, who carried the main burden of taxation and did not enjoy the townspeople's exemption from military conscription and labour dues, which on account of the hunting were particularly onerous in the regions around Aschaffenburg. Yet their discontent never progressed beyond rumour. However unimportant in itself, the Aschaffenburg episode warns against seeing every manifestation of discontent during this period as revolutionary and every popular demand as democratic.[1]

The over-anxious reaction to the Aschaffenburg disturbance was dictated not so much by the situation in the Electorate of Mainz as by the major insurrection which had erupted in the Prince-Bishopric of Liège. Wide dissatisfaction, caused by the government's incompetence and economic hardship, had led to the formation of patriotic societies and demands for the restoration of ancient liberties. The news of the fall of the Bastille intensified agitation; on 17 August 1789 the citizens of Liège took possession of the town-hall, deposed the officials and elected their own. At first the Prince-Bishop accepted their demands but soon afterwards fled to Trier. His appeal to the *Reichskammergericht* elicited an injunction which instructed his subjects to abandon their rebellion. At the same time the Court directed the Elector of Cologne, the Elector of

---

[1] Jacques Godechot, for example, has written 'In the Rhineland it was the intellectuals, notably Forster, the librarian of the University of Mainz, and Johan von Müller, secretary of the Archbishop of Mainz, who spread the revolutionary ideas. By 1790 the bourgeoisie were presenting demands and the peasants were in agitation' – *France and the Atlantic Revolution of the Eighteenth Century 1770–1799* (New York, 1965), p. 133. I do not feel that Müller would have welcomed this description of his rôle in the Elector's government. Claus Träger, an East German historian, was more specific and more inaccurate when he wrote 'In February and March 1790 the peasants rose in direct proximity to the residence of the Elector of Mainz in Aschaffenburg and brought their demands together in a remonstrance' – *Mainz zwischen Schwarz und Rot. Die Mainzer Revolution in Schriften, Reden und Briefen* (Berlin, 1963), p. 19. Agatha Ramm was perhaps simply repeating this false assertion when she wrote 'In February and March peasants rose in the neighbourhood of Aschaffenburg, one of the Elector's residences, and presented their grievances' – *Germany 1789–1919* (London 1967), p. 30.

Bavaria and the King of Prussia, as directors of the Westphalian Circle, to enforce the edict, should the insurgents refuse to submit.[1]

For political reasons Prussia was most reluctant to restore the old régime in Liège. The Prince-Bishopric occupied a vital strategic position in North-West Europe, for it cut in two the Austrian Netherlands, where another successful insurrection was now threatening the Austrian administration. Naturally eager to embarrass the Habsburgs, the Prussians had a vested interest in revolution in this part of the *Reich*.[2] When they occupied Liège at the end of November they did so as mediators, not as executors of the *Reichskammergericht* edict, and were hailed as such by the local population. The Electors of Cologne and Bavaria, Frederick William II's co-directors were enraged by this behaviour but could do nothing in the face of Prussian military might. Encouraged by Max Franz of Cologne, the Prince-Bishop of Liège refused to negotiate with his subjects. After months of wrangling, the Prussian troops were withdrawn altogether, in April 1790, leaving the rebels still in control. The *Reichskammergericht* then called on the Electoral Rhenish, Upper Rhenish, Franconian and Swabian Circles for assistance.[3]

In Mainz Prussia's policy had caused grave offence. Friedrich Karl told Max Franz of Cologne that he agreed that all the princes of the *Reich* should combine to stamp out subversion and would do all he could to accelerate the repression of Liège.[4] When directed by the *Reichskammergericht* to form part of the coercive expedition he responded with alacrity. At the beginning of May 1790, about 1500 Mainz troops marched off to join the other contingents at Maseyck, in preparation for the invasion.[5] The Prussian ambassador Stein's description of the exercise as a piece of 'Don Quixoterie' proved to be correct; the professional soldiers made no impression on the insurgents. Offensives in May and August were equally unsuccessful.[6] At the end of June Friedrich Karl published a declaration to the citizens of Liège, exhorting them to abandon their rebellion and attacking their leaders for their 'criminal deceptions' and 'perfidious and deceitful incitements'.[7] In the absence of any effective sanction the rebels could afford to disregard rhetoric of this kind. The contingents advanced and retreated and advanced and retreated but as the summer drew to a close they were no closer to suppressing the rebellion than they had been when they arrived.

[1] Lüdtke, *Oesterreich und Preußen*, pp. 87–9. The Elector of Cologne was a member of the Westphalian Circle in his capacity as Prince-Bishop of Münster, the Elector of Bavaria as Duke of Jülich and the King of Prussia as Duke of Cleves.
[2] Ibid., pp. 88–9. [3] Ibid., p. 101.
[4] Hansen, *Quellen*, vol. 1, 601–4. [5] Ibid., p. 624.
[6] Braubach, *Max Franz*, pp. 226–8, Max Franz was particularly scathing about the incompetence of the leader of the Mainz contingent, Franz Count von Hatzfeldt.
[7] *Le Moniteur Universel* (1790), no. 196.

'Revolution': Aschaffenburg and Mainz 1790

As tension mounted inside and outside the *Reich*, Friedrich Karl's despatch of the greater part of his army to Liège indicated either boundless confidence in the stability of his own country or an irrepressible urge to play the part of an international statesman. The folly of his counter-revolutionary pretensions was revealed in September 1790 when a serious insurrection broke out in the city of Mainz. The affair had its origins in a seemingly innocuous brawl between some university students and some journeymen of the carpenters' guild. The former appear to have poached some local girls at a dance, which prompted the disappointed escorts to retaliate with violence.[1] Suitably reinforced, the students exacted revenge by waylaying and mishandling some other apprentices.[2] The victims complained that their assailants had used not ordinary sticks but 'murderous weapons', including a broken-off billiard cue. The authorities were unable to discover which students had been involved and, not surprisingly, the apprentices and journeymen took the law into their own hands.

At the end of August another and similar clash led to a number of students being disarmed; when a certain student of Philosophy by the name of Marx went to reclaim his cudgel its return was refused. That evening the conflict became more serious when the students stormed into a beerhouse known to be a haunt of apprentices and, not finding the youths they were looking for, manhandled some of the other customers instead. They then attacked one of the apprentices' hostels, broke windows, furniture and glasses and inflicted considerable personal damage on the occupants. According to the official report, up till this point the apprentices had shown admirable if improbable restraint but now their patience was exhausted. On the morning after the attack on the hostel (31 August), several hundred apprentices and journeymen paraded through the streets and then marched on the University, where the students were sitting examinations.

What then ensued was described vividly by Johannes Weitzel, a student of Philosophy at the University.[3] After breaking all the windows with an assortment of missiles, the mob broke down the doors of the building and stormed into the lecture-rooms. Professor Niklas Vogt, the distinguished historian, attempted to pacify them but was beaten to the ground and left for dead. The students attempted to defend themselves with their quill-pens and pieces of wood broken off the benches but they were no match

---

[1] Johann Ignaz Weitzel, *Das Merkwürdigste aus meinem Leben und aus meiner Zeit*, vol. 1 (Leipzig, 1821), p. 127.
[2] Vienna, *MEA*, Militaria, Fasc. 102B. The documents are not paginated, but are arranged in roughly chronological order. I shall refer to them by date and destination, where possible. The account of the origins of the disturbance is based largely on the report drawn up by the *Vicedom*'s office after the attack on the University, dated *Mainz am 31ten August 1790*, and signed by *Vicedom* von Bibra and Heimes.
[3] Weitzel, *Leben*, vol. 1, pp. 127–34. He describes the events as having taken place in 1791, although this may be a misprint.

for the well-armed apprentices. Weitzel fled into the courtyard and with eight other students made a last stand on a pile of logs. They were soon surrounded, dislodged and ejected from the building amidst a hail of blows. Assisted by superior weapons and sheer force of numbers, the apprentices and journeymen had won the day and they marched off the field of battle to celebrate their victory in the neighbouring beer-halls.

By the time the news of the fracas reached the authorities, there was nothing they could do to prevent it. With the Elector away at his summer residence in Aschaffenburg, responsibility for the maintenance of order was shared by the *Vicedom*, the President of the Council and the Military Governor. The latter, the Freiherr von Gymnich, was taking luncheon with a party of nobles in Weisenau and did not return until the battle was over.[1] The military forces at his disposal consisted only of garrison troops, who were too old, incompetent or intelligent to march with their colleagues to Liège, and the Life-Guard, which was primarily decorative. Any attempt to disperse the mob by force was clearly out of the question. The authorities resorted to delaying tactics, hoping for reinforcements. A courier was despatched post-haste to Aschaffenburg and the crowds were promised satisfaction from the students.[2] Apart from a few minor incidents the night passed quietly but as dawn broke the rioting began again. The journeymen gathered in their hostels, marched through the streets with banners flying and assembled on the parade ground in front of the government offices.[3] On their insistence a number of students held to be responsible for the original riot were arrested and imprisoned in the monastery of the Jakobsberg.[4]

Hitherto only the apprentices and journeymen had been involved and their demands had not progressed beyond revenge on the students and compensation for the work they had lost. In his first report von Heimes had noted with considerable relief that the burghers had not taken any part in the disturbances.[5] On 2 September, however, the affair took a more sinister turn. The Austrian diplomat von Mölck reported to Vienna that a number of citizens had used the riots to present a number of more sophisticated demands to the government.[6] As they had no means of suppressing the insurrection by force, the unfortunate government officials were compelled to submit. They promised the journeymen that they would receive compensation for the work-days lost and promised the

---

[1] Vienna, *MEA*, Militaria, Fasc. 102B, von Stein to an unnamed person in Aschaffenburg.
[2] Ibid., *Actum d. 31ten August um 8 Uhr Abends*.
[3] Ibid., *Mainz am 2ten September 1790*, von Gymnich to the Elector.
[4] Ibid., *Vom 2ten 7br Abends 8 Uhr*, von Stein to an unnamed person in Aschaffenburg.
[5] Ibid., *Mainz am 31ten August 1790*, Heimes to the Elector.
[6] Hansen, *Quellen*, vol. 1, p. 672. Von Mölck was secretary to the ambassador Count Schlik, who was with the Elector in Aschaffenburg and did not return to Mainz until the afternoon of 2 September.

masters of the guilds that if they drew up remonstrances their grievances would be redressed as soon as possible.[1]

Meanwhile in Aschaffenburg, the Elector had not been idle. As soon as news of the insurrection reached him, he sent couriers to neighbouring princes with requests for military assistance. With the exception of the Elector of Bavaria, who regretted that he had no troops available, they responded promptly and positively. The Prince of Nassau-Usingen promised forty fusiliers, the Prince-Bishop of Würzburg a force of hussars, and the Landgraf of Hessen-Kassel even promised to come personally, should the need arise.[2] Perhaps because of the close proximity of his territory to Mainz, the most immediate and effective help came from the Landgraf of Hessen-Darmstadt. Within twenty-four hours of receiving the original request for assistance, the Landgraf despatched five hundred troops.[3] On the evening of 2 September they arrived in Bischofsheim and at 4 o'clock the next morning they marched into Mainz.[4]

Rumours of their impending arrival preceded them. But although the insurgents threatened to sabotage the pontoon bridge which linked Mainz to the right bank of the Rhine, the soldiers met with no real resistance.[5] Cowed by this show of force, the journeymen and the apprentices returned to work. There were no more parades and no more disturbances.[6] On the evening of 4 September the Elector returned to the city to find everything entirely peaceful.[7] In two published ordinances he noted the arrival of his own Aschaffenburg troops, Swiss Guards and fusiliers and the Hessen-Darmstadt and Nassau-Usingen contingents. In addition he mentioned that Würzburg hussars were on their way and that Bamberg hussars and more Hessen-Darmstadt troops were being held in reserve.[8] The insurrection was over.

Although this simple escalation of a dance-hall brawl into a full-scale riot does not appear to justify more than cursory attention, the participation of other sections of the community, the necessity of military force to restore order and above all the timing raise its significance above the pettiness of its origins. As in every other University city there had been a long tradition of conflict between town and gown in Mainz. In 1789, for example, the Elector had sent a sharp ordinance to the University on the

---

[1] Vienna, *MEA*, Militaria, Fasc. 102B, *Actum Mainz den 2ten Septbr*; *Mainz am 3ten September 1790*, von Bibra to the Elector.
[2] Ibid., *München den 7ten September 1790*; *Biebrich ce 2 Sept. 1790*; *Würzburg den 3ten September 1790*; *Weißenstein am 5ten September*.
[3] Ibid., *Darmstadt den 2ten September 1790*.
[4] Ibid., *Darmstadt den 3ten September 1790*.
[5] Hansen, *Quellen*, vol. 1, pp. 673–4.
[6] Vienna, *MEA*, Militaria, Fasc. 102B, *Mainz den 4ten Sept.*, von Gymnich to the Elector.
[7] Ibid., *Privilegierte Mainzer Zeitung*, no. 143.
[8] Ibid.

question of student discipline. Noting that recently the students' behaviour had been 'coarse, wild and riotous' ('*ein ganz unanständiges schwärmerisch-ruhestörendes Betragen*'), he called on the university authorities to exercise increased vigilance.[1] The peculiar ferocity of the attack on the University suggested that the apprentices' sexual jealousy was not the sole cause of their hostility to the institution. That they failed to kill any of the students was not through want of trying. Even after the battle in the lecture-rooms, the apprentices and journeymen roamed the streets and invaded the students' lodgings looking for more victims.[2] *En route* to Mainz from Aschaffenburg on 2 September, von Stein passed crowds of students fleeing from the city. He sympathised with their discretion because, as he pointed out, to stay invited certain death.[3] Johannes Weitzel wrote that he had considerable difficulty in leaving the city, as mobs had gathered at the city gates to catch students attempting to escape.[4]

For the conservative and pious population of Mainz the University personified all the most distasteful aspects of the Elector's policy of Enlightenment. Three monasteries had been dissolved to provide funds for its restoration, Protestant foreigners had been appointed to its chairs and through the attacks of Hermann Goldhagen's *Religionsjournal* they knew that even the Catholic professors were dangerously radical. Yet, it seemed, the heterodoxy of these intruders had been rewarded by special privileges and higher salaries than those paid to the other officials of the Electorate. Not only did they enjoy an absurdly favourable position, which the citizens themselves financed through taxation, the University authorities had proved incapable of controlling the excesses of their students, many of whom were foreigners.[5] This bitterness was of long standing. In 1784, just before the reformed University opened, Count Metternich reported that the people of Mainz were very upset by the appointment of so many 'young philosophers'.[6]

Georg Forster was in no doubt that the tension between town and University was the fundamental cause of the disturbances. In a letter to

[1] Helmut Mathy, 'Studien und Quellen zur Gerichtsbarkeit an der Universität Mainz', *Festschrift Johannes Bärmann*, Veröffentlichungen des Instituts für geschichtliche Landeskunde an der Universität Mainz, vol. 3 (Wiesbaden, 1966) p. 153. Student disorders were not of course confined to Mainz. Cf. Goethe's description of the situation at Jena and Halle, *Dichtung und Wahrheit*, pt. 2, bk. 6.
[2] Hansen, *Quellen*, vol. 1, p. 671.
[3] Vienna, *MEA*, Militaria, Fasc. 102B, *Vom 2ten 7br Abends 8 Uhr*, von Stein to an unnamed person in Aschaffenburg.
[4] Weitzel, *Leben*, pp. 137–8.
[5] In the ordinance of 21 November 1789 the Elector had mentioned that the foreign students had played a prominent part in the disorders. Dreyfus has described the proportion of students actually from Mainz as '*très faible*' – *Sociétés et Mentalités à Mayence dans la seconde moitié du 18e Siècle* (Paris, 1968), p. 467.
[6] Vienna, *Staka*, Fasc. 210, 754.

his father he conceded that the misbehaviour of the students had sparked off the riots but argued further that all classes had seized this opportunity to try to discredit the University in the eyes of the Elector. The nobility believed that higher education was unnecessary and dangerous; the officials resented the inflated salaries paid to the professors; the guilds had been incited by their priests. Forster also alleged that although the authorities knew that trouble was brewing they declined to take counter-measures, indeed connived at the plans of the apprentices, to teach the University a lesson it would never forget.[1] There is some evidence that his suspicions were well-founded. Von Stein reported to Aschaffenburg that the police knew well in advance of the apprentices' plans, because on the morning of the attack on the University a wig-maker had told the Freiherr von Coudenhove of the projected assault and this information had been passed on to the appropriate authority.[2] In part at least the riots represented a conservative reaction against the Elector's enlightened policies.

The conflict between the University and the town involved the electoral government only indirectly and, as at first only the journeymen and apprentices participated, the disturbances did not appear to be particularly serious. By the end of the second day of rioting, however, it had become clear that the burghers were using the disorders as a medium for the presentation of their own more coherent demands. This came as an unpleasant surprise to the authorities. Immediately after the attack on the University they had ordered the masters of the guilds to use their influence over their employees to restore order.[3] Yet when the apprentices and journeymen formed up on the parade ground outside the government buildings on the second day (1 September) the masters were there with them.[4] Again on the following day the masters of a number of guilds presented demands and the harassed government promised to set up a commission to investigate them.[5]

The exact nature of these grievances cannot be established. Once order had been restored by the arrival of the Hessen-Darmstadt troops, the commission was quickly forgotten. Yet some approximate estimate can be made. There is certainly no evidence that the aspirations of the masters progressed beyond their limited horizons of economic restriction. In a later ordinance the Elector noted with relief that the demands had been of a specifically guild nature; this was confirmed by Georg Forster, although

[1] Forster, *Sämtliche Schriften*, vol. 8, p. 132.
[2] Vienna, *MEA*, Militaria, Fasc. 102B, *Vom 2ten 7br Abends 8 Uhr*, von Stein to an unnamed person at Aschaffenburg. The antagonism between University and townspeople had also been shown by the dispute over the use of the Jesuit Church. See above, p. 205.
[3] Vienna, *MEA*, Militaria, Fasc. 102B, *Actum d. 31ten August*.
[4] Ibid., *Mainz am 2ten September 1790*, von Gymnich to the Elector.
[5] Ibid., *Actum, Mainz, den 2ten Septbr. 1790*.

his reaction was one of disgust.[1] Both the Austrian diplomat von Mölck and the government agreed that the complaints centred on the reorganisation of the guilds undertaken in 1782.[2] In that year the already considerable control of the guilds by the government was strengthened further by the appointment of two police commissars to supervise all their activities.[3] This measure had been justified by reference to irregularities in accounting, the keeping of minutes, the implementation of official ordinances and the admission of masters. The Elector's policy of economic expansion and social welfare had led to further clashes with the guilds.[4] Between 1782 and 1791 the government took action against the free assembly of the guilds on seven different occasions; masters rash enough to resist these and other measures were liable to three days imprisonment on bread and water.[5] By 1789 tension had reached such a peak that on 14 September of that year the *Vicedom's* office reported to the central government that in view of high prices and the French Revolution serious trouble threatened.[6] Against this background the intervention of the masters was entirely comprehensible, although it was improbable that they would progress to more radical fiscal or constitutional demands.

Like the 'insurgents' of Aschaffenburg, the citizens of Mainz appreciated that their privileged economic status was linked to the *ancien régime*. Nevertheless, there were signs during the riots that some of the characteristics of the French Revolution had penetrated the parochialism of the city. When the apprentices and the journeymen marched through the streets after the attack on the University they wore tricolour cockades and 'hats of freedom'.[7] The newspaper reports in particular dwelt on this aspect. The *Kölnische Staatsboth* described how the mob shouted 'the misunderstood word "Freedom"' and the *Hamburger Journal* added that the password of the rioters was 'Patriot!' and that anyone not giving it was assaulted.[8] The authorities suspected immediately that French agents were behind the disturbances. After order had been restored the Austrian ambassador reported to Vienna that the Mainz police sought two carpenters who, it was alleged, had already been responsible for similar insurrections in Göttingen and Strasbourg.[9] These professional revolutionaries were never apprehended, if indeed they ever existed. A good deal

---

[1] *Mainzisches Intelligenzblatt*, Nro. 73. Forster, *Sämtliche Schriften*, vol. 8, pp. 131–3.
[2] Hansen, *Quellen*, vol. 1, p. 672. Vienna, *MEA*, Militaria, Fasc. 102B, *Actum Mainz den 2ten Septbr. 1790*.
[3] Hansen, *Quellen*, vol. 1, p. 672, n. 2.   [4] See above, p. 205.
[5] Friedrich Schmitt, *Das Mainzer Zunftwesen und die französische Herrschaft* (Frankfurt am Main and Darmstadt, 1929), pp. 38, 41.   [6] Ibid., p. 42.
[7] Vienna, *MEA*, Militaria, Fasc. 102B, *Vom 2ten 7br Abends 8 Uhr*, von Stein to unnamed person at Aschaffenburg. In a letter to his brother, the Prince-Bishop of Würzburg and Bamberg, dated *Mainz den 5ten September 1790*, Friedrich Karl also alluded to this.
[8] Hansen, *Quellen*, vol. 1, pp. 673 n. 2, 675 n. 2.   [9] Ibid., p. 675.

'Revolution': Aschaffenburg and Mainz 1790

of anxiety had been expressed in the Rhineland about the possibility of French infiltration. In July 1790 the *Journal von and für Deutschland* warned its readers about a mysterious body called the *Club de la Propaganda*.[1] Although in fact there was no organised attempt by the French to distribute propaganda until 1792, revolutionary pamphlets certainly found their way into Germany. In June and August 1790 the Mainz government warned its officials about 'inflammatory brochures' and the subversive activities of German members of the French National Guard.[2]

Yet there is no clear evidence that the Mainz disturbance owed anything to outside influences; the origin and development of the affair were spontaneous and local. Nor should the importance of the slogans and cockades of the apprentices and journeymen be over-estimated. Their anger was directed only at the students, and their positive demands were confined to compensation for the work they had lost by their rioting. When they finally extracted a promise of compensation from the *Vicedom* von Bibra, they regarded it as a triumph and celebrated with a great victory parade through the streets of the city.[3] News of the disturbances in Paris, Brussels and Liège had been reported widely in the Rhineland papers and it is probable that the rioters in Mainz adopted the badges of revolution but not the substance. Had their incoherent discontent combined with an equally disaffected but well-organised bourgeoisie, with a clear political programme, and coincided with a peasant rising, a genuine revolution would have been possible. The basis for this kind of situation did not exist in Mainz.[4]

The danger of the disturbances derived less from the scale of the riots or the demands of the insurgents than from the proximity of France and the absence of electoral troops. Remembering perhaps the fate of the Prince-Bishop of Liège or Cardinal Rohan of Strasbourg, Friedrich Karl took the affair seriously. Once the foreign contingents had brought the demonstrations to an abrupt halt, the process of repression began immediately. A series of ordinances forbade all public gatherings, warned that military patrols had been ordered to break up suspicious groups with force and 'without any discrimination' and threatened dire penalties for any subversive discussion of religion, morals, the state or official ordi-

---

[1] Ibid., p. 638.   [2] Ibid.   [3] Ibid., p. 674.
[4] The myth of Mainz as a hotbed of revolution still dominates general accounts of the period. Agatha Ramm believes that the students were in *alliance* with the artisans: 'In the city of Mainz the craftsmen, led by the cabinet makers and carpenters and supported by the University students, rose in August 1790' – *Germany, 1789–1919*, p. 30. Franklin Ford's version is even more extraordinary 'Here (at Mainz) the town deputies in the hastily revived estates of the electoral archbishopric demanded an immediate end to tax exemptions' – *Europe, 1780–1830* (London, 1970), p. 143. Earlier in the same book (p. 95) he writes 'Popular agitation for democratic reforms flared up periodically in ecclesiastical states such as... Mainz.' This also is totally false.

nances.¹ All innkeepers were instructed to send in daily reports on their guests, while mere wine or beer-houses were forbidden to take in lodgers at all.²

At the same time the authorities began the prosecution of those held responsible for the riots. The compensation promised to the apprentices and journeymen was abandoned, the excuse being that *Vicedom* von Bibra had promised it only in his own name and not in that of the Elector.³ Instead the alleged ring-leaders were arrested and imprisoned. In a published ordinance the Elector ordered the commission of inquiry to proceed against the rebels 'with ruthless severity'. Privately also he announced his intention of making an example of them.⁴ The sentences announced by the commission early in November however indicated that the Elector's wrath had cooled. The sentences on the students were announced in the main hall of the University on 3 November, in the presence of the professors, the municipal councillors, the heads of the guilds and a number of burghers. Five students were sent to the fortress of Königstein for varying periods of a year, six months and a month, while five others were imprisoned in the city gaol for a month.⁵ On the following day the other section of the rioters received their punishments, amidst a combination of publicity and elaborate security precautions. Six ring-leaders were sentenced to terms of imprisonment of between three years and six months. Thirty-two other lesser offenders received light prison sentences and/or generous doses of corporal punishment.⁶

Even this relatively mild repression may have flattered the determination and aggression of the rioters. Once they had exacted revenge on the students, they were content to express what political aspirations they had in parades through the streets and drinking bouts in their hostels. A couple

---

[1] *Mainzisches Intelligenzblatt*, nos. 71, 72. [2] Ibid., no. 75.
[3] In fact the Elector was extremely displeased by what he considered to have been weakness on the part of his *Vicedom*. Von Bibra sought to justify his conduct in a number of lengthy memoranda – Vienna, *MEA*, Militaria, Fasc. 102B. von Bibra to the Elector, 3, 4, 6 September 1790.
[4] He told Count Schlick, for example, that the most guilty would receive the death penalty – Hansen, *Quellen*, vol. 1, p. 676.
[5] Max Braubach, 'Deutschland und die französische Revolution', *Historisches Jahrbuch*, 52 (1932), p. 228 n. 5. Braubach gave this information concerning the sentences during the review of Hansen's collection of documents. He had come across the information by accident in the University Library in Bonn. The commission's infringement of the traditional disciplinary autonomy of the University caused a heated dispute between the University authorities and the Elector. The behaviour of the students had not left the former in a strong position and they were forced to submit. For a detailed description of the dispute, see Mathy, 'Studien und Quellen', pp. 142–4. See also Vienna, *MEA*, Militaria, Fasc. 102B.
[6] Braubach, 'Die katholischen Universitäten', p. 229. The only other account of the sentences was published in the *Moniteur* of Paris (no. 320, 2 October 1790). It accorded roughly with that of Braubach's anonymous informant although, perhaps to emphasise the counter-revolutionary brutality of the Elector, it mentioned that some of the journeymen had been sent to the galleys, which was incorrect.

of over-enthusiastic demonstrators sustained minor bayonet wounds, a journeyman became involved in a brawl with a drunken soldier, but apart from petty incidents of this kind there was no violence.[1] The burghers were quite prepared to utilise the discontent of their employees for their own ends but were much too discreet to initiate disturbances themselves. It is clear, moreover, that the masters were not unanimous in their decision to exploit the embarrassment of the authorities. In the decree which announced the punishment of the students, journeymen and apprentices, the Elector noted with satisfaction that a number of guilds had not participated; they were to receive special congratulatory diplomas.[2] Von Bibra also reported that after the Hessen-Darmstadt contingent had arrived, a number of burghers had told him that previously they had not felt strong enough to resist the violence of the insurgents but that if trouble broke out again they would fight alongside the government troops.[3] The sincerity of their heroic offer was not put to the test, for there was no more trouble. After the leaders had been sentenced, the Hessen-Darmstadt and Würzburg troops left and the city settled back into its old routine. At the end of the year the Elector felt sufficiently secure to declare a general amnesty. The students were fetched back from Königstein and together with their former opponents were set at liberty on 1 January 1791.[4] Those considered to be particularly dangerous were deported from the Electorate but the majority were allowed to return to their studies or work-benches in peace.[5]

Probably the most important reason for the lack of any truly revolutionary momentum in the disturbances was the lack of any severe sustained economic crisis. As elsewhere in Europe, the winter of 1788–9 had been exceptionally hard. Severe cold had been followed by widespread flooding;[6] bad harvests brought high food prices. The price of a *Malter* of wheat in the city rose from 5.30 gulden in 1787, to 7 gulden in 1788 and to 9.06 gulden in 1789.[7] In October 1789, Georg Forster reported to his father-in-law that the price of a loaf of bread had risen from eight kreuzers to thirteen kreuzers. He added that although they were quiet at present, the citizens might be driven to rebellion by hunger.[8] It was also at this time that the *Vicedom* warned the government that the high prices, combined with other grievances, might provoke trouble from the guilds.[9]

Action had already been taken. On 14 August 1789 the local officials

---

[1] Vienna, *MEA*, Militaria, Fasc. 102B, *Mainz am 2ten und am 3ten September 1790*, von Gymnich to the Elector.   [2] *Mainzisches Intelligenzblatt*, no. 89.
[3] Vienna, *MEA*, Militaria, Fasc. 102B, *Mainz am 5ten September 1790*.
[4] *Mainzisches Intelligenzblatt*, no. 1 (1791).   [5] Ibid.
[6] F. Rösch, *Die Mainzer Armenreform vom Jahre 1786*. Arbeiten aus dem Forschungsinstitut für Fürsorgewesen in Frankfurt am Main, vol. 3 (Berlin, 1929), p. 165.
[7] F. G. Dreyfus, 'Prix et Population à Trèves et à Mayence au XVIIIe Siècle', *Revue d'Histoire économique et sociale*, 34 (1956), p. 251.
[8] Forster, *Sämtliche Schriften*, vol. 8, p. 98.   [9] See above, p. 258.

had been instructed to investigate the harvest in their districts.¹ Their depressing reports prompted a further ordinance on 11 September to regulate grain supplies.² Grain brought to Mainz was exempted from excise and highway dues; officials were ordered to establish communal granaries and to distribute supplies to the destitute. To prevent any recurrence of the poor harvest, officials were to ensure that the next sowing was very thorough and, where necessary, to give assistance to peasants with insufficient seed. Combined with the natural buoyancy of the Electorate's economy, these measures had the desired effect. It appears that throughout the eighteenth century commercial expansion and agricultural productivity had more than kept pace with the growing population; even in years of scarcity the Electorate produced a surplus of grain.³ In the ordinance of 11 September it was stated that the situation was not serious enough to justify a total ban on exports or the indiscriminate opening of the electoral granaries. Nor were the people of Mainz so dependent on cereals as the French, for the region produced an abundance of all sorts of vegetables, especially potatoes.⁴ For these reasons the crisis of 1789 was neither severe nor prolonged. In 1790 the price of a *Malter* of wheat fell back to 6.34 gulden.⁵ While the amount of relief paid to paupers had increased by a third in 1789, compared with 1787, in 1790 the proportional increase had declined to a quarter.⁶

The disturbances in Aschaffenburg and Mainz in 1790 may have been aggravated by memories of the hardship of the previous year, although there is no evidence even for this, but they were certainly not caused by economic distress. In the rural areas of the Electorate there were no serious outbreaks of violence, although there were some signs of tension caused by the additional burden of the *corvée* and tithe. W. A. Miles, an English visitor, wrote after a visit to Friedrich Karl's court:

> Although the spirit of liberty has not manifested itself in this neighbourhood with the degree of violence exhibited in France and in the Low Countries, the farmers in some parts of the electorate of Mayence, on being commanded to repair the roads, laconically answered that *they had not time*, and, accordingly, *corvées* were dispensed with *until they were at leisure*. The Elector has also judged it prudent to postpone those grand hunts, which require from 800 to 1,200 peasants, declaring that at this moment *il faut les laisser tranquilles*. If the *corvées* had been refused last year a detachment of Hussars would have compelled the farmers to obey the summons, and, as the indulgence of Government on this occasion is visibly the effect of fear, it is possible that concessions of greater magnitude may be exacted, since the people do not hesitate to express their discontent.⁷

---

[1] Mainz, *Kurmainzische Verordnungen*, 1te Sammlung, vol. 6, 1459. [2] Ibid., 1464.
[3] See above, Ch. 2, *passim*, and pp. 185–6. [4] See above, p. 92.
[5] Dreyfus, 'Prix et Population', p. 251. [6] Rösch, *Armenreform*, p. 165.
[7] W. A. Miles, *Correspondence on the French Revolution 1789–1817*, ed. Chas. Popham Miles, vol. 1 (London, 1890).

'Revolution': Aschaffenburg and Mainz 1790

Tension at home and the increasing belligerence of the Constituent Assembly in Paris did not inhibit Friedrich Karl's love of pomp and circumstance. At the end of September 1790 the Electors of the *Reich* gathered in Frankfurt am Main for the election and coronation of Leopold II. Amidst all the opulent pageantry which marked the occasion, the train of the Elector of Mainz stood out.[1] In 1792 the revolutionary club, established in Mainz by the French occupation force, announced that it had discovered the documents relating to the expenses of the coronation and published a summary of them, together with a suitably abusive commentary.[2] The accounts showed that the Elector had spent a total of 426,274 gulden, including 26,384 gulden on the kitchens, 15,084 on confectionery, 21,929 on wine, 37,845 on new silver, 28,544 on the Life-Guard, 37,786 on the Swiss Guard and 80,978 on new uniforms and livery. The last sum included 16,101 gulden for a Cross of the Teutonic Order and for a pair of gold and diamond buckles for the Elector's shoes.[3]

The death of the detested Joseph II was more than an opportunity for the Elector to indulge his taste for display; it also accelerated his return to the Habsburg fold. Prussia's neglect of Mainz interests in the disputes over the nuncios and the *Reichsvikare* had already strained the alliance almost to breaking-point.[4] On 8 November 1789 Johann Friedrich von Stein wrote to Johannes Müller from Potsdam: 'Let us ring down the curtain; believe me, the comedy of the League of Princes is played out.'[5] The Prussian refusal to suppress the Liège rebellion proved to be the last straw. Friedrich Karl told Frederick William II at the end of 1789 that any further procrastination would force him to abandon the league.[6] The accession of Leopold II also meant that Friedrich Karl could revive the Austrian alliance without losing face, for the new Emperor reversed his

---

[1] *Mémoires du Comte de Bray*, ed. F. de Bray (Paris, 1911), pp. 111–12, 122.
[2] *Die Krönungsrechnung bei der Wahl und Krönung Leopolds II, abgelesen in der Gesellschaft der Freunde der Freiheit und der Gleichheit zu Mainz am 11ten November von Anton Fuchs* (Mainz, 1792).
[3] It was of course in the interests of the revolutionaries to exaggerate Friedrich Karl's extravagance, although the idiosyncratic details of the document suggest authenticity. Franz Werner (*Dom von Mainz*, p. 286) quoted almost the same figures and cited as his source Girtanner's *Politische Annalen*. It is possible however that Girtanner's own information was taken from the pamphlet published by the Mainz revolutionaries. On 7 December 1791 Friedrich Karl wrote to the Cathedral Chapter that the costs of the Coronation had amounted to only 300,000 gulden – Vienna, *MEA*, GK, Fasc. 86. There is good reason to doubt the accuracy of this estimate. In 1790, before the Coronation, a treasury official reported that 300,000 gulden had been borrowed, on the authorisation of the Cathedral Chapter, but that much more would be needed (Ibid.). It is probable that no more than 300,000 gulden was borrowed on the authorisation of the Cathedral Chapter, but that additional sums were transferred from other treasury accounts or that further extraordinary sums were borrowed.
[4] See above, p. 235.
[5] K. Henking, *Johannes von Müller*, vol. 2, p. 199.
[6] Lüdtke, *Oesterreich und Preußen*, p. 95.

predecessor's policies and made a determined attempt to win the support of the *Reich*. Together with his brother, the Elector Max Franz of Cologne, Leopold wooed the Elector of Mainz with flattery and assurances of support.[1]

Their task was made a great deal easier by the appointment to the Mainz ministry of Franz Joseph Freiherr von Albini. The new arrival had wide experience of imperial affairs, having worked as an official of the *Reichshofrat*, the *Reichskammergericht* and the Prince-Bishopric of Würzburg. In 1787 Friedrich Karl had appointed him to a senior post in the Imperial Chancellery in Vienna, presumably unaware that his sympathies were entirely pro-Habsburg.[2] In January 1790 and again in the summer, during the negotiations preceding the imperial election, Albini went to Mainz to try to destroy the influence of the Elector's pro-Prussian advisers. Assisted by Friedrich Karl's disillusionment with the League and the conciliatory attitude of Austria, his initiative soon succeeded.[3] After his appointment as Chancellor and Minister of State in Mainz in the autumn, he soon elbowed aside the once omnipotent Stein-Coudenhove faction. On 25 December 1790 von Stein reported gloomily to Berlin that: 'the state of affairs and business has undergone a general and very remarkable change since Baron Albini, summoned to be Minister of Justice, unfortunately has found the way to take exclusive possession of the ear and confidence of the Elector.'[4] In a fit of pique at Albini's sudden elevation, Johannes Müller tendered his resignation. Persuaded to change his mind, he then adopted exactly the opposite position. He abandoned his old Prussian friends and, together with Albini, did his utmost to make Friedrich Karl's policy conform with the interests of Austria.[5]

Friedrich Karl's volatile temperament, in no way cooled by the failures of the 1780s, ensured that his new relationship with Austria would not be consistently harmonious. In January 1791 the Liège affair was finally brought to an end when Austrian troops suppressed the rebellion and restored the Prince-Bishop. As a source of controversy in the *Reich* its place was taken by the dispute with France over Alsace, caused by the abolition of the 'feudal régime' on 4 August 1789, the Civil Constitution of the Clergy of 1790 and the administrative reorganisation of France. These measures involved the confiscation of property and the abolition of seignorial rights in Alsace belonging to a number of German princes, and the

---

[1] Ibid., pp. 131–41.
[2] A. M. Reitzel, 'Albini, ein Mainzer Jurist und Politiker', *Mainzer Almanach* (1968).
[3] Henking, *Müller*, pp. 232–3.
[4] Hansen, *Quellen*, vol. 1, p. 753, n. 1, 756.
[5] Henking, *Müller*, pp. 239–51. Another important minister, Philipp Karl von Deel, also made the necessary adjustment to his political convictions – Lüdtke, *Oesterreich und Preußen*, p. 105.

transfer to French bishops of ecclesiastical jurisdiction previously exercised by the German episcopacy. The dispossessed princes objected that any number of treaties between France and the *Reich* had thus been broken, while the Constituent Assembly took its stand on popular sovereignty. The only way out of the impasse was financial compensation from the French, which they were prepared to pay. A number of secular princes of the *Reich* wanted to come to terms, but not the Prince-Bishops.[1]

In view of his previous record of hypersensitivity, it is not surprising that the Archbishop of Mainz was in the van of the militants.[2] When his attempt to persuade the great powers to take direct action failed, he tried to bully the *Reichstag* into threatening the Constituent Assembly with a declaration of war.[3] After the abortive flight of Louis XVI and his family to Varennes and the Declaration of Pillnitz which followed it, he urged Leopold II to undertake a punitive war against the French revolutionaries. He told Kaunitz that:

> Given all these circumstances, it seems to me that His Imperial Majesty could find no more splendid time than the present to acquire for himself immortal renown and to impose appropriate punishment on the lunacy of the French, who without any restraint continue to libel in the public press every monarch and continue to spread these libels in every country.[4]

Not for the first time, Friedrich Karl's martial ardour had outstripped his ability to act or influence. Leopold II was prepared to send stern remonstrances to the Constituent Assembly but not risk war for the sake of a minority of the *Reich*. Even at Pillnitz his threat of direct action was made conditional on the support of all European monarchs. Throughout 1791 Friedrich Karl and the other militant princes continued to bark noisily, but there was never a chance that the Emperor, the *Reichstag* or the great princes would allow them to take off their muzzles.

By this stage control of events lay elsewhere. Under the stimulus of mounting tension between Austria, Prussia and France, the tempo of events in the *Reich* began to quicken. In the Constituent Assembly the Brissotins urged war against the 'counter-revolutionary' powers with ever-increasing stridence. Even during the *Reich*'s more placid periods the grasp of the smaller princes on their destiny was only feeble; as war with revolutionary France approached they were rushed off their feet. Less than a day's march from the frontier, the Electorate of Mainz was bound to be

---

[1] Hansen, *Quellen*, pp. 800–1, n. 3.
[2] He owned no property or seignorial rights in Alsace but did exercise metropolitan jurisdiction over Strasbourg.
[3] Aretin, *Reich*, vol. 1, p. 254. Hansen, *Quellen*, vol. 1, p. 842.
[4] Alfred Ritter von Vivenot, *Quellen zur Geschichte der deutschen Kaiserpolitik Oesterreichs während der französischen Revolutionskriege, 1790–1801*, vol. 1 (Vienna, 1873), p. 249. Vivenot publishes all the most important documents relating to the Alsace dispute.

one of the first affected. Yet although the country stood on the verge of a major upheaval, the tremors did not come from within. The discontent in Aschaffenburg and the disturbance in Mainz in 1790 did not pose a serious threat to the Elector's government; their relationship with the French Revolution was largely superficial. When articulated, the demands of the participants proved to be socially discriminatory, economically restrictive and politically conservative. The only links with liberty, equality and fraternity were such externals as tricolour cockades and shouts of 'Patriot!'.

In contrast to France, the artisans did not seek or find cooperation from either their social superiors or inferiors. No Mirabeau or Lafayette emerged from the nobility, no Brissot or Robespierre emerged from the professional classes. No peasants burned *châteaux*, destroyed tithe registers, lynched officials or looted electoral granaries. This was the pattern throughout the Rhineland. Nowhere did the isolated outbreaks of discontent threaten to come together to generate a truly revolutionary momentum. Georg Forster, who was moving briskly towards a radical political position and had sympathised with the Liège revolutionaries, described the Mainz riots as 'a mere farce' ('*ein bloßes Possenspiel*'). With equal bitterness, he poured scorn on both sides; on the authorities who grovelled before the mob and then reneged on their promises; on the rioters themselves, who 'like the tame sheep and donkeys that they are' returned meekly to the fold once the whip had been brandished.[1] Forster's choice of terms may have been somewhat extreme but essentially his appraisal was correct. Revolution could only come from outside.

[1] Forster, *Sämtliche Werke*, vol. 8, pp. 132–3.

8

Revolution: Mainz 1792–3

Mainz had survived the first phase of the Revolution relatively unscathed. The cracks in the façade caused by the feeble internal tremors were sealed quickly: the disaster which was to strike the Electorate in 1792 had its epicentre in Paris. At first it appeared that the energy unleashed there in 1789 would be confined within the boundaries of France. In May 1790 the Constituent Assembly declared that the French nation renounced in general the use of force against the liberty of another people and in particular all wars aimed at conquest.[1] This pacifism was sincere but ephemeral; in the following year pressure for war increased steadily. Both the left, led by Brissot, and the right, led by Narbonne, saw in war the quickest way to achieve their political aims. Although directed at Austria and Prussia, the war declared in April 1792 also engulfed the smaller states placed by geographical accident in the path of the advancing French armies. As in earlier conflicts between the great powers, nothing the Elector of Mainz did or said could have kept the war away from his vulnerable territories. It was still within his power however to ameliorate or aggravate the effects of this unavoidable intrusion. His reaction to the crisis could have no influence on the course of events, but it did influence the opinions of his subjects. Before discussing the local population's response to the arrival of the revolutionary armies, it is necessary therefore to examine their ruler's policies and problems during this crucial phase.

As suggested by the aggressive tone he adopted towards the Constituent Assembly on the question of Alsace[2] the Elector Friedrich Karl's attitude towards the Revolution was entirely hostile. This found its clearest expression in the warm welcome he gave to the French *émigrés*. Less than a month after the fall of the Bastille the first aristocratic refugees began to appear in the Rhineland. In August 1789 three princes of the blood – the Comte d'Artois, the Prince de Condé and the Duc de Bourbon – passed through Mainz *en route* for Turin.[3] The growing radicalism of the Assembly turned

[1] *French Revolution Documents*, ed. J. M. Roberts and R. C. Cobb, vol. 1 (Oxford, 1966), p. 430.
[2] See above, p. 264.
[3] Liselotte Vezin, *Die Politik des Mainzer Kurfürsten Friedrich Karl von Erthal vom Beginn der französischen Revolution bis zum Falle von Mainz* (Dilligen, 1932), pp. 49 50.

this trickle into a flood, and their proximity to France made the Rhenish cities especially popular gathering points. The Elector of Trier, the uncle of Louis XVI and his two younger brothers, the Comte de Provence and the Comte d'Artois, was an especially generous host. Not to be outdone, his colleague in Mainz progressed from casual hospitality to official and indiscriminate assistance. In February 1791 the Prince de Condé was received in Mainz with all the honour normally reserved for a head of state. At the same time the episcopal residence in Worms was placed at his disposal. Even more opulent celebrations greeted the Comte d'Artois when he passed through the city on his way to Trier in the summer of the same year.[1] As thousands of *émigrés* streamed into the Rhineland the Electorates of Mainz and Trier came to look 'more like conquered French provinces than independent German states'.[2]

Friedrich Karl's vanity, which had influenced his foreign policy more than once in the past, was stimulated greatly by the sight of French dukes, marquises and counts soliciting and even depending on his favour. The Austrian ambassador Count Schlick reported that 'the joy the Elector takes in being surrounded by the French *émigrés* and their flatteries is beyond description'.[3] Not only were they pleased to find luxurious asylum at the Mainz court, the *émigrés* also laboured under the illusion that Friedrich Karl, as Archchancellor, would be able to persuade the *Reich* to declare war on revolutionary France. They were only too pleased to heap flatteries on their gullible host. Behind his back they called him '*l'abbé de Mayence*' and '*le gentilhomme parvenu*', but to his face he was their '*père et protecteur*.'[4]

These guests were expensive, but expense proved to be the least of the Electorate's worries. The *émigrés*' ambitions were not confined to extracting outdoor relief from the German princes; they viewed their self-imposed exile as strictly temporary. Believing the revolutionaries to be as incompetent as themselves, they looked forward to the day when they would return in a blaze of feudal chivalry to rescue their king and restore the *ancien régime*. They organised themselves into military units, recruited common soldiers to counterbalance their natural surplus of officers,

---

[1] Joseph Hansen, *Quellen zur Geschichte des Rheinlandes im Zeitalter der französischen Revolution*, vol. 1 (Bonn, 1931), pp. 774–5, 858–61.
[2] *Der Untergang des Churfürstentums Mainz, von einem churmainzischen General*, ed. J. F. Neigebaur (Frankfurt am Main, 1839), p. 16. The general in question was Franz Count von Hatzfeldt.
[3] Hansen, *Quellen*, vol. 1, p. 845. See also, for similar comments, Neigebaur, *Untergang*, p. 4, and *Denkwürdigkeiten des Generals Eickemeyer*, ed. Heinrich Koenig (Frankfurt am Main, 1845), p. 102.
[4] Prince de Ligne, *Memoirs*, vol. 2 (London, 1899), p. 148. Rudolf Eickemeyer, *Denkschrift über die Einnahme der Festung Mainz durch die fränkischen Truppen im Jahre 1792*, ed. F. C. Laukhard (Hamburg, 1798), p. 34.

bought weapons and conducted military exercises. The Constituent Assembly's reaction was predictable; no government could view with equanimity the mobilisation on its frontiers of a large body of men committed to invasion and counter-revolution. In June 1791 Louis XVI was asked to order Condé to return to France or to leave the frontier area. If he chose the latter he was also to declare that he would never engage in hostile action against France or its constitution. This was followed in October by the first of many attacks by Brissot and his supporters on the German princes who harboured the *émigrés*. On 22 November the Assembly's diplomatic committee sharply condemned the Electors of Mainz and Trier, by name, for their encouragement of the 'traitors'. The more extreme deputies began to call for punitive expeditions against them.[1]

The risks the two Electors were running were increased considerably by the cautious policy towards France adopted by the more important German princes. The Declaration of Pillnitz, issued jointly by Austria and Prussia on 27 August 1791 after the flight to Varennes, effectively ruled out armed intervention by making it conditional on the unanimous support of all the European powers. The Austrian diplomats in particular made repeated attempts to cool Friedrich Karl's counter-revolutionary ardour. In October the *Reichsvizekanzler* Prince Colloredo told him that it was both foolish and unconstitutional to allow French princes to recruit in the Electorate. Friedrich Karl replied curtly that nothing of the kind had been going on and at the same time airily dismissed the dangers of assisting the *émigrés* with the observation that France was sliding rapidly into anarchy.[2]

He soon changed his mind. On 14 December Louis XVI told the Elector of Trier that if the hostile activities of the *émigrés* had not been halted by 15 January 1792, he would be regarded as an enemy of France. He added ominously that a similar declaration would be sent to any other German prince who assisted subversion.[3] At the same time a rumour spread that three armies of 20,000 men each had been assembled for an attack on Trier, Mainz and the Archbishop of Strasbourg's territories in Baden.[4] Friedrich Karl did not waste any time checking its authenticity. If, as seemed likely, no support would be forthcoming from Austria or Prussia, a single force of 5,000 would have been enough to conquer his territories. Condé and his cohorts were told immediately to leave the Electorate.[5] Even so the expulsion was rather bogus. Many of the *émigrés* decamped to Bingen, which belonged to the Cathedral Chapter of Mainz and was not

---
[1] Hansen, *Quellen*, vol. 1, pp. 855, 998–9, 1012, 1024–5, 1033.
[2] Alfred Ritter von Vivenot, *Quellen zur Geschichte der deutschen Kaiserpolitik Oesterreichs während der französischen Revolutionskriege, 1790–1801*, vol. 1 (Vienna, 1873), pp. 263, 264–6.
[3] Hansen, *Quellen*, vol. 1, pp. 1062–4.   [4] Vivenot, *Quellen*, vol. 1, p. 563.
[5] Hansen, *Quellen*, vol. 1, p. 1071, n. 2, vol. 2, p. 28, n. 3.

subject to the Elector's jurisdiction. Later, when Austria and Prussia became involved in the war, Friedrich Karl regained his nerve and the *émigrés* were allowed to drift back.

In the event Friedrich Karl's adventurous policies did not provoke individual attention from France, but it may be doubted whether his subjects were enthusiastic about even the possibility of a punitive expedition. In Trier, where the estates gave the burghers an opportunity to make their views known, there was determined opposition to the Elector's support of the *émigrés*.[1] There were also sound economic reasons for objecting to their presence. Both Caroline Böhmer and Georg Forster, admittedly fervent supporters of the Revolution, reported that the presence of the *émigrés* had led to inflation. After an initial lucrative period, during which the *émigrés* spent most of their money, the Mainz tradesmen found it increasingly difficult to obtain payment for goods delivered.[2] Nor did the personal behaviour of the uninvited guests inspire affection. Their ability to combine immorality with condescension, bravado with languor and arrogance with penury was not calculated to win the hearts of the people they had battened on. The Danish Professor Sneedorf wrote from Mainz on 20 July 1791:

> It swarms with aristocrats here...in every inn I entered there were complaints about the French. That they don't pay can be excused to a certain extent by their unfortunate position; however, that they behave coarsely in a foreign country is – to put it mildly – very imprudent.[3]

Uncomfortably positioned on the edge of the *Reich* and flirting irresponsibly with the sworn enemies of her temporarily disabled neighbour, Mainz was drifting into dangerous waters. Navigation was made all the more difficult by the incorrigible factiousness and indecision of the court. The arrival of Albini and Friedrich Karl's desertion of the Prussian alliance had destroyed the influence of the previously dominant quartet of

---

[1] Ibid., *Quellen*. Both volumes 1 and 2 contain a great deal of material illustrating the dispute between the Elector and the estates during this period.

[2] Caroline Böhmer, *Briefe aus der Frühromantik*, ed. Erich Schmidt, vol. 1 (Leipzig, 1913), p. 250–1. Georg Forster, *Sämtliche Schriften*, vol. 8 (Leipzig, 1843), pp. 155, 186, 200, 231. Caution is advisable when assessing the economic effects of the *émigrés*' presence and the reaction they evoked from the local population. The inhabitants of Andernach, in the Electorate of Cologne, asked their government to *allow* the *émigrés* to settle there, so that they could profit from their expenditure. In a remonstrance of May 1792 the Trier estates admitted that 'a large part' of the citizens had been made blind to the dangers of the *émigrés* by the prosperity they had brought to the city. Hansen, *Quellen*, vol. 1, p. 1015, n. 3, vol. 2, p. 205.

[3] (F. Sneedorf), *Briefe eines reisenden Dänen, geschrieben im Jahr 1791 und 1792 während seiner Reise durch einen Teil Deutschlands, der Schweiz und Frankreichs* (Züllichau, 1793), p. 92. For a similar comment from another Dane, see Øjvind Andreasen and Helmut Mathy, 'Frederik Münters Reise nach Mainz (1791)', *Mainzer Zeitschrift*, 62 (1967), p. 61.

Müller, von Stein and the Baronesses von Ferrette and von Coudenhove. After a brief display of truculence Müller came to terms with the new alignment and threw in his lot with Albini.[1] But his former allies were not prepared to give up without a fight and the Elector's tortuous policies were complicated further by public bickering and private intrigue.

During these years before his state was overwhelmed by the French armies, Friedrich Karl appears to have been living in a fool's paradise. Neither at home nor abroad did he make any attempt to retrench. Convinced that the Revolution had disarmed France as a military power, he appointed himself head of the German counter-revolution, while continuing to live like a Renaissance prince. The election and coronation of Francis II in July 1792 gave him a final chance to indulge his taste for self-display. After the ceremonies at Frankfurt, the Emperor, the King of Prussia and hundreds of other German princes and nobles moved to Mainz. Never had the city seen such a brilliant gathering. The Elector's hospitality lived up to the occasion; even the French *émigrés* and the Austrian diplomats were impressed by his extravagance.[2]

In view of the enormous sums lavished on the rebuilding projects at Mainz and Aschaffenburg during the previous fifteen years, it is not surprising that two imperial coronations in quick succession, together with the costly Liège expedition, caused financial embarrassment. Tension inside the Electorate and the threat of war from outside made the crisis especially acute. As the Elector informed the Cathedral Chapter, political circumstances ruled out any possibility of increased or new taxation. Salvation was sought in loans and later, when war became inevitable, in voluntary contributions from the nobility and a levy on the clergy.[3] Superficially, loans were a relatively painless cure for over-expenditure but, as the French had discovered, they could develop into a vicious spiral when their total reached a certain point. This did not happen in Mainz. The total sum borrowed for the two coronations and the Liège expedition amounted to just over 1,000,000 gulden, or just over 50% of the Electorate's annual income. As the loans had been raised at 4%, the cost of servicing was less than 3% of the Electorate's annual income.[4] This situation contrasted

---

[1] See above, pp. 263-4.
[2] Louis Joseph Amour Marquis de Bouillé, *Souvenirs et Fragments pour servir aux Mémoires de ma Vie et de mon Temps*, vol. 2 (Paris, 1908), pp. 45-6. Vivenot, *Quellen*, vol. 2, pp. 153-4. For other descriptions of the celebrations in Mainz, see Hansen, *Quellen*, vol. 2, p. 290; Niklas Vogt, *Geschichte des Verfalls und Untergangs der rheinischen Staaten des alten deutschen Reiches* (1833), pp. 244-5; and the anonymous letter reprinted in the *Mainzer Zeitschrift*, 37-8 (1942-3), pp. 88-9.
[3] Vienna, *MEA*, GK, Fasc. 86. The 250,000 gulden borrowed to cover the cost of the Liège expedition were repaid by the Liégeois estates after their revolution had been suppressed. Only a small part of this sum however was paid in cash. Most of the repayment took the form of promissory notes. It is not known just how many of them Friedrich Karl was able to cash.
[4] Ibid., cf. Mainz, Abteilung 6, Fasc. 904.

sharply with the plight of France, where Necker had had to accept rates of 8–10%. Louis XVI was faced by a regular annual deficit of over 20% and an accumulated debt whose servicing cost more than 50% of the kingdom's annual revenues.[1] As this comparison suggests, the Electorate of Mainz was not threatened with financial collapse.[2]

This relative stability was important politically, for it meant that the Elector was not forced to go cap in hand to the Chapter to ask for increased taxation. The canons were thus denied an opportunity to exploit their sovereign's penury to their own constitutional advantage. Nor was the Elector compelled to attempt the abolition of fiscal privilege, and so he avoided exciting the nobility, clergy and other privileged groups. Neither was he obliged to seek the assistance of an Assembly of Notables or to revive the Estates General, which had not been summoned since the early sixteenth century. In Mainz there could be no *révolte nobiliaire* which in France 'provided the revolutionary movement with its initial impetus'.[3] Indeed, the years after 1789 saw greater solidarity among the privileged orders than at any other time in the Electorate's history.[4] If revolution were to come to Mainz it could not take the quasi-legal form it assumed in France, for no dissident subject, whatever his social status, was given a constitutional opportunity to express his grievances, mobilise support and seize power.

This lack of representative institutions makes it very difficult to trace the development of public opinion in Mainz between the riots of 1790 and the arrival of the French two years later. The task is made virtually impossible by the total ban imposed by the government on any other form of political activity or expression. As his attitude towards the Alsatian question and the *émigrés* suggested, Friedrich Karl was opposed to the French Revolution in all its manifestations.[5] Very soon after the fall of the Bastille it became clear that for Mainz the age of Enlightenment was over. Radical intellectuals were no longer welcomed at court, professors and schoolteachers were ordered to watch their tongues, censorship became more rigorous and the correspondence of citizens with foreigners was watched.[6]

---

[1] Georges Lefebvre, *The French Revolution from its Origins to 1793* (London, 1962), p. 97. Alfred Cobban, *A History of Modern France*, vol. 1 (Harmondsworth, 1957), p. 124.

[2] Although Kaunitz believed the Mainz finances to be in a parlous state, the Canon Count Stadion, who was in a position to know, wrote in 1792 to a personal friend that the deficit was less than people thought and could be settled without difficulty. Vivenot, *Quellen*, vol. 1, p. 412, A. Jäger, *Daniel Dumont* (Frankfurt am Main dissertation, 1920), p. 224.

[3] François Furet and Denis Richet, *The French Revolution* (London, 1970), pp. 45–6.

[4] See above, p. 245.

[5] See above, p. 265.

[6] Vogt, *Verfall*, p. 239. Similar anti-revolutionary measures were adopted in neighbouring principalities. For the policies of Max Franz of Cologne and Clemens Wenzeslaus of Trier, see Hansen, *Quellen*, vol. 1, p. 345, 417, 488–9, 534, n. 3, 535, 561–2, 574, 678–80, 690, 723–4.

The most striking illustration of this change was the persecution and eventual flight of Professor Anton Dorsch. In May 1791, while Dorsch was absent from Mainz, a letter was sent to him from Strasbourg. Spies appointed to keep watch on his home reported the arrival and origin of the letter to Chancellor Albini, who had it seized and opened. As the contents were entirely innocuous, Dorsch demanded on his return a full and written apology. Albini declined and was supported by the Elector. In November of the same year Dorsch fled to Strasbourg, where he took the oath to the new constitution, was appointed Professor of Philosophy at the University and became a prominent member of the Jacobin Club.[1]

Action was taken by all the Rhenish governments to ensure joint action against insurrection. In December 1789 a patent issued by the Electors of Mainz, Trier and Cologne warned their subjects not to imitate the subversive activities of certain neighbouring peoples and not to attempt the unilateral seizure of 'alleged rights and liberties'.[2] As usual, Friedrich Karl was in the van of the activists. It was on his initiative that discussions began at the *Reichstag* in 1790 on the need for imperial legislation to restrict the press and to stamp out revolutionary and anti-clerical publications.[3] Almost certainly this wave of conservative legislation achieved the reverse of what had been intended. Those who admired the French Revolution and were not deterred by its growing radicalism, were now compelled to adopt a much more critical attitude towards their own governments. The popular argument that the French had been obliged to seize with force what the German princes had given voluntarily lost much of its force when those same princes threw their enlightened policies into reverse. Yet however sharp the edge of their discontent became, the number of these radical dissidents remained small. Dispersed among the hundreds of German states, they could do nothing in the face of princely co-operation. Only the arrival of the French armies could help them to power.

Although the French declaration of war of 20 April 1792 mentioned only the King of Hungary, Mainz was closely involved from the start. During the months of phoney war which preceded the actual fighting, Friedrich Karl did everything in his power to further the Austrian cause. It was at Mainz in July that the newly crowned Francis II and his Prussian allies worked out the final details of their invasion plans. It was from here that the allied Commander-in-Chief, the Duke of Brunswick, issued his celebrated manifesto to the people of Paris.[4] Nor was Friedrich Karl

---

[1] Ibid., pp. 1036–9.
[2] Ibid., pp. 472, 502. The patent of the Electoral Rhenish Circle was based on that issued by the Upper Rhenish Circle the previous month.
[3] Ibid., p. 668, n. 2.   [4] Ibid., vol. 2, pp. 289–93.

The Electorate of Mainz in the Eighteenth Century

satisfied with this kind of support. Such was his desire to share in the glory and the spoils of the allied victory he expected so confidently that he agreed to send 2,000 troops to assist the invasion.[1]

This decision to send a large part of his army was extraordinarily rash, in view of the Electorate's geographical position. Less than a hundred miles from the nearest French outposts, the capital city in particular was highly vulnerable to a surprise attack. In addition, the Mainz fortifications were in a deplorable state. The cannons were all small and in poor condition, the gun-carriages were unserviceable and there were insufficient stocks of ammunition. A large part of the fortifications had been turned into an 'English garden' and military personnel were obliged to fetch the key from the court gardener. In the early summer of 1792 some desultory attempts were made to improve the defences but were abandoned when it was learnt that the Austrian and Prussian armies were marching to the Rhine.[2]

By this time events outside the Electorate were moving too fast for the hastily erected palisades to be of any avail. As he rode out of Mainz on his way to the wars, the Marquis d'Autichamps had called out to a lady who wished him luck: '*Ce n'est qu'une promenade!*'[3] His optimism soon proved unfounded. Initially the campaign went well and the allied armies advanced deep into Champagne, but a combination of stout French resistance, bad weather and incompetent leadership soon brought reverses. After the inconclusive cannonade at Valmy on 20 September the Austrians and Prussians were forced to abandon their offensive and begin the long retreat back to Germany. Meanwhile, lurking on the south-western frontier, the army of Citizen-General Custine gratefully seized the opportunity to pounce on the *Reich*'s unprotected flank. The Mainz contingent had not marched into France with the bulk of the allied army but had been stationed at Speyer, together with a thousand Austrian troops, to guard an ammunition dump. On 30 September Custine's forces surrounded the town and slaughtered or captured the entire garrison. They took Worms on 4 October and moved their advance guard into Oppenheim, a small town on the Rhine less than twenty miles from Mainz.[4]

In Mainz, the first effect of the news of the fate of the troops and the swift advance of the French was panic. The nobles, higher clergy and most commoners wealthy enough to hire transport, packed up their port-

---

[1] Ibid., p. 312, n. 4. Mainz could have been forced to participate in the war only if the *Reichstag* had declared war on France. This it never did, although on 22 March 1793 it declared that the war forced on the *Reich* by France was to be regarded as an imperial war – Karl Otmar Freiherr von Aretin, *Heiliges Römisches Reich*, Veröffentlichungen des Instituts für Europäische Geschichte Mainz, vol. 38, pt. 1 (Wiesbaden, 1967), p. 273.
[2] Hansen, *Quellen*, vol. 2, p. 156. Neigebaur, *Untergang*, pp. 33, 45.
[3] Eickemeyer, *Denkwürdigkeiten*, p. 110.
[4] Hansen, *Quellen*, vol. 2, p. 397.

able belongings and left for the German interior. The Elector returned to the city on 3 October, made hasty arrangements for the removal of government papers and the archives and left secretly the following night, with the coat of arms on his carriage obliterated.[1] There was then a curious lull of two weeks. Alarmed by reports that the Austrian general Esterhazy and the Prince de Condé were on the march with a relief force, Custine retreated towards Speyer. When this proved to be a false alarm he resumed his advance, completing the encirclement of Mainz by 19 October. After a heavy bombardment on the following day he called on the garrison to surrender.

The Mainz Commander, General Gymnich, had at his disposal only 1,500 troops, to which were added 820 Austrian reinforcements who slipped into the city from the east on the second day of the siege.[2] Although they were confronted by a French force of 13,000 men, it seems clear that the defenders could have held out for a considerable length of time. They were urged to do so by the Statthalter von Fechenbach, the Chancellor Albini and other members of the civil administration, but the military commanders decided otherwise. At a council attended by four full generals, three major-generals and one lieutenant-colonel, only lieutenant-colonel Eickemeyer advocated resistance; all the others voted for immediate surrender.[3] Eickemeyer, whose knowledge of French and low social status were ideal qualifications for the humiliating mission, was sent to the French camp to negotiate the terms of the capitulation. After agreement was reached on 21 October, the allied troops marched out and the French occupied the city gates. On the following day the bulk of the French army marched in and Custine took up residence in the Elector's palace.

At the beginning of October the Prussian ambassador von Stein had expressed the fear that the citizens of Mainz would open the gates of their city as soon as the French approached.[4] The events of the next few weeks suggested either that he had overestimated their affection for the French or had underestimated their loyalty to the Elector. In response to ringing appeals from the government, large numbers of citizens and peasants from the surrounding countryside rallied to the defences. They drew arms from the arsenal, manned the walls and went to work on the fortifications. Doubtless their enthusiasm was encouraged by the promises of generous

[1] Ibid., p. 397. Forster, *Sämtliche Schriften*, vol. 8, p. 224. Böhmer, *Briefe*, p. 269.
[2] Hansen, *Quellen*, vol. 2, pp. 450–1.
[3] Chuquet, *Guerres*, vol. 6, p. 94. Later von Gymnich felt obliged to defend himself publicly against charges of cowardice. In a pamphlet he argued that the city could not have been defended – *Beschreibung der Vestung Mainz, und der Umstände, unter welchen sie in Oktober 1792 den Franzosen übergeben ward*.
[4] Hansen, *Quellen*, vol. 2, p. 378.

compensation to themselves or their dependents if they suffered mutilation or death, but there is also substantial evidence of spontaneous patriotism.[1] The most impressive testimony to the citizens' will to resist came from a later collaborator, who attacked them in the Revolutionary Club: 'You wanted to fight for your old rulers and in the heat of the moment were even angry because the city had been handed over to the French, saying "We could have fought on".'[2] Certainly the arrival of the French was not the occasion for any public rejoicing. Georg Forster recorded that 'the people received them in a kind of gloomy silence, without any vigorous signs of opposition, but without any applause and without any rejoicing'.[3]

Despite this inauspicious start, the French appeared determined to assume the rôle of liberators rather than conquerors. No levy was imposed, the soldiers were billeted only in the palaces of the nobility and the strictest discipline was maintained.[4] On 23 October General Custine informed the representatives of the guilds that the future of the city would be determined only by the free vote of its inhabitants; if a majority wished to return to the 'old slavery', the French would bow to their prejudices.[5] Until comparatively late in the occupation, the official French picture of the Mainz population was that of a people just the same as themselves, now happily liberated from centuries of tyranny and thirsting for freedom. But the French military authorities were not inclined to leave anything to chance and mounted a propaganda offensive to convince any sceptics of the miseries of despotism and the virtues of liberty and equality. A team of German democrats was assembled to conduct the campaign. They were led by Anton Dorsch, whose return to the scenes of his former persecution symbolised the triumph of the new order.[6]

---

[1] Ibid., pp. 399 n. 2, 413. Neigebaur, *Untergang*, p. 102. (Anton Hoffmann), *Darstellung der Mainzer Revolution oder Geschichte der Stadt Mainz und umliegenden Gegend von Entstehung des französischen Revolutionskrieges bis nach der Wiedereroberung dieser Stadt, der Klubb und des in dieser Stadt eröffneten rheinisch-teutschen Nationalkonventes* (Frankfurt and Leipzig, 1794), p. 24. P. A. Winkopp, *Geschichte der französischen Eroberungen und Revolution am Rheinstrome vorzüglich in Hinsicht auf die Stadt Mainz* (n.p., n.d.), p. 49. Daniel Dumont, *Die Belagerung der Stadt Mainz durch die Franzosen im Jahre 1792 und ihre Wiedereroberung durch die teutschen Truppen im Jahre 1793* (Mainz, 1793), p. 33. Although all these contemporary observations stem from opponents of the Revolution, their number and unanimity are impressive. There is only one piece of evidence that the citizens wished to surrender – a rumour recorded in the diary of a noble living in Koblenz – Hansen, *Quellen*, vol. 2, p. 452.

[2] Karl Klein, *Geschichte von Mainz während der ersten französischen Occupation 1792–1793* (Mainz, 1861), p. 99. Daniel Dumont also wrote that the citizens were enraged by the capitulation – *Belagerung*, p. 50.

[3] Georg Forster, 'Darstellung der Revolution Mainz', *Sämtliche Schriften*, vol. 6 (Leipzig, 1843), p. 399. Niklas Vogt gained a similar impression – *Verfall*, p. 252.

[4] This was conceded even by opponents of the French – Hansen, *Quellen*, vol. 2, p. 517. Adam Gottron, 'Tagebuch des Pfarrers Turin von St. Ignaz', *Mainzer Almanach* (1958), p. 153.

[5] F. Werner, *Der Dom von Mainz nebst Darstellung der Schicksale der Stadt und der Geschichte ihrer Erzbischöfe*, vol. 3 (Mainz, 1836), p. 351.

[6] See above, p. 273.

Revolution: Mainz 1792–3

Their chief organ was the Society of the Friends of Liberty and Equality, known colloquially as 'The Club'. In his first speech Dorsch reminded its members that when he was last in the city they had been 'slaves groaning under the most abominable burden of a dissolute prince and his mob of courtiers'. It was the purpose of the Club, he announced, to spread and strengthen the spirit of liberty.[1] The members approached their task with enthusiasm. At the daily sessions in the weeks which followed, the speakers vied with each other in their abuse of the Elector's pride, dissoluteness, extravagance, hypochondria and lechery.[2] The nobility and higher clergy were subjected to similar verbal punishment, as the Electorate was portrayed as a despotism of unparalleled tyranny and corruption.[3] Simultaneously the Clubists preached the enormous benefits to be expected from a régime based on the principles of the Revolution. Georg Forster in particular stressed the universal character of these principles, arguing that *Liberté et Égalité* meant the same when spelt *Freiheit und Gleichheit*.[4]

This exercise was not intended to remain sermons for the converted; every attempt was made to spread the word to the apathetic or hostile masses outside the Club. Many of the more important speeches made there were printed and distributed throughout the city, together with dozens of original pamphlets and thousands of copies of Friedrich Cotta's summary of the new French Constitution.[5] Some of the more enthusiastic members of the Club attempted to promote the political education of the citizens through their own newpapers: Metternich's *Bürgerfreund*, Wedekind's *Patriot*, Hartmann's *Der fränkische Republikaner* and Forster's *Volksfreund*.[6] For the illiterate or less intellectual sections of the population the Club resorted to audio-visual aids. Songs of freedom, such as 'A Call to Arms to the Citizens of the Country of Mainz' and 'A Drinking-Song

---

[1] A. J. Dorsch, *Anrede an die neu gebildete Gesellschaft der Freunde der Freiheit und Gleichheit in Mainz* (Mainz, 1792).

[2] See, for example, three speeches by Georg Wedekind, the former Professor of Medicine, and a similar diatribe from Dorsch, reprinted by Claus Träger, *Mainz zwischen Schwarz und Rot: Die Mainzer Revolution in Schriften, Reden und Briefen* (Berlin, 1963), pp. 161–86. See also *Der Bürgerfreund*, ed. Mathias Metternich, no. 13, 7 December 1792.

[3] See for example *Der fränkische Republikaner*, ed. K. Hartmann and J. D. Meuth, no. 1, 16 November 1792 and A. J. Hofmann's *Der Aristokratenkatechismus*, reprinted in Träger, *Mainz zwischen Schwarz und Rot*, pp. 283–95.

[4] Georg Forster, 'Über das Verhältniß der Mainzer gegen die Franken', *Sämtliche Schriften*, vol. 6, p. 416. For other rhapsodic recommendations of the French system, see Hansen, *Quellen*, vol. 2, pp. 536–7, and a number of articles published in *Der Patriot*, a weekly journal edited by Georg Wedekind, especially 'Die Grundsätze der kriegsführenden Frankenrepublik', published in no. 5.

[5] A. Klebe, *Reise auf dem Rhein*, vol. 1 (1801), listed 121 published in or about Mainz during this period. Even this list is incomplete.

[6] H. Roth, 'Die Mainzer Presse von der Mainzer Revolution 1792 bis zum Ende der zweiten französischen Herrschaft 1814', *Quellen und Forschungen zur hessischen Geschichte*, vol. 2 (1930).

for Free Germans' were circulated and translations of the *Ça ira* published.[1] The services of the theatre were also enlisted. What plays such as 'The Aristocrat in a Jam' or 'The Aristocrat Trapped in His Lies' lacked in dramatic tension they made up for in passionate denunciation.[2] The climax of this propaganda drive came with a grand ceremony on 13 January 1793. To the accompaniment of brass bands, speeches from Custine and Forster and the firing of salutes, a 'Tree of Freedom' was erected, bedecked with a red cap and the legend 'Peace to the People, War to the Tyrants'. Around it was enacted a pageant, in which symbols of servitude and feudalism were torn from 'Slaves' and thrown on a bonfire.[3]

Both supporters and opponents of the new order were convinced that these missionary efforts would soon be successful; both Georg Forster and the Austrian diplomat von Schlick predicted imminent unanimity. Only three weeks after the arrival of the French Forster wrote that apart from a few court officials and creatures of the nobility there were no dissidents and that even the guilds had turned their backs on the past.[4] These and other similar predictions turned out to be wildly over-optimistic or pessimistic, depending on the observer's political stance. In view of the Elector's disastrous counter-revolutionary policies, which arguably could have been held responsible for the presence of the French army of occupation, disaffection with the old régime was to be expected. Its intensity or probable longevity is impossible to judge; it certainly did not amount to a warm embrace of the principles of the French. On 3 November 1792, an official still in the city reported to Chancellor Albini that only a very small number of 'intellectuals and citizens' wished to do away altogether with the Electorate's constitution. Almost everyone else wished to retain it, with the following significant modifications: the co-regency of the Coadjutor (Dalberg); popular participation in any future election of an Elector; the opening of the Cathedral Chapter to any man of 'virtue and talent'; the abolition of fiscal exemptions; a representative assembly with special responsibilities for finance and the election of canons of the Cathedral Chapter; the demolition of the city's fortifications and finally the establishment of a fixed civil list for the Elector.[5]

In the context of the pre-1792 situation in Mainz these demands were certainly radical, although equally clearly they fell a long way short of the

---

[1] Hansen, *Quellen*, vol. 2, p. 537, n. 4. *Der Patriot*, nos. 1, 6.
[2] See above, p. 68. For a detailed account of the revolutionary theatre in Mainz, see Gerhard Steiner, 'Theater und Schauspiel im Zeichen der Mainzer Revolution', H. W. Seiffert, *Studien zur neueren deutschen Literatur* (Berlin, 1964).
[3] Hansen, *Quellen*, vol. 2, p. 700.
[4] Forster, *Sämtliche Schriften*, vol. 8, pp. 242, 267. Hansen, *Quellen*, vol. 2, pp. 547–9.
[5] Vienna, *MEA*, Militaria, Fasc. 118, 49. Each bundle in this fascicle is paginated separately. This document is to be found in the first bundle.

wishes of the French and their German allies in the Club. They also represented the high-water mark of the Mainzers' political ambitions. At about that time there began a deterioration in the relations between the revolutionaries and the local population which led progressively to a state of open hostility and eventually to the rhapsodic welcome accorded by the people to the return of the Elector and the old régime.

The first indication that Forster's sanguine predictions were misguided came from the guilds. In response to Custine's proclamation of 23 October,[1] they met to consider the future of the Electorate's constitution. They agreed to abide by the decision of the guild of merchants (*Handelsstand*), which in turn deputed the task to their chairman Daniel Dumont. His proposals, presented to the occupation authorities at the beginning of November, were a grave disappointment to General Custine and his staff. Despite a lengthy panegyric of the courage and generosity of the French, Dumont rejected the idea that the French constitution could be transplanted to Mainz *en bloc*. By reference to their membership of the *Reich*, their 'German phlegm' and their peculiar traditions, he argued that the citizens of Mainz had separate problems which demanded separate solutions. He requested only a representative assembly, with the franchise predictably restricted to guild-masters, fiscal equality and a restriction of official posts to native-born Mainzers. From the French point of view what was more significant was what he left out. There was no mention of deposing the Elector, abolishing the legal privileges of the nobility or of seceding from the *Reich* and, even more ominously for the French, not even the most perfunctory homage to the principles of liberty and equality.[2] Two further approaches to the guilds produced equally disappointing results. Although a few members were persuaded to sign a declaration calling for the introduction of the French constitution, the great majority remained resolutely attached to the modified version of the old constitution. During the following months the guild-masters retained their dominant position in the city's affairs. There is no evidence that a more radical movement of journeymen and apprentices developed by their side.

This refusal to fall into the arms of the French evoked a violent reaction from the Clubists. In a number of bitter speeches and pamphlets Dumont was branded as a 'seducer of the people' and his proposals were dismissed as the 'scrawlings of a wretched armchair-politician'.[3] General Custine had also decided to adopt a more vigorous approach. On 19 November the old administration, which had been left intact when the French occupied

---

[1] See above, p. 276.
[2] Hansen, *Quellen*, vol. 2, p. 573. Of the 94 members of the *Handelsstand* in the city, 81 voted for Dumont's proposals and 13 for the French constitution.
[3] Hansen, *Quellen*, vol. 2, p. 569, n. 2. Träger, *Mainz zwischen Schwarz und Rot*, pp. 377-8.

the city, was replaced by a group of Clubists. Led by Dorsch and Forster, the new 'municipality' could be relied upon to adopt a much more purposeful attitude towards the local population.

Yet no sooner had they taken office than new regulations arrived from Paris which necessitated another revision. On 15 December the National Convention ordered the generals in charge of occupied foreign territory to obliterate the old order there in all its forms and to arrange elections to erect a new one based on liberty and equality. To supervise the execution of this decree, three deputies from the National Convention – Merlin de Thionville, Reubell and Haussmann – and two from the executive committee – Simon and Grégoire – were sent to Mainz.[1] They arranged for elections to be held on 24 February 1793 to set up a new municipal government in Mainz and the other communities under Custine's control, and to elect delegates to a Rhenish National Convention to decide the future of the entire area occupied by the French armies. As the National Convention had instructed, the electorate was confined to male citizens over the age of twenty-one and prepared to swear an oath to be 'faithful to the people and the principles of liberty and equality'.[2] On the other hand, abstentions would not be permitted; the detailed regulations for the elections warned that communities refusing to take the oath and to vote at the polls would be regarded as enemies of France and treated accordingly.

As Georges Lefebvre observed, the decree of 15 December 'instituted the dictatorship of revolutionary minorities under the protection of French bayonets, and undertook to secure the fortunes of other peoples, without consulting them, at their expense'.[3] It also had the effect of polarising opinion within the communities. The large number of Mainz citizens who wished for liberal modifications to their own constitution were not prepared to swallow whole the French import. The more the French insisted, the stronger their attachment to the old order became. The uncompromising language of the National Convention's decree and the exigencies of war left no room for men in the middle; one or two of them joined the ranks of the revolutionaries, the great majority returned to the Elector's fold.

As the day of the election approached it became clear that very few would vote as directed. Reminding the French that Custine had promised them a free choice, the guilds declared that they would neither swear the oath nor vote. Their example was followed by the electoral officials still in the city, the clergy and other informal groups who had banded together for the purpose of sending in petitions.[4] Only four days before the elec-

---

[1] Hansen, *Quellen*, vol. 2, pp. 646-8. [2] Ibid., p. 762, n. 1.
[3] Lefebvre, *French Revolution*, p. 277.
[4] Hansen, *Quellen*, vol. 2, p. 762. Erich Schreiber, *Französische Ausweisungspolitik am Rhein und die Nordfrankenlegion* (Berlin, 1929). A number of the guilds' petitions are reprinted in K. G. Bockenheimer, *Die Mainzer Klubisten, 1792-1793* (Mainz, 1896), pp. 342-55.

tions, Simon and Grégoire informed Paris that they would be forced to resort to intimidation to secure the desired result. Their worst fears were realised, for on 24 February 1793, most of the inhabitants stayed indoors. After four days of vigorous efforts at persuasion by the French and the Clubists, less than four hundred, out of a total population of 30,000, had gone to the polls. It was just as well that the deputies from the National Convention were of the opinion that 'true patriots have long got used to not bothering about the number [of supporters], however big or little it might be'.[1]

The failure of the elections was also the signal for the French to abandon finally their attempt to behave as liberators rather than conquerors. An early sign of a firmer line was the deportation at the end of January of the domicellar Emmerich Joseph Freiherr von Hettersdorff, allegedly for bribing spectators at the Club to stamp on the floor during debates.[2] As the Prussian and Austrian armies began to converge on Mainz from all sides, military considerations were added to political arguments. On the day before the election Daniel Dumont[3] and the members of the archiepiscopal Vicariate still in the city were taken across the Rhine and handed over to the Prussian front-line positions.[4] Over the next few days similar treatment was meted out to the monks, nuns, members of collegiate foundations and parish priests until the only clergymen left in the city were the handful who had taken the oath to liberty and equality.[5] Then it was the turn of ordinary citizens who had refused to take the oath or had excited suspicion in some other way. In the National Convention in Paris on 30 March, Haussmann was prepared to concede only that 'bailiffs, priests and nobles' had been deported, as enemies of the people.[6] These categories must have been exceptionally generous in their scope, for contemporary estimates of the total number who left the city varied only between 15,000 and 16,000.[7]

The voluntary or compulsory departure of about half the city's popula-

---

[1] Hansen, *Quellen*, vol. 2, pp. 756–7, 758, n. 1. There was similar resistance to the compulsory election in most other communities in the Rhineland – ibid., pp. 759–61. For a description of the events in the Cathedral Chapter's town of Bingen, see the report marked *Aschaffenburg den 8ten Mai 1793*, Vienna, *MEA*, Militaria, Fasc. 120.
[2] Schreiber, *Französische Ausweisungspolitik*, p. 44.
[3] See above, p. 279.
[4] Klein, *Geschichte von Mainz*, pp. 418–19. By January the French held only the small fortified town of Kastel on the right bank of the Rhine. The allies did not encircle Mainz from the West however until 14 April.
[5] Hansen, *Quellen*, vol. 2, pp. 768–9, 783.
[6] *Le Moniteur Universel*, No. 91, 1 April 1793.
[7] Chuquet, *Guerres*, vol. 7, p. 139. Hansen, *Quellen*, vol. 2, p. 852, n. 1. Träger, *Mainz zwischen Schwarz und Rot*, p. 539, Dumont, *Belagerung*, p. 153, *Mainz nach der Wiedereinnahme durch die verbündeten Deutschen im Sommer 1793* (Mentz, 1793), p. 39. The only estimate lower than 15,000 is that of 12,000 in Schreiber, *Französische Ausweisungspolitik*, p. 82.

tion was the clearest possible indication of the failure of the French and their German allies, as they themselves were well aware. Although encouraging reports on the progress of the Revolution were sent to Paris while Mainz remained in French hands, after the recapture by the allies there was no longer any need to dissemble. One of the military commanders, General d'Oyré, wrote afterwards: 'Despite the frequent and numerous deportations, the inhabitants were so ill-disposed [towards the French] that the electoral government could count only 150 attached to our principles, and two thirds of them refused to leave Germany for France.'[1]

The reasons for this superficial paradox were of two kinds: negative, in that they took the form of aversion to the French and their programme, and positive, in that they took the form of loyalty to the institutions and values of the old régime. One of the most important of the former category was the behaviour of the self-appointed liberators. At first strict discipline was maintained, but as the weeks passed the strain of a monotonous life in a garrison town became too much for the French soldiers. The local inhabitants took particular exception to their cavalier attitude to hygiene, which quickly turned the streets of the city into open sewers. Mainz became known locally as the 'French latrine'.[2] On their arrival at the beginning of 1793 the commissars from Paris were equally disgusted by the spectacle. Appreciating the harm it was doing to their cause, they took immediate steps to clear the mess away, but, as they lamented in their report, by that time the damage had been done.[3] Although perhaps inevitable, numerous incidents involving local girls were not calculated to promote friendly relations between conquerors and conquered.[4]

The behaviour of the upper echelons of the French administration also contributed to the growing disaffection. It cannot be denied that they found themselves in an intensely disagreeable situation: bound by their ideology to behave altruistically, yet forced by the demands of war to behave selfishly. Public opinion was outraged early in the occupation when General Custine decided to auction all the Elector's property remaining in the city. As the encirclement by the Austrians and Prussians loomed larger and the hostility of the local population became clearer, the French military authorities were both obliged and tempted to put their own

---

[1] Chuquet, *Guerres*, vol. 7, p. 139. For similar comments, see Bockenheimer, *Klubisten*, pp. 142–4, Joseph Hansen, 'Das linke Rheinufer und die französische Revolution, 1789–1801', *Mitteilungen der Akademie für wissenschaftliche Erforschung und Pflege des Deutschtums* (1927), p. 438.

[2] Klein, *Geschichte von Mainz*, p. 340, Chuquet, *Guerres*, vol. 7, p. 65, Hoffman, *Darstellung*, p. 584.   [3] Hansen, *Quellen*, vol. 2, pp. 755–8.

[4] Klein, *Geschichte von Mainz*, pp. 340–2, Hansen, *Quellen*, vol. 2, p. 753. An order of Custine of 25 January 1793 referred to the numerous complaints he had received about the behaviour of his troops towards the Mainz girls and threatened offenders with severe punishment – Hoffmann, *Darstellung*, pp. 601–3.

soldiers first.¹ Commissars Simon and Grégoire reported bitterly to Paris that the needs of the civilian population had been subordinated ruthlessly to the army, that local tradesmen found it extremely difficult to secure payment for goods delivered and that generally the 'despotic attitude' adopted by the military agents had alienated the entire population.² These complaints were echoed by Georg Forster and his colleagues in the General Administration. In a long and reproachful memorandum to the General they tendered their resignations, lamenting that they were treated as nothing more than tools of the army.³ The hapless members of the Administration were caught between two fires, for their own actions did not endear them to the citizens in their charge. Their imposition of censorship, interception of mail and interference with schools seemed hardly compatible with the dawn of liberty they themselves proclaimed.⁴ The wide gap which opened between revolutionary theory and practice gave the counter-revolutionary pamphleteers an opportunity they were not slow to exploit.

Growing opposition to the occupation authorities was accompanied by declining support for the Club. Although more than two hundred people attended its second session, the Club failed to strike roots in Mainz. Its total membership never exceeded 500; of these over fifty were French officers and a large percentage civilians from Paris, Brussels, Strasbourg and other French-speaking areas. Moreover less than a month after its foundation the minutes began to record an increasing number of resignations. On 1 January 1793 only 121 members had paid their subscriptions; by the end of February membership had dropped to 36.⁵ One powerful reason for the Club's failure to win more support was the alien religion and/or origin of its leaders. Metternich was from Trier, Hofmann from Würzburg, Wedekind, Forster, Böhmer and Blessmann from Göttingen, Cotta from Stuttgart, Pape from Westphalia, Rulffs from Bremen, Hauser from Regensburg and Stamm and Meyer from Strasbourg.⁶ It was not

---

[1] *Georg Forsters Briefwechsel mit S. Th. Sömmering*, ed. H. Hettner (Brunswick, 1877), p. 609. Even the administration Custine had appointed felt obliged to protest – Hoffmann, *Darstellung*, pp. 514–15.
[2] Hansen, *Quellen*, vol. 2, p. 755.
[3] Träger, *Mainz zwischen Schwarz und Rot*, pp. 336–47.
[4] Klein, *Geschichte von Mainz*, pp. 242–3, 259. An edict of 21 November 1792, for example, stated that freedom of the press was 'the best defence of free peoples against all kinds of secular and clerical despotism' but at the same time banned all publications which were 'contrary to the public good', might disturb public order or might mislead the people on the subject of their long-lost rights. This edict is reprinted in full in Hoffmann, *Darstellung*, p. 372.
[5] Schreiber, *Französische Ausweisungspolitik*, pp. 22–4. B. S. von Nau, *Geschichte der Deutschen in Frankreich und der Franzosen in Deutschland*, vol. 5 (Frankfurt am Main, 1794), p. 593.
[6] Klein, *Geschichte von Mainz*, p. 185. Chuquet, *Guerres*, vol. 7, p. 19. An anonymous spy of the Austrian diplomat Klemens August Count von Westphalen reported on 19 November

surprising that the well-known xenophobia of the Mainz citizens, which many times in the past had made life difficult for the Electors, should be reactivated. Speaking on behalf of all the guilds, Daniel Dumont demanded from Custine that any future constitution should reserve to native-born citizens a monopoly of public offices.[1] The counter-revolutionary propaganda also placed great emphasis on the alien character of their opponents and the programme they preached. The Clubists were depicted as foreign adventurers, out for what they could get, with no knowledge of or interest in Mainz.[2] These attacks, which were generally unjustified, were deeply resented by their targets. Georg Forster wrote to his wife at the end of January 1793 that the hatred shown by the citizens of Mainz for those unfortunate enough not to have been born in their city made itself felt in in-increasingly spiteful and degrading ways.[3]

Accident of birth was not the only reason for the Club's failure; the misguided tactics of its members were also to blame. Their attacks on the Elector and the old regime were so far removed from the actual experience of their audience that the positive benefits they promised from a new order were regarded with equal scepticism. The most striking feature of their rhetoric was an almost total lack of concrete examples of oppression or corruption.[4] Just before the elections an anonymous supporter of the Revolution admitted that the 'wild and exaggerated abuse' of the Elector had been a grave error.[5] By way of corollary, the revolutionaries' speeches and pamphlets were also excessively abstract. Perhaps on account of the academic background of most of their authors, they were characterised by a tendency to drift into high-flown rhapsodies on liberty and equality *per se*. They were also inclined to be far longer than necessary. This combination of exaggeration, vagueness and even sheer tedium was not calculated to win over the Mainz burghers. P. A. Winkopp was at least half-serious when he observed that one hundred missionaries sent to the city by the

---

1792: 'No official, no citizen of means and almost no native-born inhabitants of the Electorate have played any part in the present upheaval – only young foolish boys. And it would be most unjust if they were made to carry the blame for the evil that has been done. All the [real] participants are foreigners, brought here by the court on double-pay.' Heinrich Scheel, 'Spitzelberichte aus dem jakobinischen Mainz', *Jahrbuch für Geschichte*, 6 (1971), p. 528.

[1] Hansen, *Quellen*, vol. 2, p. 572.
[2] See, for example, the two pamphlets by P. A. Winkopp, *Über die Verfassung von Mainz oder Vergleich des alten und neuen Mainz*, and *Geschichte der französischen Eroberungen und Revolution am Rheinstrome vorzüglich in Hinsicht auf die Stadt Mainz*. Winkopp drew attention, for example, to Blessman – 'this foreigner' – who had been tutor to the three children of the Hanoverian ambassador, had then earned his living by giving German lessons to the French *émigrés* and being a toady of the Duc de Grammont, but was now an official in Custine's administration.
[3] Forster, *Sämtliche Schriften*, vol. 8, p. 323.
[4] The list of the expenditure incurred during the 1790 coronation was an exception. See above, p. 263.
[5] *Bei bevorstehender Wahl, ein Mainzer Bürger an seine Mitbürger* (Mainz, 1792), p. 14.

Elector could not have been more persuasive advocates of his cause than the revolutionaries who were preaching the opposite.[1]

The Club also paved the way for its collapse by its disunity. Custine's failure to find employment for all the members and the apparent favouritism he showed towards certain individuals divided the revolutionaries into a 'court' and 'country' party. The former, led by the President of the Administration Anton Dorsch, enjoyed the support of the French and their German employees, most of whom had been born outside the Electorate. The latter, led by Andreas Joseph Hofmann, enjoyed the support of the more radical elements – the students and those who had failed to find office under the new régime. The main demand of this group was that official appointments should be confined to native-born citizens.[2] It was not long before the sessions of the Club resounded to increasingly acrimonious disputes between the two parties. Not surprisingly, heretical revolutionaries evoked as much venom as heathen conservatives. The climax was reached on 10 January 1793 when Hofmann ascended the Club's rostrum to launch a personal attack on Dorsch of extraordinary ferocity. He accused the latter of incompetence, nepotism, theft, indiscriminate persecution of the local population, lechery, aspiring to become archbishop and concluded his diatribe by urging that Dorsch be hounded out of the city. On the following day Dorsch and his supporters returned to attack their attackers with equally abusive vigour. It was only with the greatest difficulty that the President of the Club, Georg Forster, managed to keep the Club in existence.[3] A conservative priest recorded in his diary that he welcomed the visits to the Club made by his curious parishioners, for the sight of the in-fighting there served only to confirm his flock's loyalty to the old régime.[4]

As the occupation progressed, the gap between the Clubists and the local population yawned wider. From the start there had been a group of spectators prepared to heckle the more radical speakers. A noisy demonstration in support of a speech defending the old régime prompted a request from the Club for French soldiers to maintain order.[5] As divisions widened and pressures outside increased, the spectators became more aggressive. Increasingly, speeches were interrupted by booing, whistling and the stamping of feet. On 21 January 1793 the Club repeated its request

---

[1] Winkopp, *Eroberungen*, p. 126.
[2] Helmut Mathy, *Als Mainz französisch war* (Mainz, n.d.), p. 21.
[3] At the suggestion of Forster, the relevant minutes were destroyed and thus are not to be found in von Nau. However a report on the proceedings was found later among the effects of the Club's secretary Schlemmers – Walter Grab, 'Eroberung oder Befreiung? Deutsche Jakobiner und die Franzosenherrschaft im Rheinland 1792–1799', *Archiv für Sozialgeschichte* (1970), p. 27, n. 32.
[4] Gottron, *Tagebuch des Pfarrers Turin*, p. 154.
[5] Hoffmann, *Darstellung*, pp. 177–84.

for military protection.¹ The hostility was entirely mutual: the Clubist Pape addressed the spectators as 'miserable bigots', while his colleague Cotta shouted at the hostile public gallery 'You are only Mainzers!' which was clearly the most damaging insult he could think of.² The most sweeping condemnation of his fellow-citizens came from Georg Forster, who accused them of having 'no spark of will-power or determination, no energy, no activity, no intelligence, no knowledge, no education, no feeling, no affection'.³

Eventually the French came to the conclusion that the Club had changed from a potential instrument of their policy into a liability. In February the commissars reported to Paris that it was 'worth nothing'.⁴ The refusal of many former members to swear the oath and vote in the elections was the last straw. On 16 March 1793 commissar Merlin went down to the Club and waving his sabre in the air announced its abolition.⁵ A new association was founded immediately, with fewer members and more modest aims. In a remarkably frank speech to this new 'Society of Free Germans', Charles-Jean Rougemaître admitted that many members of the old Club had been 'disguised aristocrats', that its tactics had been mistaken, that the ordinary people had regarded everything said in it as lies and that generally it had done more harm than good.⁶

The Clubists failed primarily through their factiousness, lack of political experience and simple incompetence, although it must be remembered that they were working in increasingly unpropitious circumstances. While the French retained their aura of invincibility, any citizens of Mainz wishing to embrace their principles and/or enter their employment could do so without a thought for the consequences. Collaboration became progressively less attractive as the return of the old régime in the wake of the allied counter-offensive became possible, then probable and then certain. The first stage was reached with the recapture of Frankfurt from the French on 2 December 1792. Anyone who failed to appreciate the implications of this reverse was given a sharp reminder on 19 December when the Emperor Francis II issued an official warning to subjects of the *Reich* who assisted the enemy.⁷ After 6 January, when the French were ejected from Hochheim, Prussian troops could be seen on the hills surrounding Mainz to the east.⁸

---

¹ Hansen, *Quellen*, vol. 2, p. 753, n. 3, von Nau, *Geschichte der Deutschen*, p. 560.
² Chuquet, *Guerres*, vol. 7, p. 65.   ³ Forster, *Sämtliche Schriften*, vol. 8, p. 315.
⁴ Hansen, *Quellen*, vol. 2, p. 758. As early as December an official of the municipality had commented that the Club consisted of 'out-and-out scoundrels'.
⁵ Chuquet, *Guerres*, vol. 7, pp. 112–13.
⁶ Träger, *Mainz zwischen Schwarz und Rot*, pp. 442–7.
⁷ Hansen, *Quellen*, vol. 2, p. 668.
⁸ Gottron, *Tagebuch des Pfarrers Turin*, p. 156. Even before the allied counter-offensive Count Westphalen's anonymous spy had pointed out the close relationship between the military

Revolution: Mainz 1792–3

In Mainz these events caused consternation in the revolutionary camp. Friedrich Pape's suggestion in the Club that all members should sign a defiant letter to the King of Prussia, thus publicising their allegiance to the French, was greeted by numerous resignations.[1] There was a hard core of Clubists too committed or too courageous to run for cover, but they found it difficult to arouse the same feelings in the mass of the people. The argument that the French army's strength and determination were such that no siege was possible lost much of its force when Custine began to make defensive preparations. It may also be doubted whether the citizens were convinced by another argument that an army determined to conquer or die would also be victorious.[2] The most persuasive advocate of neutrality, passive resistance or even hostility to the French was the Austrian and Prussian offensive, which by January 1793 was pushing forward on all fronts.

Explanations of this rejection of the French and their principles must not be sought only on the immediate level of their misconceived tactics or the military situation. The people of Mainz were not passive receptacles; to a large extent their reaction was determined by their political, economic, social and cultural experience in the decades preceding the occupation. This is not to deny that two individuals from identical backgrounds could respond to events very differently, but broad lines can be identified. As events in the Electorate before 1793 indicated, there were certain features of the old régime which the majority of subjects were not disposed to abandon. Of these probably the most important was the Roman Catholic religion.

By the time Custine and his army arrived in Mainz it was clear that the French Revolution was violently anti-clerical, if not anti-religious. The Constituent Assembly's suppression of the religious orders and imposition of the Civil Constitution of the Clergy had provoked a sweeping papal condemnation of both the principles and the practice of the Revolution.[3] In Mainz both conservative and progressive Catholics made clear their total opposition to the Revolution.[4] Thus the hostility evinced from the start by the Mainz clergy can have come as no surprise. After refusing to instruct parish priests to read revolutionary pamphlets from the pulpit,

---

and the political situations. On 21 November he wrote 'The Club now has a membership of 400, and 1,100 have signed the Red Book. The number of the Clubists and of those signing the Red Book will increase as soon as Hanau is in the hands of the French and Biron's reinforcements arrive here.' – Scheel, 'Spitzelberichte', p. 531. The Red Book was placed in the Club to allow people in the city to express their support for the new régime.

[1] Nau, *Geschichte der Deutschen*, p. 538.
[2] *Der fränkische Republikaner*, no. 10.
[3] Albert Soboul, *Histoire de la Révolution française*, vol. 1 (Paris, 1962), p. 231–5.
[4] *Mainzer Monatschrift von geistlichen Sachen* (1789–91), *Der Religionsjournal* (1789–91), passim.

the archiepiscopal General Vicariate was abolished.[1] Nor was opposition confined to the privileged canons, monks or nuns; in a communication to General Custine in November 1792 the lower clergy also stated that any future constitution must be compatible with 'the pure Catholic religion'.[2] Of the several hundred priests, only six joined the Club.[3] As they had opposed everything smacking of anti-clericalism under the old régime, it was natural that the clergy mobilised again when faced by a far more radical threat. They offered prayers for the Elector and his return, forbade their charges to attend the Club and did their best to obstruct the elections.[4]

The French authorities and the Clubists were keenly aware that the clergy were their most formidable opponents. Commissar Haussmann reported to Paris that those who incited the people against the Revolution were 'almost always priests'.[5] In a speech to the Club Mathias Metternich named religion as one of the three main reasons for the citizens' misguided conservatism.[6] To loosen the priests' hold on their flocks a counter-offensive was mounted to demonstrate the compatibility and even identity of Christianity and the principles of the Revolution. An anonymous pamphlet published just before the elections, for example, held that Christ's command to love one another led inescapably to the conclusion that liberty and equality, when united with obedience of the laws, formed a chief maxim of the Christian religion.[7] By an ingenious manipulation of St Paul's celebrated epistle to the Romans, Friedrich Cotta argued that it was a Christian *duty* to obey the French, for they formed the government in power.[8]

These arguments lost much of their persuasive power when simultaneously other members of the Club embarked on anti-clerical outbursts.

---

[1] K. G. Bockenheimer, 'Die Mainzer Geistlichkeit während der ersten französischen Herrschaft am Rhein, 1792–1793', *Studien aus Kunst und Geschichte*, Friedrich Schneider zum 70ten Geburtstag gewidmet, von seinen Freunden und Verehrern (Freiburg, 1906), p. 254. Gottron, *Tagebuch des Pfarrers Turin*, pp. 154–5, *Darstellung*, pp. 341, 361, 485, 533.

[2] Hansen, *Quellen*, vol. 2, p. 599.

[3] Bockenheimer, *Klubisten*, p. 70. In 1779 there were 614 clergymen in the city – C. C. W. Dohm, *Materialen für die Statistik und neuere Staatengeschichte*, vol. 2 (Lemgo, 1779), p. 170.

[4] *Der fränkische Republikaner*, nos. 7, 10. Klein, *Geschichte von Mainz*, p. 373, Chuquet, *Guerres*, vol. 7, p. 102.

[5] Ibid., p. 100.

[6] Mathias Metternich, *Rede von den Ursachen der bis itzt noch getheilten Meinungen über die Revolutionssache der Mainzer und von den Mitteln, die Meinungen und Gemüther zu vereinigen. Gehalten in der Gesellschaft der Freunde der Freiheit und Gleichheit* (Mainz, 1792), pp. 5–7. The other two were ignorance and fear of allied retribution.

[7] *Bei bevorstehender Wahl, ein Mainzer an seine Mitbürger* (Mainz, 1792).

[8] Friedrich Cotta, *An die, welche noch nicht geschworen haben*. See also, Gerhard Münch, *Der Staatsbürger kann und muß als Christ ein Patriot wie der Neufranke sein; oder Übereinstimmung der neufränkischen Staatsverfassung mit der Christusreligion* (Mainz, 1793). Part of this pamphlet is reprinted in Träger, *Mainz zwischen Schwarz und Rot*, pp. 428–34.

Citizen Bois, for example, urged the citizens to exercise great care when voting in the forthcoming elections: 'Above all watch out for the priests; they are the most dangerous, because they are the biggest hypocrites.' He added that the power of these supporters of tyranny was based on error and prejudice.[1] In a speech which purported to show the 'Union of the French Constitution and Catholicism' Friedrich Pape called the priests, among other things, 'malevolent insects', 'monsters' and 'Pharisees' and referred to the Popes as usurpers who had ushered in 'the night of human reason'. Nor is it likely that his description of the French Constitution as 'the new Gospel' and the 'Catholic Constitution' appealed to the deeply pious population.[2] They were also offended by Custine's appointment of Anton Dorsch as head of the new administration, for Dorsch was a priest who had accepted the Civil Constitution of the Clergy, had married his housekeeper–mistress and was notorious for his indiscriminate pursuit of women. The counter-revolutionary press seized the opportunity gratefully. An anonymous 'Antipatriot', for example, opined that a defrocked priest had been appointed deliberately 'so that no doubt can remain as to the moral character of the others'.[3] One of the French agents remarked: 'One hardly knows how to deal with the religious prejudices; I have seen with sorrow that the episcopal vicar of the Lower Rhine [Dorsch], recently married, administers the principal magistracy here'.[4]

After the elections of February 1793, the unflagging hostility of the clergy and the failure of attempts to destroy their influence prompted the French to take firmer action against them. Indeed they were the first to be deported. As the priests, monks and friars assembled on the banks of the Rhine, waiting for transport to the other side and the Prussian lines, they were accompanied by 'an enormous crowd of people' wishing to demonstrate their solidarity with their spiritual leaders.[5] This last round in the struggle between the clergy and the revolutionaries emphasised the degree to which Catholicism remained a dynamic force in Mainz. Unlike in France, there was no indigenous anti-clericalism.

Religious ties to the old régime were strengthened by powerful economic considerations. Mainz was first and foremost a residential city, whose *raison d'être* was the presence of the Elector, his court, his administration,

---

[1] *Der fränkische Republikaner*, no. 11.

[2] F. G. Pape, *Vereinigung der neufränkischen Verfassung mit dem Katholizismus, vorgetragen am 25ten November 1792 der Versammlung der Freunde für Freiheit und Gleichheit* (Mainz, 1792).

[3] *Der Antipatriot, Ein Gegenstück zu dem von Forster und Wedekind in Mainz herausgegebenen Patrioten* (Mainz, 1793), p. 22. See also, Hoffmann, *Darstellung*, p. 202, Dumont, *Belagerung*, pp. 99–100. In *Die Verfassung von Mainz* (p. 35) P. A. Winkopp asked his fellow-citizens rhetorically whether or not they wished to be governed by two Catholics whose orthodoxy was very much open to doubt, several Protestants and a number of others of notorious immorality.

[4] Chuquet, *Guerres*, vol. 7, p. 51.   [5] Hansen, *Quellen*, vol. 2, p. 769.

the nobility and the clergy.¹ As the opponents of the French were quick to point out, the ejection of these groups would lead – indeed, was leading – to the ruin of most people in the city. The most eloquent advocate of this point of view was P. A. Winkopp, from whom it is worth quoting at some length:

[The City of] Mainz and even the Electorate do not have their own indigenous nobility; rather all the nobles living in Mainz are Imperial Knights, who stand directly under the Emperor and the *Reich*. They draw their incomes from their family estates and fiefs, which in no way form part of the Electorate of Mainz, and to a certain extent, as in the case of the Eltz, Ostein and several other families, from Hungary and Bohemia. It is true that some of them own tithes and other forms of revenue in the Electorate itself, but these are so insignificant that I doubt whether they suffice to keep a family for a week. Their presence in Mainz is therefore very arbitrary, and they will be very welcome everywhere, even if they do not choose to live on their estates. The richest nobles in Germany were prompted to settle in Mainz by the magnificent court maintained by the Electors, who came from the same families, the hope of obtaining benefices for their younger sons and the prestige and honour the nobility enjoyed. It is true that some of them were also paid by the court, but these court appointments, these honorific positions yielded so little in the way of income that not a single nobleman was in a position to live off them for even a few months. All of them had to keep themselves from the proceeds of their hereditary estates or fiefs lying outside the Electorate. In this way, according to an estimate made a few years ago, foreign money to the tune of more than two and half million gulden was brought into circulation. As the nobility's expenditure was enormous, the market swarmed with people from the Palatinate and other vendors, who then passed on again money they realised to the citizens for articles of clothing, groceries etc.²

The most immediate effect of the capture of Mainz had been the mass exodus of the privileged orders, both ecclesiastical and secular. They left behind them an economic vacuum which the French army could not fill. To the thousands of tradesmen and craftsmen left stranded with stocks of luxury goods, as well as to the thousands in the service industries left without a clientele, the arguments of Winkopp and the other anti-revolutionary

---

¹ See above, pp. 80–4.
² Winkopp, *Die Verfassung von Mainz*, p. 15. This was a recurrent theme in anti-revolutionary pamphlets. See, for example, *Meister Johann Ehrlichs Correspondenz*, whose author claimed to be a master of the carpenters' guild. A similar situation existed in other Central European cities; see, for example, Hans Mauersberg, *Wirtschafts- und Sozialgeschichte zentraleuropäischer Städte in neuerer Zeit* (Göttingen, 1960) and Edith Ennen, 'Grundzüge der Entwicklung einer rheinischen Residenzstadt im 17. und 18. Jahrhundert, dargestellt am Beispiel Bonns', *Forschungen und Darstellungen Franz Steinbach zum 65. Geburtstag gewidmet von seinen Freunden und Schülern* (Bonn, 1960). On the very similar situation obtaining in Vienna, albeit on a larger scale, see T. C. W. Blanning, *Joseph II and Enlightened Despotism* (London, 1970), pp. 89, 148–50. Even in France, where there was only one capital city and only one main centre for the nobility, the presence of the privileged orders in a city could have a profound effect on its economy; see, for example, John McManners' brilliant study of Angers: *French Ecclesiastical Society under the Ancien Régime: A Study of Angers in the Eighteenth Century* (Manchester, 1960).

Revolution: Mainz 1792–3

propagandists made good sense. This was shown most clearly by the many petitions handed to Custine in February 1793, protesting against the impending elections. Most of them complained that the abolition of the old order would lead to the ruin of both their own particular group and the city in general. The various origins of the petitioners illustrate well the extent to which the people's livelihood depended on the privileged groups: Government officials and other individuals (120 signatures); the personnel of the Grand Chamberlain's and the Grand Marshal's office (55); the Elector's coachmen and postal servants (51); court-trumpeters (8); grooms and stable lads (27); 'the entire Mainz clergy'; 'in the name of the entire glaziers' guild'; the cobblers' guild; a joint petition from the wheelwrights', blacksmiths', armourers', nail-forgers', coppersmiths' and spurmakers' guilds; all ten members of the potters' guild; the locksmiths' guild; the bakers' guild; and so on.[1] It is particularly interesting that a petition was also received from the *Beisassenzunft*, which included some of the poorest people in the city: barge-labourers; journeymen-bricklayers, -housepainters, and -carpenters; packers, porters and all sorts of manual labourers.

The hostility shown by the guilds was not surprising, for they knew that their future under a French-sponsored régime was very uncertain. The Constituent Assembly's abolition of the guilds in France, in April 1791, had already attracted much adverse comment in the Mainz press.[2] Soon after the occupation of the city the Clubists began to demand similar measures of economic liberalisation for Mainz.[3] The anger these proposals aroused was due largely to the comparative prosperity the citizens had enjoyed under the old régime. If the city had not experienced dynamic expansion, neither had it suffered the extremes of poverty which mobilised the urban masses in France. Nor was the crisis of 1788–9 as acute or prolonged in Mainz as in its unfortunate neighbour.[4] As the anti-revolutionaries pointed out, and their opponents were obliged to concede, taxation in the city had been low.[5] The charges of gross extravagance laid

---

[1] Schreiber, *Französische Ausweisungspolitik*, pp. 31–9. Schreiber's book is marred by an extreme anti-French bias but does contain much useful material from the Darmstadt archives, which were damaged severely in the Second World War.

[2] Hansen, *Quellen*, vol. 1, pp. 776–7.

[3] *Der Patriot*, no. 3, pp. 24–31. His proposed constitution, read to the Club on 27 October 1792, also called for the abolition of all privileges and the introduction of freedom of trade – F. Valjavec, *Die Entstehung der politischen Strömungen in Deutschland 1770–1815* (Munich, 1951), p. 192. [4] See above, Ch. 2, *passim*, and pp. 261–2.

[5] Winkopp, *Verfassung von Mainz*, pp. 9, 19–21, 'Taxes in the Electorate of Mainz are extremely moderate [*sic*], and the town-dweller of Mainzi tself pays less than any other town-dweller in the world.' This was also argued by Chancellor Albini in his *Etwas über die Mainzische Konstitution in einem Sendschreiben des Gottlob Teutsch an den Verfasser des Mainzischen Bürgerfreundes* (Frankfurt and Leipzig, 1792), pp. 6–7. The point was conceded by *Der fränkische Republikaner*, no. 4, 7 December 1792. See above, pp. 85–6.

at the Elector's door by the Clubists were countered with the observation that his expenditure had brought wealth to the city but had not necessitated any increase in taxation.[1]

Only too aware of the force of these various arguments, the French and their German supporters were outraged by the selfishness of citizens whose political outlook was dictated by the aristocrat's purse. Wedekind wrote in *Der Patriot* on 12 December 1792:

> The town-dweller; who in part lived as a craftsman off the luxury, indulgence and ostentatious display of the rich and arrogant clerical nobility or who got his fodder without effort by serving their pleasures, bemoans the absence of his lords and providers and laments the fact that he is now forced to rely on his own industry, for he has learnt nothing and in the past did not need to know or do anything.[2]

A common reaction to this situation was the view that material considerations should be demoted in the citizens' list of priorities. Mathias Metternich wrote: 'So, the Elector has indulged himself wickedly; this is unjust and always will be unjust; it must stop, even if some businesses suffer in the process.'[3] The pill was sweetened by the further observation that the city's economic difficulties would be only temporary. After a painful but necessary period of transition, Mainz would benefit enormously from access to the limitless markets and trade of France. Already a start had been made on the canal-link between the Rhine and the Rhône.[4] Probably less persuasive was the argument that the city must abandon its privileged position over and against the country. It may be doubted whether the townspeople agreed that the thought of the peasants benefiting from the abolition of the *corvée* and the tithes would be adequate compensation for any hardship they might suffer themselves.[5] The citizens of Mainz were privileged members of a society based on privilege and were convinced at least that their livelihood depended on privilege. This was a situation that could be changed only by force.

Economic arguments in favour of a return to the old régime were lent

---

[1] Winkopp, *Geschichte der französischen Eroberungen*, p. 126. Friedrich Karl had in fact begun his reign by reducing taxation from 16 *Simpeln* (units of assessment) to 14.

[2] Hansen, *Quellen*, vol. 2, p. 639. In a letter to the Jacobin Club in Paris, the Mainz Club listed nine great obstacles which currently prevented the citizens' joyful acceptance of the happiness proffered them by the French: 1. the difference of origin and language, 2. debilitation resulting from the centuries of oppression, 3. superstition, 4. laziness, 5. the enervation of the town-dwellers, caused by the soft and sybaritic clerical régime, 6. mistrust of innovation, 7. the burdens caused by the war, 8. the absence of an enlightened and prosperous middle class, 9. the dependence of the city on the luxury and pleasures of its masters – Ibid.

[3] Träger, *Mainz zwischen Schwarz und Rot*, p. 268.

[4] Georg Wedekind, *Bemerkungen über die gemischten Regierungsverfassungen, In einer Volksrede, welche in der Gesellschaft der Freunde der Freiheit und Gleichheit gehalten wurde am 18. November im ersten Jahr der Republik* (Mainz, 1792), p. 22. Metternich, *Rede von den Ursachen*, p. 9.

[5] Cotta, *An die welche noch nicht geschworen haben*, p. 7, *Der fränkische Republikaner*, no. 4, 7 December 1792, *Ein Frankensoldat an die Mainzer Bürger* (Mainz, 1793).

additional weight by the economic decline of the city under the French occupation. This was due not only to the departure of the privileged orders. After the capture of Mainz the French build-up of troops continued until there were between forty-five and fifty thousand soldiers in and around the city. The strain placed on local resources of food and other essentials led to a dramatic increase in prices.[1] A substantial number of French tradesmen and craftsmen accompanied their armies into the city, thus forcing their Mainz competitors to fight all the harder for a greatly reduced market. Even when they did win French custom, they found it difficult to obtain payment.[2] As the weeks passed, destitution and later even starvation became commonplace. Much of the hardship was the inevitable result of the dislocation caused by war, although it may be doubted whether the citizens were prepared to be objective about their own impoverishment. Nor was it likely that they would be receptive to the ideas of those who appeared to be destroying their prosperity. As Georg Forster bitterly wrote:

The needs and luxury of the numerous nobles and the not less numerous priests support an enormous mob of professional idlers, agents and creatures of their wantonness; a swarm of craftsmen, shopkeepers, artists, servants and dependents, who all see in the person of their master their ideal of what a man should be and the model which they should all seek to copy. If idleness and pleasure stand at the head of the people as their standards, is it not inevitable that the morals of the working classes must deteriorate in the long run?[3]

The feeling shared by most citizens that the new order proposed by the French was alien and unsuited to their own particular needs, was reflected further in the primitive nationalism of the anti-revolutionary pamphlets.[4] The most popular argument was that which attacked '*French* liberty and equality' for being mere abstractions, bearing no relation to real life. Equality was dismissed as an impossible and dangerous ideal, while liberty was held to be not the licence and anarchy practised in France but

[1] Hansen, *Quellen*, vol. 2, pp. 679, 782, n. 1.
[2] Klein, *Geschichte von Mainz*, pp. 239–40, Dumont, *Belagerung*, p. 60.
[3] Forster, *Sämtliche Schriften*, vol. 6, p. 360.
[4] A large number of these pamphlets can be found in the *Stadtbibliothek* in Mainz. Clearly some were written on the instructions of the electoral government, but others appear to have been spontaneous creations. See, for example, *Meister Johann Ehrlichs Correspondenz* and H. T. Stiller, *An die Franken und ihre Repräsentanten in Deutschland*, Von einem freien deutschen Biedermanne ('Deutschland', 1793). It is impossible to judge how representative they were of public opinion in the city, although it seems likely that their authors would have had a good idea of which arguments were most likely to appeal to their fellow-citizens. Despite the censorship imposed by the occupation authorities, the anti-revolutionary publications appear to have circulated freely in the city – Hoffmann, *Darstellung*, p. 588, Schreiber, *Ausweisungspolitik*, p. 56, Winkopp, *Eroberungen*, pp. 165–6. As early as 30 November 1792 the pro-French *Fränkische Republikaner* complained that copies of Albini's *Etwas über die Mainzische Constitution* had been distributed to many guilds and individual citizens.

freedom from arbitrary oppression. It was claimed that the enlightened attitude of the German princes had meant that there had been a greater degree of 'true liberty' under the old régime than was promised by the new. In an open letter to General Custine, Karl Fischer, for example, maintained that 'the great German revolution' had created and was creating the only freedom worth having – 'moral freedom'. This would be a revolution more lasting and more secure than the chimerical democracy of France.[1]

These arguments, with their faint echoes of Burke and/or Kant, were supported by simple xenophobia. The anonymous author of *Aufruf eines Deutschen an seine Landsleute am Rhein* reminded his readers that this was not the first time that the wild hordes of the French *Erbfeind* had devastated their country.[2] H. T. Stiller agreed, pointing out that the Germans were open, honest, upright, prudent, chaste, disciplined, just, moderate, industrious, modest, restrained and reliable, while their French neighbours were sly, deceitful, false, rash, immoral, shameless, unjust, immoderate, lazy, boastful, dissipated and unreliable.[3] This sense of a separate national identity was far removed from the nationalism of the following century but was none the less clearly felt. The pamphlets are peppered with such statements as 'We do not wish to be united with the French, because we are Germans'; 'I desire nothing more than to be praised for being a true and genuine German in the complete sense of the word'; 'the Germans by nature have no inclination for fanaticism'.[4]

The most reasoned defence of 'local patriotism' against the cosmopolitanism of the French and the Clubists was made by the author of an open letter to General Custine, published in November 1792. He argued that what the French regarded as manifestations of feudal slavery were in fact the basis of the city's prosperity. The vast amount of money put into circulation by the privileged orders was not squeezed from a population groaning under an enormous burden of taxation. The Elector's court was financed by the produce of his own domains; the clergy derived most of their income from estates which lay outside the Electorate; and the nobility were not even subjects of Mainz – they only came to the city to spend their money. He denied that these material benefits had been acquired at the expense of justice and enlightenment. He pointed to Friedrich Karl's attempts to raise the intellectual and material level of his subjects and defied the French to produce one example of injustice. He did not suggest

---

[1] Karl Fischer, *An den Herrn Philipp Adam Custine, neufränkischen Bürger und General*, 3rd ed. ('Germanien', 1793). See also *Meister Johann Ehrlichs Correspondenz*, Stiller, *An die Franken, Gespräche über den Mainzer Freiheitsclub* (Frankfurt, 1793), Winkopp, *Verfassung von Mainz*.
[2] *Aufruf eines Deutschen an seine Landsleute am Rhein: sonderlich an den Nähr- und Wehrstand* (1792), pp. 5–6. [3] Stiller, *An die Franken*.
[4] *Der Antipatriot*, p. 26, Stiller, *An die Franken*, Hoffman, *Darstellung*, p. 174.

Revolution: Mainz 1792-3

that everything was perfect but claimed that it was infinitely preferable to the anarchy and mob-rule currently prevailing in France. He concluded:

No, the honest Mainzer knows his true advantage too well that he should exchange his old constitution, which has made him prosperous and happy, for a phantom, which never can exist and if it did would bring with it a hundred afflictions.

He ended with a ringing appeal:

Citizens of Mainz! Shout this motto at the French regicides, inscribe it on your banners:

> The German
> Fears God,
> Loves his neighbour
> And honours his King.[1]

In view of this rejection of the Revolution by most of the inhabitants of the city, the disproportionate amount of attention lavished by historians on the Clubists is explicable only in terms of the ease with which they can be adapted to suit various historiographical schools. To the nationalist historians they were black-hearted traitors, whose collaboration with the *Erbfeind* was a betrayal of the nation. To the historians of the 'Atlantic School' they were evidence of the ubiquity of the democratic spirit.[2] To Marxist historians they were the vanguard of the revolutionary bourgeoisie.[3] It is to be hoped that some sort of historical statute of limitations will allow one to ignore the charge of treason. And in view of what has been said already in this chapter, it is also to be hoped that no further comment on the unrepresentative character of the Clubists is needed. Their isolation however does not disqualify them from claiming a revolutionary-bourgeois rôle, for Marxism-Leninism has never been concerned overmuch with mere numbers.

It is possible to examine this claim in some detail, for the supporters of the old régime compiled careful lists of their opponents. The most striking characteristics of the Clubists was the diversity of their background. Of the 472 names on a list now in the *Mainzer Erzkanzler Archiv* in Vienna, the occupations of 283 are stated; the number of different trades and professions totals 77, ranging from rag-and-bone-man to dancing-master.[4]

---

[1] *Schreiben an Custine, General der französischen Armeen, veranlaßt durch seine entehrende Aufrufungen an die Bürger, und Soldaten deutscher Nation, verfaßt von einem Manne, der ein Feind von allem Despotismus ist, der aber für das Beste seines Vaterlandes, für das Wohl seiner Mitbürger, für die Ehre Deutschlands-Fürsten, sein Leben aufzuopfern bereit ist* (1792). On 23 November 1792 *Der Bürgerfreund* called on Daniel Dumont to deny that he was the author.
[2] R. R. Palmer, *The Age of Democratic Revolution*, vol. 2 (Princeton, 1964).
[3] Heinrich Scheel, 'Probleme der deutsch-französischen Beziehungen 1789–1830', *Zeitschrift für Geschichtswissenschaft*, 18 (1970).
[4] Vienna, *MEA*, Militaria, Fasc. 120. A list at Würzburg, which was compiled after the recapture of the city, includes only the 255 citizens arrested or definitely established as supporters of the French – MRA, V, 1/1.

The adoption of wider categories reveals a predominance of academics: 7 University professors, 3 school-teachers and 29 students.[1] They were supported by a group of professional men: 9 doctors of medicine, 7 lawyers, 8 clergymen and 19 employees of the Elector or Cathedral Chapter.[2] Although individual members of these élites provided the leadership, the bulk of the Club's membership was drawn from the city's tradesmen and craftsmen. For no immediately apparent reason, crafts concerned with woodwork were heavily represented: 13 cabinet-makers, 8 joiners and 1 carpenter. The largest single group was naturally enough that labelled simply 'shopkeeper' (*Krämer*) of whom there were 18. Only two other occupations raised double figures: the publicans (10) and the tailors (15). Most of the others provided only one, two or three representatives, for example: three bookbinders, three chemists, three millers, three slaters, three tobacconists, two brewers, two shoemakers, two tinfounders, two masons, one leather-dealer, one locksmith, one brushmaker, one turner, one potash-dealer, one chandler, one potter, one coppersmith, one cutler, one printer, one glazier, one grocer, one haberdasher. There were few representatives of the service industries: one barber, one chimney-sweep, one cook, two dancing-masters, one sedan-chair carrier. In view of their clientele it is not surprising that producers of luxury goods were also in short supply: one gold-beater, one gold-thread spinner, and one silversmith.

To state a man's occupation does not of course identify his economic circumstances, but although many of the tradesmen and craftsmen may have been very poor, it does not appear that the lowest classes of the city, in terms of either status or income, participated. Only one man's trade has the suffix *-knecht* to denote his labouring status. On the other hand, neither was the Club socially homogeneous. Professor Georg Forster had as little in common with a file-cutter or a flour-dealer as he had with a Canon of the Cathedral Chapter. The only possible generalisation is that the Club consisted of a small minority of the *menu peuple* of the city, led by a (proportionally) rather larger minority of the professional classes. Certainly revolutionary bourgeois seeking to abolish feudal restrictions on the development of capitalism were in short supply. Not one member of the Club was described as a manufacturer, or any kind of industrial entre-

---

[1] Even these were in a small minority, for there were over 700 students at the University – see above, p. 173. Helmut Mathy has discovered a list of 158 students who volunteered to help defend the city when Custine's army approached – 'Die Mainzer akademische Legion von 1792', *Genealogie*, 18 (1969), p. 564.

[2] Of these 9 one was 'Hofrat von Worms', another 'Amtsverweser in Höchst', another 'Richter zu Zahlbach'. Several of them held very lowly posts which hardly qualify them for the category of professional men. Of the 7 lawyers, 4 were articled clerks. Of the 8 clergymen, 1 was from Kastel, 1 from Wöllstein and 1 was a defrocked monk.

Revolution: Mainz 1792–3

peneur, while there were only ten representatives of the mercantile community (7 *Handelsmänner* and 3 *Kaufmänner*).¹

Nor was the Club, as has often been asserted, the successor of the Reading Club (*Lesegesellschaft*) of the old régime.² As more than half the Reading Club's members were nobles, army officers or clergymen, this is not surprising. Certainly Georg Forster was not impressed by its political radicalism; he reported to his wife in 1788 that it was a notorious gossip-shop.³ It does not appear that the outbreak of the French Revolution brought any substantial change. In 1791, in an open letter to the anonymous donor of French propaganda, the Reading Club stated loftily that they were concerned with more noble products of the human mind and that 'under the mild, philanthropic and paternal government of their Most Gracious Sovereign, they enjoyed the sweetest joy that legitimate freedom can bestow'.⁴ There is no doubt that some members of the Revolutionary Club had also been members of the Reading Club, and it is reasonable to suppose that they discussed politics in the latter and even argued with their more conservative colleagues, but this is far removed from seeing the former as a linear descendant of the latter.⁵

The Club's heterogeneity alone should be sufficient warning against offering any facile general interpretation of individual members' decisions to join. It is as pointless to cast them all as the vanguard of progress as it is to brand them as black-hearted traitors.⁶ As even the slightest intro-

---

¹ The various social backgrounds of the German Jacobins and the academic origin of their leadership have not deterred Marxist historians from conducting a great deal of very valuable research into the radicals of the period. As Alfred Cobban wrote, when making the same point about the French *sans-culottes*, 'current Communist theory is not Marxism but Marxism-Leninism', concerned with the 'élite of bourgeois intellectuals, whose function it is to assume leadership of the spontaneous movement of the working classes' – *The Social Interpretation of the French Revolution* (Cambridge, 1964), pp. 129–30.

² See above, pp. 195–6. This curious notion has surprising stamina. Agatha Ramm has referred to the 'Jacobin Club, originally the *Lesegesellschaft*' – *Germany 1789–1919* (London, 1967), p. 29. Even Gerteis, while pointing out that the political significance of the German *Lesegesellschaften* has been greatly overestimated, stated that the Mainz *Lesegesellschaft* developed into a political association – 'Bildung und Revolution: Die deutschen Lesegesellschaften am Ende des 18. Jahrhunderts', *Archiv für Kulturgeschichte*, 53 (1971), pp. 129–30, 136–7. The origin of the myth was the attempt by counter-revolutionaries to depict the fall of the city to the French as the result of a conspiracy of traitors – e.g. Hoffmann, *Darstellung*, pp. 1–11, Hansen, *Quellen*, vol. 2, p. 163. Subsequently the 'conspiracy theory' was seized on gladly by nationalist historians and is still in use today, although now its purpose is to emphasise the clubists' political maturity.

³ Forster, *Sämtliche Schriften*, vol. 8, p. 11.   ⁴ Hansen, *Quellen*, vol. 1, p. 843.

⁵ It is significant that the electoral government never felt obliged to close the Reading Club down, although shortly before the French captured the city the Statthalter ordered that the reading of French pamphlets should not be accompanied by overt demonstrations of support for their contents – Ibid., vol. 2, p. 410, n. 2.

⁶ For an example of the former over-simplification, see Walter Grab's introduction to Hans Werner Engels, *Gedichte und Lieder deutscher Jakobiner*, Deutsche revolutionäre Demokraten, vol. 1 (Stuttgart, 1971), and of the latter Karl Klein, *Geschichte von Mainz*.

spection should confirm, one's own motives for acting in a certain manner in a crisis cannot be articulated with any confidence. The evidence that selfishness prompted some citizens to join the Club – that Pierre, for example, sought employment as an interpreter to keep the wolf from the door, or that Wedekind's long feud with Sophie von Coudenhove contributed to his enthusiasm for the French[1] – in no way validates the counter-revolutionaries' indiscriminate picture of the Club as a nest of legalised bandits. Against the fact that membership undeniably brought material gain to some, must be set such stirring declarations of faith in the Revolution as those of Forster, contained in a letter to his friend Sömmering on 6 January 1793:

> I have decided for a cause for which I must sacrifice my peace of mind, my studies, my domestic happiness, perhaps my health, my entire belongings, perhaps my life. Yet I shall calmly let whatever happens pass over me, for it will be the inevitable result of principles I accepted long ago and still find to have stood the test of time. One thing alone, I know, is inviolably pure, because I alone can violate it, and that is my conviction.[2]

Yet Forster was as unrepresentative of his colleagues as was Pierre. His severely ethical approach to politics led first to a misunderstanding of the French Revolution and then inevitably to disillusionment. He died in Paris in 1794, bitterly lamenting that the French had proved themselves unworthy of the liberty they had claimed.

Rejected by the townspeople, the Clubists had hoped for a warmer response from the peasantry. As they often pointed out in speeches and pamphlets, the rift between town and country was as wide as that between commoner and noble. The luxury of the city was financed by the greater burden of taxation carried by the rural population.[3] To ensure that the

---

[1] Helmut Mathy, 'Jean Claude Pierre, Professor der französischen Sprache in Mainz (1734 bis ca. 1800)', *Mainzer Almanach* (1968), p. 120. Helmut Mathy, 'Georg Wedekind (1761–1831): Die politische Gedankenwelt eines Mainzer Medizinprofessors', *Geschichtliche Landeskunde*, 5 (1968), pp. 180–5.

[2] Hettner, *Forsters Briefwechsel*, pp. 570–1. This experience was common to many German intellectuals, especially those influenced by the philosophy of Kant – Jacques Droz, *L'Allemagne et la Révolution française* (Paris, 1949), pt. 2, 'La Réaction Moraliste'. For his own contemporaries and for historians since Forster personified 'The Mainz Revolution'. His collaboration with the French led to extremely hostile treatment at the hands of nationalist German historians, notably Karl Klein, whose *Georg Forster in Mainz, 1788–1793* (Gotha, 1863) reveals more about Klein's own virulent nationalism than it does about Forster. The most just general appraisal of his character and career remains that of G. P. Gooch in *Germany and the French Revolution* (New impression, London, 1965). For an excellent recent study of Forster, see Ludwig Uhlig, *Georg Forster: Einheit und Mannigfaltigkeit in seiner geistigen Welt* (Tübingen, 1965).

[3] Their arguments were based on Rousseau's observation: 'Le luxe nourrit cent pauvres dans nos villes, en fait périr cent mille dans nos campagnes' (*sic*) – quoted in Albert Soboul, *Histoire de la Révolution française*, vol. 1, p. 72. Count Westphalen's anonymous spy reported on 21 November 1792: 'Everything will soon be tried to win over the peasants, because it is on

peasants' sense of grievance took a positive form, the Club sent several of its members out into the villages to explain the virtues of liberty and equality in general and of the French Constitution in particular. They were assisted by the distribution of thousands of copies of pamphlets such as 'Concerning the Constitution of France, for the Instruction of All Citizens and Inhabitants of the Archbishopric of Mainz and the Bishoprics of Speyer and Worms'.[1]

Although the Clubists confused the peasantry's social disaffection with political radicalism, the failure of their efforts was largely the responsibility of the French military authorities. Immediately after his arrival in Mainz Custine announced that for want of other instructions he would continue to raise the old taxes and dues, including of course the tithes and *corvées*. This bitter disappointment for the peasants was followed swiftly by a positive deterioration in their position. Perhaps inevitably, the foragers of the French army were more concerned with collecting as much food as quickly as possible than with retaining the goodwill of the local population. The peasants watched with horror as their grain, wine and cattle were removed to Mainz, usually in return for virtually worthless paper *assignats*, often in return for nothing.[2] Their suffering increased when they and their draught animals were conscripted by the French for work on the city's fortifications.

The French themselves came to realise that the rural population had been alienated. Commissar Simon reported to Paris that 'by treating them with the greatest injustice, [the military authorities] have turned the inhabitants of the countryside against the French Revolution; all complain about the harassments of Commissars Villemanzy and Blanchard; several told me, with tears in their eyes, that they had suffered a thousand chicaneries'.[3] Georg Forster, on behalf of the municipal administration, complained that 'the countryman calls out, he is maltreated, he sells or slaughters his cattle, he sees want at his door'.[4] This failure of the French to win the allegiance of rural areas emerged most clearly during the elections of February 1793. Many of the Clubists sent to the villages to prepare public opinion were ejected forcibly.[5] Of the 900 communities in the

---

them that the main burden of making the revolution will fall. The citizens of Mainz have been declared by the true republicans to be cowardly and phlegmatic.' – Scheel, 'Spitzelberichte', p. 530.

[1] Chuquet, *Guerres*, vol. 7, p. 57. See also Friedrich Cotta's *Wie gut es die Leute am Rhein und der Mosel jetzt haben können* and Mathias Metternich's *Beschwerdeführung des Landmannes über die langsame Entschließung der Bürger zu Mainz*, reprinted in Träger, *Mainz zwischen Schwarz und Rot*, pp. 300–5, 315–23.
[2] Klein, *Geschichte von Mainz*, pp. 355–7. Bockenheimer, *Clubisten*, p. 16. Dumont, *Belagerung der Stadt Mainz*, pp. 58–9.
[3] Chuquet, *Guerres*, vol. 7, p. 80.
[4] Träger, *Mainz zwischen Schwarz und Rot*, pp. 336–47.
[5] Hoffmann, *Darstellung*, p. 488.

occupied zone only just over a hundred were persuaded to vote.[1] The attitude adopted by the local priest was usually of decisive importance. At Nackenheim, where the priest Melchior Arand supported the Revolution, the peasants voted for union with France, while at Bodenheim, only a few miles away, their compatriots faithfully followed the conservative views of their priest and curate.[2] It seems likely that more people voted for the Revolution in the country than in the town, but not in sufficient numbers to disturb the general pattern of rejection. Georg Böhmer, General Custine's German secretary, told the peasants that he had noted with sorrow that when their brothers the French arrived their only reaction had been to say: 'For seven years now we have sung German during the Holy Mass, but now that we are free we want to sing in Latin.'[3]

Although 'supported by bayonets', as Commissar Simon put it, the French nevertheless succeeded in securing the election of about a hundred deputies, and on 17 March 1793 the Rhenish-German National Convention opened in Mainz. Its members went to work with a will. On 18 March the territory under French occupation was declared to be a free, independent and indivisible state, whose laws were to be based on liberty and equality and whose only sovereign was the people. Three days later the delegates unanimously agreed to petition the National Convention in Paris for incorporation with the French Republic.[4] Three delegates – Forster, Lux and Patocki – were sent to Paris to announce the decision and argue in favour of its acceptance.[5]

The haste with which the Mainz Convention went to work was not caused only by revolutionary enthusiasm. Disputes between the Austrians and Prussians had delayed their advance on Mainz, but once they had

[1] Droz, *L'Allemagne et la Révolution française*, p. 210. This area, between Mainz–Bingen and Landau–Speyer, did not of course belong entirely to the Elector of Mainz, whose territory was confined to the villages surrounding Mainz and Bingen. The rest was ruled by the Elector of the Palatinate, the Duke of Zweibrücken, various Imperial Knights, the Prince-Bishops of Speyer and Worms and the Emperor, as Count von Falckenstein. In many communities a good deal of intimidation was required to persuade anyone to vote – Chuquet, *Guerres*, vol. 7, p. 106.

[2] Helmut Mathy, *Die Nackenheimer Revolution von 1792/1793*, Nackenheimer Heimatkundliche Schriftenreihe, vol. 14 (Nackenheim, 1967), Klein, *Geschichte von Mainz*, pp. 443–4. The French commissar in charge of the elections at Finthen complained that the resistance of the local priest, official and schoolmaster had seduced the people into rejecting the French – Bockenheimer, *Clubisten*, p. 337.

[3] G. W. Böhmer, *Epistel an die lieben Bauersleute zu Sarmsheim* (Mainz, 1792), p. 5. This refers to the disturbances caused by the Elector's attempt to introduce a German hymn book – See above, pp. 207–9.

[4] The text of these two decrees can be found in Hansen, *Quellen*, vol. 2, 798–800 or Träger, *Mainz zwischen Schwarz und Rot*, pp. 448–9, 464.

[5] Hansen, *Quellen*, vol. 2, pp. 812–14. In fact the National Convention agreed only to accept the 88 communities which had been represented in Mainz when the decision was taken. As the Austrians and Prussians soon reconquered the whole left bank of the Rhine, the distinction was rendered meaningless.

settled their problems in Eastern Europe, the fate of the city was sealed. The encirclement was completed on 14 April 1793, heavy siege artillery was brought up and on 18 June a massive bombardment began. For the next four weeks explosives and incendiaries rained down on the city. Hundreds of buildings were destroyed and the civilian population suffered terribly. Although the French garrison defended with great courage, making frequent sallies against their besiegers, their position was hopeless. When it became clear that there was no prospect of a relieving force even attempting to get through, the French commanders decided to surrender. After the terms of capitulation had been signed on 23 July, the remnants of the French army marched out, leaving 6,000 dead and 1,000 wounded behind them.[1]

The military success of the old régime was followed swiftly by political reconstruction. Although the French had made strenuous efforts to secure a safe-conduct for their German supporters, in the face of allied intransigence the Clubists were left to save themselves as best they could. Some succeeded in escaping disguised as French soldiers but most were rounded up by posses of Mainz citizens, beaten up and then handed over to the military authorities. They were then sent to prisons at Erfurt, Königstein and Ehrenbreitstein to await the Elector's retribution.[2] It proved to be surprisingly mild; no one was executed and no one was sentenced to a long term of imprisonment. The prisoners were offered the choice of emigrating to France or returning to their old homes. Although there was then a delay, because the French refused to recognise the surrender and release the Mainz hostages taken before the siege began, by February 1795 all the Clubists had been released and most had returned to their old occupations.[3]

The external framework of the old régime was also restored. The old administrative, judicial and ecclesiastical bodies were re-established and all measures taken under the French occupation, including marriages, were declared null and void.[4] The ordinary citizens were also eager to see

---

[1] *Mainz nach der Wiedereinnahme durch die verbündeten Deutschen im Sommer 1793* (Mentz, 1793), p. 76. The most satisfactory account of the siege is to be found in Chuquet, *Guerres*, vol. 7, pp. 144ff. See also, Goethe's day-by-day account, *Belagerung von Mainz*. Goethe was accompanying Duke Carl August of Weimar, who was attached to the Prussian army.

[2] For various reports on the arrest and imprisonment of the Clubists, see Hansen, *Quellen*, vol. 2, pp. 887–9. As the French troops were marching out, Goethe intervened personally to save some Clubists from the wrath of the mob – W. Andreas, 'Goethe und Carl August während der Belagerung von Mainz (1793)', *Sitzungsberichte der bayerischen Akademie* (1955), pp. 34–5.

[3] Chuquet, *Guerres*, vol. 7, pp. 276–7. Charles Este, an Englishman who visited Mainz in the autumn of 1793, commented that the Elector's leniency towards his political prisoners 'had continued the rational glory of Mainz!' – *A Journey in the Year 1793 through Flanders, Brabant and Germany to Switzerland* (London, 1795), p. 306.

[4] Träger, *Mainz zwischen Schwarz und Rot*, p. 532.

a return to normality and on 10 August 1793 a deputation waited on the Elector in Aschaffenburg, assuring him of their devotion and begging him to return.[1] In an effusive declaration to his 'dearest, best, most faithful and most upright citizens', Friedrick Karl agreed, promising that no effort would be spared to restore order and prosperity to the city. He concluded 'Place your trust in your father, who loves his children. I am much more happy to call myself your father than your prince.' His triumphal entry into the city he had abandoned so hastily a year before followed a month later. The entire population, drawn up in guilds, lined the streets to welcome him. A Neuwied newspaper described the scene:

At midday on 9 September the citizens gathered to greet with rapture their beloved Friedrich Karl. As his carriage approached, twenty members of the butchers' guild, dressed in white, jumped out, took the horses out of their shafts and pulled the carriage through the cheering crowds of happy people.

The 'Mainz Revolution' was over; perhaps its most fitting epitaph was provided by the Austrian ambassador Count Schlick, who reported to Prince Colloredo that:

Even if traces of discontent persist among certain sections of the population, they will be far outweighed by the need to make a living, for one begins to appreciate only too clearly how little the capital and its citizens can fend for themselves without the court and the numerous nobility attached to it.[2]

[1] Werner, *Der Dom von Mainz*, p. 424.
[2] Hansen, *Quellen*, vol. 2, p. 906. For a recent discussion of the literature on the French occupation of the city, see the long article by Heinrich Scheel, 'Die Mainzer Republik im Spiegel der deutschen Geschichtsschreibung', *Jahrbuch für Geschichte*, 4 (1969). The value of this very erudite piece is somewhat prejudiced however by Prof. Scheel's belief that only Marxists are able to understand events in Mainz during this period. Perhaps for this reason, he ignores all recent work conducted by non-Marxist historians.

Conclusion

Germany and the French Revolution

The last two decades of the *Reich* have been narrated, analysed and debated with unflagging zeal by historians of many nationalities. Other periods of German history, notably the foundation of the Second *Reich* and the infamies of the Third, have attracted even more attention, but rarely does a year pass without the publication of yet another substantial contribution to the period 1789–1806. The intense diplomatic activity and the ready availability of the appropriate sources have ensured that the *Reich*'s foreign relations during these years have been dealt with in particular detail. The massive general surveys of Sorel and von Sybel have been supplemented by innumerable studies of more limited scope, most notably that of von Srbik.[1] More recently, von Aretin has both synthesised and reinterpreted this massive weight of accumulated evidence, as well as adding the fruits of his own researches, in a work of impressive scholarship.[2] The unique greatness of German culture in this period has also inspired many distinguished works. Among others, Meinecke, Aris, Gooch, Droz and Valjavec have shown in considerable detail how German intellectuals responded to or reacted against the French Revolution, and events in their own country, during these years.[3]

For the social and economic structure of the *Reich*, 1789 was far less obviously of significance, and for this reason there are few social or economic studies directed specifically at this period. Indeed Friedrich Lütge's recent collection of essays – *Die wirtschaftliche Situation in Deutschland und Oesterreich um die Wende vom 18. zum 19. Jahrhundert* – was designed to fill

---

[1] A. Sorel, *L'Europe et la Révolution française* (8 vols, Paris, 1885–1905). H. von Sybel, *Geschichte der Revolutionszeit*, revised ed. (10 vols, Stuttgart, 1899–1900). H. von Srbik, *Das österreichische Kaisertum und das Ende des Heiligen Römischen Reiches 1804–1806* (Berlin, 1927).
[2] Karl Otmar Freiherr von Aretin, *Heiliges Römisches Reich 1776–1806* (2 vols, Wiesbaden, 1967). Vol. 2 includes a remarkably full bibliography, by far the best available for this period.
[3] Friedrich Meinecke, *Weltbürgertum und Nationalstaat; Werke*, ed. by Hans Herzfeld, Carl Hinrichs and Walther Hofer, vol. 5 (Munich, 1962). R. Aris, *History of Political Thought in Germany, 1789–1815* (London, 1936). G. P. Gooch, *Germany and the French Revolution* (Reprinted, London, 1965). Jacques Droz, *L'Allemagne et la Révolution française* (Paris, 1949). Fritz Valjavec, *Die Entstehung der politischen Strömungen in Deutschland 1770–1815* (Munich, 1951).

Conclusion

a gap.¹ Wilhelm Abel has investigated the agrarian situation, Stadelmann and Fischer the craft industries and Kuczynski the plight of the labouring poor, but when compared with England or France, German history in this sector appears distinctly underresearched.² Probably the most important reason for this relative neglect has been the *Reich's* territorial complexity, in turn responsible for the wide dispersal of sources and the difficulty of establishing general trends.

The fragmentary nature of the evidence, however, has acted as a positive incentive to political historians to examine phenomena at grass-roots level. In scores of monographs and the learned journals with which Germany has always abounded, both professional and amateur historians have kept up a large and steady output of local studies. Liesenfeld's work on Trier, Hölzle's on Württemberg, Grab's on Hamburg, Scheel's on the South-West and Kallenberg's on Sigmaringen – to name only a few of the more distinguished – have allowed a much clearer picture of German political life in general to be drawn.³ For the Rhineland, with which this present chapter will be chiefly concerned, Joseph Hansen's four massive volumes of source material retain their fundamental importance. Government papers, diplomatic reports, newspapers, memoirs, diaries, private correspondence, pamphlets and poems are all used in great profusion to show the state and development of public opinion during the last three decades of the century. Although Hansen's own interpretation emerges clearly, he is scrupulously fair in including all shades of contemporary opinion, from left to right.⁴ Yet now that different questions are being asked and fresh material has been unearthed, even this great work needs revision, or at

---

¹ Friedrich Lütge, *Die wirtschaftliche Situation in Deutschland und Oesterreich um die Wende vom 18. zum 19. Jahrhundert*, Forschungen zur Sozial- und Wirtschaftsgeschichte, 6 (Stuttgart, 1964).

² W. Abel, *Agrarkrisen und Agrarkonjunktur* (Berlin, 1966), *Geschichte der deutschen Landwirtschaft vom frühen Mittelalter bis zum 19. Jahrhundert* (Stuttgart, 1962). W. Fischer, *Handwerksrecht und Handwerkswirtschaft um 1800* (Berlin, 1955). R. Stadelmann and W. Fischer, *Die Bildungswelt des deutschen Handwerkers um 1800* (Berlin, 1955). J. Kuczynski, *Die Geschichte der Lage der Arbeiter in Deutschland von 1789 bis in die Gegenwart*, vol. 1 (Berlin, 1954).

³ F. Liesenfeld, *Clemens Wenzeslaus, der letzte Kurfürst von Trier, seine Landstände und die französische Revolution*, Westdeutsche Zeitschrift, Ergänzungsheft 17 (1912). E. Hölzle, *Das alte Recht und die Revolution: Eine politische Geschichte Württembergs in der Revolutionszeit 1789–1805* (Munich and Berlin, 1931). W. Grab, *Demokratische Strömungen in Hamburg und Schleswig-Holstein zur Zeit der ersten französischen Republik*, Veröffentlichungen des Vereins für Hamburgische Geschichte, 21 (Hamburg, 1966). Heinrich Scheel, *Süddeutsche Jakobiner* (Berlin, 1962). F. Kallenberg, 'Die Fürstentümer Hohenzollern im Zeitalter der französischen Revolution und Napoleons', *Zeitschrift für die Geschichte des Oberrheins*, 111 (1963).

⁴ J. Hansen, *Quellen zur Geschichte des Rheinlandes im Zeitalter der französischen Revolution* (4 vols, Bonn, 1931–8). This is more than can be said for most Marxist collections, which reprint only Jacobin publications. See, for example, H. Scheel, *Jakobinische Flugschriften aus dem deutschen Süden Ende des 18. Jahrunderts* (Berlin, 1965).

Germany and the French Revolution

least amplification. Given the amount of research conducted into individual areas during the past few decades, there is a pressing need for a new work of synthesis, but equally clearly this brief concluding chapter cannot supply it. All that can be done is to show that the experience of Mainz was not exceptional, but had much in common with Germany in general and the Rhineland in particular.

I

As the previous two chapters showed, two phases can be distinguished in the Mainz population's relationship with the Revolution: the more or less spontaneous disturbances of 1790, and the reaction to the presence of the French occupation–liberation forces in 1792–3. This distinction between radicalism bubbling up from below and radicalism directed from above can also be drawn in other areas which experienced the revolutionary armies directly. In one respect however Mainz differed from many of them: in not having a representative assembly which could give some sort of permanent and organised expression to public opinion. At first sight this is a difference of some importance, for in France only the Estates General could have united the conflicting forces of economic misery, social frustration and political ambition long enough to bring down the old régime. Yet although the German *Landstände* adopted a more aggressive outlook after 1789, nowhere did they seek to follow the revolutionary example of the French.[1] In the Electorates of Cologne and Trier, for example, the commoners in the estates pressed for an end to fiscal exemptions, but did not proceed to their own version of the Tennis Court Oath when rebuffed. The Trier estates even voted their ruler a substantial sum to allow him to send a contingent of 1,200 men to assist the allied invasion of France in 1792.[2]

Thus the constituted bodies would not or could not give a lead. There were growing signs however that the people they were supposed to represent would take the initiative themselves. In 1791 the French administration in the *Haut Rhin* department expressed the opinion that it was only a matter of time before the Germans living on the left bank of the Rhine threw off the yoke of tyranny: 'The people there are entirely for us... A proclamation which announced to the people that we wished to treat them as brothers...would make all of them decide to join themselves to

---

[1] F. L. Carsten, *Princes and Parliaments in Germany from the fifteenth to the eighteenth century* (Oxford, 1959). Of the Estates in Hessen he wrote: 'The new spirit...was too weak to effect any change in the distribution of power. At the last Diet of the *ancien régime*, ten years after the outbreak of the French Revolution, not the demands of the burghers, but the decisions of the landgrave carried the day, and the system of quasi absolute government prevailed' – p. 190.
[2] Hansen, *Quellen*, vol. 2, p. 309.

us.'[1] Although over-optimistic, this prediction was based on more than wishful thinking, for the two years since the fall of the Bastille had seen serious disturbances in many German towns. Their frequency was directly related to their proximity to France. In the County of Saarbrücken, for example, on the Western periphery of the *Reich*, the government was forced to make important concessions to the dissidents. After deputies from the towns of Saarbrücken and St Johann had organised popular assemblies throughout the province, a list of forty demands was sent to the Duke. Unable to mobilise sufficient repressive force, he was obliged to concede.[2] The demonstrators' success in extracting at least temporary concessions by their demonstrations was repeated in several other Rhenish cities, notably Trier, Koblenz, Cologne and Mainz.[3]

Rural areas were also affected. Reports flowed in from all over Germany, again particularly from the western areas, of refusals to pay tithes or to perform the *corvée*, deliberate contravention of the game and forestry laws and demonstrations against grain dealers suspected of hoarding.[4] In February 1792 Count Philipp Cobenzl observed gloomily that the mood of the people, especially in the frontier regions, was such that in the event of war the Austrian and Prussian soldiers would find themselves fighting their compatriots as well as the French.[5]

For all the wailing of the Germans and the great expectations of the French, these individual disturbances did not usher in a general upheaval. Although in France town and country, peasant and sansculotte, bourgeois and aristocrat did not consciously cooperate, their discontent did coincide. This was not the case in the *Reich*. The authorities were always able to deal with the insurrections one by one; never were the forces of repression stretched beyond breaking point. Even if the local difficulty proved too great for the local troops available, time was bought by tactical concessions, which were then promptly renounced when reinforcements arrived. This was the pattern of events in Saarbrücken, Trier, Koblenz, Mainz and many other cities. Paradoxically, the forces of repression at the disposal of the princes proved to be better suited for internal policing than did the French army. They were not concentrated in great barracks or frontier

---

[1] P. Sagnac, *Le Rhin français pendant la Révolution française et l'Empire* (Paris, 1917), p. 58. This verdict was echoed by Austrian observers – Hansen, *Quellen*, vol. 2, p. 119.

[2] F. Ecker, *Das Saargebiet und die französische Revolution 1789–1801*, Mitteilungen des historischen Vereins für die Saargegend, 18 (1929), pp. 27–33.

[3] W. Lüdtke, 'Der Kampf zwischen Oesterreich und Preußen um die Vorherrschaft im "Reiche" und die Auflösung des Fürstenbundes (1789/91)', *Mitteilungen des oesterreichischen Instituts für Geschichtsforschung*, 45 (1931), p. 77. Hansen, *Quellen*, vol. 1, pp. 451, 461, 469. On events in Mainz, see above, Chapter 7.

[4] Lüdtke, *Der Kampf zwischen Oesterreich und Preußen*, pp. 77–8. Hansen, *Quellen*, vol. 1, pp. 440–1. Hansen documents in considerable detail the course of a dispute over forestry rights at Boppard, in the Electorate of Trier. See the index in vol. 2 for references.

[5] Ibid., vol. 2, p. 27, n. 2.

towns but dispersed throughout the *Reich*, for even the tiniest principality maintained a military force of some description. Thus when trouble began the authorities could act immediately. If their resources were inadequate, help came promptly from neighbours anxious lest the infection should spread.[1] Indeed it was possible for the prince concerned to obtain from the *Reichskammergericht* a directive ordering the local *Kreis* to provide assistance. Only in the case of Liège did this counter-revolutionary cooperation break down temporarily, because the Prussians were more concerned to embarrass the Austrians than to restore order.[2]

The authorities' task was made a great deal easier by the insurgents' timidity. Their demands were limited, specific and invariably nonpolitical. The abolition of the tithes, the *corvées* or fiscal exemptions were of course radical changes, but could be conceded without endangering the system as a whole. Unlike their French equivalents, the individual *cahiers de doléances* were not taken to a German Estates General to acquire cumulative strength, to be given an ideological basis and to develop a revolutionary impact. Indeed, many of the disputes had a distinctly archaic flavour, especially in the Free Imperial Cities (*Reichsstädte*). Here struggles for control between the patriciate and the guilds had been a familiar feature of municipal politics for many centuries. Nor should the numerical disparity delude one into assuming that these represented an assault by 'democratic' or 'progressive' forces on a 'conservative' oligarchy. In Cologne it was the patrician *Rat* which introduced religious toleration and the guild-dominated *Deputatschaft* which rejected it.[3] Similarly, in Aachen the division between the 'Old' and the 'New' parties was not ideological but a simple contest between 'ins' and 'outs'.[4]

Nor should a natural tendency to find violent change more interesting than stability lure one into supposing that all Germany was in flames. Most areas in the interior continued as they had done since time immemorial. The predictions of imminent dissolution stemmed more from alarmism or wishful thinking than the actual pattern of events. Even in the frontier regions of the West there were large oases of calm. The council of the Electorate of Cologne reported to their ruler on 6 February 1792 that 'up till the present time no incident has occurred in your territories which could have given rise even to the remotest fear of public disorders'.[5] In another large and important state, the Duchy of Württemberg, there were unrealised fears of bread riots, but nothing more.[6]

---

[1] See above, p. 255.
[2] See above, pp. 251–2.
[3] Hansen, *Quellen*, vol. 1, pp. 209ff.
[4] Ibid., pp. 110ff.
[5] Max Braubach, *Maria Theresias jüngster Sohn Max Franz, Letzter Kurfürst von Köln und Fürstbischof von Münster* (Vienna and Munich, 1964), p. 275.
[6] Hölzle, *Das alte Recht*, p. 91.

Conclusion

Nevertheless it is clear that the first phase of the revolution in France made a powerful impact on both political thought and political action in Germany. Thinkers hitherto inexperienced in political speculation found themselves elaborating a theoretical basis to their immediate reaction to events in France. Rulers turned their backs on the Enlightenment in favour of conservatism and repression, while dissidents took heart. Yet when every disturbance has been catalogued and every forecast of revolution noted, there remains the inescapable fact that not one of the hundreds of régimes in the *Reich* was toppled by the unaided efforts of its subjects. Even the briefest of comparisons between France and Germany in 1789 suggests that this should not be surprising.

Perhaps most important was the fact that throughout the *Reich*, unlike France, the privileged orders lined up four-square in defence of the established order. The German nobles did not imitate the lemming-like plunge to destruction of their French colleagues, for the good reason that they were much more closely associated with the political establishment.[1] The greatest magnates, from whom most unrest could have been expected, were virtually sovereign rulers already and thus without ambition in this sphere. The same applied not only to the many lesser princes with direct representation in the *Reichstag*, but also to the scores of Imperial Counts with indirect representation and the hundreds of Imperial Knights with no representation. Thus the most important sections of the German nobility could not usher in a *révolte nobiliaire* because they had no one to revolt against but themselves. Only if the Emperor or the various imperial institutions had exercised real power could they have provided a focus for aristocratic hostility.

The indigenous (*landständisch*) nobles – i.e. those who were the subjects of a prince and not directly subject to the Emperor – could not supply the missing aristocratic élan, because in most cases they formed a service, not a *rentier* nobility, and had a vested interest in the continued existence of their employer. During the previous two centuries their relationship with the prince had changed significantly. Although the growth of absolutism had destroyed their political influence, at the same time the growth of bureaucracy, courts and standing armies had offered the nobles greatly expanded opportunities for employment. As a result there was neither the occasion nor the means for an 'aristocratic revolt' in the *Reich*

---

[1] In the last two or three years the notion of an 'aristocratic resurgence' in France in the late eighteenth century has been subjected to some searching criticism – see especially, François Furet, 'Le catéchisme révolutionnaire', *Annales, Économies, Sociétés, Civilisations*, 26, 2 (1971) and William Doyle, 'Was there an aristocratic reaction in pre-revolutionary France?' *Past & Present*, 57 (1972). It is not denied however that such aristocratic bodies as the Parlement of Paris and such individual nobles as Lafayette and Mirabeau led the first assault on the French monarchy.

in the late eighteenth century. The two most successful campaigns waged by German corporate groups against their ruler during this period were waged by the estates of Württemberg and Mecklenburg; the nobility were represented in neither of them.¹

Only in the very largest states – Prussia and the Habsburg Monarchy – could a confrontation of the French variety occur. In Prussia however Frederick the Great had reversed his father's hostility to the nobility. Throughout his reign he remained faithful to the principle enunciated in his Political Testament of 1752: 'A sovereign should regard it as his duty to protect the nobility, who are the first ornament of his crown and the lustre of his army.'² He reserved to them the Officer Corps and the higher ranks of the civil service, he made them all sorts of grants for the improvement of their estates and made no serious attempt to disturb their control of their serfs.³ The situation in the Habsburg Monarchy was of course very different. Even Maria Theresa succeeded in annoying her nobles by her fiscal and administrative reforms. In the more peripheral provinces natural aristocratic aversion to monarchical absolutism and centralisation was given a powerful radical twist by ethnic differences. Joseph II's administrative reorganisation and proposed fiscal reforms roused even the nobility of the central provinces from their customary torpor and brought their more volatile Magyar colleagues to the brink of revolt. Joseph's death in 1790 however improved the situation overnight. Using a combination of diplomacy, concessions and the threat of a popular insurrection, his successor Leopold succeeded in placating the opposition.⁴ Yet even had the Magyar threat materialised, it seems unlikely that their example would have been copied by the other Habsburg provinces, let alone other areas of the *Reich*. If revolution were to come to Germany it would have to come via the unaided efforts of the Third Estate.

II

The literary response of literate Germans to events in France has been the subject of many long and often distinguished studies,⁵ here only the more general characteristics can be identified. In particular there is unanimity that the initial response was overwhelmingly favourable. During the months

---

[1] F. L. Carsten, 'The German Estates in the eighteenth century', *Recueil de la Société Jean Bodin pour l'histoire comparative des institutions*, 25.
[2] G. B. Volz, *Die politischen Testamente Friedrichs des Großen* (Berlin, 1920), p. 26.
[3] Otto Hintze, *Die Hohenzollern und ihr Werk*, 8th ed. (Berlin, 1916), pp. 346, 385–6, 397–9. For a more recent account of Frederick's relations with his nobility, see H. Rosenberg, *Bureaucracy, Aristocracy and Autocracy: The Prussian Experience, 1660–1815* (Boston, 1958), especially pp. 159–61.
[4] A. Wandruszka, *Leopold II* (2 vols, Vienna and Munich, 1965), vol. 2, pp. 249–56.
[5] See above, p. 303.

Conclusion

which followed the fall of the Bastille every imaginable form of imagery was enlisted to give expression to the very genuine enthusiasm experienced. Many of those who later relapsed into indifference or changed over to hostility started out as admirers.[1] From supporting violent upheaval abroad to advocating or working for it in one's own country however has always been a giant step, and it certainly proved to be too far for most German intellectuals. There was a good deal of truth in the sneering comment of the Hanoverian conservative Brandes: 'those who are most favourably disposed towards the French Revolution are also those who are most opposed to it in their own country'.[2] A view frequently encountered held that whereas the total corruption of the established order in France had made revolution there inevitable, in Germany different conditions required a different solution. What the French had had to seize with force, the Germans had been receiving, were receiving and would continue to receive through the voluntary action of their enlightened princes.[3] Continuing reform, not revolution, was the answer. The following comment from A. L. Schlözer was typical:

Every honourable German writer will agree that the Revolution has done good to the whole race. It has taught in practice what we Germans have long known in theory, that the Sovereign is responsible to his people. They will also agree that it was a necessity for France, where the government possessed no ears for the Rights of Man or the voice of the age; and, further, that no such Revolution is in store for Germany. Abuses will be abolished by reasonable inquiries, not by gunpowder. Mild governments, aided by a free press, should bring us the same results piecemeal.[4]

Common to almost all German observers was the mistaken belief that the French revolutionaries were more concerned with the implementation of a fixed programme than with the question of how political power should be exercised. Unconcerned with constitutional forms themselves, German intellectuals failed to appreciate that not everyone would be obsessed with ends to the exclusion of means. They thus experienced no difficulty in reconciling their admiration of the Revolution in France with their trust in Enlightened Absolutism as the best system of government for their own states. The Prussian minister Hertzberg, for example, observed that the principles underlying a state ruled by an enlightened absolutist and a liberal state were identical, for in both reason not caprice governed.[5] As

[1] Gooch, *Germany and the French Revolution*, pp. 39–47. K. Epstein, *The Genesis of German Conservatism* (Princeton, 1966), pp. 435–6.
[2] Jacques Droz, 'L'Allemagne et la Révolution française', *Revue Historique* 198 (1947), p. 163.
[3] Epstein, *German Conservatism*, p. 464.
[4] Quoted in Gooch, *Germany and the French Revolution*, pp. 74–5.
[5] Droz, *L'Allemagne et la Révolution française*, p. 80. For other examples, see Ibid., p. 36; Gooch, *Germany and the French Revolution*, pp. 43, 75; Hansen, *Quellen*, vol. 1, pp. 582–5.

this comment suggests, the unpolitical character of German thought could not be changed overnight, not even by as dramatic an episode as the French Revolution. The following forthright comment from Friedrich Schlegel, for example, has an unmistakably German flavour:

> The French Revolution, Fichte's *Wissenschaftslehre* and Goethe's *Wilhelm Meister* are the greatest developments (*Tendenzen*) of our age. Anyone who takes offence at considering these of comparable importance, or anyone who considers only noisy and material revolutions to be of importance, has not elevated himself to the point where he contemplates the history of mankind as a whole.[1]

Frequently this concern to pay due attention to mankind's spiritual progress led to a condescending attitude towards the French and their involvement with the squalid world of appearances. The Germans, it was felt, had progressed beyond such ephemera to the only kind of revolution worth having – 'the revolution in the mind'.[2]

Thus most Germans qualified their support for the Revolution with reluctance to see it spread across the Rhine. This rather ambiguous phase was of short duration: as the radical drift of the Revolution gathered momentum, they began to have second thoughts. Less than three years after the storming of the Bastille, majority opinion among the literate classes of the *Reich* had acquired a distinctly anti-revolutionary bias. A. L. Schlözer, who wielded considerable influence over public opinion through his *Staatsanzeigen*, had greeted the Revolution with the words: 'How wonderful that one of the greatest nations in the world, and unquestionably the most cultured, has thrown off the yoke of tyranny. God's angels in Heaven must, for a certainty, have sounded off a *Te Deum laudamus* in jubilation.' By the end of the year however, continuing disorder had convinced him that the mob rule of the 'democratic vermin' was even less desirable than the *ancien régime*.[3] Many of his compatriots found themselves forced down the same road of disillusionment, albeit at a less precipitous pace. For some the abortive flight of the French royal family to Varennes in June 1791, which demonstrated finally that the King was a captive, was decisive; others could not stomach the executions of Louis XVI and Marie Antoinette.[4]

Given their earlier inability to appreciate that the revolutionaries were more concerned with a transfer of power than with the introduction of an enlightened programme, this progression was not surprising. Characteristically, Wieland lamented in 1791 that the Revolution had *become political*.[5]

[1] Quoted in Epstein, *German Conservatism*, p. 449.
[2] R. R. Palmer, *The Age of the Democratic Revolution* (2 vols, Princeton, 1959 and 1964), vol. 2, ch. 14. See also above, p. 294.
[3] Valjavec, *Die Entstehung der politischen Strömungen*, p. 157.
[4] Ibid.
[5] Droz, *L'Allemagne et la Révolution française*, p. 325.

Conclusion

Like so many of his fellow-countrymen he judged the Revolution from a strictly ethical viewpoint: the French, he held, had put the political cart in front of the moral horse: 'One must just go on preaching, till men listen, that mankind can only grow happier by becoming more reasonable and more moral... My eternal refrain is that reform must begin not with constitutions, but with the individual.'[1] Moral disapprobation of French 'excesses' became a common feature of German pronouncements. Lichtenberg gave this attitude its most succinct and witty expression when he wrote that in France liberty and equality had been elevated to the status of the eleventh commandment by men determined to discard the other ten.[2] The definitive statement came from Schiller in a celebrated letter to Duke Friedrich Christian von Augustenberg:

> The attempt of the French people to stand up for their sacred human rights and to win political freedom has only served to uncover their incapacity and unworthiness, and hurled back into barbarism and slavery not only this wretched people but with them a considerable part of Europe as well. Although the time was most favourable, it found only a corrupt and unworthy generation who neither appreciated nor knew how to make use of it. The use they made and are making of this great gift of providence proves incontrovertibly that the human race has not yet outgrown the guardianship of the authorities, that the liberal régime of reason comes too early when men can only barely control their brutal animal instincts and that he who lacks so much that appertains to *human (menschlich)* freedom is not yet mature enough for *civil (bürgerlich)* freedom.[3]

The concern with religion and ethics, which had distinguished the *Aufklärung*,[4] ensured that the educated members of the German Third Estate viewed the Revolution from a perspective which was very different from that of the French, or indeed any other nation. This applied particularly to those who had imbibed the philosophy of Kant, by 1789 a large number.[5] Kant remained loyal to the Revolution even after the Terror, although his lack of interest in constitutional forms enabled him to combine this with an equally sincere loyalty to the King of Prussia.[6] Even those who interpreted Kant in a revolutionary fashion, such as Georg Forster and Georg Rebmann, were increasingly disappointed by French 'immorality'. Rebmann wrote dejectedly from Paris that it was a great pity that the French rather than the Germans had initiated the Revolution, because the latter

---

[1] Gooch, *Germany and the French Revolution*, p. 152.
[2] Droz, *L'Allemagne et la Révolution française*, p. 352. For a full discussion of Lichtenberg's attitude to the Revolution see F. H. Mautner, *Lichtenberg: Geschichte seines Geistes* (Berlin, 1968), pp. 457–70.
[3] *Schillers Briefe*, ed. F. Jonas, vol. 3 (Stuttgart, Leipzig, Berlin and Vienna, n.d.), p. 333.
[4] See above, pp. 23–32.
[5] Droz, *L'Allemagne et la Révolution française*, *passim*. The importance of ethical systems in determining German responses to the Revolution is a constant theme of this book and is discussed in considerable and convincing detail.
[6] Ibid., p. 158.

were so much more profoundly moral.¹ All Kantians joined with theorists of a more traditional bent in maintaining that the creation of a *Rechtsstaat* – a state in which the sovereignty of the law prevailed – was more important than the creation of a democracy, in which the sovereignty of the people prevailed.²

Most German intellectuals did not view freedom in political terms as the right to participate in government, but in intellectual or spiritual terms, as the right to pursue their own individual self-cultivation (*Bildung*) without the interference of the authorities.³ Although the Revolution had destroyed some of the more odious forms of state interference in France, it had also brought with it violence and uncertainty, conditions particularly unconducive to *Bildung*. The Olympian figures of the *Aufklärung* found the hurly-burly of everyday politics not only distasteful but self-defeating. Goethe gave his usual magisterial expression to this attitude in three of his *Xenien*:

> Was das Luthertum war, ist jetzt das Franzthum in diesen
> Letzten Tagen, es drängt ruhige Bildung zurück.
>
> Deutschland? Aber wo liegt es? Ich weiß das Land
>   nicht zu finden,
> Wo das gelehrte beginnt, hört das politische auf.
>
> Zur Nation euch zu bilden, ihr hoffet es, Deutsche vergebens.
> Bildet, ihr könnt es, dafür freier zu Menschen euch aus.⁴

The rapture with which the Revolution was received in most quarters should not obscure the fact that there was a small but important group which condemned it from the start. Valjavec in particular has demonstrated that conservatism in Germany did not stem from opposition to the Revolution but from opposition to the Enlightenment and predated 1789 by many years.⁵ Groups such as those around Princess Gallitzin in West-

---

[1] Droz, *Revue Historique*, 198 (1947), p. 169. See also above, p. 298. This attitude was shared by those Germans who later in the 1790s preferred a 'Cisrhenan Republic' to annexation by France – J. Droz, *La pensée politique et morale des Cisrhenans* (Paris, 1940). German criticisms of the Revolution were derived from a misunderstanding of its nature, as Meinecke pointed out: 'What happened in France after 1789 was interpreted in Germany not as the work of historically conditioned and entirely concrete forces, but as the work, whether for good or ill, of the freely creating human spirit'; *Weltbürgertum und Nationalstaat*, p. 35.

[2] Droz, *L'Allemagne et la Révolution française*, pp. 47ff.

[3] For a particularly interesting discussion of the importance of *Bildung* in German culture in the modern period, see W. H. Bruford, *Culture and Society in Classical Weimar 1775–1806* (Cambridge, 1962).

[4] J. W. von Goethe, *Xenien*, Goethes Werke, hrsg. im Auftrage der Großherzogin Sophie von Sachsen, vol. 5(1) (Weimar, 1893), p. 218. What Lutheranism was, Frenchism has become, it drives back quiet cultivation. / Germany? but where is it? I don't know how to find the country; where the realm of learning begins, the political stops. / Germans, you hope in vain to form yourselves into a nation. Instead, for this you can do, develop yourselves into freer human beings.

[5] Valjavec, *Die Entstehung der politischen Strömungen*, passim.

phalia or Count Reventlow in Schleswig, journals such as Feller's *Journal Historique et Littéraire*, Goldhagen's *Religionsjournal* and the Augsburg Jesuits' *Neueste Sammlung* and individual writers such as Möser, Zimmermann, Rehberg and Brandes, although they all spoke with different voices, laid the basis for the more coherent counter-revolutionary programme which developed in the 1790s. More often than not the starting-point was religious. Protestants and Catholics alike were repelled by the anti-clericalism of the Revolution. In view of their previous record of voluntary subjection to the Prussian state, it was not surprising that the Pietists were in the vanguard of the counter-revolution.[1] Even most of those Catholics who before 1789 had outraged conservative opinion by advocating and introducing enlightened reforms had no doubts about the Revolution's impiety. Without exception, the entire German episcopate and their vicariates made their opposition known from the start.[2] Throughout the 1790s publicists of both denominations maintained a barrage of anti-revolutionary propaganda, usually combining calls for the strengthening of the throne–altar alliance with emotional appeals to the ordinary citizens' respect for religion.[3]

The most popular line of attack proceeded from disapproval of the very concept of revolution. The most influential exponents of this view were August Wilhelm Rehberg and Ernst Brandes, whose Hanoverian employment and first-hand knowledge of England made them sympathetic to gradual evolution. Their chief criticism of the Revolution concerned its supposed attachment to abstract principles. These were held responsible for a doctrinaire approach to political problems, which had had no difficulty in destroying the old régime but had found nothing durable to put in its place. Although none of the Hanoverian conservatives were opposed to change in principle, they held that reforms could only be introduced gradually and only within the context of a country's traditions.[4] They arrived at this position independently of Burke, but of course they gave his *Reflections on the Revolution in France* a warm welcome. Although this kind of attack on the Revolution was encountered especially often in the North-West, where English influence was strongest, as events in France took on a more radical complexion it became correspondingly more popular elsewhere in the *Reich*. These various anti-revolutionary strands did not acquire really potent political expression until

---

[1] Droz, *L'Allemagne et la Révolution française*, pp. 420–30. See above, pp. 26–9.
[2] Only a handful of Catholic *Aufklärer* embraced the principles of the Revolution, the most celebrated being Eulogius Schneider of Cologne and Anton Dorsch of Mainz. See above, pp. 276–7, and Hansen, *Quellen*, vol. 1, pp. 346–62, 571–5, 615–19, 729–31, 827–30, 856, 967–9, vol. 3, p. 105. Schneider was guillotined in Paris in 1794.
[3] Valjavec, *Die Entstehung der politischen Strömungen*, pt. 4, ch. 3.
[4] Gooch, *Germany and the French Revolution*, ch. 3. Droz, *L'Allemagne et la Révolution française*, pt. 4.

they re-emerged after the turn of the century in the guise of militant Francophobic nationalism, but they had been active on a local level long before that.

Although simply to describe literate commoners' responses to the Revolution goes a long way towards explaining their origins, one or two specific points need to be emphasised. In the first place it was of crucial importance that there was no national capital in which ambitious members of the Third Estate could gather. Scattered throughout the hundreds of university towns and administrative centres of the *Reich*, they could not feel part of the mainstream of politics, because no such mainstream existed. As Madame de Staël observed, the absence of a capital meant that 'the majority of writers and thinkers work in isolation, or surrounded only by a little circle which they dominate'.[1] This situation was not altered by the events of 1789. Although more intellectuals than ever before acquired an interest in politics, their disunity could not be overcome. In France there were many deep divisions within the Third Estate, but the simple ability of their delegates to meet in the Estates General gave them sufficient organisation and solidarity to bring down the old régime. In Germany no such revolutionary élan could develop: political fragmentation proved to be a source of strength for the *status quo*.[2]

Yet the stability of the German establishment cannot be ascribed simply to the disunion of its potential opponents. The whole development of German thought in the eighteenth century and before had been characterised by submission to authority, a lack of interest in the ways in which power was exercised and a predilection for religious and metaphysical problems.[3] With an increasing but still insignificant number of exceptions, this continued to be the case during the Revolutionary and Napoleonic periods. Madame de Staël, the most intelligent of foreign observers, constantly returned to this theme:

The love of freedom is not developed in the Germans; neither by deprivation nor enjoyment have they learnt the value that should be attached to it...One does not believe in the need for constitutional defences when one does not see any aggressors... They combine a great boldness of thought with a most obedient character...The enlightened men in Germany engage in lively disputes on theoretical matters and do not tolerate any restrictions on this activity; but they hand over entirely voluntarily to the powers-that-be all the practical aspects of life...In Saxony there is a completely unlimited freedom of the press; but it does not pose a danger for the government because the interest of the men of letters is not directed towards scrutiny of political

---

[1] Mme de Staël, *De l'Allemagne* (2 vols, Paris, 1958), vol. 1, p. 38.
[2] An Austrian official argued against the transformation of the Habsburg Monarchy into a unitary state, because 'the quick success of the Revolution in France had been due to the uniformity of the population' – Henry E. Strakosch, *State Absolutism and the Rule of Law: the Struggle for the Codification of Civil law in Austria 1753–1811* (Sydney, 1967), p. 168.
[3] See above, pt. 1, *passim*.

institutions; isolation makes them devote themselves to abstract speculation or poetry... German writers concern themselves only with theories, scholarship and literary and philosophical research; and the powers-that-be have nothing to fear from any of that. Moreover, although the government of Saxony is not free *de jure*, that is to say it is not representative, it is so *de facto* by virtue of the customs of the country and the moderation of its rulers.[1]

She concluded by likening the German conception of truth to the statue of Mercury which had neither hands with which to grasp nor legs with which to walk.

Although Madame de Staël's taste for lively metaphor perhaps led her to exaggerate the German intellectuals' impotence, her comments accord with the evidence of their own observations and behaviour. As she suggested, they felt that politics could safely be left to the princes, while they themselves got on with the more important intellectual business. The late Rudolf Stadelmann in particular argued forcefully and convincingly that the French Revolution was not repeated in Germany because most of the component parts of the *Reich* had experienced enlightened absolutism.[2] Just as most contemporary Englishmen took pride in their parliamentary system and declined to experiment with French democratic forms, so did most Germans remain loyal to their traditional forms of government. The French Enlightenment was born out of the chaos and misery of the closing years of Louis XIV's reign[3] and never lost its hostility to the established order; the German *Aufklärung* was born out of an alliance of academics, administrators and princes and never discarded its support of the established order.[4]

This is not the place to rake over once again the motivation of the reforms of the princes, but their reality and ubiquity can hardly be in doubt. Although illustrations are usually drawn from Austria or Prussia and such smaller principalities as Baden, Weimar and Cologne, few areas of the *Reich* escaped the attentions of their rulers. Even those princes usually singled out as examples of corruption could not resist the fashion for re-

---

[1] de Staël, *De l'Allemagne*, vol. 1, pp. 58–62, 206–7.
[2] R. Stadelmann, *Deutschland und Westeuropa* (Schloss Laupheim, Württemberg, 1948). His arguments have been supported recently by von Aretin: *Heiliges Römisches Reich*, vol. 1, p. 107. His observations have aroused the ire of Marxist and other historians of the radical left, who interpret them as a 'reactionary' denigration of the German Jacobins. See, for a particularly intemperate example, Heinrich Scheel, 'Probleme der deutsch-französischen Beziehungen 1789–1830', *Zeitschrift für Geschichtswissenschaft*, 17 (1970), p. 163. For a recent example emanating from the school led by Walter Grab, see W. Dittler, 'Johann Gottlieb Bärstecher alias Müller, Verleger und revolutionärer Demokrat im Zeitalter der französischen Revolution', *Jahrbuch des Instituts für deutsche Geschichte Tel Aviv*, 1 (1972), pp. 77–9.
[3] H. Rothkrug, *Opposition to Louis XIV: The Political and Social Origins of the French Enlightenment* (Princeton, 1966).
[4] See above, pt. 1, *passim*.

Germany and the French Revolution

form. Duke Karl of Zweibrücken, the very personification of hedonism, made a number of attempts to improve the lot of his peasants and was rewarded by rural tranquillity after 1789.[1] Landgraf Frederick II of Hesse Kassel, notorious for the sale of his subjects into British military service, was also personally responsible for an impressive programme of agricultural, judicial, social and educational reform.[2] It should also be remembered that civil servants, or indeed professional men of any description, could move elsewhere with relative ease if they found their ruler's policies repugnant.

III

If the literate members of the Third Estate could not supply the revolutionary leadership, it was even less likely to come from below. The mere territorial complexity of the *Reich* made any organisation of the dissidents virtually impossible. Although in some Free Imperial Cities (*Reichsstädte*) there were spasms of unrest, no general conflagration was ignited. The towns ruled by princes remained quiet.[3] In a recent study of the German 'Home Towns', a category he defined as including all communities which were not obviously peasant villages or great cities, Mack Walker has written 'there was no serious dissent and the community worked smoothly on the whole'.[4] Politically and culturally isolated, with an economy which operated almost entirely for its own inhabitants and the surrounding countryside, the average German town in the late eighteenth century was undynamic, parochial, but stable.[5] The new impulses which filtered through did nothing to disturb the general tranquillity: 'Only in its moderate and moralised form was the Enlightenment able to touch the German petty bourgeois; Gellert and Rabener, Salzmann and Campe, but not Voltaire, became his tutors. The light of reason shone in on the good old Lutheran domestic piety, but it sought to illuminate, not dissolve it.'[6] There was little or no contact between the merchants, manufacturers and craftsmen of the Third Estate on the one hand and the professional, academic and bureaucratic groups on the other. Membership of the reading-clubs (*Lesegesellschaften*), for example, which appeared in so

---

[1] E. Weis, *Montgelas 1759–1799: Zwischen Reform und Revolution* (Munich, 1971), pp. 170–1.
[2] O. Berge, *Die Innenpolitik des Landgrafen Friedrich II von Hessen-Kassel* (Unpublished dissertation, Mainz, 1952), pp. 118, 195, 220, 259.
[3] H. Mauersberg, *Wirtschafts- und Sozialgeschichte zentraleuropäischer Städte in neuerer Zeit* (Göttingen, 1960), p. 114.
[4] Mack Walker, *German Home Towns: Community, State, and General Estate 1648–1871* (Cornell, 1971), p. 57. He made a 'conservative estimate' that in 1800 there were some 4,000 'Home Towns' with a total population of about seven million.
[5] Ibid., pt. 1, *passim*.
[6] Stadelmann and Fischer, *Die Bildungswelt des deutschen Handwerkers*, p. 199.

Conclusion

many German cities in the second half of the century, was drawn almost entirely from the latter.[1]

In those areas of the *Reich* occupied by the French after 1792 the craftsmen were given the opportunity to make the acquaintance of radical political doctrines through the revolutionary clubs. It was an opportunity very few of them showed any inclination to take; indeed the attitude of the great majority of the German *Handwerkerstand* towards the Revolution was one of at least indifference and more often than not outright hostility. The revolutionaries' dislike of all corporate groups, and in particular their abolition of guilds, struck at the very heart of urban life in Germany. Because the guilds there were so much stronger than in France, resistance o economic liberalism was correspondingly more tenacious. Not only masters, but also journeymen and apprentices formed a united front against innovation.[2] Although this pattern applied to most towns and cities in the *Reich*, special local conditions could give rise to tension. In Vienna in the late 1780s, for example, the unsuccessful war against the Turks, the unpopular conscription and high food prices created a tense situation superficially similar to that in France. Ernst Wangermann has discovered that a number of ordinary craftsmen were receptive to radical ideas.[3] Yet even here the trouble did not progress beyond bread-riots.

Any revolution, if it were to be successful, needed literate leadership and the support of the towns. But its ultimate fate could be decided only in the countryside, for the very obvious reason that it was here that the great majority of Germans lived. Any attempt to explain why rural Germany was much more peaceful than rural France during the 1780s and 1790s is made particularly difficult by the great variety of conditions which existed in the *Reich*. The distinction between the *Gutsherrschaft* of the territories East of the Elbe and the *Grundherrschaft* of the Central and Western regions is too well known to need further discussion. These two basic categories moreover harboured all sorts of sub-divisions; Friedrich Lütge, for example, identified five main types of *Grundherrschaft* and still felt obliged to add a further group for 'special types'.[4] Yet although any generalisation must be riddled with exceptions, certain broad lines of difference can be charted.

In the first place it now seems apparent that rural Germany was better able to absorb the strains imposed by a growing population and the

[1] K. Gerteis, 'Bildung und Revolution: Die deutschen Lesegesellschaften am Ende des 18. Jahrhunderts', *Archiv für Kulturgeschichte*, 53 (1971), p. 133. See above, pp. 202–3, 296.
[2] T. S. Hamerow, *Restoration, Revolution, Reaction – Economics and Politics in Germany 1815–1871* (Princeton, 1958), p. 22. Walker, *German Home Towns*, p. 94.
[3] E. Wangermann, *From Joseph II to the Jacobin Trials*, 2nd ed. (Oxford, 1969), ch. 1.
[4] F. Lütge, *Geschichte der deutschen Agrarverfassung vom frühen Mittelalter bis zum 19. Jahrhundert* (Stuttgart, 1963), pp. 159–65.

pressure on land which inevitably followed. Throughout the eighteenth century there was a great deal of internal migration, away from the overpopulated South, Centre and West to the under-populated East. During Frederick the Great's reign, between 300,000 and 350,000 immigrants settled in Prussia, most of them on reclaimed land; by 1786 one in five of Frederick's subjects was an immigrant. With some justification he claimed that by means of this 'internal colonisation' he had won an extra province for his country.[1] A further safety-valve was provided by outright emigration to areas beyond the *Reich*, to Hungary, Galicia, Russia and the United States of America.[2]

There is also evidence to suggest that German cultivators were more prepared than their French counterparts to imitate the various agricultural innovations pioneered by the Dutch and the English. These were designed to break the 'infernal circle' of the fallow – the need to allow the land to lie fallow at regular intervals to prevent its exhaustion, which led in turn to low yields, which led in turn to the need to reserve a large proportion for arable cultivation, which led in turn to insufficient pasture, which led in turn to insufficient livestock, which led in turn to insufficient manure, which led in turn to the need to allow the land to lie fallow at regular intervals to prevent its exhaustion; and so on. Two related solutions were attempted: either a new rotation of crops was introduced, which eliminated or reduced the need for fallow, or the fallow land was sown with crops which did not lead to any further deterioration in the soil's fertility. This latter process was known as '*Sömmerung*' and can be found in many parts of Germany by the second half of the eighteenth century; in the Kurmark province of Prussia, for example, 60–70% of the fallow land was '*besömmert*' with potatoes and other root crops.[3]

Particularly important was the rapid growth in the popularity of the potato after the middle of the century, for unlike their French neighbours the Germans took to it with almost Hibernian zest. By the 1790s potatoes

[1] W. O. Henderson, *Studies in the Economic Policy of Frederick the Great* (London, 1963), pp. 128–31. Günther Franz, *Geschichte des deutschen Bauernstandes vom frühen Mittelalter bis zum 19. Jahrhundert* (Stuttgart, 1970), pp. 200, 203. There was also of course a good deal of land reclamation in France – André Armengaud, *Population in Europe, 1700–1914* (London, 1970), p. 16. It could not however be as extensive as in Germany because there was so much less waste land available. Moreover, relatively speaking France was densely populated *even before* the substantial increase of the eighteenth century – Pierre Goubert, *L'Ancien Régime*, vol. 1 (Paris, 1969), p. 38.
[2] Franz, *Geschichte des deutschen Bauernstandes*, pp. 203–7.
[3] Ibid., p. 240. Cf. Aubin and Zorn, *Handbuch*, pp. 519–20, and Abel, *Geschichte der deutschen Landwirtschaft*, p. 208. The extent to which these kinds of innovations had any impact on French agriculture in the same period remains a controversial subject. The latest view is that the impact was negligible – Michel Morineau, 'Y a-t-il eu une révolution agricole en France au XVIIIe siècle?' *Revue Historique*, 239 (1968). Cf. André Armengaud, 'Agriculture et démographie au XVIIIe siècle', *Revue d'histoire économique et sociale*, 49 (1971).

Conclusion

were grown in large quantities in every part of the *Reich*: in the Prussian province of Kurmark, for example, production increased from 5,200 *Tonnen* in 1763 to 19,000 in 1773 to 103,000 in 1801.[1] Not only did these new crops provide more food and more income for their growers, they also provided more forage and thus made possible a further solution to the problem of low yields. More forage meant stall-feeding, meant more livestock, meant more manure, meant less fallow, meant higher productivity. Together with more selective breeding, these developments produced a substantial increase in poth the quality and quantity of German livestock; in Prussia numbers increased by 150% between 1756 and the end of the century.[2]

These advances were both reflected in and assisted by the growth of a new and more positive attitude towards agriculture among literate Germans. The peasant, who at best had been ignored and at worst dismissed as a brutish sub-human, was viewed increasingly in a more favourable light: as a valuable national asset, as an individual with the same rights as his more fortunate compatriots and even as the depository of special virtues and values.[3] On the other hand there was nothing new about the friendly attitude towards the peasantry displayed by the princes and their administrations. They had long realised that the health of their treasury depended largely on the health of their tax-payers and had resisted attempts by the nobles to expropriate peasant land.[4] Under the influence of the Enlightenment however their defensive legislation acquired a more positive accent. Their propagation of new techniques, initiative in reclaiming waste land, provision of capital for agricultural improvements and abolition of the peasant's most irksome burdens all pointed to a new attitude. The achievements and failures of Joseph II and Frederick the Great in this field are well known, but their example was copied by many of their less important colleagues. Among others, Karl Theodor of the Palatinate and Bavaria, Friedrick August III of Saxony, Karl August of Weimar, Karl Friedrich of Baden and Friedrich II of Hesse Kassel were enthusiastic reformers.[5] Both urban and rural consumers benefited from the relative price stability encouraged by the granaries erected in several states in the second half of the century.[6]

---

[1] Abel, *Geschichte der deutschen Landwirtschaft*, p. 289. See also above, p. 92, and H. Grundmann, *Handbuch der deutschen Geschichte*, vol. 2 (Stuttgart, 1970), p. 512. A *Tonne* is rather less than an English ton, being 1,000 kilograms or 2,205 pounds.

[2] Aubin and Zorn, *Handbuch*, p. 521.

[3] H. Bechtel, *Wirtschaftsgeschichte Deutschlands*, vol. 2 (Munich, 1952), pp. 222–6. For a more recent discussion, see J. G. Gagliardo, *From Pariah to Patriot: The Changing Image of the German Peasant 1770–1840* (Kentucky, 1969). [4] Lütge, *Agrarverfassung*, p. 136.

[5] Grundmann, *Handbuch*, p. 514. Berge, *Landgraf Friedrich II*, pp. 118–20. Franz, *Geschichte des deutschen Bauernstandes*, pp. 237–9, 242. See above, pp. 185–7.

[6] Bechtel, *Wirtschaftsgeschichte*, pp. 219–21. Grundmann, *Handbuch*, p. 518. Braubach, *Max Franz*, p. 144.

It is impossible to gauge what effect these innovations had on the lives of the ordinary peasants. Given the vast areas involved, it seems unlikely that the individual cases of change recorded can be taken as typical. Certainly there is no clear evidence that in every part of Germany agricultural productivity even kept step with the increasing population.[1] Increased activity on the part of the governments can be shown, but there was a notorious gap between ambition and fulfilment in all spheres of legislation. Although examples of peasant prosperity can be found, notably in Southern Bavaria, the Black Forest, the Hohenlohe Plain and in parts of Hesse, Thuringia and Schleswig-Holstein, so can examples of peasant poverty.[2] Yet although the incidence of rural insurrection increased after 1789, nothing comparable to the *Grande Peur* in France developed. The German *jacqueries* never combined to acquire joint momentum, and could be dealt with individually and without difficulty.[3]

This fatal isolation was due partly to the *Reich*'s territorial fragmentation and partly to the failure of any literate dissidents of the Third Estate to exploit the peasants' social and economic discontents for more long-term political ends. It is worth repeating that there was no Estates General in Germany which might have given a revolutionary unity to the various dissenting strands. Although this lack of a corporate means of organisation and expression was certainly important, there were no signs that any members of the middle classes were prepared to give a lead. The most enthusiastic supporter of the peasantry was Justus Möser, who politically was a staunch conservative.[4] Nor was there any effective cooperation between the peasants and the urban lower classes, with whom they had most in common. Only in Silesia in 1793 did the journeymen of Breslau combine with the weavers of the surrounding countryside, and even here their effort was short-lived.[5]

Apart from these difficulties of social liaison it also seems reasonable to conclude that in the areas of the *Reich* west of the Elbe conditions around 1789 did not reach the pitch of misery prevailing in France. The comparative studies needed to support such a conclusion do not exist, but a few straws in the wind do suggest that it is based on more than the *prima facie* case that because there was less social unrest in Germany conditions there must have been better. Wilhelm Abel, for example, maintains that Ger-

---

[1] Abel, *Geschichte der deutschen Landwirtschaft*, pp. 310–11.
[2] Aubin and Zorn, *Handbuch*, p. 501. Franz, *Geschichte des deutschen Bauernstandes*, pp. 228–9.
[3] The most serious outbreak occurred in the Electorate of Saxony in 1790. See P. Stulz and A. Opitz, *Volksbewegungen in Kursachsen zur Zeit der französischen Revolution* (Berlin, 1956). There is a convenient summary in Epstein, *German Conservatism*, pp. 442–6. For a description of what peasant unrest there was, see Franz, *Geschichte des deutschen Bauernstandes*, pp. 241–9.
[4] Droz, *L'Allemagne et le Révolution française*, pp. 101–5, 343.
[5] Epstein, *German Conservatism*, p. 442.

Conclusion

man peasants paid less than their French counterparts in dues and taxes.[1] His colleague Friedrich Lütge has added that in Central and Western Germany the peasants defended successfully their hereditary tenure and secured stabilisation of services and dues.[2] More recently, Eberhard Weis has argued that, in every part of the *Reich* West of the Elbe, the system of land tenure was much more favourable to the peasant than it was in France, the princes were able to give their peasants much more effective protection against their landlords and there was virtually no exploitation of the countryside by urban capital. As a result, the alienation between noble and peasant was far more intense in France than in Germany, and moreover in the former country the rural proletariat was very much more numerous.[3] More generally, it is the case that to read a general economic history of France in the period after an equivalent volume on Germany is to move into quite a different world.[4]

IV

As this review of German reactions to the Revolution in France has suggested, the dissidents were neither numerous, nor united, nor determined enough to bring about the collapse of the old régime in their own country. They were given a second chance after 1792 in the shape of the French army, which invaded the *Reich* with the avowed intention of liberating rather than conquering. Yet what followed cannot be described as a revolutionary *movement*. It was not that the French simply removed the feudal dam and allowed the revolutionary flood to burst through; rather that small groups of Germans imposed on an apathetic and often unwilling population measures which were dictated by the invaders and ultimately enforced by them. Unlike the situation in the United Provinces–Batavian Republic or Liège, for example, the new régime was felt to be an alien imposition by its subjects and was maintained by force.

The German 'Jacobins' have been studied in careful detail by hosts of historians, but the more that is known about them, the more it is clear that they were not representative of any group, let alone the nation as a whole. Contemporaries were well aware of the fact, and a very long list of descriptions of the anti-revolutionary mood of the people could be compiled without difficulty. One would be rightly suspicious if these stemmed only from

---

[1] Abel, *Geschichte der deutschen Landwirtschaft*, pp. 233–4. Aubin and Zorn, *Handbuch*, p. 501.
[2] Lütge, *Agrarverfassung*, p. 149.
[3] Eberhard Weis, 'Ergebnisse eines Vergleichs der grundherrschaftlichen Strukturen Deutschlands und Frankreichs vom 13. bis zum Ausgang des 18. Jahrhunderts', *Vierteljahrsschrift für Sozial- und Wirtschaftsgeschichte*, 57, 1 (1970).
[4] Compare, for example, E. Labrousse and F. Braudel, *Histoire économique et sociale de la France*, vol. 2 (Paris, 1970) with F. Lütge, *Deutsche Sozial- und Wirtschaftsgeschichte*, 2nd ed. (Berlin, Göttingen and Heidelberg, 1960). The difference may of course stem more from the historians' respective approaches than the facts of the situation.

supporters of the old order, but an impressive number were recorded by the French themselves. The French minister in Zweibrücken, whose prince had reputedly been the most profligate in the *Reich*, wrote to Lebrun in December 1792:

> The French are not liked here, as we flatter ourselves they are. Some individuals and some communities may wish for liberty, but the mass of the country, always reactionary and superstitious, regard those who govern them as privileged beings. They seem to like the yoke which degrades their spirit.[1]

Longer acquaintance with French forms of government only served to exacerbate this fundamental hostility. In 1799 a senior French official made the following comment on the mood of the inhabitants of the Saar, now part of France and before 1789 one of the most restless regions of the *Reich*:

> There is great excitement in all the communities here. And because our enemies' victories have been so exaggerated, and because the news of them have so gone to the people's heads, the name of France appears to be detested everywhere...No secret is made of it – it is loudly proclaimed that within a month there will be no more talk of republicans in these regions. The agitators have already drawn up a list of houses belonging to the patriots (unfortunately a small number) which they are going to burn down, along with the names of certain individuals they are going to murder. In several communities Freedom Trees have been chopped down or mutilated, foreign newspapers circulate in abundance, posters which leave nothing to the imagination have been pasted up, and so on.[2]

Just as there had been no concerted rising against the old régime, so was there none against the new. Yet there were more incidents of spontaneous resistance to the invaders than usually is recognised. A particularly interesting case was Frankfurt am Main, for it was a Free Imperial City and in no way dependent on the privileged orders for its economic existence. The city was occupied by the French on 22 October 1792. Attempts to persuade the citizens to embrace the principles of the Revolution were rebuffed uncompromisingly. In a joint declaration the guilds informed the occupation forces that they were entirely satisfied with the municipal authorities 'who share all the burdens with us', with the wealthy citizens 'who strive with all their power to ameliorate the misery of the poor' and even with their taxes, which were low. They requested no changes and ended with the pious wish that the French nation would be as pleased with their new constitution as the Frankfurters were with their old one. Attempts by the French to seize the city's artillery were repulsed with force. The citizens

---

[1] Hansen, *Quellen*, vol. 2, p. 563, n. 1. Hansen's volumes contain many other examples, from all kinds of sources. See especially vol. 1, p. 893; vol. 2, pp. 665, 706, 743, 839; vol. 3, pp. 8, 324, 796.
[2] Quoted in Ecker, *Saargebiet*, p. 109. For a similar description of the situation in the Electorate of Cologne, see Braubach, *Max Franz*, p. 393.

Conclusion

also made an important contribution to the recapture of the city by a force of Hessians on 2 December, by attacking the defenders from behind, preventing the deployment of artillery and opening the city gates.[1]

Frankfurt was not an exception; throughout the 1790s there were reports from occupied areas of sniping at French troops, demonstrations after allied victories, the destruction of Freedom Trees, and so on.[2] In rural areas the peasants frequently used force to eject French foraging parties or commissars advocating French ideals.[3] Much more widespread of course was passive resistance, expressed in a refusal to wear *tricolore* cockades, erect Freedom Trees and particularly to vote in the elections held in accordance with the decree of 15 December 1792.[4] As in Mainz, most inhabitants of the occupied areas refused to swear the oath to be faithful to the principles of liberty and equality, which was a precondition of voting, and resisted attempts to force them to do so. A good example was the experience of the Nassau administrative district of Kirchheim, where repeated attempts by the French to persuade and then intimidate failed to have the desired effect. Only after a threat to sack their village and only after they had managed to avoid taking the oath did the inhabitants of Göllheim agree to go to the polls. The men they chose, who included their parish priest, then refused to serve.[5] The same pattern was repeated in such different and widely separated areas as the Habsburg County of Falkenstein, the Imperial Knights' territory of Hessloch and Gabsheim and the Free Imperial Cities of Worms, Speyer and Aachen.[6]

The local communities could not stop the French taking unilateral action to change their constitution or to annex them to the Republic, but they did make their protests heard. The Free Imperial Cities were particularly insistent that there should be no change in what they held to be a perfect *status quo*. The burghers of Cologne maintained that their city had been free since the days of Charlemagne, while the mayor of Aachen told the French General Desforest that 'the constitution of the city of Aachen has been purely democratic since 1450. The sovereignty resides in the people.'[7] Referring to his colleagues' reaction to the news that they were

---

[1] I. Kracauer, 'Frankfurt und die französische Revolution', *Archiv für Frankfurts Geschichte und Kunst*, 3rd series, 9 (1907), pp. 243–64.
[2] A. Karll, *Französische Regierung und Rheinländer vor 100 Jahren* (Leipzig, 1921), pp. 17–18. Braubach, *Max Franz*, pp. 393, 406. Ecker, *Saargebiet*, p. 83.
[3] Hansen, *Quellen*, vol. 2, pp. 581, 761. Ecker, *Saargebiet*, p. 49.
[4] See above, p. 281.
[5] R. Goecke, 'Zur Geschichte französischer Herrschaft am Rhein 1792, 1793, 1797', *Forschungen zur deutschen Geschichte*, 25 (1885), pp. 311–20.
[6] Hansen, *Quellen*, vol. 2, pp. 693–6, 703, 736–8, 759–61. Boos, *Geschichte der rheinischen Städtekultur von ihren Anfängen bis zur Gegenwart mit besonderer Berücksichtigung der Stadt Worms*, vol. 4 (Berlin, 1901), pp. 618–21. W. M. Becker, 'Zur politischen Stimmung in Rheinhessen während des Revolutionskrieges, 1792 bis 1794; *Der Wormsgau*, 10 (1933).
[7] Hansen, *Quellen*, vol. 2, pp. 670, 676.

to be annexed to France, a citizen of Bonn wrote: 'The general dismay which has arisen among the citizenry as a result is indescribable... [throughout the Electorate the reaction is one of] deep sorrow and general confusion, which in most people borders on despair.'[1]

Many of the reasons for this rejection of the French were listed earlier in this chapter, when the immediate response to the Revolution was discussed. There were however other sources of hostility which were created by or only became apparent after the war of 1792 and the succeeding campaigns. Most important of these was the wide gap which developed between the French invaders' professions of altruism and their actual behaviour. It was not the case, as some German nationalist historians liked to think, that the revolutionaries' claim to liberate was only a ruse to allow them to exploit all the more ruthlessly; rather that the exigencies of war obliged them to take unpopular measures. This is not to deny on the other hand a steady progression from cosmopolitan *fraternité* to national egoism. On 22 May 1790 the Constituent Assembly declared that the French nation renounced wars aimed at conquest and any coercive act against the liberty of another people. A similar statement was included in the constitution of 3 September 1791.[2] These pacific intentions soon fell victim to domestic political struggles and the war. The collapse of the 1791 constitution following the events of 10 August 1792 also cancelled the promise not to engage in wars of conquest. The decision of 24 October 1792 that the army would not go into winter quarters until the Rhine had been conquered was followed swiftly by the offer of assistance to oppressed peoples, the order to French generals to 'revolutionise' occupied areas and the annexation of Savoy, Nice, Belgium and parts of the Rhineland.[3] 1793 saw the final collapse of a foreign policy based on ideology; on 13 April the National Convention announced that it would intervene no longer in the government of foreign countries and on 15 September endorsed a recommendation from the Committee of Public Safety that their 'philanthropic' attitude should be abandoned and that their generals should in future treat occupied areas as the allies had treated France.[4] To a large extent these various decisions taken in Paris were irrelevant, for in wartime generals and common soldiers alike pay scant attention to civilian directives. The actual impact of the revolutionary armies can be gauged only by looking at those on the receiving end.

---

[1] Braubach, *Max Franz*, p. 405.
[2] J. M. Roberts and R. C. Cobb, eds, *French Revolution Documents*, vol. 1 (Oxford, 1966), pp. 364, 430. For a full account of the development of French policies, Jacques Godechot, *La Grande Nation*, vol. 1 (Paris, 1956), Ch. 3.
[3] Hansen, *Quellen*, vol. 2, pp. 518, n. 3, 601–2, 645–8.
[4] W. Grab, 'La réaction de la population de Rhénanie face à l'occupation par les armées révolutionnaires françaises 1792–9', *Occupants–Occupés* (Brussels, 1969), p. 129.

Conclusion

Usually, the first effect of a French occupation was a financial levy. After the capture of Frankfurt in October 1792, for example, General Custine demanded 2,000,000 gulden and took a number of citizens hostage to encourage payment. At Worms the figure was 600,000 gulden, although after protests it was reduced by half.[1] Levies of similar magnitude were imposed on every area seized by the French, rural as well as urban. In November 1794, for example, the enormous sum of 25,000,000 *livres* was demanded from all territories between the Maas and the Rhine.[2] The levy moreover became a recurring affliction, for the enormous appetite of the French war-machine required periodic helpings of German capital. It was intended that the heaviest burden should be borne by the privileged orders, but as most of them had fled into the German interior, it was the common people who suffered most.[3]

For most Germans far more serious than the levies were the requisitions. Permanent financial crisis at home meant that French armies abroad had to live off the land. From the moment they entered the *Reich* in the late summer of 1792 they were obliged to seize the property of the luckless inhabitants in their path. In Nassau-Saarbrücken, for example, marauding bands of French soldiers seized forage, grain, livestock and firewood, sometimes in return for worthless *bons* but usually in return for nothing. A French agent returning from this region reported that: 'the country I have just left has been treated inhumanly by requisitions; not even the most vital means of subsistence – nothing for the animals or the seed – have been left behind, and other objects in the villages have also been stolen.'[4]

As it became clear that there would be no popular insurrection in favour of the invaders, the French attitude towards the occupied areas became more ruthless. In a speech to the Convention in January 1794 Merlin de Thionville blamed the defeats of the previous year on a mistaken philanthropy and urged the adoption of a 'Prussian' attitude: 'Do not deceive yourselves, my colleagues; accustomed to the yoke, the inhabitants of Germany prefer their chains, their apathy to liberty, the torpor of servitude to the storms of freedom. There are few patriots in Germany and even they up till now have not urged the others to declare themselves.'[5] His advice that everything which might prove useful to the enemy should be seized was eagerly followed by the generals in the field. The terrible winter of 1793–4 became known locally as the '*Plünderwinter*', as Rheinhessen and the Palatinate were systematically stripped bare.

[1] Kracauer, *Frankfurt*, pp. 229–41. Hansen, *Quellen*, vol. 2, p. 439, n. 2.
[2] Ibid., vol. 3, pp. 228–9.
[3] Ibid., p. 291, n. 2. *Occupants–Occupés*, pp. 50–2.
[4] Ecker, *Saargebiet*, p. 54. Goecke, *Zur Geschichte französischer Herrschaft*, pp. 311–13
[5] Hansen, *Quellen*, vol. 3, p. 10.

The French realised of course that the surest way to alienate the local population was to reduce them to destitution. After the conquest of Luxembourg a French agent reported to the Committee of Public Safety that the local inhabitants would have to be wooed away from their Habsburg loyalties, and that 'if unfortunately you deliver this country up to a rapacious commission like those which have ravaged and desolated the country of Trier and the Palatinate you will make the name of France detested, although it is easy to make it cherished and respected'.[1] Attempts by French civilians to halt the plundering were of no avail; for any contest between military and civilian interests was decided before it started. A French gunner described in his diary the distress he and his colleagues felt at the miserable plight of the Germans, but concluded 'receiving no victuals, we were obliged to live from plundering'.[2] The most formidable self-indictment came from the Central Administration of the occupied territories at Aachen, in a remonstrance to the Directory dated 13 March 1796, in which its members reviewed the course of events since the arrival of the French armies. They complained in particular that military considerations always took precedence, and that every commander could take a decision with a simple cut of his sabre. The troops had arrived only with the rags which hung on their backs and had requisitioned grain, forage, cloth, linen, leather, lead, powder, arms, copper, shirts, wine, clothing, shoes, beds, bed-linen, medical supplies, horses, cattle and sheep: in other words anything that was not too bulky to move. Two thirds of the draught animals had been taken, only for most of them to die *en route* to the armies. The civilian authorities had watched with horror as several hundred local inhabitants had died of starvation during the first terrible winter. Also singled out for special opprobrium were the forced labour, the wholesale destruction of forests, the lavish expenditure of the generals and the damage caused by broken dams. The General Administration estimated that so far the French had seized from the area between the Maas and the Rhine foodstuff and goods to the value of 257,515,000 *livres*, while another 54,650,000 worth had been paid for only in *assignats*.[3] The complaints which rained in on the French authorities from the communities were usually ignored and at best brought only a temporary respite.[4]

Although this seizure of necessities was the chief cause of French unpopularity, grave offence was also caused by the removal to France of

---

[1] Ibid., p. 531.
[2] Ibid., p. 799, n. 3.
[3] Ibid., pp. 769–72. As Hansen comments, these figures could hardly have been precise. It can be established in detail however that between August 1794 and March 1796 the city of Trier and its immediate environs, with a total population of 47,000, delivered to the French in cash and goods 11,296,940 *livres*.
[4] See for example the protests from Bonn, Cologne and the rural areas of the Eifel reprinted in Hansen, *Quellen*, vol. 3, pp. 402, 453–62.

works of art. Again, this was official policy, not piracy on the part of individual connoisseurs. On 19 December 1793 the National Convention established a *Commission temporaire des arts* to supervise the collection in suitable regional depots of all books, instruments and any work of the sciences or the arts which might be of use to the French nation. In the following May the Committee of Public Safety set up *Agences* with the various armies to arrange the despatch of these objects to Paris. This official exploitation of conquered territories was inevitably supplemented by a great deal of free-lance work by individual soldiers. Doubtless they were no better or worse behaved than any other half-starved army of occupation, but that is saying little enough. There is a sickening familiarity about the stories of rape, murder, looting and gratuitous destruction in which the period abounds.[2] The genuine efforts by some French administrators to share out equally what food there was and by many French officers to discipline their men could do nothing to prevent all their fellow-countrymen acquiring in German eyes a group-image of diabolic malignity. This is not to deny that the French occupation could also bring certain benefits. But although the abolition of the tithe, the *corvée*, game laws and other seignorial burdens certainly improved the legal lot of the peasantry, they counted for little when compared with the devastation wrought by French foragers.[3] The removal of internal customs barriers, abolition of guilds, rationalisation of administration, introduction of uniformity to coinage, weights and measures, and other liberal economic reforms laid the basis for economic expansion but did not make themselves felt until the more settled Napoleonic period.[4]

Although the campaigns of the 1790s gave a powerful new momentum to Francophobia in the *Reich*, they did not create it. Especially in the Rhineland, memories of the depredations caused by French troops during Louis XIV's wars, the War of the Austrian Succession and the Seven Years War had faded but had never died. Not surprisingly, after 1792 anti-revolutionary publicists were careful to stress that a revolution had not changed the *Erbfeind*'s spots.[5] Clearly it is too early to identify a nationalist movement which aimed at both the expulsion of the foreign invader and the unification of Germany, but there is evidence of a more

[1] Ibid., pp. 150–1. Godechot, *Grande Nation*, p. 537.
[2] Hansen, *Quellen*, vol. 2, pp. 628, n. 2; vol. 3, 481, n. 1.
[3] In fact the French did not abolish the tithe and the seignorial dues until 1798 – Godechot, *Grande Nation*, p. 585.
[4] François Crouzet, 'Wars, Blockade and Economic Change in Europe, 1792–1815', *Journal of Economic History*, 24 (1964). Even during the Napoleonic period expansion occurred only in certain favoured industries in certain favoured areas. As Jacques Godechot has shown in considerable detail, the attitude of successive French governments to the occupied areas was entirely exploitative – *Grande Nation*, chs. 7 and 16.
[5] See above, pp. 293–5.

Germany and the French Revolution

self-conscious sense of national identity and a decline of cosmopolitanism. Even such a committed *Weltbürger* as Wieland called for national unity in 1793.[1]

Quite apart from national feelings naturally evoked by the war and the equally natural reaction to French excesses, in the long term also there had been a growth of a German consciousness. The achievements of the second half of the century, whether expressed in the poetry of Goethe, the philosophy of Kant, the plays of Schiller or the music of Mozart, gave literate Germans both a justified pride in their own culture and a less attractive taste for the denigration of that of other nations. The following extract from a work by the *Popularphilosoph* J. A. Eberhard was typical:

> France may be superior to us in the arts of luxury and taste, and the works of poetry and eloquence, and may equal us in mathematics and physics; but it has always been far behind the Protestant part of Germany in philosophic penetration [*einer gründlichen Philosophie*] and enlightened jurisprudence and theology. When could France boast of an administration of justice as humane, lenient and simple as that of several large German States? What country took the lead in eliminating torture, the crime of witchcraft and the punishment of heresy from its penal code? Where first arose a religion at once tolerant and conducive to the improvement of the human race?
>
> When the French nation – long notorious for its levity, frivolity and rashness of spirit [sought to gain liberty] there was an inevitable transition from superstition and practical immorality to atheism and theoretical immorality: a transition entirely impossible in the Protestant part of Germany.[2]

All classes of society, in the short term at least, also had good economic reasons for opposing the progress of the French. As was emphasised earlier, the destitution which followed in their wake was more the inevitable consequence of war than deliberate policy. This did not however reduce the degree of devastation. The general economic dislocation caused by the campaigns was given a special edge in the occupied areas by the destruction or confiscation of foodstuffs, livestock, raw materials, manufacturing equipment and finished goods. The compulsory circulation of *assignats*, whose purchasing power constantly and rapidly declined, also had serious effects.[3] It was reasonable for the French to argue that these were accidents of war and that once their armies had defeated the feudal forces, peace would bring prosperity to all. A large section of the German population however was opposed to the French economic system *per se*. Masters, journeymen and apprentices were opposed to the abolition of the guilds, while all sorts of tradesmen and craftsmen were alienated by the departure of their noble, clerical and government clientele, which also caused serious

---
[1] Valjavec, *Die Entstehung der politischen Strömungen*, pp. 334–8.
[2] Quoted in Epstein, *German Conservatism*, pp. 492–3.
[3] Hansen, *Quellen*, vol. 3 contains a good deal of material on the problems and protests caused by the assignats. See especially, pp. 335–40, 353, n. 2, 387. Cf. Godechot, *Grande Nation*, p. 536.

unemployment in the service industries. In the Electorate of Cologne, for example, it was the guilds which led the opposition to the proposed Cisrhenan Republic and demands for the restoration of the old order.[1] When later it became clear that annexation to France was unavoidable, the Elector Max Franz lamented that it was 'a terrible thought, because republicanisation will rob so many thousand unfortunate clerical, secular and military personnel, officials, court-servants, clergy and the citizens who lived off them of their positions, salaries, prospects, living and status'.[2] It may be doubted whether the argument that the transition from old régime to new must needs cause temporary embarrassment to some carried much weight. Even if he were able to understand, to inform a baby that the pain caused by teething would soon be forgotten and that anyway teeth were essential would not stop him crying.

One final specific cause of hostility to the French was the anti-clericalism of the invaders and the clericalism of the invaded. The vitality of religious ideals and religious institutions in eighteenth century Germany[3] ensured an appalled reaction to French excesses. This was shared by both Protestants and Catholics, although the more heavily decorated churches and more elaborate ritual of the latter offered more scope for imaginative iconoclasts. Almost immediately after the invasion of 1792, hair-raising stories of acts of blasphemy committed by French troops began to circulate. A citizen of Trier recorded in his diary reports that the 'patriots' had lit fires on altars, abused statues of the Virgin, defaced crucifixes, defecated into tabernacles, and so on.[4] That the whole revolutionary cause then suffered from guilt by association was not surprising, especially in view of the papal condemnation of its principles in March 1791 and the anti-clerical tone of its propaganda.

The effect these religious loyalties could have on the course of events became particularly clear during the elections held in the occupied areas in January and February 1793. In many places the leadership of the priests and the religious scruples of their parishioners were responsible for mass defiance of the revolutionaries' directives. At Aachen, for example, the delegates refused the oath to liberty and equality and instead adopted the following formula: 'We swear to maintain the Roman Apostolic religion in all its purity and to support with all our power the sovereignty, freedom and welfare of the people of Aachen, So help us God and his dear saints.' Jacobi wrote to Goethe on the same occasion that the Aachen citizens had shouted at their liberators: 'Our religion has been desecrated, our guilds

---

[1] Goecke, *Zur Geschichte französischer Herrschaft*, pp. 326–9.
[2] Braubach, *Max Franz*, p. 405.
[3] See above, pp. 25–32, 287–9.
[4] Hansen, *Quellen*, vol. 2, pp. 628, n. 2, 663, n. 2.

Germany and the French Revolution

have been opened, we are to become enemies of the Emperor and the *Reich*: rather we die on the spot, death is better! We'd rather have death!' Another correspondent held that French anti-clericalism had been the chief cause of the local population's hostility. According to him, the occupation authorities had alienated them finally by confiscating monastic property, converting the Jesuit Church into a bakehouse, the Capuchin Church into a granary, the Carmelite and Bernardine Churches into hospitals and the Franciscan Church into a stable. He concluded: 'Among no other people will you find more stupid superstition, among no other people more dedicated exponents or more enthusiastic supporters of clericalism [*Pfafferei*] and monkishness as here with us and in Brabant.'[1] Fear for their religion also encouraged an anti-revolutionary attitude in Protestants. As Epstein remarked: 'the high morale and complacent pharisaism of much of Germany's Protestant élite contributed to the country's immunity to revolutionary propaganda once the "true character" of the Jacobins had been exposed'.[2]

V

On 31 May 1793 the parish priest of Gabsheim, a village in Rheinhessen, wrote that his parishioners believed that the French could not be defeated by human means and that therefore they had organised a collection for masses to be said and for a pilgrimage to Walldürn to invoke divine intervention.[3] Their appeals to the Almighty went unheeded: in the face of allied disunity and incompetence, not even silver bullets could have stopped the French expansionist momentum. Five years later the left bank of the Rhine became a permanent part of France and five years after that the pagan Napoleon presided over the dissolution of the *Reich*. In the final analysis the reaction of ordinary Germans to the French and their programmes had no effect on their own political future. This was decided on the battlefields and in the chancelleries, by the generals and the diplomats. As the French won all the decisive battles they dominated all the peace negotiations and thus were able to dictate the form Central Europe was to take.

At first it appeared that the destruction of the *Reich* would come from within, not from revolutionary subversion but from the greed of the great princes. The agreements reached between Austria and Prussia at Reichen-

---

[1] Ibid., pp. 702, n. 2, 713–14, 775, n. 3. For similar opposition in Cologne see vol. 3, pp. 324, n. 1, 612, n. 1.
[2] Epstein, *German Conservatism*, p. 493. This applied to ordinary citizens as well as to the élites. See, for example, the situation in Worms – Boos, *Geschichte der rheinischen Städtekultur*, p. 607.
[3] Becker, *Zur politischen Stimmung in Rheinhessen*, p. 399. On Walldürn, see above, pp. 174–5.

bach in 1790 and Pillnitz in 1791 and the alliance concluded in 1792 raised the spectre of partition. As the Prince-Bishop of Würzburg gloomily observed: 'If Austria and Prussia unite, the end of the *Reich* is at hand.'[1] *A priori* fears were lent substance by changes of personnel at the great courts. A new generation of self-conscious *Realpolitiker* such as Bischoffwerder, Schulenburg, Cobenzl, Spielmann and Thugut, with no understanding of or interest in imperial affairs, rose to the top in Prussia and Austria. Although inevitable, a particularly severe blow was the eclipse of Kaunitz, for his clear appreciation of the advantages the imperial connection brought to the Habsburgs had not been dimmed by the intoxicating prospect of immediate territorial gain. It is clear that from a very early stage Austria and Prussia intended to gain land not only from a defeated France but also from a reorganised *Reich*.

French victories and growing discord between the two allies brought an abrupt stop to these ambitious plans, but did not diminish the danger to imperial integrity. By the Treaty of Basle of April 1795 Prussia retired from the war and effectively ceded to France her possessions on the left bank of the Rhine, leaving to some future negotiation the question of territorial compensation on the right bank. In the following year separate agreements between the French and a number of other German princes also made provision for territorial adjustment at the expense of the ecclesiastical states. Eventually even Austria, the only defence the weaker members of the *Reich* had against rapacious neighbours, was forced by the Italian victories of Napoleon to agree to the cession of the left bank. When Francis II agreed to a separate peace at Campo Formio and the summoning of the Congress of Rastatt he also signed the *Reich*'s death-warrant.

It proved to be a lingering death, for war was resumed in 1799 and it seemed at first that the coalition of Austria, Russia and Great Britain would succeed. It was the last battles which counted however and after French victories at Marengo and Hohenlinden the peace of Lunéville resumed the destruction of the *Reich*. After much complicated negotiation, the first stage was completed by *Reichsdeputationshauptschluß* of 25 February 1803, which reduced the number of ecclesiastical princes from eighty-one to three (the retitled Elector of Mainz and the Grandmasters of the Teutonic Knights and the Knights of St John) and the imperial cities from fifty-one to six (Hamburg, Bremen, Lübeck, Nuremberg, Augsburg and Frankfurt am Main). The truncated remains of imperial institutions were as fragile as the peace which sustained them and the resumption of war initiated the terminal phase. The various treaties which followed the de-

---

[1] Aretin, *Heiliges Römisches Reich*, vol. 1, p. 250. This section is based largely on chs. 4, 5, and 6 of Aretin's book and on the good, full and clear account in Agatha Ramm, *Germany 1789–1919* (London, 1967), Ch. 2.

feats of the Third Coalition at Ulm and Austerlitz transformed the *Reich* into a confederation of sovereign states. The mediatisation of the Imperial Knights had a particularly decisive quality, for their mere existence had symbolised the uniquely prescriptive character of imperial institutions. Now there was nothing left, and the formal dissolution announced by Francis II on 6 August 1806 represented only the closing of the coffin.

The rapidity with which the *Reich* collapsed found no better illustration than in the changing fortunes of the Archbishop-Elector of Mainz. In July 1792 he presided over the coronation of Francis II, entertained the cream of the German nobility at his court with lavish display and looked forward confidently to sharing in the spoils of victory after the war against France. When he died exactly ten years later, not only had his capital been in the hands of the French for more than four years and was certain to remain so, but he also knew that there were grave doubts about the future of the rest of his territories and his status as Archbishop, Elector and Archchancellor.

In July 1793 the Austrian and Prussian armies had recaptured the city of Mainz from the French and had restored the Elector and his régime.[1] Their return proved to be only temporary. In the campaign of 1794 the French reoccupied the entire left bank of the Rhine, with the sole exception of Mainz. The Elector, his court and the administration took refuge once again at Aschaffenburg, this time permanently, for his capital remained almost constantly under siege. Heavily fortified and heavily garrisoned, Mainz resisted French military assaults successfully, only to succumb eventually to French diplomacy. As part of the terms agreed at Campo Formio, the Austrians withdrew their troops from the beleaguered city, leaving the remaining defenders no choice but to capitulate. Mainz became part of France, and was to remain so for the next sixteen years, until the collapse of the Napoleonic Empire.

Although in theory the Elector Friedrich Karl continued to rule his remaining territories as he had done in the past, in practice he and his subjects were at the mercy of the fluctuating fortunes of war. His periodic attempts to influence events through the imperial institutions ended in fiasco.[2] His fate was sealed finally by the failure of the Third Coalition, although perhaps mercifully he did not live to experience the ultimate humiliation. Less than a month after his death at Aschaffenburg on 25 July 1802 the *Reichsdeputation* began work on the partition of the *Reich*. Through adroit diplomacy, Friedrich Karl's successor, Karl Anton von Dalberg, did succeed in saving something from the catastrophe. The archiepiscopal see was transferred from Mainz to Regensburg, the titles of Elector, Archchancellor, Archbishop and Primate were retained and even

[1] See above, p. 301.
[2] These are discussed fully in Aretin, *Heiliges Römisches Reich*, vol. 1.

some territory was attached to them – Aschaffenburg, Regensburg and Wetzlar.

As Dalberg was to discover, this was only the first of many such partitions. The *Reichsdeputationshauptschluß*, which became law on 27 April 1803, did however mark the end of the Electorate of Mainz, together with all the other prince-bishoprics, and the beginning of the end for the Imperial Knights, Imperial Counts and many other smaller princes. As the Elector Max Franz of Cologne had observed on an earlier occasion: 'We German princes have only laws, treaties and solemn and sworn assurances to oppose to power, which places itself above all these things; only morality can save us.'[1] In the past the amorality of the *Realpolitiker* had been restrained by a balance of greed and envy, and no one power – Bourbon, Habsburg or Hohenzollern – had acquired sufficient ascendancy to destroy the equilibrium. What preserved the Imperial Knights and Counts, with their minuscule territories; or the Prince-Bishops, with their archaic combination of temporal and spiritual; or the Imperial Cities, with their often tiny populations, was the natural strength of the anti-hegemonial forces in Europe. It was not until the armies of revolutionary and Napoleonic France achieved almost total victory on the continent that the *Reich* could be destroyed. Inefficient, backward, corrupt and oppressive it may have been, but many of its component parts still commanded the loyalty of Germans of every class. Perhaps eventually a popular movement strong enough to destroy the *Reich* from below would have developed; perhaps eventually the great German princes would have agreed to partition on their own initiative; but that was not what happened. It was of crucial importance for the future history of Germany that all change during this period was seen to lie outside the country, in Paris. Consequently, the French armies could destroy the imperial institutions, but they could not destroy the spirit which had both sustained and been created by them.

[1] Braubach, *Max Franz*, p. 207.

Appendix

The Electors and Archbishops of Mainz 1695–1802
Lothar Franz von Schönborn 1695–1729
Franz Ludwig von Pfalz-Neuburg 1729–32
Philipp Karl von Eltz-Kempenich 1732–43
Johann Friedrich Karl von Ostein 1743–63
Emmerich Joseph von Breidbach zu Bürresheim 1763–74
Friedrich Karl von Erthal 1774–1802

Bibliography

MANUSCRIPT SOURCES

The various military campaigns which have afflicted the Rhineland at regular intervals have also scattered the Electorate's archives throughout Central Europe. The most valuable material relating to the demography, economic life and social structure of the city of Mainz is to be found in the *Stadtarchiv* there.[1] Much of the old *Mainzer Regierungsarchiv*, which had found its way to the *Bayerisches Staatsarchiv* at Würzburg, was destroyed by bombing in the Second World War. Fortunately, the invaluable *Mainzer Domkapitelprotokolle* escaped this fate and are still to be found there. It is also fortunate that the *Mainzer Erzkanzlerarchiv*,[2] now part of the *Haus-, Hof- und Staatsarchiv* at Vienna, escaped unscathed, for it is the richest source for an investigation of the Electorate's domestic affairs. Its foreign affairs can best be approached through the embarrassingly rich deposits of the *Reichskanzlei* and the *Staatskanzlei*, also in the *Haus-, Hof- und Staatsarchiv*. The subsection '*Moguntina*' of the *Nationalia* section of the *Reichskanzlei* contains, among other things, some interesting material on the dispute between the Elector Emmerich Joseph and his Cathedral Chapter. I have also made use of the reports of the English and French ambassadors, in the Public Record Office and the *Archives du Ministère des Affaires Étrangères* respectively. I also used material from private archives to gain a clearer idea of the nobility's political, economic, social and cultural rôle in the Electorate. Of these the *Gräflich zu Eltzisches Archiv* and the *Freiherrlich zu Franckenstein'sches Archiv* were particularly helpful.

Abbreviations used:
Eltville	Gräflich zu Eltzisches Archiv, Eltville.
London	Public Record Office, London.
Mainz	Stadtarchiv Mainz.
Paris	Archives du Ministère des Affaires Étrangères, Paris.
Trier	Stadtarchiv, Trier, Nachlaß der Grafen von Kesselstadt.
Ullstadt	Freiherrlich zu Franckenstein'sches Archiv, Schloß Ullstadt, Neustadt an der Aisch.
Vienna	Haus-, Hof- und Staatsarchiv, Vienna.
Staka	Staatskanzlei, Berichte aus dem Reich.
Reika	Reichskanzlei, Nationalia, Moguntina.
MEA	Mainzer Erzkanzlerarchiv.
GK	Geistlich und Kirchensachen.
Waal	Fürstlich von der Leyen'sches Archiv, Waal (Schwaben).
Wiesentheid	Gräflich von Schönborn'sches Archiv, Schloß Wiesentheid.

[1] L. Falk, 'Die Bestände des Mainzer Stadtarchivs und ihre Findmittel', *De Biblioteca Moguntina* (1963).

[2] Lothar Gross, 'Mainzer Erzkanzlerarchiv', *Gesamtinventar des Wiener Haus-, Hof- und Staatsarchiv*, ed. Ludwig Bitter, vol. 1 (Vienna, 1936). Helmut Mathy, *Die Geschichte des Mainzer Erzkanzlerarchivs 1782–1815*, Geschichte und Recht, vol. 5 (Wiesbaden, 1969).

Bibliography

Würzburg Bayerisches Staatsarchiv, Würzburg.
MGKA   Mainzer Geheime Kanzlei Akten.
MDP   Mainzer Domkapitelprotokolle.
MRA   Mainzer Regierungsarchiv.

PRINTED SOURCES

(Albini, Franz Joseph Freiherr von), *Etwas über die Mainzische Konstitution in einem Sendschreiben des Gottlob Teutsch an den Verfasser des Mainzischen Bürgerfreundes* (Frankfurt and Leipzig, 1792).
Ein Paar derbe Worte des Dr. Gottlieb Teutsch an seinen tapfern Widerleger den Kaspar Hartmann (Frankfurt and Leipzig, 1793).
Andreasen, Øjvind & Helmut Mathy, 'Frederik Münters Reise nach Mainz (1791)', *Mainzer Zeitschrift*, 62 (1967).
Annalen der leidenden Menschheit, ed. A. A. F. Hennings, 10 vols. (Altona, 1795–1801).
Der Antipatriot, Ein Gegenstück zu dem von Forster und Wedekind in Mainz herausgegebenen Patrioten (Mainz, 1793).
Aretin, Karl Otmar Freiherr von, 'Dalberg zwischen Kaiser und Fürstenbund: Actenstücke zur Koadjutorwahl in Mainz 1787', *Archiv für mittelrheinische Kirchengeschichte* (1964).
Heiliges Römisches Reich 1776–1806: Reichsverfassung und Staatssouveränität, vol. 2: *Ausgewählte Aktenstücke*, Veröffentlichungen des Instituts für Europäische Geschichte Mainz, vol. 38 (Wiesbaden, 1967).
Aufruf eines Deutschen an seine Landesleute am Rhein; sonderlich an den Nähr- und Wehrstand (1792).
'Auszug eines Briefes vom Rhein', *Neue Bemerkungen in und über Deutschland von verschiedenen Verfassern*, vol. 4 (Halle, 1787).
Bahrdt, K. F., *Geschichte seines Lebens, seiner Meinungen und Schicksale*, Von ihm selbst geschrieben (Frankfurt am Main, 1791).
Becker, J. N., *Beschreibung meiner Reise in den Departmentern vom Donnersberge, vom Rhein und von der Mosel im sechsten Jahr der französischen Republik* (Berlin, 1799).
(Bedford, Francis Russell, 5th Duke of), *A Descriptive Journey through the Interior Parts of Germany and France, including Paris, with interesting and amusing anecdotes*, By a Young Peer of the Highest Rank, just returned from his travels (London, 1786).
Behlen, S., & J. Merkel, *Geschichte und Beschreibung von Aschaffenburg und dem Spessart* (Aschaffenburg, 1843).
Bei bevorstehender Wahl, Ein Mainzer Bürger an seine Mitbürger (Mainz, 1792).
Bemerkungen auf einer Reise durch Deutschland und die Niederlande, in den Jahren 1779, 1780 und 1781, Johann Bernouillis Sammlung kurzer Reisebeschreibungen, vol. 13 (Berlin, 1786).
Bentzel, Anselm Franz Freiherr von, *Neue Verfassung der verbesserten hohen Schule zu Mainz* (Mainz, 1784).
Beobachtungen und Anmerkungen auf Reisen durch Deutschland, in Fragmenten und Briefen (Leipzig, 1788).
Bergmann, Alfred (ed.), *Briefe des Herzogs Carl August an seine Mutter Anna Amalia*, Jenaer germanistische Forschungen, vol. 30 (Jena, 1938).
Böhmer, Caroline, *Briefe aus der Frühromantik*, ed. Erich Schmidt, vol. 1 (Leipzig, 1913).
Böhmer, G. W., *Epistel an die lieben Bauersleute zu Sarmsheim* (Mainz, 1792).

Bibliography

Bonjour, Edgar, *Johannes Müller: Briefe in Auswahl*, 2nd ed. (Basle, 1954).
Bouillé, Louis Joseph Amour Marquis de, *Souvenirs et Fragments pour servir aux Mémoires de ma Vie et de mon Temps*, 2 vols (Paris, 1906 and 1908).
Brandis, J. F., *Über das reichsritterschaftliche Staatsrecht und dessen Quellen* (Göttingen, 1788).
Bray, Comte de, *Mémoires du Comte de Bray*, ed. F. de Bray (Paris, 1911).
Briefe eines jungen Reisenden durch Liefland, Kurland und Deutschland an seinen Freund Herrn Hofrath K. in Liefland (Erlangen, 1777).
Brück, Anton Ph., *Kurmainzer Schulgeschichte: Texte, Berichte, Memoranden*, Mainzer Beiträge zur Pädagogik, Historische Abteilung, vol. 1 (Wiesbaden, 1960).
Der Bürgerfreund, ed. Mathias Metternich (Mainz, 1792–3).
Büsching, Anton F., *Erdbeschreibung*, 6th ed., vol. 3 (Hamburg, 1779).
Bundschuh, J. K., *Geographisches, statistisches und topographisches Lexikon von Franken*, 6 vols (Ulm, 1799–1803).
Geographisches und statistisch-topographisches Lexikon vom kur- und oberrheinischen Kreis (Ulm, 1805).
Burnet, Gilbert, *Some Letters, Containing an Account of what seemed most remarkable in travelling through Switzerland, Italy, some parts of Germany etc. in the years 1685 and 1686*, 2nd ed. (Rotterdam, 1687).
Cogan, Thomas, *The Rhine, or a Journey from Utrecht to Francfort* (London, 1793).
Compendiöse Statistik von Maynz, Trier und Cöln samt ihren Nebenländern (Leipzig, 1798).
Conrad, Hermann, *Recht und Verfassung des Reiches in der Zeit Maria Theresias*, Wissenschaftliche Abhandlungen der Arbeitsgemeinschaft für Forschung des Landes Nordrhein-Westfalen, vol. 28 (Cologne and Opladen, 1961).
Cotta, Friedrich, *An die welche noch nicht geschworen haben* (Mainz, 1793).
Von der Staatsverfassung in Frankreich zum Unterrichte für die Bürger und Bewohner im Erzbisthum Mainz und den Bistümern Worms und Speier (Mainz, 1792).
Dahl, Johannes Konrad, *Statistik und Topographie der mit dem Großherzogtum Hessen vereinigten Lande des linken Rheinufers* (Darmstadt, 1816).
Dalberg, Karl Anton Theodor Freiherr von, *The Connection between Moral and Politica Philosophy, considered by Charles Baron Dalberg; An essay, read before the Academy of Useful Sciences at Erfurt, July the 3d, 1786* (London, 1787).
Von den wahren Grenzen der Wirksamkeit des Staats in Beziehung auf seine Mitglieder, reprinted in Robert Leroux, *La Théorie du despotisme éclairé chez Karl Theodor Dalberg*, Publications de la faculté des lettres de l'Université de Strasbourg, vol. 60 (Paris, 1932).
Daniels, H., *Über das Stapelrecht zu Köln und Mainz* (Cologne, 1804).
Dankrede an Ihro Kurfürstliche Gnaden zu Mainz bey Dero Höchsten Rückkehr von Höchst nach der Residenzstadt Mainz für Dero zur Steuer allgemeiner Fruchttheuerung mildest getroffener Maasregeln und Fürsorg, abgestattet von unterthänigstdankmüthigster Bürgerschaft zu Mainz (Mainz, 1771).
Doehler, Jacob Friedrich, *Auch etwas über die Regierung der geistlichen Staaten in Deutschland* (Frankfurt and Leipzig, 1787).
Dohm, C. C. W. von, *Materialen für die Statistik und Neuere Staatengeschichte* (Lemgo, 1785).
Dorsch, A. J., *Anrede an die neu gebildete Gesellschaft der Freunde der Freiheit und Gleichheit in Mainz* (Mainz, 1792).
Erste Linien einer Geschichte der Weltweisheit (Mainz, 1787).
Dumont, Daniel, *Die Belagerung der Stadt Mainz durch die Franzosen im Jahre 1792 und ihre Wiedereroberung durch die teutschen Truppen im Jahre 1793* (Mainz, 1793).

Bibliography

Eickemeyer, Rudolf, *Denkschrift über die Einnahme der Festung Mainz durch die fränkischen Truppen im Jahre 1792*, ed. F. C. Lankhard (Hamburg, 1798).
Denkwürdigkeiten des Generals Eickemeyer, ed. Heinrich Koenig (Frankfurt am Main, 1845).
Este, C. L., *A Journey in the Year 1793 through Flanders, Brabant and Germany to Switzerland* (London, 1795).
Fischer, Karl, *An den Herrn Philipp Adam Custine, neufränkischer Bürger und General*, 3rd ed. ('Germanien', 1793).
Forster, Georg, *Sämtliche Schriften* (Leipzig, 1843).
Frank, P. A., *Beyträge zu der beständigen Wahlkapitulation für das Mainzische Erzstift* (Frankfurt am Main, 1789).
Etwas über die Wahlkapitulation in den geistlichen Staaten (Frankfurt am Main, 1789).
Ein Frankensoldat an die Mainzer Bürger (Mainz, 1793).
Füssel, Johann Michael, *Unser Tagebuch oder Erfahrungen und Bemerkungen auf einer Reise durch einen großen Theil des fränkischen Kreises nach Carlsbad und durch Bayern und Passau nach Linz* (Erlangen, 1787).
Gercken, Philipp Wilhelm, *Reisen durch Schwaben, Baiern, die angränzende Schweiz, Franken, die Rheinische Provinzen und an der Mosel in den Jahren 1779–1785*, vol. 3 (Stendal, 1786).
Girtanner, Christoph, *Historische Nachrichten und politische Betrachtungen über die französische Revolution*, 2nd ed. (13 vols, Berlin, 1794–1804).
Gönner, N. T., *Teutsches Staatsrecht* (Landshut, 1804).
Goldhagen, Hermann, *Denkbüchlein gegen die Gefahren der Zeit, um fromm zu leben und selig zu sterben* (Maynz, 1772).
Gottron, Adam, 'Tagebuch des Pfarrers Turin von St. Ignaz', *Mainzer Almanach* (1958).
Grossing, Franz Rudolph von, *Statistik aller katholisch-geistlichen Reichsstifter in Deutschland* (Halle, 1786).
Gundling, Nicolaus Hieronymus von, *Discours über den vormaligen und itzigen Stand der deutschen Churfürstenstaaten* (4 vols, Leipzig, 1747–9).
Gymnich, Klemens August Freiherr von, *Beschreibung der Vestung Mainz, und der Umstände, unter welchen sie in Oktober 1792 den Franzosen übergeben ward* (n.p., n.d.).
Hansen, Joseph, *Quellen zur Geschichte des Rheinlandes im Zeitalter der französischen Revolution* (4 vols, Bonn, 1931–8).
Hartleben, F. J., *Iurisdictio Moguntina* (Mainz, 1784).
Hassencamp, R., *Neue Briefe C. M. Wielands, vornehmlich an Sophie La Roche* (Stuttgart, 1894).
Heerdt, Franz, *Mainzer Chronik aus der Zeit von 1767 bis 1782* (Mainz, 1879).
Heinzmann, J. G., *Beobachtungen und Anmerkungen auf Reisen durch Deutschland* (Leipzig, 1788).
Herrmann, Franz, *Juristische Abhandlung der Aufnahme in die reichsritterschaftliche Genossenschaft* (Mainz, 1792).
Hettner, H., *Georg Forsters Briefwechsel mit S. Th. Sömmering* (Brunswick, 1877).
Höhler, M., *Des kurtrierischen Rats H. A. Arnoldi Tagebuch über die zu Ems gehaltene Zusammenkunft der vier erzbischöflichen Herren Deputierten* (1915).
Hof- und Staatskalender des Kurfürstentums Mainz, 1740–1792.
(Hoffmann, Anton), *Darstellung der Mainzer Revolution oder Geschichte der Stadt Mainz und umliegenden Gegend von Entstehung des französischen Revolutionskrieges bis nach*

Bibliography

Wiedereroberung dieser Stadt, der Klubb und des in dieser Stadt eröffneten rheinisch-teutschen Nationalkonvents (Frankfurt and Leipzig, 1794).
Humboldt, Wilhelm von, *Tagebücher; Gesammelte Schriften*, vol. 14 (Berlin, 1916).
Hume, David, *The Letters of David Hume*, ed. J. Y. T. Greig, vol. 1 (Oxford, 1932).
Journal von und für Deutschland, ed. Karl Anton Freiherr von Bibra (Fulda, 1784–92).
Just, Leo, 'Briefe Sömmerings an Johannes von Müller', *Jahrbuch der Vereinigung 'Freunde der Universität Mainz'* (1957).
Karamzin, Nikolai, *Letters of a Russian Traveller, 1789–90*, tr. F. Jonas (Columbia U.P., 1957).
Kerner, J. G., *Allgemeines positives Staats- und Landrecht der unmittelbaren freyen Reichsritterschaft in Schwaben, Franken und am Rheine, nebst einer Einleitung in das Staatsrecht der unmittelbaren freyen Reichsritterschaft überhaupt* (Lemgo, 1786).
Keyssler, J. G., *Travels through Germany, Bohemia, Hungary, Switzerland, Italy and Lorrain*, 2nd ed. (London, 1757).
Klebe, A., *Reise auf dem Rhein* (2 vols, Frankfurt am Main, 1801–2).
Körte, Wilhelm, *Briefe zwischen Gleim, Wilhelm Heinse und Johannes von Müller*, vol. 2 (Zürich, 1806).
Kopp, G. L. C., *Die katholische Kirche im 19. Jahrhundert* (Mainz, 1830).
Die Krönungsrechnung bei der Wahl und Krönung Leopold II, abgelesen in der Gesellschaft der Freunde der Freiheit und Gleichheit zu Mainz am 11ten November von Anton Fuchs (Mainz, 1792).
Kurfürstliche Mainzische gnädigst privilegierte Anzeigen von verschiedenen Sachen.
Kurze Beschreibung des gelobten Landes und der Mainzischen Kurlande (Mainz, n.d.).
Lang, J. G., *Reise auf dem Rhein* (von Mainz bis Düsseldorf) (Frankfurt am Main, 1790).
Lehmann, Max, 'Eine Denkschrift von Johannes von Müller aus dem Jahre 1787', *Historische Zeitschrift*, 71 (1893).
Lehne, Friedrich, *Gesammelte Schriften* (Mainz, 1837–9).
Historisch-statistisches Jahrbuch des Departments von Donnersberg für das Jahr 9 & 10 der fränkischen Republik (2 vols, Mainz, n.d.).
Lemcke, Paul, 'Ein Besuch in Mainz vor 104 Jahren', *Mainzer Anzeiger*, 100 & 101 (1883).
Lenz, Conrad, *Das Lied vom alten Veit und seinem Sohn, über den erschröcklichen und sündlichen Aufstand der Franzosen gegen ihren König und Herrn* (Mainz, 1791).
Libert, Abbé, *Voyage pittoresque sur le Rhin; d'après l'allemand de Monsieur le professeur Vogt* (Francfort, 1804).
Livet, Georges, *Recueil des Instructions données aux ambassadeurs et ministres de France depuis les traités de Westphalie jusqu'à la Révolution française*, vol. 18, États Allemands, 1 L'Électorat de Mayence (Paris, 1962).
Magazin der Philosophie und schönen Literatur (4 vols, Mainz, 1785–6).
Mainz nach der Wiedereinnahme durch die verbündeten Deutschen im Sommer 1793 (Mentz, 1793).
Mainzer Anzeigen von gelehrten Sachen (Mainz, 1785–91).
Mainzer Monatschrift von geistlichen Sachen (Mainz, 1784–91).
Mathy, Helmut, 'Ein Schriftstück zur Mainzer Universitätsreform aus dem Jahre 1779', *Jahrbuch der Vereinigung 'Freunde der Universität Mainz'* (1960).
Meister Johann Ehrlichs, Bürgers und Schreinermeisters zu R. Correspondenz mit dem Bürgerfreund zu Mainz (1792).
Metternich, Klemens Fürst von, *Aus Metternichs nachgelassenen Papieren*, ed. Fürst Richard von Metternich-Winneburg, vol. 1 (Vienna, 1880).

Bibliography

Metternich, Mathias, *Rede von den Ursachen der bis itzt noch getheilten Meinungen über die Revolutionssache der Mainzer und von den Mitteln, die Meinungen und Gemüther zu vereinigen* (Mainz, 1792).
Meusel, J. G., *Das gelehrte Teutschland oder Lexikon der jetzt lebenden teutschen Schriftsteller*, 5th ed. (Lemgo, 1796–1831).
Michel, V., *Lettres de Sophie La Roche à C. M. Wieland* (Paris, 1938).
Miles, W. A., *Correspondence on the French Revolution 1789–1817*, ed. Chas. Popham Miles (2 vols, London, 1890).
Moniteur, Gazette Nationale ou le Moniteur Universel (New Impression, Paris, 1845).
Moore, John, *A View of Society and Manners in France, Switzerland and Germany*, vol. 1 (London, 1779).
Moser, Friedrich Karl von, 'Regierungs-Geschichte des jetzigen Herrn Fürstenbishofs Heinrich des VIII zu Fulda', *Patriotisches Archiv für Teutschland*, 2 (1785).
Über die Regierung der geistlichen Staaten in Deutschland (Frankfurt and Leipzig, 1787).
Moser, J. J. von, *Beyträge zu reichsritterschaftlichen Sachen* (4 vols, Frankfurt and Leipzig, 1775).
Einleitung in das Churfürstlich-Maynzische Staatsrecht (Frankfurt am Main, 1755).
Neueste Geschichte der unmittelbaren Reichsritterschaft, unter denen Kaisern Matthia, Ferdinand II, Ferdinand III, Leopold, Joseph I, Carl VI, Franz und Joseph II (2 vols, Frankfurt and Leipzig, 1775–6).
Molitor, *Erklärung einiger Mainzischen Dikasterianten und Individuen auf die Proklamation zum Eide der Freiheit und Gleichheit* (Mainz, 1793).
Müller, Johannes von, *Sämtliche Werke*, ed. J. G. Müller (27 vols, Tübingen, 1810–22).
Müller, N., *Der Aristokrat in der Klemme* (Mainz, 1792).
Münch, Gerhard, *Der Staatsbürger kann und muß als Christ ein Patriot wie der Neufranke sein: oder Übereinstimmung der neufränkischen Staatsverfassung mit der Christusreligion* (Mainz, 1793).
Nau, B. S. von, *Geschichte der Deutschen in Frankreich und der Franzosen in Deutschland* (5 vols, Frankfurt, 1794).
Neigebaur, J. F., *Der Untergang des Churfürstentums Mainz, von einem churmainzischen General* (Frankfurt am Main, 1839).
Nicolai, C. F., *Beschreibung einer Reise durch Deutschland und die Schweiz* (12 vols, Berlin and Stettin, 1783–5).
Pacca, 'Die Denkwürdigkeiten des Kardinals Pacca', *Frankfurter zeitgemäße Broschüren*, 27–8 (1908/1909).
Pape, F. G., *Vereinigung der neufränkischen Verfassung mit dem Katholizismus* (Mainz, 1792).
Pennant, Thomas, *Tour on the Continent 1715*, ed. Sir G. R. de Beer (London, 1948).
Pfeiffer, Johann Friedrich, *Grundsätze der Universal-Cameralwissenschaft* (Frankfurt am Main, 1783).
Von der Nothwendigkeit der in den kurmainzischen Landen auflebenden Bergwerks- und Schmelzwissenschaften (Mainz, 1784).
Pilati, Carl Antonio, *Voyages en differens Pays de l'Europe en 1774, 1775 et 1776*, vol. 1 (The Hague, 1777).
Plümicke, C. M., *Briefe auf einer Reise durch Deutschland im Jahre 1791* (2 vols, 1793).
Pütter, J. S., *Über den Unterschied der Stände, besonders des hohen und niederen Adels in Teutschland* (Göttingen, 1795).
Ranke, Leopold von, *Denkwürdigkeiten des Staatskanzlers Fürsten von Hardenberg bis zum Jahre 1806* (Leipzig, 1877).
Der Religionsjournal, ed. Hermann Goldhagen (Mainz, 1776–91).

Bibliography

Republikaner, der fränkische, ed. K. Hartmann & J. D. Meuth (Mainz, 1792-3).
Risbeck, J. K., *Travels through Germany*, vol. 3 (London, 1787).
Roth, J. R., *Von dem Grundsatze, nach welchem das Verhältniß unmittelbarer reichsadlicher Einwohner reichsständischer Lande gegen reichsständische Landesherren zu bemessen ist* (Mainz, 1784).
Sartori, Joseph Edler von, *Geistliches und weltliches Staatsrecht der deutschen catholischgeistlichen Erz-, Hoch- und Ritterstifter* (7 vols, Nuremberg, 1788-91).
Statistische Abhandlung über die Mängel in der Regierungsverfassung der geistlichen Wahlstaaten und von den Mitteln, solchen abzuhelfen (2 vols, Frankfurt am Main, 1787).
Scheel, Heinrich, *Jakobinische Flugschriften aus dem deutschen Süden am Ende des 18. Jahrhunderts* (Berlin, 1965).
Scheidt, C. L., *Historische und diplomatische Nachrichten von dem hohen und niederen Adel in Teutschland* (2 vols, Hanover, 1754-5).
Schirmer, R., *Schauspielerleben im 18. Jahrhundert: Erinnerungen von J. A. Christ* (Munich, 1912).
Schnaubert, A. J., *Über des Freiherrn von Mosers Vorschläge zur Verbesserung der geistlichen Staaten in Teutschland* (Jena, 1787).
Schneider, F., 'Ein päpstlicher Gesandte über Mainz 1762 und 1764', *Mainzer Journal* (1898).
Schreiben an Custine, General der französischen Armeen, veranlaßt durch seine entehrende Aufrufungen an die Bürger und Soldaten deutscher Nation, verfaßt von einem Manne, der ein Feind von allem Despotismus ist, der aber für das Beste seines Vaterlandes, für das Wohl seiner Mitbürger, für die Ehre Deutschlands-Fürsten, sein Leben aufzuopfern bereit ist (1792).
(Schreiber, A. W.), 'Streiferei von Mainz nach Münster im Junius 1792', in *Streifereien durch einige Gegenden Deutschlands vom Verfasser der 'Szenen aus Fausts Leben'* (Leipzig, 1795).
Schrohe, Heinrich, 'Ein Reisebericht über Mainz im Jahre 1769', *Hessische Volksbücher*, 48 (1922).
Schüddekopf, Karl, *Briefwechsel zwischen Gleim und Heinse* (2 vols, Weimar, 1894, 1896).
Schulz, J. C. F., *Briefe aus Mainz während der Restaurationsfeyerlichkeiten der Universität vom 15. bis zum 19ten November 1784 geschrieben* (Frankfurt, 1784).
Schunk, D. J. P., *Beyträge zur Mainzer Geschichte mit Urkunden* (3 vols, Frankfurt and Leipzig, 1788-90).
Seyfried, J. E. von, *Statistische Nachrichten über die ehemaligen geistlichen Stiften, nebst einer historisch-politischen Übersicht der gesamten deutschen Kirchenstaaten*, ed. J. C. Freiherr von Aretin (Landshut, 1804).
Smyth, Mrs Gillespie, *Memoirs and Correspondence (Official and Familiar) of Sir Robert Murray Keith K.B.*, vol. 2 (London, 1849).
(Sneedorf, F.), *Briefe eines reisenden Dänen, geschrieben im Jahr 1791 und 1792 während seiner Reise durch einen Theil Deutschlands, der Schweiz und Frankreich* (Züllichau, 1793).
Staats Anzeigen, ed. A. L. Schlözer (Göttingen, 1782-93).
Staël, Madame de, *De l'Allemagne* (2 vols, Paris, 1958).
Stein, Freiherr vom, *Briefe und Amtliche Schriften*, vol. 1, ed. Walther Hubatsch (Stuttgart, 1957).
Stiller, H. T., *An die Franken und ihre Repräsentanten in Deutschland* ('Deutschland', 1793).

Bibliography

Swinburne, Henry, *The Courts of Europe at the Close of the Last Century*, ed. C. White, vol. 1 (London, 1841).
A Tour through Germany, containing full directions for travelling in that interesting country: with observations on the state of agriculture and policy of the different states; very particular descriptions of the courts of Vienna and Berlin, and Coblentz and Mentz (London, n.d.).
Träger, Claus, *Mainz zwischen Schwarz und Rot: Die Mainzer Revolution in Schriften, Reden und Briefen* (Berlin, 1963).
Vivenot, Alfred Ritter von, *Quellen zur Geschichte der deutschen Kaiserpolitik Oesterreichs während der französischen Revolutionskriege, 1790–1801* (5 vols, Vienna, 1873–90).
Vogt, Niklas, *Geschichte des Verfalls und Untergangs des alten deutschen Reiches* (Frankfurt, 1833).
Wedekind, Georg, *Bemerkungen über die gemischten Regierungsverfassungen* (Mainz, 1792).
Weitzel, Johann Ignaz, *Das Merkwürdigste aus meinem Leben und aus meiner Zeit* (2 vols, Leipzig, 1821–3).
Werner, Franz, *Der Dom von Mainz nebst Darstellung der Schicksale der Stadt und der Geschichte ihrer Erzbischöfe*, vol. 3 (Mainz, 1836).
Winkopp, P. A. & J. F. A. Höck, *Magazin für Geschichte, Statistik, Literatur und Topographie der sämmtlichen deutschen geistlichen Staaten* (2 vols, Zürich, 1790).
Winkopp, P. A., *Faustin oder das philosophische Jahrhundert* (n.p., 1784).
Geschichte der französischen Eroberungen und Revolution am Rheinstrome, vorzüglich in Hinsicht auf die Stadt Mainz (n.p., n.d.).
Über die Verfassung von Mainz, oder Vergleich des alten und neuen Mainz ('Deutschland', 1792).
Wohlgemeinter Rath an die Mainzer Bürgerschaft in dem glücklichen Zeitpunkt, wo Derselben die Wahl ihrer künftigen Staatsverfassung heimgestellt wurde (n.p., 1792).

SECONDARY WORKS

To list the several hundred books and articles consulted during the preparation of this book would be a pointless act of self-indulgence, since few of them would be of general interest. Only the most important are listed therefore. Fuller bibliographies can be found in the works by Dreyfus and Jung cited below and in Hans Knies, 'Mainz und Rheinhessen, eine Bibliographie für die Jahre 1939–1954', *Mainzer Zeitschrift*, 51 (1956).
On the constitutional and administrative structure of the Electorate, the most valuable works are:
Bockenheimer, Karl, *Abriß der Verfassungsgeschichte*, Beiträge zur Geschichte der Stadt Mainz, vol. 1 (Mainz, 1874).
Cremer, Josef, *Die Finanzen in der Stadt Mainz im 18. Jahrhundert* (Giessen dissertation, 1932).
Goldschmidt, Hans, *Zentralbehörden und Beamtentum im Kurfürstentum Mainz vom 16. bis zum 18. Jahrhundert*, Abhandlungen zur mittleren und neueren Geschichte, vol. 7 (Berlin and Leipzig, 1908).
Schrohe, Heinrich, *Die Stadt Mainz unter kurfürstlicher Verwaltung (1462–1792)*, Beiträge zur Geschichte der Stadt Mainz, vol. 5 (Mainz, 1920).
Veit, A. L., 'Geschichte und Recht der Stiftsmäßigkeit auf die ehemals adeligen Domstifte von Mainz, Würzburg und Bamberg', *Historisches Jahrbuch*, 33 (1912).

Bibliography

On the social and economic structure of and developments in the Electorate:
Dael, F., 'Die Bevölkerungsverhältnisse der Stadt Mainz von den ältesten bis zu den neuesten Zeiten', *Hübners Jahrbuch für Volkswissenschaft und Statistik* (1853).
Dreyfus, F. G., 'Les corporations à Mayence au XVIIIe siècle', *Cahier d'Études Comtoises*, 3 (1961).
'Prix et Population à Trèves et à Mayence au XVIIIe siècle', *Revue d'Histoire économique et sociale*, 34 (1956).
Sociétés et Mentalités à Mayence dans la seconde moitié du 18e siècle (Paris, 1968).
Kirnberger, Albert, *Die Handelsmesse in Mainz in der Zeit der merkantilistischen Politik unter der Regierung der drei letzten Kurfürsten von Mainz 1743-1793* (Mainz, 1951).
Rösch, F., *Die Mainzer Armenreform vom Jahre 1786*, Arbeiten aus dem Forschungsinstitut für Fürsorgewesen in Frankfurt am Main, vol. 3 (Berlin, 1929).
Scholl, H., *Kurmainzische Wirtschaftspolitik (1648-1802)* (Frankfurt am Main dissertation, 1924).
Schwarz, K., *Der wirtschaftliche Konkurrenzkampf zwischen der Reichsstadt Frankfurt am Main und der kurfürstlichen Stadt Mainz* (Mainz, 1932).
Veit, A. L., *Mainzer Domherren vom Ende des 16. bis zum Ausgang des 18. Jahrhunderts* (Mainz, 1924).
Zöpfl, Gottfried, *Fränkische Handelspolitik im Zeitalter der Aufklärung*, Bayerische Wirtschafts- und Verwaltungsstudien, vol. 3 (Erlangen and Leipzig, 1894).

On domestic policies and politics:
Beaulieu-Marconnay, Karl Freiherr von, *Karl von Dalberg und seine Zeit* (2 vols, Weimar, 1879).
Henking, K., *Johannes von Müller* (2 vols, Stuttgart and Berlin, 1909 and 1928).
Herse, Wilhelm, *Kurmainz am Vorabend der Revolution* (Berlin dissertation, 1907).
Illich, Hans, 'Maßnahmen der Mainzer Erzbischöfe gegen kirchlichen Gütererwerb (1462-1792)', *Mainzer Zeitschrift*, 34 (1939).
Jung, H.-W., *Anselm Franz von Bentzel im Dienste der Kurfürsten von Mainz*, Beiträge zur Geschichte der Universität Mainz, vol. 7 (Wiesbaden, 1966).
Klein, Karl, *Geschichte von Mainz unter dem letzten Kurfürsten Karl Friedrich Joseph von Erthal* (Mainz, 1870).
Michels, Adolf Carl, 'Die Wahl des Grafen Johann Friedrich Karl von Ostein zum Kurfürsten und Erzbischof von Mainz (1743)', *Archiv für hessische Geschichte und Altertumskunde*, new series, 16 (1930).
Rössler, Hellmuth, *Graf Johann Philipp Stadion, Napoleons deutscher Gegenspieler*, vol. 1 (Vienna, 1966).
Stevens, Hermann, *Toleranzbestrebungen im Rheinland während der Zeit der Aufklärung* (Bonn dissertation, 1939).

On the Electorate's cultural life:
Bach, Adolf, *Aus dem Kreise der Sophie La Roche* (Cologne, 1924).
Brück, Anton, *Kurmainzer Schulgeschichte: Texte, Berichte, Memoranden*, Mainzer Beiträge zur Pädagogik, Historische Abteilung, vol. 1 (Wiesbaden, 1960).
Die Mainzer theologische Fakultät im 18. Jahrhundert, Beiträge zur Geschichte der Universität Mainz, vol. 2 (Wiesbaden, 1955).
Coudenhove-Erthal, Eduard Graf von, 'Die Kunst am Hofe des letzten Kurfürsten von Mainz (Friedrich Carl Joseph Freiherr von Erthal) 1774-1802', *Wiener Jahrbuch für Kunstgeschichte* 10 (1935).
Gottron, Adam, *Mainzer Musikgeschichte*, Beiträge zur Geschichte der Stadt Mainz, vol. 18 (Mainz, 1959).

Bibliography

Hainebach, Hans, *Studien zum literarischen Leben der Aufklärungszeit in Mainz* (Giessen dissertation, 1936).
Jakobi, Ernst, *Die Entstehung des Mainzer Universitätsfonds*, Beiträge zur Geschichte der Universität Mainz, vol. 5 (Wiesbaden, 1959).
Jungk, Ernst, *Zur Geschichte und Rechtsnatur des Mainzer Universitätsfonds*, Beiträge zur Geschichte der Stadt Mainz, vol. 12 (Mainz, 1938).
Just, Leo & Helmut Mathy, *Die Universität Mainz: Grundzüge ihrer Geschichte* (Trautheim and Mainz, 1965).
Just, Leo, *Die alte Universität Mainz*, Beiträge zur Geschichte der Universität Mainz, vol. 4 (Wiesbaden, 1957).
Mathy, Helmut, numerous articles on the University, published in *Jahrbuch der Vereinigung 'Freunde der Universität Mainz'*, *Mainzer Almanach*, *Geschichtliche Landeskunde*.
Messer, A., *Die Reform des Schulwesens im Kurfürstentum Mainz unter Emmerich Joseph (1763-1774)* (Mainz, 1897).
Napp-Zinn, Anton Felix, *Johann Friedrich von Pfeiffer und die Kameralwissenschaften an der Universität Mainz*, Beiträge zur Geschichte der Universität Mainz, vol. 1 (Wiesbaden, 1955).
Raab, Heribert, numerous articles, mainly on ecclesiastical affairs, published in *Jahrbuch für das Bistum Mainz*, *Mainzer Almanach*, *Archiv für mittelrheinische Kirchengeschichte*. Of especial importance is his book *Die Concordata Nationis Germanicae in der kanonistischen Diskussion des 17. bis 19. Jahrhunderts*, Beiträge zur Geschichte der Reichskirche in der Neuzeit, vol. 1 (Wiesbaden, 1956).
Roth, H., *Die Mainzer Presse von der Mainzer Revolution 1792 bis zum Ende der zweiten französischen Herrschaft 1814*, Quellen und Forschungen zur hessischen Geschichte, 11 (1930).
Schweickert, K., *Die Musikpflege am Hofe der Kurfürsten von Mainz im 17. und 18. Jahrhundert*, Beiträge zur Geschichte der Stadt Mainz, vol. 11 (Mainz, 1937).
Zimmermann, Wilhelm, *Die Anfänge und der Aufbau des Lehrlingsbildungs- und Volksschulwesens am Rhein um die Wende des 18. Jahrhunderts (1770-1826)*, vol. 1 (Cologne, 1953).

On the Electorate's position in and the Electors' policies towards the *Reich*:
Aretin, Karl Otmar Freiherr von, 'Dalberg zwischen Kaiser und Fürstenbund: Actenstücke zur Koadjutorwahl in Mainz 1787', *Archiv für mittelrheinische Kirchengeschichte* (1964).
Heiliges Römisches Reich, Veröffentlichungen des Instituts für europäische Geschichte in Mainz, vol. 38 (2 vols, Wiesbaden, 1967).
'Höhepunkt und Krise des deutschen Fürstenbundes: Die Wahl Dalbergs zum Coadjutor von Mainz (1787)', *Historische Zeitschrift*, 196 (1963).
'Die Konfessionen als politische Kräfte am Ausgang des alten Reiches', *Festgabe Joseph Lortz*, ed. E. Iserloh & P. Manns, vol. 2 (Baden-Baden, 1958).
Duchhardt, Heinz, *Philipp Karl von Eltz, Kurfürst von Mainz*, Quellen und Abhandlungen zur mittelrheinischen Kirchengeschichte, vol. 10 (Mainz, 1969).
Immich, Max, 'Preußens Vermittlungen im Nuntiaturstreit 1787 bis 1789', *Forschungen zur brandenburgischen und preußischen Geschichte*, 8 (1895).
Lüdtke, Wilhelm, 'Der Kampf zwischen Oesterreich und Preußen um die Vorherrschaft im "Reiche" und die Auflösung des Fürstenbundes (1789-1791)', *Mitteilungen des oesterreichischen Instituts für Geschichtsforschung*, 45 (1931).
Schotte, H., 'Zur Geschichte des Emser Kongresses', *Historisches Jahrbuch*, 35 (1914).

Bibliography

Schulte, Albert, *Ein englischer Gesandte am Rhein: George Cressener als bevollmächtigter Gesandter an den Höfen der geistlichen Kurfürsten und beim niederrheinisch-westfälischen Kreis, 1763–1781* (Bonn dissertation, 1954).

Solf, E., *Die Reichspolitik des Mainzer Kurfürsten Johann Friedrich Karl von Ostein von seinem Regierungsantritt (1743) bis zum Ausbruch des siebenjährigen Krieges* (Frankfurt dissertation, 1936).

Vezin, Liselotte, *Die Politik des Mainzer Kurfürsten Friedrich Karl von Erthal vom Beginn der französischen Revolution bis zum Falle von Mainz, 1789–1792* (Dillingen, 1932).

On the revolutionary period:

Bockenheimer, K. G., *Die Mainzer Klubisten 1792–1793* (Mainz, 1896).

Chuquet, Arthur, *Les Guerres de la Révolution*, vols 6–7 (Paris, n.d.).

Klein, Karl, *Geschichte von Mainz während der ersten französischen Occupation 1792–1793* (Mainz, 1861).

Mathy, Helmut, *Als Mainz französisch war* (Mainz, n.d.).

'Anton Dorsch', *Mainzer Zeitschrift*, 63 (1969).

Die Nackenheimer Revolution von 1792/1793, Nackenheimer heimatkundliche Schriftenreihe, vol. 14 (1967).

'Georg Wedekind (1761–1831). Die politische Gedankenwelt eines Mainzer Medizinprofessors', *Geschichtliche Landeskunde*, 5 (1968).

Schmitt, Friedrich, *Das Mainzer Zunftwesen und die französische Herrschaft* (Frankfurt am Main dissertation, 1929).

Steiner, Gerhard, 'Theater und Schauspiel im Zeichen der Mainzer Revolution', *Studien zur neueren deutschen Literatur*, ed. H. W. Seiffert (Berlin, 1964).

Veit, A. L., *Der Zusammenbruch des Mainzer Erzstuhles infolge der französischen Revolution* (Mainz, 1927).

INDEX

Aachen, 71, 307, 324, 327, 330
Abel, Wilhelm, historian, 304, 321
Albini, Franz Joseph Freiherr von (1748–1816), Mainz minister, 264, 270–1, 273, 275, 278, 291n
Alembert, Jean Le Rond d' (1717–1783), 30, 34
Alsace, 71–2, 100, 264, 267, 272
Amorbach, 128
Arand, Melchior, revolutionary priest, 300
Aretin, Karl Otmar Freiherr von, historian, 229, 303, 316n
Aris, Reinhold, historian, 303
Artois, comte d' (1757–1836), 267–8
Aschaffenburg, 41, 90, 92, 110, 117n, 153, 184, 242, 246–51, 254–7, 302, 333–4
Aufklärung, see Enlightenment, German
Augsburg, 41, 61, 332
Austria, 4–5, 8, 31–2, 39, 47, 50, 62, 65–6, 89, 100, 108, 112, 132, 136–8, 140, 151, 161, 188–9, 192, 210–20, 228–40, 252, 263–5, 267, 269–70, 273–4, 281–2, 300, 307, 309, 315–16, 331–4

Bacon, Francis (1561–1626), 23
Baden, Karl Friedrich, Margrave of, 219–20, 239, 316, 320
Bahrdt, Karl Friedrich, radical theologian, 118
Bamberg, 43, 50, 54, 100, 221
Barker, Sir Ernest, 13, 15
Barnard, F. M., historian, 14, 18n, 20, 25
Basedow, Johann Bernard, progressive educator, 31, 122
Basle, Treaty of, 332
Bavaria, 5, 50, 84, 210–11, 233, 238
Bavaria, Karl Theodor, Elector of, 221, 223–4, 236, 240, 251–2, 255, 320
Bayle, Pierre (1647–1706), 23
Beamten, 11–15, 18
Becher, Johann Joachim, 19
Bechtel, Heinrich, historian, 10
Behrens, C. B. A., historian, 35n

Becker, Johann, 198
Belgium, 5, 100, 223, 250, 252, 325, 331
Bellarmine, Cardinal Robert, 119n
Bentzel, Anselm Franz Freiherr von (1738–85), Mainz minister, 110–11, 114–18, 121, 131–2, 135–7, 141, 143–7, 152–3, 158, 161, 168–70, 172, 185, 193, 198
Berlin, 29, 71, 227
Bettendorf, Freiherren von, 56
Bibra, Philipp Anton Freiherr von (1766–1826), Mainz *Vicedom*, 259–61
Biedermann, Karl, historian, 11
Bingen, 41, 53, 269, 281
Bischoffswerder, Johann Rudolf von, Prussian minister, 332
Böhmer, Caroline, radical writer, 270
Böhmer, Georg Wilhelm (1761–1839), clubist 283, 300
Böhmer, Georg Friedrich von, Prussian diplomat, 239
Bonn, 12, 119, 325, 327n
Boppard, 245
Brandes, Ernst (1758–1810), conservative writer, 310
Breidbach zu Bürresheim, Emmerich Joseph Freiherr von, *see* Mainz, Emmerich Joseph, Archbishop and Elector of
Braubach, Max, historian, 260n
Bruford, Walter Horace, historian, 313n
Brunswick, Karl Wilhelm Ferdinand, Duke of (1785–1806), 219, 273
Burke, Edmund (1729–97), 4, 294, 314
Butterfield, Sir Herbert, historian, 33n

Cameralism, 13, 18–19
Campo Formio, Treaty of, 332–3
Carl August of Weimar, *see* Saxony-Weimar, Carl August, Duke of
Carmer, Johann Heinrich (1721–1801), Prussian law reformer, 37
Carsten, F. L., historian, 305n
Cassirer, Ernst, philosopher, 2

Index

Catherine II ('The Great'), Empress of Russia (1762–96), 4
Charles VI, Emperor (1711–40), 55, 214
Charles VII, Emperor (1742–5), 5, 96–7
Châteaubriand, François René, vicomte de (1768–1848), 26
Clausonnette, marquis de, French diplomat, 109
Clement XIII, Pope (1758–69), 119
Clement XIV, Pope (1769–74), 109, 117
clubists, *see* Mainz, Archbishopric and Electorate of, revolutionary club
Cobban, Alfred, historian, 297n
Cobenzl, Philipp Count (1741–1814), Austrian statesman, 332
Cocceji, Samuel von (1679–1755), Prussian law reformer, 37
Colloredo, Franz Gundaker Prince von, Vice-Chancellor of the Empire, 136–7, 146, 269
Colloredo, Rudolf Joseph Prince von, Vice-Chancellor of the Empire, 135–8, 146, 148, 226
Cologne, Electorate of, 50, 60–1, 72, 177, 270n, 305, 307, 316, 330
Cologne, City of, 44–5, 48, 71–3, 75, 306–7, 324, 327n
Cologne, Max Franz, Archbishop and Elector of (1784–1801), 31, 66, 147, 214, 221, 226, 228, 236–8, 251–2, 264, 272n, 273, 334
Cologne, Max Friedrich, Archbishop and Elector of (1761–1784), 119, 121
Condé, Louis-Joseph, Prince de (1736–1818), 267–9, 275
Conrad, Father Peter, turbulent priest, 124–5, 143
Constance, 41, 50
Cotta, Friedrich (1758–1838), clubist, 277, 283, 286, 288
Coudenhove, Karl Ludwig Freiherr von, 257
Coudenhove, Georg Ludwig Freiherr von, 216, 244
Coudenhove, Sophie von, *éminence grise*, 62n, 68n, 216–18, 232, 235, 264, 271, 298
Cremer, Josef, historian, 88
Cressener, George, British diplomat, 108, 148, 150–2, 154, 159, 160
Custine, Adam Philippe comte de (1740–93), French general, 274–6, 278–80, 282–5, 287–9, 291, 294, 299–300

Dahrendorf, Ralf, sociologist, 1
Dalberg, Freiherren von, 56
Dalberg, Franz Karl Anton Freiherr von, Mainz canon, 132, 135, 147
Dalberg, Karl Anton Theodor Maria Freiherr von (1744–1817), Mainz coadjutor, 66–7, 132, 137, 149–50, 155, 169, 182, 198–201, 229–31, 234, 236, 243–4, 278, 333–4
Dalberg, Karl Joseph Freiherr von, Dean of the Mainz Cathedral Chapter, 132
Darnton, Robert, historian, 23n, 34, 36
Deel, Philipp Karl von, Mainz minister, 218–20, 226n, 232, 247, 264n
Diderot, Denis (1713–84), 26, 35
Dienheim, Christoph Freiherr von, Mainz canon, 66, 229–30, 244
Dorsch, Anton Joseph (1758–1819), clubist, 194, 273, 276, 280, 285, 289, 314
Doyle, William, historian, 308n
Dreyfus, François, historian, 39n, 40n, 70n, 72, 80, 86
Droz, Jacques, historian, 303
Dumont, Daniel (1742–1828), merchant and counter-revolutionary, 68–9, 193, 279, 281, 284, 295n

Eberbach, monastery of, 127
ecclesiastical states, 5, 240
Edelsheim, Georg Ludwig Freiherr von, Baden diplomat, 239
Edelsheim, Wilhelm Freiherr von, Baden minister, 220, 239
Eichsfeld, The, 41, 62, 154, 179
Eichstätt, 41, 50, 221–2, 225
Eickemeyer, Rudolf Heinrich (1753–1825), radical writer, 123–4, 275
Eltz, Counts von, 82–3, 154, 157–8, 244, 290
Eltz, Anselm Casimir Count von, 83, 154, 197
Eltz, Hugo Franz Karl Count von, Provost of the Mainz Cathedral Chapter, 54–5, 67, 107–8, 131, 135, 147–8, 153–4, 167
Eltz, Hugo Philipp Karl Count von, 81, 197–8
Eltz, Johann Philipp Jakob Count von, 154
Eltz, Philipp Karl Count von, *see* Mainz, Philipp Karl, Archbishop and Elector of
Emmerich Joseph Freiherr von Breidbach zu Bürresheim, *see* Mainz, Emmerich Joseph, Archbishop and Elector of
Empire, Holy Roman
Beamtenstand, 10–15
Catholic Church, 13, 29–32, 314, 330
'decadence', 3–5, 37–8, 331–4
dissolution of, 303, 331–4
economy, 6–10, 304, 317–22, 328–30
French Revolution and, 303–334
Joseph II and, 210–40
nobility, 10, 14–15, 305, 308–9, 326
nuncio dispute, 220–8, 236–40, 263
peasantry, 318–22, 326, 331
plans for reform of, 219–20, 231–6

348

Index

Empire, Holy Roman (*cont.*)
  political organisation, 3, 46–50, 59–60, 64–6, 252, 274n
  political thought, 15–23, 309–17
  population, 6, 318–19
  Protestant Church, 13, 26–9, 227, 314, 330
  society, 10–15, 304, 317–18, 321–2
  towns, 6–10, 305–7, 317–18, 322–31
  universities, 11–13, 16, 18–19, 27, 30
Ems, Congress of, 31, 104, 121n, 177–8, 194, 222–3, 226–7, 237, 239–40
England, *see* Great Britain
Enlightened Absolutism, 32–7, 139–40, 163–93, 273, 294, 310, 316
Enlightenment
  French, 2, 12, 32, 34–6, 101, 110, 316
  German, 2–3, 11–38, 309–13, 315–18
Entraigues, marquis d', French diplomat, 134–5, 137, 144, 147–8, 150–1, 154–5, 158, 160, 164
Épée, Charles Abbé de l', social reformer, 190
episcopalism, 29–31, 103–4, 118–21, 170, 220–8, 236–40
Epstein, Klaus, historian, 331
Erfurt, 41, 62, 110, 116, 118, 179–80, 186, 199, 201, 301
Erlangen, 12
Erthal, Friedrich Karl Freiherr von, *see* Mainz, Friedrich Karl, Archbishop and Elector of
Erthal, Lothar Franz Freiherr von, Mainz minister, 153, 198, 216, 243
Este, Charles, tourist, 190, 301
Etherege, Sir George, British diplomat, 3

Febronius, *see* Hontheim, Johann Nicolaus von
Fechenbach, Georg Adam Freiherr von, Dean of the Mainz Cathedral Chapter, 129–30
Fechenbach, Georg Karl Franz Freiherr von, Dean of the Mainz Cathedral Chapter, 275
Fechenbach, Philipp Franz Freiherr von, army officer, 247–8
Felbiger, Johann Ignaz (1724–88), educational reformer, 115, 164
Feller, Abbé, ultramontane journalist, 203, 314
Ferrette, Frau von, 62, 217, 244, 271
Fichte, Johann Gottlieb (1762–1814), 20, 311
Finckenstein, Friedrich Ludwig Count (1745–1818), Prussian statesman, 232, 234
Fischer, G. N., *Popularphilosoph*, 25
Fischer, Karl, anti-revolutionary writer, 294
Fischer, Wolfram, historian, 304
Ford, Franklin, L., historian, 259n

Forster, Georg (1754–94), explorer, radical writer and clubist, 170, 172, 201, 204, 241, 251n, 256–7, 261, 266, 270, 276–80, 283–6, 293, 296–300, 312
France, 2, 4–5, 10n, 11–12, 14, 23–4, 26, 29, 32, 37, 45, 64–6, 72–3, 80n, 91, 110, 112, 117, 136, 144–5, 148–51, 182, 197, 210, 219–20, 235, 290, 319n, 322, *see also under* French Revolution
Francis I, Emperor (1745–65), 10
Francis II, Emperor (1792–1835), 179, 271, 273, 332–3
Francke, August Hermann (1663–1727), Pietist, 27–8
Franckenstein, Freiherren von, 56, 157–8, 244
Franckenstein, Franz Christoph Karl Freiherr von, 154
Franckenstein, Franz Philipp Freiherr von, Mainz canon, 55, 84, 86n, 108, 112, 135, 137–8, 147–8, 151, 154, 161, 167
Franckenstein, Friedrich Joseph Karl Freiherr von, 198
Frankfurt am Main, 42, 46, 71, 74–6, 86, 97–100, 111, 113, 263, 271, 286, 323, 326, 332
Frederick I, King in Prussia (1701–13), 28
Frederick II ('The Great'), King of Prussia (1740–1786), 5, 10, 12, 18, 21, 24, 29–30, 33, 36–7, 65, 210, 219, 232–3, 239, 244, 309, 319–20
Frederick William II, King of Prussia (1786–97), 21, 28, 231, 233–4, 238, 252, 263, 271, 287, 312
Freising, 119, 214, 221
French Revolution
  émigrés, 267–8
  foreign policy, 264–7, 273, 331–4
  military campaigns, 274–5, 300–1, 331–4
  policy towards occupied territories, 276, 279–83, 286, 289, 299–300, 325–8
  response/reaction in Holy Roman Empire from
    Church, 287–9, 330–1
    governments, 273, 286, 306–7
    intellectuals, 241, 303, 309–16, 328–9
    nobles, 245, 272, 305, 308–9
    peasantry, 298–300, 306–7, 318–24, 329–31
    towns, 250–1, 258, 273, 275–302, 305–7, 317–18, 321, 323–4, 329–31
Friedrich Karl Freiherr von Erthal, *see* Mainz, Friedrich Karl, Archbishop and Elector of
Fulda, Heinrich, Prince-Bishop of, 31
Furet, François, historian, 308n

Gallicanism, 29, 223–4
Gallitzin, Princess Amalie von, 313

Index

Gellert, Christian (1715-69), 115, 317
Gentz, Friedrich (1764-1832), 20
Germany, see Empire, Holy Roman
Giessen, 12
Godechot, Jacques, historian, 161, 251n, 328n
Görres, Johannes Joseph (1776-1848), 20
Görtz, Johann Eustach Count von, Prussian diplomat, 239
Goethe, Johann Wolfgang von (1749-1832), 13, 19, 46-7, 103, 196, 201, 256n, 301n, 311, 313, 329, 330
Göttingen, 12, 22, 30, 103, 110, 146, 193, 199, 204, 258
Goldhagen, Hermann, conservative journalist, 125, 141, 206-7, 256, 314
Gooch, George Peabody, historian, 303
Gotha, see Saxony-Gotha
Goubert, Pierre, historian, 92
Grab, Walter, historian, 297n, 316n, 304
Great Britain, 22-4, 32, 61, 66, 80n, 101, 145-6, 182, 197, 234-5, 319, 332
Grégoire, Gabriel, French commissar, 280-1, 283
Groschlag, Freiherren von, 51
Groschlag, Karl Friedrich Willibald Freiherr von, Mainz minister, 110-12, 118, 121, 131-3, 135-7, 143-7, 152-3, 158, 161, 185, 193, 198
guilds, 9-10
Gundling, Nicolaus Hieronymus von, 98
Gymnich, Klemens August Freiherr von, Mainz general, 254, 275

Habsburg Monarchy, see Austria
Halle, 12, 18, 27-9, 256n
Hamerow, Theodore S., historian, 80n
Hanover, 5, 11, 30, 71, 227, 233, 236, 314
Hartmann, Kaspar, clubist, 277
Hartung, Fritz, historian, 33, 35n
Hatzfeldt, Counts von, 216, 243-4
Hatzfeldt, Charlotte Sophie Countess von, 216
Hatzfeldt, Franz Ludwig Count von (1756-1827), Mainz general, 216, 244n, 247-8, 250, 252n
Hauser, Franz Gregorius Freiherr von, Mainz diplomat, 212
Haussmann, Nicolas, French commissar, 280-1, 288
Heidelberg, 18, 199
Heimes, Valentin (1741-1806), suffragan bishop of Mainz, 170, 172-3, 177-8, 213, 218, 221-2, 225-8, 232, 247, 250, 254
Heinse, Wilhelm (1749-1803), 146
Helvétius, Claude Adrien (1715-71), 35

Herder, Johann Gottfried (1744-1803), 20-1, 25, 199, 201
Herel, Friedrich, professor at Erfurt, 118
Hertzberg, Ewald Friedrich Count von (1725-95), Prussian statesman, 234, 310
Hessen-Darmstadt, 111, 239, 255, 257
Hessen-Kassel, 255, 305n, 317, 320
Hettersdorff, Emmerich Joseph Freiherr von, Mainz canon, 281
Hinrichs, Carl, historian, 28
Höchst, 79, 100, 112, 179
Höck, J. D. A., 92-3
Hölzle, Erwin, historian, 304
Hörnigk, Philipp Wilhelm von, Austrian cameralist, 19
Hofenfels, Christian Freiherr von, Zweibrücken minister, 239
Hofmann, Andreas Joseph (1753-1849), clubist, 283, 285
Hoheneck, Philipp Karl Freiherr von, Mainz canon, 135, 147
Holborn, Hajo, historian, 1, 3, 15, 24, 26n
Holland, see United Provinces
Hontheim, Johann Nicolaus von (1701-90), suffragan bishop of Trier, 104, 119, 224, 227
Horix, Johann Baptist, episcopalist, 103-4, 106, 119
Hornstein, Franz Xaver Maria Freiherr von, Mainz canon, 114, 137, 161, 243
Humboldt, Wilhelm von (1767-1835), 171n, 192, 199, 201
Hume, David (1711-76), 26

Imperial Knights, 5, 30, 49-69, 90, 139, 196-203, 225, 290, 300n, 308, 324, 333-4
Ingelheim, Franz Karl Count von, 202
Isenbiehl, Johann Lorenz, 124, 159

Jacobi, Friedrich Heinrich (1743-1819), 13, 330
Jansenism, 29, 103, 170
Jesuits, 30, 101, 103-6, 114-17, 123, 133-4, 142-3, 156-7, 164-5, 207, 249
Johann Friedrich Count von Ostein, see Mainz, Johann Friedrich, Archbishop, and Elector of
Johann Philipp von Schönborn, see Mainz, Johann Philipp, Archbishop and Elector of
Joseph I, Emperor (1705-11), 61
Joseph II, Emperor (1765-90), 5, 32, 36-7, 46-7, 65, 117, 120-1, 134, 136, 138, 146, 148, 150, 153, 166, 168, 170, 174, 180, 185, 187, 189, 203, 210-15, 217-28, 230-3, 235, 237-9, 244, 263, 309, 320

350

Index

Josephism, 37, 121, 140, 173, 224
Julku, Kyösti, historian, 245n
Justi, Johann Heinrich Gottlieb von (1705–71), 19, 24, 36

Kallenberg, Fritz, historian, 304
Kant, Immanuel (1724–1804), 12, 20–1, 25, 294, 298n, 312, 329
Karg, Maximilian Joseph Freiherr von, Mainz diplomat, 212
Karl Theodor, Elector of Bavaria, *see* Bavaria, Karl Theodor, Elector of
Kassel, 12, 71–2
Kaunitz, Wenzel Anton Prince von (1711–94), 32, 37, 112, 140, 210–11, 215–16, 219, 223, 229–31, 265, 272n, 332
Kerpen, Hugo Franz Freiherr von, Mainz canon, 130, 132, 230
Kesselstadt, Counts von, 56, 196
Kesselstadt, Joseph Franz Count von, Mainz canon, 55
Klein, Karl, historian, 298n
Klima, A., historian, 8
Koblenz *Gravamina*, 104, 118–21, 222
Koblenz, 246, 306
Königsberg, 12
Kopp, G. L. C., historian, 174n
Krieger, Leonard, historian, 1, 14n, 16
Kuczynski, Jürgen, historian, 304

Labrousse, Ernest, historian, 2
La Roche, Georg Michael, 102–3
La Roche, Sophie, 102–3, 132
Laurens, Abbé, pornographer, 123
League of Princes (*Fürstenbund*), 65, 210–13, 218–20, 223, 227–40, 263–5
Lehrbach, Franz Sigmund Freiherr von, Austrian diplomat, 210
Leibniz, Gottfried Wilhelm von (1646–1716), 16–17, 24
Leipzig, 18, 193
Lenz, Jakob Michael (1751–92), 19
Leopold I, Emperor (1658–1705), 64
Leopold II, Emperor (1790–2), 5, 65, 178, 263–5, 309
Lessing, Gotthold Ephraim (1729–81), 22, 26, 115
Leyen, Counts von der, 51
Leyen, Damian Count von der, Provost of the Mainz Cathedral Chapter, 119, 121, 132–3, 137–8, 161, 243–4
Lichtenberg, Georg Christoph, 12, 312
Liège, 50, 61, 210, 225, 251–4, 259, 263–4, 266, 271, 307, 322
Liège, Johann Theodor, Prince-Bishop of, 31
Liesenfeld, F., historian, 304

Locke, John (1632–1704), 23, 102
Louis XVI, King of France (1774–93), 265, 269, 272, 311
Lüdtke, Wilhelm, historian, 245n
Lütge, Friedrich, historian, 303, 322
Lunéville, Peace of, 332
Lucchesini, Girolamo Marchese, Prussian diplomat, 231
Lund, 18
Luther, Martin (1483–1546), 16, 27
Lux, Adam (1765–1793), clubist, 300

Maass, Ferdinand, historian, 37n
Main, river, 41, 44, 76, 87, 188
Mainz, Archbishopric and Electorate of, archives, 39–40, 104
army, 58–9, 63, 233–4, 253–5, 278, 297
burghers, 76–80, 84–7, 98–9, 116, 158–9, 202–3, 248–51, 254–61, 275, 290
cession to France of, 332
Cathedral Chapter, 53–6, 60–9, 82–4, 90, 92, 94, 105, 126–48, 167–8, 178, 195, 228–31, 244–5, 263n, 271–2, 278, 296
censorship, 123, 170, 202–3, 283, 293n
Church, 40–3, 101, 121–2, 287–9
clergy, 85, 90, 110, 156, 176, 202–3, 208, 257, 271–2, 274, 276, 280–1, 285, 287–9, 290–1, 293–4, 296, 300n
court, 42, 57–9, 139, 241–3, 250, 263, 271, 289–90, 294, 302
economy, 42–5, 67–8, 70–95, 98–101, 112–13, 187–8, 250–1, 258, 261–3, 289–94
freemasons and *Illuminati*, 194–5, 203, 206
French émigrés, 267–72
French occupation, 84, 179, 274–302
geography, 39, 41, 70
government and administration, 41, 56–7, 61–4, 191–3, 278, 289
guilds, 76–80, 98–9, 116, 181, 188, 205, 248–51, 253–61, 276, 278–80, 283, 291, 296
Jacobins, *see* revolutionary club
Jesuits, 101, 103–6, 114–17, 123, 133–4, 142–3, 156–7, 164–5, 207, 249
Jews, 80, 85, 99, 170, 184–5, 249
judicial system, 63
monasteries, 93, 104–5, 126–33, 142, 166–8, 173–5, 182, 250, 256, 281
nobility, 42–3, 45, 49–69, 81–5, 88, 90, 93, 196–204, 243–5, 250, 257, 266, 271–2, 274, 276–7, 279, 290, 292–4, 297, 302
officials, 85–7, 116, 169–70, 191–3, 202–3, 256–7, 266, 280, 291, 296, 300n
peasantry, 87–95, 116, 125–6, 185–7, 191, 208–9, 246, 249–51, 262, 266, 292, 298–300

351

Index

Mainz, Archbishopric and Electorate of (*cont.*)
  poor, 86, 93–4, 176, 188, 261–3, 291, 293, 296
  popular conservatism, 94, 123–6, 134, 140–1, 156–7, 162, 166, 204–9, 245–66, 275–6, 279–95, 298–302
  popular radicalism, 123, 245–66, 273, 276–9
  popular enlightenment, 121–2, 193–204
  population, 41, 45, 70–1, 188, 250
  press, 193–6, 206–7, 245, 277, 283n
  Protestants, 71, 77, 85, 99, 109, 112, 170, 173, 179–83, 204–6, 244, 256, 283, 289n
  reading club, 195–6, 202, 297
  relations with the Empire, 46–9, 64–6, 97, 136–8, 144–52, 210–40, 252–3
  revolutionary club, 40, 109, 263, 276–7, 279, 281, 283–9, 295–8
  schools, 106–7, 122–6, 133–4, 141–2, 159–60, 164–6, 283
  society, 42–5, 50–9, 81–4, 113–14, 188–90, 193–204, 250–1, 261–3
  taxation and finance, 85–8, 105, 263, 271–2, 278, 291, 298
  theatre, 199, 201–2, 278
  university, 107, 114–18, 140, 159, 164, 166–73, 175, 178–9, 194, 202–3, 205–6, 253–61, 272–3, 296
Mainz, Emmerich Joseph, Archbishop and Elector of (1763–74), 47, 58, 64, 146, 150, 153, 155, 159, 161, 164, 243
  character and reputation, 108–10, 146–7
  dispute with Cathedral Chapter, 130–8
  ecclesiastical policies, 110, 118–21, 126–38, 167
  economic policies, 111–13
  educational policies, 114–18, 122, 133–4
  election, 107–8
  financial policies, 112–13
  religious toleration, 112
  social policies, 113
Mainz, Friedrich Karl, Archbishop and Elector of (1774–1802), 135, 137–8, 141
  administration, 191–3
  agriculture, 185–7
  aristocratic opposition to, 157–62, 243–5
  background, 152
  censorship, 170, 202–3, 206–7, 272–3
  character and reputation, 163–4, 212–13, 233
  counter-revolutionary policies, 246–74, 278, 301
  court, 241–3, 263, 271
  ecclesiastical policies, 31, 168–9, 173–9, 194, 207–9, 220–8, 236–40
  economic policies, 78–9, 92, 187–8
  educational policies, 164–72, 191

  election, 147–57, 161
  financial problems, 263, 271–2, 278, 291, 298
  imperial and foreign policies, 210–40, 252–3, 333
  religious toleration, 179–185, 194, 204–6
  social policies, 86–7, 188–90
Mainz, Johann Friedrich, Archbishop and Elector of (1743–63), 53, 56, 65, 74, 138
  character and reputation, 97
  ecclesiastical policies, 104–5
  economic policies, 78, 98–101
  educational policies, 106–7
  election, 96–7
  social policies, 107
Mainz, Johann Philipp, Archbishop and Elector of (1647–73), 101
Mainz, Lothar Franz, Archbishop and Elector of (1695–1729), 43, 74, 97, 242
Mainz, Philipp Karl, Archbishop and Elector of (1732–43), 54, 96–7, 197
Marburg, 12, 18, 110
Maria Theresa, Empress (1740–80), 37, 97, 148, 150, 153, 210, 309
Martini, Karl Anton Freiherr von (1726–1800), 12–13, 36
Mathy, Helmut, historian, 40n
Mauersberg, Hans, historian, 8
Mecklenburg, 3, 6
Meinecke, Friedrich, historian, 1, 303, 313n
Merlin de Thionville, Antoine-Christophe (1762–1833), French commissar, 280, 286, 326
Metternich, Counts von, 56
Metternich, Clemens Prince von (1773–1859), 52, 58, 171
Metternich, Franz Georg Count von, Austrian diplomat, 52, 137, 167, 171, 173, 211–18, 220, 256
Metternich, Mathias (1758–1825), clubist, 124, 277, 283, 288, 292
Meusel, Georg, professor at Erfurt, 118
Michaelis, Johann David, professor at Göttingen, 12
Migazzi, Christoph Anton von, Archbishop of Vienna, 32
Miles, W. A., tourist, 178n, 262
Möser, Justus (1720–94), 314, 321
Montesquieu, Charles Louis de Secondat, baron de (1689–1755), 23–4, 35, 110, 181
Moore, Dr. John, tourist, 127
Morazé, Charles, historian, 139
Mousnier, Roland, historian, 2
Müller, Johannes von, Mainz minister, 62n, 170–2, 198, 204–5, 232, 235, 239, 241, 244, 246–8, 250, 251n, 263–4, 271

Index

Münster, 12
Muratori, Lodovico Antonio (1672–1750), 23, 115, 189

Nackenheim, 166, 300
Nantes, Edict of, 181
Napoleon Bonaparte (1769–1821), 331–4
Nassau-Usingen, 255
Neipperg, Count, Austrian diplomat, 111–12, 126, 130, 134–7, 144–7, 149–54, 156, 158–9
Neller, Georg Christoph, episcopalist, 119
Netherlands, Austrian, see Belgium
Newton, Sir Isaac (1642–1727), 23

O'Kelli, Jean-Jacques, comte de, French diplomat, 216
Ostein, Counts von, 51, 290
Ostein, Johann Friedrich Count von, see Mainz, Johann Friedrich, Archbishop and Elector of
Ottoman Empire, see Turkey
Oyré, François Ignace d', French general, 282

Pacca, Cardinal Bartolomeo, Papal nuncio at Cologne, 179, 237
Palatinate, Electorate of the, 41, 48, 71, 73, 111, 149, 300n, 326–7
Palatinate, Karl Theodor, Elector of the, see Bavaria, Karl Theodor, Elector of
Papacy, 29–32, 101–4, 117, 118–21, 155, 167, 177, 179, 210, 220–8, 231, 236–40, 287, 330
Pape, Friedrich Georg (1766–1816), clubist, 283, 286–7, 289
Paris, 23, 259, 283
Passau, 213–14
Patocki, J. P., merchant and clubist, 300
Pennant, Thomas, tourist, 92, 127, 186
Pergen, Johann Anton Count von, Austrian minister, 58, 108, 131, 136–7, 145
Pfeiffer, Johann Friedrich von, cameralist and professor at Mainz, 170, 185, 188, 204
Philipp Karl Count von Eltz, see Mainz, Philipp Karl, Archbishop and Elector of
Physiocrats, 34–5
Pierre, Jean Claude, clubist, 298
Pietism, 16, 26–9, 314
Pilati, Carlantonio, 30, 67
Pillnitz, Declaration of, 236, 265, 269, 332
Pistoia, Synod of, 178–9
Pius VI, Pope (1775–99), 179, 221, 231, 236–7
Plümicke, C. M., tourist, 201
Plumb, J. H., historian, 86n
Poland, 5
Pope, Alexander (1688–1744), 26

Provence, comte de, 268
Prussia, 4–5, 10, 12, 28–30, 39, 65–6, 72, 89, 96, 182, 192, 210, 213–14, 217–20, 226, 229, 232–60, 252, 263–5, 267, 269–70, 273–4, 281–2, 286, 300, 307, 309, 316, 319–20, 331–4
Pufendorf, Samuel von (1632–94), 17–18
Pütter, J. S., 24

Quesnay, François (1694–1774), 35

Raab, Heribert, historian, 119, 159–61
Ramm, Agatha, historian, 251n, 259n, 297n, 332n
Ranke, Leopold von, 222
Rastatt, Congress of, 332
Raynal, Guillaume Thomas François (1713–96), 35
Réau, Louis, historian, 2
Rebmann, Johann Andreas Georg Friedrich (1768–1824), radical journalist, 312
Regensburg, 119, 214, 225, 333–4
Rehberg, August Wilhelm (1757–1836), conservative writer, 314
Reichenbach, Convention of, 5, 331–2
Reider, Bernard Gottfried, Mainz official, 130
Reiss, Hans, historian, 20
Reubell, Jean-Baptiste (1747–1807), French commissar, 280
Reventlow, Count, 314
Rheingau, 41, 88–9, 91, 93–4, 127, 208–9
Rhine, 44, 53, 71–5, 87, 215, 226n, 292
Riedel, Friedrich Justus, professor at Erfurt, 118
Riegger, Paul Joseph, 12–13, 37
Risbeck, J. K., 43, 57–8, 75, 83, 93–4, 127, 197
Ritter, Gerhard, historian, 1
Rome, see Papacy
Rougemaître, Charles-Jean, French clubist, 286
Rousseau, Jean Jacques (1712–78), 23, 35, 198, 298n
Rulffs, August Friedrich, Mainz official and clubist, 180–1, 189–90, 283
Russia, 3n, 4, 220

Saarbrücken, 306, 323, 326
Salzburg, Hieronymus, Archbishop of, 31, 221, 223, 226, 228
Salzburg, 50, 177, 214
Saxony, Electorate of, 5, 30, 61, 71, 233, 235–6, 315–16
Saxony, Friedrich August III, Elector of, 320
Saxony-Gotha, Ernst Duke of, 219, 239
Saxony-Weimar, Carl August, Duke of, 118, 163, 219–20, 229–35, 239, 316, 320

353

Index

Scheel, Heinrich, historian, 295, 302n, 304, 316n
Schiller, Friedrich (1759–1805), 19, 24, 199, 201, 215, 312, 329
Schlegel, Friedrich (1772–1829), 20, 311
Schlick, Joseph Heinrich Count von (1754–1807), Austrian diplomat, 244n, 268, 278, 302
Schlözer, August Ludwig, 12, 22, 24, 147, 168, 186, 310–11
Schmid, Heinrich, professor at Erfurt, 118
Schneider, Eulogius, radical priest, 314n
Schönborn, Counts von, 51–2, 90, 244
Schönborn, Johann Philipp von, *see* Mainz, Johann Philipp, Archbishop and Elector of
Schönborn, Melchior Friedrich Count von, Mainz canon, 55
Schönborn, Rudolf Franz Erwein Count von, 51
Schubart, Christian, journalist, 110
Schulenburg, Wilhelm Count von, Prussian minister, 332
Schultheiss, Philipp Adam von, Mainz official, 130, 132, 142
Shaftesbury, Anthony Ashley Cooper, 3rd Earl of, 23, 102
Sickingen, Wilhelm Count von, Mainz minister, 158, 215–16, 241
Simon, Johann Friedrich, French commissar, 280–1, 283, 298, 300
Simon, Richard (1638–1712), 23
Sömmering, Samuel Thomas (1755–1830), professor at Mainz, 170–1, 198, 201, 204, 298
Sonnenfels, Joseph Freiherr von (1732–1817), 12–14, 36–7, 198
Sorel, Albert, historian, 303
Specht zu Bubenheim, Lothar Franz Ignaz Freiherr von, Cantor of the Mainz Cathedral Chapter, 108
Spener, Philipp (1635–1705), Pietist, 27
Speyer, 41, 50, 149–50, 274–5, 300n, 324
Speyer, August Count von Limburg-Styrum, Prince-Bishop of, 225
Spielmann, Anton Freiherr von, Austrian statesman, 332
Srbik, H. Ritter von, historian, 303
Stadelmann, Rudolf, historian, 304, 316–17
Stadion, Counts von, 51, 157, 243
Stadion, Anton Heinrich Friedrich Count von (1691–1768), Mainz minister, 78, 97–107, 109–11, 121, 139, 145, 185, 193, 198
Stadion, Friedrich Lothar Count von, 156–7
Stadion, Johann Philipp Count von, Mainz canon, 94, 193
Staël, Germaine de (1766–1817), 315–16

Steigentesch, J. J. F., Director of the Mainz College of Education, 114–16, 122–4, 141–2
Stein, Johann Friedrich Freiherr von (1749–99), Prussian diplomat, 62n, 220, 239, 244, 252, 256–7, 263–4, 270, 275
Stein, Karl Freiherr von (1757–1831), Prussian diplomat, 146, 213, 220, 239
Steinberg, Georg August Freiherr von, Hanoverian diplomat, 235, 239
Stimming, Manfred, historian, 62n
Strasbourg, 41, 75, 86, 196, 258, 273, 283
Strauss, Maximilian Freiherr von, Mainz minister, 182–3, 232
Suarez, Karl Gottlieb (1746–98), Prussian law reformer, 37
Suffolk, Henry Howard, 12th Earl of, 151–2
Sweden, 4
Swieten, Gerhard van (1700–72), 37
Switzerland, 71, 100
Sybel, H. von, historian, 303

Teschen, Peace of, 4
Thomasius, Christian (1655–1728), 12–13, 17–18, 25, 28, 36
Thugut, Johann Amadeus Franz Freiherr von (1736–1818), Austrian statesman, 332
Träger, Claus, historian, 251n
Trautson, Johann Joseph von, Archbishop of Vienna, 31
Trauttmansdorff, Ferdinand Count von, Austrian diplomat, 212, 218–20, 229–31, 239, 244
Trier, 30, 48, 50, 54, 61, 111, 149, 177, 246, 251, 268, 270, 305–6, 327, 330
Trier, Clemens Wenzeslaus, Archbishop and Elector of (1739–1812), 31, 61, 119, 121, 211, 214, 221, 226, 228, 237–8, 268–70, 272n, 273
Troeltsch, Ernst, 1
Turgot, Anne Robert Jacques, baron de l'Aulne (1727–81), 35
Turin, Ernst Xaver, Mainz official, 164–5
Turkey, 3n, 4, 235

United Provinces, 9, 61, 66, 71–2, 74–5, 99–100, 146, 148, 181–3, 197, 210, 226n, 233, 235, 322

Valjavec, Fritz, historian, 22, 303
Valmy, Battle of, 274
Vienna, 12–14, 47, 71, 110, 196, 227, 290, 318
Vierhaus, Rudolf, historian, 24
Villiers, Thomas, British diplomat, 65, 97
Vogt, Niklas (1756–1836), professor at Mainz, 123, 196, 201, 253

Index

Voltaire, François Arouet de (1694-1778), 23, 26, 34, 36, 101, 112, 317
Voltelini, Hans von, historian, 36

Waldenfels, Johann Christian Freiherr von, Cologne minister, 222
Walderdorff, Franz Philipp Freiherr von, 132, 155, 243-4
Walker, Mack, historian, 317
Walldürn, 41, 174-5, 331
Wangermann, Ernst, historian, 318
Wars,
 of the Austrian Succession, 112, 328
 Seven Years War, 112, 328
Wartensleben, Count, Dutch diplomat, 150-1, 160
Wedekind, Georg Christian (1761-1839), clubist, 277, 283, 292, 298
Weimar, *see* Saxony-Weimar
Weis, Eberhard, historian, 322
Weitzel, Johann, memoirist, 171, 253-4, 256
Westphalia, Treaty of, 65, 214
Wieland, Christoph Martin von (1733-1813), 4, 12-13, 24, 101-3, 111, 116, 118, 199, 311-12

Winkopp, Peter Adolf (1759-1813), Mainz official and anti-revolutionary polemicist, 92, 203, 284-5, 289n, 290
Wolff, Christian Freiherr von (1679-1754), 12-13, 17-19, 25-9, 36
Worms, 48, 50, 119, 149-51, 173, 268, 274, 300n, 324, 326
Württemberg, 3-4, 52, 59, 71, 102, 110, 307
Würzburg, 30, 50, 54, 64, 76, 97, 100, 111, 188, 221, 264
Würzburg, Adam Friedrich Freiherr von Seinsheim, Prince-Bishop of, 100
Würzburg and Bamberg, Franz Ludwig Freiherr von Erthal, Prince-Bishop of, 31, 151, 225, 243, 255, 332

Yves, marquis d', Austrian diplomat, 142-3, 160

Zimmermann, Johann Georg, conservative writer, 314
Zinsendorf, Nicolaus Ludwig Count von, (1700-60), Pietist, 27
Zorn, Wolfgang, historian, 9
Zweibrücken, 317, 323